The Routledge Handbook of Linguistic Anthropology

The Routledge Handbook of Linguistic Anthropology is a broad survey of linguistic anthropology, featuring contributions from prominent scholars in the discipline. Each chapter presents a brief historical summary of research in the field and discusses topics and issues of current concern to people doing research in linguistic anthropology. The handbook is organized into four parts – Language and Cultural Productions; Language Ideologies and Practices of Learning; Language and the Communication of Identities; and Language and Local/Global Power – and covers current topics of interest at the intersection of the two subjects, while also contextualizing them within discussions of fieldwork practice. Featuring 30 contributions from leading scholars in the field, *The Routledge Handbook of Linguistic Anthropology* is an essential overview for students and researchers interested in understanding core concepts and key issues in linguistic anthropology.

Nancy Bonvillain teaches linguistics and anthropology at Bard College at Simon's Rock, MA. Her fieldwork and research publications focus on linguistic analyses of Mohawk, a Northern Iroquoian language. She has also written several textbooks, including *Cultural Anthropology; Language, Culture, and Communication;* and *Native Nations.*

The Routledge Handbook of Linguistic Anthropology

Edited by Nancy Bonvillain

NEW YORK AND LONDON

First published 2016
by Routledge
711 Third Avenue, New York, NY 10017

and by Routledge
2 Park Square, Milton Park, Abingdon, Oxon, OX14 4RN

Routledge is an imprint of the Taylor & Francis Group, an informa business

© 2016 Taylor & Francis

The right of Nancy Bonvillain to be identified as the author of the editorial material, and of the contributors for their individual chapters, has been asserted in accordance with sections 77 and 78 of the Copyright, Designs and Patents Act 1988.

All rights reserved. No part of this book may be reprinted or reproduced or utilised in any form or by any electronic, mechanical, or other means, now known or hereafter invented, including photocopying and recording, or in any information storage or retrieval system, without permission in writing from the publishers.

Trademark notice: Product or corporate names may be trademarks or registered trademarks, and are used only for identification and explanation without intent to infringe.

Library of Congress Cataloging-in-Publication Data
Bonvillain, Nancy, author.
The Routledge Handbook of Linguistic Anthropology / Nancy Bonvillain, Bard College at Simon's Rock.
  pages cm — (Routledge Handbooks in Linguistics)
Includes bibliographical references and index.
1. Anthropological linguistics—Handbooks, manuals, etc. I. Title. II. Title: Handbook of Linguistic Anthropology.
P35.B616 2016
306.44089—dc23
2015007379

ISBN: 978-0-415-83410-0 (hbk)
ISBN: 978-0-203-49274-1 (ebk)

Typeset in Bembo
by Swales & Willis Ltd, Exeter, Devon, UK

Printed and bound in Great Britain by
TJ International Ltd, Padstow, Cornwall

Contents

Notes on Contributors   viii
Preface   xii

1 Introduction: Intertwined Traditions   1
  Bruce Mannheim

PART I
Language and Cultural Productions   11

2 Semantic Categorization and Cognition   13
  Gerrit J. Dimmendaal

3 Gesture   27
  Jürgen Streeck

4 The Social Imaginary, Unspoken in Verbal Art   44
  Bruce Mannheim

5 New Perspectives on Kinship: Overcoming the Eurocentrism
  and Scientism of Kinship Studies through Lexical Universals   62
  Anna Wierzbicka

6 Being in the Cloud: Analysis of Discourse in Online Communities   80
  Tracy LeBlanc-Wories

PART II
Language Ideologies and Practices of Learning   93

7 Language Ideologies: Emergence, Elaboration, and Application   95
  Paul V. Kroskrity

8 Social Subordination and Language   109
  Margarita Huayhua

Contents

9	Language Socialization *Amy L. Paugh*	125
10	Studying Language Acquisition in Different Linguistic and Cultural Settings *Sabine Stoll*	140
11	Language Socialization and Marginalization *Inmaculada M. García-Sánchez*	159

PART III
Language and the Communication of Identities — 175

12	Language, Sexuality, Heteroglossia, and Intersectionality *William L. Leap*	177
13	Language, Gender, and Identity *Pia Pichler*	191
14	Discursive Practices, Linguistic Repertoire, and Racial Identities *John Baugh*	206
15	Language and Racialization *Elaine W. Chun and Adrienne Lo*	220
16	Analyzing Interactive Discourse: Conversation and Dialogue *Mary Jill Brody*	234
17	Sign Languages and Communicative Practices *Richard J. Senghas*	247
18	New and Emergent Languages *Kathleen C. Riley*	262

PART IV
Language and Local/Global Power — 277

19	Language and Political Economy *Bonnie McElhinny*	279
20	Language, Immigration, and the Nation-State *Joan Pujolar*	301

21	Language and Nationalism *Eve Haque*	317
22	Language in the Age of Globalization *Marco Jacquemet*	329
23	The Emergence of Creoles and Language Change *Salikoko S. Mufwene*	348
24	Discrimination via Discourse *Ruth Wodak*	366
25	Racism in the Press *Teun A. van Dijk*	384
26	Legal Discourse *John M. Conley*	393
27	The Language of Transitional Justice *Susan F. Hirsch*	406
28	Language Maintenance and Revitalization *Andrew Cowell*	420
29	Language Endangerment and Revitalization Strategies *Julie Brittain and Marguerite MacKenzie*	433
30	The Politics of Language Endangerment *Barbra A. Meek*	447
Index		463

Contributors

John Baugh holds the Margaret Bush Wilson Professorship in Arts at Washington University. In 2015 he was inducted as a fellow of the Linguistic Society of America, and he serves as Associate Editor of *Language*, devoted to matters related to public policy.

Julie Brittain is Associate Professor of Linguistics at Memorial University, Newfoundland, Canada. She works on syntactic issues in Algonquian languages, principally on East Cree (Quebec). Since 2004 she has been director of the Chisasibi (Cree) Child Language Acquisition Study.

Mary Jill Brody is Professor in the Department of Geography and Anthropology at Louisiana State University. She specializes in conversation and discourse in Tojol-ab'al Mayan, and is a court interpreter for monolingual Tojol-ab'al speakers in the United States.

Elaine W. Chun is Associate Professor of English and Linguistics at the University of South Carolina. Her research focuses on language, style, and identity as they relate to ideologies of language, race, racism, and gender in youth and media discourses.

John M. Conley is William Rand Kenan, Jr. Professor at the University of North Carolina School of Law. A lawyer and anthropologist, he has written numerous books and articles on the language of law, finance, and science, including *Rules Versus Relationships* and *Just Words* (with William M. O'Barr).

Andrew Cowell is Professor of Linguistics at the University of Colorado, where he specializes in endangered language documentation and linguistic anthropology. He focuses on Algonquian languages, with a secondary interest in Polynesia.

Gerrit J. Dimmendaal is Professor of African Studies at the University of Cologne, Germany. His main interests are in the description and documentation of lesser-known African languages, in particular those belonging to the Nilo-Saharan phylum, as well as the relation between language and culture.

Inmaculada M. García-Sánchez is Associate Professor of Anthropology at Temple University, PA. She is the author of *Language and Muslim Immigrant Childhoods: The Politics of Belonging* (2014), and of numerous articles and chapters on language and the immigrant experience of children and youth.

Eve Haque is Associate Professor of Applied Linguistics in the Department of Languages, Literatures and Linguistics at York University, Toronto, Canada. She is the author of *Multiculturalism in a Bilingual Framework: Language, Race and Belonging in Canada* (2012).

Contributors

Susan F. Hirsch, a cultural anthropologist, is Professor in the School for Conflict Analysis and Resolution at George Mason University, Fairfax, VA. She publishes on law's relation to conflict, reflexive research, international justice, and language in the disputing process.

Margarita Huayhua is assistant professor of anthropology at the University of Massachusetts Dartmouth. She is a first-language speaker of Quechua with extensive field research in Peru, Bolivia, and Ecuador. Her research revolves around relations of power and social domination, language, gender, race and racism, and social movements, which she approaches through the analysis of every-day social interaction.

Marco Jacquemet is Professor of Communication and Culture at the University of San Francisco. His scholarship focuses on the communicative mutations produced by the circulation of migrants and media idioms in the Mediterranean area. He is writing a book based on this research, *Transidioma: Language and Power in the Age of Globalization* (Blackwell, forthcoming). His most significant English publications to date are *Ethereal Shadows: Communication and Power in Contemporary Italy* (co-authored with Franco Berardi; Autonomedia 2009) and *Credibility in Court: Communicative Practices in the Camorra's Criminal Trials* (Cambridge University Press 2009, 2nd ed.).

Paul V. Kroskrity is Professor of Anthropology at the University of California, Los Angeles, where he has taught since earning his PhD in Anthropology from Indiana University in 1978. His books include *Language, History, and Identity* (1993); *Regimes of Language* (2000); and *Telling Stories in the Face of Danger* (2012).

William L. Leap is Professor of Anthropology at American University (Washington, D.C.). He is the author or editor of seven books and edited collections in language and sexuality studies. He is the founding co-editor of the *Journal of Language and Sexuality* and, since 1993, the coordinator of the Lavender Languages and Linguistics Conference (www.american.edu/cas/anthropology/lavender-languages).

Tracy LeBlanc-Wories is a linguistic anthropologist at Louisiana State University. She has taught courses in anthropology, gender studies, ESL composition, and linguistics. Her research focuses on discourse analysis of virtual speech communities and the linguistic and anthropological implications of online community building.

Adrienne Lo is Associate Professor of Anthropology at the University of Illinois at Urbana-Champaign. She is the co-editor of *Beyond Yellow English: Toward a Linguistic Anthropology of Asian Pacific America* (Oxford 2009) and *South Korea's Education Exodus: The Life and Times of Study Abroad*. (Center for Korean Studies, University of Washington 2014).

Marguerite MacKenzie is Professor Emerita of Linguistics, Memorial University, Canada. She assists speakers of Cree, Innu (Montagnais) and Naskapi to document and maintain their languages, which are under increasing pressure from English and French, through the production of dictionaries, grammars, texts, and language training materials.

Bruce Mannheim is a leading scholar of Native South American language, culture, and history, particularly of Southern Peruvian Quechua. His works range from a linguistic history of the Quechua language (that of the Inka since the European invasion) from the sixteenth century – and its shifting social ecology; to narrative; to ritual practices around places; and to Quechua ontology. His publications span the disciplines of anthropology, linguistics, and colonial Latin American history, and include collaborations in psychology and history of art. His distinctive methodology is to tack between the early colonial period (sixteenth and seventeenth centuries) and the present time, in the latter case drawing on extensive ethnography. His current research project is a theory of cultural replication – the ways in which cultural forms are stabilized across time and spread across populations.

Bonnie McElhinny is Associate Professor of Anthropology and Women and Gender Studies at the University of Toronto. Her research focuses on language, gender and political economy, American and Canadian colonialism, especially as they affect the Philippines and indigenous groups, and critical accounts of multiculturalism. Recent publications include *Words, Worlds, Material Girls: Language and Gender in a Global Economy* and *Filipinos in Canada*, as well as articles in *American Anthropologist*, *Philippine Studies*, and the *Annual Review of Anthropology*.

Barbra A. Meek is an Associate Professor of Anthropology and Linguistics at the University of Michigan and citizen of the Comanche Nation. She has published on language endangerment, revitalization, and the racialization of difference through language.

Salikoko S. Mufwene is the Frank J. McLoraine Distinguished Service Professor of Linguistics at the College of the University of Chicago, where he also serves on the Committee on Evolutionary Biology and on the Committee on the Conceptual and Historical Studies of Science. He is the founding editor of the Cambridge Approaches to Language Contact series. He has developed an ecological approach to language speciation that is inspired by macroecology and population genetics.

Amy L. Paugh is Associate Professor of Anthropology at James Madison University, VA. Her research investigates language socialization, children's cultures, and language ideologies in Dominica and the United States. She is the author of *Playing with Languages: Children and Change in a Caribbean Village*.

Pia Pichler is Senior Lecturer in Linguistics at Goldsmiths, University of London. She is particularly interested in linguistic/discourse analytic analysis of the interplay of gender with other sociocultural and situational practices and identities in everyday spoken interaction.

Joan Pujolar, *Llic.* Universitat Autónoma de Barcelona; MA, PhD, Lancaster University, UK, is Associate Professor of Sociolinguistics at the Universitat Oberta de Catalunya. He has studied issues of language and identity in relation to immigration and tourism in Catalonia.

Kathleen C. Riley teaches linguistic anthropology at Queens College, CUNY, and Fordham University, NY. She has conducted fieldwork in the Marquesas, France, Montreal, Vermont, and New York City, and published articles in the *Journal of Linguistic Anthropology*, *Language and Communication*, and elsewhere.

Richard J. Senghas is Professor of Linguistic Anthropology in the Department of Anthropology at Sonoma State University. His fieldwork has followed the emergence of a new sign language and Deaf community in Nicaragua, including influences from North America and Sweden.

Sabine Stoll is Research Professor of General Linguistics and Director of the Psycholinguistics Laboratory at the University of Zurich, Switzerland. Her research focus is on comparative first language acquisition in different linguistic and cultural settings.

Jürgen Streeck is a linguist and Professor of Communication Studies, Anthropology, and Germanic Studies at the University of Texas at Austin. Recent publications include

Gesturecraft. The Manufacture of Meaning (Amsterdam 2009); *Embodied Interaction. Language and Body in the Material World*, ed. J. Streeck, C. Goodwin and C. LeBaron (Cambridge 2011); and *Intercorporeality. Emerging Socialities in Interaction*, ed. C. Meyer, J. Streeck and J.S. Jordan (Oxford, forthcoming).

Teun A. van Dijk was Professor of Discourse Studies at the University of Amsterdam until 2004 and Visiting Professor at Pompeu Fabra University, Barcelona, from 1999. At present he lives and works in Rio de Janeiro. After earlier research on literary theory, text grammar, pragmatics, and the psychology of text processing, his work over the last decades has focused on racism and discourse, news discourse, ideology, context, and knowledge within the broader framework of Critical Discourse Studies. For information about his research and publications, see his website www.discourses.org.

Anna Wierzbicka, born and educated in Poland, is Professor of Linguistics at the Australian National University. Together with Cliff Goddard, Wierzbicka created the "Natural Semantic Metalanguage," based on empirical cross-linguistic investigations, which can serve as a basis for comparing meanings across languages and cultures.

Ruth Wodak is Distinguished Professor of Discourse Studies at Lancaster University, UK. She is the recipient of many prizes for her work in linguistics from universities in Europe and from the Swedish Parliament. Among her many publications are *The Politics of Fear: What Right-wing Populist Discourses Mean* (2015); *Migration, Identity and Belonging* (with G. Delanty, P. Jones, 2011); and the *SAGE Handbook of Sociolinguistics* (co-editor, 2010).

Preface

The Routledge Handbook of Linguistic Anthropology is divided into four sections representing different areas of focus within the discipline. The first, Language and Cultural Productions, includes articles summarizing some traditional concerns in linguistic anthropology and offering new insights into analyses of semantic categories (Dimmendaal), verbal art (Mannheim), and kinship terminologies (Wierzbicka). An additional chapter in this section offers an extensive review of findings in research on gesture, that important mode of communication often overlooked in linguistics studies (Streeck). And finally we are made aware of the significance of studies venturing into new frontiers in communicative interactions, i.e. the cloud (LeBlanc-Wories).

Part II of the handbook, Language Ideologies and Practices of Learning, begins with insights about the topic of language ideologies, a concern that clearly underlies and unites much of what we understand speakers know, consciously or unconsciously, about the covert meanings that they transmit and interpret when producing discourse (Kroskrity). The next contribution offers an analysis of the specific context that exemplifies the ways in which linguistic and cultural ideologies are revealed through discourse in a setting where subordinate speakers navigate their interactions with more powerful actors (Huayhua). The remaining three chapters in this section deal with different themes in language acquisition and socialization studies. The first gives us an overview of research in the field (Paugh), and is followed by an emphasis on language socialization in different linguistic and cultural contexts (Stoll), and by a focus on the way in which marginalization affects language socialization (García-Sánchez).

The next section, Part III, entitled Language and the Communication of Identities, concerns just that, i.e. how speakers transmit, embody, and enact their social and personal identities through linguistic and other communicative choices (both in what they choose and in what they do not choose). The first article, although focusing specifically on sexuality, more broadly attunes us to the significant issue of intersectionality (Leap). This reminds us that we are never conveying one identity or even an identity viewed in binary terms, but rather we simultaneously convey contextually based features of identities. The next three chapters in this section focus on specific issues: the first on gender (Pichler) and the next two on racial identities (Baugh) and the broader processes of racialization (Chun and Lo).

The last three articles in Part III are oriented towards other aspects of communication: the first on conversation and dialogue (Brody), the next on the important but often neglected topic of communicative practices in signed languages (Senghas), and the last on an exploration of new and emergent languages (Riley).

Part IV of the handbook, Language and Local/Global Power, is an extensive collection of chapters on the ways in which power, inequality, and marginalization affect language, languages, and discourse strategies. It begins with a comprehensive overview of the field of political economy and language (McElhinny). Then follow three chapters each examining separate dimensions of how contemporary global policies and social formations are intertwined with languages and discourse: immigration (Pujolar), nationalism (Haque), and globalization (Jacquemet). The next is again a comprehensive overview: of research and theories in the development of creoles and their role in language change (Mufwene).

Two articles in Part IV investigate the ways in which discourse in the press conveys discriminatory and racist meanings (Wodak; Van Dijk). Discourse practices in the United States systems of courts and justice are addressed in the next two (Conley; Hirsch). And the final sequence of three chapters in Part IV explore, from different perspectives and with different conclusions, the topic of language endangerment and revitalization (Cowell; Brittain and MacKenzie; Meek).

I would like to thank Leah Babb-Rosenfeld of Routledge Publishers for suggesting the development of this handbook and Elysse Preposi of Routledge for helping to ready it for production. I also thank Kay Hyman, a freelance editor with Swales & Willis, for coordinating the copy editing process and Tom Newman of Swales & Willis for the final production stage. And I am grateful to all of the contributors for their participation. Their work is of course central to this handbook.

Nancy Bonvillain
Professor, Anthropology and Linguistics
Bard College at Simon's Rock
Great Barrington, MA 01230

1

Introduction
Intertwined Traditions

Bruce Mannheim

As a research tradition, linguistic anthropology emerged in the United States and Canada under the aegis of Boasian "four-field" anthropology. The name itself predates Boas, and was used for the collection of texts and other linguistic materials among Native North Americans (Gal 2006: 171), but within the Boasian program, carried through by such anthropologists as Sapir, Reichard, Haas, and Voegelin, it came to denote a set of research practices in which language in all its aspects provided an opening into culture, social relations, history, and prehistory. Though located intellectually and institutionally within the field of anthropology, it draws on several intertwined traditions of anthropological and linguistic research, North American and European, beginning in the middle of the nineteenth century. These traditions can be characterized by six intellectual revolutions, each of which reshaped the way we understand language and its social, cultural, and historical reach. These are 1) the discovery of time and of regularity in change; 2) the discovery of structure; 3) the cognitive revolution; 4) understanding language as fully socially embedded; 5) language as a transindividual, interactional phenomenon; 6) a population (or populace) centered view of language. While each of these intellectual movements took place at a specific moment in time, in no sense did they supplant earlier movements; rather, the insights that have come with each transformation have been incorporated into succeeding ones.

The Discovery of Time and of Regularity in Change (Linguistics)

In the middle of the nineteenth century the study of language primarily involved the study of written texts from the past as cultural documents of the time in which they were composed, drawing especially on the classical languages of the Eurasian continents: Latin, Greek, Arabic, Sanskrit, Old Persian, and older texts in Tamil, Chinese, and Japanese. One of the major concerns of these scholars, known as *philologists,* was identifying relationships among texts, both in a single line of development and through contact with each other. Philologists were especially interested in word histories, but approached them in atomistic ways, without identifying systematic patterns of change from one historically attested stage of a language to another. It was not until the first of the revolutions – often dated to 1876 (Hoenigswald 1978) – that philologists recognized that the texts reflected systematically organized spoken languages, and that the changes from one stage of a language to another were fully systematic. A *t* sound in an older stage of a language might become a *d* between vowels, but when it did, it affected all parts of the vocabulary at the same time. The key insight of the Neogrammarians, then, was the doctrine of the *regularity of sound change*. Older scholars had also noticed that many of the classical and modern languages of Europe and Asia resembled each other, for example Danish, English, Latin, Greek, Sanskrit, and Armenian, but they were unable to show the relationships among them until they focused on systematic differences among them, in the Neogrammarian style. (We now know that all of these languages are members of an extended Eurasian language family, Indo-European, whose progenitor was spoken on the central Asian steppes between 6,000 and 8,000 years ago [Fortson 2010, Anthony 2007, Chang et al. 2015]). The *regularity of sound change* provided the key tool for understanding groupings of languages into families – not by similarities among them, but by patterned differences.

The Discovery of Structure

Linguistics and Anthropology in language unfolded over almost a half-century, independently in Europe and in America. In Europe, at the beginning of the twentieth century, one of the greatest of the Neogrammarians, Ferdinand de Saussure [1857–1913, trained in Leipzig] was tasked with organizing a course in general linguistics at the university of his home city, Geneva, Switzerland. Saussure divided the task into three domains: the Neogrammarian historical linguistics in which he was trained; linguistic geography (which was of special interest in Switzerland); and *synchronic linguistics*, the study of language in a single slice of time. Saussure modeled both dialect geography and synchronic linguistics on historical Neogrammarian linguistics, concerned not so much with similarities, as with identifying patterned, systematic differences. "In language," he wrote, "there is nothing but difference." Thus, though the French word *mouton* is translated in French–English dictionaries as *sheep*, it does not mean the same thing as sheep. In French, *mouton* is used both for the animal and for its meat; in English, *sheep* is part of a relational structure that includes the word *mutton*. Thus *sheep* in English refers only to the animal, and not to its meat; *mutton* only to the meat (in spite of its history). Both English words define each other relationally, by what they are not. Saussure's observations extend to the grammatical systems of languages: Slavic languages such as Russian have very complex aspectual systems, grammatical systems that allow you – nay, require you – to divide the time that an action takes in certain ways; French – like Russian, an Indo-European language – has a fairly simple aspectual system. In each case, the aspectual categories are defined internal to the language as part of an aspectual structure – the aspectual categories of Russian defining their values through their relationship to each other (in Russian) and the aspectual categories of French defining their values through their relationship to each other (in French). The aspectual categories of Russian do not translate easily into the aspectual categories of French, nor vice versa but neither are they random: there are recurrent patterns of value in aspectual systems of languages the world over. Saussure's famous dictum of "the arbitrariness of the linguistic sign" posited that the relative independence of sound and meaning allowed him to preserve the Neogrammarian principle of the *regularity of sound change,* since it accounted for the fact that sound change was, by and large, undeflected by the meanings or the meaning classes of words.

Saussure's posthumously published book, *Course in General Linguistics* (1916), distilled three sets of his lectures into a broad set of principles for studying language historically and synchronically, and is one of the works that shaped not only disciplinary linguistics, but also adjacent fields: social anthropology, literary analysis, and so forth. It is widely considered one of the master works of the twentieth century.

Introduction: Intertwined Traditions

Just as Saussure was a founding figure of disciplinary linguistics, Franz Boas [1858–1942] shaped the study of anthropology in North America. Trained as a psychophysicist, he began his anthropological journey through the study of observer effects in identifying the color of water in the Arctic. But his training as a student in Germany included a very large dose of pre-Neogrammarian philology, and as he turned his attention to the cultures of Native North America, language became one of the central foci of the newly emerging discipline of anthropology. Language was key to his ethnographic methodology; his students were trained to begin their ethnographic research by doing *synchronic philology* or *philology of the vernacular* (Bauman 2008), collecting oral texts, myths, and first-person accounts of cultural practices that documented the cultures that he and his students studied. On the basis of the texts, they would write grammars of Native American languages and develop synthetic, ethnographic accounts of the cultures. Many of the texts were the bases of the doctoral dissertations of his students, and were published in their original languages in collections still accessible today in libraries, especially the Bureau of American Ethnology at the Smithsonian Institute and in the text series published by the *International Journal of American Linguistics* (founded by Boas himself). Many of these texts serve as the primary documentation that some Native American peoples have of their ancestral language and social practices, and so have become primary sources for language revitalization in Native communities.

Boas's contributions to the study of language structure are as much milestones as Saussure's. In his 1889 article, "On alternating sounds," Boas dismantled the racist idea that speakers of Native American languages were congenitally unable to pronounce words in English and other European languages, and showed that instead, they were pronouncing English following the phonological (sound) canons of their own languages; the "sound blindness" that was frequently attributed to Native Americans was, in fact, an observer effect – the English speakers not understanding the systematics of Native American accents in English. Boas regarded grammatical structure as critical ethnographically, shaping not what one could say, but the way in which the speaker of a language habitually expressed her experiences, so that her experienced world was in part projected from the structure of the grammatical categories (Boas 1911), a position that was to become known as the "Sapir-Whorf hypothesis" after one of Boas's leading students, Edward Sapir and Sapir's student Whorf (see Lucy 1996, Hill and Mannheim 1992 for discussion of the history of this idea).

It was Sapir who largely molded the approach that North American anthropologists – and linguists – took to linguistic and cultural patterning. An intellectual virtuoso, Sapir was at the center of the major theoretical developments of the 1920s and 1930s in both fields, and a spokesperson for the fields among other scholars, ranging from poets to psychologists. Like Boas, Sapir specialized in the living cultures of Native North America, grounding his insights in ethnographic and linguistic fieldwork, producing analyses of the languages and linguistically related social phenomena among several of the major North American language families, with a special affinity for languages of the western United States and Canada. Sapir formulated the first precise and cogent accounts of language structure that emphasized the relationality of all aspects of linguistic form, concentrating especially on the sound system (phonology) and on grammatical categories. He was co-discoverer of the basic units of sound, along with a Southern Paiute speaker, Tony Tillohash (Sapir 1933, Fowler and Fowler 1986). And he brought his linguistic insights to culture, highlighting the relational nature of cultural *patterns*, an emphasis he shared with other Boasians such as Ruth Benedict and Robert Lowie.

A key nexus of Sapir's work was identifying the ontological status of language and culture. Early in his career, he took on A.L. Kroeber's famous article, "Culture, the superorganic," which posited that cultures (and so languages) were held by collectivities, with a rejoinder entitled

3

"Do we need a superorganic?" His reply was a resounding "no": "It is always the individual that really thinks and acts and dreams and revolts" (Sapir 1917: 442). His theoretical excursions into the nature of language and culture were shaped thereafter by two assumptions: 1) that culture and language are primarily individual phenomena; and 2) that the coherence of culture and language reflected an "innate form feeling" that individuals have for the ways in which their languages and cultures handle everyday experience. While Sapir's view of culture won the day among the Boasians, later he moved toward a position that favored the second assumption over the first. When older, Sapir treated culture and language as transindividual – culture was not "in" individuals, nor "in" collectivities, but had significant regularities that could be observed in everyday interaction *among* people (Sapir [1939] 2002, Irvine 2002, Mannheim and Tedlock 1995, Silverstein 1984).

Independently of Sapir, scholars in Europe – particularly the Russian members of the Prague, Linguistic Circle, Trubetzkoy, Karčevsky, and Jakobson – identified principles of language structure based on a Saussurean notion of "value." Like the Boasians, including Sapir, their starting point was grammatical categories (not surprisingly, in Slavic languages, Jakobson 1936), and the area that most clearly defined the nature of pattern in language was the sound system, phonology (Trubetzkoy 1939, Jakobson 1939). A leitmotif of Jakobson's work was the principle of *relational invariance,* that of identifying relational structures in language that remain constant across variable contexts.

Two influential themes emerge from the work of the Russians. The first of these is the importance of identifying principles of language structure comparatively, with the expectation that one can construct an account for the compatibilities and incompatibilities of particular linguistic structures. One of the instantiations of this program was a comparative analysis of phonological systems that attempted to account at one and the same time for: the set of phonological systems that are possible in the languages of the world; possible transitions between systems; the relative order of acquisition in phonological development; and the relative order of loss of phonological distinctions as a result of certain neurological pathologies (Jakobson 1941, Jakobson and Halle 1956). Second, the multifunctionality of all talk. Jakobson (1960) argued that talk is *not* primarily referential; rather it must be understood as a continually shifting compromise among six distinct functions: the expressive, conative, and phatic functions governing the relationship among participants in social interaction; and the referential, metalinguistic, and poetic functions establishing relationships among linguistic units and between linguistic units and the world. The second of these was especially influential in linguistic anthropology.

After migrating to the United States, Jakobson took up the work of the turn-of-the-century American philosopher Charles Sanders Peirce, and brought Peirce's "semiotic" into conversation with linguistics and linguistic anthropology. Though disciplinarily a linguist, Jakobson's influence was felt very firmly throughout the human sciences, particularly in anthropology. Jakobson was the sparkplug of the next three revolutions.

In the course of identifying structural principles of language through their roles in socially situated practices and as conceptual constructs, neither Jakobson's linguistics nor Sapir's anthropology met with much approval in North American linguistics or in the social sciences in the post-World War II period, which had become firmly behavioristic. Jakobson's linguistics, to be sure, provided the groundwork for what became known in anthropology and related fields as "structuralism" (Lévi-Strauss 1949, a work squarely within Jakobson's comparative framework; Lévi-Strauss 1980). But, increasingly, the behaviorist program in linguistics proved to be untenable, and by the middle of the 1950s was challenged by a syntactician influenced by Jakobson's work, Noam Chomsky.

The Cognitive Revolution (Linguistics and Psychology)

Chomsky's earliest work was in the mathematical models that would prove powerful enough to describe syntax and provide the analytic toolkit to account for the limits on variability among languages. It also included an important publication that reset the goals of grammatical analysis, an influential review of psychologist B.F. Skinner's *Verbal Behavior* (Chomsky 1959). Instead of limiting themselves to the largely distributional and taxonomic description of linguistic forms, Chomsky proposed that linguists establish goals more closely matching the Jakobsonian program, that is, to use syntactic analysis as a way to understand human language as a cognitive phenomenon, and to understand the constraints on possible syntactic systems (Chomsky 1965, 1988). His term for these constraints, *universal grammar*, has been the target of roughly a half-dozen frameworks that Chomsky and many of his students moved through as they sought to characterize formally human linguistic competence. Chomsky's turn to examining the cognitive apparatus underlying grammar, using grammar itself as the tool, both triggered and reflected a major shift in the goals of related fields, particularly psychology, and spurred the emergence of new fields devoted to the study of mind and brain. Chomsky (2000) himself distinguished radically between "i-language" or grammar, as a system of cognitive rules and representations, and "e-language" or linguistic behavior (using several slightly different versions of this formulation at different points in his career), bringing grammatical analysis squarely into the domain of "i-language." The "location" of grammar for Chomsky is squarely in individual minds/brains.

Attempts by some anthropologists in the 1960s and 1970s to mimic the goals of Chomskyan linguistics in anthropology largely proved to be still-births. But the cognitive turn in a broader sense reshaped views of culture and language in anthropology (for example in the work of Sperber 1996 and in comparative primatology, Cheney and Seyfarth 1988, Povinelli 1993). A version of the Chomskyan program for syntax has become the default analytic framework for grammatical analysis, and debate over the goals and consequences of grammatical analysis in the Chomskyan sense continue apace.

Language as Socially Embedded (Anthropology and Linguistics)

A counterpoint to the Chomskyan view of language as an individual-centered cognitive matter, sociolinguists of the 1960s and 1970s emphasized the social nature of language, showing how variation in languages could be gauged against a social landscape, defined politically, geographically, ethnically, and by socio-economic status. An especially influential version of this framework is the variationist sociolinguistics of Labov (1972), which has its roots in traditional dialect geography mediated especially through the work of Uriel Weinreich (see Weinreich, Labov, and Herzog 1968). Labov made efforts to align it with the emerging view of grammar in the Chomskyan framework, though variationist sociolinguistics largely stood as an elaboration of grammar. At the same time, the anthropologists John Gumperz and Dell Hymes developed a more broadly based view of talk as embedded in social action, known at the time as "the ethnography of speaking" (e.g., Gumperz and Hymes 1972, Bauman and Sherzer 1974). The ethnography of speaking took language as a critical point of entry into social analysis, and raised issues descriptive, epistemological, and analytic that were taken up by other anthropologists, often without engaging the genealogy of the ideas.

The ethnography of speaking represented a return to a Boasian view of language as the primary ethnographic entryway into culture, and linguistic anthropology as a central concern of the discipline as a whole. At the same time, it raised novel issues that were to play a central role going forward: the nature of speech communities, particularly as social and political entities (see Irvine 2006); variability in ways of speaking; the functional diversity of talk (in a Jakobsonian mold); the variability of language development among speech communities: and the centrality of the analysis of the social development of language to understanding social relationships, a research program pioneered by Schieffelin and Ochs. Increasingly sophisticated discourse-analytic tools were brought to bear on ethnographic analysis, while at the same time there was a return to the Boasian tradition of synchronic philology and a move forward to understanding textual and other discursive practices as constitutive of culture.

Language as a Constitutive Material Practice

This phrase, used by Raymond Williams, characterizes the remaining two revolutions, both of which treat language as absolutely central to, and constitutive of, social relations. Rooted in the intellectual traditions already discussed, they draw as well on currents in affine traditions: sociology, literary analysis, gender studies, political economy. These are infused at their core by Peircian semiotic, reintroduced largely through the work of Michael Silverstein, but now part of the common stock-in-trade across the human sciences. Important too was a shift in social ontology associated with language. Where it was common in the past – particularly in disciplinary linguistics – to think of the social world as divided between individuals and collectivities, and to locate language firmly in one or another camp, linguistic anthropologists took up an observation by interactionist sociologists and ethnomethodologists (such as Goffman, Garfinkel, and Sacks) in the 1960s that talk, like all social practices, is a form of *concerted action,* found neither in individuals nor in collectivities, but between individuals and constitutive of large scale social groupings. This position effectively took up Sapir's late views after a thirty-year hiatus, but developed them with a richer empirical toolkit, including conversation analysis. These views also found resonance in performance-centered folkloristics, Bakhtinian literary and social theory, work on reference and indexicality by Hanks, and the discourse-centered linguistics of Tannen. Much discussion within this framework has focused on reconstructing key analytic parameters of social analysis in an interactionist key, showing that practices that were once understood in narrowly linguistic terms, like code-switching, are infused with local, politically sensitive social meaning (Gal 1987, Woolard 1989, Zentella 1997), or showing that terms of art in social analysis, like gender, social identity, and agency, are built up out of historically situated linguistic complexes (Ahearn, Bucholtz, Duranti, Eckert, Hall, McConnell-Ginet). Linguistic anthropologists have been prominent in two major intellectual movements within disciplinary linguistics – the study of language, gender, and sexuality; and sociophonetics (with substantial overlap between them).

Language as Constitutive of Populations

Lastly, linguistic anthropologists have challenged the very idea of "a language," "a dialect," or "an idiolect" by emphasizing the fluidity and contingency of all forms of speech. Where dialect geographers of Saussure's day were concerned with mapping the boundaries of linguistic phenomena, and where sociolinguists and anthropologists of the 1960s and 1970s spoke of "speech communities," linguistic anthropologists today are more likely to engage the semiotic construction of the boundaries as constitutive of the phenomena that we all too readily called "languages" and "speech communities" in the past. Linguistic anthropologists have traced the formation of speech communities and the iconization of social differences to linguistic practices (Irvine and Gal) and have shown ways in which linguistic practices establish normative social identification – below the threshold of awareness (Hill). These observations have also brought about greater reflection on the effects that linguistic documentation has had on social relations among speakers of smaller languages – particularly languages that are now in danger of disappearing (Meek). Today, linguistic anthropology is increasingly central to all anthropological research.

References

Ahearn, Laura. 2001. Language and agency. *Annual Review of Anthropology 30*: 109–137.
Anthony, David W. 2007. *The horse, the wheel, and language. How bronze-age riders from the Eurasian steppes shaped the modern world*. Princeton, NJ: Princeton University Press
Bauman, Richard A. 1975. Verbal art as performance. *American Anthropologist 77*: 290–311.
Bauman, Richard A. 2008. The philology of the vernacular. *Journal of Folklore Research 45*(1): 29–36.
Bauman, Richard A. and Joel Sherzer (eds) 1974. Explorations in the ethnography of speaking, London: Cambridge University Press.
Boas, Franz. 1889. On alternating sounds. *American Anthropologist 2*: 47–53.
Boas, Franz. 1911. Introduction [to the] *Handbook of American Indian languages*. Washington: Bureau of American Ethnology.
Bucholtz, Mary. 2011. *White kids: Language, race, and styles of youth identity*. New York: Cambridge University Press.
Bucholtz, Mary and Kira Hall. 2004. Theorizing identity in language and sexuality research. *Language in Society 33*(4): 501–547.
Bucholtz, Mary and Kira Hall. 2005. Identity and interaction: A sociocultural linguistic approach. *Discourse Studies 7*(4–5): 585–614.
Chang, Will, Chundra Cathcart, David Hall, and Andrew Garrett 2015. Ancestry–constrained phylogenetic analysis supports the Indo–European steppe hypothesis. *Language 91*: 194–244.
Cheney, Dorothy and Robert Seyfarth.1998. Why monkeys don't have language. In *The Tanner Lectures on Human Value 19*. ed. G. Petersen. Salt Lake City: University of Utah Press.
Chomsky, Noam A. 1959. Review of B.F. Skinner, *Verbal behavior. Language 35*: 26–58.
Chomsky, Noam A. 1965. *Aspects of the theory of syntax*. Cambridge, MA: MIT Press.
Chomsky, Noam A. 1988. *Language and problems of knowledge*. Cambridge, MA: MIT Press.
Chomsky, Noam A. 2000. *New horizons in the study of language and mind*. New York: Cambridge University Press.
Duranti, Alessandro. 2015. *The anthropology of intentions: Language in a world of others*. Cambridge University Press.
Eckert, Penelope. 2000. *Linguistic variation as social practice*. Oxford: Blackwell.
Eckert, Penelope and Sally McConnell-Ginet. 2013. *Language and gender* (2nd ed.). New York: Cambridge University Press.
Fortson, Benjamin. 2010. *Indo-European language and culture. An introduction*. Chichester, UK: Wiley-Blackwell.
Fowler, Catherine S. and Don D. Fowler. 1986. Edward Sapir, Tony Tillohash and Southern Paiute Studies. *New perspectives in language, culture, and personality,* (eds William Cowan, Michael K. Foster, and Konrad Koerner), 41–65. Amsterdam: Benjamins.
Gal, Susan 1987. Codeswitching and consciousness in the European periphery. *American Ethnologist 14*: 637–53.
Gal, Susan. 2006. Linguistic anthropology. *Encyclopedia of language and linguistics*, 2nd ed., (ed. Keith Brown), 171–185. Boston: Elsevier.
Gal, Susan and Kathryn Woolard (eds). 2001. *Languages and publics: The making of authority*. Manchester: St. Jerome Publishing.
Garfinkel, Harold. 1967. *Studies in ethnomethodology*. Englewood Cliffs, NJ: Prentice-Hall.
Goffman, Erving. 1981. *Forms of talk*. Philadelphia: University of Pennsylvania Press.
Gumperz, John J. and Dell Hymes (eds). 1972. *Directions in sociolinguistics*. New York: Holt, Rinehart & Winston.
Hanks, William F.1990. *Referential practice: language and lived space among the Maya*. Chicago: University of Chicago Press.
Hill, Jane. 2008. *The everyday language of white racism*. Malden, MA: Wiley-Blackwell.
Hill, Jane and Bruce Mannheim. 1992. Language and world view. *Annual Review of Anthropology 21*: 382–406.

Hoenigswald, Henry M. 1978. The *annus mirabilis* 1876 and posterity. *Transactions of the Philological Society* 17–35.
Irvine, Judith T. (ed.). 2002. Introduction [to] *The psychology of culture* (2nd ed.). vii–xix, 1–13. Berlin: Mouton de Gruyter.
Irvine, Judith T. 2006. Speech and language community. *Encyclopedia of languages and linguistics*, 2nd ed. Boston: Elsevier.
Irvine, Judith T. and Susan Gal. 2000. Language ideology and linguistic differentiation. *Regimes of language*, (ed. Paul Kroskrity), Santa Fe, NM: School of American Research Press, 35–84.
Jakobson, Roman O. 1984 [1936.] Beitrag zur allgemeinen Kasuslehre. Gesamtbedeutungen der russischen Kasus. *Travaux du Cercle Linguistique de Prague 6*: 240–288. English trans., Contribution to a general theory of case. *Russian and Slavic grammar. Studies, 1931–1981,* (eds Linda R. Waugh and Morris Halle), 59–103. Berlin: Mouton.
Jakobson, Roman O. 1939. Observations sur le classement phonologique des consonnes. *Proceedings of the Third International Congress of Phonetic Sciences,* Ghent, Laboratory of Phonetics, 34–41.
Jakobson, Roman O. 1962 [1941]. *Kindersprache, Aphasie und allgemeine Lautgesetze,* Uppsala. Reprinted in Jakobson. *Selected writings* (vol. 1), 328–401. English trans. A.R. Keiler (1968). *Child language, aphasia and phonological universals.* The Hague: Mouton.
Jakobson, Roman O. 1960. Linguistics and poetics. *Style in language,* (ed. Thomas A. Sebeok), 350–372. Cambridge: MIT Press.
Jakobson, Roman and Morris Halle. 1956. *Fundamentals of language.* The Hague: Mouton.
Kroeber, Alfred L. 1917. The superorganic. *American Anthropologist 19*(2): 163–213.
Labov, William A. 1972. *Sociolinguistic patterns.* Philadelphia: University of Pennsylvania Press.
Lévi-Strauss, Claude. 1949. *Les Structures élémentaires de la parenté.* Paris: Presses Universitaires de France. English trans., *The elementary structures of kinship.* Boston: Beacon, 1969.
Lévi-Strauss, Claude. 1980 [1976]. Introduction [to] Roman Jakobson, *Six lectures on sound and meaning,* Cambridge: MIT Press.
Lucy, John A. 1996. The scope of linguistic relativity: An analysis and review of empirical research. *Rethinking linguistic relativity* (eds John J. Gumperz and Stephen C. Levinson), 37–69. Cambridge: University Press.
Mannheim, Bruce and Dennis Tedlock. 1995. Introduction [to] *The dialogic emergence of culture,* (eds Dennis Tedlock and Bruce Mannheim), 1–32. Urbana: University of Illinois Press.
Meek, Barbra. 2007. Respecting the language of elders: Ideological shift and linguistic discontinuity in a Northern Athapascan community. *Journal of Linguistic Anthropology 17*: 23–43.
Ochs, Elinor. 1988. *Culture and language development: Language acquisition and language socialization in a Samoan village.* Cambridge: Cambridge University Press.
Povinelli, Daniel J. 1993. Reconstructing the evolution of mind. *American Psychologist 48*(5): 493–509.
Sacks, Harvey. 1992. *Lectures on conversation* (ed. Gail Jefferson). Oxford: Blackwell.
Sapir, Edward. 1917. Do we need a superorganic? *American Anthropologist 19*(4): 441–447.
Sapir, Edward. 1949 [1933]. The psychological reality of phonemes. Reprinted in *Selected writings of Edward Sapir,* (1949) 46–60. Berkeley: University of California Press.
Sapir, Edward. 2000 [1939]. *The psychology of culture* (2nd ed.), (ed. J. T. Irvine). Berlin: Mouton de Gruyter.
Saussure, Ferdinand de. 1971 [1916]. *Cours de linguistique générale.* Paris: Payot. English trans., *Course in general linguistics* (trans. Wade Baskin). New York, Philosophical Library, 1959.
Schieffelin, Bambi B. 1990. *The give and take of everyday life: Language socialization of Kaluli children.* New York: Cambridge University Press.
Seyfarth, Robert and Dorothy Cheney. 2015. The evolution of language from social cognition. *Current Opinion in Neurobiology 28*: 5–9.
Silverstein, Michael. 1976. Shifters, linguistic categories, and cultural description. *Meaning in anthropology,* (eds Keith Basso and Henry Selby), 11–55. Albuquerque: University of New Mexico Press.
Silverstein, Michael. 1979. Linguistic structure and linguistic ideology. *The elements: A parasession on linguistic units and levels,* (eds Paul R. Clyne, William F. Hanks, and C.L. Hofbauer), 193–247. Chicago: Chicago Linguistic Society.
Silverstein, Michael. 1984. On the pragmatic poetry of prose. *Meaning, form, and use in context: Linguistic applications,* (ed. Deborah Schiffrin), 181–199. Georgetown: Georgetown University Press.
Silverstein, Michael. 2003. Indexical order and the dialectics of sociolinguistic life. *Language & Communication 23*: 193–229.

Silverstein, Michael. 2004. "Cultural" concepts and the language–culture nexus. *Current Anthropology 45*: 621–645.
Sperber, Dan. 1996. *Explaining Culture: A Naturalistic Approach*. Oxford: Blackwell.
Tannen, Deborah. 1989. *Talking voices. Repetition, dialogue, and imagery in conversational discourse*. New York: Cambridge University Press.
Trubetzkoy, Nicolai S. 1939. *Grundzüge der Phonologie, Travaux du Cercle Linguistique de Prague 7*. English trans., *Principles of phonology* (trans. C.A.M. Baltaxe, trans.). Berkeley: University of California Press, 1969.
Weinreich, Uriel, William A. Labov, and Marvin Herzog. 1968. Empirical foundations for a theory of language change. *Directions for historical linguistics*, (eds Winifred P. Lehmann and Yakov Malkiel) 97–188. Austin: University of Texas Press.
Williams, Raymond. 1977. *Marxism and literature*, London: Oxford University Press.
Woolard, Kathryn. 1989. *Double talk: bilingualism and the politics of ethnicity in Catalonia*. Stanford: Stanford University Press.
Zentella, Ana Celia. 1997. *Growing up bilingual: Puerto Rican children in New York*. Malden, MA: Blackwell.

Part I
Language and Cultural Productions

2
Semantic Categorization and Cognition

Gerrit J. Dimmendaal

1 Introduction

One crucial way in which individuals learn about the cultural practices of the community in which they grow up is through language. By gaining an understanding of the language spoken by such a community, social scientists consequently may also arrive at a better comprehension of the cultures they are interested in, as argued by one of the pioneers of linguistic anthropology, Frans Boas (1858–1942). His primary experience as an anthropologist was with the Kwakiutl and other First Nations groups in Canada. Boas saw lexical categories in languages as experience-derived classifications, as one way in which human beings can deal with the complexity of their environment. Such categories tend to be organized into semantic fields, the latter representing collections of words together covering a complete conceptual field. These words may represent concepts, they may name or refer to objects, and they may also categorize the latter.

One way of learning the semantic systems used by a specific speech community is through "folk taxonomy", defined by Mathiot (1962: 343) as "the grouping of entities according to the category labels given to them by the culture". This principle was practised first by Boas and others with respect to kinship terminology in the nineteenth century, and extended into various other lexical domains such as colour terminology or bionomenclature in the twentieth century, in particular in a branch of linguistic anthropology that has come to be known as cognitive anthropology. Section 2 below summarizes some of the results of this research tradition, whereas section 3 discusses critical issues emerging from this field of research, including the question to what extent such classifications affect cognition, more specifically "habitual thought". More recently, this kind of research has become the domain of cognitive linguists, as shown in section 4. Section 5 provides some recommendations for practice, in particular the use of multi-media for the documentation of these domains, whereas section 6 provides some future directions for research.

2 Historical Perspectives

The Cross-Cultural Survey, a project organized by the Institute of Human Relations at Yale University and aiming at a catalogue of "any known" aspect of a society's culture, in the 1930s initiated a research tradition that also had its impact on linguistic anthropology. Its originator, George P. Murdock, for example, arrived at a classificatory system for family structures through a comparison of kinship terminologies in a wide range of languages. This inductive research method in the social sciences inspired one of the most influential linguists and anthropologists of the twentieth century, Joseph H. Greenberg (1915–2001), to extend this broad comparative approach to include language (Newman 1991, in an interview with Joseph H. Greenberg), in order to reveal universal principles of human language. It was the same inductive approach used in language typology studies which inspired Berlin and Kay (1969) to investigate universals of colour terminology. Actual interest in colour was much older (as shown already in the scholarly work of Geiger or Virchow in the nineteenth century). But Berlin and Kay used the so-called Munsell colour chart to test how speakers of different languages across the world divide the colour spectrum;[1] in addition, they consulted dictionaries and other sources on as many languages as possible (all in all around one hundred different languages). By focusing on so-called "basic colour terms", i.e. terms not derived from some other lexeme (such as 'orange' in English), or part of another colour (such as 'navy blue', which is a kind of 'blue'), and known and used by a wide variety of speakers, Berlin and Kay arrived at a list of maximally 11 basic terms. Moreover, they concluded that some of these terms are more basic than others, i.e. that there are implicational universals between them reflected in seven stages. At Stage I, only two terms are found (whose best representatives are to be found in what would be called 'white' and 'black' respectively in English). At Stage II, 'red' is added, and at Stage III either 'green' or 'yellow' will be encoded, while at Stage IV, whichever of these categories was not encoded at Stage III will receive its own term. At Stage V, six term languages are found, also encoding 'blue'. Stage VI languages have a separate term for 'brown', whereas at Stage VII, with eight terms, 'purple', 'pink', 'orange' or 'grey' are lexicalized as basic colour terms.

Berlin and Kay (1969) concluded that the division of the colour spectrum is not arbitrary, but rather governed by cognitive constraints. Moreover, the implicational relations holding between the different terms imply, for example, that if a language has a basic term for 'brown' (in a corresponding English translation), it also has a basic term for 'blue', but not vice versa. Kay and McDaniel (1978) presented a slightly revised encoding sequence (Figure 2.1), with 'grue' capturing 'green plus blue' and with 'grey' operating as a "wild card", potentially popping up at any stage.

The same research tradition that led some scholars to the conviction that there are clearcut cognitive constraints on the way semantic fields such as the colour domain are organized in

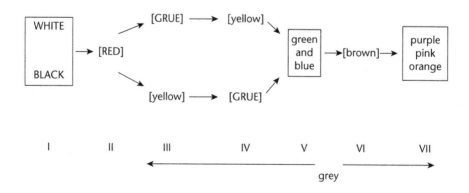

Figure 2.1 Colour-encoding sequence of Kay and McDaniel (1978)

human language led others to the conclusion that there are serious conceptual problems with this approach. As already pointed out by Berlin and Kay (1969), we find an "overdifferentiation" in languages like Russian, where there are two terms for 'blue' (*goluboj* and *sinij*), or "underdifferentiation" in Cantonese, which does not have a term for 'brown', although it does have terms for 'pink' and 'grey'. Such cases have since been replicated by different authors with examples from various other languages.

But the actual conceptual problems are more fundamental in nature. Much of the criticism was already formulated at an early point in Tornay (1978), and is still valid today. One of these concerns the question of what "basic" means, namely "basic to whom?" Pastoral communities in Eastern Africa usually have a rich vocabulary with numerous terms describing colour patterns in cattle. With respect to the Dinka in South Sudan (who speak a Nilotic language), Lienhardt (1961: 13) observes that their "very perception of colour, light, and shade in the world around them is ... inextricably connected with their recognition of colour configurations in their cattle. If their cattle-colour vocabulary were taken away, they would have scarcely any way of describing visual experience in terms of colour, light and darkness."

Hanunoo (a Malayo-Polynesian language spoken in the Philippines) is characterized as a Stage III language by Berlin and Kay (1969: 64), in that it has basic colours with foci in 'white', 'black', 'red', and 'green'. The term *(ma)raraʔ* 'red' also covers shades such as 'maroon', 'orange' and 'yellow', whereas *(ma)latuy* 'green' also covers 'mixtures of green, yellow and light brown', according to Berlin and Kay (1969: 64). In a classic contribution on colour terminology in Hanunoo, however, Conklin (1964) points out that "what appears to be color 'confusion' at first may result from an inadequate knowledge of the internal structure of a color (sic) system and from a failure to distinguish sharply between sensory reception on the one hand and perceptual categorization on the other". In actual fact, the lexical roots *raraq (raraʔ)* and *latuy* reflect an opposition between dryness or desiccation and wetness or freshness (succulence) in visible components of the natural environment respectively. Hence, it should not come as a surprise – since these are not colour terms – that both terms may cover shades of 'yellow' in the metalanguage, English. This leads us to a fundamental problem in the investigation of semantic categorizations in a cross-linguistic perspective, something that Quine (1960) referred to as the problem of the "radical translator". Translation is an interpretive task, whereby one tries to present the categories of one conceptual system in terms of another, functioning as the metalanguage, in order to make shared understandings possible. Glosses are necessary, but they should be considered neither as definitions nor as exact equivalents, as pointed out by Lounsbury (1956: 163), a view also expressed by Boas, who argued against translating the Kwakiutl principle of kin groups into any English word, for example. Instead of trying to fit the Kwakiutl system into some larger model, he tried to understand their beliefs and practices in their own terms. For example, whereas he had earlier translated the Kwakiutl word *numaym* as 'clan', he later on argued that the word is best understood as referring to a bundle of privileges, for which there is no English word. Principles underlying the semantic analysis of lexical fields should primarily be those of the speakers and not those of the investigator, an approach propagated by Hymes (1962) in his seminal contribution on "the ethnography of speaking" which has come to be characterized as "emic".

Kay, Berlin and Merrifield (1991) take recourse to so-called "fundamental neural response" categories in order to back up the biological basis of their model. These categories are derived from neurophysiological research with primates by De Valois and Jacobs (1968), showing that there are six types of colour-sensitive cells, four of which are responsible for hue (focal primary colours blue, yellow, red, and green), and two for brightness ('black' and 'white'). These are arranged in pairs (blue-yellow cells, red-green cells, and light-darkness cells). Focal non-primary colours like 'pink', for example, result from "fuzzy union" of 'red' and 'white'.

But these "biological facts" cannot account for the fact that languages may use one and the same term to describe a domain in the colour spectrum covered by three terms in English: 'green', 'blue' and 'yellow'. Foley (1997: 156) points out that such systems are attested in Asia, Australia and Oceania, North America and South America. But similar systems are common in Africa, in particular in languages in the Sahel region and neighbouring areas. For example, Tima (a Niger–Congo language spoken in the Nuba Mountains in Sudan) has the following system: [2]

(1) -tún   -tɨ́k   -rdí   -héh   -kùlùmó
     black   white   red   green   brown
                                  blue
                                  yellow

Tima also "underdifferentiates" in that it has a separate lexeme for 'brown', whereas 'green/blue/yellow' persists as "undissolved". McLaury (1992) suggests a pivotal role for the brightness dimension (rather than hue) in order to explain such systems. But as pointed out by Foley (1997: 156), "[t]his grouping of YELLOW/GRUE poses formidable problems for Kay and McDaniel's grounding of generalities of basic color terms in innate perceptual properties of the human color vision system, specifically, the subsystems based on opposing colours. Yellow and blue (member of the composite GRUE) are opposing poles of the same subsystem and, if these subsystems based on oppositions are the universal grounding for human color categorizations, it is hard to see how yellow and blue could be conflated in a single named category."

Visual physiology no doubt plays a role, setting constraints on the cultural construction of colour categories tendencies. However, our current understanding of the human cognitive system cannot help us in any way in explaining the tremendous variation between languages, also in terms of the semantic domain covered by such terms, for example, when applied to different materials such as fruits or vegetables, or the skin colour of human beings and animals. For speakers of American English, Barack Obama is their first 'black' president; the skin colour of people with a darker complexion may be referred as *axdar* 'green' by speakers of Sudanese Arabic, to mention but a few examples. Colour terms in a speech community thus do not necessarily mean Munsell colour chips. Still, Berlin and Kay and their adherents have focused entirely on the foci and ignored the range, as Wierzbicka (2005) points out. The question of "how cognition constrains culture in producing science", as Atran (1998: 547) phrased it, will thus remain unanswered until further progress has been made in the field of neurophysiology.

The inductive methods initiated for cross-linguistic research on colour terminologies inspired cognitive anthropologists to extend the lexical domain to folk biology in the 1980s and 90s. Folk biology contrasts with the theoretical programme of biology as initiated by Renaissance herbalists. The basis for subsequent systematics in biology was laid by Post-Renaissance scientists (Atran 1998: 564), who further points out:

> During the initial stages of Europe's global commercial expansion, the number of species increased by an order of magnitude. Foreign species were habitually joined to the most similar European species, that is, to the generic type in a "natural system." Enlightenment naturalists, like Jungius and Linnaeus, further separated natural history from its cognitive moorings in human ecology, banning from botany intuitively "natural" but scientifically "lubricious" life forms, such as *tree* and *grass* . . . " During the latter part of the 18th century and the beginning of the 19th century, methods for organizing plants and animals into families and orders were developed (e.g. by Lamarck), thereby laying the basis for systematics in biology and Darwin's evolutionary concepts of phyla and "the tree of life."

The global expansion also brought knowledge about alternative ways in which people classify nature, as shown in a pioneering study by Harshberger (1896), who introduced the concept of "ethnobotany" for the study of "the use of plants by aboriginal peoples". Following the inductive methods introduced to the field by Berlin and Kay (1969) for colour, Brown (1984) also arrived at implicational relations between "discontinuities" encoded by languages with respect to bionomenclature. According to his survey, systems are organized into taxonomic structures with no more than six mutually exclusive ranks expressing growth stages. With respect to botany, one may come across languages without a separate word for 'tree' (as a life-form taxon); Southern Paiute is claimed to be one such language (Brown 1984: 133–134). At "stage 2", life-form terms like 'tree' occur, whereas at "stage 3" we find terms for 'tree' and 'grerb (i.e. grass plus herb)'. "Stage 4" languages distinguish between 'tree', 'grerb' and 'vine', according to this typology, and "stage 5" languages have lexemes for 'tree', 'grerb, 'grass' and 'vine', as in Daga (a Trans-New Guinea language of Papua New Guinea):

(2) *oma*   'tree, wood'
     rarema 'grerb (herb)'
     ut   'grass (grass + weed)'
     damik   'vine'

The polysemous nature of the word translated as 'tree' in Daga, where it could also mean 'wood', is common cross-linguistically, as suggested by the examples in Brown (1984). In many African languages, the word for 'tree' may also be translated as 'medicine', as with *yaàt* in the Nilotic language Acholi (spoken in Uganda).

Similar "growth stages" are argued for in Brown (1984) with respect to zoological terms, ranging from a life-form taxon like 'fish' ("stage 1"), 'bird + snake' ("stage 2"), 'bird + fish + snake' ("stage 3"), 'bird + fish + snake + wug (worm + bug)' ("stage 4"'), 'bird + fish + snake + wug + mammal'.

The amount of data amassed by Brown (1984) is impressive, but the method used has its empirical problems in terms of observational and descriptive adequacy, and because all languages are forced into a specific template (as with colour terminology), as illustrated next for three languages that are exemplary for many languages in the database. In Ando (a Kwa language spoken in the Ivory Coast) the word *oua*, translated as 'grass', is also supposed to denote 'savannah' and 'dryness' (p. 182); though not impossible, this presumed polysemy is rather unlikely. For quite a few languages in the database, the word for 'tree' may also refer to 'wood'. But how do we know that the primary meaning is 'tree', rather than 'wood', in a language? In the Uto-Aztecan language Shoshoni, for example, the primary meaning is 'wood' (p. 146). Nevertheless, 'wood' does not appear in the list with "growth stages". Brown (1984: 183) lists Carapana (a Tucanoan language spoken in Colombia) as a "stage 5" language with words for 'tree', 'grerb', 'grass' and 'vine'. At closer inspection, the three terms in this language translated as 'grerb (grass + herb)', have a "literal meaning": *moitĩẽ* 'useless stuff', *capunirĩjẽ* 'hurtful stuff', and *cororije* 'bad stuff' (Brown 1984: 183). These three terms thus stand in meaningful paradigmatic contrast to each other. Any cross-linguistic typology of semantic categorizations in the lexicon, as represented through folk taxonomies, should take the actual meanings and semantic oppositions in languages as a basis, rather than bracketing these out.

Perceptual categories of Western researchers may systematically cause a Westerner to misperceive, or fail to perceive entirely, a meaningful element in another culture, as research in linguistic anthropology over the past century has shown. Henrich, Heine and Norenzayan (2010) introduce the concept of WEIRD people, i.e. those from Western, Educated, Industrialized,

Rich and Democratic societies, and point out (p. 1) that they are "among the least representative populations one could find among humans". In spite of this, speakers from such societies have played a key role in many psychological tests on cognitive salience. The validity of several of these tests hence may be questioned (as the authors do). The authors also provide a natural explanation of why folk genera or generic species ('starling' and 'crow', or 'oak' and 'beech') are at the basic level and the first learned by children in non-industrialized small-scale societies, whereas for children of (what the authors call) WEIRD parents, life-form taxa like 'bird' or 'tree' are more salient. Deficient input probably underpins the fact that children living " . . . in a culturally and experientially impoverished environment, by contrast to those of small-scale societies (and of our evolutionary past) tend to answer questions like "what's that?" by "that's a tree", rather than being more specific and more informative by answering "that's a maple", for example.

The standard terminology for folk biological ranking goes back to Berlin (1992), who refers to English concepts such as 'plant' or 'animal' as folk kingdom ranks. These can be divided into "life-form" ranks such as 'tree' and 'grass', or 'fish', 'bird'. Each of these contains generic ranks such as 'oak' and 'clover' or 'dog' and 'shark'. According to Berlin, these form the core of ethnobiological classifications. These generic species contain "folk-specific" ranks like 'white oak' or 'poodle', which in turn may be subdivided into "folk varietal" ranks (like 'toy poodle' or 'swamp white oak'). Taxonomies like these are hence based on relationships of contrasts and inclusion ("kind of" relations). Specific terms like 'oak' contrast with 'birch', for example, but are included within higher-level terms like 'tree' as the next hierarchical level in languages like English, where the latter term contrasts with terms like 'herb' or 'grass'.

As with Berlin and Kay's colour paradigm, models such as those defended in Brown (1984) or Berlin (1992) triggered a debate about the nature of folk taxonomies and the question of to what extent they are again culturally mediated.[3] Hunn (1985: 123) points out that there are two competing models of folk biological classification: The Taxonomic Hierarchy Model (parallel to a Linnaean taxonomy of plants, with a set of taxa specifiable by relations of affinity and contrast (defended in particular by Berlin), and the Natural Core Model (with protagonists like Hunn). With the latter conceptualization of folk biological taxonomies, one allows for gradable membership or categorial contiguity, and thereby for transitions; moreover, this model accounts for the fact that phenomena in the natural environment are not necessarily categorized (or lexicalized) and may be left unclassified instead. These two points are illustrated next.

Rather than having mutually exclusive taxa that jointly exhaust the domain, the Natural Core Model assumes that members are assigned a place in the category according to their degree of membership or to the features they share with the most typical or central members, rather than through discreteness. When looking at the category of 'birds' in English, for example, its members (e.g. 'ostrich', 'penguin', 'starling' or 'blackbird') are somewhat heterogeneous, i.e. they do not fulfil all the features on a checklist, like being able to fly. Apparently, some features are less salient than others.[4] Moreover, the same model allows for the allocation of intermediate taxa ('bats' also fly, but do not lay eggs, for example). Folk taxonomies show that life-form taxa may be biologically highly diverse, covering a wide range of generic taxa, as in Karam, a Trans-New Guinea language without a word corresponding to English 'animal' (as a unique beginner), where the term *as* refers to 'frog, small marsupial, rodent' (Bulmer and Tyler 1968). Atran et al. (2004) point out that for the Itza Maya villagers, typicality is based not on similarity but on knowledge of cultural ideals. Hence, the wild turkey is a typical bird because of its rich cultural significance, even though it is in no way most similar to other birds.

This again raises the question of to what extent classifications are essence based and reflect utilitarian factors (edible versus inedible, or poisonous versus non-poisonous). For speakers of the Central Khoisan language Khwe, the python is not a snake because it is eaten by humans, whereas (other) snakes are not (Matthias Brenzinger, personal communication).[5] For speakers of the Mayan language Tzeltal in Mexico, adult Lepidoptera (butterflies and moths) are of little interest. Their larvae, on the other hand, are carefully sorted into 16 terminal folk taxa, as some are edible, others attack crops, and still others acquire painful defensive ornamentation (Hunn 1985). Such examples support the conclusion that typicality is not based on similarity, but rather reflects the salience of or human interest in a species in a specific community. The Natural Core Model thus clearly provides a better account of folk taxonomies.

3 Critical Issues and Topics

Over the years, the "Berlin-and-Kay paradigm" on universals of colour has become a model for the nature–nurture debate in linguistic anthropology. "Universalists" hold that there are innate constraints, "relativists" hold that nature (or our cognitive system) may set its constraints but that nurture is far more important when it comes to explaining differences between languages and thereby between cultures. This also applies to the categorization of lexical domains such as bionomenclature, as we saw above. But there is another controversial issue, going back to the early days of linguistic anthropology, which has come to be known as "linguistic relativism" or the "Sapir-Whorf hypothesis", after two of its most influential protagonists, Edward Sapir (a student of Franz Boas) and his student Benjamin Whorf. Werner (1994: 3658) gives the following summary of this hypothesis:

> The categorial system of every language, including lower level grammatical and all lexical categories, points its speakers toward somewhat different evaluations of externally similar observations. Hence speakers of different languages have somewhat different views of the world, somewhat different habitual thought, and consequently their language and cultural knowledge are in a somewhat different relationship to each other. They don't live in the same world with different labels attached but in somewhat different worlds. The more dissimilar two languages are in their lexicon – that is, in conceptual and grammatical categories – the greater their tendency to embody different world views.

Whorf (1956), who was familiar with Einstein's relativity theory, referred to this phenomenon through the metaphor of "linguistic relativity". Deutscher (2010) gives a detailed historical account of this hypothesis.

It is important to keep in mind that specific concepts may exist in speech communities without a corresponding term in their language. D'Andrade (1995: 93–94) observes "that in a number of cultures there is no rank zero term for the plant domain. For example, there is no single term for "plant" in Tzeltal or Aguaruna. This does not necessarily mean that there is no concept for "plant". The evidence that such a concept can exist without a term is quite strong for both the Tzeltal and Aguaruna. First, in the systems investigated to date which lack a zero-level term, there are numerous terms for parts of plants and stages of plant growth that are applied *only* to plants. . . . In collecting more than 20,000 specimens, informants . . . never selected organisms *other* than plants . . . ; mushrooms and other fungi were not considered to fall within the domain . . . ."

And there are parallels from investigations on colours. Heider (1972) reports that Dani speakers she interviewed used the two terms whose focal meaning is 'black' and 'white' respectively, for 80 percent of the chips, with the remaining 20 percent given "non-basic" term names. These two global visual descriptors corresponding to 'white' and warmer colours like 'red' or 'yellow' on the one side, and 'black' or cooler colours like 'green' and 'blue' in English on the other, are:

(3)   *mili*   'light/warm'
       mola   'dark/cool'

In testing Dani speakers on their memory for colour, Heider (1972) found that they remembered best the colour chips that corresponded to the focals of the basic colour terms, in spite of having two basic colour terms in the sense of Berlin and Kay (1969).[6]

Nevertheless, there is also solid empirical evidence that we tend to take recourse to our primary language when it comes to assessing cognitive experiences. One piece of evidence comes from the so-called 'name strategy' of Kay and Kempton (1984). The authors asked speakers of Tarahumara, a Uto-Aztecan language spoken in Mexico, and speakers of American English to compare triads of colour chips and to come up with similarity judgements. Whereas English makes a lexical distinction between 'green' und 'blue', Tarahumara refers to these with one lexeme, *siyóname* 'grue'. The presence of the blue-green lexical category boundary caused speakers of English participating in the experiment to exaggerate the subjective distances of colours close to this boundary, whereas speakers of Tarahumara (as a language without a blue–green contrast) did not show this distorting effect.

Interestingly, such relationships between labelled categories and cognition extend beyond the lexical domain, as shown by Lucy (1992a, 1992b), who investigated the effects of grammatical distinctions on habitual thinking by conducting cognitive tests with speakers of English and the Mayan language Yucatec. English makes a clearcut distinction between countable and non-countable nouns; the former alternate between singular and plural, for example, whereas the latter do not. A language with numeral classifiers like Yucatec marks plurals only for nouns referring to animate entities. When enumerating nouns in this latter language, these require numeral classifiers (providing information about the shape and other perceptual qualities of the entity referred to), as in the following examples:

(4)   *'un-c'íit*   *há'as*   'one banana fruit'
       'un-wáal   *há'as*   'one banana leaf'
       'un-kúul   *há'as*   'one banana tree'

Nouns in Yucatec primarily denote substance (e.g. "banana-like" substance) rather than some object, as in the corresponding English translation ('banana leaf/fruit/tree'). Lucy's cognitive assessment tasks involved visual stimuli, whereby speakers were asked to describe what they saw in specific pictures and what they recalled after having viewed certain pictures; the same English and Yucatec speakers were also asked to judge which of several alternate versions of each picture was most similar to its original. Interestingly, English speakers attended relatively more to the shape of objects, in keeping with their ontological commitment to the primacy of "bodies", and Yucatec speakers relatively more to the material composition or substance of objects, again in accordance with the grammatical structure of this language.[7]

4 Current Contributions and Research

Whereas the investigation of language domains discussed above was part of the tool kit of cognitive anthropologists and anthropological linguists in the twentieth century, more recently cognitive linguists have started to play a key role.[8] This may be illustrated with a discussion of a further cognitive domain, that of spatial orientation and its linguistic reflexes. Traditionally, the conceptualization of space was thought to be a cognitive domain where little variation is found cross-linguistically. However, research on a range of languages and cultures across the world by a team of anthropologists, linguists and psychologists from the Max Planck Institute for Psycholinguistics (Nijmegen, the Netherlands) resulted in a different perspective. As shown by Levinson (2003), in his synopsis of the most important results of research initiated in the 1990s, languages use different frames of reference and non-linguistic cognition mirrors the systems available in the local language.

Speech communities may use a relative (viewer-centred) frame of reference or perspective to represent the location of objects. Hence the volume in which the present contribution is published may be found to the left or right, or in front or at the back of, the reader; alternatively, the volume may be up or down, for example on a shelf. This "egocentric" perspective contrasts with a so-called "allocentric" perspective, grouping together intrinsic and absolute frames of reference. We may, for example, project dimensions like front or back onto objects, which then receive an intrinsic front or back etc. Whereas speakers of English would refer to the side of an envelope on which the name of the addressee or receiver is written as the front, speakers of many African languages would rather call this the back, since the front is where the mouth or opening of the envelope is found. For speakers of the Dravidian language Tamil in India, turning left at the traffic lights would mean turning right for speakers of English, as for Tamil speakers traffic lights are seen as having a front (where the lights are) and consequently a left and a right.

The second type of allocentric orientation involves environment-centred perspectives, as shown in Levinson (2003). Such systems have been reported for Australian languages like Guugu Yimithirr, whose speakers prefer absolute frames of reference, i.e. roots describing spational direction, each covering quadrats of a hypothetical horizontal plane, as shown by Haviland (1998).

(5) *gungga-*   'northern edge'
    naga-   'eastern edge'
    jiba-   'southern edge'
    guwa-   'western edge'

Interesting from a typological perspective is the complete absence of relative terms and the very restricted use of intrinsic expressions like 'left' and 'right' in this language. The geocentric terms are used, not only in route directions but also to describe positions. In a standardized stimulus book shown to speakers, Guugu Yimithirr may describe a specific girl as 'crying nose to (i.e. facing) south', whereas speakers of English might describe her as 'crying while standing behind (or next to) a tree or standing next to or to the left of a tree'.[9]

Levinson (2003: 115–146) also shows how language may influence the way people think, memorize or reason about direction and spatial relations; see Foley (1997: 215–229) for a detailed discussion, also in relation to language acquisition.

Interestingly, human beings like to use these object-centred concepts (left/right, up/down, front/back) to designate cardinal directions, as shown by Brown (1983) for a variety of languages across the world. Examples include: in the Iroquoian language Mohawk 'east/down' and 'west/up', the Oceanic language Fijian 'east/upwards, 'west/down, below', or the Celtic language Cornish 'north/left', 'south/right'. The rationale behind this widespread tendency is the common (and presumably archaic) strategy in different speech communities to project oneself in a landscape and to conventionalize this projection, also in order to explain road maps, as the following example may help to show.

The Tima (whose language was discussed above with respect to colour terminology) live at the western edges of the Nuba Mountains, in Sudan. When facing east, speakers see the higher elevations of these mountains, where the sun rises, or 'where the mouth is', as Tima speakers would say. Consequently, the root for 'left' is used to designate 'north', whereas the root for 'right' (also meaning 'correct in a moral sense') also means 'south':

(6) dùkwààlí   'north, left'
    dùkòmál   'south, right'
    líŋéè   'east, up (lit. at the mouth)'
    líĥi   'west, down' (lit. on the ground)'

More recently, members of the Max Planck Institute for Psycholinguistics developed cognitive task methods (by way of stimuli kits) within the research programme "Categories across language and cognition", in order to investigate additional domains where interesting cross-linguistic differences are expected, e.g. for the perception of smell, taste, texture or geometric shape; see Senft (2012) for a discussion, also of the ecological validity (i.e. the limits) of such empirical methods. Smells have become the subject of taboo in westernized cultures, and consequently languages spoken by these communities tend to be poor in this respect, contrary to languages in, for example, the Philippines. With respect to taste, it has been claimed that we distinguish between five basic tastes: 'sweet', 'sour', 'bitter', 'salty', and 'umami' (a savoury taste). The first four of these are also distinguished in a language like Tima. This language does not have a lexeme describing 'umami', but it does have four additional terms describing other sensations (Dimmendaal 2015: 138–139):

(7) kààkààk   'bitter-sweet' (e.g. tea with little sugar)
    həlèhəlèm   'sweet' (e.g. of sugar cane)
    hùlùhùlùm   'sweet-salty' (e.g. of sour dough), 'sweet-sour' (e.g of a mango)
    dèkòdèkòk   'sourish'

What these and other examples from different lexical domains should make clear is that languages do not vary without constraint, but our current knowledge of the human cognitive system does not allow us to make interesting predictions on these variant categorizations (or the way we humans manipulate the meaning of words). Like with colour terminology or other lexical semantic fields, members of different speech communities may infuse specific distinctions with meaning and employ these in the course of "embodied practices", because they are relevant in their cultures.

5 Recommendations for Practice

Anthropology and linguistics as academic disciplines have inspired each other for more than a century now, also resulting in interesting "crossbreeding", as the seminal work of Boas, Greenberg, Lounsbury and other scientists discussed above and elsewhere in the present volume should have made clear. But protagonists of these disciplines, in their "promiscuous" scientific lifestyle, have also been looking for other "affines", to use a term from research on kinship systems, seeking comfort in disciplines such as statistics or formal logic, to mention but a few. Nevertheless, the close bond and interaction between the two disciplines remains. Visual anthropologists have used film in order to document cultural behaviour. More recently, linguists have initiated the use of new media in particular, in order to document languages that are in danger of becoming extinct in the near future.[10] Such multi-media documentation also provides new opportunities for the recording of lexical material related to semantic fields discussed in the present chapter, in combination with a visual representation by way of pictures. Transcribed and annotated video recordings provide an additional way of documenting folk biological reasoning and other relevant domains for different speech communities across the world.

6 Future Directions

Most speech communities (today as in the past) do not live "in vitro", and instead interact with speakers of other languages. Such multilingual situations usually result in the transfer or replication of linguistic features, including lexical categorizations. Hayward (1991) gives over forty examples from Ethiopia, illustrating metaphorical extensions shared between Cushitic, Omotic and Semitic languages, such as 'draw water', which also means 'copy, imitate'.[11] But this convergence also involves categorization of nature, e.g. the division between 'small birds' and 'large birds', or the description of skin colours, with separate terms for 'black, very dark', 'dark brown', and 'light brown'. These concepts are shared by these languages, although the actual terms used in these languages are not necessarily cognate; compare the words for 'small bird' in the Semitic language Amharic, *wäf*, with the corresponding word in the Cushitic language Oromo, *šimbira*, or the Omotic language Gamo, *kapó*.

State-building and the increasing role of national or official languages as well as lingua francas will probably result in a further reduction of linguistic diversity or obsolescence of languages in many parts of the world. One concomitant result of this globalization process will probably be a reduction in variation, also with regard to lexical categorizations; see Evans (2010) for a recent account. Such conceptual modifications can be observed with respect to various semantic fields in the lexicon of languages, for example with numeral systems, a domain not discussed above, again for reasons of space. Greenberg (1974) lists over fifty widespread features of numeral systems in languages, for example that there are four numbers that figure as fundamental bases in the numeral systems of the world (in order of frequency): 10, 20, 4 and 12. Kutsch Lojenga (1994) describes such a base-four system still known by older people speaking Ngiti, a Nilo-Saharan language spoken in Congo, where younger people have switched to a base-ten system. The base-four system was probably more widespread in the Central African region, as we find traces in many languages; compare, for example, the word for 'eight' in the Bantu language Swahili, *nane* from *na-ne*, 'and-four'.

Similar globalization effects may be observed with respect to colour, e.g. when languages borrow terms like 'blue' from influential lingua francas like English. Senft (2012) reports such a case from the Trobriands. As shown by Mietzner (2012), the crucial role of English in the educational system of countries like Kenya also affected the conceptualization of space, as in the Nilotic language Marakwet.

One important challenge facing the community of interested linguists and anthropologists will be the documentation, preferably by using new media, of cross-linguistic variation still observable in a quickly globalizing world.

Acknowledgment

I would like to thank Nancy Bonvillain for her comments on an earlier draft.

Notes

1 Colours vary along three dimensions: hue (or "colouredness") involving chromatic colours (like 'red' or 'yellow') and achromatic colours (those without hue, 'black' and 'white'), saturation (i.e. strength of

hue within a colour; pastel colours, for example, are desaturated) and brightness. The Munsell set of colour chips contains 320 colour chips of forty equally spaced hues and eight degrees of brightness, at maximum saturation, and nine chips of neutral hue (white, black and greys) (i.e. strength of hue within a colour; pastel colours, for example, are desaturated) and brightness.

2. Research for the documentation of the endangered language Tima was made possible through two grants from the Volkswagen Foundation (Germany) between 2006 and 2012, whose support is gratefully acknowledged.
3. Similar relativist responses have been formulated to so-called universals of kinship terminology, marking social rather than merely biological categories, and hence subject to cultural mediation, thereby supplementing biologically defined dimensions. See Chapter 5 of the present volume.
4. The notion "degree of membership" derives from fuzzy set theory in logic, whereas the concept of "most typical members" derives from prototype theory, as propagated in particular by Rosch (e.g. 1978). For a detailed discussion of these two theories (including some differences between the two), the interested reader is referred to López Rúa (2003: 60–136).
5. Matthias Brenzinger (pers. comm.) relates a further interesting experience while investigating bionomenclature in Khwe. When asking for the name of specific types of plants (as generic taxa), language helpers pointed out that they did not know, and that instead the owner of these plants should be asked.
6. The name Dani in fact refers to a cluster of languages spoken in Eastern Papua, Indonesia.
7. This raises the more general question of to what extent classifiers in languages (related to gender, or numeral, verbal, locative and deictic classifiers) reflect social order or are part of a grammatical system dividing referents into grammatical classes (expressing linguistic gender), an issue that cannot be further explored here for reasons of space. The interested reader is referred to Foley (1997: 230–245) and Aikhenvald (2012) for a discussion of these issues.
8. The research of cognitive anthropologists moved in another direction by focusing on notions of frames (representing stereotyped situations) or scripts (i.e. processing structures that help the inference of what will come next in a sequence of actions) in various cultures. See also Chapters 5 and 7 in the present volume.
9. Danzinger (2010) has argued for a fourth type of frame of reference (next to the absolutive, or numeral, verbal, locative and deictic classifiers) reflecting social order or part of a grammatical system dividing referents into grammatical classes (expressing linguistic gender), an issue which cannot be further explored here for reasons of space. The interested reader is referred to Foley (1997: 230–245) and Aikhenvald (2012) for a discussion of these issues.
10. See the documented material on various endangered languages across the world archived at the Max Plank Institute for Psycholinguistics: http://dobes.mpi.nl/archive_info/.
11. Intrafield metaphorical and metonymic extensions, i.e. extensions within the same semantic field (for example from 'eye' to 'face'), are common cross-linguistically. But so-called interfield extensions (i.e. between semantic fields, as with 'draw water' and 'copy, imitate' are usually culture specific; see Dimmendaal 2011: 115–122, 182–199) for a discussion.

References

Aikhenvald, Alexandra Y. 2012. Round women and long men: Shape, size, and the meanings of gender in New Guinea and beyond. *Anthropological Linguistics* 54(1): 33–86.
Atran, Scott. 1998. Folk biology and the anthropology of science: Cognitive universals and cultural particulars. *Behavioral and Brain Sciences* 21: 547–604.
Atran, Scott, Douglas Medin and Norbert Ross. 2004. Evolution and devolution of knowledge: A tale of two biologies. *Journal of the Royal Anthropological Institute* 10: 395–420.
Berlin, Brent. 1992. *Ethnobiological Classification: Principles of Categorization of Plants and Animals*. Princeton, NJ: Princeton University Press.
Berlin, Brent and Paul Kay. 1969. *Basic Color Terms: Their Universality and Evolution*. Berkeley and Los Angeles: University of California Press.
Brown, Cecil H. 1983. Where do cardinal direction terms come from? *Anthropological Linguistics* 25: 121–161.
_____. 1984. *Language and Living Things: Uniformities in Folk Classification and Naming*. New Brunswick: Rutgers University Press.
Bulmer, R. and M. Tyler. 1968. Karam classification of frogs. *Journal of Polynesian Society* 77: 333–385.
Conklin, Harold C. 1964. Hanunoo color categories. In Dell Hymes (ed.), *Language in Culture and Society: A Reader in Linguistics and Anthropology*, pp. 189–192. New York: Harper and Row.

____. 1980. *Folk Classification: A Topically Arranged Bibliography of Contemporary and Background References Through 1971*. Revised reprinting with author index. New Haven, CT: Department of Anthropology, Yale University.
Danziger, Eve, 2010. Deixis, gesture and cognition in spatial frame of reference typology. *Studies in Language 34*(1): 167–185.
De Valois, R. L. and G. H. Jacobs. 1968. Primate color vision. *Science 162*: 533–540.
Deutscher, Guy. 2010. *Through the Language Glass: Why the World Looks Different in Other Languages*. New York: Metropolitan Books and Henry Holt and Company.
Dimmendaal, Gerrit J. 2011. *Historical Linguistics and the Comparative Study of African Languages*. Amsterdam and Philadelphia: John Benjamins.
Dimmendaal, Gerrit J. 2015. *The Leopard's Spots: Essays on Language, Cognition and Culture*. Leiden: Brill.
Evans, Nicholas. 2010. *Dying Words: Endangered Languages and What They Have to Tell Us*. Oxford: Blackwell.
Foley, William A. 1997. *Anthropological Linguistics: An Introduction*. Oxford: Blackwell Publishers.
Greenberg, Joseph H. 1978. Generalizations about numeral systems. In Joseph H. Greenberg (ed.), *Universals of Human Language*, pp. 73–113. Cambridge, MA: MIT Press.
Harshberger, J. W. 1896. The purpose of ethnobotany. *Botanical Gazette 21*: 146–154.
Haviland, John B. 1998. Guugu Yimithirr cardinal directions. *Ethos 26*(1): 7–24.
Hayward, Richard. 1991. A propos patterns of lexicalization in the Ethiopian language area. *Afrikanistische Arbeitspapiere Sondernummer* 141–156.
Heider, E. 1972. Universals of color naming and memory. *Journal of Experimental Psychology 93*: 10–20.
Henrich, Joseph, Steven J. Heine, and Ara Norenzayan. 2010. The weirdest people in the world? *Behavioral and Brain Sciences 33*(2–3): 1–75.
Hunn, E. 1985. The utilitarian factor in folk biological classification. In Janet W. D. Dougherty (ed.), *Directions in Cognitive Anthropology*, pp. 117–140. Urbana and Chicago: University of Illinois Press.
Hymes, Dell. 1962. The ethnography of speaking. In T. Gladwin and W. C. Sturtevant (eds), *Anthropology and Human Behavior*, pp. 13–53. The Anthropology Society of Washington.
Kay, Paul, Brent Berlin and William Merrifield. 1991. Biocultural implications of color naming. *Journal of Linguistic Anthropology 1*: 12–25.
Kay, Paul and Chad K. McDaniel. 1978. The linguistic significance of the meanings of basic color terms. *Language 54*: 610–646.
Kay, Paul and Willett Kempton. 1984. What is the SapirWhorf hypothesis? *American Anthropologist 86*: 6579.
Kronenfeld, David B. 1996. *Plastic Glasses and Church Fathers: Semantic Extension from the Ethnoscience Tradition*. Oxford: Oxford University Press.
Kutsch Lojenga, Constance. 1994. *Ngiti: A Central-Sudanic Language of Zaire*. Cologne: Rüdiger Köppe.
Levinson, Stephen C. 2003. *Space in Language and Cognition: Explorations in Cognitive Diversity*. Cambridge: Cambridge University Press.
Lienhardt, G. 1961. *Divinity and Experience: The Religion of the Dinka*. Oxford: Clarendon Press.
López Rúa, Paula. 2003. *Birds, Colours and Prepositions: The Theory of Categorization and its Applications in Linguistics*. Munich: LINCOM.
Lounsbury, Floyd. 1956. A semantic analysis of Pawnee kinship usage. *Language 32*: 158–164.
Lucy, John A. 1992a. *Language Diversity and Thought: A Reformulation of the Linguistic Relativity Hypothesis*. Cambridge: Cambridge University Press.
____. 1992b. *Grammatical Categories and Cognition: A Case Study of the Linguistic Relativity Hypothesis*. Cambridge: Cambridge University Press.
MacLaury, Robert. 1992. From brightness to hue: An explanatory model of color-category evolution. *Current Anthropology 33*: 137–186.
Mathiot, Madeleine. 1962. Noun classes and folk taxonomy in Papago. *American Anthropologist 64*(2): 340–350.
Mietzner, Angelika. 2012. Spatial orientation in Nilotic languages and the forces of innovation. In Angelika Mietzner and Ulrike Claudi (eds), *Directionality in Grammar and Discourse: Case Studies from Africa*, pp. 165–175. Cologne: Rüdiger Köppe.
Newman, Paul. 1991. An interview with Joseph Greenberg. *Current Anthropology 32*: 453–467.
Quine, Willard Van Orman. 1960. *Word and Object*. Cambridge, MA: MIT Press.
Rosch, Eleanor. 1978. Principles of categorization. In Eleanor Rosch and L. Lloyd (eds), *Cognition and Categorization*, pp. 27–48. Hillsdale, NJ: Lawrence Erlbaum.

Schneider-Blum, Gertrud. 2013. *A Tima-English Dictionary. An Illustrated Lexicon of a Niger-Congo Language Spoken in the Nuba Mountains (Sudan)*. Cologne: Rüdiger Köppe.
Senft, Gunter. 2012. Referring to colour and taste in Kilivila. Stability and change in two lexical domains of sensory perception. In Andrea C. Schalley (ed.), *Practical Theories and Empirical Practice: A Linguistic Perspective*, pp. 71–98. Amsterdam and Philadelphia: John Benjamins.
Tornay, Serge (ed.). 1978. *Voir et nommer les couleurs*. Nanterre: Service de Publication du Laboratoire d'Ethnologie et de Sociologie comparative de l'Université de Paris X.
Werner, O. 1994. The Sapir-Whorf hypothesis. In R. E. Asher and J. M. Y. Simpson (eds), *The Encyclopedia of Language and Linguistics*, vol. 7, pp. 3656–3662. Oxford: Pergamon Press.
Whorf, Benjamin Lee. 1956. *Language, Thought, and Reality. Selected Writings of Benjamin Lee Whorf*, John Bissell Carroll (ed.). New York: Wiley.
Wierzbicka, Anne. 2005. There are no "color universals" but there are universals of visual semantics. *Anthropological Linguistics* 47: 217–244.

Further Reading

The intellectual and historical background to cognitive anthropology, whose adherents made important contributions to the topics discussed in the present chapter, is described in D'Andrade (1995) and Kronenfeld (1996). Conklin (1980) is a useful bibliography of references on topics such as kinship, bionomenclature, orientation, colour and sensual stimuli up to 1971. A more recent survey of these topics is found in López Rúa (2003). Readers may also want to consult Chapters 5–8 and 10–12 in Foley (1997).

3
Gesture

Jürgen Streeck

1 Introduction/Definitions

Setting aside its use in music, architecture, poetry, and visual art, the term 'gesture' is used in a number of interrelated ways:

(a) each muscular act, which may or may not be a component of a more complex muscular act, can be called a gesture: reaching for a glass is a gesture; the articulation of a language sound is an organized bundle of articulatory gestures (Browman & Goldstein 1990); a bounded intonation contour is a gesture. Gestures are the basic units of bodily action;
(b) a gesture is a discrete bodily act by which some social meaning is conveyed: bowing the head, winking, nodding;
(c) a gesture is any act that conveys social meanings of the kind body gestures also convey, i.e., showing deference or respect, recognition, or gratitude: giving flowers, sending a thank you note, forgiving a debt. It is a way of comporting oneself (cf. Latin *gerere*, to behave);
(d) a gesture is a communicative movement of the hand.

This article is only about gestures in sense (d).

Hand-gestures have recently moved center stage in the work and debates of several disciplines, including anthropology, evolutionary anthropology, linguistics, communication, psychology, philosophy, cognitive science, neuroscience, technology (human–machine interaction, robotics), design research, and research about instruction and education. A linguistic anthropologist who takes up the study of gesture at this time, however, would likely turn to the cumulative empirical research that has been conducted in the last decades about gesture as a *cultural praxis*. This could be found in historical work, as well as in the many studies of body motion and sense-making in embodied interaction in real-life settings, published by researchers in the ethnographic and 'naturalistic' (observation-based) study of social interaction. Research in this vein is informed by a view of gesture as a heterogeneous family of bodily meaning-making practices whose enactment and understanding is at each point shaped and constrained by context, firstly its place within multimodal 'packages' and sequences of action and utterance. That line of research will be the main focus of this overview.

2 Historical Perspectives

Gesture has usually played only a peripheral role in Western scholarship, relegated to a status far below spoken language. Gesture suffered the disadvantage of not being abstractable into letters. Plato was suspicious of all forms of mimesis, and so were the rhetoricians of Rome, concerned to separate the realm of persuasion, the speaker's rostrum, from that of illusion, the stage. But it was also a Roman rhetorician, Quintilianus, who, to ensure proper delivery, gave us the first, improbably precise accounts of gesture forms and their coordination with speech. Indeed, during some eras, gesture became noticed and drew attention to itself because it promised to reveal something profound about human civilization (for a more detailed and comprehensive review of the history of ideas on gesture see Kendon 1984; Bremmer & Roodenburg 1992). Until the turn of the twentieth century gesture was regarded as a property of the human species and seemed to prove universalism right: the ability to gesture-communicate with anyone, even in the absence of a common language – an experience frequently and wonderingly conveyed by explorers – demonstrated the 'psychic unity' of humankind. But then, in Boas' time, it turned into a marker of cultural difference.

Gesture has often been regarded as a phenomenon at the boundary of nature and culture: obviously intelligible to everyone in interactions across language boundaries, it seemed to transcend, and to have nothing to do with, what today is called 'culture', i.e., a people's distinct 'traits.' Inspired by reports by historians (Herodotus 1949) and reporters traveling with conquering armies (Xenophon 1962) about the success of gestural communication across language borders, guided by the ubiquitous model of the deaf, writers like Quintilianus (1922) regarded gestures of the hand as the common language of humankind. Quintilianus also subjected the *actio* (physical delivery), especially the hand-gestures, of orators to microscopic scrutiny, at a time of intense debate about bodily comportment – posture, gait, gesture – as an indicator of social class and political allegiance (Corbeill 2004). In the Middle Ages, at the time of the Inquisition, stereotypes about ethnic body motion styles served to identify non-believers, i.e., Jews (Schmitt 1990). During the Renaissance, gesture was intensely studied by painters, who developed increasingly refined methods for depicting gestures in their social contexts, using them as commonly known signs in their efforts to show 'legible interactions' (Gombrich 1982). The age of the Reformation and the Early Modern period produced ideologies of moderation and ritual exuberance dividing the Protestant North from the Catholic South, the impact of which might still be visible today (Burke 1992).

During the Enlightenment, when philosophers began to consider seriously reconstructing how humans acquired their modern faculties out of an assumed original natural state, gesture was seen as the natural state of communication at the threshold of culture- (i.e., language-) making (Condillac 1746; see Aarsleff 1974, 1976). In the nineteenth century, the idea that gesture might be the original language of humankind motivated empirical investigations into sign languages, notably those of the deaf. Gesture came into view as a window into human prehistory and the history of communication. Intrigued by the success of the Abbé de l'Épée to devise a manual communication system for his pupils at the School for the Deaf, the founders of the *Societé des observateurs de l'homme* in Paris in 1800 chose to make the collection of all sign languages of the world their first project (see Lane 1976), to uncover their common origin and traits. Tylor (1856), a founder of modern anthropology, pursued the project on a smaller scale by studying the pupils at the School for the Deaf in Berlin, in whose signs he believed to observe "survivals," i.e., vestiges from an earlier evolutionary stage. In a similar vein but with more attention to detail, Mallery investigated Plains Sign Language (1978a,b), a "savage" communication system, for the principles governing the formation of signs. He found that processes of metonymy and metaphor are abundant in the formation of sign language, anticipating insights that are also central in today's ground-breaking studies of language development and change (Heine, Claudi & Hünnemeyer, 1991; Heine & Kuteva, 2002). Similar observations had been made by the 'ethnographer of gesture' (Kendon 1995a), Andrea de Jorio in Naples in 1832 (De Jorio 2000). For Mallery and other nineteenth-century cultural evolutionists, metaphor betrays a primitive or infantile mode of thinking by analogy, but is also already a cultural phenomenon, as the diversity of metaphors in living languages and poetry demonstrates, a phenomenon 'in between', as should be expected from a 'savage culture' in between humanity's 'primitive' and 'civilized' stages of development. Darwin's (1872) theory of facial expression, that expressions originate as early parts of acts and 'project' an imminent action, became the point of departure for G. H. Mead's vision of a 'conversation of gestures', i.e., pre-symbolic interactions in which significant gestures and, eventually language, mind, and self evolve (Mead 1934). Mead (1909) developed his ideas about significant gestures and the social evolution of mind through a critique of the individualistic-psychological theory of W. Wundt (1911), who sought to explain their meanings as derived from affect-expressions.

Otherwise, in the twentieth century, beyond the occasional mention (e.g. Sapir 1991), gesture disappeared from the scientific landscape for a long time. Where it appeared, it was in the new light of Boasian 'relativistic' anthropology, not as a human universal, but as an embodiment of cultural difference. In his dissertation, originally entitled "Gesture and Environment" (1941), David Efron (1972), a student of Boas, presented the first and, for decades, unsurpassed field study of conversational gestures. Using multiple research methods including field observation, film, frequency counts, drawings, and diagrams, Efron compared the conversational handgestures made by first- and second-generation Eastern European Jews and Southern Italians in New York City. Giving precise descriptions of the movement patterns that conspire to create the phenotype of a sinuous and large gesture style among Italians, and of an angular style of more restricted movements among Jews, he typified the two styles as "physiographic" (depictive) and predominantly "ideographic" (or concrete and abstract), respectively, and attributed them as cultural group characteristics: Italians tend to depict the world; Jews trace the movement of thought. Italians and Jews of the second immigrant generation move toward local styles and make culturally hybrid gestures, so gesture style is no longer a strong predictor of ethnicity. And, being learned as it is, it cannot have any connection to a quasi-biological construct such as 'race': Efron thus succeeded in destroying the theory advanced by Nazi anthropologists that gesture and movement styles are innate properties of a 'race' (see also Boas 1932).

In the United States, after World War II, anthropologists, biologists, psychiatrists, and cyberneticists began to think about human communication as a self-regulating system; Gregory Bateson's ideas, especially, about contexts as frames, meta-communication, schismogenesis, and character formation (1936, 1972; Bateson & Mead 1942) would exert a lasting and profound influence on the development of 'naturalistic', observation-based research into interaction and bodily comportment in interaction. The 'ur-event' for the entire 'naturalistic' tradition of interaction research was the collaboration of an interdisciplinary group seeking to write the *Natural History of an Interview* (McQuown 1971), a quasi-psychiatric interview of a young woman conducted by Gregory Bateson. Bateson (1971), in his contribution to the unpublished report, entitled 'Communication', conceived of interactions as self-organizing systems within which the different bodily modalities play distinct and shifting parts; the meaning of each behavior is a function of its context, of which it simultaneously is a constitutive part. The anthropologist Birdwhistell (1979), a member of the Palo Alto group, subsequently embarked on the effort of describing 'American Movement' as if it were a language (see also Kendon & Sigmann 1996). But Birdwhistell failed to see that body motion, from gait to gesture, does not contain 'meaningless' elements equivalent to phonemes, but consists exclusively of indivisible intentional acts.

3 Critical Issues and Topics in Current Research

The following summary of the development of the field is grounded in a view of gesture as an embodied, cultural sense-making praxis that draws on all of the capacities of the human hand (Streeck 2009b, 2013b). From this perspective, a significant recent development is the increasing convergence between inquiries, not least by philosophers and anthropologists, into the cognitive or *living body* (Streeck 2013a), on the one hand, and ongoing observation-based research into the moment-by-moment organization of action and interaction, on the other. Intended to highlight the emergence of a unified perspective on the communicating human body, the following overview is divided into five sections: the first sketches the development of gesture studies in the context of interaction research; the second sketches the 'model of man', the conception of the living body, that emerges within phenomenology, 'embodied cognitive science', and 'neuro-phenomenology'; in the third section, I present a conception of gesture as distinctly *manual* cognitive and communicative activity; and in section four, I show how this conception, as well as others, account for *conceptualization* in gesture. The last section, which also serves as a limited account of methodology, shows how the praxeology of gesture and interaction meets with sociological inquiries in the wake of the *practice turn*, and describes how the analysis of gesture practices has become embedded in more-embracing studies of *multimodal* interaction, i.e., of activities in which gesture is not only coordinated with, and mediates between, other modalities (e.g. action, gaze, and speech), but operates within settings rich in meaningful artifacts and cognitive tools that offer and impose their own affordances and constraints upon the sense-making process (Streeck, Goodwin & LeBaron 2011). Everywhere, gesture shows the 'mindful' body in action, a body that, without being under the control of some 'executive system', can spontaneously perform abstract, yet meaningful, acts that provide sense for the situation and move it along.

Interaction Research

Research on hand-gestures in interaction is guided by the question 'why this now' (Schegloff & Sacks 1973: 299): what is the 'job' that the gesture accomplishes now, at this point in the interaction, where 'now' comprises such disparate concurrent behaviors as the participants' postural arrangement, their eye movements, and units of speech. The question has been approached in two very similar and yet easily compatible ways. Context analysis in the tradition of Bateson, notably by Kendon (1990), investigated how vocal and bodily communication modalities are coordinated in the production of sequences and contexts of interaction and subsequently focused on the coordination between the modalities' gesture and speech (Kendon 1972, 2004); conversation analysts sought to answer 'why this gesture now' by reference to the gesture's placement and production over time in unfolding turns at talk and sequences of action (Schegloff 1984).

In studies of movement coordination in interaction, beginning in the 1970s, Kendon (1970, 1972, 1980a, 1983) demonstrated that hand-gestures (defined as excursionary movements of the forelimbs that observers distinguish from instrumental actions) are organized into units and phrases which combine with thematic units and predications in discourse, and that the stroke of the gesture is timed so that it coincides with the main vocal accent, which in turn marks the focal word or phrase in a clause. Within extended utterances, changes in the motion pattern or hand-shape of a repetitive gesture mark changes in the speech act performed or display features of information structure (new/old information). Kendon conceives of gestures as parts of utterance action.

In Kendon's work (for an overview, see Streeck 2007), gesture has emerged as a cultural medium of communication that is functionally diverse, structured in describable ways, rich in symbolic strategies, and historically contingent (Kendon 2004). In data from England and Southern Italy, he identified 'gesture families' (such as one involving index-finger and thumb forming a ring, or one with the open hand held palm up) and showed the specific discourse function each member achieves (e.g. indicating specificity or presenting an object as an exemplar of a kind). Kendon's wide-ranging and extraordinarily precise studies encompass varieties of gesture such as pointing (Kendon & Versante 2003), and discourse-structuring gestures (Kendon 1995b), as well as ritual (alternate) and deaf sign languages (1980b, 1988).

Kendon's work reverberates across a diversity of research programs currently underway, including ethnographic studies of the conventionalization of gesture in the social life of communities (Brookes 2004); incipient sign languages (Sandler 2012); gesture-related communication systems such as Aboriginal sand stories (Green in press); the acquisition of gesture by very young children (Andrén 2010); and its roles in second-language acquisition (Gullberg 1998); as well as the production and roles of gesture in music-making (Rahaim 2008; Pearson 2013). But it has also informed the work of conversation-analytic work on gesture.

For conversation analysts, the question 'why this now' turns onto a unit's position or 'placement' in relation to emergent units of talk and sequences of action, including the turn, the turn-construction unit, and the transition place between turns at talk (for a more comprehensive overview on research on bodily action by conversation analysts, see Heath & Luff 2012). The question is how a gesture contributes to the 'project' of the turn, action, and sequence. A number of studies showed that hand gestures can be systematically deployed to manage turn-taking, for example, by foreshadowing the action for which a turn is requested (e.g. a telling, Streeck & Hartge 1992) or by displaying a participant's request for a turn (Mondada 2007a). For conversation analysts, the observation, previously reported (Dittman 1968; Kendon 1980a), that gestures which are demonstrably tied to units of speech ('lexical affiliates', Schegloff 1984), are often performed prior to the uttering of their speech affiliates, is of particular interest. A gesture may mark the opening up of a 'projection space', i.e. a stretch of talk during which something is 'in play.' Streeck (1995) has argued that the routine pre-positioning of gestures is social intelligence in action, as it offers the recipient opportunities to pre-adjust to upcoming action (the mechanism that Mead had described; Mead 1934); 'forward-gesturing' (Streeck 2009a) includes gestures that display an action type at turn-beginning, gestures that project a concept before it is uttered, and gestures that claim the turn before the speaker begins to speak.

In a seminal study, C. and M. Goodwin (1986) laid out the careful orchestration of body motion during word-searches and revealed the methodical sequential patterning of speech, gaze-shifts, and gestures in the collaborative solving of speaking problems. Streeck (1993) showed how attention to depictive gestures is organized: across language communities, depictive gestures are made salient by deictic speech elements (English '(like) this', German 'so', Japanese 'ko'), but they also receive the gaze of their maker, and two components thus combine to give the gesture prominence as object of attention (see also Gullberg & Holmqvist 1999). Interlocutors, through their gaze behavior and other responsive behaviors, can impact the ongoing construction of a gesture in collaborative efforts to work out 'what the gesture means. In sum, there are methodical practices by which interaction participants respectively mark differentially the significance of concurrent bodily action to concurrent talk (Goodwin 1986). Natural languages have evolved a number of ways of marking, indexing, or preparing embodied displays in the grammar of spoken utterances. In addition to deictic forms, these also include quotative verbs, i.e., verbs by which reported speech is launched. The recent American English quotative verb, 'be like', is an example: it prepares a bodily display (which then, literally, shows what the speaker 'was like' in the reported situation) and – impossible with its predecessor 'say' – anchors the display as a grammatical element in the talk. Today, even though more often than not 'be like' simply means 'say', the verb continues to offer the grammatical opportunity to enlist the body as narrative resource. Incidentally, 'like' is descended from a proto-Germanic word meaning 'body'; however, the lexicalization and grammaticalization of quotative forms often begin with a 'marker of embodiment' such as 'she was all like_' or 'she goes_ and I go_' (Streeck 2002).

In work by Christian Heath (1982, 1986, 1992, 2002), hand-gestures came into view as an *interaction resource*, i.e., as 'unit acts' with interactional affordances quite distinct from those of speech. (For example, they are rather immune to overlap.) Since the early 1980s, Heath has investigated how patients and doctors coordinate speech and body motion during medical encounters, specifically how patients manipulate physicians' attention through the spatial placement of gestures. To direct the attention of others is of course also the function of pointing gestures, which form the focus of an increasing number of studies across disciplines (Kita 2003). Linguistic anthropologists have played a leading role in this effort. Haviland (1993, 2000, 2003) and Levinson (Levinson & Wilkins 2006) investigated pointing and referential gestures ("small" pointing gestures indexing approximate locations of narrated events without directing visual attention to them) in communities whose languages have 'absolute' systems of spatial reference (i.e. relative locations are expressed in terms of cardinal directions) and showed that the precision in linguistic terms is matched by the precision with which gestures point to the actual locations where narrated events happened. Pointing gestures in these communities demonstrate that, as a result of ongoing dead-reckoning, members' bodies are continually attuned to where they are and in which precise cardinal direction they are facing.

The Living Body

Quite apart from these efforts to excavate the organization of sense-making in moment-by-moment interaction, philosophers, cognitive scientists, anthropologists, and sociologists since the 1990s have taken an interest in the body and its active role in social, cognitive, and cultural life. Although entirely independent endeavors, the two lines of inquiry nevertheless both trace their origin to phenomenology, that is, the sustained efforts by Heidegger (1962), and Merleau-Ponty (1962) to restitute the body to its proper place as an active, socialized, skilled, and cognizant participant in social and cognitive processes. Conversation analysts, through their ethnomethodological heritage, were more inclined to declare their indebtedness to A. Schütz' (1932) 'disembodied' phenomenology of social understanding. In contrast, the recent 'body turn' in various disciplines has led to a re-engagement with Heidegger's and Merleau-Ponty's account of human knowledge and consciousness as being grounded in the body's active, mindlessly mindful coping with the world. Bourdieu's conception of the *habitus* (Bourdieu 1977, 1990, 2000), derived from Husserl (2012) and Mauss (1973), is a case in point. Bourdieu defines habitus as

> systems of durable, transposable dispositions, structured structures predisposed to function as structuring structures, that is, as principles which generate and organize practices and representations that can be objectively adapted to their outcomes without presupposing a conscious aiming at ends or an express mastery of the operations necessary in order to attain them. Objectively 'regulated' and 'regular' without being in any way the product of obedience to rules, they can be collectively orchestrated without being the product of the organizing action of a conductor
>
> *Bourdieu (1990: 53)*

Among anthropologists, Ingold (2000, 2011) adopted a Heideggerian term to articulate a *dwelling perspective* on embodied culture, cognition, and communication, i.e., a perspective that analyzes them within the frame, and as products, of bodies' active engagements with, and transformations of, the material and social world. We do not face the objective world as observer-subjects, but become enmeshed with it in our contingent, physical, collaborative attempts to 'make do.' Gestures, as we will see, reflect this enmeshment vividly.

From the point of view of what we may call the 'new theory of embodiment', body motions are the most basic cognitive acts: cognition is motion and motion is cognition (Sheets-Johnstone 2012). Cognition is as much part of an amoeba's self-propelling away from poison (Thompson 2007) as it is of an ape's reaching for the right branch to hang from or a human making a gesture in conversation. This view of cognition as intrinsic to life is the main axiom of *neurophenomenology*, a surprising and productive collaboration between neuroscientists philosophers, among others, in which Heidegger's and Merleau-Ponty's vision enters a comfortable and mutually inspiring marriage with the biological conception of life as self-organization or auto-poesis (Maturana & Varela 1980; Varela, Thompson & Rosch 1991). One group of researchers chose the term *enaction* as a moniker for the entire research program (i.e., a view of cognition as enaction; Stewart, Gapenne & Di Paolo 2010) and emphasizes the interactional scaffolding of cognitive processes without, however, offering analyses of real-life 'socially shared cognition.' Not only gestures, then, but any living body motion 'picks out a significance' of the situation, 'couples' with selected parts of the environment, and by the same token, alters the situation for the actor. This should enable us to understand gesture on a continuum with other meaningful bodily actions performed by human bodies. In many children, the first steps that they take on their own come with a reaching action of the hands, as if grasping for the distant parent. Children's first gestures pick out, show, and shape the significances that the environment presently has for them. Zlatev (2003) has called these significances *values*. Gestures are meaningful by binding and incorporating values of the unfolding situation; this is what we can call their 'transcendence.'

Human Bodies and Their Gestures

As products of socialized living bodies, gestures are in the first place skilled physical actions, "techniques du corps" in Marcel Mauss' (1973) sense, a "manu-facture of meaning" (Streeck 2009b). To understand hand-gestures as living acts, we must understand what kind of an organ the human hand is. Four intertwined aspects of the hand are especially relevant: (a) that it has evolved as an organ of grasp (Marzke 1997; Napier 1980); (b) that it is also a complex, flexible, multi-sensory, and active cognitive organ (an organ of 'environmental cognition'; cf. Gibson 1962), which (c) does a great deal of its work autonomously, below the threshold of awareness and without executive control (Jeannerod 2006); and (d) that humans, as they invented gesture, inhabited a world made almost entirely by human hands. Provided we accept that gesture could not have evolved independently of the hands' world-making capacities, this has a number of implications for gesture: gesture should not only reflect the hands' ability to act, but also to feel and to make.

Hands are about things. They transcend themselves into the world by reaching for, taking, holding, handling, setting down, as well as making things. Their ability to hold, manipulate, and fabricate physical objects forms the arc of evolution of the human hand (Gehlen 1988), the most flexible and capable of all hands and the most distinct physical feature of the species. The grasping of an object is also one of the richest and most complex contacts that the human body has with its environment and is therefore an essential cognitive act: it is out of these acts, after all – discovering and making use of properties of matter while forming and putting together new things – that the world as we know it has arisen. Approached in this way, gestures of the hands show the living human body in its relatedness to its *Umwelt*.

Gesture is a heterogeneous medium, but it is possible to discern different *ecologies* in which gesture practices partake, and how they differentially participate in the communicative situation (Streeck 2009b). An ecological perspective gives us at least the following distinctions. Hand-gestures:

1. can reach out into the world at hand and disclose, enhance, and embellish, by handling, tapping, or otherwise 'marking up' features ('environmentally coupled gestures,' Goodwin 2007);
2. aim at the visible world and structure, disclose, and augment what is being seen (e.g., pointing, tracing);
3. conjure and depict phenomena that are not present, but referred to and described in the talk (depictive gesture);
4. conceptualize thematic content by casting it in terms of postures and actions of the hands;
5. embody and display (features of) the communicative *act* ('illocutionary' and 'discourse-structure marking' gestures, e.g. gestures of rejection and gestures projecting lists; Kendon 1995b); and
6. can be made to manage the actions of others.

For each of the orientations to the situation, there are distinct gestural practices. Thus, Wilkins (2003), Enfield (2009), and Cooperrider & Núñez (2012) have described pointing practices by body parts other than the hand (chin, lips, nose, eyes) and how members choose between them; as well as how pointing practices and linguistic practices of verbal deixis coordinate with them in situated, multimodal acts of object-identification (Enfield 2009; Stukenbrock 2009). Streeck (2008) has described various practices of gestural depiction, including handling (using), drawing, 'scaping,' modeling, and making, and argues that they reflect fundamental modes of *being* of the hand, i.e. their roles in our inhabiting a material world. Each person appears to possess a distinct, individuated repertoire of gesture practices, a gestural *habitus* (Bourdieu 1977), which may instantiate cultural and subcultural and class-based styles, but more so the *life-world* (Schütz 1932) that the individual inhabits and the way he or she makes that world through embodied communication.

For Marcel Mauss (1973), the French anthropologist, habitus was an ensemble of *techniques du corps*. It is in this sense we can apply the term *practice* to gesture: gesture is an ensemble of *techniques du corps*. For Edmund Husserl (2012), a habitus was simply a set of *I can's*, of tacitly known methods of action. A gestural practice is an "I can": a significant physical action one knows how to make and by which some other (social) act can be accomplished, or a method to complete a certain gesture task (e.g. a depiction). The gesturing hands are products and instruments of embodied cognitive activity, not signs to publicize an otherwise internal thought process.

Investigating gestures of the hands in this perspective, then, means to investigate how multiple sensory abilities and component skills, many of them derived from real-world action, come together in single meaning-making acts; to discern the effects they have and how they are understood within context; and to take stock of practices across individuals, groups, and cultures to discern some of their origins and distribution. Given that gesture is a highly individuated mode of communication, the practice approach has the advantage that it does not posit a shared code or shared rules as a precondition for understanding (Hanks 2005). Thus, it easily accommodates gesture's feature of being partly shared, partly idiosyncratic, and to likely include sediments from a wide range of sources and periods in history.

Gesture as Cultural Cognition

The hand's primordial capacity to handle, know, and make things is an essential condition for the emergence of gesture and a main source of its pictorial language and conceptualization patterns. Gesture is indeed, as Condillac (1756) had decreed, a *language of action*: apart from the fact that gesture is by definition physical action, Calbris (2011), Haviland (2013), Kendon (2009), Müller & Tag (2010), and Streeck (1996, 2009b), among others, have argued that many of its motor schemata are abstracted from *real-world* physical action: for example, many depictive, conceptual, and interaction-structuring ("pragmatic") gestures are formed by enactive schemata shared with manual actions in the world of things. In other words, gestures 'make sense of things' in terms of meaningful manual action patterns. As it were, whatever can be said, can be said by an act of the hand. Home-sign systems appear to be universally rooted in gestures that enact familiar actions of the hands (Haviland 2013). Calbris (2011), in her semiotic analysis of French conversational gestures, lays out the mechanism of metaphorical projection by which familiar action schemata (e.g. cutting) are transferred and structure diverse cognitive domains (e.g. the domain of discourse).

Cognitive linguists and psychologists see promise in gestures because they can be seen as bodily forms expressing body-based meanings, which otherwise appear as metonymies and metaphors in the lexicon of languages (Bressem & Müller 2014; Cientic & Müller 2009). What Lakoff & Johnson (1999) have called "image schemata," i.e., patterns of sensorimotor experience that also structure abstract cognitive domains, are made visible in the enacted bodily forms of gesture (Sweetser 1998). This framework is, unfortunately, occasionally stated in culture-free terms (Lakoff & Johnson 1999; Gallese & Lakoff 2005), as if 'conceptual metaphors' reflected universal experiential dispositions of the human body, rather than culture-specific ways of relying on bodily experience to structure and make sense of abstract experiential domains.

In contrast, Núñez & Sweetser (2006), studying the metaphorization of time, found, for example, that space can be used in radically different ways to represent time, depending upon the cognitive model (or "conceptual metaphor") prevailing in the culture. If the past and present are all we can know (or see), then the future must be behind us and we move backwards towards the future, keeping our constantly growing past in view. Pointing gestures that refer to the past, in Western societies always made to the back, are therefore made towards the space in front of the speaker among the Aymara of the South American highlands. Gesturing time is a rich site in which to study encultured bodies in action: Mandarin speakers are said to show time as growing from the bottom upwards, reflecting the orientation of the manual practice of writing, whereas speakers of Nheengatú in the Amazon gesture an arc with the index-finger across the sky, indicating both points in time and time's progression on the sun's path (see Cooperrider & Núñez 2009). While these practices reflect different cosmologies, they also show how cultural bodies position themselves in relation to the cosmos.

Goldin-Meadow (2003; see also Roth & Lawless 2000a,b), studied how gesture organizes conceptions of number and underwrites numerical operations. Whereas others have argued that gesture facilitates mathematical thinking by allowing subjects to "offload" cognitive matter to the hands (e.g. by "holding" a number in a positioning of fingers; cf. Wilson 2002) Núñez articulates the view that gestures demonstrate the bodily origin of mathematics (Núñez 2008; Lakoff & Núñez). Mathematics and science education are active sites of gesture research. Other cognitive domains in which metaphoric gestures have been studied include (the imagination of) language (in the explanations of university linguistics teachers discussing grammar); Mittelberg 2007).

4 Methodology and Current Research Directions

The praxeological perspective on gesture broadly aligns with the broader "practice turn" in the social sciences (Schatski, Knorr Cetina & Von Savigny 2001; Bourdieu 1990); sociologists working in this vein argue that practices are the "site of the social." What is considered a 'practice' varies widely, including what others (e.g. activity theorists) would call an 'activity' (e.g. auctioning off paintings). More often than not, the term indexes the entire *praxis* that makes up a community, such as 'writing code' or 'making Shaker furniture' (Schatzki 2001). In conversation analysis, in contrast, 'practice' means a single method by which a particular social action, or some part of it, is performed, for example, raising pitch on the penultimate syllable of a turn-construction unit to indicate imminent completion. But the scaleability of the term 'practice' is an advantage for the study of gesture, because we can meaningfully apply the term 'practice' to a variety of units of gestural action: the formation of a single gestural act, if it is routinized, is a practice. But building a gestural image by a succession of gestures is also a practice. Enlivening a diagram by gesture (Enfield 2003; Murphy 2005) is a practice (or group of practices), as is lip-pointing (Enfield 2001). What is common to all practice theories, apart from a foundation in phenomenology and Marx's historical materialism (see Engels 1963), is that they grant the body and its 'tacit knowledge' center stage as agent, repository, and reproducer of culture and social class.

But research in the wake of the practice turn does not have a discernible shared methodology to investigate embodied action. Much of the work is traditional ethnography, some of it is auto-ethnographic (Wacquant 2004), but the studies rarely capture human action at the level of detail, with the degree of precision, and supported by a growing body of empirical knowledge, as has the work of interaction researchers that follows proven methods of sequence- and context-analysis. This is why the praxeology of gesture is of wider relevance: it demonstrates the empirical scrutability of a paradigmatic domain of cultural action, a domain at the core of social life and shared practical knowledge.

Even though it has proven fruitful to focus research on only two or three communication modalities (e.g., gesture and speech, or gesture, speech, and gaze), face-to-face interaction is a *multimodal* event in which all (or most) sensory modalities are engaged. Researchers from Kendon onward have investigated gestures within the overall stream of interaction behavior. More recently the field has also realized that bodily interaction cannot be explicated without close attention to how it is embedded in, and alters, the material setting in which it takes place (Streeck, Goodwin & LeBaron 2011). Gestures often serve 'interstitial' functions, i.e. they connect diverse semiotic resources with one another, for example place-names and maps. They can also blend with the making of inscriptions such as diagrams, and with writing: the act of writing can be ritualized and thereby gesturalized; inscriptions can serve as reminders of the gestures by which they were made, and the meaning encapsulated in that act; and gestural writing motions can lend a phrase the weight of the written word (Streeck & Kallmeyer 2001). Goodwin has published a series of studies of 'environmentally coupled gestures' (Goodwin 2007), showing especially how indexical gestures link together visual perception, knowledge embodied in artifacts such as charts, maps, and computer screens, and the linguistic categories shared by the professional community (Goodwin 1994). He describes practices of tracing and highlighting by which archeologists, oceanographers, and expert witnesses structure participants' perception of a 'domain of scrutiny' (Goodwin 1995a; Goodwin & Goodwin 1996). The complexities of communication with exclusively indexical means become particularly visible in Goodwin's studies of the family interactions of an aphasic man (Goodwin 1995b, 2004), who, despite an active vocabulary of only two words, is able to continue to be a 'competent speaker' by relying on gesture, especially pointing gestures, and his family's incessant scaffolding and interpreting of his actions: making sense at every moment hinges on members' use of the entire array of semiotic resources that setting and sequence provide.

Some work-places and many instructional settings are particularly rich in environmentally coupled gestures, and various professional communities, of course, have their own 'movement vocabularies' or gesture practices. Thus, choreographers and dancers routinely rehearse pieces in the mode of 'marking', in which many energy-depleting motions are only indicated, i.e., gesturalized (Kirsh 2011). Sauer (2003) distinguishes two modes of gesturing in the communication of miners when they describe accidents or dangerous situations: a 'first person' mode, gestures made from the narrator's and/or character's viewpoint, and deployed in reports of the subjective, affect-laden experience of the life-threatening event; and a 'third person' mode, made at a distance from the speaker's body and implicated in the 'objective' analysis of the situation. Koschmann et al. (2007) and Mondada (2007b) have shown how collaborative work during surgery is mediated by 'minimized' gestures, with surgical instruments inside of, and referring to, the patient's organs. Music-making is another professional domain of great interest for research on gesture and multimodal communication: gestures, made with or without an instrument in hand, serve to manage the participation of ensemble members (Haviland 2011). Music-making is also the site of a particularly vivid manifestation of the *transmodal* capacities of gesture (Murphy 2012): the gestures of conductors synthesize desired dynamic features of sound (melody, changes in amplitude) and movement (rhythm) in motion-patterns that also direct and coordinate the action of multiple orchestra members (Sunakawa in prep); sound is construed by visible body motion, occasionally to spectacular effect (Rahaim 2008; Pearson 2013). During auctions, gestures serve to coordinate the actions of multiple participants, and they constitute 'illocutionary acts': the fall of the hammer signifies the completion of the transaction, and thus the instituting of the obligations that are implied by it (Heath 2013; Heath & Luff 2007). Few studies have been devoted to institutional uses of gesture, an indicator perhaps of the diminishing role of gesture in legal and other institutional contexts, where they were once, before the advent of print, indispensable (Hibbitts 1992; see also Allert's sociological analysis of the transaction incorporated in the Hitler salute, Allert 2008).

In the context of professional activity and instruction, gesture typically is an 'interstitial' practice that elaborates, and makes connections between, other modalities and semiotic resources. Its affordances for communication in the context of work are also grounded in their flexible temporality: a gesture can not only be slowed down or sped up to synchronize with speech and action, but also frozen and held, and thereby 'maintain' the situated sense enclosed in the gesture as long as it is required for the activity at hand. This can be of service during diagnostic, problem-solving, and instructional activities, for example, when a diagnostic category, a partial solution, or an intermediate concept is 'held' in a gesture and can 'remain active' for an extended period of time. Hand gestures thus become 'material anchors' of distributed cognitive processes, for example, by anchoring (and making accessible) 'conceptual blends' between cognitive domains (Hutchins 2005). By separating themselves from object-specific action, gestures become reusable. As Hutchins & Johnson (2009: 243) write, "putting signals into the world of action . . . creates the opportunity for the reuse of emergent structures as communicative forms. The appropriation of emergent structure is a valuable source of increased complexity in evolving systems." In other words, a situated enactive experience, once gesturalized, becomes available to be instantiated beyond the current situation, giving an emergent network of communicators another iterable sense-making device. The task for researchers is to understand *how* gestures do this work from moment to moment. Whatever the practices are in a given case, they are made possible by the unique materiality of the human hand, which, in interaction with the eye, can freely and easily alternate between, and synthesize, digital (the hand as index-finger), tactile, haptic, and visual modes of experience and representation (Deleuze 2003). The unsurpassed value of this ancient mode of communication is visible not least in such high-technology environments as airplane cockpits (Hutchins & Klausen 1996, Hutchins & Palen1997) and fMRI-scanners (Alacʸ 2011), all of which could not operate without living, spontaneous gesture.

Finally, gesture's capacities have been found to be at play wherever two or more people jointly imagine. Imagination has traditionally been conceived as a faculty of the individual mind. But many professions, as much as many lay conversations, center around joint imagining, for example, cosmetic surgeons, architects and product designers, who commonly imagine in teams and have to agree on imaginings with clients. Cosmetic surgeons manipulate the bodies of clients and mark them up by gestures in anticipation of their future shape (Mirivel 2011). Sketches rarely speak for themselves in the work of architects; the interstitial force of gesture is needed, for example, to add the third and fourth dimension to architectural blueprints by showing height and the movements of people through the structure. Arguably, part of the architectural design process takes place by sculpting volumes, suggesting walls, drawing, and landscaping 'in the air'; gesture is needed to incorporate space and to pre-experience and represent the subjective experience of a built structure (Murphy 2011). Nemirovsky, Kelton & Rhodehamel (2012: 130) define collective imagination broadly as "the embodied process of bringing objects and events into quasi-presence in social interaction" and emphasize the transformative dimension of gestures: rather than just representing or simulating (Hostetter & Alibali 2007) remembered actions, they often restructure and elaborate them, thus enabling collaborative imagining as "embodied narration of what might come to pass" (Murphy 2011).

References

Aarsleff, H. (1974). The tradition of Condillac: The problem of the origin of language in the eighteenth century and the debate in the Berlin Academy before Herder. In D. Hymes (ed.), *Studies in the History of Linguistics* (pp. 93–156). Bloomington: Indiana University Press.

Aarsleff, H. (1976). An outline of language origins theory since the Renaissance. *Annals of the New York Academy of Science, 280*, 4–13.

Alač, M. (2011). *Handling Digital Brains: A Laboratory Study of Multimodal Semiotic Interaction in the Age of Computers*. Cambridge, MA: MIT Press.

Alibali, M. W. & S. Kita (2010). Gesture highlights perceptually present information for speakers. *Gesture, 10*(1), 3–28.

Alkemeyer, T. (1997). Sport als Mimesis der Gesellschaft. Zur Aufführung des Sozialen im symbolischen Raum des Sports. *Zeitschrift für Semiotik*, 4, 365–396.

Alkemeyer, T. (2003). Bewegen als Kulturtechnik. *Neue Sammlung, 43*(3), 347–357.

Alkemeyer, T. (2004). Bewegung und Gesellschaft. Zur "Verkörperung" des Sozialen und zur Formung des Selbst in Sport und populärer Kultur. G. Klein (ed.), *Bewegung: Sozial- und kulturwissenschaftliche Konzepte*. Bielefeld: transcript, (pp. 43–78).

Alkemeyer, T. K. Brümmer, R. Kodalle, R. & T. Pille (2009). *Ordnung in Bewegung: Choreographien des Sozialen: Körper in Sport, Tanz, Arbeit und Bildung* (1st ed.). Bielefeld: transcript.

Allert, T. (2008). *The Hitler Salute. On the Meaning of a Gesture*. New York: Henry Holt & Company.

Andrén, M. (2010). *Children's Gestures from 18 to 30 Months* (Travaux de l'Institut de Linguistique de Lund, vol. 50). Lund: Lund University.

Bateson, G. (1958 [1936]). *Naven* (2nd ed.). Stanford: Stanford University Press.

Bateson, G. (1971). Communication. In N. McQuown (ed.), *The Natural History of an Interview* (vol. 95, Series XV). Chicago: Micro-fiche. University of Chicago Library.

Bateson, G. (1972). *Steps to an Ecology of Mind*. New York: Ballantine.

Bateson, G. & M. Mead (1942). *Balinese Character. A Photographic Analysis*. New York: New York Academy of Sciences.

Berger, C. & S. Schmidt (2009). Körperwissen und Bewegungslogik. Zu Status und Spezifik körperlicher Kompetenzen. In T. Alkemeyer, K. Brümmer, R. Kodalle & T. Pille (eds), *Ordnung in Bewegung: Choreographien des Sozialen: Körper in Sport, Tanz, Arbeit und Bildung* (1st ed.), pp. 65–90). Bielefeld: transcript.

Birdwhistell, R. (1972). A kinesic-linguistic exercise. In J. J. Gumperz & D. Hymes (eds), *Directions in Sociolinguistics* (pp. 381–404). New York: Holt, Rinehart, and Winston.

Birdwhistell, R. L. (1979). Toward analyzing American movement. In S. Weitz (ed.), *Nonverbal Communication. Readings with Commentary*. New York: Oxford University Press.

Boas, F. (1932). Rasse und Charakter. *Anthropologischer Anzeiger, 8*, 280–284.

Bolden, G. (2003). Multiple modalities in collaborative turn-sequences. *Gesture, 3*(2), 187–211.

Bourdieu, P. (1977). *Outline of a Theory of Practice*. Cambridge: Cambridge University Press.

Bourdieu, P. (1990). *The Logic of Practice*. Stanford: Stanford University Press.

Bourdieu, P. (2000). *Pascalian Mediations*. Oxford: Polity Press.

Bremmer, J. & H. Roodenburg (eds). (1992). *A Cultural History of Gesture*. Ithaca, NY: Cornell University Press.

Bressem, J., & Müller, C., (2014). The family of Away gestures: Negation, refusal, and negative assessment. In C. Müller, A. Cienki, E. Fricke, S. H. Ladewig, D. McNeill & J. Bressem (eds.), *Body Language Communication. An International Handbook on Multimodality in Human Interaction* (Vol. Volume 2, pp. 1592–1604). Berlin: Mouton de Gruyter.

Brookes, H. J. (2004). A repertoire of South African quotable gestures. *Journal of Linguistic Anthropology, 14*(2), 186–224.

Browman, C. P. & L. Goldstein (1990). Gestural structures: distinctiveness, phonological processes, and historical change. In I. G. Mattingly & M. Studdert-Kennedy (eds), *Modularity and the Motor Theory of Speech Perception*. Hillsdale, NJ: Lawrence Erlbaum.

Burke, P. (1992). The language of gesture in early modern Italy. In J. Bremmer & H. Roodenburg (eds), *A Cultural History of Gesture* (pp. 71–83). Ithaca, NY: Cornell University Press.

Calbris, G. (2008). From left to right: Coverbal gestures and their symbolic use of space. In A. Cienki & C. Müller (eds), *Metaphor and Gesture* (pp. 27–54). Amsterdam: Benjamins.

Calbris, G. (2011). *Elements of Meaning in Gesture*. Amsterdam: Benjamins.

Carpenter, M., J. Call, J. & M. Tomasello (2002). Understanding "prior intentions" enables two-year-olds to imitatively learn a complex task. *Child Dev, 73*(5), 1431–1441.

Cibulka, P. (2013). The writing hand: Some interactional workings of writing gestures in Japanese conversation. *Gesture, 13*(2), 166–162.

Cienki, A. & C. Müller (eds). (2009). *Metaphor and Gesture*. Amsterdam: Benjamins.

Condillac, E. (1746). *An essay on the origin of human knowledge, being a supplement to Mr. Locke's essay on the human understanding*. London: J. Noursse.

Cooperrider, K. & R. Nuñez (2009). Nose-pointing: Notes on a facial gesture in Papua New Guinea. *Gesture, 12*(2), 103–129.

Corbeill, A. (2004). *Nature Embodied: Gesture in Ancient Rome*. Princeton: Princeton University Press.

Darwin, C. (1955 [1872]). *The Expression of Emotions in Animals and Man*. New York: Philosophical Society.

De Jorio, A. (2000 [1832]). *Gesture in Naples and Gesture in Classical Antiquity*. Bloomington: Indiana University Press.

Deleuze, G. (2003). *Francis Bacon: The Logic of Sensation*. Minneapolis: University of Minnesota Press.

Dittmann, A. I. (1968). Speech and body motion. *Paper presented at the Research Conference on Interview Behavior*. Baltimore, MD: University of Maryland, April 22.

Efron, D. (1972 [1941]). *Gesture, Race and Culture*. The Hague: Mouton.

Enfield, N. J. (2001). 'Lip-pointing': A discussion of form and function with reference to data from Laos. *Gesture, 1*(2), 185–212.

Enfield, N. J. (2003). Producing and editing gestural diagrams using co-speech gesture: Spatializing non-spatial relations in explanations of kinship in Laos. *Journal of Linguistic Anthropology, 13*, 7–50.

Enfield, N. J. (2009). *The Anatomy of Meaning*. Cambridge: Cambridge University Press.

Engels, F. (1963). Über historischen Materialismus. *Marx-Engels Werke*, vol. 22. Berlin.

Gallese, V. & G. Lakoff (2005). The brain's concepts: The role of the sensory-motor system in conceptual knowledge. *Cognitive Neuropsychology, 22*(3/4), 455–479.

Gehlen, A. (1988 [1958]). *Man. His Nature and Place in the World*. New York: Columbia University Press.

Gibson, J. J. (1962). Observations on active touch. *Psychological Review, 69*, 477–491.

Goldin-Meadow, S. (2003). *Hearing Gesture: How our Hands Help us Think*. Cambridge, MA: Belknap Press of Harvard University Press.

Gombrich, E. H. (1982). *The Image and the Eye*. London: Phaidon.

Goodwin, C. (1986). Gesture as a resource for the organization of mutual orientation. *Semiotica, 62*(1–2), 29–49.

Goodwin, C. (1994). Professional Vision. *American Anthropologist, 96*(3), 606–633.
Goodwin, C. (1995a). Seeing in depth. *Social Studies of Science, 25*, 237–274.
Goodwin, C. (1995b). Co-constructing meaning in conversations with an aphasic man. *Research on Language and Social Interaction, 28*(3), 233–260.
Goodwin, C. (2004). A competent speaker who can't speak: The social life of aphasia. *Journal of Linguistic Anthropology, 14*(2), 151–170.
Goodwin, C. (2007). Environmentally coupled gestures. In S. D. Duncan, J. Cassell & E. T. Levy (eds), *Gesture and the Dynamic Dimension of Language: Essays in Honor of David McNeill* (pp. 195–212). Philadelphia: Benjamins B.V.
Goodwin, C. & M. H. Goodwin (1986). Gesture and coparticipation in the activity of searching for a word. *Semiotica, 62*(1–2), 51–75.
Goodwin, C. & M. H. Goodwin (1996). Seeing as situated activity: Formulating planes. In Y. Engeström & D. Middleton (eds), *Cognition and Communication at Work* (pp. 61–95). Cambridge: Cambridge University Press.
Green, J. (in press) *Drawn from the Ground: Sound, Sign and Inscription in Central Australian Sand Stories.* Cambridge: Cambridge University Press.
Gullberg, M. (1998). *Gesture as a Communication Strategy in Second Language Discourse.* Lund: Lund University Press.
Gullberg, M. & K. Holmqvist (1999). Keeping an eye on gestures: Visual perception of gestures in face-to-face communication. *Pragmatics and Cognition, 7*(1), 35–63.
Hanks, W. F. (2005). Pierre Bourdieu and the practices of language. *Annual Review of Anthropology, 34*, 67–83.
Haviland, J. B. (1993). Anchoring, iconicity, and orientation in Guugu Yimidhirr pointing gestures. *Journal of Linguistic Anthropology, 3*, 3–45.
Haviland, J. B. (2000). Pointing, gesture spaces, and mental maps. In D. McNeill (ed.), *Language and Gesture* (pp. 13–46). Cambridge: Cambridge University Press.
Haviland, J. B. (2003). How to point in Zinancantan. In S. Kita (ed.), *Pointing: Where Language, Culture, and Cognition Meet* (pp. 39–70). Mahwah, NJ: Lawrence Erlbaum.
Haviland, J. B. (2011). Musical spaces. In J. Streeck, C. Goodwin & C. LeBaron (eds), *Embodied Interaction. Language and Body in the Material World* (pp. 289–304). New York: Cambridge University Press.
Haviland, J. B. (2013). The emerging grammar of nouns in a first generation sign language: Specification, iconicity, and syntax. *Gesture, 13*(3), 309–353.
Heath, Christian (1982). The display of recipiency: An instance of sequential relationship in speech and body movement. *Semiotica, 42*(2–4): 147–161.
Heath, Christian (1986). *Body Movement and Speech in Medical Interaction.* Cambridge: Cambridge University Press
Heath, Christian (1992). Gesture's discreet tasks: Multiple relevancies in visual conduct and in the contextualisation of language. In P. Auer, A. di Luzio (eds), *The Contextualisation of Language* (pp. 101–128). Amsterdam: John Benjamins.
Heath, Christian (2002). Demonstrative suffering: the gestural (re)embodiment of symptoms. *Journal of Communication, 52*: 597–617.
Heath, Christian (2013). *The Dynamics of Auction: Social Interaction and the Sale of Fine Art and Antiques.* Cambridge: Cambridge University Press.
Heath, Christian & Paul Luff (2007). Gesture and institutional interaction: Figuring bids in auctions of fine art and antiques, *Gesture, 7*(2): 215–240
Heath, C. & Paul Luff (2012). Embodied action and organizational activity. In J. Sidnell & T. Stivers (eds), *The Handbook of Conversation Analysis* (pp. 283–307). Chichester: Blackwell.
Heidegger, M. (1962 [1926]). *Being and Time.* New York: Harper and Row.
Heine, B., U. Claudi & F. Hünnemeyer (1997). *Cognitive Foundations of Grammar.* Oxford: Oxford University Press.
Heine, B. & T. Kuteva. (2002). *World Lexicon of Grammaticalization.* Cambridge: Cambridge University Press.
Herodotus (1949). *Herodotus.* Oxford: Clarendon Press.
Hibbitts, B. J. (1992). "Coming to our senses": Communication and legal expression in performance cultures. *Emory Law Journal, 41*(4), 973–960.
Hostetter, A. B. & M. W. Alibali, (2007). Raise your hand if you're spatial: Relations between verbal and spatial skills and gesture production. *Gesture, 7*(1), 73–96.
Husserl, E. (2012 [1912]). *Ideas: General Introduction to Pure Phenomenology.* Hoboken: Taylor & Francis.
Hutchins, E. (2005). Material anchors for conceptual blends. *Journal of Pragmatics, 37*, 1555–1577.
Hutchins, E. & C. M. Johnson (2009). Modeling the emergence of language as an embodied collective cognitive activity. *Topics in Cognitive Science, 1*, 523–546.

Hutchins, E. & T. Klausen (1996). Distributed cognition in an airline cockpit. In Y. Engeström & D. Middleton (eds), *Cognition and Communication at Work* (pp. 15–34). Cambridge: Cambridge University Press.

Hutchins, E. & L. Palen (1997). Constructing meaning from space, gesture, and speech. In L. Resnick, R. Säljö, C. Pontecorvo & B. Burge (eds), *Discourse, Tools, and Reasoning* (pp. 23–40). New York: Springer Verlag.

Ingold, T. (2000). *The Perception of the Environment: Essays on Livelihood, Dwelling and Skill.* London; New York: Routledge.

Ingold, T. (2011). *Being Alive. Essays on Movement, Knowledge, and Description.* London: Routledge.

Jeannerod, M. (2006). *Motor Cognition. What Actions Tell the Self.* Oxford: Oxford University Press.

Kendon, A. (1970). Movement coordination in social interaction: some examples described. *Acta Psychologica, 32,* 100–125.

Kendon, A. (1972). Some relationships between body motion and speech. In A. Seigmann (ed.), *Studies in Dyadic Communication* (pp. 177–210). Elmsford, NY: Pergamon Press.

Kendon, A. (1980a). Gesticulation and speech: Two aspects of the process of utterance. In M. R. Kay (ed.), *The Relationship between Verbal and Nonverbal Behavior.* The Hague: Mouton.

Kendon, A. (1980b). A description of a deaf-mute sign language from the Enga Province of Papua New Guinea with some comparative discussion. Part II: The semiotic functioning of Enga signs. *Semiotica, 32,* 81–117.

Kendon, A. (1983). Gesture and speech: How they interact. In J. M. Wiemann & R. P. Harrison (eds), *Nonverbal Interaction* (pp. 13–45). Beverly Hills: Sage.

Kendon, A. (1984). Did gesture have the happiness to escape the curse at the confusion of Babel? In A. Wolfgang (ed.), *Nonverbal Behavior: Perspectives, Applications, Intercultural Insights* (pp. 75–114). Lewiston, NJ: C. J. Hogreve.

Kendon, A. (1988). *Sign Languages of Aboriginal Australia.* Cambridge: Cambridge University Press.

Kendon, A. (1990). *Conducting Interaction.* Cambridge: Cambridge University Press.

Kendon, A. (1995a). Andrea de Jorio – The first ethnographer of gesture? *Visual Anthropology, 7,* 371–390.

Kendon, A. (1995b). Gestures as illocutionary and discourse structure markers in Southern Italian conversation. *Journal of Pragmatics, 23*(3), 247–279.

Kendon, A. (2004). *Gesture: Visible Action as Utterance.* Cambridge: Cambridge University Press.

Kendon, A. (2009). Manual actions, speech and the nature of language. In D. Gambarara & A. Givigliano (eds), *Origine e sviluppo del linguaggio, fra teoria e storia. Società di Filosofia del Linguaggio, atti del XV congresso nazionale.Arcavata di Rende (CS), 15–17 settembre 2008* (pp. 19–33). Rome: Aracne editrice.

Kendon, A. (2012). Language and kinesic complexity: Reflections on 'Dedicated gesture and the emergence of sign language. *Gesture, 12*(3), 308–326.

Kendon, A. & S. J. Sigman (1996). Ray L. Birdwhistell 1918–1994. *Semiotica, 112*(3/4), 231–261.

Kendon, A. & L. Versante (2003). Pointing by hand in "Neapolitan". In S. Kita (ed.), *Pointing: Where Language, Culture, and Cognition Meet* (pp. 109–138). Mawah, NJ: Lawrence Erlbaum.

Kirsh, David (2011). How marking in dance constitutes thinking with the body. *Versus: Quaderni di Studii Semotici, 113–15,* 179–210.

Kita, S. (2003). *Pointing: where Language, Culture, and Cognition Meet.* Mahwah, NJ: Lawrence Erlbaum Associates.

Koschmann, T., C. D. LeBaron, C. Goodwin, A. Zemel, & G. Dunnington (2007). Formulating the triangle of doom. *Gesture, 7*(1), 97–117.

Lakoff, G. & M. Johnson (1999). *Philosophy in the Flesh.* Chicago: University of Chicago Press.

Lakoff, G. & R. E. Nuñez (2000). *Where Mathematics Comes from: How the Embodied Mind Brings Mathematics into Being.* New York: Basic Books.

Lane, H. (1976). *The Wild Boy of Aveyron.* Cambridge, MA: Harvard University Press.

Levinson, S. C. & D.Wilkins (eds). (2006). *Grammars of Space.* Cambridge, New York: Cambridge University Press.

Mallery, G. (1978a). The gesture speech of man. In D. J. Umiker-Sebeok & T. A. Sebeok (eds), *Aboriginal Sign Languages of the Americas and Australia* (pp. 407–437). New York: Plenum Press.

Mallery, G. (1978b [1880]). Introduction to the study of sign language among the North American Indians as illustrating the gesture speech of mankind. In D. J. Umiker-Sebeok & T. A. Sebeok (eds), *Aboriginal Sign Languages of the Americas and Australia* (pp. 291–310). New York: Plenum Press.

Marzke, M. (1997). Precision grips, hand morphology, and tools. *American Journal of Physical Anthropology, 102,* 91–110.

Maturana, H. R. & F. J.Varela (1980). *Autopoiesis and Cognition.The Realization of the Living.* Dordrecht: Reidel.

Mauss, M. (1973 [1935]). The techniques of the body. *Economy and Society, 2*(1), 70–88.

McNeill, D. (1992). *Hand and Mind. What Gestures Reveal about Thought*. Chicago: University of Chicago Press.
McQuown, N. (ed.) (1971). *The Natural History of an Interview* (vol. 95, series XV). Chicago: University of Chicago Library.
Mead, G. H. (1909). Social psychology as a counterpart to physiological psychology. *Psychological Bulletin*, 6, 401–408.
Mead, G. H. (1934). *Mind, Self and Society*. Chicago: University of Chicago Press.
Merleau-Ponty. M. (1962). *Phenomenology of Perception*. London: Routledge.
Mirivel, J. (2011). Embodied arguments: Verbal claims and bodily evidence. In J. Streeck, C. Goodwin & C. LeBaron (eds), *Embodied Interaction. Language and Body in the Material World* (pp. 243–254). Cambridge: Cambridge University Press.
Mittelberg, I. (2007). Percian semiotics meets conceptual metaphor. Iconic modes in gestural representations of grammar. In A. Cienki & C. Müller (eds), *Metaphor and Gesture* (pp. 115–154). Amsterdam: Benjamins B.V.
Mondada. Lorenza (2007a) Multimodal resources for turn-taking: pointing and the emergence of possible next speakers. *Discourse Studies 9*(2): 194–225.
Mondada, L. (2007b). Operating together through videoconference: Members' procedures for accomplishing a common space of action. In S. Hester & D. Francis (eds), *Orders of Ordinary Action. Respecifying Sociological Knowledge* (pp. 51–68). Guildford, UK: Ashgate.
Müller, C. & S. Tag (2010). The dynamics of metaphor: Foregrounding and activating metaphoricity in conversational interaction. *Cognitive Semiotics*, 6, 85–120.
Murphy, K. M. (2005). Collaborative imagining: The interactive uses of gestures, talk, and graphic representation in architectural practice. *Semiotica*, 156, 113–145.
Murphy, K. M. (2011). Building stories: The embodied narration of what might come to pass. In J. Streeck, C. Goodwin, & C. D. LeBaron (eds), *Embodied Interaction. Language and Body in the Material World* (pp. 243–253). Cambridge: Cambridge University Press.
Murphy, K. M. (2012). Transmodality and temporality in design interactions. *Journal of Pragmatics*, 44, 1966–1981.
Napier, J. (1980). *Hands*. New York: Pantheon.
Nemirovsky, R., M. L. Kelton, & B. Rhodehamel (2012). Gesture and imagination: On the constitution and uses of phantasms. *Gesture*, 12(12), 130–165.
Nuñez, R. (2008). A fresh look at the foundations of mathematics: Gesture and the psychological reality of conceptual metaphor. In A. Cienki & C. Müller (eds), *Metaphor and Gesture* (pp. 55–93). Amsterdam: Benjamins.
Nuñez, R. & G. Lakoff (2005). The cognitive foundations of mathematics: The role of conceptual metaphor. In J. Campbell (ed.), *Handbook of Mathematical Cognition* (pp. 109–124). New York: Psychology Press.
Nuñez, R. & E. Sweetser (2006). With the future behind them: Convergent evidence from language and gesture in the crosslinguistic comparison of spatial construals of time. *Cognitive Science*, 30, 401–450.
Pearson, L. (2013). Gesture and the sonic event in Karnatak music. *Empirical Musicology Review*, 8(1), 2–14.
Quintilianus, M. F. (1922 [100]). *The Institutio Oratoria of Quintilian* H. E. Butler (trans.), vol. IV. London: Heinemann.
Rahaim, M. (2008). Gesture and melody in Indian vocal music. *Gesture*, 8(3), 325–347.
Roth, W. M. & D. V. Lawless (2000a). Scientific investigations, metaphorical gestures, and the emergence of abstract scientific concepts. *Learning and Instruction*, 12, 285–304.
Roth, W. M. & D. V. Lawless (2002b). When up is down and down is up: Body orientation, proximity, and gestures as resources. *Language in Society*, 31, 1–28.
Sandler, W. (2012). Dedicated gestures and the emergence of sign language. *Gesture*, 12(3), 265–307.
Sapir, E. (1991 [1927]). The unconscious patterning of behavior in society. In D. Mandelbaum (ed.), *Selected Writings of Edward Sapir*. Berkeley: University of California Press.
Sauer, B. (2003). *The Rhetoric of Risk. Technical Documentation in Hazardous Environments*. Mahwah, NJ: Lawrence Erlbaum.
Schatzki, T. R. (2001). *The Site of the Social : A Philosophical Account of the Constitution of Social Life and Change*. University Park: Pennsylvania State University Press.
Schatzki, T.R., K. Knorr Cetina, & E. Eike von Savigny (eds) (2001). *The Practice Turn in Contemporary Theory*. London: Routledge.
Schegloff, E. A. (1984). On some gestures' relation to talk. In J. M. Atkinson & J. Heritage (eds), *Structures of Social Action* (pp. 266–295). Cambridge: Cambridge University Press.

Schegloff, E. A. & H. Sacks (1973). Opening up closings. *Semiotica, 8*(4), 289–327.
Schmitt, J. C. (1990). *La raison des gestes dans l'Occident médiéval*. Paris: Gallimard.
Sheets-Johnstone, M. (2012). *The Primacy of Movement* (2nd ed.). Amsterdam: Benjamins.
Skiveland, R. O. & R. Ogden (2012). Holding gestures across turns: Moments to generate shared understanding. *Gesture, 12*(2), 166–199.
Stewart, J., O. Gapenne, & E. Di Paolo (eds). (2010). *Enaction. Toward a New Paradigm for Cognitive Science*. Cambridge MA: Harvard University Press.
Streeck, J. (1993). Gesture as communication I: Its coordination with gaze and speech. *Communication Monographs, 60* (December 1993), 275–299.
Streeck, J. (1995). On projection. In E. Goody (ed.), *Social Intelligence and Interaction* (pp. 87–110). Cambridge: Cambridge University Press.
Streeck, J. (2002). Grammars, words, and embodied meanings. On the evolution and uses of *so* and *like*. *Journal of Communication, 52*(3), 581–596.
Streeck, J. (2007). Homo faber's gestures. Review article on A. Kendon, Gesture: Visible Action as Utterance. *Journal of Linguistic Anthropology*, 130–140.
Streeck, J. (2008). Depicting by gestures. *Gesture, 8*(3), 285–301.
Streeck, J. (2009a). Forward-gesturing. *Discourse Processes, 45*(3/4), 161–179.
Streeck, J. (2009b). *Gesturecraft. The Manu-facture of Meaning*. Amsterdam: Benjamins.
Streeck, J. (2013a). Interaction and the living body. *Journal of Pragmatics, 46*, 69–90.
Streeck, J. (2013b). Praxeology of gesture. In C. Müller, A. Cienki, E. Fricke, S. Ladewig, D. McNeill, & S. Tessendorf (eds), *Handbook Body Language Communication. An International Handbook on Multimodality in Human Interaction*, vol. 1 (pp. 674–685). Berlin: de Gruyter.
Streeck, J. & U. Hartge (1992). Previews: Gestures at the transition place. In P. Auer & A. di Luzio (eds), *The Contextualization of Language* (pp. 138–158). Amsterdam: Benjamins.
Streeck, J. & W. Kallmeyer (2001). Interaction by inscription. *Journal of Pragmatics, 33*(4), 465–490.
Streeck, J., C. Goodwin & C. LeBaron (2011). Embodied interaction in the material world: An introduction. In J. Streeck, C. Goodwin & C. LeBaron (eds), *Embodied Interaction. Language and Body in the Material World*. New York: Cambridge University Press.
Stukenbrock, A. (2009). Referenz durch Zeigen: Zur Theorie der Deixis. *Deutsche Sprache, 37*, 289–315.
Sweetser, E. (1998). Regular metaphoricity in gesture: Bodily-based models of speech interaction. *Actes du 16e Congrès des Linguistes (CD ROM)*. London: Elsevier.
Thompson, E. (2007). *Mind in Life*. Cambridge, MA: Belknap Press of Harvard University Press.
Tylor, E. (1856). *Researches into the Early History of Mankind*. Chicago: The University of Chicago Press.
Varela, F. J., E. Thompson & E. Rosch (1991). *The Embodied Mind. Cognitive Science and Human Experience*. Cambridge, MA: The MIT Press.
Wacquant, L. (2004). *Body and Soul. Notebooks of an Apprentice Boxer*. Oxford: Oxford University Press.
Wilkins, D. (2003). Why pointing with the index finger is not a universal (in sociocultural and semiotic terms). In S. Kita (ed.), *Pointing: Where Language, Culture, and Cognition Meet* (pp. 171–216). Mahwah, NJ: Lawrence Erlbaum Associates.
Wilson, M. (2002). Six views of embodied cognition. *Psychonomic Bulletin and Review, 9*, 625–636.
Wundt, W. ([1975] 1911). *Völkerpsychologie. Eine Untersuchung der Entwicklungsgesetze von Sprache, Mythus und Sitte*. Aalen: Scientia Verlag.
Xenophon. (1962). *Anabasis*. Norman, OK: University of Oklahoma Press.
Zlatev, J. (2003). Meaning life (+ culture). An outline of a unified bioiculturaltheory of meaning. *Evolution of Communication, 4*(2), 253–296.

Further Reading

Calbris, G. (2011). *Elements of Meaning in Gesture*. Amsterdam: Benjamins B.V.
Goldin-Meadow, S. (2003). *Hearing Gesture: How our Hands Help us Think*. Cambridge, MA: Belknap Press of Harvard University Press.
Liebal, K., Müller, C., & Pika, S. (eds) (2005). *Gestural Communication in Nonhuman and Human Primates*. Special Issue of GESTURE, 5, 1/2.
McNeill, D. (2005). *Gesture and Thought*. Chicago: University of Chicago Press.

4
The Social Imaginary, Unspoken in Verbal Art

Bruce Mannheim

> por medio de los cantares y cuentos conservan muchas idolatrías y fantásticas grandezas de sus antepasados, de que resulta aborrecer a los españoles [by means of song and story they preserve many idolatries and fantastic greatnesses of their ancestors, from which comes hatred for the Spaniards]
>
> Concolorcorvo, *El lazarillo de ciegos caminantes (1773: 369)*

1 Introduction: The Social Imaginary

Central to social life is the construction of a "social imaginary," a set of interpretive images, figures, and forms that project an implicit social ontology, sanctioning everyday understandings and making sense of them in deeply institutional terms. In a passage that recalls Sapir's (1929: 162) observation that grammatical categories project a compulsive reality for speakers of a language, Cornelius Castoriadis (1975: 293) argues that the social imaginary is radically compulsive, such that "society could not recognize itself as making itself, as institution of itself, as self-institution."[1] It is in analogy with Sapir's view that what there is – social and otherwise – is built up out of the compulsory categories with which everyday interactions are structured that I find Castoriadis compelling; analogously, the roots of the social ontology are to be found in everyday practices, some apparently inconsequential from a material standpoint, such that even the most inconsequential are imbued politically (Canessa 2012). Where I find Castoriadis less than compelling is the sense I have that the social imaginary is, for him, a substitute for what North American anthropologists traditionally called "culture," and that, for all that, he is simply proposing another arch-cultural view of social life decades after we anthropologists gave them up. I am unsettled by the claim that – according to Castoriadis – the social imaginary functions beyond any semiotic means, much as I sympathize with his observation that the language of 1960s French *sémiologie* was incapable of encompassing it. Finally, the social imaginary seems to me to be much more fragile than Castoriadis imagined it to be, much more susceptible to conjunctural events, and much more contested. Consider the following: seven years into a bloody and seemingly unshakeable military dictatorship, designed to "reorganize" Argentine society and remake the Argentine person (Feierstein 2014), when the military abruptly returned to barracks after losing the war over the Malvinas (Falkland) Islands; the cry of "*saqueo popular*" ("people's looting" – in contrast to the looting carried out by elites) as residents of the marginal slums of Caracas descended on the shops of central Caracas in February 1989 (Coronil and Skurski 1991: 316–22); and two seven-year-olds in Lima, Peru in the 1980s talking about a nearby car-bomb with the same matter-of-factness that two seven-year-olds in San Francisco would talk about – what, a temblor? – to get a sense of the fragility of the social worlds that we take for granted.

This chapter explores the construction of the social imaginary in Southern Peruvian Quechua myths and songs as both a tacit folk sociology of everyday life and a powerful critique of forms of domination in modern Peruvian society, in which Southern Peruvian Quechua speakers are oppressed linguistically, culturally, and economically. Although these myths and songs often deal in explicit fantasy, including supernatural beings, anthropomorphic animals, fantastic events, and exaggerated sorrow and loss, the social imaginary is constructed tacitly, in the background of these verbal forms. The social imaginary is multiplex, responding not only to the basic forms of social relations and agropastoral production among Quechua-speaking peasants and herders, but also to the ways in which interactions with state institutions and with non-Quechuas impinge on their everyday lives (see Huayhua, this volume), the imagery of one fading seamlessly into the imagery of the other. A Quechua-speaking peasant once explained to me that one needed to render cult to a Saint not only to make certain that the crops would continue to grow and the herds continue to increase, but also so that the Saint could act as your attorney after death. She envisioned the hereafter as a massive state bureaucracy, requiring an attorney to guide you through the maze of legal petitions and other paperwork. "Don't you know the prayer?" she asked, "'The Lord is my advocate'" (Lamentations 3: 58). It is in its multiplex nature that the social imaginary is distinctive.

When I say that the social imaginary is multiplex, I also mean to evoke W. E. B. DuBois notion of "double consciousness, the sense of always looking at oneself through the eyes of others, of always measuring one's soul by the tape of a world that looks on in amused contempt and pity" (1903: 45).[2] Like African Americans in DuBois time and today, Southern Peruvian Quechuas are forced – not requested, not encouraged, not strategically drawn, but forced – to engage a social world that, through linguistic and other forms of institutional discrimination, and through physical and sexually mediated violence, they experience as cruel and arbitrary. One result is that the contexts of their domination are taken for granted, much as the moral evaluation of Latin Peru filters through the ways in which the events that take place within these myths and songs are understood. That they are open to multiple resonances has perhaps more to do with the moral ambiguity and fragmentation of the social ontology than with ambiguity inherent in the discourses themselves (but see Mannheim 1998).

In this chapter I discuss three linguistic and literary mechanisms by which the social imaginary is shaped: (1) presupposition, in which tacit assumptions can be calculated from what is said; (2) implicature, in which the social imaginary is calculated from the way it is said; and (3) and pragmatic lamination, in which the imaginary is constructed through ambiguities in the way in which one speech event is embedded within another. All the texts that I discuss date to the late 1970s, a period in which Peru was ruled by a nationalist military government that poured forth a public rhetoric of the power of a state in which the people were united behind the armed forces. It is important that I emphasize this because the social imaginary contained within some of the texts projects a powerful state and potent civil institutions. In the years following the return of the military to the barracks, the relative power of the state was squandered by a succession of corrupt civilian governments, by utter collapse of the economy, and by a debilitating civil war. In contemporary Peru, the state might operate in ways that are just as arbitrary and bureaucratic, but which have far less potency, since over the years the state has successively yielded effective control over national territory to two insurrectionist movements, to banditry, and to concessions in favour of foreign extractive industries. In line with my argument that the social imaginary is eminently conjunctural, I would expect that work with similar verbal performances today would reveal quite a different social ontology. The texts that I discuss also represent moments of social dissonance, revealing tears in the social fabric, rather than – as Malinowski (1922: 338, 1926: 39) famously suggested – "giving dignity and importance to an institution." Verbal art has a capacity for social reflexivity; at the same time as it entertains, it stealthily unveils the tacit assumptions and moral evaluations of social fissures (Scott 1990), always partial, and always tied into the specific instances of talk and interaction, drawing on complex and subtle mechanisms of linguistic and interactional structure (Gal 1995).

2 Main Research Methods

My approach is to use texts or discourses as a sedimented archive, "because," as Sherzer (1987: 296) suggests, "discourse is the nexus, the actual and concrete expression of the language–culture–society relationship," standing in the same habitus-like relationship to the culture's ontology as grammatical categories (Hill and Mannheim 1992: 398–9). As with grammatical categories, it is not the abstract form of the texts but their existence as concrete, historically, and socially situated performances that allows them to play this role (Bauman 1975, Bauman and Briggs 1990: esp. 78–80, Hill 1995, Tedlock 1983, and Urban 1991).[3] As I hope to show here, the pragmatics of performance plays a crucial role in reproducing the social imaginary. Thus any historical reconstruction of the Quechua textual archive must interpret the texts through an ethnographically oriented hermeneutic, "over the shoulders" of the people who perform them (see Tedlock 1983: ch.4; 1987).

Since the evidence I use comes entirely from language, there is a key point of method that needs to be discussed. It has been traditional in successive generations of anthropologists to reduce evidence from language to conscious ideas about social life. A particularly influential formulation of this point of view was the philosopher Susanne Langer's (1941: 76–89) distinction between *discursive* and *presentational* forms: discursive forms explicit propositions apprehended sequentially; presentational forms tacit and apprehended simultaneously. Langer, a philosopher of art, argued that presentational forms were as available to rigorous analysis as the discursive forms that were grist for the mill for philosophers. Liberating as her analysis was for philosophers of art, her view of language was reductionist: conscious, propositional, and denotational. With the growth of linguistic anthropology since the 1980s, we have learned that these are just small parts of the complex, socially embedded, material practice – central to formulating and reproducing social relations and institutions. The problem is that Langer's formulation was absorbed into the scholarly zeitgeist and was especially influential in the formulation and growth of interpretative anthropology. It has burrowed into the methodology of social and cultural anthropologists so deeply that it has been echoed over the years – right up to the present time– in works as prominent as R. Rappaport (1974), Moore and Meyerhoff (1977), Kapferer (1991: 287–8), Tambiah (1990: 95–7), Gell (1999: 6ff.), and Descola (2013: 121–6).

In this chapter, I will show that language plays an essential role in constructing a social imaginary in Southern Peruvian Quechua narratives and songs, though one that makes hash of the distinction between discursive and presentational forms. The social imaginary is constructed directly through talk, and propositionally – in song and narrative – but below the threshold of consciousness. Although I am considering them in special circumstances – song and narrative – there is nothing special about them. They draw on pragmatic mechanisms that are fully routine – that is to say, they pervade all talk, under all circumstances.

2.1 Presupposition

The first linguistic mechanism that I discuss is formal presupposition, in which the tacit assumptions of an utterance are embedded in (and possibly tangential to) the overt assertions being made in the utterance. There is a long tradition of analysis of presupposition in philosophy and in linguistic semantics, so that its formal properties are well understood. There is a much shallower tradition among anthropologists of examining the social and cultural uses of presupposition, and here the work of Gumperz (1981) on the role of presupposition clashes in cross-cultural misunderstanding and that of McClendon (1977) on the place of cultural presupposition in the interpretation of narrative stand out. As an informal characterization of presupposition, Chierchia and McConnell-Ginet (1990: 280) describe the relationship between an utterance S and its associated presupposition p as follows:

> [an utterance of] a sentence S presupposes a proposition p if (the utterance of) S implies p and further implies that p is somehow already part of the background against which S is considered, that considering S at all involves taking p for granted.

Thus, for any utterance that has not been framed conversationally (or through specific literary devices) as contrary-to-fact, for a listener to attend seriously to the content of the utterance would be to acquiesce in its presuppositions. Here we have a conversational device that is like grammatical categories in projecting an ontology in several respects. First, the projection takes place in everyday speech, outside of the conscious awareness of the speaker. Second, under ordinary circumstances, the listener acquiesces in the ontological projection of the presupposition in a routine, automatized fashion. The major difference between grammatical categories and formal presuppositions is that grammatical categories are habitual, used over and over in countless situations, and achieve a degree of automatization that presuppositions lack. Philosophers are fond of presenting "trick sentences" like "When did you stop drinking?" as examples, but the fact of the matter is that for even the most routine utterances to be intelligible, they must be rife with presuppositions of all kinds, and in the business of everyday life we are continually buying into other people's presuppositions and other people's assumptions about what the world is like. Presuppositions are a crucial vector of contagion in the epidemiology of knowledge (Sperber 1991, Enfield 2007, Kockleman 2013).

There is a straightforward test for determining whether the implication of an utterance is a presupposition. An implication is a presupposition if it is taken for granted in an assertion, its denial when it is questioned, and when it is offered as the hypothetical assumption. Thus, not only does the question "When did you stop drinking?" presuppose that you (at the very least) used to drink, but so does the assertion, "You stopped drinking," its denial "You didn't stop drinking," and its use as a hypothetical assumption, "Were you to stop drinking, you'd face up to the misery that your life really is." Some presuppositions, such as the "drinking" one, are easier to challenge than others, but the default is to acquiesce in them.

As an example of the role of presupposition in reproducing the social imaginary, consider a Quechua popular song that could be heard frequently on the radio during the late 1970s in Southern Peru.[4] It opens with the image of a thrush that is being held in the capital city, Lima, as a prisoner, captured for gathering and spilling the flowers of the broad bean plant. The inscribed speaker then says that he too is in Lima, for "stealing" one Masiya's daughter; as he addresses himself to her he sings,

> 'Cause of you, I'm a soldier
> 'Cause of you, I'm a grunt (*cachaco*)

For a young man from rural Peru, the army is anything but a career. Only those young men who are too poor (or too out of sorts) to buy their way out of a "universal" draft actually serve; the young man's fate is closer to the thrush's than might appear at first. Here I do not want to discuss the complexities of the framing of the story line that I just told you. Rather, I want to focus on the opening quatrain.

Chuchiku   Lima–pi–ña–s   prisu
thrush   Lima–in–already–reportive prisoner
It is said that the thrush is already imprisoned in Lima

Chuchiku   Lima–pi–ña–s   prisu
thrush   Lima–in–already–reportive prisoner
It is said that the thrush is already imprisoned in Lima

Hawas–pa   t'ika–cha–n   palla–ri–sqa–n–manta,   chuchiku
Favas–of   flower–diminutive–it's   gather–begin–past participle–it's–about   thrush
For gathering fava flowers, thrush

Hawas–pa   t'ika–cha–n   wisñi–ru–sqa–n–manta,   chuchiku
Favas–of   flower–diminutive–it's   spill–purposefully–past participle–it's–about   thrush
For spilling fava flowers, thrush

To the peasant listener of the song these lines work on the presupposition that the Peruvian government can arrest birds for doing what comes naturally, for gathering and spilling bean flowers. The presupposition remains invariant even when the assertion is denied: "Chuchiku mana Limapiraqsi prisu/hawaspa t'ikachan pallarisqanmanta," "It is said that the thrush isn't yet imprisoned in Lima for gathering bean flowers" has exactly the same presupposition. In turn, the presupposition hooks the interpretation of the last couplet, in which – though not by presupposition – the arrest of birds for gathering flowers is analogized to the recruitment of peasant men into military service through a draft that equally reflects the arbitrary and unfair power of the government. I want to call your attention to the innocuousness of the figure through which a politically charged presupposition is conveyed to its listeners, below their thresholds of awareness, a point that is quite tangential to the overt content of the figure.

2.2 Implicature

The second mechanism I discuss by which the social imaginary is shaped is implicature, in which the social imaginary is calculated from the way an utterance is said. Closely related to presupposition, implicature was identified by the philosopher Paul Grice, who observed that as a socially concerted action, conversation must follow certain principles of cooperation, which when violated trigger an interpretative uptake on the part of the addressee.[5] According to Grice (1975: 45), conversation is regulated by a general principle of cooperation:

> Make your conversational contribution such as is required, at the stage at which it occurs, by the accepted purpose or direction of the talk exchange in which you are engaged.

For example, Grice defines a conversational maxim of quantity:

1 Make your contribution as informative as required (for the current purposes of the exchange).
2 Do not make your contribution more informative than is required.

Though these look like explicit social norms, they are not. Rather, they are violated repeatedly in the course of ordinary interaction, and serve as a ground for other participants in an interaction to interpret the speaker's talk. While the speaker might deliberately manipulate their speech to trigger implicatures in the other participants, ordinarily they slip beneath the threshold of awareness of all concerned. Here is an example that lies on the borderline between routine use of implicatures and conscious manipulation.

When I bought my first banjo, a friend told me to watch out if one of the features listed for a model was that it had five pegs, since it meant they were not mechanical pegs. In offering that insight, he was applying the principle of quantity, and from the absence of additional information concluded something about the quality of the banjo. Notice that like presupposition, implicatures are normally processed tacitly as part of the process of interpreting the utterance. Even though Grice's conversational maxims are flouted more often than followed, the implicatures that result from either following or flouting the maxims are inescapable if the utterance is to be attended to at all. For example, Susan Harding (1987) interviewed an evangelical minister, who testified about how his life – auto repairs and fast cars – was transformed when he was called to ministry. After the interview, she drove off in her car and skidded, prompting her to ask herself, "What is God trying to tell me?" In order for her to attend to the minister's narrative of salvation, laden with automotive imagery, she was forced – through implicature – to buy into many of its assumptions.

From an ethnographic view, the status of implicature is much more in question than that of presupposition. Grice himself regarded the cooperative principle and the maxims to be at the basis of all conversation, but as Elinor Ochs (1977) has observed, the principles and their application vary considerably across cultures and, within cultures, across contexts. From a universalist vantage, Sperber and Wilson (1986) have reformulated the Gricean mechanisms into a global model of conversational inference based on the principle of relevance. Both Ochs's and Sperber and Wilson's critiques of Grice concern his specific formulations of the maxims, though not the basic phenomenon.

My example is from a story, recorded by Alejandro Ortíz (1973: 176–83) that frames the relationship of linguistic domination of Quechua speakers by Spanish speakers as a conflict between two moral regimes with distinct ontological grounds. Quechua speakers regard their language as consubstantial with the world, and an integral part of ordinary relationships that Quechua-speaking smallholders have with each other and with their lands. Spanish, on the other hand is a language of predatory mercantilism – as we shall see, even the language is bought and sold, and control of a larger vocabulary in Spanish is a direct index of wealth. Moreover, the Spanish language itself is an instrument of coercive power. (I have discussed this story and its implications in greater detail in Mannheim 1991.)

> A community in Huanta, in highland Peru, is threatened with judicial confiscation of their very livelihood, the land, by a local landowner. The landowner is able to grab the lands because he speaks Spanish and is therefore capable of mobilizing judicial power on his behalf. The peasants, who don't speak Spanish, have no means with which to defend themselves. They recognize their disadvantage and select some members of their community to go to the capital, Lima, to buy some Spanish talk. But Spanish proves to be costly. When the peasants arrive in Lima, they stay with someone from their village, who cheats them by speaking Spanish. When they finally do manage to buy Spanish talk, they discover that they have only

enough money to buy three phrases. They head toward Huanta with their three phrases when they come upon a freshly killed corpse. When the police arrive to investigate, they, being Native Andeans on the scene of the crime, are immediately implicated. But the three peasants know what they must do to defend themselves from the accusations – they use the phrases of Spanish that they bought, thinking that they'll be rewarded for it. One police officer asks them who committed the crime, and one peasant answers, "We did." Another asks why they did it, and another peasant answers, "Because we wanted to." The third officer tells them that they are under arrest, and they answer, "That's what we deserve." The entire scene repeats itself when they are brought before a judge, and they are sentenced to prison. And what of the other villagers, who were unable to use Spanish to defend themselves?

On a superficial reading, this story is about three country rubes that go to the big city, are cheated by their countryman, and get in over their heads because they pretend to be something they are not: Spanish speakers. But there is more going on than that, as much in what the story assumes about the social world as in what it states explicitly. Spanish is associated with state and judicial power, a power that is experienced as arbitrary by the Runa. The landowner is able to pursue his ambition of seizing the lands of the community by speaking Spanish and is thereby able to mobilize judicial power on his behalf. The person in Lima from their village is able to raise the price of Spanish arbitrarily and to cheat his countrymen by switching from Quechua to Spanish. The Civil Guards speak to the Quechua speakers in Spanish, "causing us to spill out our insides," they say. They try to respond in Spanish, but are taken off by the Civil Guards anyway. The judge speaks to them in Spanish and sentences them to prison, during a court procedure that they can't understand. The Quechua speakers regard their own possession of a word and two phrases of Spanish as equally magical talismans that they can use to defend themselves from the arbitrary power of Spanish words and from Latin Peru. They assume that the power is invested in the words themselves.

Moreover, Spanish is not learned the way Quechua is. Rather, it is bought and sold. Here is where the implicature example comes in. In planning to go to Lima to buy Spanish the peasants say that they *also* will buy Spanish, a piece of information that is conveyed by a single suffix, *pis*.

Castellano rimayqa ancha caron kasqa/ It was too expensive to buy Spanish (Ortíz 1973: 176–80)

Wawqi-cha,	huq hacendado-m		
Brother-diminutive	one landlord-assertion		
común allpa-nchik-ta	huchu-yku-wa -cha-ka	-n	-chik-ña
common lands-our-accusative (includes addressee)	small-dir-to us-make-middle voice– person	3rd–	plural-already
castellanota	rima- spa	-n	chay-mi
Spanish-accusative	speak-gerund	-3rd person	that-assertion
nuqayku	-pas	hamu-rqa-ni	castellano rantiq
we (excludes addressee)	-also person	come-past-1st	Spanish buy-agentive
defende-ku	-na	-y	-paq.
defend-middle-nominal-1st person-purpose			

"Little brother, this landlord has already made us shrink our common lands by speaking Spanish, so we *also* have come to buy Spanish."

According to Grice's maxim of quantity:

Do not make your information more informative than required;

the listener can infer what the speaker has "implicated," namely that the landlord also learned Spanish by buying it, but in enormous quantities.

In this story, told to amuse rather than horrify, Quechua speakers have developed an entire social ontology, communicated tacitly, as the listeners unpack the presuppositions and implicatures lying just beneath the narrative line. Spanish is pure artifice, associated with state power, especially with the concentration of power and wealth in the capital city, Lima. Spanish can be bought and sold there so, in order to win their court case, the Huanta peasants go to the Peruvian capital Lima, not to appeal to the national political authorities, but to buy Spanish.

It is important to point out that both forms of inference that I have discussed here interpenetrate. The implicature that the landowner bought Spanish can only be understood through the associated presupposition that Spanish is indeed bought and sold, among other things making possession of Spanish a direct index of wealth and power. Similarly, in the song that I used as an example of presupposition, the analogy between the soldier and the thrush is made on the basis of the conversational maxim of relevance, triggering the analogy as a form of implicature. In both cases, the inferential processes triggered by normal semantic and pragmatic processes of interpretation play powerful roles in shaping the social imaginary of the speakers.

2.3 Interactional Lamination

Presupposition and implicature are two forms of tacit inference that are primarily propositional, although in aggregate they can have far-reaching effects in establishing the social ontology that forms a ground for the rest of social life. When we look at real time interaction, both these forms of inference operate at the same time, interlocking with each other and with tacit inferences promoted by the structure of the social interaction itself. Social interaction is layered or *laminated,* and in this section I consider the ways in which interactional lamination promotes tacit inferences in ways that are similar to presupposition and implicature, and so reproduces the social landscape in which the interaction takes place. Because the text I discuss was produced between two particular individuals, we are fully woven into the social ontology that unfolds through the narrative, in both the telling and the way it is taken up.

A traditional way of looking at talk is as "communication" between two autonomous individuals who "exchange words" (e.g. Saussure 1915: 27). In the traditional framework, talk appears to be linear and flat. In fact, even the simplest conversation is complexly organized and stratified; the participants in the conversation move through the strata in real time, calibrating – and recalibrating – their relationships to each other as they do so. Talk moves through stratified layers (Ahearn 1999, Kockelman 2013: 148ff.). Each layer has what the sociologist Erving Goffman called a "participation framework," in which the traditional "speaker" and "hearer" are decomposed into multiple roles (e.g. Goffman 1979, Levinson 1988, Hanks 1990, Irvine 1996). Goffman (1974: 517ff.), for example, advocated dividing the traditional notion of "speaker" into four:

- *author,* the person who scripts the words;
- *principal,* the party "committed to the position attested to by the content of the utterance" (Irvine 1996: 132);
- *animator,* the party who physically speaks the utterance;
- *figure,* "the character, persona, or entity projected into the audience's imagination" by the utterance (Irvine 1996: 132).

These roles are often inhabited by different individuals, though they may also be inhabited by the same individual, with different interpretations assigned to the utterance by hearers, depending on the set of roles that they identify with the animator. A politician's self-confession, for example, can be interpreted as revealing of the politician's true persona or as a cynical ploy, depending on whether hearers have projected the politician into the combined roles of *author* and *principal* or into the single role of *animator*.

Similarly, Goffman divided the traditional position of the *hearer* into several distinct sociologically framed roles:

- *addressee,* the person specifically inscribed in the discourse as a recipient;
- *bystander,* a person who is not inscribed but whose participation is ratified by other participants in the interaction;
- *overhearer,* a person who is neither inscribed nor ratified, but is acknowledged by the other;
- *eavesdropper,* a person who is neither inscribed, nor ratified, nor acknowledged in any way.

The entire configuration of roles in any given instant is called the *production format* of the utterance. Where things become complex is when one utterance is embedded in another, for example; by using quotation marks. In such situations, an entire production format is also being embedded into another, the same physical participants potentially filling distinct roles at different levels of embedding. The meaning of an utterance is an emergent property of the entire cluster of production formats and their respective configurations of roles. That is, the meaning of an utterance is produced jointly *between* roles within each production format and among roles that are distinctly assigned to the same social incumbent *among* production frames.

To see how this works, consider the following story, told to me in Quechua in the city of Cusco. The story takes place in a city that was an exact duplicate of Cusco. An elegant wedding party was taking place, and an old, hungry, ragged man came uninvited. He was dressed in rags, filthy, "*qhuñasapa*" 'encrusted in snot.' The invited guests were disgusted by the old man and physically ejected him from the party. He walked away, crying. One of the guests at the party, a woman, took pity on him and followed him, carrying food. The man was too fast for her, and though she followed him uphill and down, she could not reach him. She called to him, but he did not answer. Finally the old man warned her to keep walking and not to look back. She looked back, and saw that duplicate-Cusco had been flooded, forming a lake. Her husband and children were there – as were all the people who meant something to her. At that instant, she turned into rock, which can still be seen to this very day.

This story, first recorded in two seventeenth-century sources, is told widely in the Andean region. The story is always adaptable to the local landscape, which supplies both the spatial and moral orientation toward the events narrated in the story. When this story was told to me the lake was Lake Piwiray, in the district of Chinchero, 28 kilometers from the city of Cusco, and a major source of water for the city. The storyteller, whom I'll call "Ms Quispe" was born in Cusco, but grew up in one of the communities adjacent to Lake Piwiray. She was speaking to me. Normally, when a story is told in Quechua, the addressee and any other ratified participants join in telling it – agreeing, asking questions, and adding details (see Howard 1989, Mannheim and van Vleet 1998, Allen 2011). When Ms Quispe told me the story of Lake Piwiray, I had not yet learned how to take an active role as a listener, but she persevered in telling me the story anyway.

The Social Imaginary

She began:
1   Manas quchachu kasqan ñawpaqqa,
    ñawpaq tiempupiqa
    [riki]
    Llaqtas kasqa,
5   "llaqtan karan" ninku.
    Qusqu llaqtas kasqa chaypi
    [an]

1   It wasn't a lake in the old days,
    in the old times.
    [right]
    It was a city,
5   "It was a city" they said.
    It was the city of Cuzco there.
    [an]

We had already established that Ms Quispe was talking about Lake Piwiray. She opened the story by telling us that it was not yet a lake, and to do so opened two participation frameworks, one layered on the other. In the primary participation framework (PFI), in which she is speaking to me, she is the animator (producing the actual sounds), the principal (her point of view is expressed in the story), and the author (these are her words, even though she undoubtedly heard the story from someone else); the "figure" role is empty. I was the addressee, there was a bystander present, and we responded with the most minimal acknowledgement of those roles, marked in square brackets. (When we actually spoke, of course, the participation framework shifted – one or the other of us became the animator and Ms Quispe became the addressee. Our responses showed her that we acknowledged what she was saying, so that she could continue.)

But, in line 5, Ms Quispe opens a second participation framework (PF2), embedded in the first (Figure 4.1).

Ms Quispe is the animator in both frames, but in PF2, she is no longer the principal nor the author, roles that she assigned to unspecified others. This is marked grammatically in two ways: first, by shifting the tense marker from the past, stative *–sqa* (which is used in Quechua storytelling to narrate background information) to the simple past *–ra* (which is usually used in Quechua storytelling to describe events and to make things more immediate); and second, by shifting from the reportive evidential *–si* or *–s* to the evidential of direct assertion *–mi* or *–n*. PF2 takes the point of view of someone else (actually someone else's) – we don't know who – who can vouch for the lake having been a city once. All of this is done with a shift of two grammatical markers and a quotative.

Figure 4.1 Second participation framework (PF2), embedded in the first

As she moved through the story, Ms Quispe opened new participation frames, with new configurations of participant roles, layered deftly into her narration. For example, when she describes the guests' reactions to the old man, she took on their point of view, and they moved from being *figures* in the narrated participation framework, to being *authors* and *principals*. Again, Ms Quispe continued in the role of animator:

44 Millakusqaku machulacha disprisiyasqaku
"Ima machulan, kay qhilli machula hamun.
Chay machulata qarquychis.
Chayna millay p'achayuq,
millay qarquychis chay machuta," ñispa.
Millakusqaku chaysi qarqusqaku machulataqa, hinaspa
machulata qarquqtinku
nasqa, pasapusqa
waqayuspa
llakispa.

44 Disgusted, they insulted the little old man
"What an old man, this dirty old man came.
Throw that old man out.
He's disgusting dressed like that,
so throw the old man out disgustingly," they said.
They were disgusted, so they threw out the little old man, so
when they threw out the old man
uhh . . . he went away
crying bitterly
sadly.

In the primary participation framework, Ms Quispe repeated the insults and described the old man walking off, "crying bitterly, sadly." When she moved into the embedded framework, she embodied the point of view of the partygoers, quoting them: "He's disgusting dressed like that, so throw him out disgustingly."

I've chosen two relatively straightforward instances of layering participation framework on participation framework to illustrate the general phenomenon. Both of these are clearcut – one participation framework embedded in the other, using quotation to achieve the layering, but layering can be much more complex (framework can be embedded within framework within framework, and so on) and much less determinate. Participants in a conversation usually have little problem following shifts in participation frameworks over the course of a narrative event, and do so in real time, almost instantaneously and unconsciously, just as they track all other aspects of the interaction. But they are rarely as simple as the two examples included here. Judith Irvine (1996) points out that the problem of mapping participation frameworks onto each other and, consequently, tracing participant roles occurs not only when there are too many individuals to fit them neatly onto the traditional roles of "speaker," "addressee," and "other," but also when there are too few individuals, as when someone is talking to herself – or, as here, when Ms Quispe is moving among participant roles in different participation frameworks, both describing and embodying the several figures in the narrative. The narrative event, to quote Irvine (1996: 135), "has a relation to other [events], including the past, the future, the hypothetical, the conspicuously avoided, and so on, and these relations – intersecting frames, if you will – inform the participation structure of the moment." Within the complex web of participation frameworks that make up the narrative event there are both ambiguities and bleed-throughs between frameworks. These are calculated as deftly – as habitually and unconsciously – as the presuppositions and implicatures I discussed earlier, and similarly project assumptions about what there is in the world, and how the world works – a social ontology. The sunken city narrative very straightforwardly establishes normative claims as to appropriate relationships of hospitality – by their violation and the cruelty of their judgment (in much the way that the biblical narrative of Sodom and Gomorrah does – the similarity due to similarity of the social norms of hospitality in the two societies, the differences notwithstanding). But the narrative addressee also attends to the ambiguities among the participation frameworks and their bleed-throughs, and these play as important a role in establishing a social ontology as the more normative dimensions.

A visitor, a person who, like Ms Quispe, was an outsider to the city of Cusco, happened upon a wedding party, and was forcibly ejected by the partygoers. Among these, just one woman understood the norms of sociability and tried to feed the visitor, chasing him across the hills just outside of Lake Piwiray. Ms Quispe then broke from the primary narrative framework and, instead, for the first time, embedding a new participation framework within the old one *jumped up a level*, commented on the figure of the caring woman: *Chaypi visitachus kasqa chay warmi*, "She must have been a visitor, that woman" (line 59), a jump she marked by discarding the reportive evidential that she used in the main narrative line, which she replaced with *–chus*, an affix that marks personal conjecture.

54 Chaysi pasapushaqtinyá
    huq warmi
    huq warmilla
    khuyapayasqa
    huq [inaudible]
    (Chaypi visitachus kasqa chay warmi.)
60 Anchay warmi khuyapayasapa,
    "Akhakalláw! Chay machulachata qarqurapunku (u) yarqaysharanpaschá riki,
    qhilli kaqtinchá mana chaskita munankuchu.
    "Risaq ñuqa,
    kay mihunata pakallankupi aparusaq," nispa.
    "Khuyaramusaq" nispa.
    ayyy!
    "kay ahatawan" nispachusuna.
    Tarpasqa qhipanta.
    riki!

54 So, it's said, as he was going away
    one woman
    just one woman
    felt sorry for him
    one [inaudible]
    (She must have been a visitor there, that woman.)
60 That woman felt sorry for him,
    "Akhakalláw! They're throwing out that old man without feeding him, right.
    Since he's dirty, they don't want to offer him anything.
    "I'll go myself,

>   I'll bring him this food that I hid from them," she said.
>   "I'll go and care for him" she said.
>   ayyy!
>   "with this chicha also" she must have said.
>   She followed behind him to catch up to him.
>   riki!

Everything that the woman says is marked by direct quotation, and everything the visitor says by quotation plus a conjectural marker – "he must have said." And while the quoted speech formed an embedded participation framework, once Ms Quispe jumped up a level to comment on the woman being – like her – an outsider, the figure of the woman – as *figure* – became entangled with Ms Quispe's role as *principal* in the primary narrative participation framework and the woman's role as *principal* in the quoted, embedded participation framework. With the bleed-through of these three participant roles across two participation frameworks, the normative claims established in the narrative arc as a whole were interpolated into Ms Quispe's personal experience and her personal point of view. But the bleed-through between participant roles didn't stop there. Ms Quispe couldn't be sure that I had followed the pragmatic intricacies of the narrative, in which she folded participation framework into participation framework, in particular that I had not understood that the old man was God, and had come in disguise to test the partygoers. And so she recapitulated the story – establishing another framework like the one in which she asserted that the pitying woman was (like her) an outsider. This time she concentrated on the physical evidence of the truthfulness of the narrative – the stone pillar in the form of a woman on one of the hills near Lake Piwiray and that the old man was God.

>   113   Chaymi qaqapi?
>   Qaqamanta warmis kashan,
>   rumimanta.
>   Kashansis, ciertus.
>   Chaysi machulachaqa kasqa Dios.
>   [Arí.]
>   Risqa, prueba ruwaq.
>   Wak thantaña risqa, a proposito.
>   Wak thanta risqa.
>   "Ima nillawanqachá khayna haykuqti chay fiestakuqkuna." a . . .
>   Manas qarqullasqakuchu
>   chhaynallatachus thuqa–thuqayusqakuchushina
>   chaymantapis waqtasqakuchushina.
>   [huh!]
>   Ahá. (Chaynata millayta atisqanchá.)
>   Khaynaman tukurachipusqa chayqa
>   Dios kasqa
>   chay machula.
>
>   113   In rock?
>   There's a woman made of rock,
>   of stone.
>   There is, they say, for certain they say.

> That little old man was God, they say.
> Yes.
> He went there to test them.
> He went in rags in disguise, on purpose.
> He went in rags in disguise.
> "What would they say to me if I went to their party like this." a . . .
> They might not have thrown him out,
> they might not have spat at him like that
> and they might not have beaten him up like that.
> [huh!]
> Aha. (His power must have been fearsome.)
> He was able to transform them, like this, so
> He was God,
> that old man.

Who is Ms Quispe? She is the animator of the narrative, to be sure, and the principal in the primary participation framework, and the author (the story is widespread, but she has scripted this particular version), but is she also the figure of the woman – who like her is an outsider – or even the fearful God who metes out a terrible judgment on the city that refused him the most minimal hospitality? These are the points at which the distinct participation frameworks bleed through each other, and in which it is no longer clear that when she is taking on a new role within a new participation framework that it isn't in fact her own. She is simultaneously the aggrieved party (as the old man), the caring-woman-who-turns-to-stone, and the old-man-as-God; at the same time she is reproducing the social world in which the infraction took place (the exact double of Cusco) and her moral stance toward it, sliding them in below the listener's threshold of awareness. As she moves through the participation frames she literally inhabits these roles, and in doing so enters the social worlds associated with each of them; both she (as animator) and I (as active listener) acquiesce in the embedded, or *laminated* social worlds and their associated moral evaluations. Hill and Zepeda (1993: 212) explain, "to make an argumentative point within the 'story world' of a subnarrative probably makes the truth of such a point relatively inaccessible to challenge, compared to assertions in the interactional world." At the same time, the normative order established by the narrative line in the primary participation framework becomes so specific to the storyteller and the ethnographer in the here-and-now that both take it for granted as the way the social world works.

3 Conclusions and Future Directions

In this chapter, I discussed three linguistic and literary mechanisms by which the social imaginary is shaped: (1) presupposition, in which tacit assumptions can be calculated from what is said; (2) implicature, in which the social imaginary is calculated from the way it is said; and (3) pragmatic lamination, in which the imaginary is constructed interactionally, through ambiguities in the way in which one speech event is embedded within another. All of these are nuanced and minute aspects of linguistic interaction – the sorts of things that are often unnoted and unnoticed in ordinary interaction and in ethnography alike. But it is the very fact that they are unnoted and unnoticed – and at the same time must be taken into account for a verbal interaction to be understood in the first place – that makes them so powerful as replicators of social ontologies. Any future exploration of the social world that we take for granted must be prepared to engage the linguistic mechanisms by which that world is constituted.

Acknowledgments

An earlier version of this chapter was presented at the workshop, The Same Old Story? – Retelling and Reinventing New Traditions in South America, Albert-Ludwigs-Universität Freiburg, April 9, 2013 and to the Linguistic Anthropology Laboratory at the University of Michigan. I am grateful to Judith T. Irvine, Alaina Lemon, Michael Lempert, Barbra Meek, Perry Sherouse, and other members of the Linguistic Anthropology Laboratory for their criticisms and suggestions.

Related Topics

7 Language Ideologies (Kroskrity); **8** Social Subordination and Language (Huayhua); **11** Language Socialization and Marginalization (García-Sánchez); **14** Discursive Practices, Linguistic Repertoire, and Racial Identities (Baugh); **19** Language and Political Economy (McElhinny); **24** Discrimination via Discourse (Wodak).

Notes

1 See Hill and Mannheim (1992: 385–90) for a discussion of the claim that "grammatical categories, to the extent that they are obligatory or habitual, and relatively inaccessible to the average speaker's consciousness ... form a privileged location for transmitting and reproducing cultural and social categories ... by constraining the ontology that is taken for granted by speakers" (1992: 387). For a useful overview of Castoriadis's work, see Thompson 1984: 1–41. Key passages from Castoriadis's book, *L'institution imaginaire de la société* are excerpted in Castoriadis (1984), together with an introduction by Singer (1984).
2 There is a substantial interpretive literature on DuBois' idea of "double consciousness" (see, for example, E. Allen 1992). While I have argued elsewhere that there are moments in which strategic concealment, ambiguity, and doubling of form play a critical role in the discourses through which Southern Peruvian Quechuas position themselves (also see C. Allen 2011), I believe that the scope of these figures has been overstated, at least for Native South Americans.
3 Parallel to current research on the discourse grounding of grammatical categories (rather than their instantiation *in* discourse) is Bauman and Briggs's argument that the processes of *entextualization* are critical issues in their own right, and provide better framing of the problems of textuality in oral tradition than does the traditional view that texts are instantiated in performance. My consciousness on this point has also been raised by Ellen Basso's (1985: 11) insistence that what scholars have traditionally called "texts" are in fact the end-point of an elaborate process of editing, from the ethnographers' circumscription of the narrative event to the editor's framing within the conventions of academic expository prose (see Mannheim and van Vleet 1998 for development of this point).
4 Chuchiku appears in the anthologies of Southern Andean waynus collected by Josefat Roel Pineda (1957: 228) as "Pichiwchas," and by Gloria and Gabriel Escobar (1981: 95–97). The version transcribed here is from a recording by the Conjunto Kqempor de Cusipata, a local band from Cusipata (Province of Quispicanchi, Department of Cusco). It was recorded on Decibel LP–1148 in 1971 or 1972, and continued to be popular on Quechua-language radio broadcasts throughout the 1970s. The version published by Escobar and Escobar is more elaborate textually than the present version.
5 Virtually from the moment in which it was first proposed, anthropologists, linguists, and philosophers have developed extensions to Grice's formulation (e.g. Karttunen and Peters 1979); critiques (e.g. Davis 1998; Petrus 2010); and alternatives (Sperber and Wilson 1986 ; Levinson 2000). Since they do not materially change the analysis that I am proposing here, I use Grice's original proposal.

References

Ahearn, Laura M. 1999. A twisted rope binds my waist. Locating constraints on meaning in a Tij songfest. *Journal of Linguistic Anthropology* 8(1): 60–86.
Allen, Catherine J. 2011. *Foxboy*. Austin: University of Texas Press.
Allen, Ernest Jr. 1992. Ever feeling one's twoness. *Critique of Anthropology* 12: 261–75.

Basso, Ellen. 1985. *A musical view of the universe*. Philadelphia: University of Pennsylvania Press.
Bauman, Richard. 1975. Verbal art as performance. *American Anthropologist* 77: 290–311.
Bauman, Richard and Charles Briggs. 1990. Poetics and performance as critical perspectives on language and social life. *Annual Review of Anthropology* 19: 59–88.
Canessa, Andrew. 2012. Intimate indigeneities: race, sex, and history in the small spaces of Andean life. Durham: Duke University Press.
Castoriadis, Cornelius. 1975. L'institution imaginaire de la société. Paris: Seuil.
Castoriadis, Cornelius. 1984. The imaginary institution of society. In *The structural allegory: Reconstructive encounters with the new French thought*, ed. John Fekete, pp. 6–45. Minneapolis: University of Minnesota Press.
Chierchia, Gennaro and Sally McConnell-Ginet. 1990. *Meaning and grammar, an introduction to semantics*. Cambridge: MIT Press.
Concolorcorvo (Alonso Carrio de la Vandera?) 1773. *El lazarillo de ciegos caminantes*, ed. Emilio Carilla, 1973. Barcelona: Labor.
Coronil, Fernando and Julie Skurski. 1991. Dismembering and remembering the nation: The semantics of political violence in Venezuela. *Comparative Studies in Society and History* 33: 288–337.
Davis, Wayne A. 1998. *Implicature: Intention, convention, and principle in the failure of Gricean theory*. Cambridge: Cambridge University Press.
Descola, Philippe. 2013. *Beyond Nature and culture*, Chicago: University of Chicago Press.
DuBois, W.E. Burghardt. 1903. *The souls of Black folk*, reprinted, with introductions by Nathan Hare and Alvin F. Pouissaint, 1969. New York: Signet.
Enfield, Nicholas. 2007. *Transmission biases in linguistic epidemiology*. Leipzig: The Max Planck Institute for Evolutionary Anthropology.
Escobar, Gloria and Gabriel Escobar. 1981. *Huaynos del Cusco*, Cuzco: Garcilaso.
Feierstein, Daniel. 2014. *Genocide as social practice*. New Brunswick: Rutgers University Press.
Gal, Susan. 1995. Language and the arts of resistance. *Cultural Anthropology* 10(3): 407–24.
Gell, Alfred. 1999. *Art and agency*. Oxford: Oxford University Press.
Goffman, Erving. 1974. *Frame analysis*, New York: Harper.
Goffman, Erving. 1979. Footing. *Semiotica* 25: 1–29.
Grice, H. Paul. 1975. Logic and conversation. In *Speech acts (Syntax and Semantics 3)*, eds Peter Cole and Jerry Morgan, pp. 45–58. New York: Academic Press.
Gumperz, John Joseph. 1981. The retrieval of sociocultural knowledge in conversation. *Poetics Today* 1: 273–86.
Hanks, William F. 1990. *Referential Practices*. Chicago: University of Chicago Press.
Harding, Susan F. 1987. Convicted by the Holy Spirit: The rhetoric of fundamental Baptist conversion. *American Ethnologist* 14: 167–85.
Hill, Jane H. 1995. The voices of don Gabriel: Responsibility and moral grounds in a modern Mexicano narrative. In *The dialogic emergence of culture*, eds Dennis Tedlock and Bruce Mannheim, pp. 97–147. Urbana: University of Illinois Press.
Hill, Jane H. and Bruce Mannheim. 1992. Language and world view. *Annual Review of Anthropology* 21: 382–406.
Hill, Jane H. and Ofelia Zepeda 1993. Mrs. Patricio's trouble. The distribution of responsibility in an account of personal experience. In *Responsibility and evidence in oral discourse*, eds Jane H. Hill and Judith T. Irvine, pp. 197–225. Cambridge: Cambridge University Press.
Howard, Rosaleen 1989. Storytelling strategies in Quechua narrative performance. *Journal of Latin American Lore* 15: 3–71.
Irvine, Judith T. 1996. Shadow conversations: The indeterminacy of participant roles. In *Natural histories of discourse*, eds Michael Silverstein and Greg Urban, pp. 131–159. Chicago: University of Chicago Press.
Kapferer, Bruce. 1991 [1983]. *A celebration of demons: exorcism and the aesthetics of healing in Sri Lanka* (2nd edn.). Washington: Smithsonian Institution Press.
Karttunen, Lauri, and Stanley Peters. 1979. Conventional implicature. *Syntax and Semantics* 11: 1–56.
Kockelman, Paul. 2013. *Agent, person, subject, self*. New York: Oxford University Press.
Langer, Susanne K. 1941. *Philosophy in a new key* (1948 edn.). New York: Penguin.
Levinson, Stephen C. 1988. Putting linguistics on a proper footing: Explorations in Goffman's participation framework. In *Goffman: Exploring the interaction order*, eds P. Drew and A. Wootton, 161–227. Oxford: Polity Press.
Levinson, Stephen C. 2000. *Presumptive meanings*. Cambridge: MIT Press.
Malinowski, Bronislaw. 1922. *Argonauts of the western Pacific*. New York: E.P. Dutton.

Malinowski, Bronislaw. 1926. *Myth in primitive psychology.* New York: Norton.
Mannheim, Bruce. 1991. *The language of the Inka since the European invasion,* Austin: University of Texas Press.
Mannheim, Bruce.1998. A nation surrounded. In *Native traditions in the post-conquest world,* eds Elizabeth Boone and Tom Cummins, pp. 381–418. Washington: Dumbarton Oaks.
Mannheim, Bruce and Krista E. van Vleet. 1998. The dialogics of Quechua narrative. *American Anthropologist* 100(2): 326–346.
McLendon, Sally. 1977. Cultural presuppositions and discourse analysis. In *Linguistics and anthropology,* ed. Muriel Saville-Troike, pp. 153–90. Washington: Georgetown University Press.
Moore, Sally Falk and Barbara Meyerhoff. 1977. Introduction: Secular ritual, forms and meanings. In *Secular ritual,* pp. 3–24. Assen: Van Gorcum.
Ochs, Elinor (as Elinor Keenan). 1977. The universality of conversational implicatures. In *Studies in language variation,* eds R.W. Fasold and R. Shuy, pp. 255–68. Washington: Georgetown University Press.
Ortíz Rescaniere, Alejandro. 1973. *De Adaneva a Inkarrí: una visión indígena del Perú.* Lima: Instituto Nacional de Investigación y Desarrollo de la Educación.
Petrus, Klaus (ed.). 2010. *Meaning and analysis: New essays on Grice.* New York: Palgrave Macmillan.
Rappaport, Roy A. 1974. The obvious aspects of ritual. *Cambridge Anthropologist* 2: 3–68.
Roel Pineda, Josefat. 1957. El huayno del Cuzco. *Folklore Americano* 6–7: 129–245.
Sapir, Edward. 1929. The status of linguistics as a science. *Language* 5(4): 207–214.
Saussure, Ferdinand de. 1915. *Cours de linguistique générale.* Paris: Payot.
Scott, James R. 1990. *Domination and the arts of resistance.* New Haven: Yale University Press.
Sherzer, Joel. 1987. A discourse-centered approach to language and culture. *American Anthropologist* 89: 295–309.
Singer, Brian. 1984. Introduction to Castoriadis. In *The structural allegory: Reconstructive encounters with the new French thought,* ed. John Fekete, pp. 6–45. Minneapolis: University of Minnesota Press.
Sperber, Dan. 1991. The epidemiology of beliefs. In *The social psychological study of widespread beliefs,* eds Colin Fraser and George Gaskell, pp. 25–43. London: Oxford University Press.
Sperber, Dan and Deirdre Wilson. 1986. *Relevance.* Cambridge: Harvard University Press.
Tambiah, Stanley Jeyaraja. 1990. *Magic, science, religion, and the scope of rationality,* Cambridge: University Press.
Tedlock, Dennis. 1983. *The spoken word and the work of interpretation.* Philadelphia: University of Pennsylvania Press.
Tedlock, Dennis. 1987. Hearing a voice in an ancient text: Quiché Maya poetics in performance. In *Native American Discourse: Poetics and Rhetoric,* eds Joel Sherzer and Anthony C. Woodbury, pp. 140–75. Cambridge: Cambridge University Press.
Thompson, John B. 1984. *Studies in the Theory of Ideology.* Cambridge: Cambridge University Press.
Urban, Greg. 1991. *A discourse-centered approach to culture.* Austin: University of Texas Press.

Further Reading

On language as the location of social reproduction:
Hill, Jane H. and Bruce Mannheim. 1992. Language and world view. *Annual Review of Anthropology 21*: 382–406.

On formal analysis of narrative:
Hill, Jane H. 1995. The voices of don Gabriel: Responsibility and moral grounds in a modern Mexicano narrative. In *The dialogic emergence of culture,* eds Dennis Tedlock and Bruce Mannheim. Urbana: University of Illinois Press.
Mannheim, Bruce and Krista E. van Vleet. 1998. The dialogics of Quechua narrative. *American Anthropologist* 100(2): 326–46.

On presupposition, implicature and other forms of inference:
Bach, Kent. 2006. The top 10 misconceptions about implicature. In *Drawing the boundaries of meaning: neo-Gricean studies in pragmatics and semantics in honor of Laurence R. Horn,* eds Betty J. Birner and Gregory Ward, pp. 21–30. Amsterdam: Benjamins.
Chierchia, Gennaro, and Sally McConnell-Ginet. 1990. *Meaning and grammar, an introduction to semantics.* Cambridge: MIT Press.

Grice, H. Paul. 1975. Logic and conversation. In *Speech acts (Syntax and Semantics 3)*, eds Peter Cole and Jerry Morgan, pp. 45–58. New York: Academic Press.
Horn, Laurence. 2012. Implying and inferring. In *Cambridge handbook of pragmatics*, eds K. Jaczszolt and K. Allan, pp. 69–86.
Jang, Gijeong, Shin-ae Yoon, Sung-Eun Leec, et al. 2013. Everyday conversation requires cognitive inference: Neural bases of comprehending implicated meanings in conversations. *Neuroimage, 2013*: 51–62.
Kehler, Andrew. 2001. *Coherence, reference, and the theory of grammar*. Palo Alto: CSLI
Levinson, Stephen C. 2000. *Presumptive meanings*. Cambridge: MIT Press.
Ochs, Elinor (as Elinor Keenan). 1977. The universality of conversational implicatures. In *Studies in language variation*, eds R.W. Fasold and R. Shuy, pp. 255–68. Washington: Georgetown University Press.
Ward, Gregory and Laurence R. Horn (eds). 2006. *The handbook of pragmatics*. Malden, MA: Blackwell.
Petrus, Klaus (ed.). 2010. *Meaning and analysis: New essays on Grice*. New York: Palgrave Macmillan.
Roberts, Craige. 2012. Information structure in discourse. Towards an integrated formal theory of pragmatics. *Semantics & Pragmatics 5*, Article 6: 1–69.
Sperber, Dan and Deirdre Wilson. 1986. *Relevance*. Cambridge: Harvard University Press.

On pragmatic lamination:
Goffman, Erving. 1979. Footing. *Semiotica 25*: 1–29.
Hanks, William F. 1990. *Referential Practices*. Chicago: University of Chicago Press.
Hill, Jane H. and Ofelia Zepeda. 1993. Mrs. Patricio's trouble. The distribution of responsibility in an account of personal experience. In *Responsibility and evidence in oral discourse*, ed. Jane H. Hill and Judith T. Irvine, pp. 197–225. Cambridge: Cambridge University Press.
Irvine, Judith T. 1996. Shadow conversations: The indeterminacy of participant roles. In *Natural histories of discourse*, eds Michael Silverstein and Greg Urban, pp. 131–159. Chicago: University of Chicago Press.

5

New Perspectives on Kinship

Overcoming the Eurocentrism and Scientism of Kinship Studies through Lexical Universals

Anna Wierzbicka

1 Introduction: The Ethnocentrism of the Classic Approach to Kinship

In a wide-ranging recent debate on kinship studies in the journal *Behavioral and Brain Sciences*, linguist and cognitive scientist Stephen Levinson writes (2010: 392): "The neglect of kinship in current anthropology and in the cognitive sciences is not far short of a scandal. Humans are the categorizing species, and kinship systems categorize our own most significant others, so reflecting fundamental forms of social organization."

How did this "scandal" of the abandonment of kinship studies come about? A number of different diagnoses have been put forward. Undoubtedly, however, one critical factor was the recognition of the profound Eurocentrism of the traditional analyses of kinship terminology.

In their classic study, "The Meaning of Kinship Terms," Wallace and Atkins (1969: 364) spoke of an "almost unavoidable ethnocentrism" of kinship studies, pointing out that, traditionally, anthropological analysis of indigenous kinship systems consisted in translating 'local' kinship terminologies into a 'global' metalanguage based on symbols such as "F", "M", "Z", "B", "S", "D", "H" and "W" (usually augmented by some additions like "f", "m", "y", and "e"). All such symbols are, of course, based on English: "M" stands for the English word *mother*, "F" for *father*, "B" for *brother*, "S" for *son*, "D" for *daughter*, "H" for *husband*, "W" for *wife*, "f" for *female*, "m" for *male*, "y" for *younger* and "e" for *elder*. It was clear to Wallace and Atkins that since most of these English words have no semantic equivalents in many languages of the world, the interpretive grid offered by the traditional anthropological approach to kinship was in fact not global but 'local': it derived from English and thus imposed an Anglo perspective on the kinship systems embedded in other languages of the world. More recently, Leaf (2006: 306) made essentially the same point.

From a cross-linguistic perspective, it seems clear that, for example, the English word *brother* imposes a certain interpretation of "raw facts", rather than carving nature at its joints. It is a word that pays attention to a person's gender but is blind to their relative age, whereas in many other languages this is seen as equally important, or more important, than someone's gender. For example, the Australian language Pitjantjatjara (Scheffler 1978) does not have words for 'brother' and 'sister', but has instead the words *kuṯa, kangkuṟu,* and *maḻanypa,* glossed by Scheffler, respectively, as "B+" ("older brother"), "Z+" ("older sister") and "Sb–" ("younger sibling"). Yet many Anglophone scholars, including linguists, still seem convinced that while concepts like 'kuṯa', 'kangkuṟu' and 'maḻanypa' are culturally constructed, the concept of 'brother' simply "fits the world."

Speaking of a woman's progress through three marriages and three languages, the English writer Zadie Smith (2009: 5) describes languages as "shared words that fit the world as you believe it to be." For millions of people, including a great many writers and scholars (see, for example, Hoffman 1989; Besemeres 2002), immigrant experience has shattered the natural conviction that the words of their native language fit the world as it really is. But in the case of English, its new status as a global language and the paramount language of science has if anything strengthened the widespread illusion that English words fit the world "as it is." The concept of 'brother' is a good case in point.

In this chapter, I will try to show that while a Eurocentric perspective on the world's kinship vocabularies is indeed a major problem for the understanding of the ways in which speakers of different languages construct their social universe, this Eurocentrism is not unavoidable. In doing so, I will be building on my earlier work in kinship semantics (e.g. Wierzbicka 1986, 1992, 2010, 2013) and on the recent advances in the semantic theory known as NSM (from Natural Semantic Metalanguage), which, as I see it, allows us to overcome the Eurocentrism of the classic approach and to breathe new life into the study of kinship terminologies. I will discuss NSM methodology, assumptions, and findings very shortly, paying special attention to the developments of the last decade or so particularly relevant to kinship. Before doing so, however, it will be in order to take a closer look at what Sousa (2003) called "the fall of kinship."

2 Historical Perspectives: The Death of Kinship Studies?

Within anthropology, the strongest critique of kinship studies in the classic mode came from David Schneider, who argued that "kinship has been defined by European social scientists, and European social scientists use their own folk culture as the source of many, if not all, of their ways of formulating and understanding the world about them" (1984: 183).

Unfortunately, this critique led Schneider to throwing the baby out with the bath water and to rejecting the common sense assumption that "kinship . . . has to do with reproduction" (1984: 198). Not surprisingly, this met with strong negative reactions from many cultural anthropologists, as shown in particular by the studies in the volume entitled *The Cultural Analysis of Kinship: The Legacy of David M. Schneider* (Feinberg and Ottenheimer eds 2001).

Yet Schneider's insistence that the study of cultural phenomena needs to rely on native terms and meanings made profound good sense. Schneider argued that "the first task of anthropology, *prerequisite to all others,* is to understand and formulate the symbols and meanings and their configuration that a particular culture consists of" (1984: 196, emphasis in the original).

Cultural semantics as developed within the NSM approach (see section 3) shares this view and it provides a methodology for exploring and identifying indigenous meanings without imposing on them a Eurocentric perspective. As this chapter illustrates, NSM offers a common measure for comparing kinship terminologies across languages and cultures and provides a comparative framework for describing meanings in a way that makes sense to insiders and is intelligible to outsiders, and thus can be seen as both universal and indigenous.

In his classic account of the development of cognitive anthropology, D'Andrade (1995: 18–19) wrote: "to carry out an *emic* analysis one began with a set of categories brought in by the scientific observer and then tried to find out which of those categories really made a difference with respect to the way the natives understood and responded to things."

But the idea of a "scientific observer" bringing in his or her own categories to the analysis was at variance with the project of identifying the native speaker's "emic" categories from an insider's perspective, and it could not stand up to the arguments of critics like Schneider. As a result, the whole program of research into patterns of kinship based on this more or less collapsed in the last decade of the twentieth century, prompting, for example, Fogelson (2001: 26), to describe componential analysis of kinship as "now consigned to the dustbin of anthropological history" and to conclude, "Indeed, the study of kinship, which played such a prominent role in the development of anthropological theory, now seems to be a dead topic."

But kinship could not remain a 'dead topic' in anthropology for long and, increasingly, scholars have started to proclaim a renaissance of kinship studies. Words like *brother* and *sister* in English and *kuta* and *kangkuru* in Pitjantjatjara are so important in all languages that investigating their meaning must be seen, in the long run, as one of the priorities not only of linguistic semantics but also of any linguistic anthropology worth its salt. Yes, old-style componential analysis is dead, but the question of what such words mean will never go away. Nor can the new mathematical and computer-driven approaches to kinship (e.g. Read 2001; Jones 2010; for discussion, see Wierzbicka 2010) replace the old questions of psychological reality (Burling 1964; Romney, Kimball and D'Andrade 1964), "the native's point of view" (Geertz 1976) and the insider's understanding (Shore 1996).

3 Critical Issues and Topics: The NSM Approach to Language and Culture

'NSM' is a 'natural semantic metalanguage' based on natural language and representing the intersection of all natural languages, and 'NSM English' is an English-based version of this metalanguage. Every NSM is a tightly constrained yet flexible mini-language of simple indefinable meanings ('universal semantic primes'), along with their inherent universal grammar. To define the meaning of a word or an expression in NSM means to explain, or 'explicate' it (directly or in stages) through simple and universal human concepts that do not require further explanation themselves and that can be found as words (or word-like elements) in all languages.

The natural semantic metalanguage (NSM), built through extensive cross-linguistic investigations, is described in great detail in many publications, especially in Goddard and Wierzbicka (2002), which also contains six studies demonstrating that the posited semantic primes and their basic syntactic frames exist in a set of typologically and genetically diverse languages. A sizable bibliography is available on the NSM homepage (www.griffith.edu.au/humanities-languages/school-languages-linguistics/research/natural-semantic-metalanguage-homepage).

Thus, cross-linguistic evidence strongly suggests that alongside huge diversity there is also a shared, universal core of human thinking and knowing. This shared core includes, in effect, what Leibniz called "the alphabet of human thoughts", i.e., a fairly small set of universal semantic primes out of which an infinite number of complex meanings and ideas can be built. This set, as it has emerged from decades of NSM-based research, is presented in Table 5.1. Along with semantic primes ("atoms of meaning"), there is also a set of "semantic molecules" built out of primes. Semantic molecules, marked in explications (i.e., NSM-style definitions) with the symbol [m], function as units in the meaning of more complex concepts. All molecules can be explicated in terms of universal semantic primes.

Evidence suggests that some of these molecules (a few dozen) are universal. Universal semantic molecules relevant to the field of kinship include, above all, 'men', 'women', and 'children' (cf. Goddard and Wierzbicka 2014a). Crucially for the field of kinship studies, they also include 'mother', 'father', 'wife', 'husband' and 'be born' (cf. Wierzbicka 1992; forthcoming).

Table 5.1 Semantic primes (English exponents), grouped into 12 related categories

1	I, YOU, SOMEONE, SOMETHING~THING, PEOPLE, BODY, KINDS, PARTS
2	THIS, THE SAME, OTHER
3	ONE, TWO, MUCH~MANY, LITTLE~FEW, SOME, ALL
4	GOOD, BAD, BIG, SMALL
5	THINK, KNOW, WANT, DON'T WANT, FEEL, SEE, HEAR
6	SAY, WORDS, TRUE
7	DO, HAPPEN, MOVE
8	BE (SOMEWHERE), THERE IS, BE (SOMEONE/SOMETHING), (IT'S MINE)
9	LIVE, DIE
10	WHEN~TIME, NOW, BEFORE, AFTER, A LONG TIME, A SHORT TIME, FOR SOME TIME, MOMENT
11	WHERE~PLACE, HERE, ABOVE, BELOW, FAR, NEAR, SIDE, INSIDE, TOUCH
12	NOT, MAYBE, CAN, BECAUSE, IF, VERY, MORE, LIKE

Jointly, these two universal sets of word-like building blocks constitute a basis of human cognition, which can be accessed through the lexical core of English, or any other language.

4 The Key Issue: Lexical Universals

Donald Brown's 1991 book *Human Universals* is a milestone in the study of what he calls "the Universal People" or "UP". The reason for this is that unlike many writers on the subject of "human nature" or "human mind", Brown linked his 'human universals' with 'universal words', that is, "words or meanings [that] cut across all cultural boundaries and hence form a part of UP language" (p. 132). Some of his examples, such as 'face' and 'hand', are consistent with empirical cross-linguistic research, whereas some others, such as 'black' and 'white', are not; but Brown's overall insight that lexical universals provide evidence for conceptual universals (how PEOPLE think) is of great historical significance. The fact that Brown sought to apply this insight to the domain of kinship – pointing out, for example, that all languages appear to have different words for 'mother' and 'father' – makes his vision particularly relevant to the present chapter.

It must be said, however, that Brown's attempt to link 'human universals' with lexical universals did not go so far as to attempt to fully anchor the former in the latter. This led to an Anglocentric bias in his broad picture of 'who we (humans) are' and how we understand our connectedness with other people. For example, he wrote:

> Certain semantic components are found in UP language, even if the terms in which they are employed are not. For example, UP kin terminology includes terms that distinguish male from female (and thus indicate the semantic component of sex) and some generations from others.
>
> Brown (1991: 133)

The inherent Anglocentrism of this passage can be easily missed, yet it is so essential in the present context that it needs to be pointed out.[1]

As I have discussed in detail in *Imprisoned in English* (2014), the concept of 'sex' embedded in the English word *sex* (in the relevant sense) belongs to the English universe of meaning, not to the conceptual framework shared by all people. To attribute such a component to speakers of languages that do not have a word corresponding to *sex*, is to impose on them an Anglo/English perspective. For example, the fact that Russian has the words *mužčina* 'man', *ženščina* 'woman', *petux* 'rooster' and *kurica* 'hen' does not mean that it has the semantic component 'sex' or the semantic components 'male' and 'female'. From a cross-cultural perspective, it is a peculiarity of modern English that both men and roosters can be conceptualised in it as 'male', or both women and hens, as 'female'. From a Russian 'common sense' point of view, the difference between a man and a woman is not the same as that between a rooster and a hen. It is not an accident that Russian does not have words corresponding to 'sex', 'male' and 'female'. Rather, it is a reflection of how Russian speakers habitually think (and how they don't think) (Wierzbicka 2014).

Likewise, the fact that Russian has words matching the English words *brother* and *sister*, or *son* and *daughter*, does not establish that there is in Russian "the semantic component sex" (cf. Goddard and Wierzbicka 2014a). In fact, rigorous semantic analysis of the English words *brother* and *sister* shows that their meanings are not related through a hypothetical component 'sex', or hypothetical components 'male' and 'female', either. The presence of the words *sex*, *male* and *female* in modern English does show that the concepts embedded in them are part of the Anglo/English universe of meaning, but not that, in English, *sister* is, semantically, 'a female sibling' or *mother*, 'a female parent'. To the extent to which the traditional analysis of kinship was based on such fictitious "semantic components" it was out of kilter with ordinary human thinking – even in relation to English, let alone to languages in which the putative "semantic components" in question are not named at all.

To illustrate how meanings seemingly differing by the "semantic component sex" can be explained using ordinary and cross-translatable words, I will present here NSM explications of 'mother' and 'father' (in the primary meaning of these words):

someone's *mother*
a woman, before this someone was born
    this someone's body was for some time inside this woman's body

someone's *father*
a man, some time before this someone was born
    this man did something with a part of the body to a woman's body
something happened inside this woman's body because of this
because of this, this someone was born

As these explications illustrate, the concepts of 'man' and 'woman', which we find as words in all languages, can serve, directly or indirectly, as prototypes for contrasts that, from a modern-English point of view, may appear to be based on the semantic component 'sex', or on putative semantic components 'male' and 'female' (see Goddard and Wierzbicka 2014a).

5 "Things That Are Common to All Mankind"

In a passage from his book *Description and Comparison in Cultural Anthropology* quoted by Read (2001: 80), Goodenough (1970: 97) writes:

> We anthropologists have assumed that kinship is universal, that all societies have kinship systems. If we are correct in this assumption, if every society does have some set of relationships whose definition involves genealogical considerations of some kind, their genealogical space must be constructed of *things that are common to all mankind* (emphasis added by Read).

The key question is: what *are* those "things that are common to all mankind"? Goodenough himself speaks of "parenthood", "social recognized sexual unions", and of "parent–child relationships", but what *demonstrably* common to all mankind is not abstract concepts like "parenthood", "socially recognized sexual unions", and "parent-child relationships" but more concrete ones: 'mother', 'father', 'husband', and 'wife', which we find lexically embodied in all (or nearly all) languages of the world. (The fact that these words often exhibit language-specific patterns of polysemy does not undermine the semantic equivalence of the basic meanings; cf. Shapiro 2008; Wierzbicka 1992). Crucially, we also find in all (or nearly all) languages words corresponding to "be born" and "give birth," on which the universal concepts 'mother' and 'father' build.

The angst that anthropologists like Schneider expressed in relation to kinship as a valid area of study had at its roots a healthy desire to avoid imposing categories derived from European languages on other languages and cultures. Empirical cross-linguistic studies have shown, however, that while concepts like 'reproduction', 'genealogy', 'descent' and 'sibling', or even those like 'brother', 'sister', 'son', and 'daughter', are indeed far from universal (there are no such words in most languages), the domain of kinship *can* be grounded in genuine conceptual and linguistic universals.

In his *Description and Comparison in Cultural Anthropology*, Goodenough (1970: 2) wrote, "We have to find some set of terms that will enable us to describe other cultures with minimal distortion from ethnocentric cultural bias. And we need some set of universally applicable concepts that will enable us to compare cultures and arrive at valid generalisations about them". Evidence suggests that such a set of universally applicable terms includes, along with 'man', and 'woman' and 'child', two foundational kin terms: 'mother' and 'father' (as well as their conceptual fundament, 'be born'). As noted earlier, the presence of words with meanings 'mother' and 'father' (in the primary, biological sense of 'birth-giver' and 'begetter') in languages can be hidden from view because of the endemic polysemy of such words. However, careful semantic analysis shows that, polysemy aside, these word-meanings can indeed be found in all (or nearly all) languages.

If we do not want to fall into the trap of using "the constructions of European cultures as tools for description, comparison, and analysis" (Schneider 1984: 185), we need to articulate the putative human universals of kinship in universal human concepts, rather than in culture-specific English words (whether colloquial, like *uncle* or *brother*, or technical, like *collateral* and *male ego*).

Referring to the componential analysis of kinship terminologies as it was practiced in the 1960s, D'Andrade (1995: 30) wrote, "It is difficult to explain the beauty which a semantic analysis of kinship terms held for some anthropologists in the 1960s. In the present intellectual milieu, this type of analysis seems specialised, arcane and formalistic." It is now apparent, however, that the "specialised, arcane and formalistic" character of the analyses discussed by D'Andrade was not due to the inherent nature of the meanings of kin terms, but rather to the methodologies with the help of which these words were analysed.

Unlike the formalisms of yesteryear, NSM explications (such as those presented in section 6) allow us to bring hypothesised conceptual structures into the orbit of recognisable human ways of speaking and to present them as learnable and accessible to ordinary mortals, who, after all, rely on them in their everyday thinking and in their basic relations with other people.

In his book *Dying Words*, in which he speaks of endangered and dying languages of the world and discusses, inter alia, the semantics of kinship in the endangered Australian language Dalabon, Evans (2010: 159) says, quite poignantly, that once a language like Dalabon dies, "no one's mind will again have the thought-paths that its ancestral speakers once blazed." But if so, it is all the more important to try to understand those thought-paths as best we can; and I do not think we can understand them through academic English or through algebraic modeling. Arguably, however, we can through "things [words] that are common to all mankind."

Anna Wierzbicka

6 Current Contributions and Research: Understanding the "Thought-Paths" of a Distant Culture

Can speakers of English understand the thought-paths of speakers of Australian Aboriginal languages in the area of kinship? Can these thought-paths be *explained* to non-Aboriginal Australians, and if so, how? In what follows, I will illustrate the problems involved with some examples from one language (or dialect chain) of Northern Australia.

Kinship Verbs

Australian linguist Murray Garde opens his recent book on the language of kinship in Aboriginal Australia with a remarkable vignette. When in October 2009 the Arnhem Land plateau in the Northern Territory of Australia was declared an Indigenous Protected Area, journalists and politicians gathered on the land of the Mok clans and the 81-year-old patriarch Lofty Baradyal Nadjamerrek presided over the proceedings. Murray Garde acted as an interpreter during an interview that a journalist conducted with one of the young indigenous land management rangers.

> **Journalist**: So is old Lofty your grandfather?
>
> **Young ranger**: *Yimarnek doydoy nga-yimeninj dha nawu ngabbard nga-yime bene-modjarrk-dorrinj wanjh nungka na-kohbanj kabi-korlonhme nawu ngabbard. Wanjh nungkah Wamud ngaye mawah nga-yime.*
>
> I should call him my 'spouse bestowal' great-grandfather (MMMB), but my father is a cross cousin [of the old man] and through a [Crow-style] skewing relationship [expressed via the metaphor of 'they strike each other's nose'] that old man calls my father 'son' [literally, he 'sons' him]. Therefore [through transitive extension], I call Wamud [i.e. Lofty] my father's father.

When Garde tried to explain the intricacies of the young man's reply, the journalist was clearly bewildered and after a brief silence asked, "so is that a yes?".

Evidently, in glossing the young Aboriginal man's words in the way he did, Murray Garde was acting not only as a (cross-linguistic) interpreter, but also as a cross-cultural commentator and anthropologist. As the journalist's confused reaction indicates, however, the explanation was not entirely effective.

The vignette illustrates some profound differences between European and Aboriginal Australians. For the journalist, the key question is this: what is the (objective, knowable) relationship between Lofty and the young ranger (given who his, the ranger's, mother and father are). For the young ranger himself, on the other hand, the key question concerns different ways in which (given who his mother and father are) he can think about Lofty and what he can call him.

The young Aboriginal man's answer does not fit the journalist's question because the assumptions are in each case different. In both the question and the answer, mother and father are the major points of reference for human connectedness, but for the journalist, there is in principle only one way to articulate the connectedness between the young man and the old man, whereas for the young man there are several different ways, linked for him with different possible ways of thinking about the old man.

One important lesson from this vignette is that in trying to describe the meaning of kinship words in a language like Bininj Gunwok we often need to refer to certain ways of thinking, whereas this is seldom the case in a language like English. The so-called "kinship verbs" in Bininj Gunwok discussed by Garde are a good case in point.

Like other Australian languages, Bininj Gunwok has some nouns that can serve as what Garde calls "basic kin terms". These nouns include *karrard* 'mother' and *ngabbard* 'father'. As in other Australian languages, these nouns, which can be used for 'mother' and 'father' in the primary, biological sense, can also be used in extended senses. To distinguish between the primary and the extended senses, a variety of strategies can be used, as discussed by both Garde (2013) and Evans (2003). As the use of the symbols F and M by these authors indicates, the whole system relies on the availability of the distinct senses 'mother' ('birth-giver') and 'father' ('begetter'). This dependence on the meanings 'mother' ('birth-giver') and 'father' ('begetter') applies, in particular, to so-called "kinship verbs" like *-bornang* in Bininj Gunwok, of which Garde (2013: 60) writes:

> The verb *-bornang* rather imperfectly overlaps with the archaic English verb 'beget'. It is an imperfect translation because it is not restricted to the father-child relationship as it also includes the relationship between an individual and their father's siblings, male or female. It indexes an upper generation subject and a lower adjacent patrilineal generation object. Thus a man can refer to his son with the expression *nga-bornang* 'I am father to him/her', but a woman can refer to her brother's children with the same term. The same term can also be used by a man to refer to the children of his brother. Various subject-object pronominal prefixes on the verb are possible.

Garde cautiously chooses the verb "to index" (rather than "to mean") here: the Bininj Gunwok word in question "indexes" an upper generation subject and a lower adjacent patrilineal generation object. But what does this word *mean*? And what does it mean when a woman says *nga-bornang*, referring to her brother's children? In his English glosses, Garde uses the verbs "to father" and "to beget", and in a table presenting a "Summary of Bininj Gunwok kinship verbs" (p. 70) he describes the meaning of *-bornang* (*beget* – PP [Past Perfective]) as "be in successive patriline, beget". In the translations of particular examples, he provides, inter alia, English sentences such as "She/he fathered me" (p. 61) and "she begat me" (p. 55).

To speakers of English, such glosses as used in relation to women are deeply mystifying and appear to suggest that Bininj Gunwok ways of thinking are so exotic as to be simply beyond comprehension (they may even be taken to show that these ways of thinking are inherently illogical). From this point of view, technical explanation couched in academic English such as "she is my ascending patriline" (p. 55) may be safer: since they are not comprehensible they will not seem illogical. But clearly, such technical labels cannot serve the purpose of cross-cultural understanding. Nor do they articulate the conceptual content that speakers have in mind ('think with'). They are just place-holders. The question is: what do these words *mean*?

The gloss "she is my father's sister", which is also used by Garde (p. 55), may seem the least problematic, since it is neither incomprehensible nor illogical. It is, however, too restrictive, because *-bornang* could also refer to one's father's brother – not to mention the further complication that, as Garde's table of Bininj Gunwok "basic kin terms" (p. 32) shows, the language does not have words matching, straightforwardly, *brother* and *sister* (see also Evans 2003: 43).

Trying to devise interpretations which would avoid all the pitfalls mentioned above, I would propose trying to base the analysis of words like *-bornang* and its female counterpart *-yawmey* directly on the two solid fundamentals of 'father' and 'mother.' For instance, in Garde's examples (3.9) and (3.10) reproduced below, I would replace Garde's interpretations 1 and 2 with my own [1] and [2], as follows: [2]

(3.9) *nga-borna-ng*

    1>3-beget-PP
    1   my child (speaker is a male)
    2   my B's [brother's] child (speaker is a female)
        "I fathered him/her"

    [1] I can think about this someone like this:
         "I am this someone's father"

    [2] I can think about this someone like this:
         "I am someone like this someone's father
         because my father is this someone's father's father"

(3.10) *ngan-borna-ng*

    1>3-beget-PP
    1   my F [father]
    2   my FZ [father's sister]
        "she/he fathered me"

    [1] I can think about this someone like this:
         "this is my father"

    [2] I can think about this someone like this:
         "this is someone like my father
         because this someone's father is my father's father"

One intriguing question arising from Garde's discussion is how sentences such as his (3.9) and (3.10) should be interpreted when they refer to a person's actual father (begetter). Garde quotes Evans (2000: 14) as saying that the term *ngan-bornang* "can distinguish from within the classes of classificatory fathers known by the nominal term *ngabbard*, one's actual father", and he agrees with Evans that "in some contexts, use of this term could possibly disambiguate one's actual father from others classed as *ngabbard*". At the same time, he emphasises that "the term *ngan-bornang* can definitely be used to refer to one's father's brothers and sisters, and that such reference is quite common." (Garde p. 65)

It would seem that the only way to reconcile the observations on the common use of *ngan-bornang* to refer, specifically, to the begetter, but also, in its common use, to refer to the begetter's brothers and sisters, is to posit two distinct meanings for this word, roughly 1. a person's actual father, 2. someone (other than one's father) whose father is one's father's father.

It is not my main goal, however, to argue for a polysemy-based interpretation of kinship verbs in languages like Bininj Gunwok here. Rather, it is to show that whether or not they are analysed as polysemous, they can be plausibly interpreted through intelligible ordinary English – without sentences such as "she begat him", without phrases such as "they are in successive patriline", and without multiple disjunctive glosses. This can be done if we do two things: first, note the importance of the concepts 'father's father' and 'mother's mother' in such languages, and second, recognise an important and lexically encoded way of thinking based on these concepts that consists of the idea of viewing a person as someone whose father is one's father's father. Arguably, it is precisely this idea that underlines Garde's locutions such as "successive patriline". Similarly, Garde's glosses with the technical term "ascending generation matriline" (p. 53) can,

I would suggest, be interpreted as referring to a person viewed as someone whose mother is one's mother's mother.

In his "Summary of Bininj Gunwok kinship terms" Garde glosses the verb *-bornang* as "be in successive patriline, beget", and *-yawmey* as "be in successive matriline, conceive (literally, 'child-get')". In the approach proposed here, both these verbs would be portrayed as polysemous, but only two-way (rather than three-way) polysemous. Roughly, one meaning refers to the biological father, and the other to someone "*like* the father" (because of the specific relationship). A parallel analysis would of course apply to the "matriline term" *-yawmey*.

In sentences in which the verb *-yawmey* (or *-bornang*) is used about two people who are in "matrilineal" (or "patrilineal") relationship to somebody else, that is, sentences with a dual or "unit-augmented" subject, only the second meaning of the verb can be involved. This can be illustrated with Garde's sentence (3.16) (p. 62 this volume) (for abbreviations see note 2):

(3.16) *ben-yawme-y*

> 3 uaP-conceive-PP
> That woman and her sibling (male or female) are 'mother' to OBJ
> (literally: they 2 'mothered' OBJ)

My proposed gloss:
> these two people can think about someone [OBJ] like this:
> "my mother is this someone's mother's mother"

As these paraphrases show, what matters in Bininj Gunwok thinking is not only the distinction between a father's father and a mother's mother, but also the idea of a "shared father's father": if my father is your father's father, then I will think about you in a special way, and you will think in a special way about me. Similarly, if my mother is your mother's mother, then I will think about you in a special way, and vice versa. Such a way of thinking is foreign to speakers of English, but it is not something that they could not grasp.

Consider also the phrase *ngane-yaw*, glossed by Garde as "we two are children of our ascending generation matriline" – a gloss that can hardly be understood through ordinary English. Garde comments, somewhat more helpfully, that this locution "could possibly be translated as 'we two are her children', the propositus (i.e. the person from whose perspective the relationship is viewed) being the mother of the first-person unit-augmented referents." However, he goes on to comment that "the propositus could also be a male, i.e. brothers (sic) of one's mother, which is why I have glossed the term as "we two are children of our ascending generation matriline" (p. 53).

As already noted, however, this last paraphrase is incomprehensible, and leaves the readers with the impression that Bininj-Gunwok ways of thinking are completely inaccessible to outsiders. Such an impression would not be right, because once it is recognised that the sentence in question has two meanings, both these meanings can be stated in ordinary English, and moreover, in words cross-translatable into Bininj-Gunwok itself, along the following lines:

1. we can both think about this someone like this:
    "this is my mother"

2. we can both think about this someone like this:
    "this is someone like my mother
    because this someone's mother is my mother's mother"

And one more example: the phrase *ngandi-yawmey*, which Garde glosses as 'they conceived me' or 'they from whom I descend matrilineally' (p. 70). I would suggest that in ordinary English, the meaning of this seemingly strange sentence can be rendered as follows:

> *ngandi-yawmey*
> they can (all) think about me like this:
>> "my mother is this someone's mother's mother"

To sum up, what these kinship verbs show is that there are, in the shared conceptual vocabulary of the speakers of languages like Bininj Gunwok, some important concepts that are absent from the conceptual vocabulary of English speakers and that build on the concepts of '(someone's) father's father' and '(someone's) mother's mother'. These concepts are, potentially, understandable to English speakers, but they are not part of their shared conceptual currency.

In his paper "Kinship Verbs", to which Garde refers, Nicholas Evans (2000: 117) writes about two other languages of Northern Australia, Ilgar and Iwaidja:

> Consider the kinship verbal root *wulaŋ*, which is used in paraphrasing the nominal roots *gamu* 'mother, mother's sister', *yaja* '(maternal) uncle', and *gaɲuɲ* 'sister's child (male speaker), child (female speaker)'. On the assumption that 'mother' is the core meaning (since it is genealogically the closest to ego), I shall gloss it as 'be mother to'.

This is illustrated, inter alia, with the following two sentences:

(a) ŋan-ŋa-wulaŋ
    1SG.OBJ-3SG.FEM.ERG-be.mother.to: NON.PAST
    'my mother' (she is mother to me)

(b) ŋa-ni-wulaŋ
    1SG.OBJ-3SG.MASC.ERG-mother: NON.PAST
    'my maternal uncle' (he is (as a) mother to me)

These glosses suggest that the meaning of *wulaŋ* as used in relation to a man (one's mother's brother) is different from the meanings of the same word used about a woman (one's mother), and that the two meanings can be represented as follows:

(a) 'mother to me'
(b) 'as a mother to me'

This analysis makes a lot of sense, but presumably it was intended only as an approximation: the man in question is "as a mother to me" for a particular reason, namely, because his mother is my mother's mother. This brings us to the following NSM-based glosses for (a) and (b):

(a) I can think about her like this:
    "this is my mother"

(b) I can think about him like this:
    "this is someone like my mother
    because his mother is my mother's mother"

These glosses are of course in line with the analysis that I presented earlier in relation to Murray Garde's examples from Bininj Gunwok.

Dyadic Terms

Importantly, what applies to kinship verbs applies also to so-called "dyadic terms", such as those described by Garde (in relation to Bininj Gunwok) in the following passage:

-kunakko 'a husband and wife pair' (literally: 'two of the [same] fire/hearth')

-beyko usually 'father and child pair' but a more comprehensive definition is 'adjacent patrilineal generation pair' ('F/FB/FZ and mC/fBC' or 'person and F[Z or B])'.

-yawko usually 'mother and child pair' but a more comprehensive definition is 'M/MZ/MB' and 'wCm'ZC' or 'person and M(B or Z)' (p. 59)

It seems unlikely that, for example, *-beyko* has a unitary meaning, covering both the biological father and the biological father's brothers and sisters. As Garde says, *-beyko* usually stands for an actual father-and-child pair, and it parallels actual pairs such as husband-and-wife. At the same time, it can be used in a different sense, with reference to the "adjacent patrilineal generation pair". Assuming that the dyadic term is indeed polysemous, I would propose the following interpretation, which avoids both disjunctive analyses such as 'person and F [Z or B]' and technical and semi-technical terms such as "patrilineal", "adjacent" and "generation":

beyko$_1$
two people
people know that one of these people can think about the other like this:
  "this is my father"

beyko$_2$
two people
people can know that one of these people can think about the other like this:
  "this is someone like my father
  because this someone's father is my father's father"

Obviously the same approach would apply to the "matrilineal" dyadic term *yawko*:

yawko$_1$
two people
people can know that one of these people can think about the other like this:
  "this is my mother"

yawko$_2$
two people
people can know that one of these people can think about the other like this:
  "this is someone like my mother
  because this someone's mother is my mother's mother"

I have included in these paraphrases the framing component 'people can know that' in order to show that the dyadic term presents the relationship between the two members of the pair as a social fact. Whereas in the case of kinship verbs the speaker appears to be informing the addressee about the nature of the relationship, in the case of a dyadic term the speaker appears to be indicating how he or she is thinking about the pair (namely *sub specie* of the known relationship binding its two members).

The Notion of 'Patriline'

Finally, it is worth noting that while the literature on languages such as Bininj Gunwok is heavily dependent on the use of the technical terms *patriline* and *matriline*, these terms never seem to be defined. The adjectives *patrilineal* and *matrilineal*, from which these nouns are derived, are normally defined in dictionaries of anthropology in complex and metaphorical terms such as "descent which is traced through the male line" (Seymour Smith 1986: 218). Using NSM, we can propose the following explanation of the thinking that, as I understand, these nouns are intended to capture:

someone's patriline
many people, all these people are like one something
some of these people are men, some are women, some are children
this someone can think about these people like this:
"I am one of these people because it is like this:
my father is one of these people,
my father's father is one of these people"
all these people can think like this

7 Retrospective

The importance of the concepts of 'mother's mother' and 'father's father' in many Australian languages is often emphasised by Australianists. Evans himself writes in his grammar of Bininj Gunwok (2003: 44), to which Garde also refers:

> As in virtually all Australian languages, there is a fundamental distinction between parallel grandparents (FF, MM), in which the same type of filiative link (e.g. father-child) is repeated for two generations, and cross-grandparents (FM, MF), in which there are two types of filiative link.

The semantics of kinship verbs in Bininj Gunwok fits in well with this generalisation, as arguably does also the semantics of some "dyadic terms" described by Evans (2003) in relation to Bininj Gunwok in the following two sentences (p. 163; "Dj" stands for the dialect called Gun-dedjnjenghmi):

5.158 *guni-yau-go*
Dj 2a-child.of.female-DYAD
'you two, mother and child (or mother's brother/sister's child)'

5.159 *bani-bei-go*
Dj 3ua-child.of.male-DYAD
'father and child, father's sister and nephew/niece'

To avoid a multiply disjunctive analysis, we could assign to each of these sentences two readings, glossing them as follows:

5.158(a)
you two
people know that one of you can think about the other like this:
   "this is my mother"

5.158(b)
you two
people know that one of you can think about the other like this:
   "this is someone like my mother
   because this someone's mother is my mother's mother"

5.159(a)
two people
people know that one of these people can think about the other like this:
   "this is my father"

5.159(b)
two people
people know that one of these people can think about the other like this:
   "this someone's father is my father's father"

Presumably, no English speaker would think about a pair such as Prince William and Princess Anne, or Prince William and Prince Andrew, in terms of "father's father", so obviously the way of thinking embedded in the meaning of dyadic terms like -*beyko* or *beigo* (as in 5.1.59b) is deeply unfamiliar to speakers of English. It is not inherently incomprehensible, however, and to articulate it in English we do not need to have recourse to arcane technical language inaccessible to non-specialists, or to bend ordinary usage in peculiar ways and to say that, for example, Princess Anne either "begat" or "fathered" Prince William. What we can say is that William can think about Anne (and Andrew) like this: "this someone's father is my father's father". On the other hand, about Earl Spencer (Princess Diana's brother) William can think like this: "this someone's mother is my mother's mother". Accordingly, Prince William and Princess Anne together can be viewed as a -*beyko* or *beigo* (a pair anchored in William's father's father and Anne's father), whereas a pair composed of Prince William and Earl Spencer could be viewed as a *yawko* or *yaugo* (a pair anchored in William's mother's mother and Earl Spencer's mother).

The fact that Princess Anne's mother is also the mother of Prince William's father, or that Earl Spencer's father is also the father of Prince William's mother, would not be of interest from a Bininj Gunwok speaker's point of view: what matters is the identity of a person's father's father and their mother's mother, not of their "cross-grandparents" (father's mother and mother's father).

The concepts of 'father's father' and 'mother's mother', which are not named in (ordinary) English, clearly don't have the same role for speakers of English as they do for speakers of Bininj Gunwok – just as the concepts of 'brother' and 'sister', which are not named in Bininj Gunwok, don't have the same role for speakers of Bininj Gunwok as they do for speakers of English. But the concepts of 'father' and 'mother' are named in both these languages and can be used as stepping stones for what Jean Harkins in the title of her 1994 book about Aboriginal Australia called *Bridging Two Worlds*.

It is worth noting here that many languages outside Australia distinguish lexically between mother's mother and father's father (e.g., Mandarin does, and so does Danish), and that some languages in Australia do not (e.g., Pitjantjatjara and Pintupi; cf. Elkin 1940; Myers 1986; Goddard 1985). What is more unusual about languages like Bininj Gunwok is their way of aligning people through their fathers and fathers' fathers (or mothers and mothers' mothers). Thus, while a person's father's father (*mawah*) is distinguished lexically (and conceptually) from this person's mother's mother (*kakkak*), one word (and one concept), *-bornang*, can align a person with all the people who have the same father as this person's father; and one word (and one concept), *-yawmey*, can align him or her with all those who have the same mother as this person's mother. Such ways of thinking are unfamiliar to speakers of English but they are not totally impenetrable.

8 Concluding Remarks and Future Directions: Technical Language and Human Understanding

Given a measure of mental discipline, effort and experience, unfamiliar concepts embodied in kinship terminologies can be explained to outsiders through ordinary language. To grasp them, one does not require a tutorial in kinship studies or in arcane formalisms of any kind. One does need, however, an explanation. If this explanation is free of any technical terminology, if it is couched in words that one can understand, and if one is prepared to make an effort to get out of one's accustomed ways of thinking, then with the help of such an explanation, authentic understanding can be reached.

The issue of technical terms as an obstacle to understanding is, I think, a very serious one, as well as a very old one, and yet it is often dismissed, as well as ignored, in human sciences. Let me therefore address it here upfront, recalling some strong statements made three and a half centuries ago by Leibniz, who wrote:

> Technical terms are ... to be shunned as worse than a dog or snake.... The greatest clarity is found in commonplace terms with their popular usage retained. There is always a certain obscurity in technical terms.... Our judgments are thus rendered more reliable by this process of analyzing technical terms into merely popular ones; hence a perfect demonstration merely carries out such analysis to the ultimate and best-known elements.
>
> *Leibniz (1969 [1670], p. 123)*

Leibniz recognised, of course, that technical terminology can often allow greater brevity, but he insisted that when it is used it must rely on previous explanations offered in ordinary words used in accordance with ordinary usage. He did not accept that there are insights in human sciences that can only be expressed through technical language: " ... we have established the fact", he wrote, "that there is nothing which cannot be explained in popular terms, and that the more popular the terms, the clearer the discourse ... " (p. 125). He called this "one of the fundamental rules of philosophical style", and he lamented that it is "violated frequently, especially by metaphysicians and dialecticians" (p.125). The subjects that they deal with "occur commonly in the utterances, writings, and thoughts of uneducated people and are met with frequently in everyday life". Accordingly, ordinary people can talk about such subjects with their own ordinary words. "When such words are available, it is a sin to obscure matters by inventing new and mostly more inconvenient terms (to say nothing of the awkwardness often shown in manufacturing such words)" (p. 125).

It seems clear that what applies to the broad spectrum of human interests that Leibniz called "philosophy" applies also to linguistic anthropology in general and to kinship studies in particular. Here as elsewhere, technical discourse should be avoided, and when and where it is used, it needs to explain itself in ordinary language. When the subject matter concerns other people's ways of thinking, then it needs to explain itself in words and phrases that those involved could understand. When meanings are explained through simple and "ordinary" words, authentic understanding can be achieved – both inside groups of people bound by the same language and between such groups. This is not about a "reader-friendly style", but about clear thinking and genuine understanding.

Accordingly, cross-linguistic semantic analysis that translates complex and unfamiliar ideas into combinations of simple and familiar ones can be more than an academic exercise in linguistic anthropology: it can also serve the purposes of cross-cultural understanding and communication. In some situations, it may even serve the purposes of cross-generational education and language revitalisation.

Innumerable languages of the world are dying out and the ways of thinking embedded in them are becoming irretrievably lost to cultural outsiders, and even to the children and grandchildren of the insiders. Paradoxically, while Global English is becoming an unprecedented force for world-wide understanding, in many areas it is also becoming an instrument of conceptual and cultural homogenisation of the world. The ever-growing domination of academic English in social sciences, including anthropology and linguistics, is a good case in point.

There is a further paradox here: the fact that academic English is increasingly taken for granted as the instrument of scientific understanding for any domain means that at a time when linguistics and anthropology emphasise, as never before, the enormous cultural diversity of languages, it is also widely assumed that the ways of thinking embedded in all these diverse languages can be explained by being translated into academic English. Given the ever-growing prestige and power of English, including technical English, in international science, right across the spectrum, many anthropologists and linguists appear to be more, rather than less, inclined to assume that, for example, words like 'patrilineal' and 'matrilineal', 'ascending' and 'descending', or 'sibling' and 'generation' can be used to explain how speakers of endangered languages in Australia, Oceania and Africa think.

Apart from the inherent Anglocentrism and scientism of such approaches, they clearly exclude native speakers from the conversation. By contrast, the approach illustrated in the present paper treats indigenous speakers as potential consultants – not as the word 'consultants' tends to be used in current scholarship (as a polite euphemism for the outdated 'informants') but in a real sense, which presupposes a common language and a set of shared concepts (Goddard and Wierzbicka 2014b). Such a reinterpretation of the key notion of 'consultant' opens a space where linguistic anthropology can meet with inter-cultural communication. Arguably, in the area of kinship studies, authentic 'consultation' with native speakers would require setting aside, at least part of the time, some of the technical and academic English in which linguistic anthropology has for a long time been entrapped, and trying to think, above all, with words like 'mother' and 'father', 'be born', 'wife' and 'husband', and 'man', 'woman', and 'child'.

Related Topics

2 Semantic Categorization and Cognition (Dimmendaal); 9 Language Socialization (Paugh); 10 Studying Language Acquisition in Different Linguistic and Cultural Settings (Stoll); 22 Language in the Age of Globalization (Jacquemet); 29 Language Maintenance and Revitalization (Cowell); 30 Language Endangerment and Revitalization Strategies (Brittain and MacKenzie); 31 The Politics of Language Endangerment (Meek).

What links this chapter with Dimmendaal's is the focus on semantic categorisation considered from a cognitive point of view. The chapter is related to those by Paugh and Stoll in that it considers meanings from the point of view of their learnability; its concerns are close to those discussed in the chapters by Cowell, Brittain and MacKenzie and Meek in that it links cross-linguistic semantics with the themes of language endangerment and revitalisation, which are inseparable from what is arguably the central challenge facing anthropological linguistics today: that of overcoming Anglocentrism in exploring languages and cultures.

Notes

1 It should be noted that in addition to its half-heartedness, Brown's commitment to lexical universals had another problem: a lack of attention to lexical polysemy. One cannot establish that all languages have words meaning 'mother' and 'father' if one mistakes polysemic meanings of the relevant words for unitary ones. Brown was not unaware of this problem, but he did not bear it in mind consistently.
2 The abbreviations used in the interlinear glosses cited in this paper are as follows: 1: first person; 2a: second person augmented; 3: third person; ERG: ergative; FEM: feminine; MASC: masculine; OBJ: object; P: past; PP: past perfective; PAST: past; SG: singular; ua-: unit augmented.

References

Besemeres, Mary. (2002). *Translating One's Self: Language and Selfhood in Cross-Cultural Autobiography*. Peter Lang.
Brown, Donald E. (1991). *Human Universals*. Temple University Press.
Burling, Robbins. (1964). Cognition and Componential Analysis: God's Truth or Hocus-pocus? *American Anthropologist*, 66(1): 20–28.
D'Andrade, Roy. (1995). *The Development of Cognitive Anthropology*. Cambridge University Press.
Elkin, A.P. (1940). Kinship in South Australia: Region 4. The Aluridja Group, Western South Australia. *Oceania*, X(2): 201–233.
Evans, Nicholas. (2000). Kinship Verbs. In Petra M. Vogel and Bernard Comrie (eds), *Approaches to the Typology of Word Classes*, pp. 103–172. Mouton de Gruyter.
Evans, Nicholas. (2003). *Bininj Gun-wok: A Pan-dialectal Grammar of Mayali, Kunwinjku and Kune*, 2 vols. Pacific Linguistics.
Evans, Nicholas. (2010). *Dying Words: Endangered Languages and What They Have to Tell Us*. Wiley-Blackwell.
Feinberg, Richard and Martin Ottenheimer (eds). (2001). *The Cultural Analysis of Kinship: The Legacy of David M. Schneider*. University of Illinois Press.
Fogelson, Raymond. (2001). Schneider Confronts Componential Analyses. In Richard Feinberg and Martin Ottenheimer (eds), *The Cultural Analysis of Kinship: The Legacy of David M. Schneider*, pp. 33–45. University of Illinois Press.
Garde, Murray. (2013). *Culture, Interaction and Person Reference in an Australian Language*. John Benjamins.
Geertz, Clifford. (1976). "From the Native's Point of View": On the Nature of Anthropological Understanding. In Keith Basso and Henry A. Selby (eds), *Meaning in Anthropology*, 221–237. University of New Mexico.
Goddard, Cliff. (1985). *A Grammar of Yankunytjatjara*. Institute for Aboriginal Development.
Goddard, Cliff and Anna Wierzbicka. (2014a). *Words and Meanings: Lexical Semantics across Domains, Languages and Cultures*. Oxford University Press.
Goddard, Cliff and Anna Wierzbicka. (2014b). Semantic Fieldwork and Lexical Universals. *Studies in Language*, 38(1): 80–127.
Goddard, Cliff and Anna Wierzbicka (eds). (2002). *Meaning and Universal Grammar: Theory and Empirical Findings*, 2 vols. John Benjamins.
Goodenough, Ward. (1970). *Description and Comparison in Cultural Anthropology*. Cambridge University Press.
Harkins, Jean. (1994). *Bridging Two Worlds: Aboriginal English and Crosscultural Understanding*. University of Queensland Press.
Hoffman, Eva. (1989). *Lost in Translation: A Life in a New Language*. Dutton.
Jones, Doug. (2010). Human Kinship, from Conceptual Structure to Grammar. *Behavioral and Brain Sciences*, 33(5): 367–416.
Leaf, Murray J. (2006). Experimental-Formal Analysis of Kinship. *Ethnology*, 45(4): 305–330.
Leibniz, Gottfried Wilhelm. (1969 [1670]) Preface to an edition of Nizolius. In Leroy E. Loemker (ed.), *Philosophical Papers and Letters*, pp. 121–130. Reidel.

Levinson, Stephen. (2010). Advancing our Grasp of Constrained Variation in a Crucial Cognitive Domain. *Behavioral and Brain Sciences*, *33*(5): 391–392.
Myers, Fred. (1986). *Pintupi Country, Pintupi Self: Sentiment, Place and Politics Among Western Desert Aborigines*. Australian Institute of Aboriginal Studies; Smithsonian Institution Press.
Read, Dwight. (2001). What is Kinship? In Richard Feinberg and Martin Ottenheimer (eds), *The Cultural Analysis of Kinship: The Legacy of David M. Schneider*, pp. 78117. University of Illinois Press.
Romney, A. Kimball and Roy G. D'Andrade. (1964). Cognitive Aspects of English Kinship. *American Anthropologist*, *67*(5): 146–170.
Scheffler, Harold W. (1978). *Australian Kin Classification*. Cambridge University Press.
Schneider, David M. (1984). *A Critique of the Study of Kinship*. The University of Michigan Press.
Seymour-Smith, Charlotte. (1986). *Macmillan Dictionary of Anthropology*. Macmillan.
Shapiro, Warren. (2008). What Human Kinship is Primarily About: Toward a Critique of the New Kinship Studies. *Social Anthropology*, *16*: 137–153.
Shore, Bradd. (1996). *Culture in Mind: Cognition, Culture and the Problem of Meaning*. Oxford University Press.
Smith, Zadie. (2009). *Changing My Mind: Occasional Essays*. Penguin Press HC.
Sousa, Paolo. (2003). The Fall of Kinship: Towards an Epidemiological Explanation. *Journal of Cognition and Culture*, *3*(4): 264–303.
Wallace, Anthony F.C. and John Atkins. (1969). The Meaning of Kinship Terms. In Stephen Tyler (ed.), *Cognitive Anthropology*, pp. 345–369. Holt, Rinehart and Winston.
Wierzbicka, Anna. (1986). Semantics and the Interpretation of Cultures: The Meaning of 'Alternate Generations' Devices in Australian Languages. *Man (N.S.)*, *21*: 34–49.
Wierzbicka, Anna. (1992). *Semantics, Culture, and Cognition: Universal Human Concepts in Culture-specific Configurations*. Oxford University Press.
Wierzbicka, Anna. (2010). Lexical Universals of Kinship and Social Cognition. An Invited Commentary on D. Jones. Human Kinship, from Conceptual Structure to Grammar. *Behavioral and Brain Sciences*, *33*(5): 403–404.
Wierzbicka, Anna. (2013). Kinship and Social Cognition in Australian Languages: Kayardild and Pitjantjatjara. *Australian Journal of Linguistics*, *33*(3): 302–321.
Wierzbicka, Anna. (2014). *Imprisoned in English: The Hazards of English as Default Language*. Oxford University Press.
Wierzbicka, Anna. (forthcoming). Back to 'mother' and 'father': overcoming the Eurocentrism of kinship studies through eight lexical universals.

Further Reading

D'Andrade, Roy. (1995). *The Development of Cognitive Anthropology*. Cambridge University Press.
Evans, Nicholas. (2010). *Dying Words: Endangered Languages and What They Have to Tell Us*. Wiley-Blackwell.
Garde, Murray. (2013). *Culture, Interaction and Person Reference in an Australian Language*. John Benjamins.
Geertz, Clifford. (2000). *Available Light: Anthropological Reflections on Philosophical Topics*. Princeton University Press.
Goddard, Cliff (ed.). (2013). Semantics and/in Social Cognition. Special Issue of *Australian Journal of Linguistics*, *33*(3).
Goddard, Cliff and Anna Wierzbicka. (2014). *Words and Meanings: Lexical Semantics across Domains, Languages and Cultures*. Oxford University Press.
Levisen, Carsten. (2012). *Cultural Semantics and Social Cognition: A Case Study on the Danish Universe of Meaning*. Mouton de Gruyter.
Shweder, Richard A. (2003) *Why Do Men Barbecue? Recipes for Cultural Psychology*. Harvard University Press.
Wierzbicka, Anna. (2014). *Imprisoned in English: The Hazards of English as Default Language*. Oxford University Press.

6

Being in the Cloud

Analysis of Discourse in Online Communities

Tracy LeBlanc-Wories

Introduction/Definitions

Anthropology rests on a strong foundation of fieldwork. Since Boasian tradition has underscored getting out of the armchair and into the field, we have had many evolutions in both practice and perspective to reflect current academic trends, reinforcing the fact that anthropology is a dynamic area of study. When conducting fieldwork in anthropology, one has a plethora of choices for methods – participant observation being the most popular – but in linguistic anthropology, we have a special set of concerns and ethical quandaries to attend to before setting off into the field. Many of those concerns include understanding *who* the speaker is and *who* the audience is and from *whose* "data" exactly we are to seek permission to document, perhaps transcribe, interpret, and potentially publish. All disciplines share some fieldwork and ethical concerns, specifically acquiring the appropriate permission from institutions, communities in question, and any funding bodies; however, in linguistic anthropology, these concerns are confounding because of the question of *who*.

Even more confounding than the traditional *who* problem is the current nature of research itself – more projects are moving completely online. The discourse community is now posing much more complicated questions. Who are the proprietors? The interlocutors? The audience? The sponsors? Doing fieldwork in linguistic anthropology used to mean carrying a heavy load of equipment (usually requiring a team of graduate students or assistants) for recording data (video and audio), seeking permission of your institution and the community with whom you will be spending time, arranging living quarters, securing travel visas, applying for NIH or NSF or some other source(s) of funding, requesting Institutional Review Board approval or exemption, and even finding one or more insiders to translate and/or help guide. Now we have much more streamlined preparation and a much lighter equipment load, but the ground we have gained with lighter and better equipment is outstripped by current ethical complexities far beyond what earlier founders of and practitioners in the field ever imagined.

Ethics and methodologies of fieldwork in communities of online discourse are the main topics of this chapter. We will briefly stand on the shoulders of the giants who came before us, those who paved the way for our perceived easier time of it, and arrive at the current issues in the field, or rather, in the cloud. Fieldwork in anthropology can certainly lend its experience and successes to linguistic fieldwork, but both disciplines are lagging in the online domain of study. Many traditional anthropologists remain uncomfortable with online research for a variety of reasons, but the discomfort seems to be related to two issues: refusal to acknowledge the cloud as a legitimate field or unwillingness to confront the ethical maze that doing rich anthropological fieldwork in the cloud entails. When working on my research project (first, a linguistic ethnography and, later, discourse analysis of online communities), a few, more traditional anthropologists lamented the fact that I was not "doing" anthropology. I had not travelled afar, sought permission from a foreign government, arranged accommodation, or conducted "real" fieldwork (LeBlanc 2005). Regardless of the perceived or real differences from face-to-face interaction, online research is a worthy, valuable, and enriching endeavor to study discourse in online communities. This new frontier of the field is not at all new to other disciplines, and it can push our discipline forward, beyond traditional fieldwork. We live in a world of Twitter and Facebook, where people can connect on meaningful levels (or on superficial ones) instantly. *Hashtag* and *friend* mean different things today than a mere five years ago. Language is changing more quickly now because our vessels for communication improve daily, not over decades. Although it may seem that language has degraded as we have gone online and use fewer characters to express ourselves, linguistic anthropologists can embrace this evolution in language and language behavior, as it affords us the opportunity not only to document changes in language morphology, syntax, semantics, and pragmatics, but also gain insight into how human language is such a flexible, yet stable phenomenon.

Many of us spend significant amounts of time online. We belong to communities that may exist solely in cyberspace, so understanding how these are constructed, maintained, and re-negotiated through technological advances is vital to our study of the essence of humanity. Studying language use in these communities is a natural extension. Once we understand how language is used in discourse communities, we gain much more insight into the culture we are trying to understand. Mary Jill Brody (Louisiana State University) has always said that "language is culture and culture is language," which cannot be more appropriate an anthem for studying language in online communities of discourse. Obviously, no community is exactly like any other, whether face-to-face or online, so there is room for many approaches to analysis of a community's language use. However, current approaches may not be easily transferred to the online medium. Therefore, we are obliged as scholars to seek methods that satisfy the two most vital criteria: applicability/feasibility and ethical standards. Anthropologists have created and revised the most humanistic and holistic methods of studying the essence of being human, so it is our charge to continue that rich tradition of discourse analysis into the next generations, and this entails going online to do it.

Historical Perspectives

Many giants before us, including students of Franz Boas, Edward Sapir, and Dell Hymes, have emphasized a most important point: we cannot do discourse analysis without ethnography. Discourse analysis should include not only a transcript of the words exchanged; it needs much more depth. Discourse analysis informed by ethnography and anthropology's rich history of reflexivity enhances all analyses of not only discourse events themselves, but also discourse behavior. However, a greater number of linguistic anthropologists are examining online discourse behavior (LeBlanc 2010; Thurlow and Mroczek 2011). Many other disciplines, such as communication and media studies, have studied virtual communities (Jones 1997; Rheingold 2000; Smith and Kollock 1999), but those other disciplines do not examine language in use within the ethnographically informed context in which anthropologists work.

It is important to note here that scholars of computer-mediated communication (CMC) are the pioneers who have, since before the 1990s, provided much of our existing knowledge of how we communicate online (Bechar-Israeli 1995; Danet 1995; Jackson 1997; Mabry 1997; Morris and Ogan 1996; Paccagnella 1997; Parks and Floyd 1996). These scholars have begun the academic discussion of how the medium of the internet affects the ways in which we interact, conduct conversations or business, and create community. Each has offered different perspectives and within different areas of study. This is certainly not a complete list of CMC scholars, simply a sample of those who study how the internet affects our communicative behavior and who have influenced those of us who study CMC within linguistic and/or anthropological frameworks.

Danet (1995) chronicles early research that informed the more recent CMC scholars. She notes that before the 1990s, most study of CMC focused more on organizational efficiency and less on human (even phatic) interaction. She also introduces those new to the field of previous studies of synchronicity in online communication, such as Internet Relay Chat (IRC), some of the first interactive platforms by which everyday users convened online in real time. Danet also informs us that prior to her and others' study of CMC, scholars neglected to inquire into the potential community aspects of the internet, where users went online for recreation (phatic communion) as well as for business or educational transactional purposes. Most importantly, at the inception of the *Journal of Computer-Mediated Communication*, scholars like Danet and others succeeded in broadening the field of CMC study from primarily focusing on the technical aspects of the internet as a transactional tool to also studying the social implications of being online and how people use the internet to interact for various other reasons, some of those being purely social. Additionally, Parks and Floyd (1996) discuss social aspects of online interaction, focusing on newsgroups (specifically Usenet), where users post comments or items of interest to various newsgroups on early versions of the internet. They argue, despite earlier literature and prevailing popular opinion of that time, that people do indeed form personal and meaningful bonds with other users online. They also describe what I call accommodations: how people recreate or substitute for the communicative cues that being online removes, for example emoticons, bold type, and punctuation. This research is important because it reveals not only how people use the internet to interact socially, but also how doing so is different, yet not less impactful, than face-to-face interactions.

Related to how we interact socially, Bechar-Israeli (1995) discusses the significant ways that people create identity online, specifically nicknames on IRC. Choosing a nickname (or an avatar in later instantiations of web community interaction) necessitates much identity creation work that includes consideration of what persona someone wants to project. There is an aspect of starting fresh or even hiding or exaggerating in this naming process, which contrasts sharply with face-to-face interaction. What is significant here is that once a user plays or interacts using that chosen "nick," she builds on that intentionally and thoughtfully created persona and interacts in a community or across many communities and for a long period of time as that "nick." Bechar-Israeli also illustrates how frequent users or players have a keen appreciation of the online medium, using their knowledge of how quickly technology changes to their own advantage and playing with language in turn. This particular work is similar to my own research in that it highlights the link between techie interlocutors and their linguistic innovation and play.

Equally important is the pioneering work of Paccagnella (1997), which emphasizes the importance of fieldwork in online settings. Ethnography is the primary and most vital step in conducting holistic analysis of language use, and the validation our field now has is greatly due to works like this and others, who have remarked on how the internet is a mass medium that is as worthy of study as other media such as television and print media (Morris and Ogan

1996). The analysis of the structure of language in online contexts has been addressed by several prominent scholars (December 1996; Jackson 1997; Mabry 1997). Particularly relevant to online discourse analysis in my community of study is Mabry (1997), who discusses the structure of *flames*, or heightened discourse events that often occur in online settings. *Flames* are akin to face-to-face arguments, but not similar enough to be treated the same way. Many times in online discourse communities, just as in offline instances, people will enter into arguments that may escalate, but *flames* are special discourse events that occur only online because, although interlocutors may be arguing, they must accommodate for the lack of face-to-face encounter. So, *flames* will include special discourse markers such as quoting other members' posts before a reply, orthographic innovations like emphasizing words with asterisks, and typing "<" and ">" around words in order to convey a tone of condescension or of pretension. Much of this nuanced orthography derives from programming language because the earlier online communities of discourse consisted of gamers and/or programmers who frequently adopted conventions from their fields in order to create their own specialized language (Blashki and Nichol 2005; LeBlanc 2010; Raymond and Steele 1996).

Knowing how valuable our ethnographically informed analyses are and building upon the foundation established by CMC scholars, we can transfer our unique skill set to the cloud – bridging the gap in research on discourse communities and their interactions. This skill set is vast and unique to anthropologists. We understand the intense and extensive time requirement necessary to form valuable and trusting relationships with our communities of study, we are trained in linguistics (specifically phonology, morphology, syntax, and pragmatics), we are aware of our imprint in the field that changes it forever, and we are prepared for encountering and learning from new ways of living. With research going online, there are new skills to add to analysis (including transcription and interpretation) that are more useful to online situations. This chapter centers on these.

There are recent ethnographers of online communities, including Hutchby (2001), Holt (2004), and LeVine and Scollon (2003). Hutchby (2001) considers conversation analysis' role to be a tool for uncovering two major themes: how technology affects conversation and how communication technologies are social (like earlier technologies of the telephone and radio). These are important questions, but better left for communication theorists, because linguistic anthropology focuses on the human essence within whatever medium people are using to interact. Therefore, although the answers to the questions regarding how technology affects communication are valuable to our analysis of discourse, these insights alone are not sufficient for our endeavor, even though Hutchby does attempt to understand how we use technology to mediate and perhaps even create social bonds. The medium does indeed matter, and it affects the ways in which we reach out to one another. We are now inventing new avenues for interactions, but does that change the interaction itself? Holt (2004) studies identity creation and negotiation via virtual media. He builds on the position of previous scholars (Hutchby 2001; Wilson and Peterson 2001) that the virtual medium is just another context where humans interact and engage in the same communicative actions to form communities. So, for these scholars, interaction itself does not change regardless of the medium.

Other scholars (LeVine and Scollon 2004) disagree and believe that the medium of interaction indeed does matter as well as affect how we interact with each other. Obviously, face-to-face communication is different from online communication, both synchronous and asynchronous. Kuipers (2004) uses this notion to push anthropologists to expand the cornerstone ethnography of communication to include more flexible, multimodal means of linguistic interaction. This seems simple initially – just add a few elements to the list of concepts within the framework – but the task is much more daunting because the medium matters in an important, fundamental way. Unlike face-to-face interaction, online communicative interaction can be affected by the online medium itself in many significant ways: we cannot know what is happening, beyond the screen in the interlocutor's environment, that may have multiple effects on her. Likewise, we are not "there" with our discourse partner(s) to see what is in the immediate context of conversation, much less how it may be informing the discourse of the moment and discourse beyond the moment, and what previous contextual information that we cannot experience has influenced that particular history of discourse. This is where shared discourse histories may be confounded, as the medium is also an integral part of the discourse itself. Similar to face-to-face interactions, conversations are not solely the words and accompanying gestures exchanged. The conversation also includes what is happening surrounding the interlocutors and their words. The technological medium becomes part of the context.

Anthropologists have done fieldwork online and have produced fine ethnographies of virtual places (Boellstorff 2008; Hine 2000). The fruit from these works and the work of many virtual fieldworkers today is the realization and appreciation of how doing reflexive fieldwork yields intersubjectivity, and analyzing naturally occurring discourse (unlike scripted television shows or even naturally occurring but limited, sometimes ritualized talk) is much richer, even revealing interlocutors' metalinguistic awareness (Silverstein 1979) through their language interplay.

Boellstorff (2008) conducted years of ethnographic fieldwork through participant observation for his ethnographic project on Second Life, the virtual reality game where people create avatars, interact with other avatars, and enact lives in virtual places. One could consider these virtual worlds the latest form of an "imagined community" (Anderson 1983). The information from this ethnography is intertextual in that it streams audio and video from "real" sources while the player engages in virtual events and interactions with others. Boellstorff became a "citizen" of Second Life in order to do extensive and meaningful fieldwork, and he reflects on this dual identity as "homesteader" (Rheingold 2000) and researcher in his ethnography. This work is important because it serves as one of the first anthropologically oriented models of ethnography in a virtual space that is specifically made for creating community online. His work has brought anthropology through what was often lamented as a crisis period to re-iterate the value of ethnographic fieldwork, but that which does not necessarily require leaving home and touches on a global culture in the 21st century. Boellstorff's work and others' have now fixed anthropology within the other fields studying online human interaction, applying traditional ethnographic methods, such as participant observation and reflexivity to virtual places. Our discipline of anthropology is especially suited for studying online communities because we acknowledge the human essence of the spaces we create and their importance as integrally part of the discourses we analyze. We have an extensive and impressive foundation upon which to engage in the important work of analyzing online discourse behavior. What we need going forward is an amended method(s) for satisfying ethical concerns as well as for carrying out sound, anthropologically grounded analysis of language use that may occur completely online.

Critical Issues and Topics

American Anthropological Association's Statement on Ethics

Before setting off into the field (or the cloud), one must attend to the important task of satisfying every party involved with regard to ethical concerns. The task is never simple, but with fieldwork in the cloud, even ascertaining *who* the involved parties are is daunting. The ultimate question for anyone undertaking this task is how comfortable are we, as linguistic anthropologists, with the degree to which we have gone to satisfy our ethical concerns? We can certainly refer to the American Anthropological Association's Statement on Ethics as a starting point, but even though it is updated regularly, the authors of the statement do not directly address the complicating factors of doing research online. The AAA Statement on Ethics and Principles of Professional Responsibility (2012) has a list as follows:

1. Do no harm.
2. Be open and honest regarding your work.
3. Obtain informed consent and necessary permissions.
4. Weigh competing ethical obligations due collaborators and affected parties.
5. Make your results accessible.
6. Protect and preserve your records.
7. Maintain respectful and ethical professional relationships.

Once we attend to acquiring permission from our institution, we must focus on the community with whom we plan to spend time and from whom we will perhaps record or transcribe discourse. It is sometimes an asset, as with any kind of fieldwork, to have an extant and healthy rapport with the community. We should always gain permission from the site administrator or the community leader, but far beyond this, I feel strongly that although the observer's paradox is always present, we must still somehow make our intentions known to everyone in the community. This part of the project is where the individual scholar decides what method of obtaining informed consent works best for her project. When I outed myself as researcher, I was already a member of the community, which sometimes makes the research more difficult because boundaries may not stay erected (DeLyser 2001). I will explain that process below. However consent is obtained, despite the fact that the Institutional Review Board still leans toward more narrowly focused and offline research and that the AAA Statement on Ethics does not specifically deal with online-only projects, we need to satisfy our ethical standards as though we are setting precedent for future considerations of IRB and AAA statement revisions. The more research projects move online, the more valuable these first projects are with regard to satisfying ethical concerns.

When I began my first anthropology project, my intent was to conduct a mini-ethnography for a Master's thesis project. This quickly evolved into a linguistic ethnography because, at the time (2002–2005), one of the most fascinating traits of the community was their language and language use. *Leet speak* ("An Explanation of 1337 Speak" 2002; LeBlanc 2005; Rome 2001), or the Internet orthographic convention of adopting certain specific technological vocabulary (usually related to hacking or gaming) and interchanging some letters with numbers such as 3 for E and 7 for L (as in 1337 sp34k), was quite novel then, and the discourse community was a close-knit collection of techie-minded professionals and college students who gathered at one particular web address to bond over their shared affinity for certain items, including the latest technology. They used *leet speak* in specific contexts and conversations, not in every conversation. I became fascinated by this unique language community and their effortless code switching between mainstream English and this novel dialect. I had participated on the website long before attending graduate school, so when I approached the community about my idea, they were immediately receptive to my proposal, and gaining their permission went smoothly.

I obtained signed, written permission from the website's owner and administrator, and for all other members, I posted a new thread on the main forum of the website announcing my intentions and allowed for anyone to opt out of the project via email, whereby I would not use any threads of discourse in which they had participated. I received only one response, even though I left the "opt out" email account open for a year. Once members knew they were being studied, many took to creating the loftiest of insults to illustrate their *flaming* prowess; others engaged in posting ubiquitous quantities of banality just to be frustrating (both to me and the administrator). But eventually, threads resumed to their normal frequency and topics, and members returned to their usual hierarchy and interactions. Members sustained their community solidarity via many tacit rules of interaction. One of these rules was the knowledge of who were the elite, or leaders, and who were simply members. No one was overtly discouraged from joining in conversations, but most members knew when and how to enter into a conversation or how to begin a new one. If someone did not act appropriately within these tacit rules, other, usually high-ranking members would make it known that this particular poster was not participating correctly. Members also displayed and negotiated hierarchy through various forms of heightened discourse events, such as *flaming* and signaling. Fortunately, I was allowed to analyze threads that were initiated much earlier than my start date for research (some threads going back to 2000), so many of the usual observer's paradoxes, such as members' editing posts or acting differently because they knew they were being observed, were avoided. The owner/administrator gave me a copy of the archived discourse threads 2000–2003 so that even if members went back into older threads to edit their posts, my data displayed what was originally posted to the forum. My presence in the community as "researcher/member" and not just "member" did not affect any of the discourse I later analyzed because I had an unaltered earlier version. One advantage of online fieldwork if you have a good rapport with your community (even if you are never considered a "member") is precisely this avoidance of damaging the authenticity of the field by being in it, if provided with an archive of the discourse.

One of my other areas of concern was protecting the community's identity and safeguarding their data. I realized fairly quickly that many of my expectations of providing total anonymity would go unmet. Unfortunately, when working online, there is only a modicum of security when it comes to protecting identities, even if new or different avatars are used in lieu of the original ones. My fellow members agreed to allow me to use the name of the website where they interacted, so with a quick search, they are found. I did remove all avatars, but I provided transcripts of entire threads and this too could be easily retrieved if one searched the archives of the message board. Undeterred still, members did not seem to mind at all that their data was going public, mostly because those who regularly worked and spent time online already understood that anything they do online is public.

Yet another concern is preserving the discourse in exactly the same state as it originally appeared. In addition to using new identifiers for different interlocutors, I observed Spradley's (1980) "verbatim principle," whereby the researcher never re-phrases, re-defines, or in any way skews what is said or, in this case, posted in the original discourse. So, even if some institutional ethics standards may be outdated with regard to accounting for online research, the verbatim principle is never outdated. The current unavoidable problem is that with asynchronous data: much of the context of the discourse is ephemeral. No one can recall the exact environments of conversations that they took part in over the course of a year or even longer. Additionally, there are obvious disadvantages to not analyzing discourse in the moment that it occurs even though most discourse analysis simply cannot be conducted this way. No analyst can realistically record all minutiae of context in a discourse event, even when doing it in the moment or with video record. It is virtually impossible; however, one must ultimately choose whether one analyzes asynchronous discourse behavior that is already a bit decontextualized when reading and responding to a thread or with synchronous discourse behavior that more easily lends itself to rich analysis but in small amounts (in order to record every detail not only in the conversation itself but in the surrounding contexts – linguistic and nonlinguistic). This dilemma leads to the next focus for this chapter – methodologies. Whether we choose a very small piece of discourse or enormous threads of conversation, beyond satisfying ethical requirements the decision of how to analyze what data we have is the next logical step.

Current Contributions and Research

To quote Ottenheimer, only when we are totally immersed in the language we are analyzing, "to the point that you can speak it naturally and competently," can we or should we "compare and contrast worldviews as they are encapsulated within languages and address the larger issues of comparison on a holistic basis" (2006: 10). Doing fieldwork in linguistic anthropology requires of us, at a minimum, to learn the language of the community with whom we are living. How this translates to online communities of discourse depends on the language used. My project in online discourse analysis was in English, but a distinct dialect of it, *leet speak*. Today, most of us can read *leet speak* quite easily, but in 2005, it was still obscure to most end users of technology and took some time to learn, especially, fluent *leet speak*, where not all words were changed into alphanumeric instantiations, and much of the conversation was written in impeccable "standard" English for fear of retribution by a "grammar nazi" (LeBlanc 2005). Being online creates different layers of data that may not be present or taken into consideration vis-à-vis current methodologies. Furthermore, no single method can account for the myriad aspects of what discourse actually entails, whether online or offline. Online discourse analysis projects may vary, depending on the language in which the research is being conducted, but many projects are waiting in mainstream English. Regardless, the effort saved from learning a new language is quickly afforded to other endeavors of analysis. Building and maintaining relationships with your teachers or friends (formerly called informants) is one area that takes considerable time and effort, especially online, when you are not as easily available unless you are literally in front of a computer screen.

Another challenge to consider before beginning a project is the collection of the data itself. Some researchers may not have access to archived files with perfectly preserved discourse in whole chunks. Additionally, we must not discount the vast amount of context that is already lost. This is one hazard of working in the online medium. It is paramount that if one does receive an archive, one must either have taken part in some of the archived discourse or can be open about the fact that they were not part of the original conversation, and have therefore lost much of the surrounding and influencing contexts, beyond what the archive and distance from the event have already stripped from the data.

Main Research Methods

The ultimate goal of discourse analysis is to show how language is used in the moments of our lives and how language use is so intricately tied into other cultural facets – gender, class, age, "race," education, or religion. A different approach from doing several analyses to gain a finer-grained picture of the language/culture inextricability, a more inclusive and integrated method, such as the Ethnopragmatic Method (EPM) I explain below, could account not only for what each member is doing through language and how they are accomplishing their goals, but also for what is occurring between these interactions and what is occurring on the periphery of them in the larger discourse. Members may share knowledge or information, they may transact, or they may engage in simple phatic communion by having a conversation; however, the means by which this is accomplished is informed by many different layers of pre-established knowledge in addition to the struggle to negotiate position or status. On the periphery of all of this work taking place in mere moments of discourse, interlocutors are also affecting, informing, and using the surrounding contextual fields.

The layered aspect of the EPM is why it is different from any other discourse analytic models (Du Bois 2007, Culpeper 1996, Sperber and Wilson 1995). Many models are useful for particular kinds of analysis, especially if one is investigating specific aspects of some discourse events, for example relevance theoretic-specific exchanges (Sperber and Wilson 1995), politeness or impoliteness in use (Brown and Levinson 1987, Bousfield 2008, Culpeper 1996), or back-and-forth negotiations of stance (Du Bois 2007). Another more anthropologically minded model, the cross-cultural pragmatics approach of Wierzbicka's (1996) "natural semantic metalanguage," has succeeded in producing unbiased translations of terms found in a variety of cultural settings and in avoiding those "universal" expectations of what is considered "appropriate" language use (Grice 1989).

But we are still bound by the parameters of our methods, and therefore it is imperative that we think about even more holistic ways to analyze discourse. The EPM is meant to be a starting point for the linguistic anthropologist to create a new method in this pursuit. One important requirement of any new or augmented method should be that it is applicable to both online and offline discourse, regardless of mode or medium. I illustrate the EPM in the diagram (Figure 6.1), and it is immediately apparent that the method is cumbersome and complicated and not easily adopted. But, in order to truly appreciate and account for all aspects of discourse (granted that we all agree what is entailed in discourse events and all that is and has

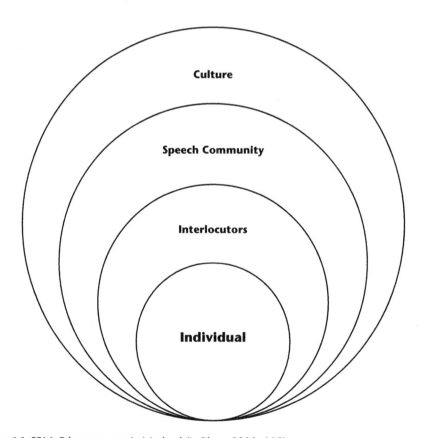

Figure 6.1 EPM: Ethnopragmatic Method (LeBlanc 2010: 118)

been informing it), we must show how and where all the aspects fit in. Where one applies this method is left for the individual analyst to decide.

I would, however, suggest the following. After traditional discourse analytic methodology, one must not only transcribe conversation, but also provide context and descriptions of the interlocutors and the situations surrounding the discourse in addition to interpretation(s). The EPM goes a bit further by visually displaying where each aspect of the discourse event may be placed and, because of that placement, be able to influence other aspects of the discourse. This of course is speculative because, especially with online discourse, much of what could be contained in the visual illustration is merely derived through extended experience with the interlocutors themselves and their discourse community and culture. This is one important deviation from nonanthropological discourse analysis: ethnography does indeed inform much of what we understand of discourse events, even if we are dealing with our native languages. I chose the stacked Venn diagram to emphasize the spheres of influence as well, but I intended the reader to conceptualize this illustration as a dynamic and fluid entity, always in flux. The individual in the center is of course at the heart of the discourse event, but this person belongs to many spheres: at a minimum, she is taking part in a conversation with at least one other person (the interlocutors) as well as being part of a potentially much larger discourse community that could contain any number of potential interlocutors. This discourse community is inevitably one part of a larger discourse community, and/or culture(s). Each of these spheres exerts influence in myriad ways and on countless levels so that by the time one particular discourse event takes place, the shared history and influence have had a massive impact on how and why and exactly in what ways this discourse takes place, as well as what the interlocutors (individual included) understand the discourse to mean (sarcasm, emoticons, *leet speak*, etc.). With each discourse event, history amasses, and interactions shape subsequent interactions and meanings, and the spheres morph into a unified and dynamic matrix of language in use. Different discourse communities impart communicative norms both from their specifically engaged community and from any other discourse communities that have ever housed or hosted discourse for a particular member. Dialects, second or fifth languages, and the multitude of otherwise "confounding" factors do not complicate but enhance the currently engaged discourse. It is an open system, where all levels of the discourse world are activated when the linguistic individual engages in any discourse event. No one individual can or is ever functioning in only one sphere at one time. Any discourse event relies on past communication(s) and triggers the dynamic interconnectedness of real, ongoing, unscripted discourse, potentially affecting a ripple-like change in the entire representation, or the Ethno-Pragmatic (EP) world. The point is that any discourse event is far larger, far more meaningful, and far more interesting than most analysts can account for with a more specifically focused methodology. Whether this model is seen as a method or simply a visualization of the discourse world, it diverges from current approaches.

Recommendations for Practice and Future Directions

Practically speaking, the EPM is not ideal. It merely attempts to illustrate just how complicated and intertextual discourse is. The next area of methodology in linguistic anthropology can focus on more streamlined, yet still encompassing, methods to analyze discourse of any medium or length or type.

Most analytical models may operate in only one sphere at a time, or in only one aspect of a combination of spheres. The EPM serves to highlight just how complicated even the simplest conversation is (whether online or offline), and anthropologists appreciate the implications of our complicated discourse behavior, all that it entails, and how it is informed. Duranti and

Goodwin (1992) have stated that in ethnopragmatics, not just meanings, but even motivations for language use are best understood only if we understand that language is informed by ethnographic history. Linguistic anthropologists have always appreciated this fact, but we have not yet been able to account for it with a practical method of analysis. That is what the future holds for this field, including the analysis of online discourse events.

Among the many methods previously employed and ones yet to be devised, it is ultimately up to the practicing anthropologist within her particular projects to decide which method best applies to her situation. However, I would urge anyone endeavoring to embark on discourse analysis, especially online discourse analysis, to remain cognizant of our larger mission of learning what it means to be human, especially as part of discourse communities within larger cultures. To "do" discourse analysis within a frame of linguistic anthropology, we should at the very least include extensive ethnography as well as linguistic and nonlinguistic contextualization, a secure and respectful relationship with the discourse community (not necessarily membership) that entails complete openness about the project, and a clear idea of what intentions about the project are for the future. All of this work, of course, rests on a carefully chosen, reliable framework for analysis that may or may not entail aspects of the EPM or other models found within this chapter.

References

American Anthropological Association. (2012) *Statement on Ethics: Principles of Professional Responsibilities.* Arlington, VA: American Anthropological Association, www.aaanet.org/profdev/ethics/upload/Statement-on-Ethics-Principles-of-Professional-Responsibility.pdf

Anderson, B. (1983) *Imagined Communities.* London: Verso.

"An Explanation of 1337 Speak." (2002). http://h2g2.com/edited_entry/A787917, electronic document.

Bechar-Israeli, A. (1995) 'FROM ‹Bonehead› TO ‹cLoNehEAd›: NICKNAMES, PLAY, AND IDENTITY ON INTERNET RELAY CHAT'. *Journal of Computer-Mediated Communication* 1(2).

Blashki, K. and S. Nichol. (2005) 'Game Geek's Godd: Linguistic Creativity in Young Males within an Online University Forum.' *Australian Journal of Emerging Technologies and Society* 3(2): 77–86.

Boellstorff, T. (2008) *Coming of Age in Second Life: An Anthropologist Explores the Virtually Human.* Princeton: Princeton University Press.

Bousfield, D. (2008) *Impoliteness in Interaction.* Amsterdam: John Benjamins.

Brown, P. and S. C. Levinson. (1987) *Politeness: Some Universals in Language Use.* Cambridge: Cambridge University Press.

Culpeper, J. (1996) 'Towards an Anatomy of Impoliteness.' *Journal of Pragmatics* 25: 349–367.

Danet, B. (1995) 'Playful Expressivity and Artfulness in Computer-mediated Communication'. *Journal of Computer-Mediated Communication* 1(2).

December. J. (1996) 'Units of Analysis for Internet Communication'. *Journal of Computer-Mediated Communication* 1(4).

DeLyser, D. (2001) 'DO YOU REALLY LIVE HERE?: THOUGHTS ON INSIDER RESEARCH'. *Geographical Review* 91(1/2): 441.

Du Bois, J. W. (2007) 'The Stance Triangle,' in R. Englebretson (ed.) *Stancetaking in Discourse.* Amsterdam: John Benjamins.

Duranti, A. and C. Goodwin (eds). (1992) *Rethinking Context: Language as an Interactive Phenomenon.* Cambridge: Cambridge University Press.

Grice, H. P. (1989) *Studies in the Way of Words.* Cambridge, MA: Harvard University Press.

Hine, C. (2000) *Virtual Ethnography.* London: Sage.

Holt, R. (2004) *Dialogue on the Internet: Language, Civic Identity, and Computer-Mediated Communication.* Westport, CT: Praeger.

Hutchby, I. (2001) *Conversation and Technology: From the Telephone to the Internet.* Cambridge: Blackwell.

Jackson, M. H. (1997) 'Assessing the Structure of Communication on the World Wide Web.' *Journal of Computer-Mediated Communication* 2(4).

Jones, S. G. (ed.) (1997) *Virtual Culture: Identity and Communication in Cybersociety.* London: Sage.

Kuipers, J. C. (2004) 'Ethnography of Language in the Age of Video: "Voices" as Multimodal Constructions in Some Contexts of Religious and Clinical Authority,' in P. LeVine and R. Scollon (eds). *Discourse and Technology: Multimodal Discourse Analysis*, Washington, D.C.: Georgetown University Press.

LeBlanc, T. (2005) *"Is There \ Translator in the House?": Cultural and Discourse Analysis of a Virtual Speech Community on an Internet Message Board*. Master's Thesis, http://etd.lsu.edu/docs/available/etd-04072005-145922/unrestricted/LeBlanc_thesis.pdf.

LeBlanc, T. (2010) *1337\/\/4YZ0F$p34K1NG: Toward a Unifying Pragmatic Theory of Virtual Speech Community Building*. Dissertation, http://etd.lsu.edu/docs/available/etd-04072005-145922/unrestricted/LeBlanc_thesis.pdf.

LeVine, P. and R. Scollon (eds). (2003) *Discourse and Technology: Multimodal Discourse Analysis*. Washington, D.C.: Georgetown University Press.

Mabry, E. A. (1997) 'Framing Flames: The structure of argumentative messages on the net.' *Journal of Computer-Mediated Communication* 2(4).

Morris, M. and C. Ogan. (1996) 'The Internet as Mass Medium.' *Journal of Computer-Mediated Communication* 1(4).

Ottenheimer, H. J. (2006) *The Anthropology of Language: An Introduction to Linguistic Anthropology*. Belmont, CA: Thomson Wadsworth.

Paccagnella, M. (1997) 'Getting the Seat of Your Pants Dirty: Strategies for Ethnographic Research on Virtual Communities.' *Journal of Computer-Mediated Communication* 3(1).

Parks, M.R. and K. Floyd. (1996) 'Making Friends in Cyberspace.' *Journal of Communication* 46(1): 80–97.

Raymond, E. R. and G. L. Steele. (1996) *The New Hacker's Dictionary*. Boston: MIT Press.

Rheingold, H. (2000) *The Virtual Community: Homesteading on the Electronic Frontier*. Cambridge, MA: The MIT Press.

Rome, J.A. (2001) 'relax we understand j00'. http://web.archive.org/web/20070216195207/http://www.case.edu/orgs/sigmataudelta/submissions/rome-relaxweunderstand.htm, electronic document.

Silverstein, M. (1979) 'Language Structure and Linguistic Ideology,' in Clyne, P. R., W. F. Hanks, and C. L. Hofbauer (eds). *The Elements: A Parasession on Linguistic Units and Levels*, pp. 193–247. Chicago: Chicago Linguistic Society.

Smith, M. A. and P. Kollock (eds). (1999) *Communities in Cyberspace*. London: Routledge.

Sperber, D. and D. Wilson. (1995) *Relevance: Communication and Cognition*, 2nd ed. Malden, MA: Blackwell Publishing.

Spradley, J. P. (1980) *Participant Observation*. Fort Worth: Harcourt Brace Jovanovich.

Thurlow, C. and K. Mroczek. (eds). (2011) *Digital Discourse: Language in the New Media*. Oxford: Oxford University Press.

Wierzbicka, A. (1996) *Semantics: Primes and Universals*. Oxford: Oxford University Press.

Wilson, S. M. and L. C. Peterson. (2001) 'The Anthropology of Online Communities'. *Annual Review of Anthropology* 31: 449–467.

Further Reading

To read further on community building in online spaces:

Baym, N. K. (1995) 'The Emergence of Community in Computer-Mediated Communication,' in *Cybersociety: Computer-Mediated Communication and Community*, S. G. Jones (ed.). Thousand Oaks, California: Sage.

Chayko, M. (2002) *Connecting: How we Form Social Bonds and Communities in the Internet Age*. Albany: State University of New York Press.

DiMaggio, P., E. Hargittai, W. R. Neuman, and J. P. Robinson. (2001) 'Social Implications of the Internet.' *Annual Review of Sociology* 27: 306–336.

To gain more background knowledge on the history of discourse analysis and how ethical considerations have changed since communities have migrated online:

Johnstone, B. (1990) *Stories, Community, and Place*. Bloomington, IN: Indiana University Press.

Lai, Y. (2014) 'Balancing Confidentiality and Transparency: A Reflexive Account of an Ethnographer in the Classroom.' *Anthropology News*. January/February: 10–11.

Part II
Language Ideologies and Practices of Learning

7

Language Ideologies
Emergence, Elaboration, and Application

Paul V. Kroskrity

1 Introduction

Simply stated, "language ideologies" are the "beliefs, feelings, and conceptions about language structure and use, which often index the political economic interests of individual speakers, ethnic and other interest groups, and nation-states" (Kroskrity 2010: 192). While this recent definition suggests the dual focus on the linguistic awareness of speakers and on their positionality within socioeconomic systems that display various kinds of social inequality, it does not reveal the contested emergence of this orientation in the late twentieth century. As used by linguistic anthropologists today, the concept of language ideologies first emerges in the work of Michael Silverstein, who defined what he called "linguistic ideologies" as "sets of beliefs about language articulated by users as a rationalization or justification of perceived language structure and use" (1979: 193). Silverstein argued that linguists needed to recognize the role of speakers' partial awareness of their language in order to understand such historical linguistic changes as the development of the Javanese honorific system or the loss of second-person pronouns like "thee" and "thou" in English. He argued persuasively that these and many other linguistic developments could not be accounted for by explanations based solely on linguistic structures. Adequate explanations could only be effected by appealing to speakers' awareness of linguistic form and their necessarily social interpretations of those forms. This claim does not seem so controversial today but at the time Silverstein made the case for including linguistic ideologies as an additional linguistic level to which linguists must attend, it refuted the theory and practice of most linguistic and anthropological linguistic models of the day. The founder of American anthropology, Franz Boas (1911: 69), had categorically dismissed what he regarded as the "misleading and disturbing factors of secondary explanations" of members of a language community. Preferring his "direct method" of analyzing linguistic categories and bypassing native interpretation, Boas ignored the social context of language in favor of reading linguistic forms as direct evidence of cultural cognition. In twentieth-century linguistics, under the influence of either Bloomfield or Chomsky, an emphasis on linguistic structures, whether surface or "deep," provided no room for considering speakers, their metalinguistic awareness, or their social worlds.

While Silverstein opened the door to the consideration of social forces on speakers' beliefs and practices regarding language, scholars still needed to connect the theme of awareness to considerations of the material world, including the role of economic value and pervasiveness of social inequality. Addressing both linguistic and cultural anthropologists, Judith Irvine (1989) argued that academic and Euro-American folk models of language have all too often linked it exclusively with the "thought" worlds of mental representation and not enough with the distribution of economic resources and political power in the material worlds of speakers. She argued effectively for recognizing this comparatively neglected side of language and developed a useful and more socially oriented definition of language ideology as "the cultural system of ideas about social and linguistic relationships, together with their loading of moral and political interests" (Irvine 1989: 255).

Before elaborating on the history suggested by these definitions, it is useful to delimit further the subject of this essay and to distinguish it from similar approaches. The theoretical notion of "language ideologies" – a default plural for reasons to be explained later – includes a body of research that simultaneously problematizes speakers' consciousness and awareness of their language, as well as their positionality (in political economic systems) in shaping their beliefs, expressed feelings, and evaluations of linguistic forms and discursive practices (Kroskrity 2000). Though a language ideologies approach is similar to Critical Discourse Analysis (e.g. Fairclough 1995, Wodak and Meyer 2001) in attempting to connect language with power and social inequality (Blommaert and Bulcaen 2000), it differs from CDA in its emphasis on awareness, its recognition of multiple and contesting ideologies, and on its preferred use of ethnographic approaches to collecting and interpreting data. Because of the significant differences in these attempts to understand language, power, and social inequality, I will devote this chapter exclusively to the approach that is clearly centered in linguistic anthropology: language ideologies.

2 Historical Perspectives

Taking Silverstein's 1979 article as the inception of a "language ideologies" approach allows us to observe two significant historical patterns. One, briefly mentioned above, is the comparatively long history, including most of the twentieth century, in which speakers' linguistic awareness, along with the social worlds that influenced their awareness, was dismissed by anthropologists and linguistic scientists. A second observation concerns the rapid acceptance, within less than three decades, of a language ideologies approach as it moved from a marginal concern to one now clearly identified as a mainstream approach, even one that has crossed over into cultural anthropology (Cody 2010: 200).

Why were speakers' understandings of their own linguistic practices so marginalized within anthropology? Much of this has to do with the Boasian agenda for language in the then newly emerging discipline of anthropology. While Boas must be credited with insisting on the inclusion of linguistics in US anthropology as both an effort to professionalize the field and, in his view, to access the native perspective, he was almost exclusively concerned with description and analysis of languages as categorization systems and with historical linguistics rather than with understanding culturally contexted speech. For him, native analyses of linguistic structure so lacked any understanding of the grammatical patterns recognizable to professional linguists that they were a kind of linguistic "false consciousness." What Boas failed to see was that any cultural "distortion" of linguistic facts was a noteworthy contribution useful to an ethnography of communication. But his preoccupation with linguistic structures as the loci of the cultural minds of natives led him to dismiss local notions about language as unworthy of anthropological attention.

In the linguistics of the early and mid twentieth century, a similar marginalization amounted to a proscription of not only speakers' linguistic ideologies but also their social worlds. Both Leonard Bloomfield's (1933) paradigmatic rejection of all meaning, and certainly of the "secondary responses" of speakers, and Chomsky's (1965) concoction of an "ideal speaker–hearer" worked to professionally proscribe any concerns for actual speakers, their linguistic ideologies, and the social meanings of their languages. Thus even though the mainstream paradigm of twentieth-century linguistics swung from behavioralist to cognitivist, the shift had no impact on rethinking language as a social phenomenon or speakers as cultural actors.

In part, as a reaction to the asocial formalism that Chomskyan linguistics represented, fields like correlational sociolinguistics (e.g. Labov) and the ethnography of communication (e.g. Gumperz and Hymes) provided a critical counterpoint and introduced the possibility of studying language, especially its actual use by speakers, as a sociocultural phenomenon. These approaches opened new horizons in exploring the social foundations of language use and in rethinking linguistic anthropology as a field of anthropology and not just a "service" discipline for other subfields. But the early formulations of these movements initially provided few resources for inclusion of speakers' language beliefs and practices as part of political economic systems. In actual practice, the ethnography of communication tended to valorize the study of language use but its "speech event" model encouraged an apolitical, broad-brush depiction of speech norms that often ignored their social distribution, or the larger political economic context. While correlational sociolinguistics clearly observed the speech variation associated with socioeconomic class, William Labov, its most famous practitioner, explicitly denigrated the importance of attending to speakers' linguistic ideologies. Based on a detailed study of a New York City English speaker, "Steve K.," Labov concluded "that a profound shift in social experience could not alter the socially determined pattern of linguistic variation" (Labov 1979: 329). Labov's objectivist model relied solely on phonological criteria and ignored lexical choice and grammar, while his dismissal of speakers' ideologies mistakenly viewed their own analyses, say about talking like the "working class," as competing with his expert perspective rather than as an ethnotheory that attends to alternative criteria for its own purposes. Even when scholars in these traditions did devote considerable attention to local language ideologies, depicting local ideologies in spectacular terms – as in Gossen's (1974) exploration of Chamula metalanguage – they were presented as cultural givens rather than understood as connected to political economic factors.

At a time when most models of meaning, including Chomsky's linguistic semantics and anthropology's ethnoscience, reduced linguistic meaning to denotation, or "reference," and predication, Silverstein (1979) recognized the need for alternative approaches and turned to semiotic models of communication based on the theories of C. S. Peirce (1931–58). For researchers, a key theoretical advantage of semiotic models was their capacity to recognize the multiple meanings of linguistic signs that emerged from "indexical" connections between those signs and the social contexts of their usage. This theoretical orientation, especially as formulated by Jakobson (1957, 1960) and later translated into a functional trope by Hymes (1964), helped to create the foundation for the ethnography of communication and its quest to explore language use and relate it to topics, institutions, settings, genres, and other aspects of their sociocultural worlds. Over time the initial zeal to explore language use in micro-contexts grew more sophisticated and confronted the mapping of linguistic forms onto patterns of social stratification, including national political economic systems. Hymes (1974: 26, 33) called for the inclusion of a speech community's local theories of speech and the study of its "communicative economy." John Gumperz (e.g. Blom and Gumperz 1972: 43; Gumperz 1982: 39) often considered the "social meaning" of dialect choices for speakers within the context of their social networks and the larger political economic context.

As linguistic anthropologists became more and more successful into the 1980s in defining language as a sociocultural phenomenon that required attention not just to linguistic theory but

Paul V. Kroskrity

also to social and cultural theories, linguistic anthropologists, like their sociocultural colleagues, became increasingly concerned with practice theory and with the agency of social actors, as well as with syncretic attempts to wed Marxist materialism with a Weberian idealism (Ortner 1984: 147), in an attempt to achieve an analytical balance in the representation of human agency within social systems (Giddens 1979), often characterized by pervasive inequality. As Marxist and other political economic perspectives became staples of sociocultural theory in the US and in Europe (Bourdieu 1977, 1984), they also inspired some of the earliest works in the linguistic anthropological tradition of language ideologies, as a way of integrating these concerns with the now legitimated interests in speakers' awareness of linguistic systems. The works included Susan Gal's (1979) *Language Shift* and "Language and Political Economy" (Gal 1989), Jane Hill's (1985) "The Grammar of Consciousness and the Consciousness of Grammar," Judith Irvine's (1989) aforementioned "When Talk Isn't Cheap: Language and Political Economy," and Kathryn Woolard's (1985) "Language Variation and Cultural Hegemony." These works adumbrated many of the key concerns that have since flourished through the remainder of the twentieth century and into the present, producing a series of important anthologies devoted to language ideological work (Schieffelin, Woolard, and Kroskrity 1998; Blommaert 1999c, Kroskrity 2000, and Gal and Woolard 2001). More recently, with the language ideological perspective more widely adopted, anthologies have appeared that specialize in the Pacific and Native American regions (Makihara and Schieffelin 2007, Kroskrity and Field 2009).

3 Critical Issues and Topics

In previous overviews (Kroskrity 2000, 2010), I have analyzed four and five key aspects of this approach but, in this condensed treatment, I will focus on what may be regarded as the three main planks of the language ideologies approach: *positionality, multiplicity and awareness.*

The first of these attributes, *positionality*, is the understanding that language ideologies represent the perception of language and discourse that is constructed in the interest, or from the perspective, of an economically positioned social or cultural group. Members' notions of what is 'true,' 'morally good,' or 'aesthetically pleasing' about language and discourse are grounded in social experience and often demonstrably tied to their political economic interests. These notions often underlie attempts to use language as the site at which to promote, protect, and legitimate those interests. Nationalist programs of language standardization, for example, may appeal to a modern metric of communicative efficiency, but such language development efforts are pervasively saturated by political economic considerations, since the imposition of a state-supported hegemonic standard will always benefit some social groups over others (see Woolard 1985, 1989; Errington 1998, 2000; Silverstein 1996; Collins 1996). State policies and practices regarding the promotion or suppression of multilingualism are differentially evaluated by linguistic minorities, like Puerto Ricans in New York City (Urciuoli 1996; Zentella 1997) or zealots of the "English-only" movement (Schmidt 2007), who both see their emblematic languages as threatened. What positionality refutes is the myth of the sociopolitically disinterested language user or the possibility of unpositioned linguistic knowledge. Though interests are rendered more visible when they are embodied by overtly contending groups – as in the struggle for airtime on Zambian radio (Spitulnik 1998), the disputes of Warao shamans (Briggs 1998), the political debates in Corsica about the institutional status or cultural role of the Corsican language (Jaffe 2003, 2007), the competing discourses linked to Mexico's vacillating language policies toward indigenous languages (Messing 2007), or the confrontations of feminists with the traditional grammarian defenders of the generic 'he' (Silverstein 1985), one can also extend this emphasis on grounded social experience to seemingly homogeneous cultural groups by recognizing that cultural conceptions "are partial, contestable, and interest-laden" (Woolard & Schieffelin 1994: 58). Even overtly shared language practices, such as Arizona Tewa kiva speech (Kroskrity 1998), can represent the constructions of particular elites who obtain the required complicity (Bourdieu 1991: 113) of other social groups and classes. Rather than accepting linguistic conservatism as an irreducible, cultural given, a language ideological approach asks how does this perspective become widely accepted, how do indexical connections to political power and religious authority promote culturally dominant beliefs?

Rosina Lippi-Green's (1997) *English with an Accent: Language, Ideology, and Discrimination* explicitly emphasizes language ideologies in her examination of contemporary educational and other institutionalized policies and practices, by demonstrating the class-based interests behind what she calls, following Milroy and Milroy (1999), the *standard language ideology*. She defines it as "a bias toward an abstracted, idealized, homogenous spoken language which is imposed and maintained by dominant bloc institutions and which names as its model the written language, but which is drawn primarily from the speech of the upper, middle class" (Lippi-Green 1997: 64). This language ideology promotes 'the language subordination process,' which amounts to a program of linguistic mystification undertaken by dominant institutions designed to simultaneously valorize the standard language and other aspects of 'mainstream culture' while devaluing the nonstandard and its associated cultural forms. For example, so-called 'double negatives' (as in "He does not have no money") may seem repulsive embodiments of ignorance to those attuned to the norms of the standard and yet the supposed deficiency is not traceable to any logical flaw that obscures its 'meaning' but rather comes from its association with a class of speakers who use it and the fact that it is grammatically proscribed by state-supported educational institutions. For Lippi-Green, in accord with a language ideological stance, the proclaimed superiority of Standard English rests not on its structural properties or its communicative efficiency but rather on its association with the political economic influence of affluent social classes who benefit from a social stratification that consolidates and continues their privileged position.

The second attribute of language ideologies is their *multiplicity*. Language ideologies are profitably conceived as multiple because of the plurality of meaningful social divisions (class, gender, clan, elites, generations, and so on) within sociocultural groups that can produce divergent perspectives expressed as indices of group membership. Language ideologies are thus grounded in social experience that is never uniformly distributed throughout polities of any scale. Thus, in Hill's (1998) study of Mexicano (Nahuatl) linguistic ideologies, when older Mexicano speakers in the Malinche Volcano area of Central Mexico say the Mexicano equivalent of "Today there is no respect," this nostalgic view is more likely to be voiced by older men. Although both genders recognize the increased 'respect' once signaled by a tradition of using Nahuatl honorific registers and other polite forms, 'successful' men are more likely to express this sense of linguistic deprivation of earned deference. Mexicano women, on the other hand, are more likely to express ambivalence; having seen their own lot in life improve during this same period of declining verbal 'respect,' some women are less enthusiastic in supporting a symbolic return to practices of former times (Hill 1998: 78–79).

Another very revealing application of multiplicity is the exploration of internal diversity as a driving force in linguistic change. In Errington's (1998, 2000) research on the complementary, if not contradictory, language ideologies underlying the development of standard Indonesian, he examines the conflicted efforts of the Indonesian government to domesticate exogenous modernity and modernize domestic traditions. Though often viewed as a success story in terms of 'the national language problem', standardized Indonesian does not readily conform to a number of facile claims by scholars and policy makers who share an instrumentalist ideology of language development in nationalism. Gellner (1983), for example, sees development of a national standard language as a key element in making the transformation to nationalism. Representing a nonideological development perspective, he portrays standardized Indonesian as an "ethnically uninflected, culturally neutral language" that is both universally available to its citizens and itself subject to development by the state.

But Errington demonstrates that though the Indonesian state's New Order attempts to efface the derivativeness of national high culture and national language by erasure of its ethnic and class sources, the language itself provides a key example of an apparent contradiction. Recent lexical change displays a proliferation of both archaic or archaized terms traceable to Old Javanese and Sanskrit, as well as the incorporation of almost one thousand terms from English. This dual development of the lexicon can hardly be defended as 'communicatively efficient' or as contributing to some neutral language widely available to all as an emblem of national identity. Rather, it represents continuity with a supposedly abandoned linguistic past in which exemplary elites rule through a language over which they have specialized control. And since knowledge of the local prestige charismatic languages (Javanese and Sanskrit) and the prestige international language, English, is socially distributed, this standardizing project joins other nationalist projects in both creating and legitimating a state-endorsed social inequality.

Another trend in this emphasis on multiplicity is to focus on contestation, clashes, or disjunctures in which divergent ideological perspectives on language and discourse are juxtaposed, resulting in a wide variety of outcomes (e.g. Briggs 1996). In one such example from Alexandra Jaffe's research on language politics in Corsica (1999a, b), she examines the ideological debate regarding the translation of French literature into Corsican – a language that has undergone language shift and has lost many functions to the state's official, written language – French. The contestation that emerges is between instrumentalists who see such translations as acts of promotion or enhancement for the symbolic value of Corsican and romanticists who adopt a more classic language and identity perspective. For them, such translations are a perversion of language and identity relationships because the act of translation suggests a common or colonized identity rather than an expression of a uniquely Corsican identity. In Jaffe's analysis, as in others that use this strategy, contestation and disjuncture disclose critical differences in ideological perspectives that can more fully reveal their distinctive properties as well as their scope and force.

Multiplicity is also an attribute that makes language ideological approaches especially appropriate for studying cultural contact and social transformation. In such cases the goal is not to identify and describe a single dominant ideology but rather to examine ideological contact, contention, and transformation. Many California Indian groups, as exemplified by the Western Mono of Central California, had indigenous language ideologies that valued multilingualism and linguistic syncretism, but did not strongly elevate particular languages as emblems of tribal identity (Kroskrity 2009a). Many of these groups were hunter-gathering communities that moved to more ideal locations seasonally and they typically maintained strong relations with neighboring groups that resulted in widespread intermarriage and multilingualism. Though these communities were more likely to emphasize the practical value of languages as economic tools rather than as vehicles of group identity prior to Euro-American domination, the influence of nationalist language ideologies from above provided a model for linking a single language with group identity that contributed symbolic resources for the ethnonationalist movements of the late twentieth-century postcolonial period (Kroskrity 2009a).

A similar pattern of influence between the language ideologies of a nation state and those of an indigenous group has been observed by Makihara (2007) for indigenous people of Rapa Nui – a Polynesian island that is part of the Chilean state. Though, in everyday speech, community members seem to prefer a linguistic syncretism of Spanish and their indigenous language, the community's growing interest in being recognized not merely as Chilean citizens but as an indigenous people with special rights has led it to marshal linguistic and other resources for the cause. On the model of official Chilean Spanish, a puristic Rapa Nui register has been adopted and deployed by political activists who call attention to their distinctive identities through its use in public contexts. But not all instances of language ideological contact result in transmission, influence, or synthesis. In her study of the interaction of 'new' and native Gaelic speakers in the Western Isles of Scotland (McEwan-Fujita 2010), the author observes how the very disparate language ideologies of these different learners result in affect-laden stance displays that render their interaction dysfunctional for language learning and can hardly be viewed as promoting Gaelic language revitalization. In the case of Galician, in northwestern Spain, the clash of new and traditional speakers of the language has resulted in confrontation and contestation over issues of ownership, legitimacy, and authenticity (O' Rourke and Ramallo 2013), showing the power of language ideologies to divide as well as to unify.

The third characteristic of language ideologies, *speakers' awareness*, is simply the observation that members may display varying degrees of awareness of local language ideologies. While Silverstein's (1979) definition, quoted above, suggests that language ideologies are often explicitly articulated by members, researchers also recognize ideologies of practice that must be read from actual usage. This research suggests a correlational relationship between high levels of discursive consciousness and active contestation of ideologies and, contrastively, between practical consciousness, or taken-for-granted beliefs and feelings about language, and relatively unchallenged, highly naturalized, dominant ideologies (Kroskrity 1998).

The types of social settings in which language ideologies are produced and commented upon constitute another source of variation in awareness. Silverstein (1998: 136) developed the notion of *ideological sites* "as institutional sites of social practice as both object and modality of ideological expression." Such sites are often the loci of religious or secular institutional rituals in which specific beliefs are inscribed. In part because of the institutional focus on language as constitutive of the law, studies of US court rooms and law school classrooms (Mertz 2007), as well as Hopi Tribal Courts (Richland 2008) and Tongan courts (Philips 2000) provide especially revealing sites for language ideologies. In cases where the government monopolizes state resources, sites of ideological production and explication are one and the same. Under the influence of Ujamaa, the socialist ideology of the Tanzanian state, explicit state language ideologies promoted Swahili and encouraged bilingual writers to develop new genres of Swahili literature (Blommaert 1999b), designed to develop indigenous forms and exclude foreign literature. Having a monopoly on publishing, the state could use controlled media to explicate endorsed language ideologies and then publish only those works that exemplified those ideologies. Lacking comparable support for indigenous languages in the US, indigenous language activists have strategically examined language ideologies as a fundamental part of revitalization programs. Loether (2009), in his study of Shoshoni language renewal, discusses the need for language planners to 'manipulate' local language ideologies in order to create a better environment for successful language revitalization. Ideologies to discard include those involving indexing the Shoshoni language exclusively to a traditional past, to images of inferiority, or to assumptions that having Shoshoni 'blood' will ensure rapid acquisition of the heritage language. In a study of a variety of Southwestern tribal communities experiencing language shift to English, researchers have noticed a new ideological development in which indigenous language speakers both revalorize their heritage languages and re-ideologize English as a 'dead' language – one which lacks the beauty, vitality, and world-view of indigenous languages. The researchers conclude, "Replacing the labels of 'dying,' 'moribund,' and 'obsolescent' for Native languages with the perspective that it is English that is dead may well be a strong step forward in Native communities' work toward reestablishing the heritage language and culture as dominant" (Gomez de Garcia, Axelrod, and Lachler 2009: 122).

Awareness is also a product of the kind of linguistic or discursive phenomena that speakers, either generically or in a more culturally specific manner, can identify and distinguish (Silverstein 1981). Nouns, our 'words for things,' display an unavoidable referentiality that makes them more available for folk awareness and possible folk theorizing than, say, a rule for marking 'same subject' as part of verb morphology. In my own analysis (Kroskrity 1993, 1998) of the contact history of the Arizona Tewa, a consistent pattern of indigenous purism can be established as both a local language ideology of the group and an established fact of language contact. But this program of purism is selectively imposed on linguistic phemonena that are more word-like, while grammatical diffusion from Apachean and Hopi seems to have evaded Tewa folk scrutiny (Kroskrity 1998). The importance of attending to awareness as a dimension of ideology is both the reversal of a longstanding scholarly tradition of delegitimating common people's views of language – a tradition extending back at least as far as Locke and Herder (Bauman & Briggs 2003) – and the recognition that when speakers rationalize their language they take a first step toward changing it (Silverstein 1979). As Coupland and Jaworski (2004: 37) have powerfully stated: "The concept of language ideology is the final rejection of an innocent, behavioral account of language and the focus of the strongest claim that sociolinguistics must engage with metalinguistic processes in the most general sense."

4 Current Research Topics

In the last two decades, as language ideological approaches have flourished, some of the key themes they have been used to investigate include: 1) "the historical production and reproduction of language ideologies" (Blommaert 1999a: 1); 2) the exploration of social identities of various sorts (national, ethnic, professional, gender, indigenous) that are produced through language ideologies; and 3) language ideological involvement in processes of subordination, marginalization, and counterhegemonic responses to such forces. Regarding the historical production and reproduction, Irvine and Gal (2000) have demonstrated the way colonial politics helped to produce language ideologies and ideologies of linguistic differentiation in Africa and Macedonia that variously rationalized the inferiority of speakers of click languages or that read multilingual adaptations as a linguistic chaos in need of regimenting along the lines of European nationalisms. Also taking the long view, Collins (1999) situates the Ebonics controversy in the historical context of evolving US national language ideologies surrounding the increasing valorization of Standard English and stigmatization of minority languages and nonstandard varieties. This historical emphasis assumes a reflexive turn as many European and Euro-American language philosophers and foundational academic figures (Herder, Locke, Schoolcraft, the Grimms, and Boas) are examined from a language ideological perspective by Bauman & Briggs (2004) in their influential book, *Voices of Modernity*.

Language ideological research has been instrumental in the further exploration of how speakers and communities marshal linguistic resources to express traditional indigenous Kaska (Canadian Yukon) identities in the modern world (Meek 2007) or newly (re-)emergent ethnolinguistic identities such as Rapa Nui (Makihara 2007) or Catalonian (Digiacommo 1999). But for many groups, local ideologies valorize hybridity as expressed through code-switching. For example, in the Puerto Rican community of El Barrio in New York City's East Harlem (Zentella 1997) speaking both Spanish and English in the form of intra-sentential code-switching is a valued expression of their status as bilingual 'Nuyoricans.' And multilingual practices can also be hybridized to create new 'Desi' identities for South Asian immigrants to California's Silcon Valley (Shankar 2008a, b). And much as linguistic ideologies have been employed to support and create identities, they can also be used to marginalize, suppress, convert, and appropriate identities. Notable achievements in this area are Kuipers' (1998) study of the Indonesian suppression of "subversive" Sumbanese rhetorical forms, Errington's (2000), and Schieffelin's (2000, 2007) studies of missionary and colonial suppression of local identities. Studies of 'crossing' (e.g. Rampton 1995) and 'styling' (e.g. Bucholtz 1999; Cutler 1999) also powerfully demonstrate the language ideological construction of linguistic otherness that motivates such acts of identity appropriation, creation, and hybridization. Often the process of language ideological construction of one's own identity is embedded in the construction of oppositional others. In Stasch's (2007) study of how members of a Papuan community construct Indonesian, he represents the ambivalent view of that community with the demonization of some aspects of Indonesian society and the admiration of others. Other topics have also received recent attention and are likely to contribute to future research as well. These will be discussed below.

5 Research Methods

Most language ideological research, especially among anthropologists, has been concerned more with theoretical development and refinement than with research methods. This is in part because most of those who do language ideological research have used a wide variety of conventional methods: participant observation, formal and informal interviewing, life history, person-centered ethnography, conversational analysis, historical linguistics, and textual analysis. Since researchers read language ideologies both from actual practice and from speakers' metalinguistic and metadiscursive responses in interviews, many researchers will collect data using two or more of the above methods. This is especially necessary for those studies in which researchers are concerned with discerning and refining the typology of speakers' awareness (Silverstein 1981, 1993; Kroskrity 1998) in order to understand the influence of structure and agency. The one exception to this general pattern of not developing specific methodological works for language ideological research is Jef Verschueren's (2012) volume that offers a rigorous pragmatics-oriented approach to studying language ideologies in written works.

6 Future Directions

In the past decade several language ideological trends have emerged that indicate productive directions for future research. Several of these can be briefly identified here. One of these is the language ideological deconstruction of linguistic racism (e.g. Bucholtz & Trechter 2001; Meek 2006; Barrett 2006; Reyes & Lo 2009). Within this literature, Jane Hill (2008) has expanded upon earlier work (Hill 1999) by using language ideological emphases on awareness to account for contrasts between stark linguistic racism (e.g. use of racial epithets) and "covert" forms of linguistic racism displayed in everyday usage by non-Hispanics of "mock Spanish." Though a speaker's use of this register is often associated with his or her attempt to be jocular or to convey a colloquial stance and not with attempts to be intentionally "racist," Hill nevertheless reveals a consistent pattern of pejoration that is indexically tied to negative stereotypes of Mexican-Americans and other Hispanics as lazy, immoral, drunken or otherwise undesirable. In her argument, American English speakers' linguistic ideologies of personalism and referentialism dilute and deflect attention away from the verbal harm done to others as a consequence of their propagation of defamatory images of Chicano/a "others." This indirection coupled with the alternative ideological emphasis combines to explain why such "covert racist" practices fly below the radar of awareness for many speakers who would find overt racist speech reprehensible.

Another trend is the application of language ideological approaches to situations of language shift and to those attempts at reversing this process that are typically called language renewal and linguistic revitalization (Bunte 2009; Cavanaugh 2004, 2009; Nevins 2004, 2013; LeMaster 2006; Meek 2007, 2010; Perley 2011; Reynolds 2009; Smith-Hefner 2009; Kroskrity and Field 2009). Because language ideological approaches can treat the interaction of multiple ideologies and not merely attend to the beliefs and practices of dominant groups, they are particularly useful in the analysis of dynamic situations involving cultural contact, socioeconomic change, evolving gender relations, and even the hegemonic influence of states on linguistic and cultural minorities.

Another relatively new interest is centered in language and the mass media. In part because the mass media represent powerful sources of persuasion and influence that can reach a vast audience and because their operation can reproduce forms of social inequality, they are an important site for language ideological research. A sample of the many topics treated in this literature are: the media globalization of Standard Spanish (Paffey 2010), the reproduction of racial stereotypes in computer game discourse (Ensslin 2010), personalist language ideologies in US media discourse (Hill 2007), media discourses about language shift in Corsica (Jaffe 2007), and changing forms of mass mediated speech-making by politicians in Madagascar (Jackson 2013). In addition to these topics, it is also appropriate to give brief mention to other topics like language ideologies of specific professions (law, medicine, academia), of translation, and of verbal, visual, and musical aesthetics (Kroskrity 2009b; Black 2012).

Related Topics

4 The Social Imaginary, Unspoken in Verbal Art (Mannheim); **8** Social Subordination and Language (Huayhua); **11** Language Socialization and Marginalization (García-Sánchez); **14** Discursive Practices, Linguistic Repertoire, and Racial Identities (Baugh); **15** Language and Racialization (Chun, Lo); **19** Language and Political Economy (McElhinny); **20** Language, Immigration, and the Nation-State (Pujolar); **21** Language and Nationalism (Haque); **22** Language in the Age of Globalization (Jacquemet); **24** Discrimination via Discourse (Wodak); **25** Racism in the Press (van Dijk); **26** Legal Discourse (Conley); **30** The Politics of Language Endangerment (Meek).

References

Barrett, R. (2006). Language Ideology and Racial Inequality: Competing Functions of Spanish in an Anglo-owned Mexican Restaurant. *Language in Society 35*: 163–204.
Bauman, R. & C.L. Briggs (2003). *Voices of Modernity: Language Ideologies and the Politics of Inequality*. Cambridge University Press.
Black, S. (2012). Laughing to Death: Joking as Support amid Stigma for Zulu-speaking South Africans Living with HIV. *Journal of Linguistic Anthropology 22*: 87–108.
Blom, J.P. & J.J. Gumperz (1972). Social Meaning in Linguistic Structures: Code-switching in Norway. In J.J. Gumperz & D. Hymes (eds), *Directions in Sociolinguistics* 407–434. Holt, Rinehart & Winston.
Blommaert, J. (1999a). The Debate is Open. In J. Blommaert (ed.), pp. 1–38. Mouton de Gruyter.
——. (1999b). *State Ideology and Language in Tanzania*. Rudiger Köppe Verlag.
Blommaert, J. (ed.) (1999c). *Language Ideological Debates*. Mouton de Gruyter.
Blommaert, J. & C. Bulcaen (2000). Critical Discourse Analysis. *Annual Review of Anthropology 29*: 447–466.
Bloomfield, L. (1933). *Language*. Henry Holt.
Boas, F. (1911). Introduction. In F. Boas (ed.), *Handbook of North American Indian Languages*, pp. 1–83. *Bulletin of the Bureau of American Ethnology*, vol. 40.
Bourdieu, P. (1977). *Outline of a Theory of Practice*. Cambridge University Press.
——. (1984). *Distinction. A Social Critique of the Judgement of Taste*. Harvard University Press.
——. (1991). *Language and Symbolic Power*. Harvard University Press.

Briggs, C.L. (1996). Conflict, Language Ideologies, and Privileged Arenas of Discursive Authority in Warao Dispute Mediation. In C.L. Briggs (ed.), *Disorderly Discourse: Narrative, Conflict, and Inequality*, pp. 204–242. Oxford University Press.

——. (1998). "You're a Liar – You're Just Like a Woman!": Constructing Dominant Ideologies of Language in Warao Men's Gossip. In B.B. Schieffelin et al. (eds), pp. 229–255.

Bucholtz, M. (1999). You da man: Narrating the Racial Other in the Linguistic Production of White Masculinity. *Journal of Sociolinguistics* 3(4): 443–460.

Bucholtz, M. & S. Trechter (eds) (2001). *Discourses of Whiteness*. Special issue of *Journal of Linguistic Anthropology* 11(1).

Bunte, P.A. (2009). "You Keep Not Listening With Your Ears": Ideology, Language Socialization, and Paiute Identity. In P. Kroskrity & M. Field (eds), pp. 172–189.

Cavanaugh, J.R. (2004). Remembering and Forgetting: Ideologies of Language Loss in a Northern Italian Town. *Journal of Linguistic Anthropology* 14: 24–38.

——. (2009). *Living Memory: The Social Aesthetics of Language in a Northern Italian Town*. Wiley-Blackwell.

Cody, F. (2010). Linguistic Anthropology at the End of the Naughts: A Review of 2009. *American Anthropologist* 112: 200–207.

Collins, J. (1996). Socialization to Text: Structure and Contradiction in Schooled Literacy. In M. Silverstein & G. Urban (eds), *Natural Histories of Discourse*, 203–228. University of Chicago Press.

——. (1999). The Ebonics Controversy in Context: Literacies, Subjectivities, and Language Ideologies in the United States. In J. Blommaert (ed.), 201–234. Mouton de Gruyter.

Coupland, N. & A. Jaworski (2004). Sociolinguistic Perspectives on Metalanguage: Reflexivity, Evaluation, and Ideology. In A. Jaworski, N. Coupland & D. Galasinski (eds), *Metalanguage: Social and Ideological Perspectives*, pp. 15–51. Mouton de Gruyter.

Cutler, C.A. (1999). Yorkville Crossing: White Teens, Hip Hop, and African American English. *Journal of Sociolinguistics* 3(4): 428–442.

Digiacommo, S.M. (1999). Language Ideological Debates in an Olympic City: Barcelona 1992–1996. In *Language Ideological Debates*, J. Blommaert (ed.), pp. 105–142. Mouton deGruyter.

Ensslin, A. (2010) "Black and White": Language Ideologies in Computer Game Discourse. In Sally Johnson & Tommaso M. Milani (eds), Language Ideologies and Media Discourse: Texts, Practices, Politics, pp. 205–222. Continuum.

Errington, J. (1998). Indonesian('s) Development: On the State of a Language of State. In B.B. Schieffelin et al. (eds), pp. 271–284.

——. (2000). Indonesian('s) Authority. In P.V. Kroskrity (ed.), pp. 205–227.

Fairclough, N. (1995). *Critical Discourse Analysis: The Critical Study of Language*. Longmans.

Gal, S. (1979). *Language Shift: Social Determinants of Language Change in Bilingual Austria*. Academic Press.

——. (1989). Language and Political Economy. *Annual Review of Anthropology* 18: 345–367.

Gal, S. & K. Woolard (2001). *Languages and Publics: The Making of Authority*. St. Jerome Publishing.

Gellner, E. (1983). *On Nations and Nationalism*. Cornell University Press.

Giddens, A. (1979). *Central Problems in Social Theory*. University of California Press.

Gomez de Garcia, J., M. Axelrod & J. Lachler (2009). "English is the Dead Language." In P. Kroskrity & M. Field (eds), pp. 99–122.

Gossen, G.H. (1974). To Speak With a Heated Heart: Chamula Canons of Style and Good Performance. In *Explorations in the Ethnography of Speaking*, Richard Bauman and Joel Sherzer (eds), pp. 389–413. Cambridge University Press.

Gumperz, J.J. (1982). *Discourse Strategies*. Cambridge University Press.

Hill, J.H. (1985). The Grammar of Consciousness and the Consciousness of Grammar. *American Ethnologist* 12: 725–737.

——. (1998). "Today There is No Respect": Nostalgia, "Respect." and Oppositional Discourse in Mexicano (Nahuatl) Language Ideology. In B.B. Schieffelin et al. (eds) pp. 103–122.

——. (1999). Language, Race, and the White Public Space. *American Anthropologist* 100: 680–689.

——. (2007). Crises of Meaning: Personalist Language Ideology in US Media Discourse. In Sally Johnson & Astrid Ensslin (eds), *Language in the Media*, pp. 70–88. Continuum.

——. (2008). *The Language of Everyday White Racism*. Wiley-Blackwell.

Hymes, D.H. (1964). Introduction: Toward Ethnographies of Communication. In J.J. Gumperz & D.H. Hymes (eds), *The Ethnography of Communication*, pp. 1–34. *American Anthropologist* 66(6), Part 2.

——. (1974). *Foundations in Sociolinguistics: An Ethnographic Approach*. University of Pennsylvania Press.

Irvine, J.T. (1989). When Talk Isn't Cheap: Language and Political Economy. *American Ethnologist* 16: 248–267.

Irvine, J.T. & S. Gal (2000). Language Ideology and Linguistic Differentiation. In P.V. Kroskrity (ed.), pp. 35–83.
Jackson, J. (2013) *Political Oratory and Cartooning: An Ethnography of Democratic Process*. Blackwell.
Jaffe, A. (1999a). *Ideologies in Action: Language Politics in Corsica*. Mouton de Gruyter.
——. (1999b). Locating Power: Corsican Translators and their Critics. In J. Blommaert (ed.), pp. 1–38.
——. (2003). Misrecognition Unmasked? "Polynomic" Language, Expert Statuses and Orthographic Practices in Corsican Schools. *Pragmatics 13*: 515–537.
——. (2007). Corsican on the Airwaves: Media Discourse in a Context of Language Shift. In Sally Johnson and Astrid Ensslin (eds), *Language in the Media*, pp. 149–172. Continuum.
Jakobson, R. (1957). *The Framework of Language*. University of Michigan Press.
——. (1960). Concluding Statement: Linguistics and Poetics. In T. Sebeok (ed.), *Style in Language*, pp. 350–373. MIT Press.
Kroskrity, P.V. (1993). *Language, History, and Identity: Ethnolinguistic Studies of the Arizona Tewa*. University of Arizona Press.
——. (1998). Arizona Tewa Kiva Speech as a Manifestation of a Dominant Language Ideology. In Schieffelin, Woolard, and Kroskrity (eds), pp. 103–123. Oxford University Press.
——. (2000). Regimenting Languages. In P. Kroskrity (ed.), pp. 1–34. School of American Research.
——. (2009a). Embodying the Reversal of Language Shift: Agency, Incorporation, and Language Ideological Change in the Western Mono Community of Central California. In P.V. Kroskrity & M. Field (eds), pp. 190–210.
——. (2009b). Narrative Reproductions: Ideologies of Storytelling, Authoritative Words, and Generic Regimentation. *Journal of Linguistic Anthropology 19*: 40–56.
——. (ed.) (2000). *Regimes of Language: Ideologies, Polities, and Identities*. School of American Research.
Kroskrity, P.V. & M.C. Field (eds) (2009). *Native American Language Ideologies: Beliefs, Practices, and Struggles in Indian Country*. University of Arizona Press.
Kroskrity, P.V. (2010). Language Ideologies – Evolving Perspectives. In *Language Use and Society (Handbook of Pragmatics Highlights)*. Jurgen Jaspers (ed.), pp. 192–211. John Benjamins.
Kuipers, J.C. (1998). From Miracles to Classrooms: Changing Forms of Erasure in the Learning of Ritual Speech. In *Language, Identity, and Marginality in Indonesia: The Changing Nature of Ritual Speech on the Island of Sumba*, pp. 125–148. Cambridge University Press.
Labov, W. (1979). Locating the Frontier between Social and Psychological Factors in Language Variation. In *Individual Differences in Language Abilities and Behavior*, Charles J. Fillmore, William S.-Y. Wang, and Daniel Kempler (eds), pp. 327–339. Academic Press.
LeMaster, B. (2006). Language Contraction, Revitalization, and Irish Women. *Journal of Linguistic Anthropology 16*: 211–228.
Lippi-Green, R. (1997). *English with an Accent: Language, Ideology, and Discrimination in the United States*. Routledge.
Loether, C. (2009). Language Revitalization and the Manipulation of Language Ideologies: A Case Study. In P.V. Kroskrity & M.C. Field (eds), pp. 238–255.
McEwan-Fujita, E. (2010). Ideology, Affect, and Socialization in Language Shift and Revitalization: The Experiences of Adults Learning Gaelic in the Western Isles of Scotland. *Language in Society 39*: 27–64.
Makihara, M. (2007). Linguistic Purism in Rapa Nui Political Discourse. In M. Makihara & B. Schieffelin (eds), pp. 46–69.
Makihara, M. & B. Schieffelin. (eds) (2007). *Consequences of Contact: Language Ideologies and the Sociocultural Transformation of Pacific Societies*. Oxford University Press.
Meek, B.A. (2006). And the Injun Goes "How!": Representations of American Indian English in White Public Space. *Language in Society 35*: 93–128.
——. (2007). Respecting the Language of Elders: Ideological Shift and Linguistic Discontinuity in a Northern Athapascan Community. *Journal of Linguistic Anthropology 17*: 23–43.
——. (2010). *We Are Our Language: An Ethnography of Language Revitalization in a Northern Athabaskan Community*. University of Arizona Press.
Mertz, E. (2007). *The Language of Law School: Learning "to Think a Lawyer"*. Oxford University Press.
Messing, J. (2007). Multiple Ideologies and Competing Discourses: Language Shift in Tlaxcala, Mexico. *Language in Society 36*: 555–577.
Milroy, J. & L. Milroy (1999). *Authority in Language: Investigating Language Prescription and Standardisation*. Routledge.

Nevins, M. E. (2004). Learning to Listen: Confronting Two Meanings of Language Loss in the Contemporary White Mountain Apache Speech Community. *Journal of Linguistic Anthropology* 14: 269–288.
——. (2013). *Lessons from Fort Apache: Beyond Language Endangerment and Maintenance*. Wiley-Blackwell.
O'Rourke, B. and F. Ramallo. (2013). Competing Ideologies of Linguistic Authority amongst Speakers in Contemporary Galicia. *Language in Society* 42: 287–305.
Ortner, S.B. (1984). Theory in Anthropology Since the Sixties. *Comparative Studies in Society and History* 26: 126–166.
Paffey, D. (2010). Globalizing Standard Spanish: The Promotion of "Panhispanisms" by Spain's Language Guardians. In Sally Johnson & Tommaso M. Milani (eds), *Language Ideologies and Media Discourse: Texts, Practices, Politics*. pp. 41–60. Continuum.
Peirce, C.S. (1931–58). *Collected Papers of Charles Sanders Peirce*. Harvard University Press.
Perley, B.C. (2011). *Defying Maliseet Language Death: Emergent Vitalities of Language, Culture and Identity in Eastern Canada*. University of Nebraska Press.
Philips, S. (2000). Constructing a Tongan Nation-state through Language Ideology in the Courtroom. In P.V. Kroskrity (ed.), pp. 229–257.
Rampton, B. (1995). *Crossing: Language and Ethnicity among Adolescents*. Longman.
Reyes, A. & A. Lo (2009). *Beyond Yellow English*. Oxford University Press.
Reynolds, J.F. (2009). Shaming the Shift Generation: Intersecting Ideologies of Family and Linguistic Revitalization in Guatemala. In P.V. Kroskrity & M.C. Field (eds), pp. 213–237.
Richland, J.B. (2008). *Arguing with Tradition: The Language of Law in Hopi Tribal Court*. University of Chicago Press.
Schieffelin, B.B. (2000). Introducing Kaluli Literacy: A Chronology of Influences. In P.V. Kroskrity (ed.), pp. 205–227.
——. (2007). Found in Translating: Reflexive Language across Time and Texts in a Bosavi, Papua New Guinea. In M. Makihara & B. Schieffelin (eds) pp. 140–165.
Schieffelin, B.B., K.A. Woolard & P.V. Kroskrity (eds) (1998). *Language Ideologies, Practice and Theory*. Oxford University Press.
Schmidt, R. (2007). Defending English in an English Dominant World: The Ideology of the "Official English" Movement in the United States. In Alexandre Duchene & Monica Heller (eds), *Discourses of Endangerment*, pp. 197–215. Continuum.
Shankar, S. (2008a). Speaking Like a Model Minority: "FOB" Styles, Gender, and Racial Meanings among Desi Teens in Silicon Valley. *Journal of Linguistic Anthropology* 18: 268–289.
——. (2008b). *Desi Land: Teen Culture, Class, and Success in the Silicon Valley*. Duke University Press.
Silverstein, M. (1979). Language Structure and Linguistic Ideology. In P. Clyne, W. Hanks & C. Hofbauer (eds), *The Elements*, pp. 193–248. Chicago Linguistics Society.
——. (1981). The Limits of Awareness. Working Papers in Sociolinguistics, no. 84. Southwest Educational Development Library. [Reprinted in A. Duranti (ed.) *Linguistic Anthropology: A Reader*, pp. 382–402. Blackwell.].
Silverstein, M. (1985). Language and the Culture of Gender: At the Intersection of Structure, Usage, and Ideology. In *Semiotic Mediation*, Elizabeth Mertz and Richard J. Parmentier (eds), pp. 219–259. Academic Press.
——. (1993). Metapragmatic Discourse and Metapragmatic Function. In J. Lucy (ed.), *Reflexive Language: Reported Speech and Metapragmatics*, pp. 33–58. Cambridge University Press.
——. (1996). Monoglot A Standard in America: Standardization and Metaphors of Linguistic Hegemony. In *The Matrix of Language: Contemporary Linguistic Anthropology*, Donald Brenneis and Ronald, K.S. Macaulay (eds), pp. 284–306. Westview Press.
——. (1998). The Uses and Utility of Ideology: A Commentary. In B.B. Schieffelin et al. (eds), pp. 123–145.
Smith-Hefner, N.J. (2009). Language Shift, Gender, and Ideologies of Modernity in Central Java, Indonesia. *Journal of Linguistic Anthropology* 19: 57–77.
Spitulnik, D. (1998). Mediating Unity and Diversity: The Production of Language Ideologies in Zambian Broadcasting. In B.B. Schieffelin et al. (eds), pp. 163–188.
Stasch, R. (2007). Demon Language: The Otherness of Indonesian in a Papuan Community. In M. Makihara & B. Schieffelin (eds), pp. 96–124.
Urciuoli, B. (1996). *Exposing Prejudice: Puerto Rican Experiences of Language, Race, and Class*. Westview Press.
Verschueren, J. (2012) *Ideology in Language Use: Pragmatic Guidelines for Empirical Research*. Cambridge University Press.

Wodak, R. & M. Meyer (2001). *Methods of Critical Discourse Analysis*. Sage.
Woolard, K.A. (1985). Language Variation and Cultural Hegemony: Toward an Integration of Sociolinguistics and Social Theory. *American Ethnologist 2*: 738–748.
——. (1989). *Double Talk: Bilingualism and the Politics of Ethnicity in Catalonia*. Stanford University Press.
Woolard, K. & B. Schieffelin.1994. Language Ideology. *Annual Review of Anthropology 23*: 55–82.
Zentella, A.C. (1997). *Growing Up Bilingual: Puerto Rican Children in New York*. Blackwell.

Further Reading

Hill, J.H. (2008). *The Language of Everyday White Racism*. Wiley-Blackwell.
In this book the author develops an approach to linguistic racism that utilizes language ideological theory.

Kroskrity, P.V. (ed.) (2000). *Regimes of Language: Ideologies, Polities, and Identities*. School of American Research.
A collection of research on language ideologies that moves the field toward a more "reflexive" examination of academic and Western language ideologies.

Lippi-Green, R. (1997). *English with an Accent: Language, Ideology, and Discrimination in the United States*. Routledge.
A collection of interesting applications of a language ideological approach to various US institutions – from legal to Disney animated films. A useful introduction to the politics of language standardization.

Schieffelin, B. B., K.A. Woolard and P.V. Kroskrity (eds) (1998). *Language Ideologies, Practice and Theory*. Oxford University Press.
The foundational collection of articles on the then emerging research area of language ideologies.

8

Social Subordination and Language

Margarita Huayhua

Introduction

Q'upakama kashan, lliwta pichana mamita. It is full of garbage, you *mamita* need to sweep.
Mana q'upa kananchu, limphiw kanan, mana There must be no garbage, it has to be clean.
qhillipi tiyanachu[1] You should not live in the middle of filthiness.

As I listened to the above assertion made by a visitor to the household that was hosting me, I thought it was a disrespectful way to behave as a guest. But, to my surprise, the host responded to the visitor's remark by quickly saying: *ya siñurita* ('yes, miss'). My first thought was that the host was allowing herself to be patronized, but her quick answer was a formulaic one. After the visitor left she jokingly said: "***quwichaq mihunan q'upalla paykunapaqqa***" ("they always see the guinea pigs' food as garbage").

In the highlands of Peru, more than three million speakers of Southern Peruvian Quechua, the language of the Inka, continue to live cheek-by-jowl with descendants of their conquerors, strangers in their own land. Social subordination is built into the most mundane activities, reproducing macro levels of dominance over Native Andeans. Subordination is also channeled institutionally through schools, clinics, and other government-run institutions and programs.

Subordination – a habitual form of dominance by one party over another – happens on a daily basis in formal and nonformal situations, across racial/ethnic, gender, and class lines. Subordination is not only a consequence of abstract ideas about how a society must be organized; social subordination is also a consequence of mundane, daily, embodied practices in which individuals are enmeshed above and below the threshold of awareness.

Native Andeans, together with other impoverished groups, are the primary target of public policies orchestrated by the state. The Peruvian state has instituted public policies to mitigate structural socioeconomic inequalities across different governments (e.g., Fujimori, Toledo, and Garcia). These policies include social programs such as comprehensive health insurance and allocations of food for school children. The programs are administered by local branches of government or municipalities. Under the leadership of the Ministerio de Desarrollo e Inclusión Social, the policies seek to improve the quality of life for the poorest citizens by promoting their rights and giving them access to opportunities and the means to develop their own abilities.[2]

However, despite the well-intentioned state policies to address socioeconomic inequalities via social programs, such policies infringe directly on people's private lives. The social programs actually foster the very social subordination they were designated to ameliorate.

The following section will examine one such program, called the 'Expansion and Enhancement of Water and Drainage in the village of Uqhupata'[3] managed by the municipality of Santiago (Department of Cuzco). This includes a home visit program called Saneamiento Intradomiciliario (intra-domiciliary sanitation, hereafter *visita domiciliaria* or *visita*). The program actively intervenes in the homes of Quechua-speaking villagers to promote sanitary domestic habits. Municipal agents go door to door to inspect households. The agents inspect the homes and determine the levels of cleanliness according to criteria listed on the program's surveillance form (hereafter SF).[4] The SF has five headings for scoring the hygiene habits of villagers and their households: water, personal care, latrine, kitchen tidiness, and garbage.

The Kitchen: The Heart of the Quechua Household

The use of space in the home follows the logic of the villagers themselves. The kitchen is key to a villager's sense of interiority. In a typical Andean household, the kitchen and the patio are places where household members spend most of their time. Quechua speakers take their meals, converse about their daily activities, and attend to their kin and co-villagers in the kitchen. The kitchen usually has a clay stove, a **musk'a** (stone mortar) and small corrals for **quwi** (guinea pigs). Each morning the female head of household will sit on a small wooden bench as she feeds the mouth of the clay stove with firewood. She places pots filled with the ingredients for the morning soup over each eye of the stove.

The distribution of material things within the kitchen and the patio lead household members to handle their business in a certain way. As Keane 2005: 194 suggests, material things instigate "(by virtue of [their] form, that is, iconic suggestion) ... certain kinds of action," but they do not determine them. The woman is prompted to sit on the bench that is present and the action of sitting close to the clay stove may further encourage carrying out other actions. Actions are thus constituted by the interplay of human agency and the surrounding material things (signs) that are components of the objective contexts for human action. The things that are part of the woman's objective contexts (e.g., the bench, the pots, and the clay stove) have led her to adopt particular ways of accommodating and handling her body. These objects shape human beings "through comfort, demarcations of space, channeling movement and posture" (Keane 2006: 200).

Before examining how agents as guests and Quechua-speaking hosts handle the *visita domiciliaria* program in face-to-face interactions in Quechua-speaking households in Uqhupata, let me briefly outline the way households have been conceptualized in anthropology more generally.

Households: Brief Review

Since the beginnings of anthropology, the household was considered a structure that organizes social relations (Morgan 2003 [1881]). For example, Bourdieu (1990) considers the household a structure that itself structures bodily practices. Following Bourdieu, Carsten & Hugh-Jones (1995: 46) suggest that the household is a way buildings are connected to people and ideas – bringing together "architecture, kinship and cultural categories." Mueggler (2001) conceptualizes the household as a structure that creates differential social relations and hierarchy. And Fox (2006: 5) suggests that households are animate entities that are important expressions of the kinship unit. Households are a forum for social relationships, and reflect power and dynamics of growth.

In Latin America, the house is an organized set of material practices described by "the vocabulary for the physical dwelling: the house as shelter is a metaphor for the house as economy" (Gudeman & Rivera 1990: 2). In addition, the home demonstrates the relationship between social practice and meaning (Gose 1990). In the Andes, the space surrounding the household has been understood as an extension of the personal space of its members. That is, unspoken "rules concerning the approach of visitors – whether they remain at the gate or enter the yard, patio, porch or house – reflect [strangeness or] social distance from household members" (Carsten & Hugh-Jones 1995: 3). Thus, the household can be understood as a sovereign space within which social and moral values are contained.

What it Means for a Quechua Household to Receive a Visit

For Quechua villagers the household is the space of all sociability. Villagers observe strict ceremonial behavior when properly receiving a guest in order to maintain boundaries and the sovereignty of the household, as well as to protect the household's sacred interiority from exposure to "social critique." The relationships between hosts and guests are also marked fairly strictly (Allen 1981).

Following the villagers' own conventions about appropriate behavior on the part of both the guest and host is central to villagers' sense of self, and sense of self-esteem. It is appropriate to offer food to guests, whether they are co-villagers or strangers. To omit to offer food would be considered a sign of rudeness or bad manners; just like for American Indian hosts, omitting to offer food "would have been a discourtesy amounting to an affront. If hungry, [the visitor] ate; if not hungry, courtesy required that he should taste the food and thank the giver" (Morgan 2003 [1881]: 45–48). Hospitality "creates a moral space in which outsiders can be treated as provisional members of the house, as aspects of" its sacred interiority (Shryock 2004: 36), because hospitality, as Shryock (2004: 37) points out, "creates a momentary overlap of the inner and outer dimensions" of a household. Offering cups of coffee, or food to welcome and please a guest configures the relationship between the host and guest.

Family Visits

Work-related visits among relatives occur early in the morning. Visitors would usually find their female relative busy cooking the morning meal. If a female relative is visited unexpectedly by a kinsman or kinswoman looking to confirm the exchange of work, she may deal with the sudden disruption of her sense of "interiority" by quickly facing her kin then returning to her task at hand. She would signal cordiality through short phrases suitable for the situation, thus keeping in line with social values of consideration if there is a visitor.

Visits take longer when relatives cross the threshold of the household. These visits can be characterized by generosity, warmness, and conviviality. Visits among kin follow the norms of hospitality, which include conventions and expected forms of behavior (Pitt-Rivers 1968: 16). Being hospitable and respectful are constituents of the social and moral values shared by relatives as members of the household and the village at large (Herzfeld 1987).

Partaking in hospitality can become risky to the extent that both guests and hosts could overstep their limits. Violations can occur, as I show in the Andean village of Uqhupata, when municipal agents rush into villagers' households to carry out the *visita*. Let us examine two examples of interactions between agents and household members to show whether or not the way language is used undermines Quechua-speaking hosts.

Strangers' Visits to Households

When a nonvillager steps into a household unexpectedly, announcing their presence with the word *visita* (visit), a household member runs toward the patio to attend to the visitor. The host keeps the visitor on the patio. Household members put a lot of energy into pleasing the visitor by offering a place to sit and by offering food. Sometimes, a nonvillager such as a municipal agent fails to reciprocate respect and consideration.

Agents demand that villagers comply with the *visita* program's outline of cleanliness and attempts to inspect the household. Villagers maintain a hospitable attitude to reduce the chances of failing the inspection. Agents' injunctive attitude (Goffman 1967: 25) toward their hosts compromises the values and code of conduct held by the household. The visits from municipal agents can interrupt to the point of invading the household's interiority and the household members' personal interiorities.

As has been explained, agents – under the umbrella of the *visita* – inspect households to evaluate villagers' level of cleanliness. The inspection is carried out based on criteria listed on the surveillance form (SF): consumption of water, personal and household hygiene, use of the latrine, kitchen tidiness, and garbage. Let us examine an example where the host openly challenges the *visita*.

Being Caught on the Patio

I am on the patio with my host Ñaña and her daughter Ususi, along with Ñaña's sister Pani. We are chewing some **kuka** leaves. The patio has no fence and is visible to everybody from the road. Ususi is telling us about being scolded by an angry nurse. An agent appears on the road leading to the house, and is greeted as Ms Gas (G):[5] "*winus diyas siñurita* Gas" ("good morning *siñurita* Gas"). The host does not stand up to receive the agent, who enters the patio and glances around, carrying a clipboard with the SF in order to check cleanliness. Gas walks fleetingly by the unused toilet, the washing sink, and the kitchen door. She opens and closes the tap above the sink, and says "*muy bien, la pila funciona*" ("very good, the faucet works").

After this comment she turns toward the host and adds:

9 G: **Limphiw kayqa kanan. LIMPHIWTA MAQCHIRUNKICHIS.**
[. . .]

G: This must be clean. You have to clean it.

The agent pushes the latrine door to open it but a startled chicken noisily emerges from inside. Gas notes something on the SF and turns to the host to speak:

11 G: <u>Miren</u> pues(.) mana kayqa wallpa puñu- nanpaqchu. **KAYQA BAÑUN USANAYKICHISPAQMI HISP'ANAYKICHISPAQMI.**

Ya doña chay bañutawan limphiwta pichachiwanki AH (,) mañana voy a volver

G: Look at this. This is not for chickens to sleep in. This is a bathroom; you must use it. You must pee there. Okay *doña*, you will make somebody clean this bathroom; ah, it has to be done ((leaving)) I'll come back tomorrow.

The agent was not welcome and was ignored by the host. Ñaña does not invite the agent to sit down and she does not stand to show the agent the kitchen. Ñaña silently observes and only the daughter responds laconically to the agent's commands: "*Ya siñurita*" ("okay *siñurita*").

The host's unwillingness to receive the agent does not preclude the inspection. The agent inspects the sink and the latrine located on the patio. Her phrase "**limphiw . . . kanan**" (line 9) denotes that the sink must be cleaned with urgency. Ususi's response is noncommittal. The hen in the latrine prompted a louder injunction from the agent: "***HISP'ANAYKICHISPAQMI***" ("you must pee in the latrine" [line 11]). The injunctive and threatening last phrase " . . . ***limphiwta pichachiwanki AH***" expresses the authoritative demand in the name of cleanliness, and exposes the agent's patronizing attitude that undermines the host in her own house.

Despite the host's refusal to acknowledge the agent as a guest and her refusal to allow the scrutinizing visitor access to her kitchen, Ñaña could not prevent the agent from coming in and intruding on the household. The agent carries out her inspection and demands cleanliness in both Quechua and Spanish (line 11). Ñaña is scolded and humiliated. Her lack of response to the injunctions can be read as a stance against the agent's actions, or as an act of giving up and allowing the agent to continue with her course of action.

Ñaña cannot escort her unwanted visitor out to the road as the Greek Glendiots did with guests from Texas who failed to recognize that "hospitality is not only a privilege, but one that confers a reciprocal obligation to offer *respect*" (Herzfeld 1987: 80–81). Ñaña is made powerless by the agent, who enters the house without consent. As an official, the agent can be bold and inspect every corner of the household if she wishes. The *visita* reaffirms the agent's superordinate stance, while it subordinates the host.

The "law of hospitality," in Pitt-Rivers's (1968: 26) sense, is broken during the *visita*. The agent's entry beyond the gate and attempt to enter the kitchen breaks the normative "social distance" that should be kept with strangers (Carsten & Hugh-Jones 1995: 3). The agent's means of interrupting – and her use of language when demanding cleanliness – exceeds the bonds of a proper Quechua guest–host relationship. Such an interruption violates the household's interiority.

The *visita domiciliaria* inadvertently reinforces the perception that villagers live in unhygienic conditions. Hence, villagers require professional assistance to change their habits and adopt a "clean" lifestyle. In the above examined interaction, villagers are depicted as filthy and in need of acquiring clean habits. This need to cleanse "unclean" Quechua practices, according to urban policies of cleanliness, is a "civilizing" project that aims to include villagers as members of the Peruvian citizenry. Let us examine a further example in which the civilizing project of cleanliness – embedded in the *visita* – violates not only villagers' household sovereignty, but the host's personal interiority as well.

A Friendly Visit

It is around 9:30 a.m. Sasiku and I are chewing **kuka** leaves in her kitchen. We hear a female voice (A) calling out:

12 A: *Doña(,) Doña Sasiku(?)*   A: *Doña(,) Doña* Sasiku(?)

Wrapping up her bag of **kuka** leaves, Sasiku hurries to the patio to attend to the unexpected visitor. The municipal agent is already standing on the patio. Sasiku (Sa) greets her: "***winus diyas siñurita***" ("good morning *siñurita*"), takes her sweater off to lay it on a rock, and says: "***chaychapi tiyakuy siñurita***" ("please *siñurita* sit down over there"). The visitor sits down, smiles, and says "*gracias*" ("thanks"). She points out:

[. . .]

15 A: *Mamita **visita** AH (,) VISITA*   A: Little mama [this is] a visit ah(.) [This is a]
       *DOMICILIARA **ña yachankichisña***   house visit (,) you are familiar with this
       ***riki**(?)*   already right(?)

Margarita Huayhua

The visitor warns the host that the *visita* is necessary to ascertain whether her household meets municipal guidelines for a "hygienic house." The agent will examine the organization of the household and check for cleanliness, inspecting the tableware, kitchen and latrine. In this context, the Spanish word *"mamita"* signals that the host is in a lower position and has to comply with this official surveillance. The phrases *"visita AH"* and *"VISITA DOMICILIARA"* convey the purpose of the visit and give it legitimacy (line 15). To avoid any doubts, the agent explains using Quechua that everybody in the village is familiar with the *visita domiciliaria* program. The host utters *"aha"* ("yes"), implying that she cannot reject an official visit.

While the agent fills in some general data on the SF (information like the geographical location and date), the host grabs a stick from a pile of eucalyptus firewood and walks toward her kitchen, with the agent following behind her. There, the agent stands near the threshold of the door and says:

16 A: Y::: este- como se llama- <u>de una vez</u>   A: And::: this- how can I say- I will proceed
       <u>seguimien**tuta ruwayrusayki**</u> mama [6] (.)   right away with the supervision *mama*(.)
[...]

After some hesitation, the visitor informs the host of her intention to proceed with the inspection *"de una vez ..."*; the agent uses Quechua towards the end to soften the nature of the intrusion (line 16). The use of Quechua, however, does not bring the agent "closer" to the villagers and it does not lead to her acceptance as a temporary member of the household. The agent notices the **quwi** that Sasiku is preparing and remarks that it looks delicious.[7] Sasiku looks for a bench to offer her guest and places her sweater on the doorway in response to a request from the visitor. The visitor manages to sit where she likes. The guest is offered a plate of cooked **muraya**.[8] After saying thanks, the visitor eats a couple of **muraya** and puts the rest in a plastic bag to store in her backpack. Returning to the list in the SF, the agent translates the Spanish into Quechua and announces:

18 A: **Imaynataq** *practikashankichis wasipi*   A: *Doñita* I'll ask you about how you are exer-
       chayllatan tapuyusayki *doñita ya*(?)   cising ((cleanliness)) okay(?) ((follows the
                                                     SF written guide))
19 Sa: °*Ya siñurita*°   Sa: Okay *siñurita* ((feeds the stove's mouth with
                                                      firewood))
20 A   Ya doña Sa:: Sasiku no(?)   A: Okay doña Sa:: Sasiku, right(?)
[...]
22 A: <u>Muy bien</u>, **kaypi ununchismanta**   A: Very well, now we'll talk about our water(.)
       rimariyusun khunan(.) **unu- batiyan-**   we have our washbowl and our water right(.)
       chispis(.) **ununchispis kashan riki**(.) now you have to practice cleanliness-
       khunanqa qankuna *limpiesata-limpiesa-*   cleanliness right(?)
       tan riki practikanaykichis(?)
23 Sa: °*Ah*°   Sa: Yes ((peeling **muraya** and putting them into
                                                      a pot))
24 A: *Orden* **wasipipis**(.) **wawakunapis**   A: The house has to be organized(.) and the
       limphiw kananku(.) **timpuchata**   children must be clean (.) you find the time
       hap'iyrukuspaqa munayta wawakuna-   to clean the children nicely okay *mamita*(?)
       tapas allinta alistana *mamita ya*(?)
25 Sa: °*Ya*° *(siñurita)*   Sa: Yeah *(siñurita)*
26 A: *Primera* **visitapiqa asta- mana allinta* A: In this first visit un- I'm not finding you all
       tarishaykichis (.) *pero* **huq visitapiqa** organized and cleaned, but in the next visit
       ñacha mihurña *visita* **kamunqa** *ya*(?) everything has to be better okay(?)
[...]

114

Social Subordination and Language

28 A:	Ya(,) **Nuqanchis- ununchista khunan klurasqatachu tumashankichis manachu**(?)	A:	Now we- are you drinking our water chlorinated or not(?)
[...]			
31 Sa:	**Kluramushankucha riki** *siñurita* **diriktiwakuna**(.) *nusi imaynacha kakunpas* °*siñurita*°(.) *mana imaynapis riparanichu chaytaqa*(.)	Sa:	I assume it is being chlorinated by the board of directors *siñurita*(.) I have no idea *siñurita*(.) I have not paid attention to that (.)
32 A:	Ya, **manachu unu tumasqaykipipas riparanki**(,) *imayna unu kasqanta*	A:	Okay didn't you notice the quality of water(,) when you drink it
33 Sa:	**Mana** *siñurita* **chaytaqa riparanichu**	Sa:	I didn't notice that *siñurita* ((pours water into a pot))
34 A:	*Ah ya, a la* **vistallan kluruyuq hampisqa unu kaqtinqa**(,) *siempre saburchan as midisinama ima ahh* **tumpa**/	A:	Okay, it is noticeable when the water is chlorinated(,) it tastes like medicine ahh like/
35 Sa:	/**Mana** *siñurita* **chaytaqa riparanichu**	Sa:	I didn't notice that *siñurita* ((rotating the guinea pig to roast it uniformly))
36 A:	**manachu**(?)	A:	No(?)
[...]			
39 Sa:	**Qaynakuna, qayna unaykunaña asway** *ah- chhayna unuta* (,) **chay sirkachalla kluramunku chayqa lichi hina**:: *unu* °*tukurupun*°	Sa:	A long time ago, a long time ago a- they did(,) they chlorinated the water and it looked like milk
40 A:	Ya, **chaya chay- chaya chay hampimusqanku**	A:	Yes it is- it- that is when they have chlorinated the water
41 Sa:	°*Ya siñurita*°	Sa:	Okay *siñurita*
42 A:	*Manaya mana ninki- mana riparanichu nispa*(.) **chaya chay hampisqa unu klurasqa riki**(?)	A:	You don't say no- you don't say I have not noticed(.) that is the chlorinated water ((fills in the SF)) it is chlorinated right(?)

The agent sets the topics of the conversation (line 18). She points out that the house has everything needed to "cultivate" hygienic practices (line 22). The agent finds the host's house and children are not sufficiently neat or clean. She demands more obvious effort at cleanliness on her next visit. Most of the time the host assents to what the agent is recommending. If we follow the interaction between the agent and Sasiku, we learn how the host is subordinated despite the interaction occurring in Saskiku's own house. The agent addresses the host as "*doñita*," "*doña*," "*mamita*" (lines 18, 20, 24); these address forms place individuals in a lower position in relation to their interlocutors. The Spanish diminutive "ita" in the first and third words denotes a condescending attitude towards the host. The host addresses her interlocutor consistently as *siñurita* (lines 19, 25, 31, 33, 35, 41), which denotes distance and respect. By doing this the host expects the agent to behave kindly, as is expected from an educated professional. The forms of address used in this interaction reinforce the host's lower position vis-à-vis the agent.

In line 22 the agent implies that in the past the household and its members were not clean. But the use of "*khunanqa*" ("now") signals that this should no longer be the case. The household now has the means to practice hygiene. Hence, hygiene should be the "norm"; the children and the household should be clean and tidy respectively: "*limpiesata* . . . **praktikanaykichis**" ("you must practice cleanliness"). Such activities should be obvious to any visitor such as the agent. The phrase in line 26 denotes that the household and its members do not meet the criteria for cleanliness. The agent expects to find conditions improved on the next visit.

Margarita Huayhua

The focus on the task at hand downplays the encroachment of the agent into the house. Throughout the conversation, the host continues to feed the mouth of the stove with firewood and tends to the roasted guinea pig. She also peels **muraya**, and so forth. The host responds laconically to her interlocutor's questions and injunctions while carrying out her tasks. She tries to keep her sense of interiority, thus her lack of interest in the agent's enquiries. The lack of interest is noticeable in the host's response to the question about the regular chlorination of the water (line 28), for example "**nusi imaynacha kakpunpas**" ("I have no idea"), and "**mana . . . riparanichu**" ("I haven't noticed") (lines 31, 33).

It is the agent's insistence (lines 32, 34, 36) that compels the host to pay attention to the agent's question on water quality. The host recalls a past event from months ago when the water appeared "milky" (line 39). The milky appearance provides proof that the water has been chlorinated. The agent uses the opportunity to scold the host: "**Manaya mana ninki-mana riparanichu**" (line 42). The host should not say "I haven't noticed"; she should speak "the truth," given that she is able to notice whether or not the water has been chlorinated. It implies that the host's responses in lines 31 and 33 are not accurate answers. The agent continues asking:

43 A: **Unuykita** este- **waqaychankichu icha diriktamente pilitamantachu tumanki**(?)

A: Your water, eh- do you keep water in buckets or do you drink it straight from the faucet(?)

44 Sa: **Ummm- pilitamanta** siñurita **purunguchapi aysayakamuspalla tumaykuqa**(.)

Sa: Mmm- in order to drink water we fetch it in a gourd-shaped vessel(.)

45 A: **Ya**(,) muy bien(.)

A: Okay(,) very good(.)

[. . .]

47 A: **Ya**(,) **batiyayki khunan::** funcionashanchu limphiwchu **kashan**(?)

A: Okay(,) is your sink clean and in working condition now(?) ((keeps filling in the SF))

48 Sa: >**Khunallanmi chikuchay** siñurita **papata maychhiramuran chaypi**<

Sa: Just now my child has washed potatoes there

49 A: **Ya**(.) voy a ver ahorita ya (.) higiene personal dice si se había limpiado la señora (.) se habia base habia peinado uu- **tutamantan ñaqch'arukusqankiña umaykita** he(?)

A: Okay(,) I'll check that in few minutes ((reading the SF)) it said personal hygiene if the woman has cleaned herself up(.) If she- if she has combed- at dawn you have already combed your hair right(?)

50 Sa: **Ya** °siñurita°

Sa: Yes siñurita

51 A: **Allinmi**(,) **allinmi**(.) **chay** practikana **mamá sapa unchay chay** limpie**sata wawakunawanpas ya**(?)

A: Very good(,) very good(.) Mamá that kind of hygienic habit has to be practiced everyday also with the children, okay(?)

52 Sa: °**Ya** siñurita°

Sa: Yeah siñurita

53 A: **Makichanchista imakunapaq maqchikunchis** mamita(?)

A: Why do we wash our little hands mamita(?)

[. . .]

56 Sa: **Wayk'unapaq primirta** siñurita **maqchikuna**(.)

Sa: We have to wash our hands before cooking siñurita(.)

57 A: **Ya**(.) muy bien(.) lavador**pi hap'ispachu**(.) **pilitapichu** directamente(?)

A: Yes(.) very good. Do you wash them in a bucket or right in the sink(?)

58 Sa: **Aywis** siñurita **pilitapi**(.) aywisqa lavador**pipas**

Sa: Siñurita sometimes we wash in the sink(.) and sometimes in the bucket

59 A: **Ya** muy bien(.)

A: Okay, very good(.)

[. . .]

116

Social Subordination and Language

61 A: *Ya muy bien*(,) na- **WAWAKUNATA ASTAWAN** mamita idukana ya(?)	A: Okay, very well(,) the- *mamita* children have to be educated more and more, okay(?)
62 Sa: °*Ya siñurita*°	Sa: Yeah *siñurita*
63 A: <u>Siempre mihunapaqqa</u> llipin chiku- **wawachaykikunata** phaway makichaykichista maqchikamuychis nispa	A: Always before eating, all chil- you make your children wash their hands by telling them to do so
[. . .]	
65 A: *Makinchispi* contaminación **kashan** imaymana unquykuna ya(?)	A: "Our" hands are contaminated, they are the source of many diseases, okay(?)
66 Sa: °*Ya siñurita*°/	Sa: Yeah *siñurita*
67 A: /*Ya* **wawakunapaq** mas que nada(.) uu- tutaymanta hatarimuspapas simichankuta ima maqchikunanku(.) primeramente **paykuna**(.)	A: Okay, we have to be careful for the sake of the children(.) early in the morning they have to wash their mouths before anybody else
68 Sa: *Aha*	Sa: Yes
69 A: *Taytamamata* rikuspaqa paykuna a la vistallata- ña yachankuña imata ruwanankuta(,) ya doñita(?)	A: If the children see that their parents keep hygienic practices- for sure- they will know what to do every morning(,) okay doñita(?)
[. . .]	
72 A: [. . .]*letrinayki kashan* eh(?)	A: [. . .]you have a latrine right(?)
73 Sa: °**Kashanmi** *siñurita*°	Sa: Yes, there is one *siñurita*
74 A: *Ya*(.) **limphiwchu** mamita kunallan **kashan**(.) manachu(?) ((keeps filling in the SF))	A: Okay(.) right now it is clean(.) or not(?) ((keeps filling in the SF))
75 Sa: *Ma*:: na:: i- **wawakunaq hisp'asqan** siñurita **kashan**(,) unuwanqa hich'ayamunkun(.) hisp'aspankuqa	Sa: No:: ne:: e- the children have used it *siñurita* (,) but when they use it(.) afterwards they pour water
76 A: *Ya*(.) kunallan qhawaramusaq ya(?)	A: Okay(.) I'll check it in a moment(?)
77 Sa: °*Ya siñurita*°	Sa: Okay *siñurita*
78 A: *Ya*(.) usashankichisña entonces(?)	A: So you use the latrine
79 Sa: *Aha usashaykuñan*	Sa: Yes, we use it
80 A: *Ya*(.) letrinamanta hisp'akuspa señora- kutiramuspa imata ruwankichis?	A: Okay(.) when you are done in the latrine señora- what you do?
81 Sa: <u>Makitaya</u> siñurita **maychhikuyku**(,) kasqan uhupi pilapas **kashan** siñurita	Sa: Of course we wash our hands *siñurita*(,) the faucet is also there *siñurita*
[. . .]	
84 A: *Chaytaq* kachariyuwashaqchis **hisp'ay** apayunanpaq(.) manacha(?)	A: I expect you are not opening the faucet to make the stool pass(.) right(?)
85 Sa: *Mana* siñurita(,) °baldipi hap'ikuspaykupuniya hich'ayuyku°	Sa: No *siñurita* (,) we fetch water in a bucket to pour water in the latrine
86 A: *Ya*(.) <u>muy bien</u>, chay allin **kashan** ya(.) **wawakunata** primeramente bañuta haykuqtinkuqa makiykichista maqchikuychis(.) paykunata primiruta ninayki	A: Okay(.) very good, that is good(.) you have to say to children first that after using the latrine they have to wash their hands
87 Sa: °*Ya siñurita*°	Sa: Okay *siñurita*

117

At this point in the interaction, the host responds attentively to the agent's questions (e.g., line 44 and onward). The host's answers satisfy the agent, which is denoted by "very good" and "okay" (e.g., lines 45, 49, 57, 59). Following the SF, the agent shifts attention to the working condition of the sink and its cleanliness (line 47). The sink may not be "clean" given that the host's child had washed potatoes there, leaving traces of soil (line 48). This answer prompts the agent to check the hygienic conditions of the sink (line 49). In line 49, again following the SF, the agent makes sure that the host's hair is combed by asking if she combed it early this morning. The agent's injunctive phrase "***praktikana* . . . *sapa unchay chay limpiesata*"** (line 51) denotes that combing your hair is a sign of hygiene, a practice that must be embraced by all the household's members. Such a routine is interlaced with awareness on why "we" must wash our hands. To ask the host why she should wash her hands would be regarded as disrespectful behavior in any guest–host relations. Nonetheless, the host is subject to the agent's questioning (e.g., line 53) despite the fact that all this is taking place in Sasiku's house.

The agent's repeated questions about hand washing lead the host to remark that "of course one washes ones hands to cook" (line 56). After the agent asks where one should wash one's hands, the host quickly informs the agent that she and her family wash them in the sink or in a bucket, depending on how much time they have. The injunction that the host's children must be taught about hygienic habits implies that children have to be habituated to washing their hands before meals (lines 61, 63). "Our" hands are contaminated; they are the source of different illnesses (line 65). The agent goes on to stress that children must also brush their teeth as soon they get up (line 67). Children would fall into the habit of washing their hands and face if their parents do the same (line 69). The implication is that currently children are not socialized to adopt hygienic habits because of their parents neglecting to teach them.

The agent continues to review the SF and asks about the latrine and its cleanliness (lines 72, 74). The latrine has been used by the host's children and the host is not sure if water was poured properly (line 75). Thus, it will be inspected by the agent (line 76), who asks whether they are washing their hands after using the latrine (line 80), which prompts a strong response "*makitaya . . . maychikuyku*" (line 81). This sentence connotes that people know for sure they have to wash their hands after using the toilet. What is more, they know that water should be fetched in a bucket to pour in the toilet and keep it clean (line 85). Despite the host's confident responses to the questions about hand washing, the agent stills maintains a patronizing attitude and insists that the host instructs the children to wash their hands after using the latrine (line 86). Finally, the agent shifts attention to the cleanliness of the kitchen.

88 A: [. . .]*utensilio* **kusaskunata maypi waqaychanki** *mamá*(?)

89 Sa: ***Sirvishu kusasniykuna*** *siñurita* **anchaychallapi** °*siñurita*(.) ***misachaypi kashan*°**

90 A: Ya (,)*aschatawan* **mihurayusun** *mamá ya*(?)

91 Sa: °***Ya*** *siñurita*°

92 A: ***Phurarunki plastikuchawan*(,) *chayman p'aqtinki platukunata, huq laduchaman tasatapas*(.) *mihuytataq huq larupi hap'inki ya*(?)**

93 Sa: **ya** *siñurita su/*

A: [. . .]where do you keep your utensils *mamá*(?)

Sa: *Siñurita* my plates, mugs and other things are over there *siñurita*(.) by the small table ((points toward a wooden crate))

A: Okay ((pulls aside a plastic curtain to check the utensils)) you need to improve this okay *mamá*(?)

Sa: Okay *siñurita*

A: You line the crate with a plastic (,) and on that you place the plates face down, and next to them the mugs (.) and you keep the raw food in another space okay(?)

Sa: ((rotating the guinea pig again)) Okay *siñurita su/*

Social Subordination and Language

94 A:	/*Huqpi mihurta nuqa rikuyta munani*(,) **chaychakunata** *mamá* **arreglaykunk**i *ya*(?)	A:	/Next time I would like to see some improvement(,) you will fix that okay mama(?)
95 Sa:	*ankiy na- ankiy pachan kaqcha siñurita platuwan tasawan waqaychanayku*(.) *anchiy hawanpitaq virdurachakunata waqaychakuyku*(.)	Sa:	((pointing with her index finger)) this a- this space below is to keep plates and mugs siñurita(.) and the space above is to keep vegetables(.)
96 A:	*Ya muy bien*(.) *ahí hay carne también creo que- ya está bien-* **huqpi aqnata** *pruti***hiyunki**, *nachawanpas-* **plastikucha**/	A:	Okay very good ((continues checking)) I think there is also meat that- all right- next time you will protect it like this with- you will cover it with a/
97 Sa:	/**Ya** *siñurita*	Sa:	/Okay siñurita ((squeezes a handful of **muraya** from the water))
98 A:	**wanpis tapayunki** *mamá ya*(?) **chaychata ordenayukusun astawan**(.)	A:	Plastic mamá okay(?) we need to tidy up these little things(.)

[. . .]

The agent's self-response in Spanish "*la cocina . . . no está ordenada*" shows the kitchen is not tidy according to official standards. The agent asks about the tableware. She is directed to a table and a wooden crate (line 89) placed at the left side of the doorway. After pulling aside a plastic curtain to inspect the tableware, the agent states that there needs to be improvements made (line 90). The crate must be covered with plastic, with the plates placed face down. The mugs should be placed next to them. The raw food has to be stored separately[9] (line 92). The host is instructed she should make these changes before the next *visita* (line 94). However, the host indicates with her index finger that the tableware is kept in the crate and the food is stored on the ledge above it (line 95). The agent stands up to check the utensils and approves of their state, but she highlights that things need more organization to comply with cleanliness criteria (lines 96, 98). The food should also be protected with a piece of plastic. The agent sits in the doorway again and continues asking:

100 A:	**Kurral animalniykikunapaq kan** *eh*(?)	A:	You have a pen for your animals right(?)
101 Sa:	*Kaypiqa mana siñurita* **animalniyku** °*kanchu*° *Llawlliq'asa larupi animalniykuqa*(.)	Sa:	Siñurita I don't have any animals here(.) they are in Lawlliq'asa(.)
102 A:	*Ya*(.) *muy bien*(.)	A:	Okay, very good
103 Sa:	*Kaypiqa tiyayku quwichallantinya siñurita*(.) *quwichantin michichallantin*(.)	Sa:	Siñurita we live here with guinea pigs and cats (.) only with these animals(.)
104 A:	*Ya*(.) *el patio alrededor* **limphiwchu**(?) *falta*(,) *falta mamá limpieza*(.) **ama chhaynachu tiyaychis**(.) *chay nata este- latakunatapas siq'akunatapas* **huk laduman k'uchunay**(,) *wawakunaq libre purinanpaq ya*(?)	A:	Okay(.) the yard around is clean(?) ((checking the patio)) it is not(,) it lacks cleanliness mamá(.) you must not live like that(.) that- this- you must keep cans and plastic bags in a corner(,) so children can walk without obstruction okay(?)
105 Sa:	*Ya siñurita*	Sa:	Okay siñurita ((continues peeling **muraya**))
106 A:	**Por favor**(.) *basurata imata ruwashankichis* doña:: Sa- Sasiku(?)	A:	Please(.) what are you doña Sa- Sasiku doing with the garbage(?)
107 Sa:	*Mm*:: *qayninpa siñurita* **karru kasqa**(,) *chaymanya dispachayku*(.)	Sa:	Mm:: siñurita a few weeks ago there was a garbage car(,) so we throw the garbage there(.)
108 A:	*Ya*(,) *aqnatapuni siq'akunapi por favor* **huñunkichis** *ya*(?)	A:	Okay(,) please you'll always gather the garbage in plastic bags okay(?) ((keeps filling in the SF))

[. . .]

119

On having animals and keeping them penned in, the host informs the municipal agent that her animals are kept elsewhere, which the agent approves of readily. Regarding guinea pigs and cats, the host is self-assured and asserts that all villagers share their kitchen with them: "*kaypiqa . . . quwichantin michillantin tiyayku*" (line 103). These animals are not a problem for them. Faced with this response, the agent makes no further comments, instead she asks about the patio's cleanliness. Glancing at the patio, the agent forcefully highlights that it is by no means clean: "*falta . . . limpieza*" (line 104). The authority with which she is vested to guide villagers towards a "hygienic life" is denoted in the injunctive phrase "***ama chhaynachu tiyaychis***" (line 104). The phrase connotes that the host has to develop hygienic habits and that the villagers change their "unclean" houses. Even cans and plastic bags should be kept in one place. The host's response on the collection and disposal of garbage satisfies the agent (line 106), who asserts approvingly that garbage must always be collected (line 108). After filling in Sasiku's name on the SF, the agent goes on to inspect the latrine, the sink and the faucet. She comes back to the kitchen doorway and points out the following:

112 A: *No deben de echar tierra al baño*(.)   A: You shouldn't put soil in the latrine(.) there
       MANA ALLPA KANANCHU(?)   shouldn't be soil(?)
[. . .]

The agent's scolding, first in Spanish and then in Quechua, denotes that the addressee must "understand" that soil is a sign of filthiness and a latrine must be free of any traces of soil. The louder voice denotes the authority of the agent to proceed as she wants. The procedures subordinate the host to the *visita* requirements of cleanliness. The host, however, is more interested in roasting the ***quwi*** than addressing the agent's concerns. The agent asks the host for her fingerprint in lieu of a signature on the SF, after which the agent assigns a score to the level of the household's cleanliness. She is not asked to stay to share the ***quwi***. Not sharing food would be unthinkable for villagers under other circumstances. The visitor maintains her condescending attitude while leaving, warning that the tableware has to be kept clean. After the agent departs, Sasiku pulls out her ***kuka*** leaves and we continue chatting.

Even though the municipal agent has trespassed upon the boundaries of the household, the host manages to connote her lack of interest by continuing her activities even while she is policed on how the housekeeping should be handled. The terms of the relationship between the host and the visitor were established at the onset of the visit. The visitor assumed an official presence in order to carry out the *visita domiciliaria*. The host villager cannot decline an official visit, and as a consequence the host is forced to resign herself and open her household for the inspection. The inspection disrupts the household's and its members' interiority, which undermines the power of the host's stewardship over her own household.

Coda

In both official visits the hosts are treated as subjects of subordination, i.e., contentious relations of domination are produced in the interactions between hosts and guests that are evident in the languages used (spoken Quechua and Spanish). In the first case, the *visita* is carried out despite the host not explicitly granting permission to have the house inspected. The agent goes ahead and inspects the sink and the toilet anyway, but she could not inspect the kitchen nor ask the host about cleanliness more generally in order to complete the information necessary on the SF. The host ignores the official visitor's surveillance, which can be read as act of resistance.

In the second example, the visitor does not subordinate herself despite the hospitality offered, although this would be normal custom and expected behavior in a Quechua household.

Rather, it is the host who is subordinated despite being in her own home. The host acquiesces, but doesn't fully engage with the visitor's agenda by continuing to cook and replying with short responses. That is, the host's actions play down the *visita*.

The construction of the sewage system and accompanying latrines to improve villagers' lives transgress the heart of the villagers' households (and consequently, the personhood of the householders) through the *visita domiciliaria*. The construction unknowingly led villagers to submit themselves to the demands of cleanliness, which reinforced the ideology that Quechua-speaking people live enmeshed in filthiness and "stench" by nature. To "remedy" this situation the *visita* seeks to make sure that water is chlorinated and kept clean; that households' members practice cleanliness; that latrines are used and kept clean; that kitchens are tidy and free of **quwi**; that patios have no feces around; and that garbage is collected.

The discourse on cleanliness connotes that villagers live in unhygienic conditions and that their life is full of filth, which is instantiated through spoken Quechua and Spanish. In such a discourse the "stench" of households must be removed by sanitizing measures, that is, by regimenting households to urban ideologies of housekeeping and cleanliness.[10] The *visita* is invasive and it infringes on the host's intimate life and the household's sovereignty. In both cases the *visita* reveals relations of subordination that unfolds during the inspection.

Quechua-speaking women are placed in the lowest social position within the Peruvian social hierarchy; they are seen as objects of subordination by those placed in a superordinate position. This subordination is channeled unintentionally by institutions such the municipality of Cuzco. For instance, the large-scale subordination of Quechua women is not inverted in the *visita* when they receive visitors in their households. Hospitality is not "a means of [articulating and inverting] a pattern of domination at one and the same time," as is proposed by Herzfeld 1987: 77. Or better, relations of domination are articulated in both visits but domination is not inverted. Rather, open and conflicting ways of subordinating hosts take place through the enactment of the scripted words of the SF, and agents' superordinate stance.

What is more, interactions between the agents as guests and the villagers as hosts in Quechua households do not yield "some approximation to equality" (Dresch 2000: 117). In the household-centered events, interactions are most of the time under the visitor's control. In both events the set of conventions that combine the "rule of self-respect and the rule of considerateness" are not maintained (Goffman 1967: 10). The conduct of the visitors is not considerate, nor do they reciprocate respect. Rather, the patterns of hospitality that normally engender respect are demoted in the Quechua households.

The *visita* violates Quechua-speaking women's own interiority and the sacred interiority of households. The hosts understanding of households' space, organization, distribution, and use is affected. Even the act of chewing **kuka** leaves[11] is affected. The *visita* is a process of changing household members' own personal organization and relationships with the household's space and forms of housekeeping. The household, particularly the kitchen, is the center where main events of life take place, events that include cooking, birthing, raising children and acquiring, adulthood, attending to a kin, agreeing or disagreeing with a mutual work obligation, and learning the everyday basis of being a member of a Quechua-speaking village.

The moral foundations and social values of households is eroded by the *visita*, affecting the code of conduct of households' members and violating Quechua norms of reciprocity. This in turn affects the village at large. It is an assault on the host's sovereign territory and the host's autonomy; it is also a system of regulating villagers' social and cultural practices. The "civilizing" (and discriminatory) effects of well-intentioned, state-supported programs, be they local or national, affect villagers' sovereignty to live on their own terms. The desire to regiment the living space and household members' moral behavior is a civilizing process, in which the *visita* is a medium and a strategy to subordinate villagers to "standards" of what is considered as clean and hygienic life in the Peruvian southern Andes.

The pervasiveness of relations of subordination, evident in face-to-face interactions within the village households, undermines the right of the host to organize her life in her own home, in spite of the small acts of resistance. Given the facts, it is plausible to assert that, in general, widespread relations of dominance, evident when visitors violate hospitality and subordinate villagers within their own households, are not just residual effects of a colonial past (for historical insights see Méndez 1996; Larson 2004), but are produced by the actions of individuals in everyday situations. Everyday interactions between hosts and visitors inform national understandings about those who do not conform to an imaginary of a homogenous nation. In these interactions, domination and subordination are produced, as well as patterns that project a high level of domination (Gamson 1985), in which rural Quechua speakers are enmeshed.

Recommendations for Practice

To learn to speak a second language includes not only learning the formal grammatical structure, but it also means learning social and cultural cues in order to behave appropriately and show respect in any situation. In the southern Andes, government and NGO employees, together with acquiring the language, should learn respectful behavior, as well as observe the boundaries of social respect in both Spanish- and Quechua-speaking cultures. In any other Latin American country where there are social groups that speak other Native languages than Spanish, individuals should learn a second language together with the cultural nuances to respect the society that speaks the language.

Future Directions

Based on my study I suggest pursuing additional thorough research to uncover the systemic ways by which dominance and social subordination are perpetuated. For instance, research on how this perpetuation is reproduced, or challenged at micro- and macro-scale levels, to maintain a hierarchical system that maintains privilege would be useful; as well as a study of how language is used to build boundaries among interlocutors and how these boundaries refract national racial imaginaries about individuals who have no access to a "national" language. The focus on social practices of interaction shifts the attention to how relations of social oppression are produced and how they are part of the interactional order beyond individuals' ethnic or identity self-ascription. This focus moves the discussion on to relations of subordination beyond debates on racial/ethnic categories that do not reveal how such relations are built and reproduced. The systematic ways by which relations of domination are produced and challenged across cultures, across linguistic boundaries, and across the world can be revealed by paying attention to the interactional order.

Acknowledgments

An earlier version of this chapter was presented on May 21, 2013 at the LASA Congress as "Hierarchical Relations among Women in the Southern Andes." I am grateful to Claire Insel, Sabine MacCormack, Gillian Feeley-Harnik, Bruce Mannheim, Amy Mortensen, and Andrew Shryock for their insightful comments. Any errors remain mine.

Related Topics

15 Language and Racialization (Chun & Lo); **24** Discrimination via Discourse (Wodak); **25** Racism in the Press.

Notes

1 Italic bold: **Quechua**; italic: *Spanish*. Capital letters denote a louder voice. Words within double parentheses are comments of the author. Translations made by the author.
2 For details see www.midis.gob.pe/index.php/es/nuestra-institucion/sobre-midis/quienes-somos (accessed May 16, 2014).
3 To run the project villagers had to resettle their houses. Houses were rebuilt next to another in straight paths. Small water springs were diverted, and swamps dried. Currently, the main brook is polluted by the sewage that runs straight into it before reaching the sewage collector.
4 The sheet shows logos of the Swiss Agency for Development and Cooperation (knows as COSUDE in Peru), the Regional Government of Cuzco, and the Ministry of Health.
5 Villagers had a difficult time saying the agent's Spanish name and they ended up pronouncing it as "Gas."
6 Regarding transcription conversations, in addition to the details highlighted in note 1, I follow Goodwin (1990) and Sack et al. (1979). A dot (.) shows falling, or final, intonation, underlined words is emphatic stress, hyphen (-) indicates a cut-off or self-interruption, colons (::) indicate elongation, comma (,) indicates a short pause, a question mark (?) indicates a rising intonation, an oblique (/) indicates a point at which a current speaker's talk is overlapped by an interlocutor's talk, two degree signs (° ... °) indicate that the exchange between them is low or very low in volume. Words within more than and less than symbols (< ... >) indicate that the talk is rushed, and words within parentheses indicates a likely possibility. Some transcription conventions accompany the English translated version to facilitate the reading.
7 Sasiku's child is crying and the agent tries to quiet the child by saying: 'Don't cry, okay? We'll eat roasted **quwi**, okay?'
8 **Muruya** are dehydrated potatoes.
9 This picture differs from London. As a guest I was introduced to the house's rules of conviviality and communal use of the kitchen. The host showed me the cabinets in which tableware and pots are kept, as well as what kind of cutting boards I should use to cut bread, meat or vegetables. I was put on a schedule to clean the house although I was not staying for free. I have to follow my host's rules and organization.
10 Kitchen organization responds to different necessities and views on what is tidiness or cleanliness.
11 **Kuka** leaf is a symbol of proper hosting, a form of amusing and sweetening conversation (for further details see Allen 2000). It is seen by nonindigenous people as a sign of filthiness. On many occasions I witnessed villagers throw away their ball of chewed **kuka** and rinse out their mouths as they approached a health center or a town.

References

Allen, Catherine. 1981. "To Be Quechua: The Symbolism of Coca Chewing in Highland Peru." *American Ethnologist* 8(1): 157–171.
Allen, Catherine J. 2002. *The Hold Life Has: Coca and Cultural Identity in an Andean Community*. Washington: Smithsonian Institution Press.
Bourdieu, Pierre. 1990. *The Logic of Practice*. Translated by Richard Nice. Cambridge: Polity Press.
Carsten, Janet & Stephen, Hugh-Jones. 1995. "Introduction." In Janet Carsten & Stephen Hugh-Jones (eds), *About the House: Levi-Strauss and Beyond*, pp. 1–46. Cambridge: Cambridge University Press.
Dresch, Paul. 2000. "Wilderness of Mirrors: Truth and Vulnerability in Middle Eastern Fieldwork." In Paul Dresch, Wendy James, & David Parkin (eds), *Anthropologist in a Wider World: Essays in Field Research*, pp. 109–127. New York: Berghahn Books.
Fox, James. 2006. "Comparative Perspectives on Austronesian Houses: An Introductory Essay." In James Fox (ed.). *Inside Austronesian Houses: Perspectives in Domestic Design for Living*, pp. 1–29. Canberra: ANU Press.
Gamson, William. 1985. "Goffman's Legacy to Political Sociology." *Theory and Society* 14: 605–622.
Goodwin, Marjorie. 1990. *He-Said-She-Said: Talk as Social Organization among Black Children*. Bloomington: Indiana University Press.
Goffman, Erving. 1967. *Interaction Ritual: Essays on Face-to-Face Behavior*. Chicago: Aldine. Gose, Peter. 1990. "House Rethatching in an Andean Annual Cycle: Practice, Meaning, and Contradiction." *American Ethnologist* 18(1): 39–66.
Gudeman, Stephen & Alberto Rivera. 1990. *Conversations in Colombia: The Domestic Economy in Life and Text*. Cambridge: Cambridge University Press.

Herzfeld, Michael. 1987. "'As On Your Own House': Hospitality, Ethnography, and the Stereotype of Mediterranean Society." In David Gilmore (ed.), *Honor and Shame and the Unity of the Mediterranean*, pp. 75–89. Washington DC: American Anthropological Association.

Keane, Webb. 2005. "Signs are Not the Garb of Meaning: On the Social Analysis of Material Things." In Daniel Miller (ed.), *Materiality*, pp. 182–205. Durham: Duke University Press.

———. 2006. "Subjects and Objects." In Christopher Tilley, Webb Keane, Susan Kuechelr-Fogden, Mike Rowlands, & Patricia Spyer (eds), *Handbook of Material Culture*, 197–202. London: Sage Publications.

Larson, Brooke. 2004. *Trials of Nation Making. Liberalism, Race, and Ethnicity in the Andes, 1810–1910.* Cambridge: Cambridge University Press.

Méndez Cecilia, G. 1996. "Inkas Sí, Indios No: Notes on Peruvian Creole Nationalism and its Contemporary Crisis." *Journal of Latin American Studies 28*: 197–225.

Morgan, L. Henry. 2003 [1881]. *House and House-Life of the American Aborigines.* Chicago: University of Chicago Press.

Mueggler, Erik. 2001. "The Valley House." In Erik Mueggler, *The Age of Wild Ghosts: Memory, Violence and Place in Southwest China*, pp. 95–126. Berkeley: University of California Press.

Pitt-Rivers, Julian. 1968. "The Stranger, the Guest and the Hostile Host." In J.G. Peristiany (ed.), *Contributions to Mediterranean Sociology*, pp. 13–30. Paris: Mouton & Co.

Sacks, Harvey, Emanuel A. Schegloff, & Gail Jefferson. 1974. A Simplest Systematics for the Organization of Turn-Taking for Conversation. *Language 50*(4): 696–735.

Shryock, Andrew. 2004. "The New Jordanian Hospitality: House, Host, and Guest in the Culture of Public Display." *Society for Comparative Study of Society and History 46*: 35–62.

Further Reading

Bourque, Susan & Kay Warren. 1981. *Women of the Andes: Patriarchy and Social Change in Two Peruvian Towns.* Ann Arbor: University of Michigan Press.

Derrida, Jacques. 2000. "Step of Hospitality/ No Hospitality." In Jacques Derrida & Anne Dufourmantelle (eds), Rachel Bowlby (trans.), *Of Hospitality: Anne Dufourmantelle Invites Jacques Derrida to Respond*, 75–155. Stanford: Stanford University Press.

Eckert, Penelope & Sally McConnell-Ginet. 2013. *Language and Gender*, 2nd ed. Cambridge: Cambridge University Press.

Elias, Norbert. 2000. *The Civilizing Process. Sociogenetic and Psychogenetic Investigations.* Edmund Jephcott (trans.). Malden, Oxford: Blackwell Publishers.

Esch, Elizabeth & D. Roediger. 2006. "Non-racialism through Race (and Class)." *New Socialist: Ideas for Radical Change 56*: 6–10.

Escobar, Arturo. 1995. *Encountering Development: The Making and Unmaking of the Third World.* New Jersey: Princeton University Press.

Fausto, Carlos 2012. "The Friend, the Enemy, and the Anthropologist: Hostility and Hospitality among the Parakanã (Amazonia, Brazil)." *Journal of the Royal Anthropological Institute* S196–S209.

Goodwin, Charles. 2000. "Action and Embodiment: Within Situated Human Interaction." *Journal of Pragmatics 32:* 1489–1522.

Huayhua, Margarita. 2013. "Racism and Social Interaction in a Southern Peruvian Combi." *Ethnic and Racial Studies 37*(13): 2399–2417.

Pagliai, Valentina. 2011. "Unmarked Racializing Discourse, Facework, and Identity in Talk about Immigrants in Italy." *Journal of Linguistic Anthropology 21*(S1): E94–E112.

9
Language Socialization

Amy L. Paugh

Introduction

Language socialization research investigates how children and other novices are socialized through language, and how they socialize others, as they learn to use language via interactions with more knowledgeable relatives and friends. This approach considers linguistic and cultural learning to be interrelated processes that extend from infancy throughout the lifespan. Employing longitudinal ethnographic research methods, language socialization researchers explore how novices actively gain communicative competence as they acquire linguistic form, discursive practices, embodied stances, and the ideologies that render them meaningful within their cultural contexts. The first wave of language socialization research examined such processes in monolingual societies. A second wave of research extended this approach to the study of multilingual speech practices and language contact phenomena (Garrett and Baquedano-López 2002). This essay reviews the development and central concerns of the language socialization paradigm. It then examines current work on language socialization in multilingual settings, situations of language shift and migration, and in peer contexts.

Historical Perspectives

The language socialization paradigm emerged as a sociocultural approach to language learning in the 1980s (Ochs and Schieffelin 2008). It is rooted in linguistic anthropology, but draws on and contributes to multiple disciplines, including linguistics, developmental psychology, sociology, philosophy, and education. This approach was established amidst debates over the roles of "nature" versus "nurture" in language learning, and in response to socialization studies that did not take language into account as a critical vehicle of cultural transmission (Ochs and Schieffelin 1984; Kulick and Schieffelin 2004). Grounded in anthropological theory and methods, language socialization research considers language acquisition to be embedded in and vital to the acquisition of culture, and situated within culturally salient patterns of social interaction and sociability. Language acquisition and language socialization are viewed as interdependent developmental processes that must be studied together and contextualized within local ideologies about children, learning, personhood, and language (for comprehensive reviews of language socialization, see Duff and Hornberger 2008; Duranti et al. 2012; Garrett and Baquedano-López 2002; Kulick and Schieffelin 2004; Ochs and Schieffelin 1995, 2008, 2012; Riley 2008; also Riley 2014 on language socialization in the Romance world).

Early language socialization research expanded the contextual scope of language acquisition study beyond the mother–child dyad that was the focus of psycholinguistics, and carefully considered the role of discursive practices in cultural and linguistic learning within their local contexts. Foundational studies by Ochs (1988) in Samoa and Schieffelin (1990) in Papua New Guinea exemplify the first wave of language socialization research. Ochs (1988) situated Samoan children's grammatical development within their sociocultural environments and in relation to local understandings of rank and the status of children. With careful attention to linguistic structure and how it encodes sociocultural information, her ethnography demonstrates children's socialization into culturally appropriate affective expression, respectful conduct, and a sense of performance. Schieffelin (1990) similarly contextualized language acquisition within cultural conceptions of child development with a focus on the socialization of assertion and appeal, two interactional strategies fundamental to the system of reciprocity in Kaluli social life. Kaluli caregivers concentrated on the socialization of assertive stances, largely through εlεma "say like this" routines, because they believed that children know how to appeal. In a classic volume edited by Schieffelin and Ochs (1986), leading scholars in this burgeoning field explored language socialization in Kwara'ae, Basotho, Kaluli, Samoan, Japanese, and North American communities, examining culturally relevant interactional routines such as teasing, shaming, prompting, and calling out, among others.

Also foundational to the development of language socialization study was Heath's (1983) research on early socialization into narrative skills at home and its relation to literacy development and educational outcomes among children in three North American communities. Heath found that approaches toward literacy varied considerably across the white working class (Roadville), black working class (Trackton), and suburban middle class (Maintown) communities in the Piedmont Carolinas of the United States that she observed. These strategies cultivated different pathways of learning and demonstrating knowledge, which were compatible with each group's norms of social interaction and understandings of children. However, while these socialized "ways of taking" meaning from the world around them fostered a relatively seamless transition into formal schooling for Maintown children, Roadville and Trackton children struggled as their skills mismatched expectations in mainstream educational institutions.

Following from this early work was a second wave of research extending the language socialization approach to the study of multilingual speech practices and language contact phenomena like language shift, an intergenerational process whereby a social group intentionally or unintentionally gives up one language for a usually more dominant one. Kulick (1992) and Zentella (1997) are exemplary models of early language socialization work on multilingualism, language shift, and code-switching practices (also Schieffelin 1994). These studies contextualized micro-level socializing interactions within both local social structures and institutions, and larger macro-level sociopolitical and economic processes such as globalization and modernization. Kulick (1992) elucidated the process of language shift in Gapun, Papua New Guinea, teasing out how local ideologies and interpretations of a changing world influence language vitality. As Gapuners experienced external contact, Christian influence, and cultural change, the lingua franca Tok Pisin came to represent the valued side of the self known as *save* (knowledge, social awareness), along with a host of other meanings including modernity, progress, and masculinity. The village vernacular, Taiap, which formerly expressed both sides of the self, became associated with *hed* (personal will, autonomy) and more negatively valenced meanings related to tradition, paganism, and femininity. This was contributing to a language shift from Taiap to Tok Pisin through child-rearing practices that heavily privileged Tok Pisin, despite adults blaming their children for refusing to speak Taiap.

Zentella (1997) reported on her detailed longitudinal language socialization study of children's English/Spanish bilingualism and code-switching practices in a New York Puerto Rican (NYPR) immigrant community. She followed a network of five female friends from childhood through early motherhood, carefully documenting interactions between the girls and their families and later with their own children. These exchanges were contextualized within ethnographic study of the community as it changed over time, giving insights into how the girls both lost and maintained aspects of Spanish as they struggled through educational institutions, the labor market, and the urban environment. Spanish was ultimately rendered less necessary than English for child rearing, community membership and NYPR identity, and simply surviving. What remained significant regardless of language choice was acting with *respeto* (respect) and in age- and gender-appropriate ways; the fact that Spanish was not necessary to convey these contributed to language loss by the third generation.

Critical Issues and Topics

A central concern of language socialization research is elucidating how novices become culturally intelligible members, or not, of their social groups. This entails gaining understanding of the social organization and linguistic practices that support this process. There is a focus on how the novice–expert relationship is constructed through everyday interactions and routines, with attention to both social constraints and individual agency. Language socialization is viewed as an *interactional* process (Ochs and Schieffelin 2012: 5) that is collaborative, dynamic, and multidirectional. Novices may act in accordance with normative expectations or vary from them, leading to cultural reproduction as well as transformation over time. Researchers have examined such processes over the lifespan and across such settings as the home in infancy and early childhood, school and peer contexts in childhood and adolescence, and occupational or academic contexts in adulthood (see the broad scope of studies covered in Duranti et al. 2012). Language socialization attends to shifting roles from novice to expert over time, as in one's professional field (e.g., novice African American hair stylists studied by Jacobs-Huey 2007, or jazz students examined by Duranti 2009; see also Mertz 2007; Roberts 2010).

Language socialization researchers have engaged productively with Bourdieu's notion of *habitus*, which encompasses taken-for-granted assumptions about the world and learned dispositions to act in particular ways, including verbal and nonverbal communication, social practices, and ways of carrying oneself related to class, gender, ethnicity, and so on (Bourdieu 1977; Ochs and Scheiffelin 2012). Such acquired ways of thinking and being engender the capacity to act routinely, but also allow for creativity in social life. Novices actively contribute to both reproduction and transformation of cultural and linguistic practices within the structural limitations imposed by their societies or social groups. Further, language socialization can result in unexpected or undesirable outcomes, so researchers must account for cultural reproduction but also "why socializing messages to behave and feel in particular ways may also produce their own inversion" (Kulick and Schieffelin 2004: 356).

A critical issue engaged by initial language socialization research was the extent to which the interactional patterns observed among middle-class Euro-American families with their children, which characterized research on language acquisition at the time, were representative of cultures worldwide. Ochs and Schieffelin (1984) explored variations among US, Samoan, and Kaluli patterns of caregiving and talking with infants and young children. They identified a continuum of approaches ranging from child centered to situation centered, and questioned the universality of child-directed speech or baby talk. For example, Kaluli caregivers do not grammatically simplify language to children, as this simplification is thought to inhibit language acquisition (Schieffelin 1990). Caregivers studied by Ochs (1988) in stratified Samoan society did not employ a baby talk register either, but for different reasons. For Samoans, grammatical simplification and social accommodation is appropriate for high-ranking addressees and not for children. Researchers have continued examining how local theories of child rearing and expectations of children affect social interactions with them, including to what extent adults and other experts modify their language use with novices (Paugh 2012a; Solomon 2012). For example, recent scholarship suggests that use of certain baby talk features that are part of a group's habitus and commonly assumed to be beneficial for young children could be problematic for autistic children's linguistic and social development (Ochs et al. 2005; Solomon 2012).

At a fundamental level, language socialization research gives insights into the construction of identities and social roles and relationships through detailed examination of moment-to-moment social interaction across settings and persons (Ochs 1996; Ochs and Schieffelin 2008). It is grounded in an understanding of the indexicality of language, whereby linguistic forms like grammatical and discourse features index or point to a multitude of contextually specific sociocultural information, including ethnicity, race, class, gender, religion, rank, status, age, child/adult, nationality, and regional origins, as well as culturally recognizable activities, social relationships, and affective stances. Learning to interpret and convey these social meanings is critical to the development of communicative competence, in other words, the knowledge of grammatical rules and how to use language varieties appropriately and pragmatically in social interaction. Across societies, experts apprentice novices into the inference and display of culturally intelligible emotional stances and actions, including when and how to be respectful, polite, deferent, bold, etc. (Ochs and Schieffelin 1989; Schieffelin and Ochs 1986). Researchers attend to both the direct and indirect socialization of affective expression and social comportment through varied linguistic possibilities, such as languages, dialects, registers, and styles.

The study of socializing activities and interactions illuminates how children and other novices come to understand the social order and (re)produce similarities and differences, group membership or lack thereof, and relations of power, inclusion, and exclusion. In other words, using language in social context plays a key role in enacting or bringing into being social identities and relations of subordination, dominance, and hierarchy. Howard (2007, 2009a, 2012), for instance, analyzed the socialization of Muang children in Northern Thailand into hierarchy through acquisition of person reference terms and other communicative practices. Burdelski (2012) demonstrated how Japanese caregivers model and provide verbal and embodied guidance in politeness forms, transmitting to children an understanding of how hierarchy organizes social relationships in Japanese society. Among Vietnamese children, Shohet (2013) illustrated how the concept of *hy sinh* ("sacrifice") is socialized through routine linguistic and corporeal displays of respect, thus reinforcing the "asymmetrical reciprocity" that underlies the sociomoral order.

Shaming as a vehicle for normative moral socialization has been shown to have varying meanings and strategies across cultures (Lo and Fung 2012). Miller and colleagues' long-term fieldwork has compared the construction of self and morality through narrative socialization among middle-class families in Taipei, Taiwan, and Chicago, United States, finding that Taiwanese families tend to tell stories about children's misdeeds while American families are more likely to minimize them (Miller et al. 2012). Lo and Fung (2012) suggested that among urban Taiwanese families, South Koreans, and Korean Americans, a sense of shame is an essential part of individual morality, with caregivers held responsible for cultivating children's moral development through direct negative assessments and embodied shaming practices.

Attention to the socialization of morality via language gives insights into social organization and local understandings of the self and subjectivity.

While language socialization research attends to routine practices, or what is repeated in social life (Moore 2012), it also addresses the novel. Studies of bi/multilingualism from a language socialization perspective offer insights into the complexities of micro- and macro-level processes that affect linguistic and cultural learning and broader societal change, as in contexts of colonialism, postcolonialism, or migration (Baquedano-López and Mangual Figueroa 2012; Garrett 2012; Garrett and Baquedano-López 2002; Kulick 1992; Paugh 2012b; Zentella 1997). Language ideologies, or the ideas that language users hold toward and assessments they make about their language(s) and the language(s) of others, impact linguistic practice with novices as users evaluate language according to cultural values and ideas about contextually appropriate expression (Riley 2012a). Attention to language ideologies and their links to socialization practices are critical, particularly when communicative codes are differentially valued and practiced. Unequal power relations, while ever present in novice–expert interactions, are particularly salient in social groups facing rapid change or socioeconomic and political subordination. What "counts" as a language can vary within and across populations, thus language socialization researchers attend to the complex language ideologies and heterogeneous, fluid language practices that they encounter.

Current Contributions and Research

While there are many current directions in language socialization research, this section highlights several areas that have received recent attention, particularly linguistic and cultural contact situations, peer socialization, and children's agency. Many of these studies share similar concerns about multilingual practices, tensions between social groups and nation-states, and enduring themes in language socialization research like morality, respect and deference, and age- or generation-inflected expectations of child and adult linguistic practice. Recent studies offer insights into the mundane micro-level socializing practices, broader language ideologies, and macro-level sociopolitical contexts that shape the development of two or more languages from birth or in second or heritage language acquisition, as well as language shift (useful reviews include Duff 2012; Friedman 2012; Garrett 2012; Nonaka 2012).

Recent work on multilingual socialization attends to local conceptions of the status of children and how these views mediate linguistic practice, exploring the impact of age-graded language ideologies and codes on the longevity of local languages within their historical and current sociopolitical contexts (Garrett 2007, 2012; Paugh 2012b). Beliefs about respect, age-appropriate demonstration of knowledge, and child autonomy permeate adult expectations about when a child may begin producing a second language, with implications for its actual use. Garrett (2007, 2012), for example, found that in St Lucia, age and childhood expectations have intersected to facilitate a language shift toward English while also aiding in some maintenance of the Afro-French creole, Kwéyòl, through age-appropriate communicative practice. Code-specific genres like cursing may also play a role in language maintenance, as children are permitted in some circumstances to use Kwéyòl forms that index assertive stances (Garrett 2005).

Social interactions involving language-learning children can contribute to language shift in ways that are unexpected or not compatible with official efforts at preservation and revitalization. Paugh (2005b, 2012a, 2012b) explored language shift in Dominica in the Eastern Caribbean through children's home, school, and peer interactions, contextualized within a national language revitalization movement. Rural adults discourage children from speaking Patwa, an Afro-French creole, in favor of English, the official national language, while urban intellectuals promote Patwa's preservation as a symbol of national identity. Through language socialization practices in the course of the shift, however, Patwa has become indexically linked to adult roles and status, creating a powerful resource for dominantly English-speaking children to use in navigating peer interactions and enacting adult roles in imaginative play. Through everyday socializing activities and peer play, emotionally charged aspects of Patwa are being maintained in a separate set of circumstances far removed from formal language revitalization efforts, which encourage formal spelling bees and an annual creole celebration.

Meek's (2007, 2010) research in a northern Athapascan community in the Yukon Territory, Canada, similarly noted the transformative role played by children in a process of language shift from Kaska to English. Through the course of the language shift and related language revitalization efforts, children have come to re-conceptualize Kaska as the language of elders. Because of this, the children interact with elders passively rather than actively in order to display appropriate respect, so they do not take advantage of the opportunity to speak the language during traditional Kaska activities when elders could help them learn. In spite of widespread revalorization of Kaska, then, language revitalization efforts have reinforced the language shift by shoring up age-graded language ideologies linking differential language use to notions of respect, authority, and status asymmetries. At the same time, Meek (2007) found that children use Kaska to direct one another in peer contexts where its use does not challenge expectations of respect toward elders.

Multilingual language socialization studies illuminate what is altered or lost in situations of sociolinguistic contact and change, but also identify what is maintained, such as discourse structures and ways of using a threatened language even with diminished use of the code itself (Bunte 2009; Field 2001; Kulick 1992), or blended varieties and stylistic innovations (Fader 2009). Makihara (2005), for example, found that intergenerational language shift from Rapa Nui to Chilean Spanish on Easter Island was mediated by heritage tourism efforts. From this came a revival of Rapa Nui as an emblem of island identity, but also the emergence of new varieties of Rapa Nui Spanish and syncretic Rapa Nui speech styles among children. Riley's (2007) analysis of language socialization, language shift, and cultural identity in the Marquesas in French Polynesia similarly showed how language socialization practices can lead to syncretic language varieties among youth. In this case, such co-mingling may help to preserve the indigenous code, Enana, even if it is not as "pure" as elite language activists would prefer.

Howard (2009a) explored how children are socialized into expressing respectful speech in and through Standard Thai in the Muang community in Northern Thailand, with implications for the vitality of the local vernacular Kam Muang. In classroom interactions with teachers, children are expected to use Standard Thai politeness particles, which index respect but also appropriate Thai citizenship. At the same time, children at the village school appear to have access to more opportunities for use of their vernacular language than middle-class children sent to school in the city. Further, Howard (2010) demonstrated that perceptions of syncretic linguistic practice among youth are interpreted differently across class distinctions and in relation to local understandings of social relationships. Many younger Muang speakers employ syncretic language practices for language play and supporting culturally valued "fun" interactions with friends.

Through formal education and other institutions, multilingual practices often come to the fore as foci in the socialization of national identities and desired forms of citizenship (Friedman 2010, 2012; Howard 2009a; Minks 2013; Moore 2006; Paugh 2012b), many times at the expense of one code over another. Friedman (2010, 2012) documented the role of formal schooling in language revitalization efforts in Ukraine. With Ukrainian a focus of purism and nation-building efforts, in contrast to language revivalists' views of Russian as having a perceived "polluting" effect by language revivalists, schoolchildren in the language classroom are socialized into dominant language ideologies supporting state language revitalization efforts, such as through error correction routines and explicit socialization of linguistic pride by describing Ukrainian as a "pure and beautiful language" (Friedman 2012: 642). Often such corrections and a strict separation of codes contrast with everyday community language practices, and many children continue to use Russian outside of the classroom, leaving the fate of Ukrainian uncertain (Friedman 2010).

Language socialization research also examines links between multilingual practices and religious identities, with associated tensions between "tradition" and "modernity," and relations with the nation-state. Moore (2006, 2012) examined how guided repetition was used in Cameroon to socialize Fulbe children, who spoke Fulfulde, into use of Arabic in Qur'anic schools and of French in public schools. In addition to linguistic form, children were socialized into the identities indexed by them: a devout religious "traditional" Muslim identity through Arabic, and the "modern" Francophone and Cameroonian identities indexed by French. As Moore (2006: 122) states, in both contexts "second-language socialization entailed two intertwined processes: the formation of linguistic habits and the transformation of heart and mind." Fader (2007, 2009, 2012) considered religious and gender socialization, literacy practices, and language change through gendered use of Hebrew, Yiddish, and English in a Hasidic Jewish community in Brooklyn, New York. Socialization into appropriate gender roles was resulting in girls increasingly speaking Hasidic English over Yiddish as they mediated communication between the orthodox Hasidic community and the secular non-Hasidic world, while boys continued acquiring Yiddish and Hebrew through religious study in protective spaces within the community (Fader 2007).

The language socialization paradigm has been employed productively in situations of migration and diaspora for understanding identity negotiation, exclusionary practices, and the role of children in mediating interactions between the family and outside institutions (Baquedano-López and Mangual Figueroa 2012; Baquedano-López et al. 2010; Mangual Figueroa 2011, 2012; Orellana and Reynolds 2008; Zentella 1997). García-Sánchez (2010, 2012, 2014) employed a language socialization perspective to understand racialization and the politics of childhood in an immigrant community in Spain. Her research detailed how Moroccan immigrant children were being socialized into marginalized identities through exclusionary linguistic and nonverbal practices in peer and other contexts like school and medical encounters. Mangual Figueroa (2011, 2012) probed how mixed-status Mexican families in the New Latino Diaspora made sense of and socialized ideas about citizenship and their migratory status through routines regarding homework and planning for the future in the home.

Heritage language socialization practices in diasporic settings shape children's transnational identity formation, as illustrated in several studies of diverse groups in the United States. Baquedano-López (2000) documented the socialization of Spanish and cultural links to Mexico through *doctrina* (Catholic catechism) classes among Mexican-American children. Kattan (2009) demonstrated how Israeli children temporarily living in the United States were socialized through metalinguistic commentary in home and school settings both to recognize differences between Israeli and American pronunciations of Hebrew and to understand how those phonological differences indexed (in)authenticity. He (2012) outlined a multifaceted view of heritage language development and provided an illustrative case study of one Chinese heritage language learner and his complex and varied trajectory of socialization over time, including how his own socialization transformed others involved in the process. Finally, language and moral personhood intertwined in Sikh education classes in an American diasporic community studied by Klein (2013). Here, religious classes using archaic Punjabi and Sikh youth discussion classes employing modern Punjabi both constructed "a view of heritage language as moral action that represents and socializes transnational and generational continuity and ethno-religious identification" (Klein 2013: 36).

Learners of second languages often face particular social challenges, as they may find restricted access to the target language if they are not accepted, or are even opposed, by the dominant community, or conversely they may not embrace a new language and culture for various reasons, such as when trying to maintain their heritage language and identity (Duff 2012; Duff and Talmy 2011: 97–98). Talmy (2008, 2009) explored ideologies and classroom practices impacting the socialization of high school English-as-a-second-language (ESL) students, and their teachers, in Hawai'i. Through teacher–student interaction concerning respect, students were socialized into classroom control as well as mainstream ideologies stigmatizing ESL identities vis-à-vis "regular" students (Talmy 2009). At the same time, "oldtimer" students socialized new ESL teachers into reproducing ineffective classroom practices through their oppositional behavior and alternative identity construction. Similarly, Cekaite (2013) documented the creation of a "bad subject" (Kulick and Schieffelin 2004) in a Swedish school as a Somali girl learning Swedish as a second language was deemed to exhibit noncompliance with teachers' directives, thus creating over time a "problematic" and "unwilling" student identity through student–teacher as well as peer interactions in the classroom. Studying adult foreign language learners, Cook (2008) examined the socialization of Japanese and related social identities through style shifts using the *masu* honorific form, versus plain verb endings.

As demonstrated by many of the studies described above, language socialization researchers have turned a more focused lens to children's agency and impact on cultural and linguistic practices and ideologies, especially in peer-controlled contexts (Goodwin and Kyratzis 2012). Documentation and analysis of children's social interactions and play offer insights into identity construction, multilingual practices, verbal play and improvisation, and linguistic and cultural transmission, loss, and revitalization (Aronsson 2012; García-Sánchez 2010; Garrett 2007; Howard 2007, 2009b; Kyratzis et al. 2010; Minks 2013; Paugh 2005a, 2012b). Goodwin's (1990, 2006) extensive research on children exploring peer inclusion and exclusion and children's understandings of social class and ethnicity serves as a model for research on peer socialization. Children's language play is viewed as a forum for exploring and often challenging dominant ideologies and social structures, including age-graded hierarchies and family roles (De León 2007; Reynolds 2008, 2010). Paugh (2005a, 2012b) documented how children in Dominica were covertly contributing to Patwa maintenance through their unsupervised peer play, challenging the formal and informal English-only policies of their teachers and caregivers (also see Garrett 2007 on St Lucia). Similarly, Minks (2010, 2013) illustrated how indigenous Miskitu children on Corn Island, Nicaragua, exploited their heteroglossic repertoires and developed intercultural voices by mixing Spanish and Kriol English with the Miskitu language during expressive activities like vocal play and song. Children can also influence their own literacy socialization, as Sterponi (2007) demonstrated among children in two California classrooms who engaged in clandestine reading practices, both acquiring and transforming school-sanctioned literacy forms. Children's communicative practices when not in the presence of adults, the presumed experts, demonstrate their interpretations of local ideologies and may considerably impact sociolinguistic reproduction and change.

Main Research Methods

Language socialization research is ethnographic in orientation. It investigates social interactions in naturalistic home, community, and institutional contexts, such as classrooms and professional spheres. Often caregivers and other experts comment on cultural rules and linguistic ideologies for novices through explicit corrections, directives, accounts, and running commentary on novices' behavior, comportment, practices, and skills. However, ways of interacting, feeling, and behaving are implicitly socialized as well, occurring over time through participation in mundane social interaction and activities. As Ochs and Schieffelin (2012: 12) state:

> Language socialization studies tend to layer levels of analysis, looking at children and other novices' involvement in social life from the top down, looking into the organization of involvement itself for the socializing potentialities of semiotic forms and communicative arrangements, and looking up from micro-movements of bodies, gestures, and verbal acts to longer-term sociocultural and political implications.

In addition to examining caregiver–child interaction, which is often the focus of language acquisition studies, language socialization researchers investigate the impact on linguistic and sociocultural learning of multiple family members (such as sibling caregivers), as well as members of novices' social networks outside the family (such as peers and teachers).

Garrett (2008: 192–194) and Ochs and Schieffelin (2012: 11–12) highlight several key features of language socialization methodology: it uses field-based data collection, employing such tools as audio/video recordings and other ethnographic techniques; it takes a holistic ethnographic perspective; and it attends to both micro- and macro-levels of analysis (see also Duff and Talmy 2011; Garrett and Baquedano-López 2002; Kulick and Schieffelin 2004). Language socialization studies exhibit a longitudinal design with observation and recordings across multiple contexts of daily life; this permits analysis over time of the incremental, co-constructed transmission and modification of language varieties, cultural and linguistic ideologies, and social identities. However, cross-sectional and brief case studies have also employed the language socialization approach (Ochs and Schieffelin 2012: 12).

Any locus of novice–expert interaction is open to language socialization study. For example, communicative events involving food and eating have emerged as fruitful sites of study, both in terms of language socialization generally and as explicit foci of analytic attention. For instance, Ochs and colleagues probed American family dinnertime interactions for, among other issues, how family identities and gendered family roles are enacted and socialized through personal storytelling (e.g., Ochs and Taylor 1995). Blum-Kulka (1997) examined the socialization of sociability through dinner talk among Native Israeli, American Israeli, and Jewish American families. Paugh (2005b, 2012c) analyzed how ideologies, moralities, and ways of talking about paid work were socialized through children's overhearing of and participation in parents' work narratives at the dinner table in the United States. Examination of food-related interactions themselves gives insights into socialization of food preferences, eating practices, and human sociality (Cavanaugh et al. 2014). Ochs, Pontecorvo, and Fasulo (1996) offered a foundational comparative analysis of American and Italian ways of "socializing taste," regarding both foods and culturally specific habitus (also see Ochs and Shohet 2006). Paugh and Izquierdo (2009) explored dinnertime interactions in Los Angeles, studying how middle-class American families managed food-related conflicts and socialized strategies of negotiation over eating practices and individual autonomy. Riley (2012b) considered food socialization of both the children that she studied as well as herself in the Marquesas. Karrebæk (2012, 2013) examined language socialization and the stigmatization of immigrant identities in teacher–student interactions about food choices (especially what non-Danish children carried to school in their lunch boxes) in an ethnically diverse primary classroom in Copenhagen, Denmark. Interactions involving food and eating are just one site of language socialization, but a rich one due to the importance of food and how it is distributed and consumed across cultures.

Documentation of discursive practice is critical, as expectations and ideologies expressed in conversation and interviews do not always match actual language use (Kulick 1992; Schieffelin 1990). Transcription of video/audio recordings is ideally done in consultation with participants or other local experts in order to elicit valuable commentary on verbal and nonverbal practices. Data collected through ethnographic observation and recordings across contexts are deepened and expanded through use of interviews, questionnaires, life histories, and other tools. Through such a longitudinal ethnographic approach, language socialization research develops "a processual account of how individuals come to be particular kinds of culturally intelligible subjects" (Kulick and Schieffelin 2004: 351). Its theoretical and methodological tools provide for socially grounded investigation of the transmission as well as the disruption of linguistic and cultural practices across generations and lifetimes.

Future Directions and Recommendations for Practice

Language socialization research continues to expand as indicated by the range of topics and approaches considered in the *Handbook of Language Socialization* (Duranti et al. 2012). While normative ideologies and practices remain a focus, researchers have begun attending more to the creative and unexpected in language socialization (Kulick and Schieffelin 2004). As Duranti, Ochs, and Schieffelin (2012: 421) question: "there remains a challenge for the language socialization paradigm: how are creativity and conformity integrated into the lives of children and novices as well as into our theory of their development?" (see also Aronsson 2012; Duranti and Black 2012; Kulick and Schieffelin 2004). A prime way to accomplish this is to increase attention to the multiple contexts of children's lives, especially children's cultures and play frames in which they creatively employ and test out the linguistic boundaries and cultural rules of their societies. Children and other novices can redefine dominant ideologies, languages, and forms of interaction, even reconstituting "heritage" or other vernacular codes in the process of learning aspects of them and how to use them.

Children's participation in the research process may be augmented through use of participatory methods, such as giving children the tools to document and explain their own experiences through photography and audio-recording (see Montgomery 2009: 43–48). For example, García-Sánchez (2014) sought to avoid the pitfalls of either romanticizing or abnormalizing Muslim immigrant children's childhoods in Spain in part by attending to children's own perspectives through interviews, pictorial narrations (termed lifemaps), and by observation and recording of their everyday interactions. As she describes: "Listening to children's ongoing reflections on their lives has been the main compass I have used when I felt I was being pulled too far in one of those two directions [as described above]" (García-Sánchez 2014: 10). Situated within the multifaceted contexts and interactions of everyday life, attention to children's voices broadens and deepens our understandings of language socialization processes on the ground.

Recent work suggests a growing focus on teasing out language socialization processes across contexts, modalities, and temporal scales ranging from immediate interactional moments to intermediate time periods (days, months, years) to much broader and longer sociohistorical processes (Howard 2012; Reyes 2013; Wortham 2005). As Howard (2012: 345, emphasis added) states regarding social hierarchy in particular, the language socialization approach can explicate "when socializing practices and discourses occur *sequentially* within an interaction, *developmentally* within the child's or novice's trajectory of changing participation over time, and *historically* over longer durations, generations, and eras." Follow-up research tracing longer time scales and trajectories of language socialization, though possibly challenging for individual researchers to accomplish and thus suggesting the value of team-based projects, would aid in understanding sociolinguistic transformation and processes of intergenerational change over time. This is particularly needed in studies of language shift and revitalization given that language loss is a dynamic process, the outcome of which cannot be well predicted given shifting political and social climates, the unevenness at which it takes place across communities and societies, and the ebbs and flows of bi/multilingualism over the life course of individual language users.

Ultimately, language socialization studies have much to offer in understanding the minute socializing practices and longer trajectories involved in becoming a culturally recognizable subject, even when such a subject is deemed undesirable or incomplete. Following in the anthropological tradition, this approach offers deep insights into processes of inclusion, exclusion, and the reproduction of social inequality, as well as challenges to it through the discursive practices of everyday life. Perhaps in the future language socialization researchers will find increasing ways to make their findings accessible and applicable to those involved in structuring children's and other novices' daily lives.

Acknowledgments

The completion of this chapter was facilitated by a summer grant from the Department of Sociology and Anthropology at James Madison University, Harrisonburg, VA. I am grateful to Nancy Bonvillain and Kate Riley for their useful comments and editorial suggestions.

Related Topics

7 Language Ideologies (Kroskrity); **13** Language, Gender and Identity (Pichler); **14** Discursive Practices, Linguistic Repertoire, and Racial Identities (Baugh); **15** Language and Racialization (Chun, Lo); **23** The Emergence of Creoles and Language Change (Mufwene); **28** Language Maintenance and Revitalization (Cowell); **29** Language Endangerment and Revitalization Strategies (Brittain, MacKenzie); **30** The Politics of Language Endangerment (Meek).

References

Aronsson, Karin. (2012). Language socialization and verbal play. In Alessandro Duranti, Elinor Ochs, and Bambi Schieffelin (eds), *The Handbook of Language Socialization*, pp. 464–483. Malden, MA: Wiley-Blackwell.

Baquedano-López, Patricia. (2000). Narrating community in *doctrina* classes. *Narrative Inquiry* 10(2): 1–24.

Baquedano-López, Patricia and Ariana Mangual Figueroa. (2012). Language socialization and immigration. In Alessandro Duranti, Elinor Ochs, and Bambi Schieffelin (eds), *The Handbook of Language Socialization*, pp. 536–563. Malden, MA: Wiley-Blackwell.

Baquedano-López, Patricia, Jorje Solís, and Gabino Arredondo. (2010). Language socialization among Latinos: Theory, method and approaches. In Enrique Murillo et al. (eds), *Handbook of Latinos and Education*, pp. 329–349. New York: Routledge.

Blum-Kulka, Shoshana. (1997). *Dinner Talk: Cultural Patterns of Sociability and Socialization in Family Discourse*. Mahwah, NJ: Lawrence Erlbaum.

Bourdieu, Pierre. (1977). *Outline of a Theory of Practice*. Richard Nice (trans.). Cambridge: Cambridge University Press.

Bunte, Pamela. (2009). "You keep not listening with your ears!": Language ideologies, language socialization, and Paiute identity. In Paul Kroskrity and Margaret Field (eds), *Native American Language Ideologies*, pp. 172–189. Tucson, AZ: University of Arizona Press.

Burdelski, Matthew. (2012). Language socialization and politeness routines. In Alessandro Duranti, Elinor Ochs, and Bambi Schieffelin (eds.), *The Handbook of Language Socialization*, pp. 275–295. Malden, MA: Wiley-Blackwell.

Cavanaugh, Jillian, Kathleen Riley, Alexandra Jaffe, Christine Jordan, Martha Karrebæk, and Amy Paugh. (2014). What words bring to the table: The linguistic anthropological toolkit as applied to the study of food. *Journal of Linguistic Anthropology* 24(1): 84–97.

Cekaite, Asta. (2013). Socializing emotionally and morally appropriate peer group conduct through classroom discourse. *Linguistics and Education* 24: 511–522.

Cook, Haruko Minegishi. (2008). *Socializing Identities through Speech Style: Learners of Japanese as a Foreign Language*. Tonawanda, New York: Multilingual Matters.

De León, Lourdes. (2007). Parallelism, metalinguistic play, and the interactive emergence of Zinacantec Mayan siblings' culture. *Research on Language and Social Interaction* 40(4): 405–436.

Duff, Patricia. (2012). Second language socialization. In Alessandro Duranti, Elinor Ochs, and Bambi Schieffelin (eds), *The Handbook of Language Socialization*, pp. 564–586. Malden, MA: Wiley-Blackwell.

Duff, Patricia, and Hornberger, Nancy H. (eds) (2008). *Encyclopedia of Language and Education, Vol. 8. Language Socialization* (2nd ed.). New York: Springer.

Duff, Patricia, and Steven Talmy. (2011). Language socialization approaches to second language acquisition: Social, cultural, and linguistic development in additional languages. In Dwight Atkinson (ed.), *Alternative Approaches to Second Language Acquisition*, pp. 95–116. London: Routledge.

Duranti, Alessandro. (2009). The relevance of Husserl's theory to language socialization. *Journal of Linguistic Anthropology* 19(2): 205–226.

Duranti, Alessandro and Steven Black. (2012). Language socialization and verbal improvisation. In Alessandro Duranti, Elinor Ochs, and Bambi Schieffelin (eds), *The Handbook of Language Socialization*, pp. 443–463. Malden, MA: Wiley-Blackwell.

Duranti, Alessandro, Elinor Ochs, and Bambi Schieffelin (eds). (2012). *The Handbook of Language Socialization*. Malden, MA: Wiley-Blackwell.

Fader, Ayala. (2007). Reclaiming sacred sparks: Linguistic syncretism and gendered language shift among Hasidic Jews in New York. *Journal of Linguistic Anthropology* 17(1): 1–22.

——. (2009). *Mitzvah Girls: Bringing up the Next Generation of Hasidic Jews in Brooklyn*. Princeton, NJ: Princeton University Press.

——. (2012). Language socialization and morality. In Alessandro Duranti, Elinor Ochs, and Bambi Schieffelin (eds), *The Handbook of Language Socialization*, pp. 322–340. Malden, MA: Wiley-Blackwell.

Field, Margaret. (2001). Triadic directives in Navajo language socialization. *Language in Society* 30(2): 249–263.

Friedman, Debra. (2010). Speaking correctly: Error correction as a language socialization practice in a Ukrainian classroom. *Applied Linguistics* 31(3): 346-367.

——. (2012). Language socialization and language revitalization. In Alessandro Duranti, Elinor Ochs, and Bambi Schieffelin (eds), *The Handbook of Language Socialization*, pp. 631–647. Malden, MA: Wiley-Blackwell.

García-Sánchez, Inmaculada M. (2010). Serious games: Code-switching and gendered identities in Moroccan immigrant girls' pretend play. *Pragmatics* 20(4): 523–555.

——. (2012). Language socialization and exclusion. In Alessandro Duranti, Elinor Ochs, and Bambi Schieffelin (eds), *The Handbook of Language Socialization*, pp. 391–419. Malden, MA: Wiley-Blackwell.

——. (2014). *Language and Muslim Immigrant Childhoods: The Politics of Belonging*. Malden, MA: Wiley-Blackwell.

Garrett, Paul B. (2005). What a language is good for: Language socialization, language shift, and the persistence of code-specific genres in St. Lucia. *Language in Society* 34(3): 327–361.

——. (2007). Language socialization and the (re)production of bilingual subjectivities. In Monica Heller (ed.), *Bilingualism: A Social Approach*, pp. 233–256. New York: Palgrave Macmillan.

——. (2008). Researching language socialization. In Patricia Duff and Nancy Hornberger (eds), *Encyclopedia of Language and Education. Vol. 10. Language Socialization* (2nd ed.), pp. 189–201. New York: Springer.

——. (2012). Language socialization and language shift. In Alessandro Duranti, Elinor Ochs, and Bambi Schieffelin (eds), *The Handbook of Language Socialization*, pp. 515–535. Malden, MA: Wiley-Blackwell.

Garrett, Paul B. and Ariana Mangual Figueroa. (2002). Language socialization: Reproduction and continuity, transformation and change. *Annual Review of Anthropology* 31: 339-361.

Goodwin, Marjorie Harness. (1990). *He–Said–She–Said: Talk as Social Organization among Black Children*. Bloomington: Indiana University Press.

——. (2006). *The Hidden Life of Girls: Games of Stance, Status, and Exclusion*. Malden, MA: Blackwell.

Goodwin, Marjorie Harness, and Kyratzis, Amy. (2012). Peer language socialization. In Alessandro Duranti, Elinor Ochs, and Bambi Schieffelin (eds), *The Handbook of Language Socialization*, pp. 365–390. Malden, MA: Wiley-Blackwell.

He, Agnes Weiyun (2012). Heritage language socialization. In Alessandro Duranti, Elinor Ochs, and Bambi Schieffelin (eds), *The Handbook of Language Socialization*, pp. 587–609. Malden, MA: Wiley-Blackwell.

Heath, Shirley Brice. (1983). *Ways with Words: Language, Life, and Work in Communities and Classrooms.* New York: Cambridge University Press.
Howard, Kathryn M. (2007). Kinterm usage and hierarchy in Thai children's peer groups. *Journal of Linguistic Anthropology* 17(2): 204–230.
———. (2009a). "When meeting *Khun* teacher, each time we should pay respect": Standardizing respect in a Northern Thai classroom. *Linguistics and Education* 20(3): 254–272.
———. (2009b). Breaking in and spinning out: Repetition and decalibration in Thai children's play genres. *Language in Society* 38(3): 339–363.
———. (2010). Social relationships and language shift in Northern Thailand. *Journal of Sociolinguistics* 14(3): 313–340.
———. (2012). Language socialization and hierarchy. In Alessandro Duranti, Elinor Ochs, and Bambi Schieffelin (eds), *The Handbook of Language Socialization*, pp. 341–364. Malden, MA: Wiley-Blackwell.
Jacobs-Huey, Lanita. (2007). Learning through the breach: Language socialization among African American cosmetologists. *Ethnography* 8(2): 171–203.
Karrebæk, Martha Sif. (2012). "What's in your lunch box today?": Health, respectability, and ethnicity in the primary classroom. *Journal of Linguistic Anthropology* 22(1): 1–22.
———. (2013). Lasagna for breakfast: The respectable child and cultural norms of eating practices in a Danish kindergarten classroom. *Food, Culture and Society* 16(1): 85–106.
Kattan, Shlomy. (2009). "Because she doesn't speak real Hebrew": Accent and the socialization of authenticity among Israeli Shlichim. *Crossroads of Language, Interaction, and Culture* 7: 65–94.
Klein, Wendy. (2013). Speaking Punjabi: Heritage language socialization and language ideologies in a Sikh education program. *Heritage Language Journal* 10(1): 36–50.
Kulick, Don. (1992). *Language Shift and Cultural Reproduction: Socialization, Self, and Syncretism in a Papua New Guinean Village.* Cambridge: Cambridge University Press.
Kulick, Don and Bambi Schieffelin. (2004). Language socialization. In Alessandro Duranti (ed.), *A Companion to Linguistic Anthropology*, pp. 349–368. Malden, MA: Blackwell.
Kyratzis, Amy, Jennifer Reynolds, and Ann-Carita Evaldsson. (2010). Introduction: Heteroglossia and language ideologies in children's peer play interactions. *Pragmatics* 20(4): 457–466.
Lo, Adrienne and Heidi Fung. (2012). Language socialization and shaming. In Alessandro Duranti, Elinor Ochs, and Bambi Schieffelin (eds), *The Handbook of Language Socialization*, pp. 169–189. Malden, MA: Wiley-Blackwell.
Makihara, Miki. (2005). Rapa Nui ways of speaking Spanish: Language shift and socialization on Easter Island. *Language in Society* 34: 727–762.
Mangual Figueroa, Ariana. (2011). Citizenship and education in the homework completion routine. *Anthropology and Education Quarterly* 42(3): 263–280.
———. (2012). "I have papers so I can go anywhere!": Everyday talk about citizenship in a mixed-status Mexican family. *Journal of Language, Identity, and Education* 11: 291–311.
Meek, Barbra A. (2007). Respecting the language of elders: Ideological shift and linguistic discontinuity in a northern Athapascan community. *Journal of Linguistic Anthropology* 17(1): 23–43.
———. (2010). *We are Our Language: An Ethnography of Language Revitalization in a Northern Athabascan Community.* Arizona: University of Arizona Press.
Mertz, Elizabeth. (2007). *The Language of Law School: Learning to "Think Like a Lawyer."* New York: Oxford University Press.
Miller, Peggy J., Heidi Fung, Shumin Lin, Eva Chian-Hui Chen, and Benjamin R. Boldt. (2012). *How Socialization Happens on the Ground: Narrative Practices as Alternate Socializing Pathways in Taiwanese and European-American Families.* Boston, MA: Wiley-Blackwell.
Minks, Amanda. (2010). Socializing heteroglossia among Miskitu children on the Caribbean Coast of Nicaragua. *Pragmatics* 20(4): 495–522.
———. (2013). *Voices of Play: Miskitu Children's Speech and Song on the Atlantic Coast of Nicaragua.* Tucson: University of Arizona Press.
Montgomery, Heather. 2009. *An Introduction to Childhood: Anthropological Perspectives on Children's Lives.* Malden, MA: Wiley-Blackwell.
Moore, Leslie. (2006). Learning by heart in Qur'anic and public schools in Northern Cameroon. *Social Analysis* 50(3): 109–126.
———. (2012). Language socialization and repetition. In Alessandro Duranti, Elinor Ochs, and Bambi Schieffelin (eds), *The Handbook of Language Socialization*, pp. 209–226. Malden, MA: Wiley-Blackwell.

Nonaka, Angela M. (2012). Language socialization and language endangerment. In Alessandro Duranti, Elinor Ochs, and Bambi Schieffelin (eds), *The Handbook of Language Socialization*, pp. 610–630. Malden, MA: Wiley-Blackwell.

Ochs, Elinor. (1988). *Culture and Language Development: Language Acquisition and Language Socialization in a Samoan Village*. Cambridge: Cambridge University Press.

——. (1996). Linguistic resources for socializing humanity. In John Gumperz and Stephen Levinson (eds), *Rethinking Linguistic Relativity*, pp. 407–437. New York: Cambridge University Press.

Ochs, Elinor and Bambi Schieffelin. (1984). Language acquisition and socialization: Three developmental stories and their implications. In Richard Shweder and Robert LeVine (eds), *Culture Theory: Essays on Mind, Self, and Emotion*, pp. 276–320. Cambridge: Cambridge University Press.

——. (1989). Language has a heart. *Text* 9(1): 7–25.

——. (1995). The impact of language socialization on grammatical development. In Paul Fletcher and Brian MacWhinney (eds), *The Handbook of Child Language*, pp. 73–94. Cambridge: Blackwell Publishers.

——. (2008). Language socialization: An historical overview. In Patricia Duff and Nancy Hornberger (eds), *Encyclopedia of Language and Education. Vol. 8. Language Socialization* (2nd ed.), pp. 3–15. New York: Springer.

——. (2012). The theory of language socialization. In Alessandro Duranti, Elinor Ochs, and Bambi Schieffelin (eds), *The Handbook of Language Socialization*, pp. 1–21. Malden, MA: Wiley-Blackwell.

Ochs, Elinor, and Merav Shohet. (2006). The cultural structuring of mealtime socialization. *New Directions for Child and Adolescent Development* 111: 35–49.

Ochs, Elinor, and Carolyn Taylor. (1995). The father knows best dynamic in dinnertime narratives. In Kira Hall and Mary Bucholtz (eds), *Gender Articulated*, pp. 97–120. New York: Routledge.

Ochs, Elinor, Clotilde Pontecorvo, and Alessandra Fasulo. (1996). Socializing taste. *Ethnos* 61(1–2): 7–46.

Ochs, Elinor, Olga Solomon, and Laura Sterponi. (2005). Limitations and transformations of habitus in child-directed communication. *Discourse Studies* 7(4–5): 547–583.

Orellana, Marjorie Faulstich and Jennifer Reynolds (2008). Cultural modeling: Leveraging bilingual skills for school paraphrasing tasks. *Reading Research Quarterly* 43(1): 48–65.

Paugh, Amy L. (2005a). Multilingual play: Children's code-switching, role play, and agency in Dominica, West Indies. *Language in Society* 34(1): 63–86.

——. (2005b). Learning about work at dinnertime: Language socialization in dual-earner American families. *Discourse and Society* 16(1): 55–78.

——. (2012a). Local theories of child rearing. In Alessandro Duranti, Elinor Ochs, and Bambi Schieffelin (eds), *The Handbook of Language Socialization*, pp. 150–168. Malden, MA: Wiley-Blackwell.

——. (2012b). *Playing with languages: Children and change in a Caribbean village*. New York: Berghahn Books.

——. (2012c). Speculating about work: Dinnertime narratives among dual-earner American families. *Text and Talk* 32(5): 615–636.

Paugh, Amy and Carolina Izquierdo. (2009). Why is this a battle every night?: Negotiating food and eating in American dinnertime interaction. *Journal of Linguistic Anthropology* 19(2): 185–204.

Reyes, Angela. (2013). Corporations are people: Emblematic scales of brand personification among Asian American Youth. *Language in Society* 42(2): 163–185.

Reynolds, Jennifer F. (2008). Socializing puros pericos (little parrots): The negotiation of respect and responsibility in Antonero Mayan sibling and peer networks. *Journal of Linguistic Anthropology* 18(1): 82-107.

——. (2010). Enregistering the voices of discursive figures of authority in Antonero children's sociodramatic play. *Pragmatics* 20(4): 467–493.

Riley, Kathleen. (2007). To tangle or not to tangle: Shifting language ideologies and the socialization of Charabia in the Marquesas, French Polynesia. In Miki Makihara and Bambi Schieffelin (eds.), *Consequences of Contact*, pp. 70–95. New York: Oxford University Press.

——. (2008). Language socialization. In Bernard Spolsky and Francis Hult (eds), *The Handbook of Educational Linguistics*, pp. 398–410. Malden, MA: Blackwell.

——. (2012a). Language socialization and language ideologies. In Alessandro Duranti, Elinor Ochs, and Bambi Schieffelin (eds), *The Handbook of Language Socialization*, pp. 493–514. Malden, MA: Wiley-Blackwell.

——. (2012b). Learning to exchange words for food in the Marquesas. In Leo Coleman (ed.), *Food: Ethnographic Encounters*, pp. 111–126. Oxford: Berg.

——. (2014). Language socialization. In Christiane Fäcke (ed.), *Manual of Language Acquisition*, pp. 69–86. Berlin: Walter De Gruyter.

Roberts, Celia. (2010). Language socialization in the workplace. *Annual Review of Applied Linguistics 30*: 211–227.
Schieffelin, Bambi (1990). *The Give and Take of Everyday Life: Language Socialization of Kaluli Children*. Cambridge: Cambridge University Press.
———. (1994). Code-switching and language socialization: Some probable relationships. In J. F. Duncan, L. Hewitt, and R. M. Sonnenmeier (eds), *Pragmatics: From Theory to Practice*, pp. 20–42. Englewood Cliffs, NJ: Prentice Hall.
Schieffelin, Bambi and Elinor Ochs (eds). (1986). *Language Socialization across Cultures*. New York: Cambridge University Press.
Shohet, Merav. (2013). Everyday sacrifice and language socialization in Vietnam: The power of a respect particle. *American Anthropologist 115*(2): 203–217.
Solomon, Olga. (2012). Rethinking baby talk. In Alessandro Duranti, Elinor Ochs, and Bambi Schieffelin (eds), *The Handbook of Language Socialization*, pp. 121–149. Malden, MA: Wiley-Blackwell.
Sterponi, Laura. (2007). Clandestine interactional reading: Intertextuality and double-voicing under the desk. *Linguistics and Education 18*: 1–23.
Talmy, Steven. (2008). The cultural productions of the ESL student at Tradewinds High: Contingency, multidirectionality, and identity in L2 socialization. *Applied Linguistics 29*(4): 619–644.
———. (2009). A very important lesson: Respect and the socialization of order(s) in high school ESL. *Linguistics and Education 20*: 235–253.
Wortham, Stanton. (2005). Socialization beyond the speech event. *Journal of Linguistic Anthropology 15*(1): 95–112.
Zentella, Ana Celia (1997). *Growing up Bilingual: Puerto Rican Children in New York City*. Oxford: Blackwell Publishers.

Further Reading

Duranti, Alessandro, Elinor Ochs, and Bambi Schieffelin (eds). (2012). *The Handbook of Language Socialization*. Malden, MA: Wiley-Blackwell.
This state-of-the-art volume brings together a collection of 27 chapters by prominent scholars in language socialization research. Each chapter reviews a topic or approach and original research by the author(s). The chapters explore current language socialization research and theory with case studies from home, community, and institutional contexts, across multiple cultures, and across the lifespan. It is an indispensable collection for language socialization researchers.

10
Studying Language Acquisition in Different Linguistic and Cultural Settings

Sabine Stoll

1 Introduction

It is undisputed that every child learns the language(s) of her social environment in the first years of life. However, what are the cognitive processes that enable children to learn language and which environmental processes are involved has been a matter of continuous dispute. This century-old debate of nature vs. nurture has also moved center-stage in the field of language acquisition research, resulting in two major strands of theories: nativist vs. empiricist/constructivist.

Nativist theories assume an innate linguistic module with an innate core grammar, which makes language acquisition possible. Assumptions about the nature of this linguistic module vary from a complex system of parameters (Chomsky 1981) to a single mechanism of recursion in the latest versions of generative theories of grammar (Hauser et al. 2002; for a summary see Ambridge & Lieven 2011). Even though the parameter-setting approach was abandoned in newer versions of generative theory, it is still assumed by some acquisition researchers (e.g. Hyams 2012).

The other major type, constructivist theories, also known as usage-based theories, assume a set of innate abilities, which in their combination enable humans to learn language, but these cognitive abilities are not assumed to be specific to language nor necessarily even specific to humans (Tomasello 2003). This approach emphasizes that these cognitive abilities are also found in other species, but the specific combination of them is responsible for the human-specific ability to understand, produce, and learn language in all its different varieties.

Currently there are around 7000 languages spoken and several hundred thousand have existed before they became extinct or developed into other languages. The ability of children to acquire any of these systems and contexts emphasizes the great flexibility of the human mind. This flexibility is the focus of this chapter.

Independent of the linguistic theory assumed, it is undisputed that language acquisition requires input. The amount of input necessary, however, is again a matter of theoretical dispute. Nativist accounts assume that minimal input is sufficient, whereas constructivist theories assume the necessity of an extensive and elaborate input to build up the vocabulary and the grammar of the language over several years. Both, languages in their grammatical build-up and the social environments in which they are learned, however, vary to an extreme degree and so far we know relatively little about the impact of different cultural backgrounds and different linguistic systems on the acquisition process.

Thus, one of the challenges of language acquisition research is to find out exactly what are the common variables across cultures and languages that allow children to learn the linguistic system of their respective culture and socio-communicative environment. To find these variables has become the greatest challenge in acquisition research because according to recent work there are hardly any substantial linguistic universals (Bickel 2007, Evans & Levinson 2009) on which children can rely in learning language. If there are commonalities, they occur on the most abstract level, which would still not account for the abilities required to link these abstract concepts to the individual language-specific features expressing these concepts.

Further, so far, there is very little research comparing the socio-communicative environments in which children acquire their native languages. However, at least, there seems to be one crucial and universal feature of language acquisition common to all cultural contexts in which children grow up: the involvement of children in communicative interactions (e.g. Snow 1984). From a number of experimental studies we know that listening to communication alone without taking part in communicative interactions (or observing language in the case of sign language) is not enough to learn a language (e.g., Sachs & Johnson 1976, Kuhl et al. 2003). Thus, communicative interaction seems to be the driving force behind language learning and can even lead to the development of new linguistic systems. This has been shown in the development of Nicaraguan sign where, over several generations, children and older signers turned a rudimentary, inconsistent system of home signs into a fully fledged language (Senghas & Coppola 2001). Thus, there seems to be a human drive toward the development of systematic communication systems and transmitting such a system in personal interaction. The central research question is how children extract the necessary linguistic information from these interactions.

Acquisition research, therefore, aims to discover the cognitive, innate mechanisms in interrelation with factors in the environment such as the linguistic system and the input that enables children to learn language. In other words, we still try to solve the old puzzle of the interaction of nature and nurture. Redirecting our focus on nurture, however, might help in better understanding the role of nature. Given the fact that interaction and input are foundational for acquisition, it seems unavoidable to take a more empirical bottom-up approach in comparing the acquisition of as many different languages as possible. This is a very demanding task if we take into account the large design space of languages without substantial linguistic universals (Bickel 2007, Evans & Levinson 2009). The first step in such an approach, then, is to analyze development in tracing naturalistic interactions in as many diverse languages as possible. The second step is to compare the different developments in the various languages. This chapter tries to trace these research tasks from a cross-linguistic perspective. The main focus is on the role of the ambient language, concentrating on features such as the amount and kind of input children receive. Two main topics of this chapter are:

- How can we systematically study the impact of grammar on the acquisition process?
- How can we study the role of the socio-communicative context for learning a language?

The chapter is organized as follows. To give an overview of how acquisition is studied, it starts out with a short presentation of the major methods commonly used in language acquisition studies. The focus is on sampling issues that are intertwined with these methods. Second, some potentially universal milestones of early language learning are presented before paying attention to environmental features relevant for learning language. Third, the chapter illustrates how cross-linguistic research contributes to our understanding of the mechanisms of language acquisition and why the input plays a central role for understanding acquisition.

2 Main Research Methods and Sampling Issues

To study language acquisition both within and across languages there are several established methods to gather and analyze data. I discuss the major methods used in acquisition research and concurrent sampling issues: (1) naturalistic, observational data and (2) experiments. There is a third method, namely questionnaires, which are used to study specific questions such as early vocabulary. The most commonly used questionnaire is the MacArthur-Bates Communicative Development Inventories (Fenson et al. 1993), which has been adapted to a number of different languages. The focus in this chapter, however, is on naturalistic vs. experimental methods, whereby the following sampling issues take center-stage: choice of languages, choice and number of participants, and recording scheme.

2.1 Naturalistic/Observational Data

Naturalistic studies are conducted to learn about the child's behavior in her natural environment. In contrast to experiments, naturalistic studies are correlational in nature and can merely contribute to hypothesizing about cause and effect. The main advantage of observational studies is that they provide insights into what children do spontaneously in their natural environment.

There are two main types of observational studies. In cross-sectional studies a large enough number of children of a specific age range is recorded, usually at one or a few points in time, to conduct a statistical test. In longitudinal studies, usually a small number of children is recorded over a longer time period at regular intervals. Both in cross-sectional and in longitudinal studies, recordings constitute a snapshot of a specific context, which can potentially bias our results.

Longitudinal studies are the main method for gathering comprehensive data about the developmental path of individual children and we will focus on this type of data collection in the following, since longitudinal studies are usually the starting point in cross-linguistic comparisons and the first type of data we collect in a hitherto unstudied language. Longitudinal studies are either diaries or audio-visual recordings.

2.1.1 Diaries

The earliest acquisition studies conducted around the end of the nineteenth century were diary studies of a small number of European languages such as French, Russian, English, and German (for a good summary, see Ingram 1989). These focused on the individual linguistic development of a child observed by a parent interested in language acquisition. The diary studies varied greatly in detail and focus and also in the age range of documentation.

Diary studies are especially useful in the early phases of acquisition when children speak very little, at unpredictable times and intervals during the day. The study needs to be conducted by the main caregiver who spends the day with the child. In diary studies of very early development nearly all utterances of the child can be recorded. This, however, becomes unfeasible as soon as the child starts to talk more. During this time, then, only newly emergent structures can be noted down. As a result diary studies usually cannot be used to answer questions about frequency distributions or quantitative questions in general. However, the exact qualitative development can be traced in noting down all occurrences of specific individual words or constructions. This allows us to find errors, which are sometimes very rare and difficult to detect otherwise. Further, we gain a comprehensive picture of nearly every new construction or the precise development of a specific grammatical category.

The greatest problem with this method is the interpretation of how the child's constructions relate to her environment. In diary studies there is generally a lack of information about the surrounding language, i.e., we usually do not know whether the utterance was a repetition of a preceding utterance by a conversation partner or indeed a spontaneous, unprompted occurrence. Further, we rely on the exact memory of the researcher who notes down the exact wording of the utterances. This can be challenging at times when the researcher is simultaneously the caregiver who has to look after the child. Modern recording devices, such as small dictaphones into which one can quickly repeat the exact utterance, can nowadays be of enormous help in the difficult logistics of such studies.

Diary studies have long been very useful in documenting the development of individual children, often resulting in hypotheses for developmental processes in general. Thus, even today such studies can have an immense impact, as shown by Tomasello's diary study of his daughter's language development (Tomasello 1992). This data led Tomasello to the insight that children start out with rigid, item-specific constructions, which only later in development become more flexible and are generalized to other constructions. These findings have strongly influenced subsequent experimental research and in fact have led to a paradigm change in acquisition research. Nowadays item-based learning is discussed on a par with rule-based learning, which was predominantly taken for granted before this study.

For comparative research diary studies are useful to acquire an overview of the first constructions learned. Further, they are very useful in learning about qualitative changes in the development of categories and constructions to compare them across languages. Thus, diary studies provide an excellent first step, especially in describing very early development. Further, they are useful for developing hypotheses about general learning processes, which then can be followed up in more detail and in a quantitative manner in longitudinal corpora or experiments.

2.1.2 Audio-Visual Corpora

In modern acquisition research, especially if we are interested in hitherto underresearched languages, we usually start out with longitudinal studies consisting of video/audio recordings of children in their natural contexts. Longitudinal studies usually follow the development of a handful of children at regular intervals over a specific time period. Ideally, the social and communicative environment of the child is covered in the recordings. This allows us to study the role of extralinguistic factors in language acquisition, such as the role of input and speech surrounding the child in general. Nowadays recordings are nearly exclusively made with video, but there are also some earlier studies that are audio only. Longitudinal studies are extremely time and labor intensive and consequently very costly. The recordings alone usually stretch from about a year to several years. Then, as a first step all the utterances by all the participants need to be transcribed, translated if necessary, and then annotated, e.g., morphological glossing, parts-of-speech glossing and/or other features of interest. These annotations involve both native speakers and linguists specialized in the language. In contrast to experiments, however, such studies can be used to investigate a wide range of research questions on various issues of grammar, vocabulary, socio-communicative behavior, pragmatics etc. There are several factors that play a crucial role in interpreting longitudinal studies. Sampling issues are relevant both for analyzing the acquisition process of an individual language and for cross-linguistic comparisons with other longitudinal studies. There are three main types of variation, which have an important impact on the interpretation of longitudinal data in addition to the selection of target children:

- Individual variation: number of children recorded, age span of recordings etc;
- Contextual variation: number and kind of people present, types of situations recorded etc;
- Distributional variation: intervals and length of recording;
- Selection of target children.

Individual Variation

Longitudinal studies are always case studies of individual children. It is well known that there is large individual variation in development (e.g., Fenson et al. 1994, Bates et al. 1995) and without knowing the norm it is difficult to interpret what the behavior of an individual child tells us about the population. Just to give an illustration of the extreme variation shown in a large-scale cross-sectional study of English acquisition including 659 babies (8–16 months) and 1130 toddlers (16–30 months): "children reported scoring at the 10th percentile are reported to comprehend fewer phrases at 16 months than children scoring at the 90th percentile do at 8 months" (Fenson et al. 1994: 33). In this study similar variation was encountered for all linguistic variables tested. Thus, without knowing about the norm it is difficult to interpret the development of a small number of children, i.e., we do not know how their development compares to the population. These individual differences also make it problematic to pool the children of the same age and generalize the developmental path or time scale if we only have a small number of participants. Consequently it is difficult to generalize from the sample to the whole population for which the norm is unknown.

There are, however, ways to circumvent these difficulties. One possibility is to conduct incremental comparisons (Stoll & Gries 2009). In such an incremental approach, individual differences are placed center-stage. The idea here is to first analyze each child individually over the respective longitudinal period. Second, the child is compared to his/her surrounding adults. Then, in a third step, the individual child-adult dyads/polyads are compared. This allows us to determine whether there are similarities in the case studies both within and also across languages. This method also allows us to take into account the different age spans investigated in different studies. We know that age is a poor predictor of development and the incremental approach takes care of this variable by individually comparing the path of development independent of the exact age. Incremental comparisons thus allow a step-by-step comparison and subsequent potential generalizations of developmental paths.

Contextual Variation in Recordings

A further challenge with case studies is that recordings usually constitute only small snapshots of the activities in the daily life of a child. These specific contexts are not necessarily representative of the typical activities a child is engaged in during her day. This is highly relevant because we know that both conversational partners and activities taking place during recording have an impact on the speech of the child and the caregivers. They influence the type of constructions children and adults produce and they have a strong impact on how explicit the interaction partners are.

In an early study of communicative skills of 4-year-olds, Shatz and Gelman (1973) have found that the children in their study adjusted their speech to their interlocutors. If they talked to adults their constructions were longer and more complex than if they talked to their 2-year old siblings. This shows that talk to peers or also younger siblings varies significantly from talk to adults, not only in what is said but also in how it is said. It seems that this sensitivity starts very early on in development, even at a younger age than found in the Shatz & Gelman study. Ochs (1988) found that 2-year-old Samoan children switch register as indicated by different pronunciations depending on their interactional partners. This shows a very early meta-awareness of socio-communicative contexts. A recent experimental study by Hoff (2010) confirmed that both the context and the interactional partners had an influence on children's speech, even though the individual differences remained constant across contexts. Compared to free play and mealtime, during book reading the language of the children (age range 1.5–3.0) was more complex with respect to vocabulary and overall more coherent. Further, there were significant effects on the speech of the children depending on their conversational partner. If children spoke to their mother their speech was much richer in vocabulary and they were more likely to reply to questions than if interacting with a sibling (Hoff 2010: 468). These observations show that the recorded contexts indirectly influence our results.

In many of the available longitudinal corpora, however, children interact exclusively with their mother or their primary caregivers. The caregiver plays with the child or engages him/her in conversation or play for the duration of the recording. Often no other adults or children are present. This makes the transcription and the preparation of the data easier but such a setting has the great disadvantage that the recordings are not necessarily representative of a child's "normal" activities and conversation partners during her day. Further, all other contexts and conversational partners of the child and the parent, which are part of the natural context of growing up, are excluded. Thus, with such recordings we can only study child-directed speech in a very specific context, namely the child interacting with the caregiver. The role of other interactions or the influence of child-surrounding speech cannot be studied. Features of the context thus need to be counted as variables in comparing different corpora within and across languages.

Distributional Variation

We know that the frequency of occurrence of linguistic items and constructions correlates with acquisition. Tomasello & Stahl (2004) have illustrated impressively that the recording scheme and the amount of recording has an enormous impact on our results. Since linguistic features differ strongly in their frequency of occurrence in conversation, our sample size, in addition to the recorded variation of contexts, influences our chances of recording a phenomenon. Consequently, our results about the interrelation of acquisition and occurrences in the input largely depend on the reliability of our sampling regarding both content and size. If we are interested in a phenomenon that occurs only rarely, the probability of catching it when first produced correlates positively with the amount of recording per session in addition to the recording scheme.

Recording schemes vary from weekly to biweekly or monthly recordings. Usually, children are recorded for an hour per week or every fortnight at least. This recording scheme has severe sampling problems, as illustrated in detail by Tomasello & Stahl (2004). Rare phenomena are difficult to catch in such small corpora. As a result they are often caught only several months after their real first occurrence, which happens not to be during recording time. Rowland & Fletcher (2006) have confirmed the role of sampling size in the detection of errors and item-specificity in constructions. Following Tomasello & Stahl (2004), it turns out that the traditional recording scheme of 1 hour per week is much less suitable for characterizing overall development than, say, recording once for 5 hours per month. These five hours can be distributed over several recording sessions within a single week but the chance of catching rare phenomena rises significantly. The change in sampling strategy has the additional positive effect that we might gather different situations in the daily life of the child. This recording scheme is also much easier to apply in fieldwork situations and will give a broader picture of the daily life of a child than weekly snapshots of 30 minutes to 1 hour, which tend to be repetitive in contexts if there is always a fixed schedule when the child is recorded.

Ideally of course, the amount of hours in weekly recordings is increased. This has been done in a few so-called high-density studies with up to 10 hours of recording per week (see Lieven & Behrens 2012). They even provide a better picture and less time lag in the detection of items learned by the child. Further, there is also one extreme study called the Human Speechome Project (Roy et al. 2009), in which all the language of one target child from birth to three years and the language he hears at home is recorded, resulting in several hundred thousand hours of home recording. This is an exceptional study with challenging data preparation, which is still ongoing. So far, it is not feasible to conduct such ultra-high-density studies in other languages or with a larger sample of children, which would of course constitute a great step forward in acquisition research. Our main challenge to date in working with naturalistic data is to take care of sampling variables and contexts of sampling to make sure the speech we collect is as representative as possible of the child and the environment of the child.

Selection of Target Children

We know from a number of studies that in addition to individual variation the socio-economic status (SES) of the families has an effect both on child-rearing behavior, which affects the development of the child (Hart & Risley 1995, Huttenlocher et al. 2002, Hoff 2003). Effects of SES on cultural attitudes and child-rearing behavior seem to occur across cultures. This, at least, is the case in societies with significant differences in income and education. The effects of SES might be less pronounced in societies with less educational stratification, such as rural societies living on subsistence farming. Nevertheless, this potentially biasing factor needs to be counted in when choosing children for a study.

2.1.3 Available Data: Cross-linguistic Sample of Longitudinal Corpora

A very important initiative by MacWhinney & Snow (1985) resulted in the collection of a large database of acquisition corpora that are openly available to the community (http://childes.psy.cmu.edu). This has been a great step forward for comparative language acquisition research and actually for the first time has made possible comparative studies on a wider range of languages. Still, the sample of languages for which we have corpora is relatively small, constituting not even 1 percent of the languages of the world (Lieven & Stoll 2010, Stoll 2009). For 39 languages corpora are openly available and for approximately a dozen other languages there exist corpora that are not open to the public. The goal of language acquisition research, however, is to make general statements about how children learn language. Thus, we need to be sure that our claims hold for all languages, and not only for a potentially biased subset.

In the currently available corpora there is indeed a strong family bias, of which we need to be aware in order to interpret and generalize our findings adequately. The family bias concerns the type of languages for which we have corpora. There are around 400 language families and a large number of isolates, all of which are learned by children growing up in their respective environments. Acquisition mechanisms or processes need to apply to any of these languages. Given the fact that only a tiny fraction of some features of the world's languages have been studied with regard to their acquisition and 54 percent of the 39 open access corpora on Child Language Data Exchange System (CHILDES) are from the Indo-European language family, mainly spoken in Western Europe, generalizations are tentative so far. These languages are very similar in many respects and this leads to an overrepresentation of structures typical of Europe but rare elsewhere (e.g., relative clauses introduced by relative pronouns, cf. Haspelmath 2001).

2.1.4 A New Approach to Cross-linguistic Sampling

Given these current data limitations, we are not yet in a position to make statements about language acquisition in general but, rather, primarily about some acquisition processes in a few languages, mainly of the same family. No acquisition theory has so far been tested, therefore, against a representative sample of languages. This, however, is definitely the main goal we need to aim for in future research. Since it is very unlikely that in the near future we will ever be in a position to have an adequately stratified sample of acquisition corpora, including all language families and important features, more creative sampling procedures are required. Only then will we be able to find out whether fundamental differences in grammar have repercussions on the nature of language acquisition processes. There are two constraints on sampling languages for comparative acquisition research:

- Maximize the diversity of linguistic structures in our sample. The reason is that we are interested in finding out what constitutes the flexibility of the human mind and whether there are some universal cognitive mechanisms that apply independent of the grammatical build-up of individual languages.
- Minimize the number of languages for which we have to sample new corpora. The reason behind this constraint is a practical one, because gathering a longitudinal corpus is a highly time- and cost-intensive endeavor, especially if fieldwork of hitherto undescribed languages is involved.

To escape this methodological impasse we recently proposed a new typological approach with a new sampling method (Stoll & Bickel 2012). The method is called Maximum Diversity Sampling with the purpose of maximizing the diversity of grammatical structures in our sample. For this we apply a fuzzy clustering algorithm (Kaufman & Rousseeuw 1990) to large typological databases (from the AUTOTYP system, http://www.autotyp.uzh.ch, and from the World Atlas of Language Structures, http://wals.info, following standard procedures in typology). This clustering algorithm focuses on ten variables that are important for acquisition, such as the presence and absence of agreement, case marking, word order, degrees of synthesis, polyexponence, inflectional compactness of categories, syncretism, and existence of inflectional classes. The clustering was set to find five maximally diverse language groups, which seems to be a reasonable number of language groups to deal with and, if necessary, to collect corpora (Stoll & Bickel 2012). This corpus of maximally diverse languages then allows us to test potentially universal acquisition mechanisms and draw more general conclusions than has been possible so far. Currently a large-scale cross-linguistic comparative project has started working with 10 languages from these five maximally diverse groups of languages (two languages per cluster so far). The project aims to find general features of the input and learning mechanisms that allow the child to learn languages by extracting information from the input (see www.acqdiv.uzh.ch/index.html).

2.2 Experiments

Experiments are the other main method used in acquisition studies and for a number of questions they are the only option. For instance, for comprehension studies testing prelinguistic children, or studies about cognitive or socio-communicative abilities in very early development, experiments are unavoidable.

Experiments allow us to test clear hypotheses, clearly control for potentially relevant variables, and ultimately make claims about cause and effect. Further, we have large enough groups to gloss over individual differences and test for age differences, which is important in developmental studies. Controlling variables is an important and already difficult issue, but in cross-linguistic research, to hold this control constant across different cultural groups can be a challenge. For instance, in an experiment in which the stimuli are short video clips with people acting on some objects, we need to make sure that there is no difference in the familiarity with these objects, clothes people wear in the film, or even the fact of being familiar with films in general. Stimuli that are adequate for one cultural group are not necessarily equally adequate for other groups; this needs to be considered as well. Further, instructions need to be held constant across languages but this can be difficult with languages having or lacking specific grammatical features. If we study a language with classifiers vs. another language without classifiers, for example, the instructions themselves can influence the results. All these variables can have an impact on the answers of the child and hence on the results we obtain. Further, experiments about linguistic development are usually impossible to conduct in languages for which we have not yet studied the acquisition process at all. Experiments are, therefore, usually a second step after we have gained some overall knowledge about the acquisition process.

3 Critical Issues and Topics: Factors Influencing the Acquisition Process

We have seen that there are substantial individual differences in linguistic abilities across children of the same age groups within the same culture. These individual differences concern not only the size of the vocabulary but also when, how, and maybe even whether a grammatical construction is learned at all. It is well known that there are substantial differences in the vocabulary of children and even adult native speakers. Up to very recently, grammar was assumed to be uniform in all native speakers. Recent research, however, has challenged this claim by showing that we also find a large amount of heterogeneity in grammatical competence among adult native speakers (Dąbrowska & Street 2006). There are two potential reasons that have taken center-stage in the literature to account for such individual differences, both in language learning and in resulting adult language competence: innate differences in cognitive capabilities on the one hand and differences in the environmental variables of learning opportunities on the other. Innate abilities relevant to vocabulary and grammar learning could, for instance, consist of attention span, memory abilities including both short-term and long-term memory, pattern detection abilities, differences in processing speed etc., which are relevant for abstracting and generalizing lexical patterns into grammar. Other reasons might be differences in environmental factors such as the structure of the language to be learned and the amount and kind of input children receive. We start with some universal, probably innate milestones and then move on to environmental factors influencing acquisition.

3.1 Milestones: Early Predispositions for Language

We know from acquisition studies of a number of typologically different languages that there are some very basic cognitive, linguistic, and socio-communicative milestones that seem to be reached around the same time window in development, no matter which language a child is exposed to. These milestones mainly consist of prelinguistic abilities, on the one hand, and some very general observations about the time course of acquisition, such as the time span within which children learn the basic grammar of their language, on the other.

Good candidates for innate predispositions to acquire language are: categorical speech perception, pattern recognition, statistical learning, intention reading, joint attention, and imitation. Infants are born with the ability to perceive human speech sounds categorically (Eimas et al. 1971), but this ability is not specific to humans. However, the perceptual learning in the first year of life as a result of language input is presumably unique to humans (Fernald & Marchman 2006: 1038). This specific and constant input of their mother tongue/s presumably also leads to the loss of the earlier ability to discriminate all possible phonemes at around 10 months of age (Werker & Tees 1984). We also know that this massive input already has an impact on the phonetic perception of 6-month-old infants (Kuhl et al. 1992). Another extremely important capability has been discovered by Saffran et al. (1996), namely the ability, at 8 months, to learn statistically, i.e. to learn to segment syllables into words merely on the basis of transition probabilities. This is clearly a prerequisite for finding recurring patterns in the input, which is the basis of all word and grammar learning. Further, to ultimately learn language, patterns need to be remembered as well. There are some general developments of long-term memory in the first year of life. Rovee-Collier (1999) found that short-term memories of 2- and 18-month-old children tested in a nonlinguistic task were similar, but long-term retention develops significantly in the first year. Interestingly retention can be improved by adapting the training schemes (Rovee-Collier 1999: 81), which is very relevant for the role of linguistic input to the child.

At the same time a number of socio-cognitive abilities develop. This period has become known by the term '9-month revolution' (Tomasello 1995). Around 9–12 months of age, children start to recognize symbolic gestures and that words are symbols (Bates et al. 1979), further understand joint attentional triadic frames, and develop the comprehension of intentions (Tomasello 1995). In addition, children around that age start imitating with role reversal (see Tomasello 2003 for a summary). This implies that children understand others as intentional agents, whose actions are then imitated. Role reversal is important for language learning: for instance, personal pronouns cannot be simply imitated if used by another speaker but need to be adapted to the perspective of the speaker. Another milestone relevant for communication is the child's understanding and her own use of pointing, which is one of the earliest and probably universal steps in communicating with the environment. In an experimental study of children growing up in very different cultures, including two rural communities, one in India, the other in Peru, and an urban community in Canada, Callaghan et al. (2011) found very similar behavior regarding a number of socio-communicative skills, such as pointing and joint attention. Similar results were obtained in a longitudinal study comparing children in rural Germany with children growing up in Chintang, a village in Eastern Nepal (Lieven & Stoll 2013). In this longitudinal study of two very different cultures, no correlation was found between the onset and the amount of pointing, and the pointing directed to the child.

Usually around their first birthday, children also learn their first words, after going through some universally similar stages of babbling. Around 6 months of age they start with reduplicated babbling and around 9 months their babbling sounds somewhat similar to their native language (Oller 2000), i.e., they imitate its intonation and stress patterns.

Independent of language, vocabulary strongly increases in the second and third year of life. Around age 4 most children master the basic grammar of their native language. However, how children extract the necessary information from the input to build up grammar is far from being understood and research is just at the beginning.

3.2 Environmental Factors Influencing the Acquisition Process

The role of environmental influence on language learning has been one of the hot topics of language acquisition research. We know from studies of a wide range of languages and cultures that there is a large variation in the interactional patterns between adults and children, both in the type and amount of interactions and in cultural attitudes expressed in ethno-theories about child rearing (e.g. Ochs & Schieffelin 1984, Keller 2007). The relevant question is whether these differences have an impact on how and when language is learned. In the following I concentrate on two features that take center-stage in acquisition studies: (i) linguistic characteristics of the input and (ii) amount and type of input.

3.2.1 Linguistic Features

The world's languages vary to an extreme degree on all linguistic levels. Even though there is a substantial number of language families with similar grammatical features, linguistic typology has recently forcefully questioned the idea of absolute universals that are valid for all languages (Bickel 2007, Evans & Levinson 2009). Even the most basic candidates for universals have been called into question lately.

Not even phonemes (duality of patterning, Sandler et al. 2011), nor words (Schiering et al. 2010), nor the distinction of nouns and verbs (Peterson 2010) are universal. It appears that each language has a unique combination of features, none of which seem to be universal. This means a huge design space for human language, which in principle every child can cope with. For instance, the number of sounds in languages ranges from a very minimal inventory of six consonants in Rotokas (West Bougainville, Papua New Guinea) to a very large inventory of 122 consonants in !Xóõ (Southern Khoisan; Botswana) (Maddieson 2005). Some of these sounds, such as clicks, are very complex to produce and are learned late. On the morphological level there is again huge variation ranging from languages with hardly any morphology, such as Chinese with zero verb forms, to extremely complex morphology such as Chintang (Nepal), with more than 1800 verb forms (Bickel et al. 2007). Both of these languages are from the Sino-Tibetan family, thus, even within language families, there can be extreme diversity. The challenges for children learning Chintang vs. Chinese vary to an extreme extent. Whereas a Chinese-learning child does not have to generalize a verbal paradigm at all, the task of a Chintang child is to extract the verbal paradigm in somehow encountering all 1844 forms and then generalizing the paradigm. Recent research on the acquisition of the verbal paradigm in Chintang suggests that children learn verb forms in an item-specific way before becoming productive verb users (Stoll & Bickel 2013).

Children learning languages with conjugation classes, as for instance in Polish (Dąbrowska 2001) or Finnish (Kirjavainen et al. 2012), still have different learning challenges to meet. These studies on languages with different types of morphologies suggest that complexity is an important factor for the learning process and needs to become the focus of future comparative work.

3.2.2 Input

One of the most burning questions in acquisition studies has been how much input is necessary for a child to build up the grammar and the vocabulary of her native language. There are several strands of research that provide insights into this question. First, there are cross- and within-cultural differences in how much children are addressed. Second, there are some potentially universal features in the structure of the input.

Amount of Input

We know from a number of influential longitudinal studies and also experiments focusing on the input children receive that there are enormous differences in the amount of language children hear per day. There are two main factors that have been shown to play a role in differences in input: cultural differences and socio-economic differences.

The way infants are addressed in different cultures and the ethno-theories behind these behaviors vary widely. As shown by Ochs & Schieffelin (1984) in an ethnographic study comparing how infants are addressed in three very different cultures during their first two years of life, "the biological predispositions constraining and shaping the social behavior of infants and caregivers must be broader than thus far conceived in that the use of eye gaze, vocalization, and body alignment are orchestrated differently in the social groups . . . " (Ochs & Schieffelin 1984: 299). In comparing the socialization of Anglo-American white middle-class babies with Samoan and, Kaluli they find wide-ranging differences in the amount and kind of interactions with prelinguistic infants. Children growing up in US middle-class families are usually the center of attention and treated as full interactional partners right after birth. Adults in this culture accommodate their speech and behavior to the children and apply a self-lowering strategy in constantly interpreting possible intentions, even though the infants are far from being able to express any of these "intentions" themselves. This is very different from the environment of Kaluli and Samoan children, who are widely ignored in their prelinguistic phase and only start to be treated as interactional partners when they utter some culture-specific words (Ochs & Schieffelin 1984). The studies of these three cultures were based on participant observation. These children, however, are not only surrounded by their primary caregiver and other adults but also by a large number of other children. So far, we know very little about how much interaction in direct input they indeed receive. We also know that there are at least some greeting rituals and there is also information about some explicit teaching strategies, which include prelinguistic infants in interactions. When other children address the infant in Kaluli, mothers face the baby toward the interlocutors and speak for the baby in a high-pitched voice (Ochs & Schieffelin 1984: 289). To fully understand the linguistic environment that infants in Kaluli and also Samoa encounter, quantitative studies, including the behavior of other children, would be instructive. Studies on a wider variety of cultures are clearly a desideratum in this area of research.

One other important factor found to correlate with the amount of input children receive is the socio-economic status (SES) of the families in which the children grow up. There has been a number of studies on the amount of input English children of families with different socio-economic status receive (Hart & Risley 1995, Hoff-Ginsberg 1991, 1998, Huttenlocher et al. 2002). Hart & Risley (1995), in a large-scale longitudinal study, have shown that the difference in terms of words that children of different SES groups encounter over a period of three years amounts to more than 3 million words for each child. Children of lower SES have a much lower input than children from higher SES groups. These studies also suggest that the overall amount of language children hear has an impact on the size of vocabulary and also on the grammatical development of the child. Hoff-Ginsberg (1991) has shown that there is not only a difference in speech directed to children in the different SES groups but she also found parallel social class differences in adult-to-adult speech. A further important finding of Hoff-Ginsberg's study was that the context of recording (mealtime, dressing, book reading and toy-play) had a significant effect on the language addressed to children. For instance, in contexts like book reading there were fewer differences among the different SES groups than in, for example, free play. Thus, the variable context plays an important role in the amount and also the type of language children receive. A recent study by Fernald et al. (2013) has shown that SES differences even have a strong impact on early processing and also on vocabulary learning: differences in processing were already evident at the age of 18 months. At 24 months of age the differences in the size of vocabulary were striking. Children from lower SES families lagged around 6 months behind their peers, both in processing skills and in vocabulary. Also, at later stages, with respect to the development of complex syntax there, is a significant correlation between the number of complex sentences a child hears and the child's mastery of multi-clause sentences (Huttenlocher et al. 2002).

All these studies strongly indicate that the amount of language a child hears has an impact on her linguistic development. This fact seems to be related to differences in adult competence, which turns out to be heterogeneous as well. Dąbrowska & Street (2006) have shown that we might have to revise the assumption that adults have a unified grammatical system. In comparing the ability to understand complex sentences, they found considerable individual differences correlating with education and socio-economic status of the speaker.

Type of Input

It is well known that not only the amount of input children receive varies considerably but also the kind of input for children of different ages and social groups.

One of the prerequisites for learning language seems to be participation in interactional communicative frames. As claimed by Snow (1984), frequent adjacent dyadic interactions with the child by the mother or a caregiver allow the child to predict the relevance of such interactions and ultimately understand the purpose of language. The question is whether these early interactions somehow facilitate language learning. It has been claimed that there are some prominent linguistic and potentially universal linguistic features of child-directed speech in these interactions, namely: frequent repetitions, prompting, slower speech, expansions of what the child said, shorter and fewer ungrammatical utterances (e.g. Snow & Ferguson 1977, Brown 1998). In many cultures very direct markers of such interactions in the form of prompts ('say X') and recasts (immediate use of the same word in a different construction or form) have been found; and features of early child-directed speech might help the child to parse and remember individual words and grammatical features (Farrar 1990, 1992). Interaction has thus been claimed to play a key role in helping children to understand that words have meaning. Then, later on, they learn words and grammatical constructions in repetitive interactions. Such interactions make use of all the of the milestones children acquire around 9–12 month of age, i.e. joint attention, intention reading and imitation.

As shown by Kuhl et al. (2003), even phonetic perception requires interaction. On the level of verb learning the importance of interaction for acquiring Tzeltal (Mayan, Mexico) verbs has been shown by Brown (1998), who states that Tzeltal mothers rarely talk to their prelinguistic infants and there is hardly any motherese observed. However, later on, verbal interactions between child and caregiver become crucial in learning Tzeltal grammar. Brown claims that to learn verbs children have to rely exclusively on "distributional facts about the linguistic context" (Brown 1998: 199). She hypothesizes that dialogic repetition is an important feature for learning the complex verbal system of Tzeltal. Prompts, expansions, and repetitions are a feature of the dialogic exchanges between the child and the caregiver. A similar observation was made by Küntay & Slobin (1996), focusing on what they call "variation sets," i.e. repetitive variations of the same theme in interactions between a caregiver and a child (for further elaboration of this observation see Onnis et al. 2008). A recent quantitative study on the role of interactions looked at Chintang children learning the ergative case (Stoll & Bavin 2013). In this large-scale longitudinal study it was shown how repetition has a quantitative effect in learning the ergative case. First, children use the ergative case predominantly as an exact repetition of the form used by an interlocutor in the same interactional frame. Then, later on, they use ergatives, which are not a direct repetition but prompted by the preceding utterance of an interlocutor that includes an ergative. Then, as a last step they use the ergative more frequently and spontaneously, without being prompted in any way. These direct interactions thus seem to have an impact on the learning process.

Further, the input itself seems to be structured in such a repetitive way that it potentially facilitates language learning. We know from the analysis of at least three languages (for English see Cameron-Faulkner et al. (2003), for a comparison of English, German, and Russian see Stoll et al. (2009)) that the input children receive is very repetitive, at least at the beginning of utterances. To see whether this is a specific feature of child-directed speech we would need some comparisons with the speech surrounding the child. These are tasks for the future, however, which will have an important impact in showing whether there are indeed strong linguistic differences between child-directed vs. adult-to-adult speech.

Not only do interactions themselves have structure but also the way in which these interactions are carried out. Since the early 1960s (Ferguson 1964) it has been well known that both the language addressed to infants (infant-directed speech), also known as motherese or baby talk, and the language addressed to small children, nowadays most often referred to as child-directed speech (CDS), differs significantly from the speech adults use among each other. These differences concern both prosodic and linguistic features and, of course, the content. The most prominent prosodic features are: higher pitch, larger pitch contours, longer pauses, slower tempo (Snow & Ferguson 1977, Fernald & Simon 1984, Fernald et al. 1989). Fernald & Simon (1984) found a significant difference between the language mothers addressed to their newborns and the language they used to address other adults; in particular, prosodic patterns rarely found in adult-to-adult speech were used frequently in infant-directed speech. Fernald et al. 1989 have argued for a universal set of prosodic modifications in infant-directed speech. In comparing speech modifications directed to British English, American English, German, French, and Japanese infants, they conclude that there is a universal set of features based on innate predispositions in the speech addressed to infants.

Bernstein-Ratner & Pye (1984), by contrast, argue that conventionalized, culture-specific features determine or at least influence the way adults address infants (for a summary of the controversy see Ingram 1995). In analyzing the speech addressed to Q'uiche Mayan infants Bernstein-Ratner & Pye found no higher pitch in child-directed speech, but rather, on the contrary, higher pitch was used in adult-to-adult speech. Higher pitch in this culture is reserved for people with higher status, so there seems to be at least a tendency to use a different pitch for adults than for infants: whether it is higher or lower pitch depends on other cultural variables. Reports on Tzeltal (Mayan) by Brown (1998) suggest that mothers do not use motherese in this other Mayan language. Instead of talking in high pitch they whisper to their prelinguistic infants if they address them at all. Thus, these features of child-directed speech are not universal and hence also not necessary in the sense that not each and every one of them needs to occur in a language for children to be successful in learning this language. However, when occurring, these features are most likely to be helpful for the acquisition process (Nelson et al. 1989). At the very least they help catching and directing the attention of the child, which is a prerequisite to learning. This hypothesis is strengthened by the fact that infants seem to prefer infant-directed speech to adult-directed speech (Cooper & Aslin 1990, Fernald & Kuhl 1987) and this even holds if the adult speaks in a different language than the mother tongue of the baby (Werker et al. 1994).

Even if there is no clearly delimited number of features characterizing the input of any language, there is a strong suggestion that a combination of a number of these features in the input facilitates the acquisition process. To learn more about such a potential set of universal features that could be a construction kit for the input to the language-learning child, we need to know more about the input in maximally diverse languages. This is indeed the most pressing task for future research as I see it.

4 Future Directions

Cross-linguistic language acquisition research is a relatively young field and it has made great progress in recent decades, starting out with initiatives like Slobin's cross-linguistic studies of a wide range of typologically different languages (e.g., Slobin 1985, 1992, 1997), Berman & Slobin's (1994) comparative study of narrative structures, and a large number of other cross-linguistic studies.

Further, the availability of a number of different corpora on CHILDES, including some languages from different language families, has had a major impact on the field. The available data is only a tiny sample, however, a fraction of what constitutes the design space for human languages. To truly understand acquisition we need a systematic picture of how the most diverse features of grammar are learned. Now, one of the most important future goals is to learn more about the flexibility of the language-learning mind. This entails concentrating systematically on languages with maximally diverse structures rather than studying languages of one family only or choosing languages by convenience sampling. This will then ultimately allow us to make claims about language acquisition processes in general rather than only about language-learning processes of individual languages. A first step in this direction was the development of a sampling method to identify maximally diverse languages (Stoll & Bickel 2012), which was a prerequisite to systematically studying the flexibility of the human mind. The next step, which has been undertaken, is a large comparative project actually comparing acquisition processes in these languages (see http://www.acqdiv.uzh.ch/index.html).

As detailed above, we know that children learn from their environment. To find out how they really do this, we need to know their socio-communicative environment in rich detail. To achieve this we should move away from classical studies focusing on semi-natural recordings of the child with her mother or some other close caregiver. Rather, we need to widen our research space by recording as much of the daily lives of the language-learning child as possible. This will expand our knowledge about the role and the structure of the input in general rather than focusing on a more or less artificial snapshot of dyadic interactions with her mother, a context that is often only a small part of the daily life of a child.

These goals, however, entail going out to the field and collecting acquisition data in as many diverse languages as possible, thereby taking into account the sampling issues mentioned in this chapter. For this we need close collaboration with linguists, psychologists, and anthropologists. Such an interdisciplinary approach was pioneered in a large-scale longitudinal study of Chintang, an endangered Sino-Tibetan language spoken in Nepal (cf., http://www.clrp.uzh.ch).

Related Topics

7 Language Ideologies (Kroskrity); **8** Social Subordination and Language (Huayhua); **9** Language Socialization (Paugh); **11** Language Socialization and Marginalization (García-Sánchez); **22** Language in the Age of Globalization (Jacquemet).

References

Ambridge, Ben & Elena V. M. Lieven. 2011. *Child language acquisition: contrasting theoretical approaches.* Cambridge: Cambridge University Press.

Bates, Elizabeth, Laura Benigni, Inge Bretherton, Luigia Camaioni, Virginia Volterra et al. 1979. *The emergence of symbols: cognition and communication in infancy.* Academic Press.
Bates, Elizabeth, Philip S. Dale, & Donna Thal. 1995. Individual differences and their implications for theories of language development. In P. Fletcher & B. MacWhinney (eds), *Handbook of child language,* 96–151. Oxford, UK: Basil Blackwell.
Berman, Ruth A. & Dan I. Slobin. 1994. *Relating events in narrative: A crosslinguistic developmental study.* Hillsdale, NJ: Lawrence Erlbaum Associates.
Bernstein-Ratner, Nan & Clifton Pye. 1984. Higher pitch in BT is not universal: acoustic evidence from Quiche Mayan. *Journal of Child Language 11,* 515–522.
Bickel, Balthasar. 2007. Typology in the 21st century: major current developments. *Linguistic Typology, 11,* 239–251.
Bickel, Balthasar, Goma Banjade, Martin Gaenszle, Elena Lieven, Netra Paudyal, Ichcha P. Rai, Manoj Rai, Novel K. Rai, & Sabine Stoll. 2007. Free prefix ordering in Chintang. *Language 83,* 44–73.
Brown, Penelope. 1998. Conversational structure and language acquisition: The role of repetition in Tzeltal adult and child speech. *Journal of Linguistic Anthropology 8,* 197–221.
Callaghan, Tara C., Henrieke Moll, Hannes Rakoczy, Felix Warneken, Ulf Liszkowski, Tanya Behne, & Michael Tomasello. 2011. *Early social cognition in three cultural contexts.* Wiley-Blackwell.
Cameron-Faulkner, Thea., Elena Lieven, & Michael Tomasello. 2003. A construction based analysis of child directed speech. *Cognitive Science 27,* 843–873.
Chomsky, Noam. 1981. Principles and parameters in syntactic theory. In Norbert Hornstein & David Lightfoot (eds), *Explanation in linguistics: The logical problem of language acquisition,* 32–75. London: Longman.
Cooper, Robin Panneton & Richard N. Aslin. 1990. Preference for infant-directed speech in the first month after birth. *Child Development 61,* 1584–1595.
Dąbrowska, Ewa. 2001. Learning a morphological system without a default: The Polish genitive. *Journal of Child Language 28,* 545–574.
Dąbrowska, Ewa & James Street. 2006. Individual differences in language attainment: Comprehension of passive sentences by native and non-native English speakers. *Language Sciences 28,* 604–615.
Eimas, P. D., E. R. Siqueland, Peter Jusczyk, & J. Vigorito. 1971. Speech perception in infants. *Science 171,* 303–306.
Evans, Nicholas & Stephen C. Levinson. 2009. The myth of language universals: Language diversity and its importance for cognitive science. *Behavioral and Brain Sciences 32,* 429–448.
Farrar, J. 1990. Discourse and the acquisition of grammatical morphemes. *Journal of Child Language 17,* 607–624.
Farrar, J. 1992. Negative evidence and grammatical morpheme acquisition. *Developmental Psychology 28,* 90–98.
Fenson, L., P. S. Dale, J. S. Reznick, D. Thal, E. Bates, J. P. Hartung, S. Pethick, & J. S. Reilly. 1993. *The MacArthur communicative development inventories: user's guide and technical manual.* Baltimore: Paul H. Brokes Publishing Company.
Fenson, L., P. S. Dale, J. S. Reznick, E. Bates, D. J. Thal, & S. J. Pethick. 1994. *Variability in early communicative development,* vol. 59, Monographs of the Society for Research in Child Development. Chicago: University of Chicago Press.
Ferguson, Charles A. 1964. Baby talk in six languages. *American Anthropologist 66,* 103–114.
Fernald, Anne & Thomas Simon. 1984. Expanded intonation contours in mothers' speech to newborns. *Developmental Psychology 20,* 104–113.
Fernald, Anne & Patricia Kuhl. 1987. Acoustic determinants of infant preference for motherese speech. *Infant Behavior and Development 10,* 279–293.
Fernald, Anne & Virginia A. Marchman. 2006. Language learning in infancy. In *Handbook of psycholinguistics,* vol. 2, 1027–1071. New York: Academic Press.
Fernald, Anne, Virginia A. Marchman & Adriana Weisleder. 2013. SES differences in language processing skill and vocabulary are evident at 18 months. *Developmental Science 16,* 234–248.
Fernald, Anne, Traute Taeschner, Judy Dunn, Mechthild Papousek, Bénédicte de Boysson-Bardies, Ikuko Fukui et al. 1989. A cross-language study of prosodic modifications in mothers' and fathers' speech to preverbal infants. *Journal of Child Language 16,* 477–501.
Hart, B. & T. R. Risley. 1995. *Meaningful differences in the everyday experience of young American children.* Baltimore, MD: Paul Brookes Publishing.

Haspelmath, Martin. 2001. The European linguistic area: standard average European. In Martin Haspelmath, Ekkehard König, Wulf Oesterreicher & Wolfgang Raible (eds), *Language typology and language universals: an international handbook,* 1492–1510. Berlin: Mouton de Gruyter.

Hauser, Marc D., Noam Chomsky, & W. Tecumseh Fitch. 2002. The faculty of language: What is it, who has it, and how did it evolve? *Science 298,* 1569–1579.

Hoff, Erika. 2003. The specificity of environmental influence: Socioeconomic status affects early vocabulary development via maternal speech. *Child Development 74,* 1368–1378.

Hoff, Erika. 2010. Context effects on young children's language use: The influence of conversational setting and partner. *First Language 30,* 461–472.

Hoff-Ginsberg, Erika. 1991. Mother–child conversation in different social classes and communicative settings. *Child Development 62,* 782–796.

Hoff-Ginsberg, Erika. 1998. The relation of birth order and socioeconomic status to children's language experience and language development. *Applied Psycholinguistics 19,* 603–629.

Huttenlocher, J., M. Vasilyeva, E. Cymerman & S. Levine. 2002. Language input and child syntax. *Cognitive Psychology 45,* 337–374.

Hyams, Nina. 2012. Missing subjects in early child language. In J. De Villiers & T. Roeper (eds) *Handbook of generative approaches to language acquisition,* 13–52. Springer.

Ingram, David. 1989. *First language acquisition: method, description and explanation.* Cambridge: Cambridge University Press.

Ingram, David. 1995. The cultural basis of prosodic modifications to infants and children: A response to Fernald's universalist theory. *Journal of Child Language 22,* 223–223.

Kaufman, Leonard & Peter J. Rousseeuw. 1990. *Finding groups in data: an introduction to cluster analysis.* New York: Wiley.

Keller, H. 2007. *Cultures of infancy.* Lawrence Erlbaum Associates Publishers.

Kirjavainen, M., A. Nikolaev & E. Kidd. 2012. The effect of frequency and phonological neighbourhood density on the acquisition of past tense verbs by Finnish children. *Cognitive Linguistics 23,* 273–315.

Kuhl, Patricia K., Karen A. Williams, Francisco Lacerda, Kenneth N. Stevens, & Björn Lindblom. 1992. Linguistic experience alters phonetic perception in infants by 6 months of age. *Science 255,* 606–608.

Kuhl, Patricia K., Feng-Ming Tsao, & Huei-Mei Liu. 2003. Foreign-language experience in infancy: Effects of short-term exposure and social interaction on phonetic learning. *Proceedings of the National Academy of Sciences 100,* 9096–9101.

Küntay, A. & D. I. Slobin. 1996. Listening to a Turkish mother: Some puzzles for acquisition. In D. I. Slobin, J. Guo, & A. Kyratzis (eds), *Social interaction, social context, and language: Essays in honor of Susan Ervin-Tripp,* 265–286. Hillsdale, NJ: Erlbaum.

Lieven, Elena V. M. & Sabine Stoll. 2010. Language. In Marc H. Bornstein (ed.), *Handbook of cultural developmental science,* 143–160. Psychology Press.

Lieven, Elena V. M. & Sabine Stoll. 2013. Early communicative development in two cultures: A comparison of the communicative environments of children from two cultures. *Human Development 56,* 178–206.

Lieven, Elena & Heike Behrens. 2012. Dense sampling. In Erika Hoff (ed.), *Research methods in child language: a practical guide,* 226–239. Wiley-Blackwell.

MacWhinney, Brian & Catherine E. Snow. 1985. The child language data exchange system. *Journal of Child Language 12,* 271–296.

Maddieson, Ian. 2005. Consonant Inventories. In Martin Haspelmath, Matthew S. Dryer, David Gil & Bernard Comrie (eds), *The world atlas of language structures,* 10–14. Oxford: Oxford University Press.

Nelson, Deborah G. Kemler, Kathy Hirsh-Pasek, Peter W. Jusczyk, & Kimberly Wright Cassidy. 1989. How the prosodic cues in motherese might assist language learning. *Journal of Child Language 16,* 55–68.

Ochs, Elinor. 1988. *Culture and language development: Language acquisition and language socialization in a Samoan village.* Cambridge: Cambridge University Press.

Ochs, Elinor & Bambi B. Schieffelin. 1984. Language acquisition and socialization: three developmental stories and their implications. In Richard A. Shweder & Robert A. LeVine (eds), *Culture theory: Essays on mind, self, and emotion,* 276–320. Cambridge: Cambridge University Press.

Oller, D. Kimbrough. 2000. *The emergence of the speech capacity.* Psychology Press.

Onnis, Luca, Heidi R. Waterfall, & Shimon Edelman. 2008. Learn locally, act globally: Learning language from variation set cues. *Cognition 109,* 423–430.

Peterson, J. 2010. *A grammar of Kharia: A South Munda language.* Leiden: Brill.

Rovee-Collier, Carolyn. 1999. The development of infant memory. *Current Directions in Psychological Science 8,* 80–85.

Rowland, Caroline F. & Sarah L. Fletcher. 2006. The effect of sampling on estimates of lexical specificity and error rates. *Journal of Child Language 33*, 859–877.
Roy, Brandon C., Michael C. Frank, & Deb Roy. 2009. Exploring word learning in a high-density longitudinal corpus. In *Proceedings of the Thirty-First Annual Conference of the Cognitive Science Society*, CogSci 2009.
Sachs, Jacqueline & Marie Johnson. 1976. Language development in a hearing child of deaf parents. *Baby Talk and Infant Speech,* 246–252.
Saffran, Jenny R., Richard N. Aslin, & E. L. Newport. 1996. Statistical learning by 8-month-old infants. *Science 274*, 1926–1928.
Sandler, Wendy, Mark Aronoff, Irit Meir, & Carol Padden. 2011. The gradual emergence of phonological form in a new language. *Natural Language and Linguistic Theory 29*, 503–543.
Schiering, R., B. Bickel, & K. A. Hildebrandt. 2010. The prosodic word is not universal, but emergent. *Journal of Linguistics 46*, 657–709.
Senghas, Ann & Marie Coppola. 2001. Children creating language: How Nicaraguan Sign Language acquired a spatial grammar. *Psychological Science 12*, 323–328.
Shatz, Marilyn & Rochel Gelman. 1973. The development of communication skills: Modifications in the speech of young children as a function of listener. *Monographs of the Society for Research in Child Development 38*, 1–38.
Slobin, Dan Isaac. 1985. *The crosslinguistic study of language acquisition. Vol. 2: Theoretical issues*. Hillsdale, NJ: Lawrence Erlbaum Associates.
Slobin, Dan Isaac. 1992. *The crosslinguistic study of language acquisition. Vol. 3*. Hillsdale, NJ: Lawrence Erlbaum Associates.
Slobin, Dan Isaac. 1997. *The crosslinguistic study of language acquisition. Vol. 4*. Mahwah, NJ: Lawrence Erlbaum Associates.
Snow, Catherine. 1984. Parent-child interaction and the development of communicative ability. In R. I. Schiefelbusch & J. Pickar (eds), *The acquisition of communicative competence*, 69–107. University Park Press.
Snow, Catherine E. & Charles A. Ferguson. 1977. *Talking to children: language input and acquisition*. Cambridge: Cambridge University Press.
Stoll, S. 2009. Crosslinguistic approaches to language acquisition. In Bavin, E. (ed.) *The Cambridge handbook of child language*, 89–104. Cambridge: Cambridge University Press.
Stoll, Sabine & Stefan Gries. 2009. An association-strength approach to characterizing development in corpora. *Journal of Child Language 36*, 1075–1090.
Stoll, Sabine & Balthasar Bickel. 2012. How to measure frequency? Different ways of counting ergatives in Chintang (Tibeto-Burman, Nepal) and their implications. In Frank Seifart, Geoffrey Haig, Nikolaus P. Himmelmann, Dagmar Jung, Anna Margetts, Paul Trilsbeek, & Peter Wittenburg (eds), *Potentials of language documentation: methods, analyses, utilization*, 84–90. Manoa: University of Hawai'i Press.
Stoll, Sabine & Edith L. Bavin. 2013. The acquisition of ergativity. In Edith L. Bavin & Sabine Stoll (eds), *The acquisition of ergativity*, 1–14. Amsterdam: John Benjamins.
Stoll, Sabine & Balthasar Bickel. 2013. The acquisition of ergative case in Chintang. In Edith L. Bavin & Sabine Stoll (eds), *The acquisition of ergativity*, 183–208. Amsterdam: John Benjamins.
Stoll, Sabine & Elena Lieven. 2014. Studying language acquisition cross-linguistically. In Heather Winskel & Prakash Padakannaya (eds), *South and Southeast Asian psycholinguistics*. Cambridge: Cambridge University Press.
Stoll, Sabine, Kirsten Abbot-Smith, & Elena Lieven. 2009. Lexically restricted utterances in Russian, German and English child-directed speech. *Cognitive Science 33*, 75–103.
Tomasello, Michael. 1992. *First verbs: a case study of early grammatical development*. Cambridge: Cambridge University Press.
Tomasello, Michael. 1995. Joint attention as social cognition. In Chris Moore & P. J. Dunham (eds), *Joint attention: Its origins and role in development*, 103–130. Lawrence Erlbaum Associates.
Tomasello, Michael. 2003. *Constructing a language: a usage-based theory of language acquisition*. Harvard, MA: Harvard University Press.
Tomasello, Michael & Daniel Stahl. 2004. Sampling children's spontaneous speech: how much is enough? *Journal of Child Language 31*, 101–121.
Werker, J. F. & R. C. Tees. 1984. Cross-language speech perception: evidence for perceptual reorganization during the first year of life. *Infant Behavior and Development 7*, 49–63.
Werker, Janet F., Judith E. Pegg, & Peter J. McLeod. 1994. A cross-language investigation of infant preference for infant-directed communication. *Infant Behavior and Development 17*, 323–333.

Further Reading

Bavin, E. L. & S. Stoll (eds). 2013. *The acquisition of ergativity*. Amsterdam: John Benjamins.
Berman, R. A. & D. I. Slobin.1994. *Relating events in narrative: A crosslinguistic developmental study*. Hillsdale, NJ: Lawrence Erlbaum Associates.
Bickel, Balthasar. 2007. Typology in the 21st century: major current developments. *Linguistic Typology*, *11*, 239–251.
Bowerman, M. & P. Brown (eds). 2007. *Crosslinguistic perspectives on argument structure: Implications for learnability*. Mahwah, NJ: Lawrence Erlbaum Associates.
Pye, C., B. Pfeiler, L. de León, P. Brown, & P. Mateo. 2007. Roots or Edges? Explaining variation in children's early verb forms in five Mayan languages. In B. Pfeiler (ed.), *Learning indigenous languages: Child language acquisition in Mesoamerica*, 15–47. Berlin, New York: Mouton de Gruyter.
Slobin, D. I. (ed.). 1985–1995. *The crosslinguistic study of language acquisition* (vols. 1–5). Hillsdale, NJ and Mahwah, NJ: Lawrence Erlbaum Associates.

11
Language Socialization and Marginalization

Inmaculada M. García-Sánchez

1 Introduction

Language socialization, with its traditional attention to culturally preferred subjectivities and ways of being in the world, and marginalization, as a relationally liminal sociocultural positionality and/or power status, are processes that have not often been considered in relation to each other. Yet this chapter is concerned with the value and usefulness of studying issues of marginalization from a language socialization paradigm. The chapter charts the past and present contributions of language socialization to the study of marginality, and considers how these contributions, even if limited, offer exciting possibilities for future scholarship that can open up new paths for the exploration of complex and dynamic language socialization trajectories in contexts of social, political, and economic marginalization.

In the first part of the chapter, I consider why, in language socialization studies, attention to marginalization work has been relatively limited. I argue that while the language socialization paradigm has ample theoretical breadth and methodological flexibility to enrich our understandings of the everyday and institutionalized ways in which individuals, or entire groups, come to occupy marginal subject positions and how these positions are shaped dialogically by power relations, the field has tended to foreground other sociocultural conundrums of language socialization processes. In these first sections I attempt to shed more direct light on some of these implicit historical inclinations so that the paradigm can be opened up to new issues and topics. I then describe how, for the last two decades in particular, and in spite of the paucity of marginalization studies mentioned above, language socialization scholars have made important contributions to our understandings of marginalization processes. Lastly, I describe how I have built on this previous scholarship and on insights from the language socialization paradigm in my own work among Moroccan immigrant children in Spain, further addressing some of the challenges and paradoxes that I have encountered along the way.

2 Historical Perspectives: "Competent" Membership as an Idealized Endpoint of Language Socialization

In their early formulation of language socialization, Ochs and Schieffelin (1984) observed that "the process of acquiring a language is deeply affected by the process of becoming a competent member of a society" (p. 277). This defining focus on sociocultural practices, knowledge, and ideologies that allow individuals to be recognized as intelligible cultural actors and competent members of communities has remained a central part of programmatic statements about language socialization studies well into the mid-2000s (e.g. Garrett and Baquedano-López 2002; Garrett 2006; Schieffelin and Ochs 1986; Ochs 2002; Schieffelin 1990). While, from their inception, language socialization studies were sensitive to the agency of children and other novices, and elegantly struggled with the tension of continuity and change that permeate even the most normative of developmental trajectories, the focus on competent membership did tend to foreground those normative developmental trajectories at the expense of other possible endpoints of socialization. While this emphasis was particularly true in the first wave of language socialization studies, often conducted in relatively homogeneous, monolingual – sometimes also relatively isolated – communities, this trend was also present in later studies carried out in more heterogeneous, multilingual, and culturally syncretic settings.

At this point, it may be useful to recognize how the emphasis on culturally preferred practices and trajectories is a legacy of the historical development of language socialization. The field arose in the early 1980s to address important lacunas in psycholinguistic studies of language acquisition, developmental psychology studies of child development, and anthropological studies of socialization (see Ochs and Schieffelin 2008 for a historical overview of language socialization). Not coincidentally, those three lines of inquiry, especially during that period of time, had developed strong traditions of centering much of their scholarship around the description either of universal and/or culture-specific normative developmental milestones, whether linguistic, cognitive, psychosocial, or sociocultural. In effectively critiquing the gaps left in these other disciplines and examining sociocultural and communicative aspects of social engagements involving novices, some of the theoretical and descriptive concerns of those disciplines seem to have carried over, giving many language socialization studies an implicit, if not explicit, focus on normative trajectories. This direction may have been reinforced by the use of elements of practice theory, such as Bourdieu's notion of habitus, that were also crucial in the formulation of the paradigm, but that have long been noted for their focused attention to practices of reproduction of culturally predictable and preferred subjectivities. The end result is that other types of language socialization experiences, such as those having to do with difference or marginality, while sometimes acknowledged and even analyzed to varying degrees, remained in the background of many language socialization studies.

Despite this trend, by the early and mid-2000s, when the field had developed its own strong research agenda and had expanded its scope to consider the communicative practices of novices in more diverse and contested sociopolitical contexts, such as among formerly colonized nations and populations and/or immigrant and diasporic communities, scholars within the paradigm itself started to recognize the dangers of focusing too narrowly on normative language socialization trajectories and experiences. For example, Ochs (2000) discussed the problem of how a heavy emphasis on these types of generalizations in language socialization processes can obscure, and even sometimes erase, the considerable variation in communicative practices and in socialization experiences that can be found in any community, an observation that was later picked up and further developed by Garrett and Baquedano-López (2002).

It is also around this time period that Kulick and Schieffelin (2004) produced one of the most theoretically elaborated examinations to date of language socialization in relation to issues of marginality and deviance. In this, they presented some productive and necessary ways for language socialization to move away from accounting only for normative trajectories, or in their own words "culturally predictable and desirable outcomes" (p. 354), to include other types of socialization trajectories related to undesirable and dispreferred subject positions.

Following Althusser and other French poststructuralist thinkers, they widened the horizons of the paradigm to include the examination of bad subjects, or individuals who engage in conduct considered culturally deviant, who display culturally unexpected traits, or who otherwise possess attributes associated with what in other brands of scholarship has been called "social stigma" (Goffman 1963). Furthermore, they challenged future scholarship in the paradigm to take up questions crucial to the study of "culturally problematic subjectivities" (Kulick and Schieffelin, 2004, p. 365) and marginalization, such as: how social actors come to understand certain positions and social identities as (un)desirable; how certain individuals come to occupy, or end up being positioned in, these differentially regarded positions; and how these processes are mediated by mechanisms and relations of power.

3 Crucial Issues and Topics: Studying Marginalization Across Contexts and Analytic Scales

Currently, the idea of normative trajectories associated with competent membership is seen more as a desired, or even something of an idealized, developmental endpoint among a number of language socialization trajectories (see Ochs and Schieffelin 2012 for a state-of-the-art formulation of the paradigm), and among a number of differently valued forms of societal membership and cultural subjectivities. While the ways in which this more recent scholarship has refocused, and attempted to overcome, the early theoretical limitations of this field of inquiry have been very helpful, there is still much room for both theoretical and empirical development of language socialization in relation to marginalization and related forms of sociocultural, linguistic, political, and economic disenfranchisement. Let me point out here some directions this development could take.

Theoretically, it would be important to continue to build upon, but simultaneously move beyond, the notion of bad subjects, or "cases in which socialization does not occur, or where it occurs in ways that are not expected or desired" (Kulick and Schieffelin, 2004, p. 355). By all means, we should continue documenting cases where the endpoints of language socialization trajectories are culturally "problematic," for example cases involving individuals' resistance and other modes of praxis that promote or hinder sociocultural change. This is particularly important because empirically we still do not know much about how these marginal subjectivities come into being.

It is also important, however, to recognize that getting a handle on the mechanisms of marginalization involves understanding how some individuals, or groups of people, are ascribed negative social identities and come to inhabit, often with varying degrees of possibility for resistance against, positions culturally recognizable and recognized as devalued and marginal in the social order. This is the case, for instance, when certain kinds of individuals or groups of people are actively discriminated against at various levels of sociopolitical life and are routinely positioned in structurally marginal categories, often being blocked from more desirable positions and identities by hegemonic ideologies and power relations. In liberal nation-states, in particular, the deep irony is that the marginal positionalities of certain groups are often covertly promoted through unequal structural arrangements, even though they are often ideologically deplored as undesirable outcomes. Indeed, there are usually a number of ideologies manufactured precisely in the service of justifying why many marginalized individuals or groups often "fail" to achieve preferred sociocultural trajectories, such as deficit theories that explain the educational failure of poor minority children as the result of environmental family and community factors. Yet it behooves us to be sensitive to these power mechanisms that mask how marginal positionalities and devalued identities can become de facto socialization endpoints for children and other novices who belong to marginalized communities.

There are a number of theoretical orientations and methodological features of language socialization that make it a productive intellectual tool to probe the mechanisms and tensions involved in the study of marginalization. To conclude this section, I mention three dimensions that are not only paradigmatically key, but that I have also found particularly useful in my own work among Moroccan immigrant children in Spain. First, language socialization is deeply process oriented, focusing heavily on *how* sociocultural practices are promoted, discouraged, negotiated, acquired, resisted, subverted . . . etc. This is a great strength because, unlike other paradigms in the social sciences where complex phenomena, such as discrimination or social reproduction, are often just assumed, language socialization research can show empirically the intricate architecture of socially organized practices that position certain groups as marginal members of the social group. Moreover, it can account for both practices that are explicitly organized as exclusionary and practices that are implicitly organized as marginalizing through indirect indexicality and other similar semiotic mechanisms, as well as for all the range of language-socializing practices that lies in between.

A second dimension of language socialization that helps illuminate how the marginalization experiences of children and other novices are mediated by (in)direct semiotic practices and other modes of social action is the way in which the field has paid attention to how micro-interactional social phenomena are embedded within, and are to a certain extent constitutive of, macro social conditions and ideologies. For example, considering the tensions between local interactional exchanges and larger sociocultural phenomena, such as language ideologies or ideologies of personhood, has been another traditional strength of the paradigm. An important caveat to consider here, however, is that to address the theoretical and empirical issues implicated in the study of marginalization, scholarship within the field needs to pay more attention to how interactional negotiations of local power relations or of group membership are shaped by sociohistorical and macro-political dynamics regulating hierarchal categories of belonging, mechanisms of citizen subject-formation, and other processes related to membership. This caveat has also been noted recently by other scholars in the field (i.e. Baquedano-López and Mangual Figueroa 2012; Fader 2012).

Finally, while language socialization scholars have productively utilized a variety of ethnographic methodologies, a most valuable orientation has been its longitudinal, cross-context perspective. This integrated approach is especially effective when studying processes of marginalization for several reasons. On the one hand, studying children's and novices' social engagements across situations of language use allow us to chart the relative constraints and affordances that novices experience in different settings. This is important because processes of marginalization and exclusion are very rarely totalizing across areas of social life. While it is possible to find examples of extreme cases of absolute social disenfranchisement, most often novices are likely to encounter varying degrees of marginalization in different contexts and spheres of their social lives. Even within a given context, an aspect I will elaborate later in relation to my own work, it is possible to find contradictions among different mechanisms of inclusion/exclusion, or among different social actors' actions and stances regarding constraints and affordances for participation. Furthermore, equally important in this regard is the fact that novices' agency to resist and subvert their own marginal positioning in favor of more advantageous forms of social participation is also likely to vary across sociocultural contexts. The power of a cross-context perspective in being able to determine the degree of *redundancy* (in Bateson's sense 1972) with which children and novices experience marginalization and social exclusion cannot be underestimated. On the other hand, a longitudinal orientation powerfully combines with this cross-context perspective to allow us to trace what Wortham (2005) has called "trajectory of socialization," or how language socialization takes places intertextually across speech events and interactional encounters.

Taking into account multiple analytic- and time-scales in a variety of contexts is crucial to making robust generalizations about relative routinization or exceptionality of novices' participation in marginalizing discursive events over time, and how this (in)consistent participation may lead to individuals' development of more or less enduring marginal and negative forms of social identification.

4 Current Contributions and Research: Marginalization as Trajectories of Language Socialization

While issues of marginalization may not have been an overriding focus in most language socialization scholarship to date, as a wider variety of communities and research topics have been explored, there has been an increasing sensitivity to the everyday and institutional production of negatively marked categories and forms of membership. In particular, I have identified four areas of inquiry in which a language socialization perspective has already enriched our knowledge of marginalization and the social processes that underpin it, such as ostracism, discrimination, and exclusion: (a) marginalization as structural product of institutional policies and practices towards individuals with stigmatized identities, such as students from racial and linguistic minorities and students with disabilities; (b) marginalization as production of social difference in children's and youth's peer networks; (c) marginalization as community ostracism in orthodox, nonliberal religious communities; and (d) marginalization as sociocultural and sociopolitical exclusion in migration settings. This section is not intended to be an exhaustive literature review on scholarship conducted on these four lines of inquiry (see Duranti et al. 2012 for wide-ranging coverage of language socialization). My purpose here is to showcase a few important examples of language socialization research in these thematic areas, pointing out specifically their contributions to our current understandings of marginalization processes.

Marginalization as Structural Product of Differential Participation in Institutional Policies and Practices

Historically, one of the first domains in which language socialization researchers paid attention to issues pertaining to processes of marginalization was in the documentation of linguistic and interactional practices sanctioned as legitimate in formal schooling activities. Most often this legitimization came at the expense of other productive patterns of language use that, while devalued in institutional practices, were fundamental in the primary socialization of children in their homes and communities, particularly for children from indigenous, minority, and/or working-class backgrounds (e.g. Cook-Gumperz 1977; Heath 1983; Miller 1982; Moore 2006; Philips 1983; Watson-Gegeo 1992). The now classic studies of Philips (1983) and Heath (1983), for example, make a powerful case for how the routine marginalization within the classroom of interactional and literacy practices favored in minority and working-class communities impacts not only these children's differential participation in school activities, but also their overall academic achievement. Focusing on forms of classroom participation, in particular, Philips (1983) examined how the communicative arrangements consistently favored by teachers on the Warm Spring Reservation were at odds with how their Native American students were encouraged to participate in learning activities in their homes and communities. Complementarily, Heath (1983) investigated the richness of literacy events across a number of diverse communities in the US, including African-American and white middle- and working-class communities. In comparing children's early literacy socialization in their communities to literacy socialization in schools, she found that the literacy practices treated as legitimate in school tasks were those most closely aligned with literacy practices actively socialized in white, middle-class households. These studies inspired a second generation of researchers to continue to explore how the mismatch between children's early language socialization and preferred institutional language practices, in addition to the routine devaluing of the *cultural funds of knowledge* (Moll 1992) and literacy skills of certain groups of students, greatly contribute to marginal educational trajectories among poor, minority, and immigrant students (e.g. Ballenger 1992; Delpit 1995; Pease Alvarez and Vasquez 1994). The critical mass of research accumulated throughout the last twenty-five years in this regard has been an important force in counteracting deficit ideologies that blame the educational "failure" of children from communities who experience multiple levels of sociocultural exclusion on their supposed linguistic and sociocultural deprivation, demonstrating instead how institutional practices and policies do not allow space for children from these communities to build on the rich bodies of social and linguistic knowledge already in their repertoires.

More recently, the area of disability studies, particularly those of children with autism spectrum disorders, has also allowed language socialization researchers to explore additional aspects of how institutional practices and policies, including culture-specific interactional habitus and ideologies about human communication and sociality, may hinder or promote the social and educational participation of individuals with marginalized identities (e.g. Ochs 2002; Ochs, Solomon, and Sterponi 2005). An interesting perspective on the multiple dimensions of institutional inclusion comes from Ochs et al.'s (2001) study of the interplay between institutional policies of inclusion and the everyday realities of what negotiating meaningful inclusion means for children with autism in public school contexts. While in his seminal paper on the discursive processes by which a student comes to be labeled *learning disabled,* Mehan (1996) had already shown that this category of identity may construct social facts about people, very often social facts that can marginalize a person, Ochs et al. (2001) went on to examine how these social facts organize, and emerge in, everyday interactions involving children with autism with their teachers and peers. Exploring how children with autism attempt to position themselves in these interactions in relation to what categories and subject positions they are allowed or encouraged to occupy, Ochs et al. concluded that, while educational laws and policies may guarantee access and physical placement of students with disabilities in US public schools, the degree of success to which these children experience inclusion in the social life of the school is highly dependent on the outcome of their daily engagements with their unaffected peers.

Marginalization as Production of Social Difference in Children's and Youth's Peer Cultures

An area of language socialization research that has been the focus of intense elaboration in the last couple of decades is how children and youth negotiate status, identities, and relationships as they construct forms of social organization within their own peer cultures (e.g. De León 2007; Evaldsson 2005; Garrett 2007; Goodwin and Kyratzis 2007; Howard 2007; Loyd 2012; Minks 2010; Paugh 2012; Reynolds 2008). Important dimensions of this negotiation often involve establishing group boundaries of inclusion and exclusion, while simultaneously positioning oneself and others in the local peer social order. Researchers studying those dimensions, in particular, have made important contributions to our understandings of children's sophistication at deploying interactional moves and strategies to ascribe negative categories to their peers, as well as to bar other children from occupying socially prominent roles, or to exclude them completely from participating, in the activities of the peer group. This research has demonstrated that children can be crucial agents in the social marginalization of other children in powerful ways, even from a very young age. Preschool girls studied by Sheldon (1996), for example, effectively obstructed the participation of another girl in their games, by assigning the role of an unborn baby brother to this girl within the pretend-play frame. Among preadolescents, Goodwin (2006), studying the consistent exclusion of one particular African-American girl, whom she calls Angela, in a multi-ethnic, multi-class peer group in Southern California, documented in great micro-detail the many linguistic resources and forms of *transmodal stylization* (Goodwin and Alim 2010) mobilized by the other girls to co-construct the degraded status of an at best devalued and pesky *tag-along* that Angela occupied in the peer group. In my own work among Moroccan immigrant children in Spain, on which I elaborate below, I have examined how, during the school day, Spanish peers routinely enact linguistically-mediated forms of racialized exclusion towards Moroccan immigrant children in the form of tattle-tales, peer directives, and fueling the fire. Through these practices, which belie official curricular principles built around the notion of inclusion, Spanish children mark the behavior of their Moroccan immigrant peers as deviant and, furthermore, are able to perpetuate with their actions larger historical-political realities concerning social and ethnic relations in their immediate environment (García-Sánchez 2014).

If language socialization studies have shown how interactions with peers can be a source of alienation, crucial in the development of negative forms of social identification for many children and youth, closely related research has also analyzed a complementary aspect of this phenomenon that is also important to mention here, namely how the peer group can also be an important community of practice for the development of what Bucholtz (1999) has called *positive identity practices*. This seems to be particularly the case among youth who inhabit stigmatized subjectivities or social identities, such as being a *nerd* (Bucholtz 1999), and youth who are routinely framed as *problems* (an educational problem, a delinquency problem, a teen-pregnancy problem . . . etc.), such as Latino female gang members (Mendoza-Denton 2008) or youth in alternative educational programs for "at-risk" students (Rymes 2001). As these scholars have suggested, in these cases active engagement in semiotic resources for constructing their own *difference* (e.g. speech, make-up and clothing styles, taste in music, or embrace/rejection of formal education) within the context of the peer group offers them a path of resistance to build alternate social networks, as well as to pursue alternate identities. By allowing them to opt out of the disenfranchised subject positions offered to them, these positive forms of membership can, therefore, counteract wider mechanisms of marginalization that these youth are experiencing in other domains of their social lives.

Marginalization as Community Ostracism in Nonliberal Religious Communities

Because of its central role in the development of morality, the formation of subjectivities, and processes of community membership and affiliation, language socialization into religious practices and orientations has traditionally been a fruitful focus of research within the paradigm (e.g. Baquedano-López 2008; Benor 2012; Ek 2005; Fader 2009; García-Sánchez 2010; Moore 2013; Schieffelin 2014). Schieffelin and Fader, working respectively on Evangelical Christian communities in Papua New Guinea and on Hasidic Jewish communities in the US, have additionally considered issues of marginalization as community ostracism directed at those individuals who fail to embrace or remain on the religious path.

Among the newly converted Bosavi in Papua New Guinea, for example, Schieffelin (2014) has reported how strong exclusion lines emerged, separating *insiders*, those who embraced the new Evangelical Christian faith, from *outsiders*, those who refused to convert to Christianity and maintained traditional Bosavi ways, or those who "fell" after conversion. Placing themselves at the physical, social, and moral center of communities, Bosavi Christians positioned non-Christians on the periphery of villages and mission enclaves, and regarded them as living "to the side" (p. S232). Schieffelin (2014) has argued that this expression not only denoted spatial configurations, but increasingly also indexed marginal social identities and reconfigured kinship relationships, as many Christians came to assume positions of power and authority over their non-Christian relatives in what had traditionally been a fairly egalitarian society with few hierarchical divisions of this kind. Among Hasidic Jews in Brooklyn, Fader (2009, p. 83) has also discussed the specter of community exclusion for those young women who do not adhere to Hasidic technologies of the self, and who therefore may not comply with community standards for modesty or obedience. In later work, Fader (2014) has further elaborated that many Hasidic youth who have stopped believing very commonly decide to remain within the faith nonetheless for fear of the social and familial marginalization they will have to endure if they leave. In these cases, some youth start leading a "double life," turning to social media and other spaces where they can express themselves and their dissenting beliefs without endangering their membership in the community.

Marginalization as Sociocultural and Sociopolitical Exclusion in Migration Settings

Given the global nature of contemporary migrations, the study of immigration has become a focal concern across the social sciences, and language socialization has been no exception. Indeed, in the last decade there has been a growing number of scholars who have made use of the language socialization paradigm to illuminate issues of language as it relates to the immigrant experience (e.g. Baquedano-López 2000, 2004; Bhimji 2005; García-Sánchez 2014; García-Sánchez and Orellana 2006; Lo 2009; Klein 2009; Kyratzis, Tang, and Koymen 2009; Mangual Figueroa 2011; Relaño Pastor 2005; Talmy 2008; Zentella 2005). While a number of themes have been taken up in this growing body of literature, two research foci that are particularly relevant to this exploration of language socialization and marginalization are the politics of belonging in relation to how immigrant groups are able to negotiate membership and participation in their multiple communities, and the sociocultural and linguistic categorization and stratification of immigrants. With regards to structures of membership and belonging, Baquedano-López's (2000, 2004) studies of Catholic catechism classes at two parishes in California analyzed religious literacy practices that socialize the children of Mexican immigrants to affiliate positively with an ethnoracial collective identity that is often disenfranchised by societal hierarchies, that of dark-skinned Mexicans living in the US. As the politics of the English Only movement swept through these parishes, however, the opportunities for Mexican immigrant children to attend these Spanish-language Catholic *doctrina* classes, in which they received empowering messages relevant to their identities as Mexicans and US immigrants, also dwindled. Instead, Mexican immigrant children were increasingly encouraged to attend English-language catechism lessons in which they participated in religious literacy practices that promoted ideologies of belonging strongly aligned with assimilationist US ideals of the melting pot, *e pluribus unum*.

Relatedly, in her study of mixed-status families (i.e. households with undocumented and documented members in the same family unit) in the New Latino Diaspora in Pennsylvania, Mangual Figueroa (2011) has investigated the impact of the legal and political codification of immigrants on the everyday lives of, and language socialization practices in, immigrant households. She has examined, for example, the contested meanings of citizenship as articulated by the children and their immigrant parents during homework completion routines specifically for their citizenship class. Manual Figueroa has insightfully captured the poignancy of these family interactions in which, while all family members conceive of themselves as *good citizens*, parents and siblings still have to struggle to position themselves differently in relation to notions of civic participation and still have to strive to imagine different ways in which they could one day contribute to the nation, depending on their legal categorization as either *citizens*, *residents*, or as *undocumented immigrants* who can be deported any time. Outside of the US, I (García-Sánchez 2013) have explored a complementary aspect of the politics of citizenship and belonging, that of cultural citizenship as a product of everyday practice in institutional contexts. I have shown how teachers in a Spanish public school play on essentialist notions of Moroccan immigrant and Roma children's ethnolinguistic identities, upholding notions of sociopolitical belonging that are predicated on ideologies of homogeneity and monolingualism. While these discursive constructions of difference have the potential to exacerbate immigrant and minority children's marginalization, crucially, however, in this research I have also emphasized how Moroccan immigrant and Roma children are sometimes able to contest teachers' essentialist formulations, effectively resisting these forms of multi-cultural cooption by asserting multiple, hybrid forms of membership and belonging.

5 A Case Study of Marginalization and Its Paradoxes: Moroccan Immigrant Children in Spain

I now turn to consider how I have built on the three dimensions of language socialization identified above (theoretical focus on process; attention to different levels of analytic scale; and a longitudinal, cross-context methodological perspective) in my own research among Moroccan immigrant children in a rural community in southwestern Spain (García-Sánchez 2014). In this study, I have focused specifically on how local and larger sociocultural and economic structures, as well as historically informed politics of inclusion/exclusion, impact these children's sense of belonging and emerging processes of identification as they negotiate membership and forms of participation across linguistic and community boundaries in familial, neighborhood, and institutional contexts. In examining forms of participation available, allowed, and encouraged for these children, I quickly realized that Moroccan immigrant children often came to occupy a relatively liminal sociocultural positionality and/or degraded status in certain social spheres of their lives. It also became increasingly apparent to me that the marginalization these children experienced in some settings was hardly an all-encompassing trajectory operating concurrently across contexts of their everyday lives, or with the same level of intensity and impact. Thus, I became particularly interested in understanding the paradoxes of marginalization and how they might affect sociocultural trajectories of children and other novices in contexts of social exclusion and disenfranchisement.

Indeed, the marginalization of individuals and/or communities almost always involves different, and often diverse, sources of exclusion (e.g. economic, legal, political, linguistic, religious). These multiple sources translate themselves into various social and semiotic mechanisms of marginalization (e.g. employment and housing practices, media (mis)representations, institutional policies, interactional encounters). I have come to believe that it is when we study the variable interplay between sources and mechanisms of marginalization on the ground and in the most immediate contexts of people's everyday lives, that important paradoxes in how mechanisms may contradict or reinforce one another across contexts become particularly obvious. Moreover, in some cases, mechanisms at different levels of sociopolitical life can be clearly at odds in their inclusion or exclusion effect on individuals and communities. This is because, while these mechanisms are very often firmly held in place by unequal structural arrangements and hegemonic forces, in certain cases they can also be challenged and offset by some forms of social and political (both institutional and more quotidian) praxis. This is especially the case in contexts of marginalization where these mechanisms of inclusion/exclusion emerge from the dialectic tension of two opposing sociocultural forces: forces of reproduction of unequal structural arrangements, historical discourses of discrimination, and exclusionary legal frameworks and forces of change that seek to lever open spaces for more social equity and justice.

In this regard, Spain is clearly a society deeply ambivalent about the prospect of cultural change and the multi-cultural politics of belonging provoked by recent migratory trends. And this ambivalence resonates particularly forcefully in the lives of Moroccan immigrant children, not only because of the current geopolitical climate of suspicion surrounding Muslim and North African immigrant communities in Europe, but also because of the problematic association of contemporary Moroccan immigration with the historical figure of *the Moor*, a model of personhood that has been consistently portrayed as diametrically opposed to authentic Spanishness in discourses and narratives of national belonging and formation (García-Sánchez 2014, pp. 28–60). In my analysis, I address how these various negative ideological positionings impinge upon Moroccan immigrant children's lives in complex and powerful ways. Thus, while the analytical cornerstone of the study centers on how children attempt to position themselves and are positioned by others as they participate in micro-level communicative practices with extended family, friends, and peers, teachers, religious figures, medical doctors, and sport coaches, I always consider these everyday interactional practices against the larger sociopolitical backdrops of increased levels of disenfranchisement and problematization of Muslim and North African immigrants in Europe, in general, and of the more context-specific negative ideologies about, and legal codification of, Moroccan immigrant communities in Spain.

Bringing together these different levels of analytic scale and forms of sociocultural semiosis has allowed me to identify and discuss an important paradox in Moroccan immigrant children's lives that I have characterized as negotiating membership as the "outsiders inside" (García-Sánchez 2014, p. 297). I have delineated how Moroccan immigrant children in Spain are able to negotiate the boundaries of simultaneous inclusion and exclusion at different levels of sociopolitical life and across different quotidian contexts. At the level of legal codification of belonging, this inherent contradiction stems from a restrictive set of citizenship laws, according to which children of immigrant parents are not considered Spanish nationals, even if they are born in Spain or brought to the country when they are toddlers (as was the case for all the children in my study). This paradox widens, particularly at the level of social and institutional policy, when, in spite of being legally defined as Moroccan nationals, because of their status as minors, by law they have the same legal protections as their Spanish peers, independently of their parents, immigration status. Therefore, they have access to the same free and public social, educational, and health services as other, Spanish, children, although only until their late teens (16 or 18 years old, depending on the type of social service and institution). The mismatch of being treated like insiders at the level of social policy but legally disenfranchised from citizenship, and ideologically degraded as immigrant children from a particularly undesirable and "*unassimilable*" group, also reverberates in children's everyday social engagements.

Moroccan immigrant children encounter this simultaneous inclusion and exclusion, for example, when they have to come to terms with the juxtaposition of institutional and pedagogical practices of inclusion in school settings (such as bilingual Arabic–Spanish signs on walls, the institutionalization of a multi-cultural curriculum specifically designed to "teach" children tolerance), and the quotidian technologies of surveillance and racialized exclusion (such as tattles and peer directives) that Moroccan immigrant children face in school. Pedagogical practices attempt to emphasize interculturality and friendship. Yet, Moroccan immigrant children face negative recognition from their Spanish peers, who routinely abnormalize the Moroccan children's behavior in their everyday social activities at school (García-Sánchez 2014, pp. 125–167). This abnormalization often intensifies beyond the walls of the school. Moroccan immigrant children acutely felt their marginalization when Spanish children never invited them to their birthday parties or did not want to become their friends and play with them in the neighborhoods and parks of this town (García-Sánchez 2014, pp. 88–124).

Another powerful contradiction that Moroccan immigrant children had to contend with in school contexts had to do with educational classroom practices that, although intended to foster interculturality and class participation by immigrant and minority children, as realized in actual student–teacher interactions, had the paradoxical consequence of positioning Moroccan immigrant children outside of the national collectivity. Teachers and administrators were aware of the value of not marking others as overtly different and diligently took steps to prevent explicit exclusion and discrimination. Yet, they ironically took part in excluding immigrant children from a sense of sociocultural belonging, when, in class discussions and other forms of classroom discourse, they upheld traditional notions of membership predicated on a single shared culture and language (García-Sánchez 2013).

Moroccan immigrant children also navigated paradoxical positionalities of their ambiguous status as relative insiders and outsiders in other contexts of their daily lives. When translating for their families and for Spanish medical staff at the state-run health clinic in this town, children came to enact a double role as agents of the clinic, but also as advocates for their families. In their dual role acting for the clinic and as representatives of their families and neighbors, these children functioned as medical institution insiders when they conveyed institutional views and values to Moroccan families, but they also acted as outsiders when they took interactional steps in their translations to protect Moroccan immigrant adults from institutional surveillance (García-Sánchez 2014, pp. 222–256).

Children's complex negotiation of simultaneous inclusion and exclusion was also visible in neighborhood play when Moroccan immigrant girls played together and rehearsed alternative processes of identification linked to valued forms of societal membership. In their games, for example, Moroccan immigrant children constructed desirable social identities for their play characters that positioned them as fully fledged insiders in Spanish society. Yet throughout these games, the children also displayed their understanding of some of the constraints in achieving this sense of membership. In their fantasy games, they challenged and transformed the marginalization and discrimination they often experienced in their everyday lives. They also contested subaltern socioeconomic positions and other structural marginal categories of Moroccan immigrant families within Spanish society more generally. Play frames often functioned as powerful counternarratives to the marginalizing constraints Moroccan immigrant girls encountered. Thus the play narratives allowed them to reject the disenfranchised subject positions offered to them and enabled them to fantasize about more desirable subjectivities and positions of power (García-Sánchez 2014, pp. 221–288).

In addition to tracing the nuances of Moroccan immigrant children's experiences of marginalization, the cross-context, multi-scalar, and processual perspective of the language socialization paradigm has also been important in helping me identify different interactional frameworks and arrangements that enable children to become more active participants in negotiating their own positioning and sense of belonging. A key realization in this sense is that children's interactional affordances to challenge their negative and/or differential positioning varied not only depending on the social context, but sometimes also on the type of interactional encounter and the participants involved, even within the same setting. Therefore, taking seriously the examination of immigrant children's capacity to act on their own behalf and creatively produce interactional affordances to counter their own marginalization involves being sensitive, at the very least, to two different types of variability in forms of social organization and structural arrangements: intercontextual and intracontextual variability. For example, in my own study, I encountered the children in contexts where power disparities between them and their interlocutors were very pronounced (i.e. educational institutions), but also in contexts that allowed them to exercise greater interactional agency to challenge how they were being discursively constructed by others and where they had more space to define their own forms of identification (i.e. medical clinics or neighborhood play with friends). In the first type of setting, the forms of agency available to Moroccan immigrant children were more limited, and, therefore, it was more difficult for them to counter their exclusion and how they were being defined as marginal outsiders. Being able to investigate immigrant children's socioculturally mediated capacity to negotiate their positions in their social worlds across a wide variety of contexts is crucial to capturing the complex interplay between the constraints and affordances children experience in different settings. This holistic, intercontextual perspective is important for our understandings of how trajectories of marginalization emerge and become more or less enduring, as well as how they can be disrupted.

Similarly, examining intracontextual variability in participation affordances and forms of social organization is critical to investigating how marginalized individuals may be able to take up interactional opportunities to actively negotiate their social positioning and identity, even in contexts involving large power differentials, where social relations are clearly asymmetrical. For example, one of the contexts where Moroccan immigrant children had fewer opportunities to stand up for themselves and redefine the subject positions to which they were very often relegated by their classmates, was at the school. As mentioned above, Moroccan immigrant children routinely faced a set of linguistically mediated technologies of exclusion, consisting of quotidian discursive practices, such as tattling, blaming, accusing, and shaming sequences, in which racialized and exclusion boundaries were instantiated through aggravated peer directives and other linguistic structures that encode unmitigated, negative types of agency and responsibility, and in which Moroccan immigrant children were either not ratified as full participants or were negatively ratified. A key aspect to consider here, and one of the reasons why Moroccan immigrant children often reported feeling lack of institutional support to be able to stand up to these forms of exclusion, is that these practices were so much part of the fabric of everyday social interaction in the classroom that they were rarely recognized by teachers as actual forms of exclusion. Thus, teachers often became unwitting collaborators in these practices: Spanish children's accusations against Moroccan classmates were ratified, even if less than consciously, by teachers. It is noteworthy to point out in this regard, however, that even the most insignificant action of a teacher against a Spanish tattler (i.e. when teachers did not ratify the accusations, but rather negatively align with them) was enough for Moroccan immigrant children to defend themselves, often confrontationally, against their peers' degrading characterizations and to reassign these negative social identities to the original perpetrators (García-Sánchez 2014, pp. 168–178). Indeed, a crucial common dimension of all of the examples where Moroccan immigrant children were able to counter these forms of exclusion, by overtly challenging their classmates, is that they all follow teachers' explicit disalignment with the tattling action performed by their Spanish classmates. These examples speak not only to the decisive role that teachers can have in the everyday social inclusion/exclusion of Moroccan immigrant children at school, but also, more generally to how, even within contexts in which marginalized individuals face enormous constraints, the actions and stances of specific social actors, particularly those in hierarchically more powerful positions, can change the dynamics in participation frameworks so that marginalized individuals are not rendered so socially vulnerable and have more interactional opportunities to redefine the trajectory of marginalizing social encounters.

6 Future Directions and Concluding Thoughts

In this chapter, I have discussed some productive ways in which a language socialization perspective can illuminate marginality as a relationally liminal sociocultural positionality and/or power status. This paradigm can be especially effective in revealing how processes of marginalization emerge from the complex, dialectic intersection between individuals' developmental trajectories of socialization and larger sociocultural, structural, and ideological arrangements that shape and constrain those trajectories. While experiences involving difference and marginality may not have been the central analytic focus of many language socialization studies to date, in this chapter I have shown how scholarship within the paradigm has been sensitive to the importance of sociocultural, linguistic, and other semiotic mechanisms by which marginalization is (re)produced in a variety of institutional, everyday, religious, and sociopolitical contexts.

Theoretically and methodologically, I have elaborated specifically on three traditional dimensions of language socialization (theoretical focus on process; attention to different levels of analytic scale; and a longitudinal, cross-context methodological perspective) that I consider extremely valuable in capturing the everyday and institutionalized ways in which individuals, or entire groups, come to occupy marginal subject positions and how these positions are shaped dialogically by power relations. One of the ways in which these intellectual tools can expand our understandings of marginalization processes is by allowing us to trace the relatively totalizing impact of marginalization mechanisms, precisely by exploring contradictions and paradoxes in these mechanisms, and how these paradoxes play out in quotidian social practice. I find the exploration of the paradoxes of marginalization an especially fertile ground for the ethnographic exploration of how individuals come to develop more or less enduring marginal and devalued forms of social identification because, from a theoretical perspective, paradoxes enable us to consider the multiple, and varying, levels of exclusion with which individuals from disenfranchised groups are confronted in different spheres of their social lives, and how different contexts may reinforce or contradict one another. Studying these paradoxes is also important from a more applied perspective, since it can allow us to discover arenas where it is more feasible to lever open spaces, or where marginalized individuals themselves are already creating those spaces, for more equitable forms of social action and practice.

Investigating the paradoxes of marginalization is, however, only one possible path for future scholarship in the paradigm to follow. As I have also discussed in this chapter, there is still much room for both theoretical and empirical development of language socialization in relation to marginalization, such as how marginal subjectivities come into being, how semiotic mechanisms of membership shape the ways in which individuals or entire groups are routinely blocked from socially desirable positions and identities, or how the social (re)production of structures of discrimination underpins the organization of marginalizing interactional encounters and institutional engagements that can lead to socialization trajectories of disenfranchisement, as well as how these forms of social reproduction can be disrupted.

Related Topics

7 Language Ideologies (Kroskrity); **8** Social Subordination and Language (Huayhua); **9** Language Socialization (Paugh); **10** Studying Language Acquisition in Different Linguistic and Cultural Settings (Stoll); **19** Language and Political Economy (McElhinny); **20** Language, Immigration, and the Nation-State (Pujolar); **22** Language in the Age of Globalization (Jacquemet).

References

Ballenger, C. (1992). Because you like us: The language of control. *Harvard Educational Review, 62*, 199–208.
Baquedano-López, P. (2000). Narrating community in doctrina classes. *Narrative Inquiry, 10*(2), 1–24.
Baquedano-López , P. (2004). Traversing the center: The language politics of language use in a Catholic religious education program for immigrant Mexican children. *Anthropology and Education Quarterly, 35*(2), 212–232.
Baquedano-López, P. (2008). The pragmatics of reading prayers: Learning the act of contrition in Spanish-based Catholic religious education classes (Doctrina). *Text & Talk, 28*(5), 582–602.
Baquedano-López, P. and Mangual Figueroa, A. (2012). Language socialization and immigration. In A. Duranti, E. Ochs, and B. Schieffelin (Eds), *The Handbook of Language Socialization* (pp. 564–586). Oxford: Wiley-Blackwell.
Bateson, G. (1972). Steps to an Ecology of Mind: Collected Essays in Anthropology, *Psychiatry, Evolution, and Epistemology*. Chicago: University of Chicago Press.
Benor, S. B. (2012). *Becoming Frum: How Newcomers Learn the Language and Culture of Orthodox Judaism*. New Brunswick, NJ: Rutgers University Press.
Bhimji, F. (2005). Language socialization with directives in two Mexican immigrant families in south central Los Angeles. In A. C. Zentella (Ed.), *Building on Strength: Language and Literacy in Latino Families and Communities* (pp. 60–76). New York: Teachers College Press.
Bucholtz, M. (1999). "Why be normal?": Language and identity practices in a community of nerd girls. *Language in Society, 28*, 203–223.
Cook-Gumperz, J. (1977). Situated instruction: Language socialization of school age children. In S. Ervin-Tripp and C. Mitchell-Kernan (Eds), *Child Discourse* (pp. 103–121). New York: Academic.
De León, L. (2007). Parallelism, metalinguistic play, and the interactive emergence of Zinacantec Mayan siblings' culture. *Research on Language and Social Interaction, 40*(4), 405–436.
Delpit, L. (1995). *Other People's Children: Cultural Conflict in the Classroom*. The New Press: New York.
Duranti, A., Ochs, E., and Schieffelin, B. B. (Eds) (2012). *The Handbook of Language Socialization*. Oxford: Wiley-Blackwell.
Ek, L. D. (2005). Staying on God's path: Socializing Latino immigrant youth to a Christian Pentecostal identity in Southern California. In A. C. Zentella (Ed.), *Building on Strength: Language and Literacy in Latino Families and Communities* (pp. 77–92). New York: Teachers College Press.
Evaldsson, A. C. (2005). Staging insults and mobilizing categorizations in a multiethnic peer group. *Discourse and Society, 16*(6), 763–786.
Fader, A. (2009). *Mitzvah Girls: Bringing up the Next Generation of Hasidic Jews in Brooklyn*. Princeton, NJ: Princeton University Press.
Fader, A. (2012). Language socialization and morality. In A. Duranti, E. Ochs, and B. B. Schieffelin (Eds), *The Handbook of Language Socialization* (pp. 322–340). Oxford: Wiley-Blackwell.
Fader, A. (2014). The internet, ultra-orthodox Jews and the interiority of faith. Paper presented at the 113th American Anthropological Association Annual Meetings. Washington, DC.
García-Sánchez, I. M. (2010). The politics of Arabic language education: Moroccan immigrant children's socialization into ethnic and religious identities. *Linguistics and Education, 21*(3), 171–196.
García-Sánchez, I. M. (2013). The everyday politics of 'cultural citizenship' among North African immigrant school children in Spain. *Language and Communication, 33*, 481–499.
García-Sánchez, I. M. (2014). *Language and Muslim Immigrant Childhoods: The Politics of Belonging*. Oxford: Blackwell-Wiley.
García-Sánchez , I. M. and Orellana , M. F. (2006). The construction of moral and social identity in immigrant children's narratives-in-translation. *Linguistics and Education, 17*(3), 209–239.
Garrett, P. (2006). Language socialization. *Elsevier Encyclopedia of Language and Linguistics* (2nd ed.), vol. 6 (pp. 604–613).
Garrett, P. (2007). Language socialization and the reproduction of bilingual subjectivities. In M. Heller (Ed.), *Bilingualism: A Social Approach* (pp. 233–256). New York: Palgrave Macmillan.
Garrett, P. and Baquedano-López, P. (2002). Language socialization: Reproduction and continuity, transformation and change. *Annual Review of Anthropology, 31*, 339–361.
Goffman, E. (1963). *Stigma: Notes on the Management of Spoiled Identity*. London: Penguin.
Goodwin, M. H. (2006). *The Hidden Life of Girls: Games of Stance, Status, and Exclusion*. Malden, MA: Blackwell Publishing.

Goodwin, M. H. and Kyratzis, A. (2007). Children socializing children: Practices for negotiating the social order among peers. *Research on Language and Social Interaction, 40*(4), 279–289.

Goodwin, M. H. and Alim, H. S. (2010). "Whatever (neck roll, eye roll, teeth suck)": The situated coproduction of social categories and identities through stancetaking and transmodal stylization. *Journal of Linguistic Anthropology, 20*(1), 179–194.

Heath, S. B. (1983). *Ways with Words: Language, Life, and Work in Communities and Classrooms*. Cambridge: Cambridge University Press.

Howard, K. (2007). Kinship usage and hierarchy in Thai children's peer groups. *Journal of Linguistic Anthropology, 17*(2), 204–230.

Klein, W. L. (2009). Turban narratives: Discourses of identification and differences among Punjabi Sikh families in Los Angeles. In A. Lo and A. Reyes (Eds), *Towards a Linguistic Anthropology of Asian-Pacific America* (pp. 111–130). New York: Oxford University Press.

Kulick, D. and Schieffelin, B. (2004). Language socialization. In A. Duranti (Ed.), *A Companion to Linguistic Anthropology* (pp. 349–368). Malden, MA: Blackwell.

Kyratzis, A., Tang Y. T., and Koymen, B. S. (2009). Codes, code-switching and context: Style and footing in peer group bilingual play. *Multilingua, 28*, 265–290.

Lo, A. (2009). Evidentiality and morality in a Korean heritage language school. In A. Reyes and A. Lo (Eds), *Beyond Yellow English: Towards a Linguistic Anthropology of Asian Pacific America* (pp. 63–83). New York: Oxford University Press.

Loyd, H. (2012). The logic of conflict: Practices of social control among inner city Neapolitan girls. In S. Danby and M. Theobald (Eds), *Disputes in Everyday Life: Social and Moral Orders of Children and Young People* (pp. 325–353). *Sociological Studies of Children* and Youth, vol. *15*. Emerald Group.

Mangual Figueroa, A. (2011). Citizenship and education in the homework completion routine. *Anthropology & Education Quarterly, 4*(3), 263–280.

Mehan, H. (1996). The construction of an LD student: A case study in the politics of representation. In Silverstein and Urban (Eds), *Natural Histories of Discourse*, (pp. 253–276). Chicago: University of Chicago Press.

Mendoza-Denton, N. (2008). *Homegirls: Language and Cultural Practice among Latina Youth Gangs*. Oxford: Wiley-Blackwell.

Miller, P. (1982) *Amy, Wendy, and Beth: Learning Language in South Baltimore*. Austin: University of Texas Press.

Minks, A. (2010) Socializing heteroglossia among Miskitu children on the Caribbean Coast of Nicaragua. *Pragmatics, 20*(4), 495–522.

Moll, L. C. (1992). Funds of knowledge for teaching: Using a qualitative approach to connect homes and classrooms. *Theory into Practice, 31*(2), 132–141.

Moore, L. C. (2006). Changes in folktale socialization in a Fulbe community. *Studies in African Linguistics*, Suppl. *11*, 176–187.

Moore, L. C. (2013). Qur'anic school sermons as a site for sacred and second language socialisation. *Journal of Multilingual and Multicultural Development, 34*(5), 445–458.

Ochs, E. (2002). Becoming a speaker of culture. In C. Kramsch (Ed.) *Language Socialization and Language Acquisition: Ecological Perspectives* (pp. 99–120). New York: Continuum Press.

Ochs, E. (2000). Socialization. *Journal of Linguistic Anthropology, 9*(1–2), 230–233.

Ochs, E. and Schieffelin, B. B. (1984). Language acquisition and socialization: Three developmental stories. In R. Shweder and R. LeVine (Eds), *Culture Theory: Mind, Self, and Emotion* (pp. 276–320). Cambridge: Cambridge University Press.

Ochs, E. and Schieffelin, B. B. (2008). Language socialization: A historical overview. In P. Duff and N. Hornberger (Eds), *Encyclopedia of Language and Education*, vol. 8, Language Socialization, 2nd ed. (pp. 3–15). New York: Springer.

Ochs, E. and Schieffelin, B. B. (2012). The theory of language socialization. In A. Duranti, E. Ochs, and B. B. Schieffelin (Eds) *The Handbook of Language Socialization* (pp. 1–21). Oxford: Wiley-Blackwell.

Ochs, E., Kremer-Sadlik, T., Solomon, O., and Sirota, K. (2001). Inclusion as a social practice: Views of children with autism. *Discourse Studies, 10*(3), 399–419.

Ochs, E., Solomon, O., and Sterponi, L. (2005). Limitations and transformation of habitus in child-directed communication. *Discourse Studies, 7*(4–5), 547–583.

Paugh, A. L. (2012). *Playing with Languages: Children and Change in a Caribbean Village*. New York and Oxford: Berghahn Books.

Pease-Alvarez, C. and Vasquez, O. (1994). Language socialization in ethnic minority communities. In F. Genesee (Ed.), *Educating Second Language Children: The Whole Child; The Whole Curriculum; The Whole Community* (pp. 82–102). New York: Cambridge University Press.

Philips, S. U. (1983). *The Invisible Culture: Communication in Classroom and Community on the Warm Springs Indian Reservation*. New York: Longman.
Relaño Pastor, A. M. (2005). The language socialization experiences of Latina mothers in southern California. In A. C. Zentella (Ed.), *Building on Strength: Language and Literacy in Latino Families and Communities* (pp. 148–161). New York: Teachers College Press.
Reynolds, J. F. (2008). Socializing Puros Pericos: The negotiation of respect and responsibility in Antonero Mayan sibling and peer networks. *Journal of Linguistic Anthropology, 18*(1), 82–107.
Rymes, B. (2001). *Conversational Borderlands: Language and Identity in an Alternative Urban High School*. New York: Teachers' College Press.
Schieffelin, B. B. (1990). *The Give and Take of Everyday Life: Language Socialization of Kaluli Children*. Cambridge: Cambridge University Press.
Schieffelin, B. B. (2014). Christianizing language and the displacement of culture in Bosavi, Papua New Guinea. *Current Anthropology, 55*(10), S226–S237.
Schieffelin, B. B. and Ochs, E. (1986). Language socialization. *Annual Review of Anthropology, 15*, 163–191.
Sheldon, A. (1996). You can be the baby brother but you aren't born yet: Preschool girls' negotiation for power and access in pretend play. *Research on Language and Social Interaction, 29*(1), 57–80.
Talmy, S. (2008). The cultural production of the ESL student at Tradewinds High: Contingency, multidirectionality, and identity in L2 socialization. *Applied Linguistics, 17*(1), 1–22.
Watson-Gegeo, K. A. (1992). Thick explanation in the ethnographic study of child socialization: A longitudinal study in the problem of schooling for Kwara'ae (Solomon Islands) children. *New Directions for Child Development, 58*, 51–66.
Wortham, S. (2005). Socialization beyond the speech event. *Journal of Linguistic Anthropology, 15*(1), 95–112.
Zentella, A. C., (Ed.) (2005). *Building on Strength: Language and Literacy in Latino Families and Communities*. New York: Teachers College Press.

Further Reading

This section includes highlights from the References section (first three entries), as well as additional readings (final two).
Kulick, D. and Schieffelin, B. (2004). Language socialization. In A. Duranti (ed.), *A Companion to Linguistic Anthropology* (pp. 349–368). Malden, MA: Blackwell.
García-Sánchez, I. M. (2014). *Language and Muslim Immigrant Childhoods: The Politics of Belonging*. Oxford: Wiley-Blackwell.
Ochs, E., Kremer-Sadlik, T., Solomon, O., and Sirota, K. (2001). Inclusion as a social practice: Views of children with autism. *Discourse Studies, 10*(3), 399–419.
García-Sánchez, I. M. (2012). Language socialization and exclusion. In A. Duranti, E. Ochs, and B. B. Schieffelin (eds.), *The Handbook of Language Socialization* (pp. 391–420). Oxford: Wiley-Blackwell.
Goodwin, M. H. (2008). The embodiment of friendship, power and marginalization in a multi-ethnic, multi-class preadolescent U.S. girls' peer group. *Girlhood Studies: An Interdisciplinary Journal, 1*(2), 72–94.

Part III
Language and the Communication of Identities

Part II

12

Language, Sexuality, Heteroglossia, and Intersectionality

William L. Leap

Introduction

Anthropological interests in language and sexuality began with studies that explored linguistic representations of differences, e.g., male vs. female speech, "third gender" categories, the "language(s)" of same-sex identities. Since the late 1990s, and inspired by emerging developments in queer linguistics (see Further Reading below), these interests have been reconfigured to ensure that linguistic inquiry is no longer anchored in single identities or in binary contrasts. Today's studies examine connections between language and sexuality in relation to topics as diverse as embodiment (Hennen 2005, King 2008, Vidal-Ortiz 2011, Weinberg and Williams 2010), articulation (Podesva 2007, 2011, Zimman 2013), erotic practice (Adams-Thies 2012, Leap 2011, Morrish and Sauntson 2007a,b), public performance (Barrett 1999, Mann 2011, Motschenbacher 2012), homophobic/transphobic oppression (Edelman 2011, 2014, Murray 2009, Peterson 2010), migration and diaspora (Murray 2013), and sexual citizenship (Boellstorff 2005, Gaudio 2009, Provencher 2007, Rahman 2010, Leap and Boellstorff 2004).

Similarly, scholars in feminist studies have moved away from discussing race, gender, and class as isolated, identity-centered formations, and have begun to foreground attention to their "intersectionality" (Crenshaw 1989, 1991). In fact, current discussions extend these "intersections" of race, gender, and class to include sexuality, age, ability, mobility, place, and other social descriptors that, together with meanings of race, gender, and class, are now considered mutually constitutive rather than compartmentalized. Importantly, these discussions also show that the resulting intersections of social meaning unfold unevenly across the local social terrain. As Nash explains, intersectionality " ...secur[es] privilege and domination simultaneously" (2008: 10, citing Wing 1990: 191).

Anthropological studies of language and sexuality, like those cited above, provide ample indications that sexuality, along with age, ability, and similar descriptors, is implicated within the intersectional accumulations of race, class, and gender in the sense suggested in Nash's discussion. Those studies also suggest that the details of intersectionality cannot be fully contained within single forms of linguistic practice or even within studies of "particular choices and combinations of linguistic forms drawn from several distinct linguistic varieties" (Barrett 2003: 558). What are required are discussions of language and sexuality that " . . . differentiate carefully between different kinds of difference" (Yuval-Davis 2006: 198) and also specify "how many social divisions are involved and/or which ones should be incorporated into the intersectionality process" (Yuval-Davis 2006: 201) within any given setting. I propose that an analysis of language and sexuality that is attentive to heteroglossia (Vološinov 1972, Bakhtin 1981) will provide useful starting points for locating the social divisions that are relevant to local conditions of intersectionality. And, as this chapter shows, such an analysis connects studies of heteroglossia and intersectionality with current interests in queer linguistics and queer theory.

Historical Perspectives

Introducing Language, Sexuality, and Heteroglossia

Writing about gay life in Manhattan during the 1940s, Donald Vinning shares the following anecdote. A gay man at that time could say something like the following in a public gathering:

> "I adore seafood. Gorge myself whenever the fleet is in. But I can't abide fish", and any gay man would instantly know that the speaker was turned on by sailors and turned off by women, while the puzzled Mr. and Mrs. Readers Digest, listening in, would assume this was a discussion about food preferences.
>
> Vinning (1986: 55)

Chauncey (1986: 286–287) and others refer to the lexical practice displayed in this example as double entendre. That is, the speaker's references to "seafood" and "fish" offers one set of messages to those who recognize the coded, sexualized distinction between seafood and fish; these references provide an entirely different message to those who are unfamiliar with the coded distinction and are left to respond to the statement strictly on face value. Similarly, the speaker uses the term "Mr. and Mrs. Readers Digest" to identify persons "unfamiliar" with the coded distinction, citing the publication that for years occupied a central place in a certain category of American homes to index a naiveté about sexual sameness. Those included within that category would likely agree that the phrase "Mr. and Mrs. Readers Digest" accurately captured their reading preferences. However, they might not recognize the more subtle sexualized allusion implied by that reference to middle-class American taste. So here, too, is another instance of double entendre, this time marking or disguising a particular moral evaluation. Think how differently the anecdote would read, if the couple had been named "Mr. and Mrs. National Geographic," "Mr. and Mrs. New Yorker," or "Mr. and Mrs. National Enquirer."

But describing the references to sexuality in Vinning's example as double entendre captures only part of the social message captured by this example. The pairing of *seafood* and *fish* is recognized by all three parties to the speech event, but is recognized in somewhat different ways in each case. Thus the use of double entendre marks a site where references to gender and sexuality combine with considerations as varied as class position and relative social naiveté to create interlocking social connections and social contrasts. In other words, references associated with sexuality in Vinning's example are expressed variably – or, and more to the point, heteroglossically – in this example; and the use of double entendre itself takes the form of a heteroglossic formation. That is, the example's references to sexuality are "not merely reflected but refracted through sign ... [as] determined by an intersecting of differently oriented social interests within one and the same sign community" (Vološinov 1972: 23).

Identifying these overlapping distinctions as heteroglossia suggests that relationships between language and sexuality are refracted across, among, and between linguistic and social relationships that are attested within the given setting. Studies of heteroglossia then examine messages about sexuality indicated through particular refractions while paying attention to how refraction as a whole displays facts about sexuality within the social moment. But, to do this, studies of heteroglossia must avoid foregrounding any single linguistic feature and the social importance of its message, while neglecting the significance of other features and their contributions to the message. To cite the most obvious example: noting that double entendre was "about sexuality" erases the subtle, but substantial, distinctions between the speaker's work of disclosure and the acts of reception that characterize the informed listener's participation in this example – and distinguish it from the participation of Mr. and Mrs. Reader's Digest.

Heteroglossia and Intersectionality: Feminist Theory with Queer Implications

Crenshaw (1989, 1991) raised a similar argument in her classic discussion of intersectionality, where she cautioned against building discussions of gender that refuse to address attendant inflections of race and class. Crenshaw explained:

> many of the experiences Black women face are not subsumed within the traditional boundaries of race or gender discrimination as the boundaries are currently understood, and that the intersection of racism and sexism factors into Black women's lives in ways that cannot be captured wholly by looking at the race or gender dimensions of those experiences separately.
>
> *Crenshaw (1991: 1244)*

Understandably, conditions shaping Black women's experiences of racism and sexism in one social location are unlikely to apply in exactly the same way in other locations. In fact, Crenshaw cautions:

> a focus on the most privileged group members marginalizes those who are multiply burdened and obscures claims that cannot be understood as resulting from discrete sources of discrimination.
>
> *Crenshaw (1989: 140)*

Crenshaw's arguments prompted considerable discussion in feminist studies, but a review of this work led McCall to observe: " . . . despite the emergence of [this] major paradigm of research . . . , there has been little discussion of how to study intersectionality, that is, of its methodology" (2005: 1771).

Yuval-Davis (2006) responds helpfully to that challenge, noting that race, gender, and class each have " . . . a different ontological basis" and thus are "irreducible to other social divisions" as well as to each other. So race, gender, and class are each shaped by conditions of social oppression – although, in some cases, they mutually contribute to that oppression, and they are never attested in social settings entirely in isolation. Thus,

> Being oppressed . . . "as a Black person" is always constructed and intermeshed in other social divisions (for example, gender, social class, disability status, sexuality, age, nationality, immigration status, geography, etc).
>
> *Yuval-Davis (2006: 195)*

For Yuval-Davis, what results is an analysis of intersectionality that " . . . differentiates carefully between different kinds of difference" (2006: 198) but also specifies "how many social divisions are involved and/or which ones should be incorporated into the intersectionality process"

(2006: 201). And, as Nash (2008) explains, what results is an analysis that highlights the mutually productive relationships connecting the privileged and the multiply burdened, even when the discussion addresses a particular formation of difference:

> If intersectionality is solely an anti-exclusion tool designed to describe "the multiplier effect" or "the lifelong spirit injury of black women" then it is incumbent upon both feminist theory and antiracist work to develop a conceptualization of identity that captures the ways in which race, gender, sexuality, and class, among other categories, are produced through each other, securing both privilege and oppression simultaneously.
>
> Nash 2008: 10, citing Wing (1990: 191)

What also results is an analysis of intersectionality that refuses to be defined by self-evident categories of social reference or oppression. In fact, by showing that privilege and oppression are simultaneously produced through the interconnectedness of race, gender, class, and related formations, an analysis of intersectionality undermines the orderly logics that those categories and their neatly bounded references so often proclaim. In this sense, studies of intersectionality have much in common with the language-centered studies of heteroglossia (like that outlined in the preceding section). Adding discussions of intersectionality to discussions of heteroglossia enriches the analytical power of both modes of inquiry, as the examples in the following sections will suggest.

Critical Issues and Topics

Who Goes to a Lesbian Bar?

One of the shortcomings in earlier studies of language and sexuality was the practice of organizing the discussion of linguistic practices around a single category of social reference. Abe (2010, 2011) addressed this issue successfully in her studies of language use in the "lesbian bars" in Shinjuku Ni-choome, the "second block area" of Tokyo. At issue here are linguistic practices that are refracted variously across details of gender and sexuality, but also the fact that a category like "lesbian" submerges evidence of local heteroglossia and intersectionality beneath a single, inclusive sign, creating an appearance of uniform reference when the local linguistic practices actually indicate otherwise. Moreover, in the case that Abe describes, the inclusive category has US/European affiliations that apply uneasily to the urban Tokyo bar scene. As Halberstam (2012: 343) observes, only "when we refuse to verify the seemingly inevitable priorness of US/European sexual economies," does it become possible " . . . to recognize and learn from other modes of gender identification embedded in other kinds of sexual practice and productive of alternative forms of sociality and community and identity." Abe's research shows how studies of heteroglossia position these modes of identification and alternative forms not just as single formations, but as intersectional practices.

The sites in Shinjuku Ni-choome were called "lesbian bars" in popular descriptions of the area's sexual geography. But Abe (2011: 376) admitted, " . . . the community served by [these] lesbian bars turned out to be much broader than I had expected." In the main, the "lesbian bars" served a female, same-sex identified or bisexual clientele. However, some "lesbian bars" were frequented by *rezu* or *rezubian*, a female-bodied subject who maintains a female identity while being attracted to other women. Other "lesbian bars" were popular with *onabe*, a female-bodied subject who "loves women and who chooses a woman as partner, but [whose] social and emotional identity is male" (2011: 377). *Rezu* were less likely to frequent these sites.

And other "lesbian bars were meeting places for *rezu, onabe, nyuu haafu* (transgender people), *nonke* (straight women), and *okame* (gay male friends of any of the above).

Rezu, onabe, nyuu haafu, nonke, and *okame* spatialize particular linkages between desire and identity within the sexual geography of Shinjuku Ni-choome – but not in identical ways. So a "lesbian"-centered description is distortive, but so is a description that treats the Japanese categories as if they too are unified domains.

In the case of *rezu*, the linkages circulate around female identification; however, *rezu* linguistic practices do not rely on the linguistic markers that ordinarily indicate "female identity" in Japanese speech. Instead, *rezu* draws on references to chronological age and social seniority, object choice/preference, and gendered authority, while suspending widely circulating associations between language, gender, and sexuality.

For example, Abe found that employees at *rezu* bars (of younger age and *rezu* identified) prefer to use the pronoun *jibun* ("one's self") for first person reference. As they explained to Abe, using the first person pronouns *boku* or *washi* would index close connections with masculine identity, and *rezu* do not self-describe as *onabe*. At the same time, these employees preferred using *jibun* over *watashi* and *atashi*, because they found those pronouns to be associated with "too much femininity" (Abe 2011: 379). In effect, using *jibun* allows these employees to self-enregister as *rezu*, hence as female, but also outside of the conventional heteronormative masculine/feminine binary.

A different refraction of gender, sexuality, age, and economic status was reported by a *rezu* who was a bit older (mid-thirties) than the bar employees and who worked at a graphic design firm. Unlike the bar employees, she was willing to use a first person pronoun (*atashi*) with more feminine associations in ordinary conversation, but then shift to *boku*, a first person pronoun with strongly masculine associations when a forceful, persuasive message or a message with strong emotion was required. So, rather than being suspended, the heteronormative male/female binary has been incorporated into *rezu* discourse, in this case organizing the basis for heteroglossic distinctions between ordinary and emotionally charged conversational reference.

That a difference in blue collar vs. white collar employment coincides with the contrast in age and linguistic practice here is also worth noting. This is additional evidence that those who claim *rezu* "identity" may also occupy different relationships to structures of (heteronormative) power and privilege; here again, while *rezu* may appear to be a single category of desire, appearances alone do not provide an adequate basis for social or linguistic analysis. What is needed is an analysis that will " . . . differentiate carefully between different kinds of difference" (Yuval-Davis 2006: 198) and then specify "how many social divisions are involved and/or which ones should be incorporated into the intersectionality process" (Yuval-Davis 2006: 201). As Abe's analysis suggests, paying attention to heteroglossic linguistic practice – that is, to linguistic differences " . . . intersecting [with] differently oriented social interests within one and the same sign community" (Vološinov 1972: 23) – provides a useful entry point for such analysis.

"Theorizing" Penetrative Sex in Delhi

Bakhtin alluded to some of these properties of heteroglossic refraction in his discussion of the dialogic properties of text. He wrote, for example: "the living utterance" – that is, concrete discourse that takes shape within a specific social and historical moment – " . . . cannot help but brush up against thousands of living dialogic threads, woven by socio-ideological consciousness around the given object of an utterance" (1981: 276–277). Of interest to Bakhtin are the cumulative properties of such encounters and also their diachronic implications: "The utterance arises out of this dialogue as a continuation of it and as a rejoinder to it; it does not approach the object from the sidelines" (1981: 277). Or, in Jaffe's wording, "all utterances carry the traces of past utterances [as well as] the social and cultural contexts of talk and action in which they were embedded" (2009: 20).

Lawrence Cohen's report of a "remarkable conversation" (2005: 286) between a group of same-sex identified men in Delhi (India) in 1993 shows how traces of past utterances combine with the social/cultural contexts of talk and action in current time, and how the resulting heteroglossic fusion of antecedent and current practice created a critical moment of intersectionality.

The conversation in question centered around the management of (safe) sex practice in response to the AIDS pandemic. Two people were the key participants in that conversation: Giti Thadani and Shivananda Khan. Thadani was a writer-philosopher and actively involved in a project aimed at retrieving nonpatriarchal themes in Vedic scripture. The project's goal was to recover fragments of heritage now absent from current discussions of Indian sexuality. Shivananda Khan, initially a self-styled mystic and ascetic, had recently become an AIDS activist and was now seeking innovative ways to fuse sexual identity and pan-Asian citizenship. Khan's wilful transgression of national boundaries made him a person of interest in the eyes of the Indian state. While he had been residing in India for some time, he was born in London and was of Pakistani heritage. Still, Khan saw his project as similar to Thadani's, in that both of them were attempting to develop a "critical non-western genealogy of relation, subject, object, and sex" (Cohen 2005: 286). Their shared modernist interests provided a starting point for the evening's discussion, even if Thadani and Khan approached modernist issues on quite different historical terms.

Cohen was also a participant in the conversation. He is an anthropologist who had spent several years becoming familiar with local cultures and sexualities in Varanasi and other locations in India; AIDS activism was a part of his research agenda and also his personal politics. Finally, there were also several younger men who were searching for a "gay life" in locations other than Delhi's public parks (the city's popular sites for gay cruising) or its party circuit (elite locations where these young men usually felt out-of-place). Alok, one of the young men, was also a local gay activist, but someone whose politics was shaped by practical experiences of struggle and not by abstract political discourse.

As the conversation began, Khan started praising the virtues of nonpenetrative sexual practice and soon Thadani and Khan began discussing the usefulness of nonpenetration as a strategy for HIV protection. They saw nonpenetration as an alignment with a primordial, but now forgotten Vedic logic (Thadani) but also as a strategy for diffusing lingering traces of patriarchal violence in their personal lives (Khan). Cohen internationalized the discussion by introducing a (Western) feminist critique of patriarchal violence, which strengthened the emerging intellectual consensus against penetrative sex.

The young men in the room had been sitting quietly as Thadani and Khan abstractly theorized diverse forms of male nonpenetrative intercourse. Alok was made increasingly uncomfortable by this discussion – so much so that he finally interrupted the two men mid-sentence, to exclaim: "But I like to be fucked" (Cohen 2005, 286).

Cohen's description of the conversation ends with Alok's spontaneous comment. While we do not know whether Alok's remark affected what was said about safe sex, Vedic restoration, and anti-patriarchal practice during the remainder of the evening's conversation, there are ample indications that it heightened the heteroglossic inflections that were already present in the exchange, and reshaped *how* the remainder of that conversation unfolded in other ways.

Both Thadani and Khan were (in Cohen's words), "radically self-made persons" (2005: 286) and, like Cohen, were familiar with the conventional logics of same-sex geography in Delhi. Like his friends, Alok had placed himself at distance from that geography and its logics, eschewing both the parks and the elite party circuit. And being actively engaged in locating and creating a new politics of place, Alok understandably did not find erotic intimacy to be a site that was for abstract, intellectual musings, much less a site amenable to temporal displacement. And Thadani and Khan, for their part, were busy making statements about appropriate sexual practice that paid no attention to what real-life sexual subjects (like Alok) had to say about desire, object choice, or satisfaction.

There is more at stake in Alok's comment than the message conveyed by the explicit statement of desire, and Halberstam's (2005) discussion of queer temporality offers a useful entry point for looking beyond appearances. As noted, Thadani and Khan are part of a social terrain shaped by willful compliance with normative authority and regulation, while Alok and his friends have placed themselves at a distance from that terrain. As Halberstam reminds us, there are "all kinds of people" who, like Alok and his friends,

> will and do opt to live outside of reproductive and familial time as well as on the edges of logics of labor and production, [and . . .] outside the logic of capital accumulation . . . ravers, club kids, HIV-positive barebackers, rent boys, sex workers, homeless people, drug dealers, and the unemployed.
>
> *Halberstam (2005: 10)*

This positioning "outside" and "on the edges" of conventional practice makes it unlikely that any of these people would voluntarily subordinate their sexual freedom to demands of consent and compliance coming from mainstream authority. For that reason,

> [they] could productively be called "queer subjects" in terms of the way they live (deliberately, accidentally, by necessity) during the hours when others sleep, and in the spaces (physical, metaphysical, and economic) that others have abandoned; and in terms of the ways they might work in the domains that others assign to privacy and family.
>
> *Halberstam (2005: 10)*

And, in some instances, a "queer" status is confirmed not only by spatial/temporal positioning but "by the risks they take, either by choice or by necessity." Halberstam includes here "the transgender person who risks his life by passing in a small town" and also "the queer performers who destabilize the normative values that make everyone else feel safe . . . " (2005: 10).

Alok qualifies as a "queer subject" under Halberstam's definition. Like his friends (who might also be termed "queer" here), Alok has placed himself outside of the conventional domains of Delhi's homosexual geography. Moreover, the effect of Alok's comment "destabilize[d] the normative values that were making everyone else (in the conversation) feel safe" (Halberstam 2005: 10). Stated more accurately, perhaps, Alok and his friends represent a particular type of queerness, one that " . . . stands against homogenizing and contests normativity, whether such practices descend from hegemonic heterosexual discourses or mainstream lesbian and gay politics" (Fotoupoulou 2012: 25, citing Seidman 1997).

The writer-philosopher and the ascetic-activist (plus the anthropologist) are excluded from Halberstam's rendering of "queer" in this case. Given what Cohen's remarks reveal about discursive practice, their freedom to transgress boundaries stems from their "insider" status – as established figures in the Delhi artistic and countercultural scene and from the protected visibility and privilege that this status affords them. Even if they self-identified as "queer," their claims to queerness would not be based on allegiance to marginal location, or on any other component of queerness as Halberstam describes them. Indeed, the refractions of linguistic and social practice attested throughout the conversation – who spoke, who was silent, whose arguments aligned, whose arguments conflicted, and so on – confirm that heteroglossic queerness can be powerfully dissident , even as it is one part of a larger intersectional display.

Current Contributions and Research

Racializing Erotic Desire in Gauteng

As Abe's and Cohen's examples have indicated, intersectionalities are connected to broader formations that Yuval-Davis calls "different kinds of difference" (2006: 198), which do not always correspond neatly with categories of sexual identity or with other predetermined points of social reference. Studies of heteroglossic refraction, as just suggested, provide useful entry points for specifying "how many [such] social divisions are involved and/or which ones should be incorporated into the intersectionality process" (Yuval-Davis 2006: 201).

This was one of the tasks that Milani addressed in his study of preferred terms for "self" and "other" used in personal advertisements posted to *Meetmarket*, a South African "on-line . . . meeting place for men who are seeking other men." *Meetmarket* charges no membership fee to those who use the website, thereby ensuring that the site "attract[s] as wide a pool of users as possible in the context of South Africa's high poverty rate" (2013: 616). To create a manageable corpus for this analysis, Milani limited his focus to postings from South Africa's Gauteng province (specifically from the Johannesburg-Pretoria area). A computer-assisted corpus scan then determined the most frequently used terms to describe the person posting the advertisement ("self") and the object-of-desire that was the target of the intended search ("other").

Milani's analysis of these terms and frequencies showed that MAN and GUY featured prominently as terms for *self* and for *desired other* in these personal ads (2013: 623). Importantly, part of what gave each term prominence was its distinctive collocation with references to racial identity. For example, in contexts of *self*-reference, "GUY collocates with *Indian* and *black*, whereas MAN is linked to *black* and *white*, "although "the collocational strength of the phrase *black man* (320.24) is much higher than that of *white man* (43.59)." The collocation link between MAN and the adjective *African* is also statistically strong in this corpus (log-likelihood value of 72.450).

MAN retained " . . . [its] robust tendency to co-occur with *black*" *in instances where* personal ads referred to the *desired other*. In those references, MAN also collocated regularly with references to men who are older and more mature, and with references to *real, hairy, strong,* and *married*. In contrast, GUY as a reference to *desired other* also collocated with "a plethora of racial descriptors (*white, black, Indian*), physical attributes (*hot, slim, good-looking*) and general characteristics (*decent, nice, fun, next-door*)." Moreover, GUY collocated regularly with references to younger men and with references to (*straight/str8*) *acting* and to *top* (the penetrating partner in anal sex).

That the personal ads make repeated references to this heavily masculinized framework of power, dominance, and control is understandable, perhaps, given that *Meetmarket* is an "on-line . . . meeting place for men who are seeking other men" (2013: 616); masculine men usually figure prominently in on-line homoerotic discourses of desire. Importantly, Milani finds, references to segregated racial preference has an even greater salience in these personal ads. Of the men who self-identified as Black in the personal ads, 59 percent " . . . overtly refer to blackness in their descriptions of the desired other," Milani reports, while a comparable 64.9 percent of the men who identified as white " . . . . explicitly state that they are looking for white men" (2013, 628).

To say that masculinity is racialized in roughly 60 percent of these on-line postings is to suggest that apartheid era practices of racial segregation are still being maintained in some sectors of postapartheid South African gay society – Black as well as white, Milani argues. Given how greatly South Africa has changed since the 1990s, the continuity of racial exclusion is troublesome. For Milani, this means that "queers" are not really "queer" in the South African case (2013: 629–630); if they were, desire would not embrace such strict segregation.

But roughly 40 percent of those posting ads on *Meetmarket* show a refusal to define desire in racially segregated terms. Instead, those ads use terms like GUY that embrace multiple racial categories or they refer to physical attributes without assigning them any racial coding. If, instead of generalizing, the analysis " . . . differentiates carefully between different kinds of [queer] difference" (Yuval-Davis 2006: 198), as attested within these texts, the analysis begins to suggest that homoerotic interests unfold heteroglossically across indications of race, gender, age, class, privilege, and other social refractions.

Intersectionality, Desire and Social Difference

But, more than that, differentiating between types of difference requires that the analysis explain *how* notions of shared desire become embedded within particular sites of linguistic and social difference.

While language and sexuality studies may be concerned with "fantasy, repression, pleasure, fear and the unconscious" and the other features that "arguably make sexuality sexuality" (Cameron and Kulick 2003: 105), these features and their linguistic representations cannot be discussed as if they were independent, self-contained elements of social experience. Fantasy, repression, pleasure and the like are "not merely reflected . . . through sign"; they are "refracted . . . by an intersecting of differently oriented social interests within one and the same sign community" (Vološinov 1972: 23). These context-specific refractions, along with the social interests that organize these refractions and assign them value, are part of the research agenda in language and sexuality studies.

As it is used in this argument, the reference to "community" has normative, regulatory associations, more so than references to spatial and physical locations. Cohen's example shows that participants and researchers may hold expectations of a cohesive, unified social group, but those expectations are all too often fractured by conflicting claims to belonging that include and exclude membership from each site. In homoerotic desire and pleasure, but quickly dissolved into competing discourses that pit Alok's enthusiastic endorsement of penetration against Vedic and feminist endorsements of sexual abstinence, and also pit those forms of abstinence against each other. Abe's and Milani's examples addressed the same issue. Both examples demonstrate that common interests disguise refractions, and that the social group seemingly united by common interests may prove, upon closer inspection, to be shaped by a refraction of interests rather than by their unified circulation.

Under these circumstances, discussion of (socio-)linguistic processes that ignore details of refraction – or submerge evidence of refractions in favor of references to a more inclusive linguistic process – are likely to be discussions that accept normative practices on face value. Nonnormative linguistic practices and the intersectionalities associated with them will likely be omitted from that discussion. And the same is true for an "intersectional analysis that has the potential to reveal both privilege and oppression" (Nash 2008: 10).

To cite one such example: Agha uses the following Lakhota (Sioux) sentence to make a distinction between enregistered and entextualized voice:

wąlewą	*hiyu*	*wele:*
male	female assertion	
interjection he came	of surprise	

Agha 2005: 48, citing Trechter (1995: 10)

The sentence contains an opening interjection ordinarily associated with "male speech" in Lakhota (*wąlewą*) and an adverb-final particle ordinarily associated with "female" speech (*wele:*). As in other linguistic contexts (Hall 2005), Lakhota syntax indicates a speaker's rejection of a rigidly defined gender-binary by allowing differing gender markers within the same syntactic form. Anticipating that linguistic fact, Trechter (1995) introduced her discussion of this example with the caption: "Lakhota atypically gendered speech." But Agha's commentary does not address atypicality. Instead, he explains how a bystander observing the comment is able to normalize its contradictory material, to ensure that "the enregistered voice associated with the form *wele:* – namely, that the speaker is female – is detachable" and "the entextualizing voicing effect – that *male speaker is maternal, affective etcetera* – is recoverable" (Agha 2005: 48, emphasis in original).

Trechter describes the social context surrounding this Lakhota sentence in the following terms: "a man sees his two-year-old nephew who he was not expecting at his house that evening and he calls to the child" (1995: 10). Agha's discussion of audience reception is consistent with that context, yet Agha's discussion does not consider the message that the bystander is constructing. And, as in any audience reception context, that message is multiple and refracted. There could be a "mixed gender" message, whereby a male speaker is enacting/embodying a typically female role; if so, that message might invite the bystander to implement the work of "repair" (e.g. some form of normalization along the lines that Agha describes). A "mixed gender" message might also invite the listener to accept the speaker's self-representation as a claim to sexuality rather than as a momentary disruption of gendered linguistic norms. Trechter provided examples (1995: 13–16) where associations between "mixed gender" clinic usage and "sexual preference of speaker" were the likely outcomes. In one of those examples, a female speaker of Lakhota in her mid-forties overheard her brother claim that "men say yo, and women say ye," and she replied: "Yeah, well I say *yo* and *yelo*, but I'm not gay. . . . " (1995: 14).

An entirely different reading is also possible: that a male-bodied subject is momentarily adopting attributes stereotypically associated with women. In the uncle/nephew example cited above, these can be labeled attributes of "caring," whose presence is indexed linguistically in this setting by *yele*. Importantly, however, the indexing has occurred in specific circumstances: the uncle expresses "caring" in relation to the nephew, in a setting where the presence of the nephew was unexpected, and where the uncle was able to voice his affective reactions to his surprise. In a public location – a grocery store, a religious meeting house, a government building – the uncle's reaction might have been phrased differently. In this sense, *yele* indicates performative and iterative as well as affective dimensions of the social moment, rather than attributes that are intrinsic to the social subject or attributes that copy practices of his gender-opposite. Trechter's (1995) comments are again worth citing. She recognizes that Lakhota scholars commonly describe *wąlewą as* a "male" interjection and describe *yele:* as a marker of "female" affect. But Trechter cautions against relying too heavily on predetermined gendered usage or on references to a predetermined gender binary as the sole framework for linguistic description. She explains: " . . . [I]t is clearly difficult to generalize the meaning of . . . affective and social connotations" associated with *wąlewą* and *yele:* .

> [T]he use of the clitics is dependent upon the age of the speaker and addressee, their kinship relation, knowledge of the language, social stance, and the perception of a third party (audience) in addition to the content of the utterance and affective disposition of the speaker in the speech event.
>
> *Trechter (1995: 16)*

Trechter continues, anticipating the appeal to intersectionality argued throughout this chapter:

> An operative scheme of gender deixis in Lakhota would necessarily require . . . [that] the particles which index gender must be interpreted in the overall ground of the speech event, which . . . is constantly created and changing according to the factors listed above and the interactive influence that constitutive gender exerts over the speech event.
>
> *Trechter (1995: 16)*

In other words, rather than simply commanding entextualized voicing or enregistered voice, as Agha proposes, forms like *wa̧lewa̧* and *wele:* identify sites where "kinds of difference" cluster, only one of which may be properly encoded in gendered or in gender-transgressive/sexualized terms. Foregrounding "gender" – or any type of entextualized/enregistered binary when multiple kinds of difference are evidenced at the site of refraction ignores the presence of heteroglossic refractions and their intersectional significance. Worse yet, it endorses speaking – and speech community – as a singular, normative formation.

Future Directions

Intersectionality as Queer Linguistics

Queer linguistics begins by refusing to make such singular endorsements. Instead, while work in queer linguistics often studies relationships between language and sexuality, it always addresses a broader question: how do structures of power assign vulnerability to some forms of sexuality while surrounding other forms of sexuality within privilege and protection (Motschenbacher 2011, Leap 2013, Milani 2013)?

Sexuality's alignments with race, ethnicity, class, age, citizenship, and other forms of heteroglossic refractions, as examined in this chapter's discussion of intersectionality, are some of the means through which vulnerability and privilege/protection are secured in those instances. Recall here how Abe's (2011) example shows linguistic differences combining with differences in appearance, and other social ascription, to distinguish the *rezu* working at the bar and the *rezu* working in a white collar setting. Language marks the distinction in this case, but linguistic practice is not the only element encoding difference, and queer linguistic inquiry cannot be defined solely by studies that connect the specifics of sexuality to the specifics of linguistic practices. Indeed, as Barrett (2003: 558) has argued, where sexuality is concerned, " . . . identity (and desire) might be found not in the use of a particular variety but rather in the particular choices and combinations of linguistic forms drawn from several distinct linguistic varieties."

Still, the discussion in this chapter has pushed for an analysis that moves beyond choices and combination across distinct varieties. The point has been to use heteroglossic refractions as an entry point for situating linguistic practice, linguistic choices, and combinations of forms within socially and historically constructed intersections of difference. It is through attention to intersectional formations that anthropological linguistics is able to determine (in Barrett's wording), "when and how language itself becomes an important resource for indexing one's sexual identities and desires" (2003: 558) but also why certain types of linguistic resources are shared unevenly within the same linguistic/social setting.

Acknowledgments

My thanks to Laura Jung, Nikki Lane, Elijah Edelman, and Riddhi Bhandari (American University, Washington, D.C.), David Peterson (University of Nebraska-Omaha), and Lucy Jones (Hull University, UK) for helpful comments during the preparation of this chapter.

Related Topics

7 Language Ideologies (Kroskrity); **8** Social Subordination and Language (Huayhua); **13** Language, Gender, and Identity (Pichler); **14** Discursive Practices, Linguistic Repertoire, and Racial Identities (Baugh); **15** Language and Racialization (Chun, Lo); **19** Language and Political Economy (McElhinny); **24** Discrimination via Discourse (Wodak).

References

Abe, Hideko. 2010. *Queer Japanese: Gender and Sexual Identities through Linguistic Practices*. New York: Palgrave-Macmillan.

Abe, Hideko. 2011. "Lesbian Bar Talk in Shinjuku, Tokyo." In *Language & Gender. A Reader* (2nd ed.), ed. Jennifer Coates and Pia Pichler, 375–383. Malden MA: Wiley-Blackwell.

Adams-Thies, Brian. 2012. "Fluid Bodies or Bodily Fluids: Bodily Reconfigurations in Cybersex." *Journal of Language and Sexuality* 1(2): 179–204.

Agha, Asif. 2005. "Voice, Footing, Enregisterment." *Journal of Linguistic Anthropology* 15: 38–59.

Bakhtin, Michael. 1981. "Discourse in the Novel." In *The Dialogic Imagination*, ed. Michael Holquist, transl. Caryl Emerson and Michael Holquist, 259–422. Austin: University of Texas Press.

Barrett, Rusty. 1999. "Indexing Polyphonous Identity in the Speech of African American Drag Queens." In *Reinventing Identities: The Gendered Self in Discourse*, eds. Mary Bucholtz, A.C. Liang, and Laurel A. Sutton, 313–332. New York: Oxford University Press.

Barrett, Rusty. 2003. "Models of Gay Male Identity and the Marketing of 'Gay Language' in Foreign-Language Phrasebooks for Gay Men." *Estudios de Sociolingüística* 4(2): 533–562.

Boellstorf, Tom. 2005. *The Gay Archipelago*. Princeton: Princeton University Press.

Cameron, Deborah and Don Kulick. 2003. *Language and Sexuality*. New York: Cambridge University Press.

Chauncey, George. 1986. *Gay New York*. Chicago: University of Chicago Press.

Cho, Sumi, Kimberlé Crenshaw, and Leslie McCall. 2013. "Toward a Field of Intersectionality Studies." *Signs* 38(4): 811–845.

Cohen, Lawrence. 2005. "The Kothi Wars: AIDS, Cosmopolitanism and the Morality of Classification." In *Sex in Development: Science, Sexuality and Morality in Global Perspective*, eds. Vincanne Adams and Stacy Leigh Pigg, 269–303. Durham: Duke University Press.

Crenshaw, Kimberlé. 1989. *Demarginalizing the Intersection of Race and Sex: A Black Feminist Critique of Antidiscrimination Doctrine, Black Feminist Theory and Antiracist Politics*. University of Chicago Legal Forum, 139.

Crenshaw, Kimberlé. 1991. "Mapping the Margins: Intersectionality, Identity Politics and Violence against Women of Color." *Stanford Law Review* 43(6): 1241–1299.

Edelman, Elijah Adiv. 2011. "'This Area Has Been Declared a Prostitution-Free Zone': Discursive Formations of Space, the State, and Trans Sex Workers' Bodies." *Journal of Homosexuality* 58(6–7): 848–864.

Edelman, Elijah Adiv. 2014. "'Walking While Transgender': Necropolitical Regulations of Trans Feminine Bodies of Colour." In *Queer Necropolitics*, eds. Jin Haritaworn, Adi Kuntsman, and Sylvia Posocco, 172–190. London: Routledge.

Fotopoulou, Aristea. 2012. "Intersectionality, Queer Studies and Hybridity: Methodological Frameworks for Social Research." *Journal of International Women's Studies* 13(2): 19–32.

Gaudio, Rudolph Pell. 2009. *Allah Made Us: Sexual Outlaws in an Islamic African City*. Malden MA: Wiley-Blackwell.

Halberstam, Judith. 2005. "Queer Temporalities and Post-Modern Geographies." In *In a Queer Time and Place: Transgender Bodies, Subcultural Lives*, 1–21. New York: New York University Press.

Halberstam, Judith. 2012. "Global Female Masculinities." *Sexualities* 15(3/4): 336–354.

Hall, Kira. 2005. "Intertextual Sexuality: Parodies of Identity, Class and Desire in Liminal Delhi." *Journal of Linguistic Anthropology* 15(1): 125–144.

Hennen, Peter. 2005. "Bear Bodies, Bear Masculinity: Recuperation, Resistance, or Retreat." *Gender and Society* 19(1): 25–43.

Jaffe, Alexandra. 2009. "Introduction: The Sociolinguistics of Stance." In *Stance: Sociolinguistic Perspectives*, ed. Alexandra Jaffe, 1-28. New York: Oxford University Press.

Jones, Lucy. 2010. *Dyke/Girl: Language and Identities in a Lesbian Group*. Basingstoke: Palgrave Macmillan.

King, Brian. 2008. "'Being Gay Guy, That's the Advantage': Queer Korean Language Learning and Identity Construction." *Journal of Language, Identity and Education* 7: 230–252.

Leap, William L. 2011. "Language, Gay Pornography, and Audience Reception." *Journal of Homosexuality* 58(6–7): 932–952.

Leap, William L. 2013. "Commentary II: Queering Language and Normativity." *Discourse and Society* 24(5): 643–648.

Leap, William L. and Tom Boellstorff, eds. 2004. *Speaking in Queer Tongues: Globalization and Gay Language*. Urbana: University of Illinois Press.

Levon, Erez. 2010. *Language and the Politics of Sexuality: Lesbians and Gays in Israel*. Basingstoke: Palgrave Macmillan.

Mann, Stephen L. 2011. "Drag Queen's Use of Language and the Performance of Blurred Gender and Racial Identities." *Journal of Homosexuality* 58(6–7): 793–811.

McCall, Leslie. 2005. "The Complexity of Intersectionality." *Signs* 30(3): 1771–1800.

Milani, Tommaso. 2013. "Are 'Queers' Really 'Queer'? Language, Identity and Same-Sex Desire in a South African Online Community." *Discourse and Society* 24(5): 615–633.

Morrish, Liz and Helen Sauntson. 2007a. "Discourse and Identity in a Corpus of Lesbian Erotics." In *New Perspectives on Language and Sexual Identity*, 112–136. Basingstoke: Palgrave Macmillan.

Morrish, Liz and Helen Sauntson. 2007b. *New Perspectives on Language and Sexual Identity*. Basingstoke: Palgrave Macmillan.

Motschenbacher, Heiko. 2011. "Taking Queer Linguistics Further: Sociolinguistics and Critical Heteronormativity Research." *International Journal of the Sociology of Language* 212: 149–179.

Motschenbacher, Heiko. 2012. "Negotiating Sexual Desire at the Eurovision Song Contest: On the Verge of Homonormativity?" In *Let's Talk about (Texts about) Sex*, eds. Marietta Calderón and Georg Marko, 287–299. Frankfurt am Main: Peter Lang.

Murray, David A. B., ed. 2009. *Homophobias: Lust and Loathing across Time and Space*. Durham: Duke University Press.

Murray, David A. B., ed. 2013. "Special Issue: Queering Borders – Language, Sexuality and Migration." *Journal of Language and Sexuality* 3(1): 1–155.

Nash, Jennifer. 2008. "Rethinking Intersectionality." *Feminist Review* 89: 1–15.

Peterson, David James. 2010. "'The Basis for a Free, Just and Stable Society': Institutional Homophobia and Governance at the Family Research Council." *Gender & Language* 4(2): 257–320.

Podesva, Robert. 2007. "Phonation Type as a Stylistic Variable: The Use of Falsetto in Constructing a Persona." *Journal of Sociolinguistics* 11(4): 478–504.

Podesva, Robert. 2011. "The California Vowel Shift and Gay Identity." *American Speech* 86(1): 32–86.

Provencher, Denis. 2007. *Queer French: Globalization, Language and Sexual Citizenship in France*. Aldershot: Ashgate.

Rahman, Momin. 2010. "Queer as Intersectionality: Theorizing Gay Muslim Identities." *Sociology* 44(5): 944–961.

Seidman, Steve. 1997. *Difference Troubles: Queering Social Theory and Sexual Politics*. Cambridge: Cambridge University Press.

Trechter, Sara. 1995. "Gender Myths in Native America: Gender Deictics in Lakhota." *Issues in Applied Linguistics* (Special Issue: Sociolinguistics and Language Minorities) 6(1): 5–22.

Vidal-Oriz, Salvador. 2011. "'Maricón,' 'Pájaro,' and 'Loca': Cuban and Puerto Rican Linguistic Practices, and Sexual Minority Participation, in U.S. Santería." *Journal of Homosexuality* 58: 901–918.

Vinning, Donald. 1986. *How Can You Come Out If You've Never Been In?* Trumansburg, NY: Crossing Press.

Vološinov, V.N. 1972. *Marxism and the Philosophy of Language*, transl. Ladislav Matejka and I.R. Titunik. New York: Seminar Press.

Weinberg, Martin S. and Colin J. Williams. 2010. "Men Sexually Interested in Transwomen (MSTW): Gendered Embodiment and the Construction of Sexual Desire." *Journal of Sex Research* 47(4): 374–383.

Wing, A.K. 1990. "Brief Reflections Toward a Multiplicative Theory and Praxis of Being." *Berkeley Women's Law Journal* 6: 181–201.

Yuval-Davis, Nira. 2006. "Intersectionality and Feminist Politics." *European Journal of Women's Studies* 13(3): 193–209.

Zimman, Lal. 2013. "Hegemonic Masculinity and the Variability of Gay-Sounding Speech: The Perceived Sexuality of Transgender Men." *Journal of Language and Sexuality* 2(1): 5–43.

Further Reading

Crenshaw (1989, 1991) are classic discussions of intersectionality. Cho et al. (2013) and Fotopoulou (2012) review general directions in theory. Motschenbacher (2011) outlines current and future directions in queer linguistics. Abe (2010), Levon (2010) and Jones (2010) are case studies that connect sexuality/intersectionality with queer linguistic practice.

13
Language, Gender, and Identity

Pia Pichler

Introduction

Whereas the ideology of women's and men's language use as categorically and innately different remains significant in popular debate, most language and gender research in the last couple of decades has problematized the view that we are somehow pre-programmed to speak in a specific way because we are either women or men. The notion that gender is neither fixed nor homogeneous but that it is 'constructed' in specific sociocultural, historical and situational contexts is not entirely new but has constituted an ever-increasing influence on language and gender theory, methodology and research.

This chapter will capture some of the complexity, heterogeneity and even contradictory nature of gender performances that are at the core of the social constructionist approach to language and gender, with a particular focus on the rich and varied talk of adolescents and young adults. This focus will allow for a fresh perspective on many of the most important developments in the field at the same time as presenting data from an age range of speakers that will be of particular interest to many of the readers of this handbook.

The first section of the chapter will trace the development of social constructionist thinking about language and gender. The second section will clarify the main two aspects of language that this chapter will focus on, (conversational) style and discourse, providing a brief overview of early language and gender research on conversational style. The third and main section considers a range of important issues on the basis of recent language and gender research. It introduces language and gender studies that highlight what can be gained from moving beyond a discussion of conversational style to include a focus on discourse. It discusses the interplay of gender with other sociocultural variables and the contributions ethnographic and community of practice studies have made to capture the heterogeneity of gendered performances. The section will also highlight how scholarship on language and sexuality, as well as on gender structures, has shaped our recent understanding of language, gender and identity. The chapter will conclude with some recommendations for future practice in language and gender research.

Historical Perspectives

Several different approaches have influenced the thinking of language and gender scholars adopting a 'social constructionist' approach to their work, including post-structuralist theories about subject positions created in discourse (Foucault 1972) and about performativity (Butler 1990) but also ethnomethodological ideas about people's own sense-making of everyday action and identities (Garfinkel 1967).[1] Both Conversation Analysis (CA, e.g. Schegloff 1997), rooted in ethnomethodology, and Judith Butler's (1990) performative model of gender have been particularly influential, but differ vastly in their understanding of and approach to the study of language and gender. The latter is interested in gendered performances and their constraints, thereby inviting an engagement with gendered ideologies and structures that may not be directly visible in spoken interactional data but nevertheless shape the talk and identity constructions of social actors. CA takes a decidedly bottom-up approach to the discussion of (gender) identity and warns against analysts imposing their a priori assumptions (e.g. about the relevance of macro-social categories such as gender) on the data. It aims to focus the analysis mostly on the interactional data (and not beyond) in order to examine participants' own understanding of the interaction, the relevant context and (interactional) positions in their talk. The debate between proponents of CA vs. performativity studies has been a lively and often antagonistic one in the language and gender field (e.g. Benwell and Stokoe 2006; Cameron 2005; Holmes 2007; Wetherell 1998). CA has contributed valuable micro-analyses of turn-taking, of the way speakers position themselves from one turn to another in interaction, and, together with Membership Categorisation Analysis (e.g. Benwell and Stokoe 2006: 64–86) of interactional stances and local identity positions that may have been overlooked in discussions of macro-social categories of gender, social class, ethnicity, etc. Of course, micro-linguistic discourse analysis of natural talk has never been the exclusive territory of CA. Moreover, both linguistic anthropological/ethnographic research, with its focus on cultural context (e.g. Hall 2009), and pragmatic understandings of language concentrating on inferential meaning (e.g. Cameron 2005), argue that a pure CA restriction to speakers' explicit orientations to the relevance of gender misses out on important levels of meaning-making.

In their seminal paper on sociocultural linguistics Bucholtz and Hall (2005) resolve some of these methodological debates by drawing on the concept of indexicality to show that there are many different ways in which gender can emerge as relevant in language, including overt references to gender as well as very indirect ideological associations between language forms and gender. Elinor Ochs (1992) famously argued that there are only very few linguistic forms (such as kinship terms) in the English language that index the gender of a speaker directly. Much more common is the occurrence of indirect indexicality, which relates "gender to language through some other social meaning indexed" (Ochs 1992: 342–343). Thus, for example, linguistic forms first index different stances, such as toughness, or acts such as 'swearing', or activities such as 'gossip'. These stances, acts and activities then in turn come to index macro-identities such as gender. Although unrelated, one of Judith Butler's most frequently quoted explanations of the concept of performativity can shed light on the formation of indexical links over time: "Gender is the repeated stylization of the body, a set of repeated acts within a rigid regulatory frame which congeal over time to produce the appearance of substance, of a 'natural' kind of being" (Butler 1990: 33). The congealing that Butler refers to can also be thought of as the emergence of indexical ties that link linguistic practices to stances and, ultimately, to gender.

Critical Issues and Topics

The various extracts from language and gender studies discussed in this chapter will exemplify many different identity relations and indexical processes summed up by Bucholtz and Hall (2005). Some will attend to gendered meanings of phonological or grammatical variation, although the central focus of the chapter will be on conversational style and discourses.

Language and gender studies' interest in conversational style was already very well developed before current social constructionist scholarship began to view it as a resource for identity construction. It is already evident in Robin Lakoff's (1975) pioneering work on what she sees as women's tentative use of language. Subsequent critiques of her introspective work are framed as empirical studies of recorded and transcribed extracts of women's and men's talk, focusing on interruptions and minimal responses such as 'mhm', (tag) questions such as 'isn't it' and hedges such as 'maybe' and 'you know'. Several studies explore patterns of conversational dominance exerted by men over women in heterosexual couples, arguing that interactional asymmetry in private contexts reflects power differences between women and men at large (e.g. Fishman 1980; DeFrancisco 1991; Zimmerman and West 1975). This so-called 'dominance' model of language and gender stands in opposition to what has become known as the 'difference model', which highlights and even celebrates gendered (conversational) styles, i.e. women's collaboration and men's competition (Coates 1996; Goodwin 1988; Pujolar 1997; Tannen 1990).

This interest in conversational style remains at the centre of much current language and gender research taking a social constructionist approach and will feature prominently in the discussion of specific examples of research into the language of young women and young men in this chapter. However, some of these studies have extended their focus to other aspects of communicative and even non-verbal style and several have incorporated a focus on different types of discourse (e.g. sexist, feminist . . .) that speakers voice when they interact with one another. 'Discourse' here refers to language practice that is shaped by and has the potential to shape or even constitute ideologies, social practices and identities (e.g. Gee 1996: 127). By examining discourses and features of (conversational) style in the talk of usually comparatively small groups of speakers, language and gender scholars have been trying to capture how speakers 'construct' identities or are constructed (as gendered), as the remainder of this chapter will demonstrate.[2]

Current Contributions and Research

From Conversational Style to Discourses

Both Deborah Cameron (1997) and Jennifer Coates (1999) combine an interest in conversational style with an analysis of (gendered) discourses in their work on the informal talk of young speakers. Coates highlights the interplay of language, gender and age by showing how the talk of a group of young, white, middle-class women changes as they get older. When the girls are 12 years old their talk does not exhibit much conversational support, nor any mitigation or hedging; moreover, the girls interrupt one another when they want to speak. By the time the girls are 15 years old they have acquired the type of collaborative conversational style that Coates's (1996) pioneering research found to be characteristic of white, middle-class, adult women friends. They develop topics jointly over several minutes and mirror one another's self-disclosures; they also show their support with minimal responses and take each other's face needs into consideration with the use of hedges such as 'sort of' and 'like'. The girls' talk at different ages contains traces of a range of different discourses, including scientific, maternal, romantic, repressive and feminist discourses, which allow them to experiment with different and frequently contradictory femininities. However, Coates also argues that the data of the girls at 15 contains much less resistance to and subversion of dominant discourses (e.g. about their bodies or about being 'a bitch') than when they were younger. Coates therefore asks whether the gender positions the girls in this particularly privileged group construct for themselves in their talk are in fact as liberated as one may assume.

Deborah Cameron (1997) discusses the talk of five 21-year-old, white, male, US university students from suburban, middle-class backgrounds. Despite engaging in gossip and using some features of conversational support such as hedging, repetition and latching onto the utterance of the previous speaker, the young men are far from resisting dominant gender norms, as Cameron points out. On the contrary, their gossip about women or fellow students, including one they call 'that really gay guy', shows their clear alignment with hegemonic masculinity, which informs the young men's views about the speech, clothing and bodies of "real" men (Cameron 1997: 53–54). Cameron's analysis demonstrates that conversational collaboration and competition are not necessarily mutually exclusive (see also Eckert 1993; Sheldon 1997). Above all, the study highlights the importance of considering discourse(s) in language and gender studies: "I hope that it might make us think twice about the sort of analysis that implicitly seeks the meaning (and sometimes the value) of an interaction among men or women primarily in the style, rather than the substance, of what is said" (Cameron 1997: 62).

The importance of a heterosexuality discourse for the construction of hegemonic masculinities is also evident in Scott Kiesling's (2002) work on male US fraternity members. By participating in a weekly ritualised narrative event that relies on the telling of 'fuck stories', or by using gendered and frequently derogatory address terms such as 'honey', 'Hazel', 'bitch' or 'bitchboy', the young men's gender performances display both their hetereosexuality and their superiority over women and other men.

The research discussed in this section captures what can be gained from introducing a focus on discourses into a discussion of gender and conversational style. The next section will show what can be gained from moving beyond the talk of young, white, middle-class speakers.

The Interplay of Gender with Other Sociocultural Identities

Social constructionist critiques of what have been branded 'essentialist' notions of language and gender (see Holmes 2007) encourage us to think about how gender interacts with other factors and aspects of identity, including social status and ethnic culture. Early research on conflict negotiation among adolescents found that, unlike (white) middle-class girls, working-class girls make use of face-threatening acts such as playful disputes and insults (Eder 1990; Goodwin 1990; Hasund and Stenström 1997). These findings suggest that the lack of direct, unmitigated challenges found in Coates's (1999) research in older adolescent girls could be attributed at least partly to their middle-class background.

Pichler's (2006, 2009) research captures the use of multifunctional teasing in a group of Bangladeshi girls from a working-class area of the East End of London. In their teasing episodes the girls display verbal toughness, but teasing also allows them to bond and it constitutes a fun activity in its own right.

Extract 1: *I don't think so*:: (Pichler 2009: 117–119)[3]

(1)
Rahima   {*mocking*}[WE AIN'T **THAT**] **DUMB**

(2)
Ardiana   [we know Rahima you are]
Rahima   we're (in comprende) {*mock Spanish/French accent*}
Varda   YOU WAS TAL[KING QUITE DUMB]

(3)
Ardiana   (1) we know you are {teasing}
Rahima   (1) /what   (-) **oh::** that's because **you** are

(4)
Ardiana   I don't think so somehow I (get) **good** grades {sl. provoc.}
?   {faint chuckle}

(5)
Ardiana   in English you know (.) I've got A-star (.)   [/right]
Rahima   {mock impressed} (.) wo: [::w]

(6)
Ardiana   .hhh {nasal} [I think] I (said yo[u:-)]   [(are
Rahima   [wow]   [yeah] that's [why

(7)
Ardiana   you doing that)]
Rahima   you're doing *Found]ation yeah I understand (-)
Dilshana   {laughs}
*foundation level of exam

(8)
Ardiana   I did *Higher **tu janishne (-)   really >what do
Rahima   {higher pitch}\really
?   {yawn}
*higher level of exam; **Bengali: "do you know?"

(9)
Ardiana   you [mean really<]   [REALLY REALLY]   did /I::
Rahima   [you done Founda]tio[n with me /right]

(10)
Ardiana   >I don't [think] so (somehow)< {teasing}   >I don't think soo:: ::<
Rahima   [yeah]   yeah you di::d {teasing}

It is tempting to interpret the use of competitive teasing captured in this extract as simply reflecting the speakers' working-class backgrounds (for an in-depth discussion of this transcript see Pichler 2006; Pichler 2009: 119–120). From a constructionist perspective it becomes more appropriate to ask how the girls use competitive (and other types of) teasing to construct their identities. For the girls in this group, who frequently comment on the 'loudmouth' culture of their peers in their form-group, teasing constitutes a resource to construct themselves as tough. This toughness, together with the girls' pronounced anti-school stances, indexes a type of ladette femininity, which is valued in their immediate peer group. It is also worth noting that these tough femininities allow the British Bangladeshi girls in this group to position themselves in opposition to stereotypical notions of young "Asian" femininity.

This tough femininity is neither the only important subject position for these young Bangladeshi girls nor is it equally valued by all young British working-class women. Another group of Anglo-Irish young working-class girls from the same school does not only refrain from tough teasing but also distances itself from stereotypical representations of working-class femininity, e.g. the school truant, the promiscuous girl or future teenage mother (see Pichler 2009).

Instead the girls present themselves as sheltered and responsible, aspiring to what Skeggs (1997) describes as respectable middle-class femininity.

Ironically, this respectable and sheltered middle-class femininity is positioned as much less desirable in a third group of young women from one of the most prestigious private schools in the UK (Pichler 2009). The talk of these young women highlights their efforts to index what to them are alternative forms of cultural capital, in the form of 'cool' non-conformity with school values or streetwise knowledge of music and drugs. This amount of coolness needs to be pitched carefully, in order not to be mistaken for 'toughness'. That is, familiarity with soft drugs is acceptable, as is moaning about school, whereas drug addiction or truanting are not. Moreover, the girls' gendered performances as 'cool' and 'real' are balanced by their displays of dominant cultural capital (Bourdieu 1984; see also Skeggs 1997) in their conversations about literature, arts and science, which have to be seen in the context of their privileged (economic, social) backgrounds and life styles as well as their trajectories towards elite university education.

Research that aims to capture some of the ways in which gender intersects with other social categories has often been designed as small-scale, ethnographic studies of 'communities of practice', as the next section will show.

Heterogeneity of Gender Identities: Ethnography and Communities of Practice

The concept of the community of practice (Lave and Wenger 1991) was introduced to language and gender research by Penelope Eckert and Sally McConnell-Ginet (1992). Penny Eckert's now classic ethnographic study of jocks and burnouts, the two most prominent communities of practice in US high schools, exemplifies this practice-based, local view of gender. Eckert describes both linguistic (phonological and grammatical) and social practices (including clothing, participation in sports and/or extra-curricular activities, use of alcohol and/or drugs). Differently from what might be expected from previous variationist research that showed women using more standard variants than men (e.g. Trudgill 1974), burnout girls actually use more advanced, that is vernacular (or non-standard) variants of the variables (uh), (ay) and (ae) than any of the other (jock or burnout) boys (Eckert 2011). Eckert argues that for the burnout girls, who lack some of the more physical resources (including street fights) available to their male peers, the linguistic capital in the form of the (local) vernacular of Detroit becomes particularly important in the construction of their burnout identities. Clearly, gender interacts with the local identity categories of jocks and burnouts, which themselves represent local interpretations of social class, with jocks displaying the very pro-school values aimed at middle-class trajectories that are so vehemently rejected by the burnouts.

Mary Bucholtz's (1999) subsequent work on a third community of practice in the US high school shows how young Californian women identifying as nerds avoid the use of certain linguistic practices (including slang and non-standard lexis) to distance themselves from 'cool' teenagers such as the burnouts and jocks. At the same time nerds use other linguistic practices such as Greco-Latinate lexical items and hypercorrect phonological forms to construct their identities as intelligent.

Robert Lawson's ethnographic work on young Scottish masculinities explores the identity constructions of fourteen 15-year-old pupils, identifying four different communities of practice in the school, which he labels "the Alternatives, the Sports, Neds and Schoolies" (Lawson 2013: 373). In his 2013 paper Lawson focuses on the masculinity of the Neds, which relies on (frequently also physical) displays of traditional working-class toughness, especially in their talk about fights.

Lawson's discussion of his data is at pains to avoid a characterization of the young men's talk as purely competitive. For example, in the following extract Phil's friend Nathan needs to resolve the dilemma of insisting that he actually does remember Phil crying ('greeting') whilst preserving his friend's face by allowing him to hold on to his performance of tough masculinity.

Extract 2: 'I really wasn't greeting' (from Lawson 2013: 382)[3,4]

1	Phil:	So I- I re:ally really wasn't greeting,
2		just because-
2		(.)
4		[S-
5	Nathan:	[Aye, but it did look like it.
6		I- I- I wasn't saying you were greeting,
7		but it did look like you were greeting.
8	Phil:	(.)
9		No, it's think- it's just cause my eyes,
10		it looks like [I'm greeting.
11	Nathan:	[Ah but-
12	Phil:	Do I look as if I'm greeting now?
13	Nathan:	(.)
14		N:o but-
15		No but I did see something coming [out-
16	Phil:	[No, it's
17		because of the colour
18		of my eyes are always [like all thingied.
19	Nathan:	[I know.
20	Phil:	Look as if I'm greeting now?
21	Nathan:	No, but I did see something.

What may stand out for many readers of Lawson's data is the dominance of hegemonic masculinity based on (physical) toughness in this group of Glaswegian Neds. However, Lawson's main point is that the young men avoid direct and open confrontation in various ways, including Nathan mitigating some of his challenges and subsequently offering support to his friend's version of events by stating that he is familiar with Phil's problem of watering eyes being misinterpreted as crying by others. Lawson highlights the importance of tracing subtle shifts in the positioning of speakers (see also Wetherell 1998), caused by their efforts to preserve their friendship whilst contesting one another's version of events in their performance of tough masculinities.

Recent ethnographic research has also provided insight into performances of tough femininities, which may at times offer young women alternative gender positions (e.g. Moore 2004; Pichler 2009; Mendoza-Denton 2008). In Germany, Inken Keim (2007) captures the performance of tough, rebellious femininities in a group of German-Turkish girls, the 'Powergirls', from a Turkish migrant neighbourhood in Mannheim's inner city.

Drawing on ethnographical data including biographical interviews and long-term observation, Keim (2007) argues that the identity performances of young Turkish-German women are heavily interconnected with their educational trajectories. The Powergirls belong to a 10–20 percent minority of young Turkish-Germans who commute out of their local immigrant neighbourhood to pursue better educational and professional pathways. Particularly in Gymnasium (grammar school) the percentage of pupils of migration backgrounds is extremely low and "for the first time in their lives, they experience the negative image of the Turkish migrants in terms of abuse such as *scheiß ausländer* ('fucking foreigner') and *dreckiger* ('dirty') or *dummer Türke* ('stupid Turk')" (Keim 1997: 159). Together with their new linguistic and educational demands, the experience of this new environment is described by many as *Schock des Lebens* ('shock of their lives') and it is against this backdrop that the Powergirls formed as a group at the age of 12–13.

Whereas much recent work on language and ethnicity has celebrated the performance of hybrid ethnic cultures (e.g. Pichler 2009), Keim's data and discussion also focus on the struggle of the Powergirls against the alienation they experience both from their German school and from models of deferential Turkish femininity they associate with their parents' generation.

Extract 3: 'they are so terribly obsequious' (Keim 2007: 164) [5]

1   AR: die sind so furschbar unterwürfig * bedienen die älteren *
      'they are so terribly obsequious they wait on the older ones

2   AR: servieren tee↓ * und gehn wieder still in die ecke↓
      serve them tea and then they go quietly into their corner

3   AR: des findisch einfach schre"cklisch↓
      I think that is really terrible'.

The Powergirls' rebellion is expressed at different levels of style, including clothing, make-up and piercings, dating of boys, clubbing and experimenting with drugs. Their linguistic style includes disruptive turn-taking behaviour, ritual insults and coarse language. It includes formulas such as *halts maul langer* ('shut up, man'), *verpiss dich* ('piss off') and *siktir lan* ('fuck you, man'), or terms of abuse such as *orospu* ('whore') and *orospu çocuğu* ('child of a whore') (Keim 2007: 168). Several of these practices orient to the talk of young Turkish men, including the use of verbal duelling and coarse sexual formulas, positioning the girls in opposition to traditional Turkish femininity at the same time as distancing them from teachers and their school. Their opposition to their German school world is also expressed in their choice of language varieties, particularly their choice of 'Mannheim Turkish', used by second- and third-generation speakers, especially in interaction with their elders, and German-Turkish mixing, which was the preferred in-group code choice for the Powergirls. Monolingual German only gradually gains in importance for the Powergirls and frequently goes hand in hand with the acquisition of a more polite conversational style. The girls first accept this style into their repertoire in interaction with their favourite German-Turkish youth worker in their youth club and monolingual German then gained in prominence as they became older and began to enter professional and higher educational domains.

Keim's work shows how the Powergirls' repertoire of style develops over time, and how they were increasingly able to mobilize different styles appropriate to the requirements of the context. Hand in hand with this change of style went a change in the girls' self-perception from the rebellious Turkish Powergirl "to a socially and professionally successful" young German-Turkish woman (Keim 2007: 171).

There are now several examples of ethnographic studies of ethnic minority femininities that investigate young women's performances of rebelliousness and (verbal) toughness, which position them in opposition to traditional models of femininity encouraged by their parents' generation (e.g. Keim 2007; Mendoza-Denton 2008; Pichler 2009). However, there does not appear to be a consensus about the extent to which this toughness ultimately empowers the girls. Mendoza-Denton's (2008: 169) discussion of Latina gang girls in a Californian high school highlights the emancipatory potential of a discourse of "being macha", which is all about "taking charge of one's own self". On the other hand, Keim's study suggests that whilst the Powergirls retain many of their original markers of their adversarial and mixed language style for their in-group communication, it is their acquisition of a more mainstream style of (polite monolingual) German that ultimately empowers them by allowing them access to higher education and professional success.

Indexing Gender and Sexuality

The interplay of gender and sexuality has already been captured in several of the studies discussed above, for example in Cameron's 1997 analysis of the talk of male US college students, which positions the speakers as "red-hot blooded heterosexual males" (Cameron 1997: 61). Celia Kitzinger (2005) demonstrates that more subtle displays of heterosexuality are contained in many everyday conversations, for example in references to spouses and (pronominal) positioning of the speaker as part of a couple. Language and gender studies have begun to extend their scope to include what could be described as performances of non-normative (gender and sexual) identities. Kira Hall (2003: 375) sums up this important shift to include what she calls 'exceptional speakers' in the following way:

> The practice-based and ideological models of language and gender that developed in response to these critiques, such as queer linguistics, seek not to describe how women's language use differs from men's, or how homosexuals' language use differs from heterosexuals', but to document the diverse range of women's and men's linguistic repertoires as developed within particular contexts.

This focus on the heterogeneity of gender performances, on queering gender, stands out in Rusty Barrett's now seminal (1999) paper on African American drag queens. In this paper Barrett highlights the difference between 'performed gender' and 'self-categorized gender' on the basis of drag queens who "maintain 'male' gender identity alongside 'female' gender performances" (Barrett 1999: 318). Barrett also shows that it would be a mistake to interpret the drag use of white women's style as performance of white femininities. White women's style, in addition to African American Vernacular English and gay male speech, are all used in the performance of 'polyphonous' drag queen identities in this specific context.

Barrett's work thus asks us to consider how (gender) identities are indexed in a specific situation. This question of indexicality is central to Kira Hall's (2009) ethnographic work in New Delhi with young women who identify as 'boys' rather than as 'lesbians'. Both 'boys' and 'lesbians' participated in a support group for 'women who are attracted to women' at a New Delhi non-government organisation, the 'Centre' (Hall 2009: 140). Whereas all the participants were bilingual and from what can be described as middle-class backgrounds, the performance of their sexualities intersected in interesting and different ways with gender and social class.

Extract 4: *'She calls me woman!* (Hall 2009: 146–147)[6]

```
1 Liz:    I'm saying for the individuals in this group.
2         today.
3         who we are (.) sitting with.
4         Is there no room to be a fe:male
5         and yet to be: (.) masculine.
6         in that role.
```

7		to ↑b<u>e</u>: like that.
8 Jess:		I th[ink]-
9 Liz:		[Why] doesn't society allow for that.
10		Why can't we b<u>e</u> like tha[t.]
11 Jess:		[Well] because
12		that's -ss uh one of those things,
13		You have to follow a p<u>a</u>ttern.
14		You're a woman so you have to
15		↑[BE::: this this this] this.
16 Liz:		[Yeah but ↑WHY::.] Why?
17		You're- you're also- you're a woman,
18		but you are attracted to other w<u>o</u>men.
19		That's not acceptable to society,
20		But you <u>a</u>re b<u>e</u>ing like that,
21 Jess:		<quietly, rapidly> <gālī detī hai.
22		mujhe wom<u>a</u>n [boltī hai.]>
23 Liz:		<falsetto> <[↑Well just]> [[feh-]]
24 Jess:		<loudly, rapidly> <[[gālī]] detī hai.
25		wom<u>a</u>n boltī hai mujhe.
26		tereko abh<u>i</u> ag lagtī hũ mai͂.>
27 Sarvesh:		[<laughs>]
29 Priti:		[<laughs>]
30 Bijay:		[<laughs>]
31 Liz:		<rapidly> <NO. GUYS.>
32		I am just asking the question

Hindi translation (for lines 21–32)

Jess:	<quietly, rapidly> *She insults me.* *She calls me* woman!>
Liz:	<falsetto> <[↑Well just]> [[feh-]]
Jess:	<loudly, rapidly> <*She insults me.* Woman *she calls me!* *Now you think I'm fire (to burn you alive)*>?

In this extract Jess performs a particular type of masculinity that is, as Hall argues, recognized by the other boys. Male physicality is important to the boys, who long for moustaches and sexual reassignment surgery. Liz, the group facilitator, on the other hand offers to the boys a very Western, post-modern understanding of gender, suggesting that masculinity does not necessarily require male bodies. Jess's rejection of this model of performed (sexual and gender) identity goes hand in hand with a switch to Hindi. This switch does not only index a particular adversarial stance, but it exploits ideological associations of the use of Hindi (vs. English) to index a masculinity that is marked by "its defiance of upper class norms of politeness" (Hall 2009: 159) and therefore stands in opposition to the lesbian-identified participants of the Centre, whose language preference is English.

Hall's linguistic anthropological research design allows her to see how language ideologies (about Hindi vs. English) play out at the local level and are used by speakers as resources to index sexual, gender and class identities in specific contexts. Like Keim's work it presents an important example of (language and gender) research that balances a focus on local language (and gender) practices with an interest in larger-scale structures, ideologies of language, gender and social class.

Gender Structures

Although studies of situated, local performances of gender have dominated the field for a long time, debates about gender structures (e.g. ideological, political and economic) have never entirely gone away and have featured particularly in language and gender studies interested in institutional settings. Pioneering studies of institutional talk, such as West (1984) on doctor–patient talk, orient to the 'dominance' model of gender and are framed as studies of (asymmetrical) turn-taking rights and practices, frequently aiming at establishing if gender overrides occupational roles or vice versa (e.g. Woods 1989). Although studies of institutional practices of turn-taking or interactional dominance remain significant, the social constructionist model of gender has encouraged researchers also to explore the many different ways in which gender interacts with occupational or institutional roles in specific settings, or communities of practice (e.g. Holmes and Schnurr 2006; Ostermann 2003; Shaw 2006). Some of this research has focused particularly on the gender structures that frame and constrain the performances of speakers. For example, Susan Ehrlich's work on Canadian trial discourse in sexual assault or sexual harassment cases demonstrates how the agency of the speaker is constrained by identities being imposed onto the speaker (e.g. as 'participants in consensual sex', Ehrlich 2006) or by powerful gender stereotypes (e.g. of women not communicating their lack of sexual consent clearly enough, Ehrlich 1998). This type of research shows how gender ideologies can have "the effect of obscuring and neutralizing the power dynamics between women and men" in situations of sexual assault (Ehrlich 1998: 169).

Language and gender research in educational settings allows for an insight into ideological constraints on gender performances of young speakers. Julia Davies's (2003) work on 14-year-old pupils in the north of England analyses the ways in which single sex groups tackle work set by the teacher in their English lessons. Whereas the girls adopt a highly collaborative style that allows everyone to engage fully with the literary work, boys who want to do the same are frequently met with a display of what Davies calls 'Macho discourse', which, for example, positions an in-depth exploration of a poem as 'gay' or 'queer'. Davies presents evidence of what appears to be an overarching gendered conversational style in the English classroom, constrained by dominant gender ideologies that position "conformity to educational expectations [as] feminine" (Davies 2003: 129). Davies's research, or that of Sian Preece (2009) on performances of laddish masculinity by young working-class British Bangladeshi men in higher educational settings, is very much concerned with the constraints on gendered behaviours that are likely to affect not only the discourse practices but also, potentially, the educational success of the speakers, particularly if the display of laddishness cannot be compensated by a display of more traditional cultural capital, a balancing act that may be easier for students from elite backgrounds, as Preece (2009: 134) observes (but see Keim 2007).

Future Directions

Social constructionist language and gender research in the last couple of decades has foregrounded the heterogeneity of gender performances, highlighting the ways in which gender interacts with other aspects of (sociocultural) identity such as ethnicity, age, social class and sexuality. Frequently the focus of this research has been on interactional stances or the local, situated practices of speakers that have been studied from an ethnographic and/or community of practice perspective. This research varies in the extent to which it balances an exploration of the local (gender) performances of identities in spoken interaction with an examination of macro-social constraints on these performances. The fact that the prime source of data for most language and gender scholars is precisely language (rather than, for example, data on women's representation in politics or managerial posts, gendered access to education or distribution of wealth – see Mills and Mullany 2011: 23–24) may well explain the recent focus on speaker agency in language and gender studies,[7] particularly in work on informal spoken interaction. However, as Cameron (2009: 15) argues: "To make sense of what [humans] are doing as creative, agentive language users, we also have to consider the inherited structures (of belief, of opportunity or the lack of it, of desire and of power) which both enable and constrain their performances".

Language and gender research may do well to examine more closely the relationship between the agency that speakers display on a micro-linguistic level and the (constraints on the) agency of speakers beyond the local context of their interactions. For example, we may want to ask to what extent the instances of interactive resistance to dominant gender norms and performances (e.g. of heterosexist or tough masculinity, of respectable or even servile femininity) that were evident in the data of many of the studies discussed above are indicative or constitutive of grander-scale disruptions of the gender order. Equally we may want to evaluate the performances of the cool or tough stances adopted by young women and men that have been described in this chapter against the background of the social norms, physical acts, spaces and structures that frame the 'performances' of gender and sexual identities. Some of the studies discussed in this chapter have already managed to balance these micro- and macro-perspectives on gender performances. Other language and gender scholars may feel that cross-disciplinary collaborations will allow us to explore the complexities of gender performances more fully.

Related Topics

12 Language, Sexuality, Heteroglossia, and Intersectionality (Leap); **14** Discursive Practices, Linguistic Repertoire, and Racial identities (Baugh); **16** Analyzing Interactive Discourse (Brody).

Notes

1 For a more detailed overview see Bucholtz and Hall 2005: 588 and Cameron 2005: 323.
2 Although many language and gender students interpret the term 'construction' to connote speaker agency above the level of consciousness, it is important to bear in mind that this can, but does not necessarily have to be, the case; see Bucholtz and Hall's excellent summary (e.g. 2005: 606); or Cameron and Kulick (2003) who adopt the differentiation between 'identity' (conscious) and 'identification' (non-conscious).
3 Extract 1 (Pichler 2009) and Extract 2 (Lawson 2013) use the same symbols for transcription. However, only Extract 1 is based on the stave system: sequential talk is represented from left to right rather than from top to bottom, i.e. whatever is said first is found on the very left within a stave, rather than at the very top. Simultaneous speech is represented by vertically aligned utterances within one stave. Detailed transcription conventions for Extracts 1 and 2 are:

?	identity of speaker not clear
{laughter}	non verbal information
xxxxxx{laughing}	paralinguistic information qualifying underlined utterance
[.....]	beginning/end of simultaneous speech
(......)	doubt about accuracy of transcription
CAPITALS	increased volume
bold print	speaker emphasis
>...<	faster speed of utterance deliver

/	rising intonation
yeah:::::	lengthened sound
-	incomplete word or utterance
=	latching on (no gap between speakers' utterances)
(.)	micropause
(-)	pause shorter than one second
(1); (2)	timed pauses (longer than one second)
*Bengali	translation of Bengali or Sylheti *utterance* into English

4   Extract 2 does not use the stave system. Transcription conventions are as given for Extract 1 above.
5   Extract 3 uses the following conventions (see Keim 2006: 181):

*, **	short pause, longer pause
↓	falling intonation
"	strong accent

6   Extract 4 uses the following transcription conventions (quoted from Hall 2009: 159):

a colon (:) indicates lengthening; an equals sign (=) indicates latching (no gap between utterances); brackets ([ ]) indicate overlapping speech; a hyphen (-) indicates self-interrupted speech; an upturned arrow (↑) indicates pitch accent in the syllable that follows; a downturned arrow (↓) indicates lowered pitch in the syllable that follows; underline indicates emphasis; CAPS indicate heightened volume; a period indicates falling contour; a question mark indicates rising contour; a comma indicates continuing contour; single parentheses enclose unintelligible speech; parenthetical carrots (< >) enclose transcriber's commentary on the interaction as well as paralinguistic detail regarding the way in which an utterance is produced; x's in parentheses (xxx) indicate unintelligible talk; *italics* indicate Hindi; standard font indicates English. Short pauses under 0.5 seconds are identified in parentheses by a period and longer pauses by a specific numerical value.

7   I accept Bucholtz and Hall's (2005: 606) argument that agency should not be confused with intentionality, but I wish to highlight that language and gender studies would benefit from an increased/renewed interest in the larger social constraints of local (gender) identity performances.

References

Barrett, Rusty (1999) Indexing polyphonous identity in the speech of African American drag queens. In Mary Bucholtz, A.C. Liang and Laurel Sutton. (eds), *Reinventing Identities: The Gendered Self in Discourse*, 313–331. New York: Oxford University Press.
Benwell, Bethan and Elizabeth Stokoe (2006) *Discourse and Identity*. Edinburgh: Edinburgh University Press.
Bourdieu, Pierre (1984) *Distinction: A Social Critique of the Judgement of Taste*, R. Nice (trans.). London: Routledge.
Bucholtz, Mary (1999) 'Why be normal?': language and identity practices in a community of nerd girls. *Language in Society* 28: 203–223.
Bucholtz, Mary and Kira Hall (2005) Identity and interaction: a sociocultural linguistic approach. *Discourse Studies* 7(3): 585–614.
Butler, Judith (1990) *Gender Trouble: Feminism and the Subversion of Identity*. New York: Routledge.
Cameron, Deborah (1997) Performing gender identity; young men's talk and the construction of heterosexual masculinity. In Sally Johnson and Ulrike Hanna Meinhof (eds), *Language and Masculinity*, 47–64. Oxford: Blackwell.
Cameron, Deborah (2005) Relativity and its discontents: language, gender, and pragmatics. *Intercultural Pragmatics* 2–3: 321–334.
Cameron, Deborah (2009) Theoretical issues for the study of gender and spoken interaction. In Pia Pichler and Eva Eppler (eds), *Gender and Spoken Interaction*, 1–17. Houndmills: Palgrave Macmillan.
Cameron, Deborah and Don Kulick (2003) *Language and Sexuality*. Cambridge: Cambridge University Press.
Coates, Jennifer (1996) *Women Talk. Conversation between Women Friends*. Oxford: Blackwell.
Coates, Jennifer (1999) Changing femininities: the talk of teenage girls. In Mary Bucholtz, A.C. Liang and Laurel A. Sutton (eds), *Reinventing Identities. The Gendered Self in Discourse*, 123–144. Oxford: Oxford University Press.

Davies, Julia (2003) Expressions of gender: an analysis of pupils' gendered discourse styles. *Discourse and Society* 14(2): 115–132.
DeFrancisco, Victoria Leto (1991) The sounds of silence: how men silence women in marital relations. *Discourse and Society* 2(4): 413–424.
Eckert, Penelope (1993) Cooperative competition in adolescent "girl talk". In Deborah Tannen (ed.), *Gender and Conversational Interaction*, 32–61. Oxford: Oxford University Press.
Eckert, Penelope (2011) Gender and sociolinguistic variation. In Jennifer Coates and Pia Pichler (eds), *Language and Gender. A Reader* (2nd ed.), 57–66. Oxford/Malden, MA: Wiley-Blackwell.
Eckert, Penelope and Sally McConnell-Ginet (1992) Think practically and look locally: language and gender as community-based practice. *Annual Review of Anthropology* 21: 461–490.
Eder, Donna (1990) Serious and playful disputes: variation in conflict talk among female adolescents. In Allen Grimshaw (ed.), *Conflict Talk*, 67–84. Cambridge: Cambridge University Press.
Ehrlich, Susan (1998) The discursive reconstruction of sexual consent. *Discourse and Society* 9(2): 149–171.
Ehrlich, Susan (2006) Trial discourse and judicial decision-making: constraining the boundaries of gendered identities. In Judith Baxter (ed.), *Speaking Out: The Female Voice in Public Contexts*, 139–158. Houndmills: Palgrave Macmillan.
Fishman, Pamela (1980) Conversational insecurity. In Howard Giles, Peter W. Robinson and Philip M. Smith (eds), *Language: Social Psychological Perspectives*, 127–132. Oxford: Pergamon.
Foucault, Michel (1972) *The Archaeology of Knowledge, and the Discourse on Language*, A. M. Sheridan Smith (trans.). New York: Pantheon Books (trans.).
Garfinkel, Harold (1967) *Studies in Ethnomethodology*. Englewood Cliffs, NJ: Prentice Hall.
Gee, James Paul (1996) *Social Linguistics and Literacies. Ideology in Discourses* (2nd ed.) London: Routledge.
Goodwin, Marjorie Harness (1988) Cooperation and competition across girls' play activities. In Sue Fisher and Alexandra Todd (eds), *Gender and Discourse: The Power of Talk*, 5594. Norwood, NJ: Ablex.
Goodwin, Marjorie Harness (1990) *He-said-she-said: Talk as Social Organisation among Black Children*. Bloomington: Indiana University Press.
Hall, Kira (2003) Exceptional speakers: Contested and problematized gender identities. In Miriam Meyerhoff and Janet Holmes (eds), *Handbook of Language and Gender*, 352–380. Oxford: Blackwell.
Hall, Kira (2009) Boys talk: Hindi, moustaches and masculinity. In Pia Pichler and Eva Eppler (eds), *Gender and Spoken Interaction*, 139–162. Houndmills: Palgrave Macmillan.
Hasund, Ingrid Kristine and Anna-Brita Stenström (1997) Conflict talk: a comparison of the verbal disputes between adolescent females in two corpora. In Magnus Ljung (ed.), *Corpus-based Studies in English. Papers from the Seventeenth International Conference on English Language Research on Computerized Corpora*, 119–132. Amsterdam: Rodopi.
Holmes, Janet (2007) Social constructionism, postmodernism and feminist sociolinguistics. *Gender and Language* 1(1): 51–66.
Holmes, Janet and Stephanie Schnurr (2006) "Doing femininity" at work: more than just relational practice. *Journal of Sociolinguistics* 10(1): 31–51.
Keim, Inken (2007) Socio-cultural identity, communicative style, and their change over time: A case study of a group of German-Turkish girls in Mannheim/Germany. In Peter Auer (ed.), *Style and Social Identities. Alternative Approaches to Linguistic Heterogeneity*, 155–186. Berlin/NewYork: de Gruyter.
Kiesling, Scott (2002) Playing the straight man: displaying and maintaining male heterosexuality in discourse. In Kathryn Campbell-Kibler, Robert Podesva, Sarah J. Roberts and Andrew Wong (eds) *Language and Sexuality: Contesting Meaning in Theory and Practice*, 2–10. Stanford, CA: CSLI Publications.
Kitzinger, Celia (2005) Speaking as a heterosexual: (How) does sexuality matter for talk-in-interaction? *Research on Language and Social Interaction* 38(3): 221–265.
Lakoff, Robin (1975) *Language and Woman's Place*. New York: Harper and Row.
Lave, Jean and Etienne Wenger (1991) *Situated Learning: Legitimated Peripheral Participation*. Cambridge: Cambridge University Press.
Lawson, Robert (2013) The construction of "tough" masculinity: negotiation, alignment and rejection. *Gender and Language* 7(3): 369–395.
Mendoza-Denton, Norma (2008) *Homegirls. Language and Cultural Practice among Latina Youth Gangs*. Malden, MA/Oxford: Blackwell.
Mills, Sara and Louise Mullany (2011) *Language, Gender and Feminism: Theory, Methodology and Practice*. London: Routledge.
Moore, Emma (2004) Sociolinguistic style: A multidimensional resource for shared identity creation. *Canadian Journal of Linguistics* 49: 375–396.

Ochs, Elinor (1992) Indexing gender. In Alessandro Duranti and Charles Goodwin (eds), *Rethinking Context: Language as an Interactive Phenomenon,* 335–358. Cambridge: Cambridge University Press.

Ostermann, Ana Cristina (2003) Communities of practice at work: Gender, facework and the power of habitus at an all-female police station and a feminist crisis intervention center in Brazil. *Discourse and Society 14*(4): 473–505.

Pichler, Pia (2006) Multifunctional teasing as a resource for identity construction. *Journal of Sociolinguistics 10*(2): 226–250.

Pichler, Pia (2009) *Talking Young Femininities.* Houndmills: Palgrave Macmillan.

Pujolar, Joan i. Cos (1997) Masculinities in a multilingual setting. In Sally Johnson and Ulrike Hanna Meinhof (eds), *Language and Masculinity,* 86–106. Oxford: Blackwell.

Preece, Sian (2009) "A group of lads, innit?" Performances of laddish masculinity in British Higher Education. In Pia Pichler and Eva Eppler (eds), *Gender and Spoken Interaction,* 115–138. Houndmills: Palgrave Macmillan.

Schegloff, Emanuel (1997) 'Whose text? Whose context?' In *Discourse and Society 8*(2): 165–187.

Shaw, Sylvia (2006) *Governed by the rules? The female voice in parliamentary debates.* In Judith Baxter (ed.), *Speaking out: the Female Voice in Public Contexts,* 81–102. Houndmills: Palgrave Macmillan.

Sheldon, Amy (1997) Talking power: girls, gender enculturation and discourse. In Ruth Wodak (ed.) *Gender and Discourse,* 225–244. London: Sage.

Skeggs, Beverly (1997) *Formations of Class and Gender.* London: Sage.

Tannen, Deborah (1990) *You Just Don't Understand. Women and Men in Conversation.* London: Virago Press.

Trudgill, Peter (1974) *The Social Differentiation of English in Norwich.* Cambridge: Cambridge University Press.

West, Candace (1984) When the doctor is a "lady": power, status and gender in physician-patient encounters. *Symbolic Interaction* 7: 87–106.

Wetherell, Margaret (1998) Positioning and interpretive repertoires: conversation analysis and post-structuralism in dialogue. *Discourse and Society 10*(3): 293–316.

Woods, Nicola (1989) Talking shop: sex and status as determinants of floor apportionment in a work setting. In Jennifer Coates and Deborah Cameron (eds), *Women in their Speech Communities,* 141–157. London: Longman.

Zimmerman, Don H. and Candace West (1975) Sex roles, interruptions and silences in conversations. In Barrie Thorne and Nancy Henley (eds), *Language and Sex: Difference and Dominance,* 105–129. Roweley: Newbury House.

Further Reading

Coates, Jennifer and Pia Pichler (eds) *Language and Gender. A Reader* (2nd ed.) Oxford/Malden: Wiley-Blackwell.
This reader provides a very good overview of language and gender research, including classic and more recent papers discussed in this chapter.

Eckert, Penelope and McConnell-Ginet (2013) *Language and Gender,* (2nd ed.) Cambridge: Cambridge University Press.
This textbook will be particularly valuable with respect to the social constructionist model of gender.

Holmes, Janet and Miriam Meyerhoff (2003) (eds) *The Handbook of Language and Gender.* Oxford: Blackwell.
This is a rich resource, offering some chapters that are very accessible and suitable as introductory reading, and others that require previous knowledge on the subject.

Mills, Sarah and Louise Mullany (2011) *Language, Gender and Feminism. Theory, Methodology and Practice.* London: Routledge.
This book presents a range of theoretical perspectives, methodological and analytical approaches, linking language and gender studies firmly to their feminist roots.

Pichler, Pia (2009) *Talking Young Femininities.* Houndmills: Palgrave Macmillan.
This book presents a discourse analytic exploration of the interplay of gender with social class and ethnicity on the basis of the talk of three groups of British girls from different socio-cultural backgrounds.

14

Discursive Practices, Linguistic Repertoire, and Racial Identities

John Baugh

1 Introduction

"Discursive practices" correspond to the ways in which people throughout the world use a combination of language and symbols in expressive and communicative ways. Discursive practices vary from culture to culture, and frequently differ within a speech community depending upon the groups of people who may share knowledge of a common language. Their means of expression and interpretation may be dissimilar, however, due to factors that lead to the relative isolation of groups within a speech community based, say, on region, religion, sexual orientation, or race – among others. Here we focus on the ways in which discursive practices intersect with racial identities, along with descriptions of why different linguistic repertoires can either enhance or restrain the ways in which racial identities are affirmed overtly through language usage.

A discussion of this kind could easily fall prey to the misleading implication of linguistic supremacy, that is, in the sense that discursive practices are dominated by language usage, which is why our discussion begins with a powerful illustration of nonverbal discursive practice with overt racial symbolism. During the 1968 Olympics two African American athletes, Tommie Smith and John Carlos, won gold and bronze medals respectively in the men's 200 meter race. Tommie Smith set a world record for the event on that day, and Australian Peter Norman took second place in the event, sharing the winner's podium with the two African American athletes.

Tommie Smith (2007) would later write about this iconic and controversial victory celebration in his autobiography, *Silent Gesture*. The relevance of that episode to the present discussion is due in large measure to the fact that the raised fists of the African American athletes, who wore black gloves and removed their shoes to symbolize black poverty in their homeland, did not employ language; however, they did engage in a symbolic discursive practice that was highly communicative. Indeed, all three athletes wore human rights badges on their jackets. Peter Norman did so in solidarity with the American black athletes, while simultaneously conveying his own disagreement with the mistreatment of Aboriginal people in his native Australia.

These symbolic gestures raised huge objections at the time: Tommie Smith and John Carlos were banished from the Olympic Village and were subject to death threats upon their return to the United States. No words were necessary to communicate their racial identity and solidarity with impoverished African Americans, who took pride in their accomplishment and the

Discursive, Linguistic, and Racial Issues

Figure 14.1 1968 Olympic Games, Mexico City, Mexico, men's 200 meters final. US gold medallist Tommie Smith (center) and bronze medallist John Carlos give the black power salutes as an anti-racism protest as they stand on the podium with Australian silver medallist Peter Norman. (Credit: Rolls Press/Popperfoto/Getty Images)

courageous defiance that they displayed to a global audience that was forcibly reminded of the discriminatory plight of many black people in the United States.

Tommie Smith was reacting, at least in part, to the legacy of discrimination against African Americans, which was frequently on vivid historical display by the Ku Klux Klan, whose practices of burning crosses while wearing their iconic white robes and pointed hoods were symbolic nonverbal discursive practices designed to invoke black racial fear and to assert white supremacy. These symbolic nonlinguistic images were, of course, accompanied by racist linguistic discursive practices including hateful speeches and racist publications that utilized language to promote white supremacy overtly.

There are several reasons why this discussion emphasizes at the outset symbolic racial representations of discursive practices: the vast majority of discursive practices employ linguistic behavior in one way or another and the role of nonverbal symbols might easily be subsumed when compared with racial identities that are affirmed through linguistic content.

Figure 14.2 Ku Klux Klan rally, Maryland, USA (1986) (Credit: Paul Souders/Getty Images)

"Linguistic repertoire" corresponds not only to representations of communicative competence and linguistic competence; individuals have differential access to the languages and dialects that thrive in their midst. Bilingual speakers, for example, may express racial identities quite differently, depending upon the language they employ. Latinos in the United States who are fluent in Spanish and English may reserve depictions of "La Raza" (i.e. the race) for Spanish usage, while rarely doing so in English. Bidialectal African Americans may employ vernacular black dialect to evoke racial solidarity, while rarely doing so with mainstream Standard American English.

Depictions and descriptions of racial identity vary greatly among people from different racial backgrounds throughout the world, where matters of racial identity tend to be strongly pronounced by those who either experience or acknowledge the existence of racial oppression, and it is often free from consideration by those who believe that racial discrimination is a relic of the past that has been replaced by circumstances where – in their opinion – racial differences no longer account for social disparities that may have existed in bygone times.

2 Relevant Research Perspectives

Evaluations of discursive practices are not the province of any one particular research discipline. Scholars in many fields have explored the ways in which people are expressive, and while the current remarks emphasize anthropological perspectives, where cultural considerations related to discursive practice are paramount, it is important to recognize that research in the humanities and social sciences frequently evaluates discursive practices through their respective disciplinary lenses. Educational researchers have also contributed substantially to our understanding of discursive practices in schools (see Young 2009). Philosophers who have formulated studies of speech acts are among the leading scholars devoted to specialized forms of discourse, where utterances have consequences, particularly when stated by those in positions of authority (see Austin 1962, Grice 1989, Searle 1969).

Walter Ong and some who have been inspired by his studies of the transition from orality (i.e. speech) to literacy (i.e. the acquisition of reading and writing) have also evaluated discursive behavior in academic and social settings (see Ong 1982, Farrell 1983, Tannen 1990). Heath (1983) links all three of these traditions in her studies of language usage in the American South among blacks and whites, observing a combination of cultural differences as well as educational disparities that have a direct impact on discursive practices in the communities and schools she studied. The communities that Heath evaluated, called Roadville and Trackton, are not merely segregated on the basis of race, but also by differences in discursive linguistic practices that reflect cultural dissimilarities in the ways that speech and literacy are employed, as well as how they are transmitted to the children who live in racial isolation, but who attend the same schools.

Both groups, the whites who live in Roadville, and the blacks who live in Trackton, are working class folks, but the ways in which they tell stories and use combinations of figurative and literal language owe much to the fact that Roadville residents trace their ancestry to the hills of Appalachia, where literal storytelling and rote memorization are valued, whereas Trackton residents are the descendants of field slaves who were historically denied access to schools and literacy, and they relied heavily on oral traditions that were often embellished to enhance their content and meaningful expression. Heath rightly resists dichotomous racial categorization in favor of complex cultural differences that owe their existence to historical segregation and differential access to the written word.

Sociolinguists and dialectologists have routinely studied language usage in a variety of social contexts and different regions by speakers from diverse backgrounds, sometimes working with monolingual speakers (see Labov 1966, Rickford and Rickford 2000, Wolfram and Schilling-Estes 1998) and on other occasions evaluating the speech of speakers who employ more than one language (see Myers-Scotton 1993, Poplack 1979, Valdés 1996, and Zentella 1997).

A combination of sociologists and anthropologists have studied "talk" through conversation analyses that often utilize evaluations of video or audio recordings of day-to-day interactions among people in various social settings (see Goffman 1972, Sachs, Schegloff and Jefferson 1974, Goodwin 1981). Similarly, broader studies of discourse analyses that include and occasionally exceed conversation have been evaluated by scholars whose training incorporates aspects of sociology, anthropology, and linguistics (see Schiffrin 1988, Tannen 1990, Bucholz and Hall 2005).

Critical discourse analysts have been quite explicit about the consequences of speech and writing that have social and political relevance (see Wodak 2001, Fairclough 1989). Some have addressed the content of racist discourse directly, noting the divisive nature of remarks that serve to elevate some racial groups while disparaging others (see Van Dijk 1992, Kochman 1983). Whereas some linguists and anthropologists have evaluated language usage in a variety of social settings, proponents of critical discourse analyses (CDA) recognize that social and economic disparities within a given speech community have direct impact on human interaction and dialogue. CDA scholarship often evaluates power dynamics that are evident through linguistic characterization, and studies of gender inequality are illustrative in this regard. Women in many different speech communities do not have the same opportunities as men, and often this lack of opportunity is embodied in discursive practices that employ language as a means of maintaining discriminatory practices. For example, some employers deny opportunities to younger women based on the belief that they may need maternity leave, which may or may not be stated explicitly. The United States military, until very recently, excluded woman from combat roles based on assumptions that their male colleagues would be in greater danger derived from their (i.e. the men's) desire to be more protective of women serving in combat.

CDA also evaluates other power dynamics that are displayed through language, such as when a police officer gives commands, or bosses admonish their workers. The language usage of racists has also been the object of scholarly inquiry using CDA, because many racist texts or comments tend to demonize the group that is the object of scorn, while praising the group(s) that often convey racially insensitive or hurtful comments.

Language educators, including those who teach English, writing, and foreign languages have long been devoted to helping students expand their discursive linguistic capacities in academic contexts from pre-schoolers to graduate students in higher education. Some of these studies, from different disciplinary perspectives, evaluate how language operates in workplaces, as well as gathering perceptions of the languages and dialects that people encounter within the speech communities where they live (see Preston 1989, Purnell, Idsardi and Baugh 1999).

Some scholars devote primary attention to the teaching and acquisition of reading in first or second languages, and these analyses also provide insights into a realm of discursive practice that is related to the ways in which people can encode the written word (see Bernhardt 1992, Brantmeier 2009). Students of semiotics have also grappled with the ways in which language and other forms of symbolic representations correspond to human communicative capacities (see Sebeok 2001). In addition, the field of the "sociology of language" represents a specialized branch of sociology where language serves as the primary means through which social demarcation within communities is identified (see Fishman 1972, Bernstein 1971).

These observations about diverse research that is devoted to alternative forms of discursive practices are by no means comprehensive; rather, they are representative of an array of studies that explore the full range of human communicative expression, spanning purely introspective linguistic analyses such as those proposed by Chomsky (1957, 1965) as well as the ethnographic perspectives espoused by Hymes (1964, 1972) and Hymes and Gumperz (1972).

On some occasions these studies explicitly evaluate racial identities, and some speech pathologists have been explicit in this regard, seeking to differentiate pathological speech disorders from vernacular dialects employed by members of minority groups (see Seymour and Seymour 1997, Washington and Craig 1999, Wyatt 1997, Stockman 2006, Vaughn-Cook 1976, Peña 2007).

In addition to the studies cited thus far, which tend to be grounded in different academic disciplines, there are many scholars who have described discursive practices in their own right. Most of these evaluations consider the ways in which discursive practices operate in different social circumstances, including schools (see Lemon 1995, 2002, Young 2009, Stoughton and Siverston 2005), and regarding social identity (Wilson 1999). Unlike many of the disciplinary oriented studies of human communicative endeavors, explicit studies of discursive practices share evaluations of expressive ways in which people affirm group affiliations or other forms of categorization or classification.

As indicated, no one discipline can claim to provide a comprehensive approach to studies of discursive practices, and those who strive to produce new studies of discursive behaviors will need to take care in designing their research, taking into account the theoretical assumptions that are inherent in the corresponding analytical methods that are employed, as well as the means and circumstances through which corresponding data are gathered. Anyone who attempts to evaluate discursive practices will no doubt find their task to be somewhat daunting, but the vast majority of scholars cited thus far are careful to identify their research domain with empirical evidence that justifies their alternative modes of analysis.

3 Historical Perspectives

In order to understand the history of racial identities it is first important to acknowledge the ways in which humans have come to classify themselves and others in both biological and sociological terms. Depending upon the nation and communities in question, matters of racial diversity, disparities, and identity will vary substantially, as will relationships among those who are members of different racial groups. Biologists are quick to point out that racial differences among humans are quite minor, in terms of skin color, hair texture, and other physical traits that are associated with people of different racial backgrounds. Sociologists, on the other hand, and historians frequently observe that human behavior is often determined by race, resulting in privilege for some and hardship for others.

The matter of membership within racial groups is also relevant, depending upon someone's personal racial identity, as well as the ways in which racial classifications are constructed by those who are not members of that particular racial group. That is, some people are "insiders" to a specific racial group, while others are "outsiders" to that race. A current controversy in the United States is highly emblematic of this situation. More specifically, the Washington, D.C. professional football team is called "The Redskins," which is a racist term that was used historically in disparaging ways to refer to Native Americans from any Indian nation; Cherokee, Cree, Arapaho, Navajo, Apache, and Cheyenne (among others) were lumped together under the "Redskin" label. American Indians (i.e. insiders) never referred to themselves in this manner: it was only non-Indians (i.e. outsiders) who adopted this terminology. The current owner of "The Washington Redskins" has resisted calls to change the name of the team, citing tradition; however, the historical discursive practice that referred to Native Americans as "Redskins" is unquestionably racist and remains offensive to American Indians, and others who find the term to be objectionable.

There is a degree of racial relativity that comes into play in this regard, to say little of the fact that many people today claim mixed racial heritage, which began along with the historical colonization and conquests previously described, and racially mixed children continue to be born in different parts of the world. In some cases, like my own, racial mixing was forced upon enslaved women who were denied the dignity of choosing the men who impregnated them. It is now far more common for children with biracial or multiracial backgrounds to be the product of loving, mutually supportive unions. Regardless of the positive or negative circumstances that gave rise to racially mixed populations, many people who are the product of racial mixing often employ their own discursive practices to affirm their multiracial heritage.

It is also important to note that a great many of these historical episodes transpired long before the industrial revolution. Wind provided the power for sailing vessels at that time, and guns capable of firing a single shot before reloading played a huge role in the conquest of populations that did not possess firearms. With the advent of the industrial revolution, circumstances began to change regarding the speed with which people could travel, and the creation of new guns capable of firing multiple shots before reloading added greatly to the power of those, typically white people who had ready access to those highly sophisticated weapons.

These were the evolutionary circumstances that gave rise not only to in-group and out-group racial identities; they frequently defined lines of social demarcation that were easily maintained in societies where racial differences came to define one's social and political standing, to say little of corresponding access to education for oneself or one's children. Although linguists and anthropologists know well that all living cultures support spoken languages, writing systems are not equally universal. Moreover, the communities where written forms of languages exist are further stratified by those who have learned to read and write, in contrast to those who have been unable to acquire literacy.

Access to education has, throughout the world, much more to do with economic circumstances than racial heritage per se. Nevertheless, in the communities that have historically (or currently) exhibited racial discrimination, the subordinate racial group(s) tend to be poor and therefore lack access to adequate educational opportunities. Those who do not have the ability to read and write usually rely on oral traditions to communicate. At times these oral events are highly ritualized, where storytelling and poetry are engaged for various reasons, similar to those previously described related to studies by Heath (1983). In some instances these oral traditions intersect with spoken discourse related to racial identities, but language devoted to matters of race in cultures without written forms of language are fleeting by nature since speech, unless recorded, vanishes at the moment it is produced.

Those who have access to literacy also have the means by which they can record discourse for posterity, and the existence of written records has been a distinctive hallmark of human evolution for those languages that have come to include viable writing systems that convert speech to a visual format. Speech is universal to every human society, while writing is limited to those who gain access to education in cultures that practice literacy. Human discourse, in the form of either speech or writing, is the vehicle through which discursive practices embracing racial identities are typically conveyed. As noted at the outset, many symbolic forms of racial identity exceed language usage, but the vast majority of discursive episodes that reflect racial matters are contained in utterances or writing.

Discursive practices that evoke racial symbolism and identity have varied greatly throughout human history, and they remain as evidence of instances of racial division or solidarity in different communities throughout the world. Immigration patterns have, in some cases, exacerbated these trends as newcomers to a nation who may be of a different racial background than the majority of native citizens can often become the object of racial scorn, particularly in circumstances where economic pressures are such that they are perceived to threaten occupational opportunities for local native groups. History has also revealed some remarkable people, such as Gandhi, Martin Luther King Jr., and Nelson Mandela, who have employed discursive practices to combat racism, elitism, and the injustices born of racial subjugation. India, South Africa, and the United States were all once ruled by British monarchs, and their soldiers governed with brutality against local populations. The legacy of racial oppression still lingers in India, South Africa, and the United States; however, Gandhi, Martin Luther King Jr., and Nelson Mandela utilized a combination of inspirational speeches as well as acts of political defiance to promote racial equality in their respective countries. Again, we find that discursive practices are not the product of linguistic behavior alone; rather, it is the combination of symbolic activities, which frequently include inspirational language, that complements other events to achieve justice and racial liberation.

4 Analytical Procedures

Scholars who seek to examine discursive practices associated with racial identity have many options, depending upon the era and evidence to be considered to evaluate these communicative or symbolic events. Those who wish to study historical examples of racial identity are frequently at the mercy of differential records in this regard. Since "time travel" is not possible, archaeologists and anthropologists do their very best to reconstruct the lives and cultures of people from bygone days, based on the array of artefacts they leave behind, which offer the keys and clues to reconstructing the lives of past cultures. Tools, pottery, and clothing are common evidence for these purposes, but the discovery of the "Rosetta Stone" hints at the rarity with which written records are recovered; even rarer is the appearance of an ancient tome that makes explicit or indirect references to race.

Those who wish to study discursive activities regarding racial identities after the advent of the printing press have the advantage of access to superior documentation: many of these books or records contain specific racial information. For example, the sale of African slaves in North and South America was frequently accompanied by documents regarding the purchase price of the slaves, along with descriptions of their sex, age, language abilities, and other characteristics such as mixed racial heritage. Those interested in these events within the United States have the added advantage of recordings that were gathered by John and Alan Lomax; their field recordings are now available on-line, and they contain a wealth of oral history by Americans from different racial backgrounds, including black prisoners who would sing while working on Mississippi chain gangs.

Any effort to reconstruct the nature of discursive practices related to racial identities in historical terms will be more or less challenging, depending upon the communities of interest and the quality of the records available. In the modern era a host of new procedures can be employed to study discursive practices that correspond to racial identities, including experiments, surveys, and participant observation. Social psychologists have already conducted experiments with significant racial salience, including Steele's (1999) formulation of "stereotype threat," which is manifest as a result of racial preconceptions.

Educators, political scientists, and sociologists have all explored racial behavior and classifications, using a variety of analytical procedures that are tailored to their specific research interests and goals. Educators have been fixated on differences in academic performance based on race (see Banks 2002, Ladson-Billings 1994, Darling-Hammond 2004). Political scientists have concentrated on political engagement by different racial groups at different points in history (see Dawson 2011, Cohen 2010, Barker 1994, Fraga 1995). Sociologists, such as Myrdal (1944), Moynihan (1965) and Wilson (1978, 1996) have also evaluated racial characteristics related to employment, welfare, and a myriad of social traits such as crime, drug use, and symbolic racism (see Sears 1988, Bobo 1983, 2012). When viewed collectively each branch of social science has embraced alternative forms of discursive practices with racial salience, and those who wish to study these practices as they exist today can utilize an array of methodologies that can shed light on different dimensions of racial identities for various populations throughout the world.

Surveys may be useful in some circumstances, and some may be well suited to utilizing the internet in ways that were simply unavailable several years ago. Experimental studies of racial identity are also possible, where matters of racial membership and identity can be evaluated through controlled studies among people from different backgrounds. Anthropologists may wish to observe these practices, which might include careful recordings of accounts pertaining to racial identities. Alexander (2010) has employed some of these methods in her book on the excessively high rates of African American incarceration. Santa Ana (2002) has evaluated portrayals of Latinos in print media, along with some unflattering metaphors that have been used to depict people of Mexican ancestry. Indeed, the title of Santa Ana's (2002) book, *Brown tide rising*, is a phrase that he discovered in a news story about the growing Latino population in the United States, that is, including both documented and undocumented residents. His work describes other metaphorical depictions of "wetbacks" and "beaners" that are demeaning to people of Latino descent.

Alexander (2010), who is an attorney by training, was able to look at a range of legal evidence in support of her research. Santa Ana (2002) used discourse analyses to gather the metaphorical comparisons that he found in print media. Anthropologists and ethnographers may also find it useful to employ "Conversation Analysis" to examine discursive practices regarding racial identities, which might be done directly or indirectly (Goodwin 1990). The "direct" approach, which may be better suited to studies where the analyst is already familiar with racial terminology and nomenclature, might include interviews or recordings of conversations where racial topics are explicit. Such interviews could address racial labels and classifications directly, or field recordings could minimize the participation of the observer in favor of recording local citizens who are engaged in discussion about racial identities amongst themselves. Indirect evaluation might take the form of ethnographic interviews or inquiries where the analyst does not introduce any racial classifications in an a priori manner, but rather crafts a series of questions related to the ways in which people in a given community refer to themselves. Thus, in the case of ethnographic inquiries, the fieldworker will not ask about specific racial labels in an explicit manner, but will approach the topic by making inquiries about different groups in a community, while hoping to elicit the corresponding racial labels that are employed.

The internet also offers new and alternative means of exploring racial identity because "YouTube" and "Twitter", among other social media, are often explicit in their racial portrayals and characterizations. In these cases the anthropologist could take advantage of new advances in technology that, under ideal circumstances, might serve as a supplement to traditional fieldwork where a combination of (in)direct data collection procedures are utilized.

5 Anticipated Findings

Just as there are many languages that differ throughout the world, we also know that they possess linguistic universals in order to operate effectively for human communication (see Chomsky 1957, 1965). Similarly, the discursive practices that embody racial identities will have diverse manifestations in different cultures at different points in time. When matters of racial identity are concerned, however, discursive practices will always contain direct or indirect racial characterizations, or some combination thereof.

Depending upon the community and the symbolic representation(s) for racial identity, the analyst of corresponding discursive practices may expect to locate evidence in speech, writing, and visual representations, such as paintings (from long ago) or internet video recordings (which utilize more recent advanced technology).

Historical accounts of racial identities will be tied, in all likelihood, to the corresponding technology from the era when these depictions were created. Cave dwellers who left drawings of their livelihoods on the walls of their cavern homes did so to the best of their abilities, occasionally depicting wars with antagonists whose group affiliations differed from theirs. Paintings that represent the crusades often take on symbolic, if not explicit, racial representations that are occasionally supported by written records with racial significance. Hitler's rise to power in the wake of World War I and the terrible atrocities that he inflicted on Jewish (and other) victims of the Holocaust reflect Nazi propaganda, the complex mixture of speech, writing, and visual symbolism that was intended to bolster the "master race."

South Africa's apartheid policies have been somewhat transformative in this regard, drawing upon historical practices to distinguish between white, colored, and black populations, along with the corresponding advantages or disadvantages derived from these racial classifications. To illustrate this legacy the creators of the Apartheid Museum in Johannesburg provide all visitors with tickets that randomly assign guests to one of the three apartheid era racial groups. Thus, upon purchasing a ticket, the visitor is randomly designated to enter the museum through one of three entrances; that is, for whites, for coloured people, or for blacks. The entrances are separated by see-through barriers that allow each visitor to witness, at a distance, the alternative experiences of other visitors whose museum admission classifications differ from their own. As such, the curators of this museum remind all who enter that South Africa was once overtly divided by race, so much so that authorities resorted to "a pencil test" to assist them with their racial classification. Briefly, a pencil would be inserted into a person's hair – male or female – and, depending on whether the pencil fell from the hair, they were then classified as being white, colored, or black, along with other considerations, such as skin color. Whites, for the most part, were not able to place pencils in their hair without them falling out. Black people could insert a pencil into their hair and it would remain fixed. Anthropologists will recognize that this particular discursive practice need not require any linguistic accompaniment whatsoever, yet the relevance to racial identity is overt.

An illustration of another discursive practice that has racial significance and has taken on mythical stature resulted from Gandhi's "Salt March" in 1930 to protest the British salt tax. Gandhi left his home in Ahmedabad and within 24 days he walked nearly 240 miles to the Arabian Sea, whereupon he made salt in defiance of British law and its salt monopoly throughout India. This famous nonviolent act of civil disobedience was not explicit in its racial portrayals, but the racial relevance of this act is inescapable because Gandhi's race and that of his fellow Indians differed from that of their British rulers.

Leaping forward to the present, the legacy of "Rap" and "Hip Hop," which are no longer the exclusive province of African American spoken word artists, often describe circumstances with racial relevance, and the oral skills and carefully crafted dialog included in support of Hip Hop worldwide often embraces a defiant tone in opposition to authorities that are viewed as oppressive (Alim 2006, Morgan 2009). While youthful resistance to authority is not limited to racial contexts, the spoken word traditions evolved in African American communities that have given rise to the global Hip Hop nation stem from the racial oppression born of slavery, and the numerous social maladies associated with American enslavement.

That early oppression, based on race, resulted in secret discursive practices among the slaves to find disparaging ways to refer to white Americans, and many derogatory terms grew from this process. Some recent evidence of this legacy was on display during the George Zimmerman murder trial pertaining to the wrongful death of Trevon Martin, an African American 17-year-old whom Zimmerman considered to be suspicious, and whom he shot during a confrontation.

Testimony was provided by a young African American woman, Rachel Jeantel, who was the last person to speak with Trevon Martin before he was shot. As she recounted the conversation that she shared with Trevon, under oath, Don West – a defense attorney for George Zimmerman – did his best to discredit Rachel Jeantel through a series of questions that were intended to cast her in a negative light. More precisely, when asked to repeat the conversation she shared with Trevon Martin she mentioned that he stated that he was being followed by a "creepy ass cracker." Mr. West pounced on this statement, claiming that it confirmed that Trevon Martin had initiated a racist remark. Rachel Jeantel asserted through single word replies that she strongly disagreed with Mr. West's assertion.

Mr. West:	Describing the person is what made you think this was racial?
Ms. Jeantel:	Yes.
Mr. West:	And that's because he described him as a "creepy ass cracker"?
Ms. Jeantel:	Yes.
Mr. West:	So it was racial, but it was because Trevon Martin put race in this?
Ms. Jeantel:	No.
Mr. West:	You don't think that's a racial comment?
Ms. Jeantel:	No.
Mr. West:	You don't think that "creepy ass cracker" is a racial comment?
Ms. Jeantel:	No.
Mr. West:	Are you okay this morning?
Ms. Jeantel:	Yes.
Mr. West:	You seem so different than yesterday.

On the previous day Ms. Jeantel's testimony was defiant in tone and demeanor, whereas her remarks during this exchange, all reflected in single word responses, were stated in a calm and quiet voice. Of direct relevance to matters of racial identity is the phrase "creepy ass cracker." Mr. West was surely mindful of the fact that this expression has racial relevance, because African Americans often use the term "cracker" as a disparaging way to refer to a white person. Yet Ms. Jeantel denied that she thought this term was racial.

In light of the circumstances under which these remarks were made, during a high stakes murder trial, it would appear that Ms. Jeantel was attempting to protect Trevon Martin's reputation by trying to deflect any suggestion that his comment might have been considered to be "racist," rather than "racial." In other words, it would appear that Rachel Jeantel was asserting that Trevon Martin's comment was merely descriptive, and not intended as a racially demeaning remark. Without question, the phrase "creepy ass cracker" has unmistakable racial relevance, and suggested that Trevon Martin considered Mr. Zimmerman's pursuit to be "creepy"; that is, unwelcome and causing an uneasy feeling of fear. The transcript confirms that Mr. West did not choose to emphasize the "creepy" part of the comment but favored the suggestion that Trevon Martin's remarks introduced the specter of race.

Although the preceding illustration is taken from discourse produced during a murder trial, there are many other occasions where racially charged comments take place in institutionalized settings with significant consequences. For example, there have been many allegations pertaining to direct and indirect comments about minority employees that either explicitly or indirectly made reference to the race of workers. School administrators in the state of Delaware were discovered to have shared racist text messages when cell phones that they used were replaced by district employees who happened to stumble on the racially offensive text messages while transferring data to new cell phones.

Whenever discourse is produced under circumstances where people from different racial backgrounds interact, we may find a combination of discursive practices that have racial significance. Racial remarks need not be "racist" per se, although racist comments have been prevalent throughout history; rather, some racial commentaries may be benign or intended to dispel negative stereotypes associated with various groups that might otherwise be characterized in racial terms. References to African Americans, Native Americans, or Latinos may not be racist, although they have racial relevance. Comments referring to Niggers, Redskins, and Wetbacks are almost always racist, derogatory, and disrespectful.

6 Preliminary Implications for Future Research

Although we have intentionally concentrated on racial considerations, human identity is far more complicated when viewed in its totality, and particularly so when inherited historical hardships are taken into account (see Baugh 2006). While it is true that different forms of racial discrimination abound globally, so too do discursive practices that are intended to bolster alternative identities, based on a person's sex, age, disability, or sexual orientation, among others.

Offensive language frequently occurs when insensitive people refer to someone with mental challenges as "retarded," or if someone who is profoundly deaf is characterized as being "dumb." As with discursive practices that are racially charged, comments that disparage members of other groups that may have nothing whatsoever to do with race are also subject to the range of negative and positive commentaries, which often change over time.

When making reference to homosexuals, for example, the term "queer" was once considered to be highly offensive and was routinely used in derogatory ways that were explicit in their discriminatory intent. Over time the term "queer" has now been embraced by gay men and lesbians, who will often proudly exclaim, "We're queer and we're here." The transformation of terminology that was once offensive into contemporary interpretations that are now embraced by those these terms were originally intended to offend remains complicated; "insiders" may be able to use this terminology within the in-group with positive intent, while "outsiders" who employ the very same terminology may still be viewed as making offensive remarks from the standpoint of group insiders. The use, or lack thereof, of the term "nigger" by blacks or whites in the United States reflects similar patterns of in-group or out-group usage, along with corresponding controversies about the relative offensiveness of the term. Some younger African Americans have gone so far as to suggest that the pronunciation of the final syllable of the word is crucial: a final vocalic schwa syllable /ə/ is considered by them to be positive, whereas the historical /-ɜːr/ final syllable pronunciation is still deemed to be highly offensive.

Discursive practices, like all living languages, are constantly undergoing change, and anthropological linguists are in an outstanding position to observe and document these trends as they adapt to new situations and circumstances in speech communities around the world. The combination of speech, writing, and other artefacts that have discursive relevance are particularly well suited to anthropological analyses because they often exceed linguistic behavior and include cultural commodities that symbolize various groups that coexist within a given community. It is my hope that future research in this realm may be of benefit to humanity, serving our better nature in years to come.

Related Topics

7 Language Ideologies (Kroskrity); **8** Social Subordination and Language (Huayhua); **11** Language Socialization and Marginalization (García-Sánchez); **15** Language and Racialization (Chun, Lo); **19** Language and Political Economy (McElhinny); **24** Discrimination via Discourse (Wodak); **25** Racism in the Press (Van Dijk).

References

Alexander, Michelle (2010) *The New Jim Crow: Mass Incarceration in the Age of Colorblindness*. New York: New Press.
Alim, H. Samy (2006) *Roc the Mic Right: The Language of Hip Hop Culture*. London: Routledge.
Austin, John L. (1962) *How to Do Things with Words*. Cambridge, MA: Harvard University Press.
Banks, James (2002) *An Introduction to Multicultural Education*. Boston: Allyn and Bacon.
Barker, Lucius (1994) *African Americans and the American Political System*. Englewood Cliffs, NJ: Prentice Hall.
Baugh, John (2006) "It ain't about race": Some lingering (linguistic) consequences of the African slave trade and their relevance to your personal historical hardship index. *Du Bois Review* 3(1): 145–159.
Bernhardt, Elizabeth B. (ed.) (1992) *Life in Language Immersion Classrooms*. Philadelphia: Multilingual Matters.
Bernstein, Basil (1971) *Class, Codes, and Control*. London: Routledge.
Bobo, Lawrence (1983) Whites' opposition to busing: Symbolic racism or realistic group conflict? *Journal of Personality and Social Psychology* 45(6): 1196–1210.
Bobo, Lawrence (2012) The real record on racial attitudes. In Peter V. Marsden (ed.), *Social Trends in American Life: Findings from the General Social Survey since 1972*, 38–83. Princeton, NJ: Princeton University Press.
Brantmeier, Cindy (ed.) (2009) *Crossing Languages and Research Methods: Analyses of Adult Foreign Language Reading*. Greenwich, CT: Information Age Publishing.
Bucholtz, Mary and Kira Hall (2005). Identity and interaction: a sociocultural linguistic approach. *Discourse Studies* 7: 585–614.
Chomsky, Noam (1957) *Syntactic Structures*. Paris: Mouton.
Chomsky, Noam (1965) *Aspects of a Theory of Syntax*. Cambridge, MA: M.I.T. Press.
Cohen, Cathy (2010) *Democracy Remixed: Black Youth and the Future of American Politics*. New York: Oxford University Press.

Darling-Hammond, Linda (2004) What happens to a dream deferred? The continuing quest for equal educational opportunity. In James A. Banks (ed.), *Handbook of Research on Multicultural Education* (2nd ed.), 607–630. San Francisco: Jossey-Bass.
Dawson, Michael (2011) *Not in our Lifetimes: The Future of Black Politics*. Chicago: University of Chicago Press.
Fairclough, Norman (1989) *Language and Power*. London: Longman.
Farrell, Thomas (1983) IQ and Standard English. *College Composition and Communication* 34(4): 470–484.
Fishman, Joshua (1972). *The Sociology of Language: An Interdisciplinary Social Science Approach to Language in Society*. Nowley, MA: Newbury House Publishers.
Fraga, Luis Ricardo (1995). *The Declining Significance of Rights: Civil Rights in a Multicultural Society*. Stanford, CA: Stanford Center for Chicano Research.
Goffman, Erving (1972) *Relations in Public: Microstudies of the Public Order*. New York: Harper and Row.
Goodwin, Charles (1981) *Conversational Organization: Interaction between Speakers and Hearers*. New York: Academic Press.
Goodwin, Marjorie Harness (1990) *He-said-she-said: Talk as Social Organization among Black Children*. Bloomington, IN: Indiana University Press.
Grice, H. Paul (1989) *Studies in the Way of Words*. Cambridge, MA: Harvard University Press.
Gumperz, J. J. and Hymes, D. (eds) 1972 *Directions in Sociolinguistics: The Ethnography of Communication*. New York: Holt, Rinehart, and Winston.
Heath, Shirley Brice (1983) *Ways with Words: Language, Life, and Work in Communities and Classrooms*. Cambridge: Cambridge University Press.
Hymes, D. (ed.) (1964) *Language in Culture and Society: A Reader in Linguistics and Anthropology*. New York: Harper & Row.
Hymes, D. (ed.) (1972) *Reinventing Anthropology*. New York: Pantheon.
Kochman, Thomas (1983) *Black and White Styles in Conflict*. Chicago: University of Chicago Press.
Labov, William (1966) *The Social Stratification of English in New York City*. Washington, D.C.: Center for Applied Linguistics.
Ladson-Billings, Gloria (1994) *The Dreamkeepers: Successful Teachers of African American Children*. San Francisco: Jossey-Bass.
Lemon, Alaina (1995) 'What are they writing about US blacks?': Roma and race in Russia. *Anthropology of East Europe Review* 13(2): 34–90.
Lemon, Alaina (2002) Without a "concept"? Race as discursive practice. *Slavic Review* 61(1): 54–61.
Morgan, Marcyliena H. (2009) *The Real Hiphop: Battling for Knowledge, Power, and Respect in the LA Underground*. Durham, NC: Duke University Press.
Moynihan, Daniel Patrick (1965) *The Negro Family. The Case for National Action*. Washington, DC: United States Department of Labor, Office of Policy Planning and Research.
Myers-Scotton, Carol (1993) *Duelling Languages: Grammatical Structure in Codeswitching*. New York: Oxford University Press.
Myrdal, Gunnar (1944) *An American Dilemma: The Negro Problem and Modern Democracy*. New York: Harper.
Ong, Walter J. (1982) *Orality and Literacy: The Technologizing of the Word*. London: Routledge.
Peña, Elizabeth (2007) Lost in translation: Methodological considerations in cross-linguistic research. *Child Development* 78: 1255–1264.
Poplack, Shana (1979) *Sometimes I'll Start a Sentence in English y Termino en Español: Toward a Typology of Code-switching*. New York: Centro de Estudios Puertorriqueños.
Preston, Dennis (1989) *Perceptual Dialectology: Nonlinguists' Views of Areal Linguistics*. Dordrecht: Foris Publications.
Purnell, Thomas, William Idsardi, and John Baugh (1999) Perceptual and phonetic experiments on American English dialect identification. *Journal of Language and Social Psychology* 18(1): 10–30.
Rickford, John R. and Russel J. Rickford (2000) *Spoken Soul: The Story of Black English*. New York: John Wiley & Sons, Inc.
Sachs, Harvey, Emanuel A. Schegloff, and Gail Jefferson (1974) A simplest systematics for the organization of turn-taking for conversation. *Language* 50: 696–735.
Santa Ana, Otto (2002) *Brown Tide Rising: Metaphors of Latinos in Contemporary American Public Discourse*. Austin: University of Texas Press.
Schiffrin, Deborah (1988) *Discourse Markers*. Cambridge: Cambridge University Press.
Searle, John R. (1969) *Speech Acts: An Essay in the Philosophy of Language*. London: Cambridge University Press.

Sears, David O. (1988) Symbolic racism. In P. A. Katz and D. A. Taylor (eds), *Eliminating Racism: Profiles in Controversy*, 53–84. New York: Plenum Press.
Sebeok, Thomas (2001) *Global Semiotics*. Bloomington, IN: Indiana University Press.
Seymour, Harry and Charlena Seymour (1977) A therapeutic model for communicative disorders among children speaking black English. *Journal of Speech and Hearing Disorders* 42: 247–256.
Smith, Tommie (2007) *Silent Gesture: The Autobiography of Tommie Smith*. Philadelphia: Temple University Press.
Steele, Claude (1999) Thin ice: Stereotype threat and black college students. *The Atlantic* (August).
Stockman, Ida (2006) Evidence for a minimal competence core of consonant sounds in the speech of African American children: A preliminary study. *Clinical Linguistics and Phonetics* 20(10): 723–749.
Stoughton, Edy Hammond and Connie Siverston (2005) Communicating across cultures: discursive challenges and racial identity formation in narratives of middle school students. *Race, Ethnicity and Education* 8(3): 277–295.
Tannen, Deborah. *You Just Don't Understand: Women and Men in Conversation*. New York: Morrow.
Valdés, Guadalupe (1996) *Con Respeto: Bridging the Distances between Culturally Diverse Families and Schools: An Ethnographic Portrait*. New York: Teachers College Press.
Van Dijk, Teun (1992) Discourse and the denial of racism. *Discourse and Society* 3(1): 87–118.
Vaughn-Cooke, Anna Fay (1976) The implementation of a phonological change: the case of resyllabification in Black English (dissertation). Washington, D.C.: Georgetown University.
Washington, Julie A. and Holly K. Craig (1999) Performances of at-risk, African American preschoolers on the Peabody Picture Vocabulary Test. *Language, Speech, and Hearing Services in Schools* 30(1): 75–82.
Wilson, Eirt H. (1999) Towards a discursive theory of racial identity: The souls of black folk as a response to nineteenth-century biological determinism. *Western Journal of Communication* 63(2): 193–215.
Wilson, William Julius (1978) *The Declining Significance of Race: Blacks and Changing American Institutions*. Chicago: University of Chicago Press.
Wilson, William Julius (1996) *When Work Disappears: The World of the New Urban Poor*. New York: Knopf.
Wodak, Ruth (2001) *Methods of Critical Discourse Analysis*. London: Sage.
Wolfram, Walt and Natalie Schilling-Estes (1998) *American English*. Malden, MA: Blackwell.
Wyatt, Toya (1997) The Oakland Ebonics debate: implications for speech, language, hearing professionals and scholars. *Perspectives on Language, Learning and Education* 4: 15–18.
Young, Richard (2009) *Discursive Practice in Language Learning and Teaching*. Malden, MA: Blackwell.
Zentella, Ana Celia (1997) *Growing up Bilingual: Puerto Rican Children in New York*. Malden, MA: Blackwell.

15
Language and Racialization

Elaine W. Chun and Adrienne Lo

1 Introduction

It may be commonly heard in social science discourses that race is a social construct. This pithy assertion does not mean that race is merely an illusion but that racial categorization is an ideological process that defines the material conditions and embodied experiences of many (Omi and Winant 1994, Smedley 1998). Race remains a basic dimension of social differentiation in many cultures because racialization is a semiotic process that naturalizes social difference: signs that point to race, such as skin color, hair texture, and voice quality, are thought of as self-evident visible, tangible, or audible cues that differentiate human types on a primordial, genetic basis.

In this respect, race is often thought to be different from seemingly flexible social dimensions like sexuality, nationality, or class; you can change your nationality, but not your race. Yet racial differences necessarily intertwine with cultural, geo-political, or economic configurations (see McElhinny 2010, and in this volume), and the slippage between "racial" terms and "ethnic," "national," or "class" ones (e.g., *black/African American, Asian/Chinese, white/American/privileged*) in contexts such as the United States reflects complex convergences across sociocultural axes (see Leap, this volume; Baugh, this volume). In other settings, naturalizing and structured forms of discrimination may be talked about in terms of "immigration," "ethnicity," or "nation," not "race" (see Lemon 2002; Huayhua, this volume; Pujolar, this volume). We thus use the term "ethnoracial" to refer to a historically situated local ideology of human distinctiveness, and "racialization" to emphasize the naturalizing character of this process.

Language plays a key role in semiotic processes of racialization (Alim, Ball, and Rickford, forthcoming), and scholars' assumptions about the relationship between language, race, and ideology have undergone important conceptual shifts over the past fifty years. In this chapter, we provide a brief overview of the three main approaches, noting the basic questions, objects, sites, methods, and objectives of this body of work. We highlight research on *linguistic racialization*, or the sociocultural processes through which race – as an ideological dimension of human differentiation – comes to be imagined, produced, and reified through language practices. Such an approach shows how the material and experiential reality of race is kept alive; it also provides nuanced insights about how language can convey sociocultural meanings that are often implicit, complexly layered, and dynamically shifting.

2 Historical Perspectives

2.1 Approaches to Understanding Language, Race, and Ethnicity

Linguistic anthropology as a field owes its origins to ideas about race and language that were developed by American anthropologists. Working alongside sociologist W.E.B. Du Bois, anthropologist Franz Boas rejected the racist beliefs of his time that some races were inferior to others and that certain languages were "primitive." In particular, he showed that scholars' inability to hear distinctions in Native American languages reflected their habits of perception rather than deficiencies of the language being studied (Hill and Mannheim 1992). For Boas, language alone thus provided a privileged window into cultural patterns that were otherwise distorted by "secondary explanations" (Bauman and Briggs 2003). Documentation of the linguistic practices of populations threatened by racism was an important focus of early work in linguistic anthropology that continues today (see Brittain and MacKenzie, this volume; Meek, this volume).

Scholarship on race in linguistic anthropology and sociolinguistics has reflected varied assumptions about what language is and where language is to be studied. The DISTINCTIVE ETHNORACIAL LANGUAGE perspective attends primarily to linguistic patterns that distinguish ethnoracial groups. It locates language as an abstract system of communication shared by group members that can be characterized in terms of linguistic features or discourse strategies. The ACTS OF ETHNORACIAL IDENTITY (cf. Le Page and Tabouret-Keller 1985) perspective shifts attention to the moment-to-moment construction of ethnoracial identities within speech events, treating linguistic elements not as features of groups but as resources for achieving interactional ends. Here, too, language remains a relatively abstract object, but one recruited by speaking subjects who creatively and performatively exercise agency. A final RACIALIZATION approach expands the focus to include the "listening subject" (Inoue 2006): language is an object only insofar as it has come to be understood as such; it is necessarily subject to situated interpretation, cultural production, and regimes of power, emerging and circulating over various scales of space and time in interactional events and cultural institutions. While our identification of three trends may misleadingly suggest discrete theoretical ruptures, we emphasize that most studies are, at least peripherally, concerned with the full range of analytical objects and sites mentioned here.

2.2 Distinctive Ethnoracial Language

One early line of research on language and race examines how ethnoracial groups use language in distinctive ways, approximating a one-to-one mapping of people, linguistic varieties, and cultures (Bauman and Briggs 2003). Under this *Distinctive Ethnic Language* paradigm, which emerged in the 1960s, ethnolects, such as African American English (AAE), are internally cohesive and systematically patterned structures of sound, grammar, words, and discourse (Green 2002). This conception aligns with a structuralist view of language as an abstract system of speaker competence, where linguistic units (phonemes, morphemes, words, phrases) combine according to complex rules.

By adopting a language of structuralism to describe language-internal distinctions (e.g., voiced/voiceless) as well as language-external ones (e.g., black/white), scholars mobilized tools of science to provide intellectually compelling arguments of moral, cultural, and linguistic equality: working-class blacks used a system of communication that was as referentially logical, structurally complex, and culturally sophisticated as that used by middle-class whites (Bucholtz 2003). This body of research was aimed at exposing the workings of linguistic racism, an important legacy that continues today (Purnell, Idsardi, and Baugh 1999).

While work in sociolinguistics has sought to describe the distinctive phonology, syntax, and lexicon of ethnolects such as AAE (Labov 1972, Smitherman 1977, Baugh 1983), Chicano English (Fought 2003), and Native American English (Leap 1993), anthropological studies have attended to distinctiveness in discourse. For example, this research has highlighted how African Americans, Asian Americans, European Americans, and Native Americans may have varied discourse practices with respect to bedtime narratives (Heath 1983), oral narratives (Au 1980), classroom interactions (Michaels 1981, Philips 1983, Cazden 1988), game disputes (Goodwin 1990), and indirect critique (Mitchell-Kernan 1972). As noted in these studies, differing communication styles can lead to misunderstandings in institutional settings, whether as a result of contrasting participation frameworks (Philips 1983), narrative sequences (Michaels 1981), prosodic cues (Gumperz 1982), causal ordering (Young 1994), or expectations of sociability (Bailey 1997).

Yet the concept of ethnic distinctiveness in language has remained undeniably slippery (Eckert 2008, Jaspers 2008, Benor 2010). After all, no linguistic element is exclusive to a single variety and all dialects are historically and contextually variable (Agha 2007, Wolfram 2007). In addition, the tacit equivalence of "ethnically distinct" and "non-white" has been challenged in studies that have examined white ethnic communities (e.g., Schiffrin 1984, Benor 2012). In its focus on the ethnolect as an abstract system that can be objectively described, it has overlooked a key question: *Who hears language as "ethnoracial"?* As noted by Bucholtz (2003), the linguist – often an outsider to the group being studied – has ultimately served as the arbiter of which features to classify as ethnically distinctive. In addition, descriptions typically refer to linguistic difference from a white, middle-class standard (e.g., copula *deletion* [from Standard English], monophthong*ization* [of Standard English diphthongs]), presupposing the normativity of Standard English and erasing the linguist's own subjectivity in the process (Silverstein 1996).

2.3 Acts of Ethnoracial Identity

In the 1980s, some language scholars turned their attention to *identity* as an object of investigation, conceptualizing language not in terms of characteristic features of groups but as resources that individuals draw upon to construct ethnoracial selves. Scholars of the *Acts of Ethnoracial Identity* approach concentrate on how linguistic elements index (Ochs 1992, Silverstein 2003) – that is, point to and create – ethnoracial meanings. Aligning with social constructionism more generally, this view frames identity as an outcome of linguistic practice (Bucholtz and Hall 2004). This turn to the performative subject reflects a political recognition that speakers are not bound to a singular biographical fate; their linguistic agency allows them to contest hegemonic ascriptions of ethnoracial identity.

Rather than identifying linguistic norms across a group, this approach has theorized moment-to-moment negotiations of identity among co-participants in everyday conversations and public performances. Research on code-switching and style-shifting, for example, has highlighted the multiple possibilities of ethnoracial identifications when racialized speakers strategically deploy their varied linguistic repertoires. Studies of Puerto Rican American children (Zentella 1997), Dominican American high school students (Bailey 2002), and white middle-class American boys (Cutler 1999) have depicted multilingual and multidialectal speakers as flexible and creative interlocutors, celebrating linguistic heterogeneity as the outcome of speaker choice and virtuosity rather than disorder or confusion. For example, Barrett (1999) has shown how African American drag queens adopt multiple styles – namely the use of a "white woman" style in addition to an African American and gay male styles – in ways that challenge racist and homophobic ideologies even while maintaining certain misogynistic assumptions. Similarly, Alim and

Smitherman (2012) have illustrated how US President Barack Obama adopted various linguistic strategies in order to "Whiten," "Blacken," "Americanize," and "Christianize" himself, thus hitting a cultural "sweet spot," despite marginalizing discourses of language, citizenship, religion, and race (p. 23). In addition, one subset of this research has attended to speakers who use language understood as belonging to ethnic outsiders, a practice called "crossing" (Rampton 1995), which may be leading to the emergence of new language varieties in urban youth communities (Alim, Ibrahim, and Pennycook 2009, Rampton 2011).

In its focus on the performative subject, this approach acknowledges that identity is an outcome of language rather than prior to it. However, such work maintains the assumption that languages are classifiable, nameable, juxtaposable objects (Woolard 2004) and may attribute more agency to individuals than is often the case, by describing speakers who *construct* identities, *deploy* linguistic forms, and *determine* their attendant ethnoracial meanings. Thus, while an *Acts of Ethnoracial Identity* approach recognizes the heterogeneous complexity of language, it sometimes lacks reflexive attention to linguists' and community members' language ideologies that underlie these acts of identity. In the next section, we describe an approach that places such ideologies at the center of its analysis.

2.4 Racialization

A final body of work, grounded in a linguistic anthropological tradition, brings *language ideologies* to the analytical foreground, namely, how languages become enregistered (Agha 2007) as racialized objects, how linguistic differences are created and mapped onto social differences, including race, gender, class, and sexuality (Irvine and Gal 2000), and how these webs of social meaning are mapped onto interactions. Under the *Racialization* view, scholars attend to the cultural processes by which such associations emerge and move across various scales of space and time – across interactional and institutional sites. Indeed, some of the most stimulating work in linguistic anthropology has examined the complex relationship between racialization and language, tracing how ideologies of authentic ethnolects and universal standards point to the workings of standard language ideology, how ideologies of language and race are reproduced and disrupted, and how racialized indexical values and identities are complex and indeterminate.

3 Critical Issues and Current Contributions

3.1 Ethnolect as Ideology

A key contribution of linguistic anthropology is its recognition of ethnolects as ideological – namely, a component of standard language ideology (Silverstein 1996, Walters 1996). According to this ideology, produced through European encounters with linguistic and racial others (Bauman and Briggs 2003), some languages – "authentic" nonstandard languages – are well-suited to expressing one's identity, anchoring the self in a particular time, place, and community, while others – "anonymous" standard languages – represent "a voice from nowhere" (Gal 2006, Woolard 2008). One important strand of this research examines, from a historical perspective, how ethnoracial difference is projected onto forms of linguistic difference, whether in European efforts to describe the peoples and languages of Africa (Irvine and Gal 2000, Irvine 2001); Spanish attempts to write grammars and prepare dictionaries in the colonial Yucatan (Hanks 2010); or the creation of the category of Standard American English, which located authentic English in the white rural Midwest, away from racialized urban centers (Bonfiglio 2002).

Framing racialization as an encounter between a listening subject and a speaking subject (Inoue 2006), rather than as a self-evident production, has revealed how racializing ideas about linguistic difference are embedded in the idea of the Indo-European language family (Olender 1992) and the creation of the categories of creole and pidgin (Bolton 2000). In other words, what we hear as a distinct ethnolectal variety is not based on a pre-existing empirically verifiable linguistic reality but on the ways that we are socialized to recognize certain distinctions while erasing others (Irvine and Gal 2000) in the service of specific ideological interests (Woolard and Schieffelin 1994). For example, many Americans have been socialized to hear "double negatives" as a distinctive feature of African American language, although many white speakers in the US South also use this feature, and black speakers employing it do so in particular discourse contexts. Moreover, what counts as a vernacular as opposed to a standard can shift (Gal 2006, 2012): Standard American English can be framed as a timeless, placeless standard when contrasted against AAE, for example, but as a temporally and regionally specific vernacular against British English.

3.2 Ideological Production/Disruption

Linguistic anthropologists have investigated how discursive processes play a key role in producing, and sometimes disrupting, ideologies of language, race, power, and authenticity – that is, how linguistic and other semiotic acts can produce racial categories and assign moral value to them in ways that benefit certain groups, often at the expense of others. As Jane Hill (2008) has argued in her book *The everyday language of white racism,* a single linguistic moment can index both overt and covert social meanings, such that racist ideologies can be reproduced in relatively hidden yet mundane ways (see also Dick and Wirtz 2011). White English monolinguals who draw on hyper-Anglicized Spanish may portray themselves as playful or cosmopolitan, yet this portrait covertly depends on racist images of lazy Latino others (Hill 1998). Similarly, male European Americans or Asian Americans who use AAE-influenced elements may perform masculine toughness or youthful coolness, yet they simultaneously reinforce stereotypes of black hypermasculinity (Bucholtz 1999, Chun 2001, Bucholtz and Lopez 2011). While racializing discourses are likely to depend on hegemonic ideologies of race, these ideologies can be contested, for example, when nonwhite speakers construct whiteness as a non-normative category (Gaudio 2001, Trechter 2001, Jacobs-Huey 2003, Chun 2004).

While racist discourse may emerge in explicit forms in some settings (Billig 2001, Lo forthcoming), explicit talk about race – a genre known as "race talk" – can be sanctioned as inappropriate. Consequently, speakers engage in extensive metalinguistic labor when participating in it, for example rationalizing the mention of race (Anderson 2008), seeking alignment from others (Pagliai 2009), or claiming a nonracist identity (Van Dijk 1992) by positioning others as racist (Reyes 2011, Koven 2013, Pardo 2013, Tetreault 2013). In other cases, participants position themselves as not talking explicitly or willingly about race through strategies of inarticulateness (McElhinny 2001, Bucholtz 2011a) or the claim that they are merely talking about "language" or "culture," as illustrated in Urciuoli's (1996) book *Exposing prejudice: Puerto Rican experiences of language, race, and class.* Her important work illustrates how what is understood as "ethnic," as opposed to "racial," in US discourses is primarily a matter of framing, respectively as "acceptable, non-threatening difference" or as "unacceptable, threatening difference." Linguistic acts that covertly reproduce racial stereotypes occur in a range of culturally significant everyday and institutional genres, including narratives (Bucholtz 1999, 2011a, Wortham 2011b), pretend play (García-Sánchez 2014), rap battles (Alim, Lee, and Carris 2010), and government documents (Dick 2011). Racializing processes also intersect with related ideologies about individual agency, intentionality, and authenticity as participants reconcile what is "said" with what is "meant" (Hill 2008, Pardo 2013); which signs are "natural" and which ones are "acquired" (Bucholtz 1995, Hill 2008, Roth-Gordon 2011); whether ethnic identity is about "being" or "doing" (Kang and Lo 2004); whether an interaction is "naturally occurring" vs. "performed" (Hall 1995, Barrett 1999, Bucholtz 2003); and whose knowledge is "authentic" or "expert" and whose is not (Jacobs-Huey 2006).

3.3 Indexical Indeterminacy

As the cultural value of language is produced by those who listen from different ideological positions, what language indicates about the sociocultural context (e.g. its social indexicality) is not always shared (Agha 2007). Indexical values are multiple and often indeterminate (Silverstein 1992, Irvine 1996, Jaffe 2009). One of the earliest works in this vein was Basso's (1979) *Portraits of "the Whiteman": Linguistic play and cultural symbols among the western Apache*, which illustrated how linguistic practices that were understood by whites as perfectly normal were seen by Western Apache as intrusive and overbearing. Similarly, Morgan (1991) investigated how white women and African American women had sharply differing interpretations of African American expressions of indirectness. Such work built upon earlier studies of cross-cultural miscommunication (e.g., Twitchin 1979, Gumperz 1982) that illustrated how the same linguistic sign could have variable interpretations across listeners. Research on out-group talk has demonstrated how linguistic practices considered inappropriate in some settings (e.g. whites speaking AAE) may be ratified in local contexts (Cutler 1999, Sweetland 2002). Experimental research on race and language has made similar claims, documenting how the speech of African Americans and Asian Americans is not heard by everyone as indicating a speaker's race (Hanna 1997, Lindemann 2003, Wolfram 2007).

Whereas early ethnolectal work presumed that language reflects a speaker's genuine identity – "who they really are" – and that a clear line can be drawn between when I'm "being me" and when I'm "performing someone else," linguistic anthropologists have shown that participants are positioned in relation to their language and to social others through complex footings (Goffman 1981) or stances (Du Bois 2007, Jaffe 2009). People can fluidly position themselves in relation to figures of personhood (Reyes 2007) – distancing themselves from these figures in moments of mockery (e.g., Ronkin and Karn 1999, Kiesling 2001), adopting them in acts of alignment (e.g., Barrett 1999, Lo 1999), or commenting ironically on them in satire (e.g., Chun 2004, Bucholtz and Lopez 2011), as the performance frame itself can come to the fore (Barrett 1999). Analyses at the interactional scale have also revealed the nuanced negotiations of indexical value when multiple ideologies co-exist. For example, Lo (1999) has shown that participants negotiate whether an individual is a legitimate speaker of an ethnic variety or whether something counts as homage, alignment, or overperformance. In her study, she illustrates how a Korean ethnic slur is used by a young Chinese American in order to affiliate with his Korean American interlocutor, yet the use of this slur is rejected by the Korean American, given their different ideologies of language and ethnicity related to this term. Because indexical meanings are emergent and negotiated, terms like "Asian American" or "Black" do not necessarily have stable values across events (Reyes 2005, 2011), items that may be identified by linguists as "African American slang" can point to distinctions of race in one moment but age, region, and class in other moments (Reyes 2005), and Asian American stereotypes can serve as oppressive homogenizations as well as celebratory resources across a single interaction (Reyes 2007). Likewise, the value of discursive acts also unfolds moment by moment, as an act that appears to be accommodation can subsequently be transformed into mockery (Chun 2009). Whether a speaker is challenging or reproducing hegemonic ideologies of language is therefore not always evident, as Chun's (2004) analysis of Margaret Cho's performances of Mock Asian demonstrates.

In recent years, scholars have examined how divergent interpretations of cultural signs, linked to local cultural figures, produce particular identity positions within and across institutions and communities. For example, in her book *White kids: Language, race, and styles of youth identity*, Bucholtz (2011c) shows how European American youth at a California high school in the 1990s position themselves in relation to local figures of coolness by variably aligning with AAE or Standard English. White hip-hop fans, for example, adopted terms used by their African American peers, such as *patna,* while preppies more readily used terms such as *hella,* which originated from AAE but was no longer associated with blackness. Nerds generally rejected AAE-origin terms, aligning themselves with Standard English instead. Bucholtz (2009) also analyzes how Chicano youth, adult teachers, and the US popular media position themselves in relation to the Spanish word *güey*; while students associate the term with cool, working-class masculinity, teachers and the media associate it with vulgarity and middle-class masculinity, respectively. Wortham has similarly demonstrated how residents in a Pennsylvania town variously interpreted racialized, plastic collectible figurines called "Homies," viewed by some as celebrations of a Mexican gangster lifestyle yet viewed by others as authentic versions of their own Mexican experience (Wortham, Mortimer, and Allard 2009, Wortham 2011a).

Such work has shown that the constitution of ethnoracial identities does not depend on the use of ethnolects. Rather, it depends on how participants position themselves and become positioned in relation to racialized styles and figures of personhood, as in Rosa's (forthcoming) discussion of the complex voicing involved in "Inverted Spanglish," where Latino high school students speak Spanish in two different ways: mockingly vocalizing white figures attempting to use Spanish and performing "themselves" in cool, youth-oriented slang. In particular, research on Asian Americans has noted that while a recognizable variety of Asian American English may not circulate (Reyes and Lo 2004, Lo and Reyes 2009), participants can position themselves in relation to figures of Asian immigrants (Bucholtz 2004, Chun 2004, Talmy 2004, Reyes 2007, Shankar 2008b, Reyes forthcoming) or African American youth (Chun 2001, 2013, Reyes 2005, Bucholtz 2004). The production of an Asian American identity thus does not depend upon "distinctive" Asian American linguistic features, but on stances that speakers produce towards various kinds of ethnic figures.

Indexicality determines that racial meanings always come bundled together with other meanings (Keane 2003), so signs that point primarily to race for some listeners can index age, place, class, and/or gender to others (Morgan 1994, Shankar 2008a, Sharma 2011, Wong and Hall-Lew 2014), and signs enregistered as indexes of regional or class dialects, like Pittsburghese or Standard English, can also be associated with speakers defined in racial terms (Lippi-Green 1997, Eberhardt 2012). Research on how signs and meanings are complexly bundled has analyzed the workings of implicit reference. For example, scholars have examined talk that alludes to but does not name race – discourse about culture, like "hard-working/lazy" or "diverse/non-diverse" (Urciuoli 1996, 2009); language, like "slang/standard" (Urciuoli 1996, Roth-Gordon 2009, Urciuoli 2009); place and class, like "urban," "suburban," "ghetto," and "prep" (Modan 2007, Chun 2011, LaDousa 2011); or lifestyles, like "playboys," "migrants," or "FOBs" ("fresh-off-the-boat") (Roth-Gordon 2007, Shankar 2008b). This research has also investigated how linguistic signs work together with non-linguistic signs. For example, in *Homegirls: Language and cultural practice among Latina youth gangs,* Mendoza-Denton (2008) illustrates how Latina gang girls rely on a "lexicon" of make-up (lipstick, eyeliner, foundation) and language to identify either as Norteña or Sureña gang members.

4 Future Directions

Linguistic anthropological research has made significant contributions to our understanding of language and race, elucidating not only why race continues to be viewed as a natural dimension of human difference but also how linguistic markers of race are linked to complex ideological configurations. An issue that remains to be investigated is how scholars can best conceptualize this process across time and space, for example how can we connect what happens in face-to-face moments with what happens in media or legal discourses or how events of the past are brought to bear on those of the present or future. Some of the most stimulating work in this area has begun to address this very issue of language and race across *temporal and spatial scales*.

Moving beyond earlier research, which tended to provide post hoc explanations of how "micro" moments relate to "macro" structures or how "local" discourses draw on "global" ones, newer work has investigated how racialized signs are taken up along trajectories of speech events, moving across powerful institutions, including schools, the legal system, and the media (Wortham 2005, Dick 2011, Wortham 2011a, Reyes 2013, Chun forthcoming). As researchers investigate how racialized personas and varieties get linked to times and spaces (Dick 2010, Blanton 2011, Wirtz 2014), such as those that are "modern," "backwards," or "rural," they have also focused increasing attention on how these ensembles are mediatized, or packaged and circulated as objects for media consumption, whether in live performances (Chun 2004, Wirtz 2014), television and film (Bucholtz 2011b, Bucholtz and Lopez 2011, Lo and Kim 2011, 2012), corporate advertisements (Limerick 2012, Shankar 2015), YouTube videos (Chun and Walters 2011, Walton and Jaffe 2011, Chun 2013), songs, or video games (Mendoza-Denton 2011). For example, Shankar (2015) describes how advertising executives craft ads that imagine, appeal to, and create Asian American consumers in ways that reproduce racist ideologies of white normativity, while Wirtz (2014) examines how folklore performances present images of Blackness, the past, and the present in Cuba. This new work attends to the ways that different participants take up and interpret media images, as in Chun's (2013) analysis of how YouTube commenters evaluate an Asian American's use of "black" linguistic features when performing racialized figures of "gangster" and "ironic" cool. Scholars have begun to attend to the ideological consequences of these mediatizing processes; Bucholtz (2011b), for example, has analyzed how cultural interpretations of white users of linguistic features linked to blackness were "indexically regimented," or shaped over time, in American films from the mid-1990s to the 2000s.

The media is an especially persuasive and powerful institution, shaping ideas about our ethnoracial landscape, interpolating us to position ourselves within it, and guiding interpretations of the past and present (see Van Dijk, this volume; Wodak, this volume). As racialization involves both the centrifugal and the centripetal – moving outward as much as inward and backward as much as forward – the task remains for the scholar to unpack these layers and trajectories of time and space. By doing so, we might come to better understand what it is that we are doing with racialized language, how it relates to what we believe about race and language, and where it is that things might go from here.

Acknowledgments

We thank Angela Reyes and Nancy Bonvillain for their helpful comments on an earlier version of this paper. All remaining errors are ours.

Related Topics

8 Social Subordination and Language (Huayhua); **12** Language, Sexuality, Heteroglossia, and Intersectionality (Leap); **13** Language, Gender, and Identity (Pichler); **14** Discursive Practices, Linguistic Repertoire, and Racial Identities (Baugh); **19** Language and Political Economy (McElhinny); **20** Language, Immigration, and the Nation-State (Pujolar); **24** Discrimination via Discourse (Wodak); **25** Racism in the Press (Van Dijk).

References

Agha, Asif. 2007. *Language and social relations*. Cambridge: Cambridge University Press.
Alim, H. Samy and Geneva Smitherman. 2012. *Articulate while Black: Barack Obama, language, and race in the U.S.* New York: Oxford University Press.
Alim, H. Samy, Arnetha Ball, and John Rickford, (edited by). Forthcoming. *Racing language, languaging race*. Stanford, CA: Stanford University Press.
Alim, H. Samy, Awad Ibrahim, and Alastair Pennycook. 2009. *Global linguistic flows: Hip hop cultures, youth identities, and the politics of language*. New York: Routledge.
Alim, H. Samy, Jooyoung Lee, and Lauren Mason Carris. 2010. " 'Short, fried-rice-eating Chinese emcees' and 'good-hair-havin Uncle Tom niggas': Performing race and ethnicity in freestyle rap battles." *Journal of Linguistic Anthropology* 20(1): 116–133.
Anderson, Kate. 2008. "Justifying race talk: Indexicality and the social construction of race and linguistic value." *Journal of Linguistic Anthropology* 18(1): 108–129.
Au, Kathryn Hu–pei. 1980. "Participation structures in a reading lesson with Hawaiian children: Analysis of a culturally appropriate instructional event." *Anthropology and Education Quarterly* 11(2): 91–115.
Bailey, Benjamin H. 1997. "Communication of respect in interethnic service encounters." *Language in Society* 26(3): 327–356.
Bailey, Benjamin H. 2002. *Language, race, and negotiation of identity: A study of Dominican Americans*. New York: LFB Scholarly Publishing.
Barrett, Rusty. 1999. "Indexing polyphonous identity in the speech of African American drag queens." In *Reinventing identities: The gendered self in discourse*, edited by Mary Bucholtz, A. C. Liang, and Laurel A. Sutton, 313–331. New York: Oxford University Press.
Basso, Keith H. 1979. *Portraits of "the Whiteman": Linguistic play and cultural symbols among the western Apache*. New York: Cambridge University Press.
Baugh, John. 1983. *Black street speech: Its history, structure, and survival*. Austin: University of Texas Press.
Bauman, Richard and Charles L. Briggs. 2003. *Voices of modernity: Language ideologies and the politics of inequality*. New York: Cambridge University Press.
Benor, Sarah Bunin. 2010. "Ethnolinguistic repertoire: Shifting the analytic focus in language and ethnicity." *Journal of Sociolinguistics* 14(2): 159–183.
Benor, Sarah. 2012. *Becoming frum: How newcomers learn the language and culture of Orthodox Judaism*. New Brunswick, NJ: Rutgers University Press.
Billig, Michael. 2001. "Humour and hatred: The racist jokes of the Ku Klux Klan." *Discourse & Society* 12(3): 267–289.
Blanton, Ryan. 2011. "Chronotopic landscapes of environmental racism." *Journal of Linguistic Anthropology* 21(S1): E76–E93.
Bolton, Kingsley. 2000. "Language and hybridization: Pidgin tales from the China coast." *Interventions* 2(1): 35–52.
Bonfiglio, Thomas Paul. 2002. *Race and the rise of standard American*. New York: Mouton de Gruyter.
Bucholtz, Mary. 1995. "From mulatta to mestiza: Passing and the linguistic reshaping of ethnic identity." In *Gender articulated: Language and the socially constructed self*, edited by Kira Hall, and Mary Bucholtz, 351–373. New York, NY: Routledge.
Bucholtz, Mary. 1999. "You da man: Narrating the racial other in the production of white masculinity." *Journal of Sociolinguistics* 3(4): 443–460.
Bucholtz, Mary. 2003. "Sociolinguistic nostalgia and the authentication of identity." *Journal of sociolinguistics* 7(3): 398–416.
Bucholtz, Mary. 2004. "Styles and stereotypes: The linguistic negotiation of identity among Laotian American youth." *Pragmatics* 14(2–3).

Bucholtz, Mary. 2009. "From stance to style: Gender, interaction, and indexicality in Mexican immigrant youth slang." In *Stance: Sociolinguistic perspectives*, edited by Alexandra M. Jaffe, 146–170. New York: Oxford University Press.

Bucholtz, Mary. 2011a. "'It's different for guys': Gendered narratives of racial conflict among white California youth." *Discourse and Society* 22(4): 385–402.

Bucholtz, Mary. 2011b. "Race and the re-embodied voice in Hollywood film." *Language and Communication* 31: 255–265.

Bucholtz, Mary. 2011c. *White kids: Language, race, and styles of youth identity.* Cambridge Cambridge University Press.

Bucholtz, Mary and Kira Hall. 2004. "Language and identity." In *A companion to linguistic anthropology*, edited by Alessandro Duranti, 369–394. Oxford: Basil Blackwell.

Bucholtz, Mary and Qiuana Lopez. 2011. "Performing blackness, forming whiteness: Linguistic minstrelsy in Hollywood film." *Journal of Sociolinguistics* 15(5): 680–706.

Cazden, Courtney B. 1988. *Classroom discourse: The language of teaching and learning.* Portsmouth, NH: Heinemann.

Chun, Elaine. 2001. "The construction of White, Black, and Korean American identities through African American Vernacular English." *Journal of Linguistic Anthropology* 11(1): 52–64.

Chun, Elaine. 2004. "Ideologies of legitimate mockery: Margaret Cho's revoicings of Mock Asian." *Pragmatics* 14(2/3): 263–289.

Chun, Elaine. 2009. "Speaking like Asian immigrants: Intersections of accommodation and mocking at a U.S. high school." *Pragmatics* 19(1): 17–38.

Chun, Elaine. 2011. "Reading race beyond black and white." *Discourse and Society* 22(4): 403–421.

Chun, Elaine W. 2013. "Ironic blackness as masculine cool: Asian American language and authenticity on YouTube." *Applied linguistics* 34(5): 592–612.

Chun, Elaine. Forthcoming. "The meaning of *Ching-Chong*: Language, racism, and response in new media." In *Racing language, languaging race*, edited by H. Samy Alim, Arnetha Ball, and John Rickford. Stanford: Stanford University Press.

Chun, Elaine and Keith Walters. 2011. "Orienting to Arab Orientalisms: Language, race, and humor in a YouTube video." In *Digital discourse: Language in the new media*, edited by Crispin Thurlow and Kristine R. Mroczek, 251–273. Oxford: Oxford University Press.

Cutler, Cecilia. 1999. "Yorkville Crossing: A case study of hip hop and the language of a white middle class teenager in New York City." *Journal of Sociolinguistics* 3(4): 428–442.

Dick, Hilary Parsons. 2010. "Imagined lives and modernist chronotopes in Mexican nonmigrant discourse." *American Ethnologist* 37(2): 275–290.

Dick, Hilary Parsons. 2011. "Making immigrants illegal." *Journal of Linguistic Anthropology* 21(S1): E35–E55.

Dick, Hilary Parsons, and Kristina Wirtz, edited by. 2011. *Racializing discourses. A special issue of the Journal of Linguistic Anthropology 21(S1)*.

Du Bois, John W. 2007. "The stance triangle." In *Stancetaking in discourse: Subjectivity, evaluation, interaction*, edited by Robert Englebretson, p. 323. Amsterdam; Philadelphia: John Benjamins.

Eberhardt, Maeve. 2012. "Enregisterment of Pittsburghese and the local African American community." *Language and Communication* 32(4): 358–371.

Eckert, Penelope. 2008. "Variation and the indexical field." *Journal of Sociolinguistics* 12(4): 453–476.

Fought, Carmen. 2003. *Chicano English in context.* New York: Palgrave Macmillan.

Gal, Susan. 2006. "Contradictions of standard language in Europe: Implications for the study of publics and practices." *Social Anthropology* 14(2): 163–181.

Gal, Susan. 2012. "Sociolinguistic regimes and the management of 'diversity'." In *Language in Late Capitalism: Pride and Profit*, edited by Monica Heller, and Alexandre Duchêne, 22–37. Routledge.

García-Sánchez, Inmaculada Ma. 2014. *Language and Muslim immigrant childhoods: The politics of belonging.* Malden, MA: Wiley.

Gaudio, Rudolf P. 2001. "White men do it too: Racialized (homo)sexualities in postcolonial Hausaland." *Journal of Linguistic Anthropology* 11(1): 36–51.

Goffman, Erving. 1981. "Footing." In *Forms of talk*, 124–159. Philadelphia: University of Pennsylvania.

Goodwin, Marjorie Harness. 1990. *He–said–she–said: Talk as social organization among Black children.* Bloomington: Indiana University Press.

Green, Lisa J. 2002. *African American English: A linguistic introduction.* New York: Cambridge University Press.

Gumperz, John J. 1982. *Discourse strategies.* New York: Cambridge University Press.

Hall, Kira. 1995. "Lip service on the fantasy lines." In *Gender articulated: Language and the socially constructed self*, edited by Kira Hall and Mary Bucholtz, 183–216. New York: Routledge.
Hanks, William F. 2010. *Converting words: Maya in the age of the cross*. Berkeley: University of California Press.
Hanna, David B. 1997. "Do I sound 'Asian' to you? Linguistic markers of Asian American identity." In *University of Pennsylvania Working Papers in Linguistics*, edited by Charles Boberg, Miriam Meyerhoff, and Stephanie Strassel, 141–153. Philadelphia, PA: Department of Linguistics, University of Pennsylvania.
Heath, Shirley Brice. 1983. *Ways with words: Language, life, and work in communities and classrooms*. New York: Cambridge University Press.
Hill, Jane. 1998. "Language, race, and white public space." *American Anthropologist* 100(3): 680–689.
Hill, Jane H. 2008. *The everyday language of white racism*. Malden, MA: Wiley–Blackwell.
Hill, Jane H. and Bruce Mannheim. 1992. "Language and world view." *Annual Review of Anthropology* 21: 381–404.
Inoue, Miyako. 2006. *Vicarious language: Gender and linguistic modernity in Japan*. Berkeley, CA: University of California Press.
Irvine, Judith T. 1996. "Shadow conversations: The indeterminacy of participant roles." In *Natural Histories of Discourse*, edited by Michael Silverstein and Greg Urban, 131–159. Chicago: University of Chicago Press.
Irvine, Judith T. 2001. "The family romance of colonial linguistics: Gender and family in nineteenth century representations of African languages." In *Languages and publics: The making of authority*, edited by Susan Gal and Kathryn A. Woolard. Manchester: St. Jerome Press.
Irvine, Judith T. and Susan Gal. 2000. "Language ideology and linguistic differentiation." In *Regimes of language: Ideologies, polities, and identities*, edited by Paul V. Kroskrity. Santa Fe, NM: School of American Research Press.
Jacobs-Huey, Lanita. 2003. "Remembering Chrissy: EnGendering knowledge, difference, and power in women's hair care narratives." *Transforming Anthropology* 11(2): 30–42.
Jacobs-Huey, Lanita. 2006. *From the kitchen to the parlor: Language and becoming in African American women's hair care*. New York: Oxford University Press.
Jaffe, Alexandra M. 2009. *Stance: Sociolinguistic perspectives* New York: Oxford University Press.
Jaspers, Jürgen. 2008. "Problematizing ethnolects: Naming linguistic practices in an Antwerp secondary school." *International Journal of Bilingualism* 12(1–2): 85–103.
Kang, M. Agnes and Adrienne Lo. 2004. "Two ways of articulating heterogeneity in Korean-American narratives of ethnic identity." *Journal of Asian American Studies* 7(2): 93–116.
Keane, Webb. 2003. "Semiotics and the social analysis of material things." *Language and Communication* 23(3): 409–425.
Kiesling, Scott F. 2001. "Stances of whiteness and hegemony in fraternity men's discourse." *Journal of Linguistic Anthropology* 11(1): 101–115.
Koven, Michele. 2013. "Antiracist, modern selves and racist, unmodern others: Chronotopes of modernity in Luso-descendants' race talk." *Language and Communication* 33(4, part B): 544–558.
Labov, William. 1972. *Language in the inner city: Studies in the Black English vernacular*. Philadelphia,: University of Pennsylvania Press.
LaDousa, Chaise. 2011. *House signs and collegiate fun: Sex, race, and faith in a college town*. Bloomington, IN: Indiana University Press.
Le Page, R. B. and Andrée Tabouret-Keller. 1985. *Acts of identity: Creole-based approaches to language and ethnicity*. New York: Cambridge University Press.
Leap, William. 1993. *American Indian English*. Salt Lake City: University of Utah Press.
Lemon, Alaina. 2002. "Without a 'concept'? Race as discursive practice." *Slavic Review* 61(1): 54–61.
Limerick, Nicholas. 2012. "Recontextualizing ideologies about social difference in New York Spanish-language newspaper advertising." *Language and Communication* 32(4): 312–328.
Lindemann, Stephanie. 2003. "Koreans, Chinese or Indians? Attitudes and ideologies about non-native English speakers in the United States." *Journal of Sociolinguistics* 7(3): 348–364.
Lippi-Green, Rosina. 1997. *English with an accent: Language, ideology, and discrimination in the United States*. London, New York: Routledge.
Lo, Adrienne. 1999. "Codeswitching, speech community membership, and the construction of ethnic identity." *Journal of Sociolinguistics* 3: 461–479.
Lo, Adrienne. Forthcoming. "'Suddenly faced with a Chinese village': Racialization and Asian Americans in a California suburb." In *Racing language, languaging race*, edited by H. Samy Alim, Arnetha Ball, and John Rickford. Stanford, CA: Stanford University Press.

Lo, Adrienne and Angela Reyes. 2009. "On yellow English and other perilous terms." In *Beyond yellow English: Toward a linguistic anthropology of Asian Pacific America*, edited by Angela Reyes, and Adrienne Lo, 3–20. New York: Oxford University Press.
Lo, Adrienne and Jenna Kim. 2011. "Manufacturing citizenship: Metapragmatic framings of language competencies in media images of mixed race men in South Korea." *Discourse & Society* 22(4): 1–18.
Lo, Adrienne and Jenna Kim. 2012. "Linguistic competency and global citizenship: Contrasting portraits of multilingualism in the South Korean popular media." *Journal of Sociolinguistics* 255–276.
McElhinny, Bonnie. 2001. "See no evil, speak no evil: White police officers' talk about race and affirmative action." *Journal of Linguistic Anthropology* 11(1): 65–78.
McElhinny, Bonnie. 2010. "The audacity of affect: Gender, race and history in linguistic accounts of legitimacy and belonging." *Annual Review of Anthropology* 39: 309–328.
Mendoza-Denton, Norma. 2008. *Homegirls: Language and cultural practice among Latina youth gangs*. Malden, MA: Blackwell.
Mendoza-Denton, Norma. 2011. "The semiotic hitchhiker's guide to creaky voice: Circulation and gendered hardcore in a Chicana/o gang persona." *Journal of Linguistic Anthropology* 21(2): 261–280.
Michaels, Sarah. 1981. "'Sharing time' Children's narrative styles and differential access to literacy." *Language in Society* 10(3): 423–442.
Mitchell-Kernan, Claudia L. 1972. "Signifying and marking: Two Afro-American speech acts." In *Directions in sociolinguistics*, edited by John J. Gumperz, and Dell Hymes, 161–79. New York: Blackwell.
Modan, Gabriella G. 2007. *Turf wars: Discourse, diversity, and the politics of place*. Malden, MA: Blackwell.
Morgan, Marcyliena. 1991. "Indirectness and interpretation in African American women's discourse." *Pragmatics* 1(4): 421–451.
Morgan, Marcyliena. 1994. "Theories and politics in African American English." *Annual Review of Anthropology* 23: 325–345.
Ochs, Elinor. 1992. "Indexing gender." In *Rethinking context: Language as an interactive phenomenon*, edited by Alessandro Duranti, and Charles Goodwin, 335–358. Cambridge: Cambridge University Press.
Olender, Maurice. 1992. *The languages of Paradise: Race, religion, and philology in the nineteenth century*. Cambridge, MA: Harvard University Press.
Omi, Michael and Howard Winant. 1994. *Racial formation in the United States*. New York: Routledge.
Pagliai, Valentina. 2009. "Conversational agreement and racial formation processes." *Language in Society* 38(5): 549–579.
Pardo, Rebecca. 2013. "Reality television and the metapragmatics of racism." *Journal of Linguistic Anthropology* 23(1): 65–81.
Philips, Susan Urmston. 1983. *The invisible culture: Communication in classroom and community on the Warm Springs Indian reservation*. New York: Longman.
Purnell, Thomas, William Idsardi, and John Baugh. 1999. "Perceptual and phonetic experiments on American English dialect identification." *Journal of Social Psychology* 18(1): 10–30.
Rampton, Ben. 1995. *Crossing: Language and ethnicity among adolescents*. New York: Longman.
Rampton, Ben. 2011. "From 'multi-ethnic adolescent heteroglossia' to 'contemporary urban vernaculars'." *Language and Communication* 31(4): 276–294.
Reyes, Angela. 2005. "Appropriation of African American slang by Asian American youth." *Journal of Sociolinguistics* 9(4): 509–532.
Reyes, Angela. 2007. *Language, identity, and stereotype among Southeast Asian American youth: The other Asian*. Mahwah, NJ: Lawrence Erlbaum Associates.
Reyes, Angela. 2011. "'Racist!': Metapragmatic regimentation of racist discourse by Asian American youth." *Discourse & Society* 22(4): 458–473.
Reyes, Angela. 2013. "Corporations are people: Emblematic scales of brand personification among Asian American youth." *Language in Society* 42(2): 163–185.
Reyes, Angela. Forthcoming. "The voicing of Asian American figures." In *Racing language, languaging race*, edited by H. Samy Alim, John Rickford, and Arnetha Ball. Stanford, CA: Stanford University Press.
Reyes, Angela, and Adrienne Lo. 2004. "Language, identity, and relationality in Asian Pacific America: An introduction." *Pragmatics* 14(2/3): 115–125.
Ronkin, Maggie and Helen E. Karn. 1999. "Mock Ebonics: Linguistic racism in parodies of Ebonics on the Internet." *Journal of Sociolinguistics* 3(3): 360–380.
Rosa, Jonathan. Forthcoming. "From Mock Spanish to Inverted Spanglish: Language ideologies and the racialization of U.S. Latinas/os." In *Racing language, languaging race*, edited by H. Samy Alim, John Rickford, and Arnetha Ball. Stanford, CA: Stanford University Press.

Roth-Gordon, Jennifer. 2007. "Racing and erasing the playboy: Slang, transnational youth subculture, and racial discourse in Brazil." *Journal of Linguistic Anthropology* 17(2): 246–265.

Roth-Gordon, Jennifer. 2009. "The language that came down the hill: Slang, crime, and citizenship in Rio de Janeiro." *American Anthropologist* 111(1): 57–68.

Roth-Gordon, Jennifer. 2011. "Discipline and disorder in the Whiteness of Mock Spanish." *Journal of Linguistic Anthropology* 21(2): 210–228.

Schiffrin, Deborah. 1984. "Jewish argument as sociability." *Language in Society* 13(3): 311–335.

Shankar, Shalini. 2008a. *Desi land: Teen culture, class, and success in Silicon Valley*. Durham: Duke University Press.

Shankar, Shalini. 2008b. "Speaking like a model minority: 'FOB' styles, gender, and racial meanings among Desi teens in Silicon Valley." *Journal of Linguistic Anthropology* 18(2): 268–289.

Shankar, Shalini. 2015. *Advertising diversity: Producing language and ethnicity in American advertising*. Durham, NC: Duke University Press.

Sharma, Devyani. 2011. "Style repertoire and social change in British Asian English." *Journal of Sociolinguistics* 15(4): 464–492.

Silverstein, Michael. 1992. "The indeterminacy of contextualization: When is enough enough?" In *The contextualization of language*, edited by Peter Auer, and Aldo Di Luzio, 55–76. Philadelphia: John Benjamins.

Silverstein, Michael. 1996. "Monoglot 'standard' in America: Standardization and metaphors of linguistic hegemony." In *The matrix of language: Contemporary linguistic anthropology*, edited by Donald Brenneis and Ronald K.S. Macaulay, 284–306. Boulder, CO: Westview Press.

Silverstein, Michael. 2003. "Indexical order and the dialectics of sociolinguistic life." *Language and Communication* 23(3): 193–229.

Smedley, Audrey. 1998. "'Race' and the construction of human identity." *American Anthropologist* 100(3): 690–702.

Smitherman, Geneva. 1977. *Talkin and testifyin: The language of Black America*. Boston: Houghton Mifflin.

Sweetland, Julie. 2002. "Unexpected but authentic use of an ethnically-marked dialect." *Journal of Sociolinguistics* 6: 514–536.

Talmy, Steven. 2004. "Forever FOB: The cultural production of ESL in a high school." *Pragmatics* 14(2/3): 149–172.

Tetreault, Chantal. 2013. "Cultural citizenship in France and le Bled among teens of pan-southern immigrant heritage." *Language and Communication* 33(4, part B): 531–543.

Trechter, Sara. 2001. "White between the lines: Ethnic positioning in Lakhota discourse." *Journal of Linguistic Anthropology* 11(1): 22–35.

Twitchin, John. 1979. Crosstalk. In *Multi-racial Britain* BBC.

Urciuoli, Bonnie. 1996. *Exposing prejudice: Puerto Rican experiences of language, race, and class*. Boulder, CO: Westview Press.

Urciuoli, Bonnie. 2009. "Talking/not talking about race: The enregisterments of culture in higher education discourses." *Journal of Linguistic Anthropology* 19(1): 21–39.

Van Dijk, Teun A. 1992. "Discourse and the denial of racism." *Discourse & Society* 3(1): 87–118.

Walters, Keith 1996. "Contesting representations of African American Language." In *SALSA III: Proceedings of the Third Annual Symposium about Language and Society*, edited by Risako Ide, Rebecca Parker, and Yukako Sunaoshi, 137–151. Austin, TX: Department of Linguistics, University of Texas.

Walton, Shana and Alexandra M. Jaffe. 2011. "'Stuff White People Like': Stance, class, race and internet commentary." In *Digital discourse*, edited by Crispin Thurlow, and Kristine R. Mroczek, 199–219. New York: Oxford University Press.

Wirtz, Kristina. 2014. *Performing Afro-Cuba: Image, voice, spectacle in the making of race and history*. Chicago: University of Chicago Press.

Wolfram, Walt. 2007. "Sociolinguistic folklore in the study of African American English." *Language and Linguistics Compass* 1: 292–313.

Wong, Amy Wing-mei and Lauren Hall-Lew. 2014. "Regional variability and ethnic identity: Chinese Americans in New York City and San Francisco." *Language and Communication* 35(1): 27–42.

Woolard, Kathryn A. 2004. "Codeswitching." In *A companion to linguistic anthropology*, edited by Alessandro Duranti, 73–94. Malden, MA: Blackwell.

Woolard, Kathryn A. 2008. "Language and identity choice in Catalonia: The interplay of contrasting ideologies of linguistic authority." In *Lengua, nación e identidad. La regulación del plurilingüismo en Espana y América Latina*, edited by Kirsten Süselbeck, Ulrike Mühlschlegel, and Peter Masson, 303–323. Frankfurt am Main, Madrid: Vervuert/Iberoamericana.

Woolard, Kathryn A. and Bambi B. Schieffelin. 1994. "Language ideology." *Annual Review of Anthropology* 23: 55–82.
Wortham, Stanton. 2005. "Socialization beyond the speech event." *Journal of Linguistic Anthropology* 15(1): 95–112.
Wortham, Stanton. 2011a. "Homies in the New Latino Diaspora." *Language and Communication 31*: 191–202.
Wortham, Stanton. 2011b. "Racialization in payday mugging narratives." *Journal of Linguistic Anthropology* 21: E56–E75.
Wortham, Stanton, Katherine Mortimer, and Elaine Allard. 2009. "Mexicans as model minorities in the new Latino diaspora." *Anthropology and Education Quarterly 40*: 388–404.
Young, Linda Wai Ling. 1994. *Crosstalk and culture in Sino–American communication*. New York, NY: Cambridge University Press.
Zentella, Ana Celia. 1997. *Growing up bilingual: Puerto Rican children in New York*. Malden, MA: Blackwell.

Further Reading

Bucholtz, Mary. 2011. *White kids: Language, race, and styles of youth identity*. Cambridge: Cambridge University Press.
This compelling ethnography examines how white youth at a California high school use language to perform local styles and to construct their identities, positioning themselves in relation to adults and peers and often reproducing ideologies of race, gender, and class.

Hill, Jane H. 2008. *The everyday language of white racism*. Malden, MA: Wiley-Blackwell.
This provocative book provides a theoretical framework for understanding how white racism in the United States is achieved in covert, everyday ways, including the appropriation of non-white language and the labeling of racist language as "gaffes."

Morgan, Marcyliena. 1994. "Theories and politics in African American English." *Annual Review of Anthropology 23*: 325–345.
This article reviews studies of African American English, showing how these studies are embedded in political and ideological issues about the place of African Americans in US history and culture, and calling for greater consideration of African American women, language attitudes, and identity.

Reyes, Angela. 2007. *Language, identity, and stereotype among Southeast Asian American youth: The other Asian*. Mahwah, NJ: Lawrence Erlbaum Associates.
This richly detailed ethnography of Southeast Asian American youth in Philadelphia illustrates how ethnic stereotypes, such as those of Asian newcomers and African American youth, can be appropriated for various and dynamic interactional purposes.

Urciuoli, Bonnie. 1996. *Exposing prejudice: Puerto Rican experiences of language, race, and class*. Boulder, CO: Westview Press.
This book examines language prejudice experienced by Puerto Ricans in New York by illuminating processes through which people are racialized, race and class are conflated, race and ethnicity are contrasted, and linguistic perceptions are mapped onto race and class.

Zentella, Ana Celia. 1997. *Growing up bilingual: Puerto Rican children in New York*. Malden, MA: Blackwell.
This insightful ethnography describes Spanish-English bilingual strategies and patterns among several Puerto Rican youth in a New York community, illuminating both the situated particularity and patterned generality of their language practices.

16

Analyzing Interactive Discourse
Conversation and Dialogue

Mary Jill Brody

1 Introduction and Historical Perspectives

There are myriad reasons for considering conversation or interactive discourse important for linguistic anthropology, despite the fact that, until recently, monologue narrative has been the default genre of examination. Monologue narrative in the form of folktales from Native American languages filled the notebooks and publications of many early linguistics anthropologists.[1] Yet these same scholars also paid attention to the content (if not the structure) of conversation for their ethnographic bread and butter. Boas, for example, encouraged Zora Neale Hurston to be attentive to conversation in the African American communities to which she had unique access (Lewis 2001). Malinowski relied on Trobriand conversation for much of his understanding of that society,[2] and his emphasis on the importance of phatic communion and language as action showed that the mundane content of everyday conversation was not outside what he considered to be important (1922, 1923). Yet, as Moerman (1988) points out, anthropologists have typically focused on truncated renditions of the content of conversations for their data, rather than on conversational data itself. Conversational data has been coded for content, and the occasional pithy quote has been extracted for a title or a heading, but actual conversation has not until recently been considered to be primary data as such. An important pioneer in this endeavor is Hortense Powdermaker, in her 1962 ethnography *Copper Town: Changing Africa*, where she found conversation an invaluable tool added to her multiple methods including "survey, essay writing, interviewing, casual visiting, attending social affairs," when she was frustrated in her attempt to access the perspective of those living in the segregated African township to which she had limited access:

> Although I drove to it almost daily, I was missing the intimate knowledge and feeling-tone of daily life which comes from actually living in a community, seeing and hearing much that goes on, and participating in daily life, all of which is so essential to an understanding of any society. It occurred to me that I might get a vicarious sense of personal daily life if an assistant recorded everything that people said and did in [their] home and its immediate neighborhood, from the time they got up in the morning until they went to bed; so I asked one to stay home for a week and do just this . . . . At the end of the week, when he brought

me the recorded conversations, I realized that these were really the stuff of life and that they provided what I had been missing. They gave much more than that: attitudes, opinions, and behavior, some of which I had not known existed. Its richness naturally prompted a continuation of the method, not only in this household and neighborhood, but in others and at the beer hall, the public washing stands, the welfare hall, the union meetings, on the road, and wherever Africans met . . . . Knowledge was shared, gossip exchanged, and traditional and modern points of view argued. These conversations about the trivial and the significant, which make up the fabric of personal and social life, had a quality of intimacy which was invaluable to me.

Powdermaker (1962: xix–xx)

These African voices are quoted directly throughout her ethnography: "In the book, they give a personal dimension to an objective study. The reader hears individual Africans talk, as well as listening to the author's description and interpretation" (Powdermaker 1962: xx). It is surprising that other ethnographers did not quickly follow her research methodology guidelines. Certainly the advent of portable tape-recorders made possible this and other types of linguistic fieldwork in conversation.

The extensive overlapping of the sometimes delicately fractional labels for what scholars do who work with interactive discourse in its cultural context can make for confusion. As part of my attempt to discover who linguistic anthropologists are and what they do with interactive discourse, I made an inventory of the first twenty years of the *Journal of Linguistic Anthropology*, to see the frequency and type of use of conversational data in the articles published there. Of course, linguistic anthropologists publish in other journals and those who may describe themselves and their work as other than linguistic anthropology may have their work published in the *Journal of Linguistic Anthropology*; however, I consider this survey as a rough metric of recent trends in the field.[3] I found that fully one quarter of the articles were based entirely or in part on conversational data. Some included lengthy conversational transcripts (e.g., Brody 1991). While some (e.g., Farris 1991) are concerned to present a list of transcriptional conventions in a footnote, most do not. This treatment of transcription conventions points to the fact that some linguistic anthropologists continue to participate in the taken-for-granted nature of transcription discussed below. Given the new concentration on conversational structure, the articles in the *Journal of Linguistic Anthropology* show that linguistic anthropologists continue to pay attention both to the form and to the content of conversation as important data.

Below, I will introduce various threads of analysis of interactive discourse, highlighting their similarities and differences. Next, I will discuss the various systems of transcription that each of these threads has developed; transcription is by no means a neutral act (Bucholtz 2000, Ochs 1979), and the choices made in each case are important. I have chosen to avoid discussion of both mediated and reported (reconstructed) conversation, in order to focus on face-to-face interaction. Not surprisingly, most of the work reviewed will be on analysis of English, with several outstanding exceptions (see below). I have also chosen to avoid discussion of two modes of interactive discourse found in linguistic anthropology: elicitation (see Moore 1993) and, with some exceptions, interview (see Briggs 1986). Both of these modes of dialogue are peculiar controlled and task-specific types of interaction that are to a greater or lesser degree distant from the natural interactions on which I focus.

There are, however, three works based on specialized interview data that merit mention despite my general exclusion of interview here: *The First Five Minutes* by Pittenger, Hockett, and Danehy (1960), Labov and Fanshel's (1977) *Therapeutic Discourse*, and Erickson and Schultz' (1983) *The Counselor as Gatekeeper*. They are important because they were carried out so early in the stream of research reviewed here, because each developed a specialized transcription for their corpus, and because they influenced later work on interviews, conversation, and transcription. *The First Five Minutes* was a truly pioneering work, based on a tape-recording of the first five minutes of an initial session of a patient seeing an experienced psychiatric practitioner. Their transcription was a fine-grained linguistic (phonemic) and paralinguistic one presented in a unique format: pages are cut at the mid-point, with the transcription appearing in the top half of the page and the analysis in the bottom half. The techniques of analysis were explicitly based on "psychiatry and anthropological linguistics" (1960: 207). Like Pittenger et al., Labov and Fanshel developed a micro-analysis of the first five minutes of a psychiatric clinical interview, which they characterize as a "comprehensive discourse analysis," paying attention to "implicit communication," not only "in the form of vocal gestures" but in "the unexpressed social and psychological propositions" as well (1977: 29). Erickson and Schultz were more ambitious in breadth of scope, in that they made video as well as audio recordings of 25 interviews between students and college counselors, and developed a transcription system that included nonverbal (proxemics and eye contact) behavior.

2 Current Contributions and Research

It is challenging to try to organize more than 40 years of different trends in the analysis of interactive discourse. Many disciplines and sub-disciplines have contributed to the study of face-to-face interaction through talk, including Conversation Analysis, Linguistic Anthropology, Discourse Analysis, Sociolinguistics, Interactional Sociolinguistics, Rhetoric, Sociology, Communications, Dialogue Analysis and others. I will discuss the major trends below.

2.1 Interactional Sociolinguistics in Linguistic Anthropology

It is difficult to pinpoint a beginning for the explicit study of conversation within linguistic anthropology. In the 2005 edition of *Conversational Style: Analyzing Talk among Friends* (originally published 1984), Tannen identifies the type of work she does as interactional sociolinguistics, and looks to the early work of John Gumperz (1982) as its antecedent. Schiffrin (1994: 97) identifies interactional sociolinguistics as representing a distinct thread of scholarship working with conversation within the field of discourse analysis, with roots in anthropology, linguistics, and sociology.[4]

Essays within Gumperz 1982 are on topics such as "The sociolinguistics of interpersonal communication," "Conversational code-switching," "Prosody in conversation," "Contextualization conventions," "Socio-cultural knowledge in conversational inference," and "Interethnic communication." At the outset of this work, Gumperz states that he "seeks to develop interpretive sociolinguistic approaches to the analysis of real time processes in face to face encounters" (1982: vii) and defines communication as "a social activity requiring the coordinated efforts of two or more individuals" (1982: 1)

In her preface to the 2005 edition of *Conversational Style*, Tannen states that her work

> is intended for scholars who wish to delve into the theoretical underpinnings of an interactional sociolinguistic approach to analyzing conversational discourse; for students who wish to observe how the microanalysis of conversational discourse is done and try their hand at doing it; and for those interested in how the microanalysis of everyday conversation can play a role in understanding and addressing cross-cultural communication
>
> Tannen (2005: xv)

One premise of interactional sociolinguistics is that talk is incomplete, and hence interlocutors must rely on extralinguistic knowledge and features such as accent, intonation, or gaze to interpret interactions. Such features have been labeled "contextualization cues" by Gumperz (1982). Interactional sociolinguistics has been most interested in the "implicit or indirect" cues that "acquire meaning when interpreted in a specific context" (Jaspers 2012: 137). Contextualization cues take on different meanings in different cultural communication systems, leading to problems in cross-cultural communication (Scollon and Scollon 1981).

2.2 Conversation Analysis

The origins of Conversation Analysis (or CA, always and distinctively with a capital C and a capital A) are in Garfinkle's ethnomethodology (1967) and the sociologically grounded attempt to rigorously analyze behavior, in this case ordinary conversation, as routine replicable social interaction: "for participants, and hence for conversation analysts, the point of departure for the analysis of any utterance is the talk, or other action, that it emerges from" (Goodwin and Heritage 1990: 287). Detailed discussion of the deeper roots of CA can be found in Maynard (2013) and Goodwin and Heritage (1990). The founders of CA were Gail Jefferson, Harvey Sacks, and Emanuel Schegloff, who individually and collectively published a large number of articles. The significance of early work in CA for linguistic anthropology is indicated by the inclusion of papers by Sacks and Schegloff in the important linguistic anthropology collection edited by Gumperz and Hymes *Directions in Sociolinguistics: The Ethnography of Communication* (1972). C. Goodwin (1981) pioneered a thorough introduction to the engagement of interlocutors in conversation that included analysis of gaze. There are several collections of papers in CA, including Atkinson and Heritage (eds) (1984), Boden and Zimmerman (1991), Button, Drew, and Heritage (1986), Button and Lee (1987), Schenkein (1978), and Sudnow (1972), among others.

Michael Moerman's *Talking Culture: Ethnography and Conversation Analysis* (1988) must be considered as the pioneering work of CA meets Linguistic Anthropology; in it he laments that little CA work has been done on languages other than English (p. 3, note 4), and calls for a "culturally contexted conversational analysis" (1988: 5), which he accomplishes through analyses of numerous conversations in English and in Thai, all appropriately contextualized. Its publication spurred a series of papers in the journal *Research on Language and Social Interaction* (vol. 24, 1990), devoted to discussing this work and its impact. Since then extensive CA research has been undertaken in other languages such as Japanese (Hayashi 2003, Maynard 1989, Tanaka 1999), Korean (Kim 1992, 1993, 1999), Dutch (Mazeland 2013), Finnish (Sorjonen 2001), and others. Several linguistic anthropologists have adopted or adapted CA for their analytic and transcriptional purposes (e.g., M. H. Goodwin 2006; see below).

2.3 Dialogue

The "dialogic turn" refers to an endeavor, centered prominently in Europe beginning in the 1990s, that takes as its premise that communication is a "two-way or multidirectional interaction among participants" (Phillips 2011: 3). Such investigations typically (but not always) involve public discourses rather than face-to-face conversations (e.g., Fairclough 1992) and emphasize models (e.g., Weigand 2010); many authors look to Bakhtinian notions of dialogue (Bakhtin 1981, 1984) and Buber's I–thou relationship (Buber 1970). The International Association of Dialogue Analysis initiated their journal *Language and Dialogue* with the injunction that "language means language use in dialogue" (Weigand 2011: 5). This is more than a commitment to conversation, but a philosophical position: "Language as dialogue is not restricted to the dialogic form but means the dialogic function or orientation, in principle, of any language use" (Wiegand 2010: 3).

3 Issues and Topics

There are a number of notable issues that are foci of scholarly work in conversations and dialogue, some of which overlap. I list and discuss some of the important topics of this work below.

Some of the earliest work on conversation has been on socialization and child language acquisition; Ochs (1979), Ochs and Schieffelin (1983), and others have analyzed the conversation of children with their caregivers and with each other (Bloom 1993, Brown 1998, Dorval (ed.) 1990, M. H. Goodwin 1990, 2006, Ochs 1988, Schieffelin 1990). Tannen has published influential books on conversations among friends (Tannen 1984/2005, 1986, 1989) and the stylistic differences in their speech. A great deal of work has been done on conversation and gender (Barrett (forthcoming), Bucholtz, Laiang, and Sutton (eds) 1999, Hall and Bucholtz (eds) 1995, Wodak (ed.) 1997, and others). Early and influential work on gendered conversation has come from the Conversation Analysis perspective (Fishman 1983, Zimmerman and West 1975, West 1979, West and Zimmerman 1983). Investigations of gender in conversation have also revealed cross-cultural differences (Brown 1990, Tannen 1990, (ed.)1993, 1994a, 1994b). Some of the generic characterizations of gender differences in conversation have been challenged by work on individuality (Johnstone 1996, Sawyer 2001). Feminist approaches to gendered conversation include work by McIlvenny (ed.) (2002), Speer (2005), Speer and Stokoe (eds) (2010) Stokoe (2000). The issue of emergent identity in Conversation Analysis has been investigated, especially in relation to gender, but also to other social identities (Antaki and Widdicombe (eds) 1998, Bucholz 2011, Holmes 2006).

Blum-Kulka (1997) investigated Israeli families' dinner-time conversations and Varenne et al. (1992) used data from conversations to examine US families as cultures, taking into consideration issues of power and socialization. Conflict in discourse has been another theme, with focus both on the conflict itself and also its resolution (Brown 1990 and 2011, Grimshaw (ed.) 1990, Haviland 1986, 1996, 1998). Gossip conversations (Brody 1991, 2006, M. H. Goodwin 1990, Haviland 1977a, 1977b, 1998, 2007) are particularly rich in both ethnographic and structural information.

On a more grammatical level, there have been investigations of questions and answers as they operate in conversation and in socialization (Brody 2004, Brown 2010) and on indexicality (Hanks 1990). Repetition in conversation has been investigated for English (Tannen 1987) and for Mayan languages (Brody 1986, 1993, 1994; Brown 1998). Study of the relation between grammar and interaction understands grammar as being emergent from the interaction of social participants (Du Bois 2014, Ochs, Schegloff, and Thompson (eds) 1996). "Grammar's integrity and efficacy are bound up with its place in larger schemes of organization of human conduct, and with social interaction in particular" (Ochs, Schegloff and Thompson (eds) 1996: 3). As early as 1952, Charles Fries developed a usage-based grammar of English from a corpus of recorded telephone conversations. "With the recent development of mechanical devises for the easy recording of the speech of persons in all types of situations there seems to be little excuse for the use of linguistic material not taken from actual communicative practice when one attempts to deal with a living language" (p. 3, note 2).

Formulaic speech in general (Coulmas (ed.) 1981) and greetings in particular (Duranti 1997) have been the focus of cross-cultural investigation. The early paper "Opening up closings" by Schegloff and Sacks (1973), which investigates the termination of telephone calls could be considered in this context as well. There have been a number of important conversational studies in code-switching (Auer (ed.) 1998, Mishoe 1998, Myers-Scotton 1993, Poplack 1980).

One particularly interesting theme of investigation has been the conversational behaviors of those with brain damage that affects their speech (Goodwin (ed.) 2003, Yearly and Brewer 1989). This work is important for what it can tell us about language in the brain and about normal interactions. The focus of this work is on interactions between aphasics (or people whose language has been affected by neurological damage) and others.

> On the one hand, people with fairly intact syntactic and semantic ability have difficulty in engaging in social interaction outside the laboratory. On the other hand, parties with very severe language impairments are nonetheless able to say quite complicated things by successfully using the social and cognitive resources provided by the sequential organization of conversation to tie their talk to the talk of their interlocutors.
>
> Goodwin (2003: 3)

I have mentioned above several themes that analyses of conversation have centered on. This is by no means an exhaustive list but, rather, representative of the kinds of work carried out with conversation and dialogue.

4 Main Research Methods: Transcription

As previously noted, presentation of spoken language on the page has sometimes been taken for granted by linguistic anthropologists (see above). Yet serious consideration of transcription is crucial for all those who engage in the analysis of conversation or interactive discourse, in that spoken language differs from the ways it is written down in numerous significant ways (Bucholtz 2000, Lapadat and Lindsay 1999, Ochs 1979). The impermanent nature of speech makes oral data evanescent, requiring thoughtful application of transcription regarding its analysis and presentation. Issues unique to transcription of multi-party interactions include the identification of individual speakers, overlap and timing of speech, and indication of laughter and other nonverbal sounds. There are several disciplinary threads of transcription for spoken language that include considerable overlap, especially in the serious attention which they pay to the uniquely complex issues of accurately conveying multi-party interaction. I have chosen not to deal with coded transcripts from corpus data in various languages but rather to focus on transcriptions as presented in publications for readers and guidelines for preparing these. I also confine discussion to systems that are used commonly, rather than idiosyncratically.

Of course the IPA and the Americanist systems of phonetic transcription were those first used to record spoken data (Kelly and Local 1989). The detail that these kinds of transcriptions provide, however, is often cumbersome, and only highly trained readers can easily access data transcribed in this way. Transcribers and readers interested in discourse and conversation structure generally find that phonetic transcriptions carry too much information. More highly favored are systems that use common orthographic conventions and specialized indicators of features important to the analysts (e.g., timing of pauses, overlap of speech, etc.).

Edwards (1993) identifies two overarching principles behind transcription systems:

> (1) that the transcript preserve the information needed by the researcher in a manner which is true to the nature of the interaction itself . . . and (2) that its conventions be practical with respect to the way in which the data are to be managed and analyzed, for example, easy to read, apply to new data sets, and expand if needed for other purposes.
>
> Edwards (1993: 4); see also Du Bois (1991), Edwards (2001)

4.1 Georgetown Transcription System

In that the three editors of *The Handbook of Discourse Analysis* are all at Georgetown University, and all claim allegiance to a common model for research at some level (Schiffrin, Tannen, and Hamilton (eds) 2003: 1–10), it is perhaps not unfair to label the transcription initiated by Tannen (1984) and adopted and adapted by Schiffrin, Hamilton, and others as the Georgetown Transcription System. It first appears in Tannen (1984), *Conversational Style: Analyzing Talk among Friends* as "Key to Transcription Conventions" (p. xix). A modified version can be found in Tannen 1989, Appendix II "Transcription Conventions," where she acknowledges the influence of Chafe (1986) in its use of intonation units as lines, and of Preston (1982) in using standardized spelling. It includes approximate pause indication, notations for stress, pitch, intonation, and volume, along with means of indicating overlapping and latched speech (speech of the interlocutor that follows without pause or overlap), as well as conventions for speech that is difficult or impossible to transcribe, and brackets "for comments on quality of speech and context" (Tannen 1984: xix).[5]

4.2 CA Transcription

The transcription system used by CA was developed by Gail Jefferson (Atkinson and Heritage (eds) 1984: ix–xvi), and pays special attention to the sequential nature of talk. There are bracket codings for simultaneous and overlapping utterances, linking for contiguous utterances, indications for timing intervals both within and between utterances, a series of indications for "characteristics of speech delivery" (including lengthening, intonation shifts and contours, speed of speech, volume, emphasis, and vocal qualities such as aspirations, inhalations, gutturalness, and a double parentheses convention for indicating nonverbal sounds, e.g., ((sniff)). Doubtful transcriptions are indicted by single parentheses. Additional features in the CA transcription include representations for gaze direction, applause, and indicators for pointing out the transcriptional items of interest for discussion. Jenks (2011) is a short volume dedicated to teaching the CA transcription system (see also Hepburn and Bolden 2013).

4.3 Du Bois et al.: Santa Barbara Discourse Transcription

The Santa Barbara Discourse Transcription system (Du Bois et al. 1992, Du Bois et al.1993) was developed in conjunction with the Santa Barbara Corpus of Spoken American English (http://www.linguistics.ucsb.edu/research/santa-barbara-corpus). Du Bois (1991: 76) describes exactly what constitutes this transcription system:

> the words spoken, written so as to allow each lexical item to be recognized; an identification of the speaker of each turn; the temporal sequencing of utterances, whether these follow each other in succession or are simultaneous (as when speakers overlap), basic units in which the utterances were articulated, such as turns and intonation units; intonation contour, whether functionally or phonetically classified; accent; fluctuations in timing such as tempo, pause and lengthening; nonverbal noises made by speech event participants, such as laughter, throat-clearing, inhalation; special qualities of voice that extend over a stretch of speech; non-utterance events that become relevant to the interaction, such as a participant's serving food, or a sudden thunderclap in the background; metatranscriptional and "evidential" comments on the transcription itself, indicating where the transcriber is uncertain of the words spoken, and so on; and other features as appropriate.

Notations for the system are included in Appendix 1 Symbols for Discourse Transcription (Du Bois et al. 1991: 104–105). Du Bois et al. 1993 outlines the transcription system, and Du Bois et al. 1992 provides meticulous details for using the system. The Santa Barbara website "Transcription in Action: Resources for the Representation of Linguistic Interaction" (Bucholtz and Du Bois, www.linguistics.ucsb.edu/projects/transcription/representing) provides Du Bois' current materials from his book manuscript *Representing Discourse*, further amplifying Du Bois et al. 1993. The Santa Barbara Discourse Transcription system is by far the most detailed and most effective of all the systems reviewed here.

4.4 Others

Chafe's (1993) transcription system emphasizes prosodic features of speech (specifically, "words, pauses, lengthenings, terminal pitch contours, and both primary and secondary accents" (p. 34) as they operate to indicate cognitively significant "intonation units" and "accent units" (p. 33) that function to indicate information flow in spoken discourse. He generally uses standard spelling, with the exception of *gonna* and *wanna*. In his "Appendix: Summary of Transcription Conventions" he indicates that his system is linked to that of Du Bois et al. 1993.

John Gumperz identifies his transcription system as "a way of transcribing and otherwise preparing for systematic analysis audio- and videotaped oral performances of all kinds, ranging from chat to formal discussion and ritual event, from within a sociolinguistic and functional perspective" (Gumperz and Berenz 1993: 91); his best-known applications have been to cross-cultural conversation within institutional contexts (Gumperz 1982, 1992). His system is designed to display the interpretation of "verbal and nonverbal signs or contextualization conventions, that is, systems of cues that guide conversational management" (Gumperz and Berenz 1993: 91–92), paying particular attention to pauses, overlap, latching, lengthening, volume, pitch, and relative timing. He emphasizes the importance of using standard orthography, with the exception of *gonna* and *wanna*. He makes allowances for transcription of languages other than English and their translation into English (p. 112–113), in the context of having a system amenable to computer keyboard (see Gumperz 1992 for an extended analysis of a discourse segment). "A Note on Conventions" appears at the beginning of *Discourse Strategies* (Gumperz 1982: xi–xii) and "Transcript Notation" appears as an Appendix to Gumperz and Berenz (1993: 121); these systems differ considerably, but maintain the same goals.

This inventory of transcription systems is by no means comprehensive, but concentrates on those systems used by groups of scholars in the US. It turns out that many authors who use transcript data do so without indicating transcription conventions, while others who do so list those used in an ad hoc fashion in a footnote or appendix.

5 Future Directions

Conversation is the matrix of all other speech genres. With the advent of portable recording technology, the means to study conversation became available. Linguistic anthropologists embraced the technology and began to take seriously the fleeting conversational contributions of all kinds of interlocutors: first, for its content, later as a structured form of human communication. The study of conversation forced linguistic anthropologists to rethink the importance of transcription, which they adapted to meet the needs presented by conversational data. Future work will continue to expand the realm of study of interactive discourse among specific groups such as youth and the elderly, variously abled individuals such as those who are autistic or speech-impaired, and a wider range of languages and specialized speech communities. Cross-cultural universals of conversation will be posited and challenged by findings of such investigations. There is much yet to be understood about this most basic form of human communication.

Related Topics

3 Gesture (Streeck); **6** Being in the Cloud (LeBlanc-Wories); **7** Language Ideologies (Kroskrity); **8** Social Subordination and Language (Huayhua); **12** Language, Sexuality, Heteroglossia, and Intersectionality (Leap); **13** Language, Gender, and Identity (Pichler); **14** Discursive Practices, Linguistic Repertoire, and Racial Identities (Baugh); **15** Language and Racialization (Chun, Lo); **17** Communicative Practices in Signed Languages (Senghas); **18** New and Emergent Languages (Riley); **23** The Emergence of Creoles and Language Change (Mufwene); **24** Discrimination via Discourse (Wodak); **26** Legal Discourse (Conley); **27** The Language of Transitional Justice (Hirsch).

Notes

1 Of course these monologue folktale texts are replete with reported conversation, which is outside the scope of this paper.
2 For example "Kula conversations will predominate on such occasions ..." (Malinowski, 1922: 214).
3 I have chosen not to engage the overwhelmingly daunting task of reviewing the contents of the much lengthier run of *Anthropological Linguistics*.
4 The other approaches identified by Schiffrin are speech act theory, ethnography of communication, pragmatics, conversation analysis, and variation analysis.
5 In the 2005 new edition of *Conversational Style*, the transcription conventions appear as Appendix 1.

References

Antaki, C. and S. Widdicombe (eds) (1998) *Identities in Talk*. London: Sage Publications.
Atkinson, J. M. and J. Heritage (eds) (1984) *Structures of Social Action: Studies in Conversation Analysis*. Cambridge: Cambridge University Press.
Auer, P. (ed.) (1998) *Code-Switching in Conversation: Language, Interaction, and Identity*. London and New York: Routledge.
Bakhtin, M. M. (1981) *The Dialogic Imagination. Four Essays*, M. Holquist (ed.), Austin: University of Texas Press.
Bakhtin, M. M. (1984) *Problems of Dostoevsky's Poetics*, C. Emerson (ed. and trans.), Minneapolis: University of Minnesota Press.
Barrett, R. (Forthcoming). *From Drag Queens to Leathermen: Language, Gender, and Gay Male Subcultures*. New York: Oxford University Press.
Bloom, L. (1993) "Transcription and coding for child language research: The parts are more than the whole," in J. A. Edwards and M. D. Lampert (eds) *Talking Data: Transcription and Coding in Discourse Research*, Hillsdale, NJ: Lawrence Erlbaum, pp. 149–168.
Blum-Kulka, S. (1997) *Dinner Talk: Cultural Patterns of Sociability and Socialization in Family Discourse*. Mahwah, NJ: Lawrence Erlbaum.
Boden, D. and D. H. Zimmerman (eds) (1991) *Talk and Social Studies in Ethnomethodology and Conversation Analysis*. Cambridge: Polity Press.
Briggs, C. L. (1986) *Learning how to Ask: A Sociolinguistic Appraisal of the Role of the Interview in Sociolinguistic Research*. Cambridge: Cambridge University Press.
Brody, J. (1986) "Repetition as a rhetorical and conversational device in Tojolab'al (Mayan)," *International Journal of American Linguistics 52*(3): 255–274.
Brody, J. (1991) "Indirection in the negotiation of self in everyday Tojolab'al women's conversation," *Journal of Linguistic Anthropology 1*(1): 78–96.
Brody, J. (1993) "Mayan conversation as interaction," *Texas Linguistics Forum 33*: 234–243.
Brody, J. (1994) "Multiple repetitions in Tojolab'al conversation," in B. Johnstone (ed.) *Repetitions in Discourse*, vol. II, Norwood, NJ: Ablex, pp. 3–14.

Brody, J. (2004) "'Why was I late?' 'I don't know': Tojolab'al answers to questions in context," *Proceedings of the Conference on Indigenous Languages of Latin America I.* (12 pp.) www.ailla.utexas.org/site/cilla1_toc.html.

Brody, J. (2006) "Responsibility in Tojolab'al gossip: Indirect speech, modal orientation, and metalinguistic terms as used to construct self and other in a moral landscape," *Ketzalcalli 2*: 2–21.

Brown, P. (1990) "Gender, politeness and confrontation in Tenejapa," *Discourse Processes 13*: 123–141.

Brown, P. (1998) "Conversational structure and language acquisition: The role of repetition in Tzeltal adult and child speech," *Journal of Linguistic Anthropology 8*(2): 197–221.

Brown, P. (2010) "Questions and their responses in Tzeltal," *Journal of Pragmatics 42*: 2627–2648.

Brown, P. (2011). "Everyone has to lie in Tzeltal" [reprint], in B. B. Schieffelin and P. B. Garrett (eds) *Anthropological Linguistics: Critical Concepts in Language Studies*, Vol. III *Talking about Language*, London: Routledge, pp. 59–87.

Buber, M. (1970) *I and Thou*, W. Kaufmann (trans.), New York: Charles Scribner's Sons.

Bucholtz, M. (2000) "The politics of transcription," *Journal of Pragmatics 32*: 1439–1465.

Bucholtz, M. (2011) *White Kids: Language, Race, and Styles of Youth Identity*, Cambridge: Cambridge University Press.

Bucholtz, M. and J. W. Du Bois. *Transcription in Action: Resources for the Representation of Linguistic Interaction.* www.linguistics.ucsb.edu/projects/transcription/index.html.

Bucholtz, M., A. C. Liang and L. A. Sutton (eds) (1999) *Reinventing Identities: The Gendered Self in Discourse*, New York: Oxford University Press.

Button, G., P. Drew and J. Heritage (eds) (1986) "Interaction and Language Use," Special Double Edition, *Human Studies, 19*: (2–3).

Button, G. and J. R. E. Lee (eds) (1987) *Talk and Social Organization*, Clevedon: Multilingual Matters.

Chafe, W. (1986) "How we know things about language: A plea for catholicism," in D. Tannen (ed.) *Language and Linguistics: The Interdependence of Theory, Data, and Application, Georgetown University Round Table on Languages and Linguistics 1985*, Washington, D. C.: Georgetown University Press, pp. 124–125.

Chafe, W. (1993) "Prosodic and functional units of language," in J. A. Edwards and M. D. Lampert (eds) *Talking Data: Transcription and Coding in Discourse Research*, Hillsdale, NJ: Lawrence Erlbaum, pp. 33–44.

Coulmas, F. (ed.) (1981) *Conversational Routine: Explorations in Standardized Communication Situations and Prepatterned Speech*, The Hague: Mouton Publishers.

Dorval, Bruce (ed.) (1990) *Conversational Organization and its Development*, Norwood, NJ: Ablex.

Du Bois, J. W. (1991) "Transcription design principles for spoken discourse research," *Pragmatics 1*: 71–106.

Du Bois, J. W. (2014) "Towards a dialogic syntax," *Cognitive Linguistics 25*(3): 355–410.

Du Bois, J. W. et al. (1992) "Discourse transcription," *Santa Barbara Papers in Linguistics 4*: 1–225.

Du Bois, J. W. et al. (1993) "Outline of discourse transcription," in J.A. Edwards and M.D. Lampert (eds) *Talking Data: Transcription and Coding in Discourse Research*, Hillsdale, NJ: Lawrence Erlbaum, pp. 45–89.

Duranti, A. (1997) "Universal and culture-specific properties of greetings," *Journal of Linguistic Anthropology 7*(1): 63–97.

Edwards, J. A. (1993) "Principles and contrasting systems of discourse transcription," in J. A. Edwards and M. D. Lampert (eds) *Talking Data: Transcription and Coding in Discourse Research*, Hillsdale, NJ: Lawrence Erlbaum, pp. 3–32.

Edwards, J. A. (2001) "The transcription of discourse," in D. Schiffrin, D. Tannen, and H. E. Hamilton (eds) *The Handbook of Discourse Analysis*, Oxford: Blackwell Publishing, pp. 321–348.

Erickson, F. and J. Shultz. (1983) *The Counselor as Gatekeeper: Social Interaction in Interviews*. New York: Academic Press.

Fairclough, N. (1992) *Discourse and Social Change*, Cambridge: Polity Press.

Farris, C. (1991) "The gender of child discourse: Same-sex peer socialization through language use in a Taiwanese preschool," *Journal of Linguistics Anthropology 1*(2): 198–224.

Fishman, P. (1983) "Interaction: The work women do," in B. Thorne, C. Kramerae and N. Henley (eds) *Language, Gender and Society*, Cambridge, MA: Newbury House, pp. 89–101.

Fries, C. (1952) *The Structure of English: An Introduction to the Construction of English Sentences*, New York: Harcourt Brace.

Garfinckle, H. 1967 *Studies in Ethnomethodology*, Englewood Cliffs, NJ: Prentice-Hall.

Goodwin, C. 1981. *Conversational Organization: Interaction between Speakers and Hearers*, New York and London: Academic Press.

Goodwin, M. H. (1990) *He–Said–She–Said: Talk as Social Organization among Black Children*, Bloomington, IN: Indiana University Press.

Goodwin, M. H. (2006) *The Hidden Life of Girls: Games of Stance, Status, and Exclusion*, Oxford: Blackwell.
Goodwin, C. and J. Heritage (1990) "Conversation Analysis," *Annual Review of Anthropology* 19: 283–307.
Goodwin, C. (ed.) (2003) *Conversation and Brain Damage*, Oxford: Oxford University Press.
Grimshaw, A. D. (ed.) (1990) *Conflict Talk: Sociolinguistic Investigations of Arguments in Conversations*, Cambridge: Cambridge University Press.
Gumperz, J. L. (1982) *Discourse Strategies*, Cambridge: Cambridge University Press.
Gumperz, J. L. (1992) "Contextualization and Understanding," in C. Goodwin and A. Duranti (eds) *Rethinking Context: Language as an Interactive Phenomenon*, Cambridge: Cambridge University Press, pp. 229–252.
Gumperz, J. L. and N. Berenz (1993) "Transcribing conversational exchanges," in J. A. Edwards and M. D. Lampert (eds) *Talking Data: Transcription and Coding in Discourse Research*, Hillsdale, NJ: Lawrence Erlbaum, pp. 91–122.
Gumperz, J. L. and D. Hymes (eds) (1972) *Directions in Sociolinguistics: The Ethnography of Communication*, New York: Holt, Rinehart, and Winston.
Hall, K. and M. Bucholz (eds) (1995) *Gender Articulated: Language and the Socially Constructed Self*, New York: Routledge.
Hanks, W. F. (1990) *Referential Practice: Language and Lived Space among the Maya*, Chicago: University of Chicago Press.
Haviland, J. B. (1977a) "Gossip as competition in Zinacantan," *Journal of Communication* 27(1): 186–191.
Haviland, John B. (1977b) *Gossip, Reputation and Knowledge in Zinacantan*, Chicago: University of Chicago Press.
Haviland, J. B. (1986) "'Con Buenos chiles': Talk, targets and teasing in Zinacantán,' *Text* 6(3): 249–282.
Haviland, J. B. (1996) "'We want to borrow your mouth": Tzotzil marital squabbles,' in C. Briggs (ed.), *Disorderly Discourse: Narrative, Conflict, and Inequality*, Oxford: Oxford University Press, pp. 158–203.
Haviland, J. B. (1998) "'Mu`nuk jbankil to, mu`nuk kajvaltik': 'He is not my older brother, he is not Our Lord.' Thirty years of gossip in a Chiapas village," *Etnofoor* 11(2/2): 57–82.
Haviland, J. B. (2007) "Person reference in Tzotzil gossip: Referring dupliciter," in N. J. Enfield and T. Stivers (eds) *Personal Reference in Interaction: Linguistic, Cultural, and Social Perspectives*, Cambridge: Cambridge University Press, pp. 226–252.
Hayashi, M. (2003) *Joint Utterance Construction in Japanese Conversation*, Amsterdam/Philadelphia: John Benjamins.
Hepburn, A. and G. B. Bolden (2013) 'The conversation analytic approach to transcription,' in J. Sidnell and T. Stivers (eds) *The Handbook of Conversation Analysis*, Malden, MA: Blackwell Publishing, Ltd., pp. 57–76.
Holmes, J. (2006) *Gendered Talk at Work: Constructing Gender Identity through Workplace Discourse*, Malden, MA: Blackwell Publishing.
Jaspers, J. (2012) "Interactional sociolinguistics and discourse analysis," in *The Routledge Handbook of Discourse Analysis*, 135–146. New York: Routledge.
Jenks, C. J. (2011) *Transcribing Talk and Interaction: Issues in the Representation of Communication Data*, Amsterdam/Philadelphia: John Benjamins.
Johnstone, B. (1996) *The Linguistic Individual: Self-expression in Language and Linguistics*, Oxford: Oxford University Press.
Kelly, J. and J. K. Local (1989) "On the use of general phonetic techniques in handling conversational material," in D. Roger and P. Bull (eds) *Conversation: An Interdisciplinary Perspective*, Clevedon: Multilingual Matters, pp. 197–212.
Kim, K. (1992) "Topicality in Korean conversation: A conversation analytic perspective," in P. M. Clancy (ed.) *Japanese/Korean Linguistics* 333–354, Stanford: CSLI Publications.
Kim, K. (1993) "Other-initiated repair in Korean conversation as interactional resources," in S. Choi (ed.) *Japanese/Korean linguistics 3*: 3–19, Stanford: CSLI Publications.
Kim, K. (1999) "Phrasal unit boundaries and organization of turns and sequences in Korean conversation," *Human Studies* 22: 425–446.
Labov, W. and D. Fanshel (1977) *Therapeutic Discourse: Psychotherapy as Conversation*, New York: Academic Press.
Lapadat, J. C. and A. C. Lindsay (1999) "Transcription in research and practice: From standardization of technique to interpretive positioning," *Qualitative Inquiry* 5(1): 64–86.
Lewis, H. S. (2001) "The passion of Franz Boas," *American Anthropologist* 103(2): 447–467.
Malinowski, B. (1922) *Argonauts of the Western Pacific: An account of native enterprise and adventure in the Archipelagoes of Melanesian New Guinea,* London: Routledge and Kegan Paul.

Malinowski, B. (1923) "The problem of meaning in primitive languages," in C. K. Ogden and I. A. Richards (eds) *The Meaning of Meaning: A Study of Influence of Language upon Thought and of the Science of Symbols*, New York: Harcourt, Brace and World, pp. 296–336.

Maynard, D. W. (2013) "Everyone and no one to turn to: Intellectual roots and context for Conversation Analysis," in J. Sidnell and T. Stivers (eds) *The Handbook of Conversation Analysis*, Malden, MA, Oxford: Blackwell Publishing Ltd., pp. 11–31.

Maynard, S. K. (1989) *Japanese Conversation: Self-contextualization through Structure and Interactional Management*, Advances in Discourse Processes, Vol. XXXV. Norwood, NJ: Ablex.

Mazeland, H. (2013) "Grammar in conversation," in J. Sidnell and T. Stivers (eds) *The Handbook of Conversation Analysis*, Malden, MA: Wiley–Blackwell, pp. 475–491.

McIlvenny, P. (ed.) (2002) *Talking Gender and Sexuality*, Amsterdam, Philadelphia: John Benjamins.

Mishoe, M. (1998) "Styleswitching in Southern English," in C. Myers-Scotton (ed.) *Codes and Consequences: Choosing Linguistic Varieties*, New York, Oxford: Oxford University Press, pp. 162–177.

Moerman, M. (1988) *Talking Culture: Ethnography and Conversation Analysis*, Philadelphia: University of Pennsylvania Press.

Moore, R. E. (1993) "Performance form and the voices of characters in five versions of the Wasco Coyote Cycle," in J. Lucy (ed.) *Reflexive Language: Reported Speech and Metapragmatics*, Cambridge: Cambridge University Press, pp. 213–240.

Myers-Scotton, C. (1993) *Social Motivations for Codeswitching: Evidence from Africa*, Oxford: Clarendon Press.

Ochs, E. (1979) "Transcription as theory," in E. Ochs and B. Schieffelin (eds) *Developmental Pragmatics*, New York: Academic Press, pp. 43–72.

Ochs. E. (1988) *Culture and Language Development: Acquisition and Language Socialization in a Samoan Village*, Cambridge: Cambridge University Press.

Ochs, E. and B. B. Schieffelin (eds) (1983) *Acquiring Conversational Competence*, London: Routledge & Kegan Paul.

Ochs, E., E. A. Schegloff and S. A. Thompson (eds) (1996) *Interaction and Grammar*, Cambridge: Cambridge University Press.

Phillips, L. (2011) *The Promise of Dialogue*, Amsterdam: John Benjamins.

Pittenger, R. E., C. F. Hockett and J. J. Danehy (1960) *The First Five Minutes: A Sample of Miscroscopic Interview Analysis*, Ithaca, NY: Paul Martineau.

Poplack, S. (1980) "Sometimes I'll start a sentence in Spanish Y TERMINO EN ESPAÑOL: Toward a typology of code-switching," *Linguistics 18*: 581–618.

Powdermaker, H. (1962) *Copper Town: Changing Africa*, New York, Evanston: Harper & Row.

Preston, D. (1982) "Riting fowklower daun 'rong: Folklorist's failures in phonology," *Journal of American Folklore 95*(377): 304–326.

Sawyer, R. K. (2001) *Creating Conversations: Improvisation in Everyday Discourse*, Cresskill, NJ: Hampton Press.

Schegloff, E. and H. Sacks (1973) "Opening up closings," *Semiotica 8*: 289–327.

Schenkein, J. N. (1978) *Studies in the Organization of Conversational Interaction*, New York: Academic Press.

Schieffelin, B. B. (1990) *How Kaluli Children Learn What to Say, What to Do, and How to Feel*, New York: Cambridge University Press.

Schiffrin, D. (1994) *Approaches to Discourse*, Oxford, Cambridge, MA: Blackwell.

Schiffrin, D., D. Tannen and H. E. Hamilton (eds) (2001) *The Handbook of Discourse Analysis*, Oxford: Blackwell Publishing.

Scollon, R. and Scollon S. B. K. (1981) *Narrative, Literacy and Face in Interethnic Communication*, Norwood, NJ: Ablex.

Sorjonen, M. L. (2001) *Responding in Conversation: A Study of Response Particles in Finnish*. Amsterdam: John Benjamins.

Speer, S. A. (2005) *Gender Talk: Feminism, Discourse and Conversation Analysis*, New York: Routledge.

Speer, S. A. and E. Stokoe (eds) (2010) *Conversation and Gender*, Cambridge: Cambridge University Press.

Stokoe, E. H. (2000) "Toward a conversation analytic approach to gender and discourse," *Feminism and Psychology 10*: 552–563.

Sudnow, D. (ed.) (1972) *Studies in Social Interaction*, New York: Free Press.

Tanaka, H. (1999) *Turn-taking in Japanese Conversation: A Study in Grammar and Interaction*, Amsterdam, Philadelphia: John Benjamins.

Tannen, D. (1984/2005) *Conversational Style: Analyzing Talk among Friends*, Norwood, NJ: Ablex.

Tannen, D. (1986) *That's Not What I Meant!: How Conversational Style Makes or Breaks Relationships*, New York: Ballantine Books.

Tannen, D. (1987) "Repetition in conversation: Towards a poetics of talk," *Language* 63(3): 574–605.
Tannen, D. (1989) *Talking Voices: Repetition, Dialogue, and Imagery in Conversational Discourse*, Cambridge: Cambridge University Press.
Tannen, D. (1990) *You Just Don't Understand: Women and Men in Conversation*, New York: William Morrow.
Tannen, D. (1994a) *Gender and Discourse*, New York and Oxford: Oxford University Press.
Tannen, D. (1994b) *Talking from 9 to 5: How Women's and Men's Conversational Styles Affect Who Gets Heard, Who Gets Credit, and What Gets Done at Work*, New York: William Morrow.
Tannen, D. (ed.) (1993) *Gender and Conversational Interaction*, New York and Oxford: Oxford University Press.
Varenne, H. et al. (1992) *Ambiguous Harmony: Family Talk in America*, Advances in Discourse Processes, Vol. XLIV. Norwood, NJ: Ablex.
Weigand, E. (2010) *Dialogue: The Mixed Game*, Amsterdam: John Benjamins.
Weigand, E. (2011) "Preface of the first issue," *Language and Dialogue* 1(1): 5.
West, C. (1979) "Against our will: Male interruptions of females in cross-sex conversation," *Annals of the New York Academy of Sciences 327*: 81–100.
West, C. and D. Zimmerman (1983) "Small insults: A study of interruptions in cross-sex conversations between unacquainted persons," in B. Thorne, C. Kramare and N. Henley (eds) *Language, Gender, and Society*, Cambridge, MA: Newbury House, pp. 102–117.
Wodak, R. (ed.) (1997) *Gender and Discourse*, London: Sage.
Yearly, S. and J. D. Brewer (1989) "Stigma and conversational competence: A conversation analytic study of the mentally handicapped," *Human Studies* 12(1–2): 97–115.
Zimmerman, D. H. and C. West (1975) "Sex roles, interruptions, and silences in conversation," in B. Thorne and N. Henley (eds) *Language and Sex: Difference and Dominance*, Rowely, MA: Newbury House, pp. 105–129.

Further Reading

Auer, P. and A. di Lusio (eds) (1992) *The Contextualization of Language*, Amsterdam, Philadelphia: John Benjamins.
Cooren, F. and A. Létourneau (eds) *(Re)presentations and Dialogue*, Amsterdam, Philadelphia: John Benjamins.
Duranti, A. and C. Goodwin (1990) *Rethinking Context: Language as an Interactive Phenomenon*, Cambridge: Cambridge University Press.
Maranhão, T. (ed.) (1990) *The Interpretation of Dialogue*, Chicago: University of Chicago Press.

17
Sign Languages and Communicative Practices

Richard J. Senghas

Introduction

Sign languages are articulated in three-dimensional space (rather than oral/aural speech), involving especially the hands, arms, and face, but also incorporating body movement, eye-gaze, and other important conventionalized forms, such as the systematic referential use of space. In contrast to spoken languages, sign languages are ideal for communication among people who do not hear or produce speech. Typically, these languages emerge to meet the needs of deaf groups or communities. Some sign languages or signing systems are indeed related to spoken languages (in which case they are usually considered *artificial* sign languages, see section 1.1 below), but many, if not most, sign languages are independent of the grammatical structures of spoken languages, and therefore have their own linguistic and "speech" communities that warrant linguistic anthropological study. Sign languages allow anthropologists and linguists to explore the nature of language and culture more generally, as well as aspects of language and culture specific to signing communities and deaf people.

A growing body of ethnographic and linguistic studies reveals that the circumstances surrounding the use of sign languages do vary significantly cross-culturally. These studies document a wide range of cultural associations, patterns in social interaction, and ideologies involving language. Historical change in the sign languages themselves, as well as attention to when, where, and how they are used, has demonstrated that the study of communicative practices in sign languages will be a dynamic area of inquiry for quite some time to come. Attitudes about sign languages vary, both internally and externally to the signing communities. While still relatively under-documented, the increasing amount of cross-cultural and cross-linguistic studies of signing communities around the globe already present data that have required us to update our theories and descriptions of language, as well as our models of deafness so often implicated in those theories and descriptions. These changing understandings, in turn, seem to be affecting the discourse about deafness and signing, both within the signing communities and at political and policy-making levels.

1.1 Types of Sign Language

Scholars have developed a number of terms for the description and analysis of sign languages, as well as the practices and communities of those who use them. Some of the terms are unique to this topic of study, while others are adaptations or extensions of relevant concepts used elsewhere in anthropology, linguistics, and other disciplines. The development of the terms themselves reflects the theoretical changes in this field over time. Let us start with some of the more commonly used terms, saving some of the more esoteric ones for later when addressing specific topics.

The terms for *types* of sign languages include *natural sign language, artificial sign language* (or *manually coded language*), *contact signing, fingerspelling*, and *homesign*. Defining these different terms will help dispel the most common misperceptions about sign languages.

Natural sign languages are complex, grammatical systems with all the core ingredients common to other human languages (Klima and Bellugi 1979). The fundamental distinction between spoken and signed language is that the sets of articulators are different; speech creates sounds via the oral tract, while sign uses hands, arms, face, and other parts of the body to make linguistic utterances.[1] Widespread linguistic recognition of natural sign languages as true, distinct languages in their own right is relatively recent, triggered primarily by the pioneering work of Stokoe and his colleagues (1976/1965) in the 1960s. As far back as the nineteenth century, Tylor (1878) recognized that sign languages used in communities of deaf people do not necessarily match the linguistic patterns of the spoken languages, but not much linguistic work on sign languages followed until the latter part of the twentieth century. Stokoe's description of what is now called American Sign Language (ASL) revealed systematic linguistic structures and principles that had been previously overlooked, even by its signers and by most professionals in deaf education. ASL clearly demonstrates linguistic principles operating at all the familiar analytic levels seen in spoken language: phonetics and phonology (i.e., articulation), morphology (word formation), syntax (sentence-level organization), as well as semantics (meaning) and pragmatics (language as action) – the levels often of most interest to anthropologists, as these levels provide ethnographers insight into the worldviews and social dimensions of human interaction. Once ASL began to be systematically described linguistically, comparable work in other sign languages soon followed. *Ethnologue* (Lewis, et al. 2014) now identifies at least 138 sign languages around the world, and many linguists see evidence that several others exist that are not (yet) identified in *Ethnologue* or other catalogues of languages.

Artificial sign languages (such as Signed English, Signed Spanish, and Signed Swedish) are simply *versions* of spoken languages whose linguistic structures are mapped to visual forms to make them accessible to those who cannot hear them. In effect, artificial languages are codes of the corresponding spoken languages, much as Morse code and semaphore are.[2] Artificial sign languages retain the word order of the corresponding spoken language, and often incorporate sign elements for typical prefixes and suffixes that mark morphology or syntax (e.g., pluralization, part of speech (adverb/adjective), tense). One reason natural sign languages are so frequently overlooked and not recognized in their own right is because artificial sign languages have often been developed to help deaf individuals learn to read, write, and sometimes even speak the spoken languages dominant in their societies, displacing the use of the natural sign language.

Signers will often modify their signing to accommodate those not fully fluent with sign language (or, perhaps, for those *unwilling* to use a natural sign language; more on that topic below), resulting in *contact signing*. Like other language contact phenomena, contact signing can involve changing word order or adopting features of another language to make signed communication across a language barrier easier (Lucas and Valli 1989; Lucas, et al. 2001). Such linguistic accommodations are inevitably linked to cultural expectations and social circumstances, and often interact with ideological issues of identity or power, and are likely another reason natural sign languages so frequently go unrecognized as distinct languages.

Fingerspelling is, in effect, another language contact phenomenon. Manual alphabets are particularly common where sign languages are used in highly literate societies. A fairly common misconception is that sign language is simply a spoken language spelled out on the hands, and brief reflection will see that this naïve assumption is similar to the one that conflates artificial sign languages with natural ones, as previously described. Some manual alphabets use one-handed forms (e.g., ASL, Nicaraguan Sign Language, Swedish Sign Language), while others may require two (e.g., British Sign Language). Fingerspelling is frequently used between deaf and (non-signing) hearing individuals when writing on paper is inconvenient, and the nonsigner is familiar with the fingerspelling alphabet, which is usually fairly easily and quickly learned.[3]

A feature common to many contemporary sign languages (both natural and artificial) that are used in literate societies is the incorporation of fingerspelling letters into signs as parts of those words. For example, the ASL sign for LIBRARY involves the L-handshape moved in a vertically circular motion in front of the body; or in Nicaraguan Sign Language, POLICIA (police officer) is a P-handshape tapped on the upper arm opposite the signing hand.[4]

Homesigns are idiosyncratic systems that emerge in circumstances where households or communities have only one or a few deaf individuals, and there is little or no contact with signing communities. Because these deaf individuals are isolated from exposure to established sign languages, new signs are invented to facilitate communication, but these systems are typically very limited, both in vocabulary and complexity. Morford (1996), among others, has explored homesigns, which in some cases have proved more complex than previously believed possible.

When discussing sign language, the term *gesture* sometimes refers to nonlinguistic body movements and facial expressions, but also, depending on context, may refer to movements and facial expressions that do indeed carry linguistic content. For that reason, we often see the qualified terms *linguistic gesture(s)* and *nonlinguistic gesture(s)*. Of course, that raises the inevitable question of where that distinction can and should be made (and how), including the possibility of overlap.

1.2 deaf, Deaf, and d/Deaf

Turning away from terminology used for the signing itself, and towards the communities of signers using such languages, we encounter terms associated with deafness: *deaf, Deaf, d/Deaf*.

The uncapitalized term *deaf* is often used in a way limited to actual audiological status, and generally refers to a (measurable) level of hearing that does not accommodate conversation. Profound deafness can mean little or no hearing capacity at all, but often individuals will have limited hearing in different frequency ranges, only some of which are in the typical range of the human voice. The capitalized form, *Deaf,* has been widely, but not universally, adopted in the social science literature on deafness and sign languages since Woodward (1972) and others introduced it. This latter term generally invokes some cultural or identity elements, which can be entirely distinct from an individual's actual capacity to hear. For example, an individual with little or no capacity to hear but unfamiliar with sign language, without an explicit identity involving deafness shared with a community of others and without social contact with other deaf individuals might be deaf without being Deaf. However, another individual with some hearing capacity but having a strong sense of community with other deaf individuals, especially if that community has an explicit sense of identity associated with their deafness, might not be considered very deaf, but would be Deaf.

Because the audiological and sociological phenomena of deafness are so often inextricably intertwined, the orthographically awkward form *d/Deaf* has been adopted to reflect that. Eventually, discussions inevitably have had to address the many kinds of Deaf identities that have been documented around the world, given the range of cultural associations with deafness that prevail in various societies. This is an area where linguistic anthropology has been able to make important contributions. Breivik (2005) and Monaghan et al. (2003), among others, have highlighted international and local dimensions of Deaf identities.

2 Historical Perspectives on Sign Languages and Signing Communities

Earlier perspectives on deafness highlight deaf individuals' often problematic situations within their encompassing hearing societies. Plann 1997 takes us as far back as sixteenth-century Spain, Lane (1984) explores the intertwined history of sign language and deafness in France and the United States, and Baynton (1996) provides an engaging sociohistorical account of sign language throughout US history, and especially as influenced by the international movement to suppress "manualist" pedagogies in favor of oralist approaches intended to develop speech, lip-reading, and writing to best normalize deaf individuals and integrate them into hearing society. (Many of Lane's contributions address this movement, including the Second International Conference on Education of the Deaf, known as the Milan Conference of 1880, which had broad influence in deaf education.)

Even where signing was acknowledged, it was often assumed to be either of limited or lower linguistic status, or as simply another version of the dominant spoken language (i.e., not as distinct, natural sign languages as discussed above). Later, studies of sign language and deaf interactions have revealed patterns familiar to anthropologists: culturally distinct groups and communities with their own sets of shared identities, traditions, and language, with the linguistic relativity effects that would inevitably follow.

2.1. Linguistic Recognition of Sign Language

In the 1960s and 1970s, we begin to see systematic linguistic attention to sign language and its use. As already mentioned in 1.1 (above), Stokoe and colleagues (1976/1965) demonstrate that sign languages do reveal linguistic principles at all levels, including phonological, morphological, syntactic, and semantic. Following Stokoe's groundbreaking work, we see sociolinguistic and psycholinguistic inquiry into sign language (primarily of American Sign Language), much of it addressing variation (Woodward 1976; Fischer 1975, 1978; Frishberg 1975). Woodward in particular focuses on regional variation (Woodward 1973b, 1976; Woodward and DeSantis 1977a, 1977b; Woodward et al. 1976). Woodward also describes what he originally calls *Pidgin Sign English* (1973a), and is later explored as *contact signing* (Lucas and Valli 1989; Lucas et al. 2001). Cross-linguistic and historical comparisons begin to broaden the view (Woodward and DeSantis 1977a, 1977b; Woodward and Erting 1975).

During the 1960s and 1970s, the attention paid to sign language(s) revealed that not only are there significant populations of deaf people who use sign languages, but also patterns of practice within these populations that indicate identifiable communities who share norms and have developed sets of cultural traditions. Deaf identity becomes more than an audiological difference "managed" (à la Goffman 1959, 1963) with respect to hearing norms. Sometimes framed in terms of *sub*cultures, at other times as *different* cultures (and even in terms of bilingualism/biculturalism; cf. Parasnis 1996), the discourse both in academic circles and in Deaf communities begins to change: what it *means* to be d/Deaf becomes a focus of concern. Sign language becomes both a means of communication within the Deaf communities, as well as a marker of cultural membership.

2.2 Recognition of the Culture(s) of Signing Communities

In the 1980s and 1990s, we see a swell of interest in sign language, and especially the beginnings of fieldwork involving sign languages and deafness in many parts of the globe. Padden (1980), Markowicz and Woodward (1982/1978), Lane (1984, 1992; Lane et al. 1996), Groce (1985), Foster (1989, 1996), Padden and Humphries (1988), and Schein (1992) give a good sense of the sociocultural dimensions, especially in North America. Accounts from the Caribbean (Washabaugh 1986), Ireland (LeMaster 1990), the Yucatán (Johnson 1991), and Kenya (Devlieger 1994) expand the horizons internationally. By the 2000s, we begin to see an even broader international sampling. Monaghan et al. (2003) includes chapters from a range of scholars examining signing and Deaf communities in the UK, Austria, Sweden, Switzerland, Ireland, Brazil, South Africa, Japan, Taiwan, Russia, Nicaragua, Thailand and Viet Nam, Nigeria, as well as regions of the US. Other accounts from Belgium (De Clerck and Goedele 2007), Nepal (Hoffmann-Dilloway 2008), South Africa (McIlroy and Storbeck 2011), and India (Friedner 2013, 2014) continue the trend towards richer, cross-cultural and cross-linguistic analyses. Extended ethnographies from Nicaragua (Polich 2005), Thailand (Reilly and Reilly 2005), Japan (Nakamura 2006), provide nuanced and complex insights into not only familiar topics regarding sign languages and Deaf communities, but also more general cultural and ideological issues as they intersect locally with signing and deafness.

3 Critical Issues and Topics

While much of the earlier literature on sign languages and Deaf culture highlights a hearing/Deaf opposition, and is framed in ways most salient to North American audiences, the trend towards a variety of coverage has brought with it increasingly diverse theoretical and disciplinary perspectives. Several of these echo themes from many of the chapters in this volume.

3.1 Language Variation in Sign Languages

As mentioned above in 2.1, the recognition of signing as linguistic led to studies of linguistic variation. Many of these studies examine expected sociolinguistic dimensions, how much variation and at what levels (e.g., phonological, syntactic) there is by location, age, ethnicity, or racial identity (Woodward and Erting 1975; Woodward 1976; Lucas and Schatz 2003), socioeconomic status, and gender (LeMaster 1990, 2003), but also some factors particular to deafness, including contact with other deaf individuals, membership in Deaf communities, presence of other deaf family members, and age of first exposure to signing or to Deaf communities (e.g., Woodward and Erting 1975; Woodward and DeSantis 1977b). In the psycholinguistic world, many of the studies focus on cognitive and developmental factors (e.g., Senghas et al. 2005), especially age of first exposure to signing, but also of perceptible forms of articulation, memory, and grammaticization.

As made clear in the Monaghan et al. 2003 volume (among several other sources), special education and deaf schools play central roles in a very large number of the cases studied around the world, in part because they create circumstances for speech communities to form and endure, and also to explain historical connections among the various dialects of sign languages. The concepts of linguistic communities and speech communities, linguistic competence, and communicative competence are usefully applied to sign languages and their communities of "speakers" (cf. Gumperz 1968; Hymes 2001/1972). Documentation of patterns in linguistic forms and practices themselves then leads us to useful comparisons along the familiar range of theoretical issues shared with studies of so many other languages, including spoken ones.

3.2 Models of Deafness

Responding to changing understandings of the socially constructed nature of deafness, the concept of *models of deafness* emerged in the 1980s and 1990s as a rich area of discussion, focusing at first on distinctions between so-called *medical* (or *biomedical*) and *cultural* models of deafness (Markowicz and Woodward 1978; Padden 1980, 1996; Padden and Humphries 1988; Lane 1984, 1992; Parasnis 1996). Medical models of deafness assume the implicit, default perception of deafness as a "defect" or abnormality in hearing, one that ought to be "fixed" by one or more methods. Oralist pedagogies (see 2 above), mechanical devices such as hearing aids, and more recently surgical-prosthetic interventions such as cochlear implants (CI), are adopted as mitigations to help "normalize" and integrate deaf individuals into their larger societies, thereby ameliorating what is perceived (however accurately or inaccurately) as their otherwise inevitably isolated and socially impoverished lives.

Cultural models explicitly incorporate the socially constructed nature of deafness, addressing factors beyond audiological capacity, including ideologies of language, "normal" physiological and cultural human variation, and hegemonic social relations that can and should be questioned, if not reorganized. Not surprisingly, a wide range of scholars and activists draw on ethnographic and linguistic data to challenge uncritically assumed medical models of deafness. Cochlear implants (CIs), especially their implantation in very young children when success rates are higher, have become a flashpoint, as well encapsulated in the documentary video *Sound and Fury* (Weisberg et al. 2000). Some scholars and activists espousing cultural models of deafness describe CIs as a typical medical model response. They argue that CIs are often only marginally successful, but more importantly, are seen as a response to a *perceived* absence of language and sociocultural interaction only because sign languages and Deaf communities are not recognized and accepted as natural and appropriate responses to deafness by the hegemonic hearing society (cf. Fjord 1999–2000, 2001). When deaf children are allowed to join the communities of Deaf signers, the cultural model holds, their language acquisition and cultural identity develop normally. The tension over CIs is particularly acute because those in favor of CIs point out that early interventions (when deaf children do not understand the implications nor have control over their own implantations) permit more "typical" (spoken) language acquisition, and greater integration with general society. Those opposed to CIs, especially those who have experienced or are aware of Deaf communities and their rich sign languages, sometimes argue that implantations are, in effect, a form of cultural "ethnocide" (Hladek 2002).

Not surprisingly, the simple binary oppositions of hearing/Deaf, and medical/cultural models of deafness are later challenged as insufficient. With evidence from the range of circumstances already identified in 2.1 above, we see that various analytic approaches are needed to explain the cross-linguistic, cross-cultural differences of various circumstances. For example, Polich (2005) proposes *eternal dependent* as another model of limited deaf personhood distinct from the medical and cultural ones previously applied in North America and elsewhere. In this model, Polich focuses on the social agency of deaf individuals and groups, rather than a cultural identity, and explores the often limited agency of deaf people despite their age and cognitive or linguistic capacities; deaf individuals may be relegated to socially dependent positions their whole lives, hence *eternal* dependent. Others see analogies between deafness or Deaf identity and the social and cultural patterns of other kinds of groups and communities. Solomon (2012) proposes the concepts of *vertical identities* (those handed down from generation to generation, with ethnicity, race, and nationality as archetypical), and *horizontal identities* (those adopted and developed through experience and association with peers or others with shared traits and circumstances, among them Deafness, Down syndrome, autism, prodigies, gay/lesbian/transgender). Clearly, these identity dimensions will continue to unfold with further cross-cultural ethnographic and linguistic documentation and comparison, including the notion of *deafnicity*, as discussed in 4.2 below.

3.3 Language and Ideology

Linguistic anthropology is noted for demonstrating that language plays ideological roles, both as markers *of* identity, as well as the medium *through which* ideological processes occur. Examination of both form and content of sign language practices continues this disciplinary tradition, and we can see patterns at the macro-level of the ethnographic documentation that bear striking resemblances to what we have seen occur for other languages. As so often seen in inventories of other local languages and their cultures (whether colonial and hegemonic records, or postmodern existential critiques, or even activist lists of languages needing recognition), sign languages have also been categorized as not "real languages" (only gesture or mime, or perhaps broken versions of "proper" [spoken] languages), or "primitive," or at best expedient means to eventually acquire the target, dominant spoken and written languages. To use signing has sometimes been interpreted as a performative act (cf. Kulick 2003) that marks a deaf individual as an "oral failure" (Monaghan 2003), incapable of mastering the speech of proper society, but that has also brought the inevitable covert prestige of using sign as an anti-hegemonic marker of opposition, perhaps part of the reason ASL was so often cited as a central trait of American Deaf culture (e.g., Padden and Humphries 1988; Parasnis 1996).

Within sign languages themselves, we find signs with ideological associations, both explicit and implicit. For example, the ASL sign for HEARING-IN-THE-HEAD certainly marks a negative association with a cultural identity linked to hearing society. The NO-SABE sign used in Nicaragua refers to deaf individuals incapable of using sign language, or even language altogether, which thereby limits their perceived social agency (Senghas 2003). Other signs might appear to be relatively arbitrarily assigned (as are most words in most languages), but might convey some implicit associations that are arguably socially hierarchical (such as the many ASL signs involving gender distinctions made by using base locations higher or lower on the head, such as the corresponding contrastive locations of FATHER/MOTHER and BOY/GIRL).

To help explain ideological behavior associated with languages, Irvine and Gal (2000) have identified the three concepts of *iconization* (one linguistic form indexing a linguistic or social group), *erasure* (the ideological "disappearing" of problematic differentiations), and *fractal recursivity* (patterns in identity/distinction made at one level being applied recursively at higher or lower levels, thus providing a resource for uniting or dividing groups). These ideological concepts can be usefully applied to sign languages, explaining why certain dialects of sign language may receive recognition (whether positive or negative), while others remain overlooked. These concepts can be applied even to cases examining homesign systems in the Yucatán, as Haviland (2014) indicates (see 4.1 below). Irvine and Gal's (2000) concepts help explain why the patterns of ideologies associated with sign languages and deafness play out in locally specific ways that are inherently part of larger local and regional ideological systems.[5]

3.4 Literacy, Language Policies, and Pedagogy

Literacy has long been a problematic issue in deaf education (Monaghan 2003; Plann 1997). For deaf individuals, the phonological basis of many writing systems (however idiosyncratic) makes mapping of written forms to spoken ones difficult, at best. For those deaf individuals who acquire sign language as their first language, literacy in the society's dominant language(s) involves the simultaneous acquisition of a second language. Most ASL signers write in English, and those two languages have markedly different structures and features. Because of the practicality of literacy, as well as the prevalent ideological associations of literacy with being educated and, therefore, intelligent and civilized, deaf education often uses literacy as a primary measure of educational success. However, many deaf students find themselves in a Catch-22 bind: because their literacy may be limited, the means of learning (books, etc.) are often less accessible to them, or the methods of assessment (written tests) do not adequately measure their actual skills and content knowledge (Bagga-Gupta and Domfors 2003 discusses this particular conundrum as it plays out in Swedish deaf education).

Mainstreaming, especially in the US and some European countries, is another recurring topic of concern in deaf education; in an effort to treat deaf students as equal to their hearing peers, schools have policies of including these deaf students as much as possible in regular classrooms, with varying levels of special support. Most residential deaf schools in the US have closed over the last fifty years, and many deaf students no longer have separate special deaf education day schools available as options. Ironically, deaf students can often feel socially isolated even while physically situated within classrooms of (mostly or entirely) hearing students. These deaf students may be limited to the interpretations provided by interpreters (when available) or teachers, or what limited conversation their peers are able and willing to sign (if any). Even students with Cochlear implants may have only limited ability to follow conversations under ideal interactive conditions, and so these students face communicative challenges that they would not experience if they were in classes with deaf peers.

Nationalist issues are also a factor in the language policies that affect sign languages. Policies meant to encourage fluency and literacy in certain languages associated with national identity, especially in formerly colonial states, will often exclude the local sign languages as an acceptable language for instruction or public use.[6]

4 Current Contributions and Research

The current geographic range of linguistic anthropology involving sign languages continues to expand, as well as the range of theoretical approaches to studying these cases. Deafness and signing often intersect with other sociocultural phenomena in ways that reveal a number of principles that otherwise remain implicit and obscure. We touch on a few representative examples here; a number of other projects that have been the topic of recent PhD dissertations are beginning to appear as scholarly articles and monographs.

4.1 Linguistic Ethnography of Signing Practices

Ideologies of linguistic practices have been a recurring theme in recent articles appearing in the *Journal of Deaf Studies and Deaf Education*. For example, Pizer et al. (2013) explore the expectations as linguistic intermediaries of hearing adults whose parents are Deaf,[7] a topic also addressed previously by Preston (1996). They find an ideology among such families that these hearing signers would naturally accommodate deaf signers through inclusive bilingual practices, a pattern that contrasts with those observed in spoken-language bilingual families. Moving geographically outside of North America and Europe, Hoffman-Dilloway (2008, 2010, 2011) has been exploring the ethnolinguistic politics of Deafness and signing in Nepal, including issues of language standardization and regimentation. Two other interesting cases come from the Yucatán.

Taking Gumperz' notions of speech communities to their logical minimum, Haviland (2014) examines social interaction within a single family with multiple deaf members. The family has developed an idiosyncratic homesign system, yet Haviland observes familiar ideological patterns even in this "miniscule speech community" that are consistent with Irvine and Gal's (2000) principles of iconization, erasure, and fractal recursivity. MacDougall's 2012 dissertation describes the second Yucatecan case, a Chican community with a high rate of deafness, and among which the use of signing is so common and unmarked among both deaf and hearing community members that a distinct Deaf identity does not form. (This Chican case is reminiscent of Groce's (1985) descriptions of signing practices on the island of Martha's Vineyard, as well as the accounts of signing among the Bedouins of the Negev Desert [A. Senghas 2005]).

4.2 Deafnicity *and* Deaf Sociality – *Revisiting the Nature of Ethnicity*

While Erting (among others) proposed a concept of Deaf ethnicity as far back as 1978, more recently, Eckert (2010) draws on classical Greek philosophical distinctions of *hómaemon* (common origin), *homóglosson* (common language), and *homóthreshkon* (common worldview/cosmology), to clarify the theoretical concept of ethnicity itself, and explain why its application to American Deafness in the form of *deafnicity* is both useful and appropriate. Eckert's argument supports previous claims by Erting (1978), Padden and Humphries (1988, 2005), and Lane (1992; Lane et al. 1996; Lane et al. 2011), among others, but also helps clarify why and how ethnicity might be useful in anthropological and sociological studies not involving deafness.

In contrast to Eckert's deafnicity, which might arguably apply only to situations where ethnicity is recognized locally as salient, Friedner (2014) argues that *sociality* provides another analytic framework that explains discursive practices of deaf individuals and groups, including Deaf churchgoers in Bangalore, India. The concept of deaf sociality is not mutually exclusive with Eckert's deafnicity, but may apply better where deaf people "come together to create local moral worlds [. . .] through communities of practice" (Friedner 2014: 43).

4.3 Orthography – *Writing in Sign Language*

As previously mentioned (3.4 above), literacy has often been a problematic issue for signers. Most signers write in a second language, the dominant spoken language of their encompassing hearing societies (e.g., ASL signers typically write in English, Nicaraguan Sign Language signers write in Spanish, Swedish Sign Language signers write in Swedish [or even English!]). However, Valerie Sutton and others have been developing the Sutton SignWriting system (SW) (http://www.signwriting.org), which is intended for general use (not just linguistic transcription), and communities of signers from at least 30 countries have been adopting SW for written communication in their respective sign languages, including online communities. SW is a visually iconic form of writing that represents the face and body movements used in sign languages (in effect, a visually phonetic writing system).

In addition to her studies in Nepal, Hoffman-Dilloway (2011) has also been analyzing these SignWriting texts, their circulation among those who write and use them, and the metalinguistic discourse about these texts conducted via an e-mail listserv. She argues that the use of SW allows its users to articulate and challenge dominant assumptions and ideologies about language and writing. In one curious twist, Hoffman-Dilloway (2011) discusses the ideological implications of writing SW texts from either the perspective of the signer or from the perspective of the audience observing (and participating with) the signer, essential when performing certain traditional genres recognized within Deaf communities. These particular orthographic distinctions cannot easily be made for spoken languages, but are among those that can be chosen in SW as a way of performing genre through text.

5 Main Research Methods

In much of the anthropological study of sign languages, classic participant observation (with ethnographic interviews) is typically combined with closer linguistic analysis (cf. Bernard 2011): from phonology through morphosyntactics, semantics, and the pragmatic level of discourse analysis and critical discourse analysis. The circumstances of many linguistic anthropologists documenting signing practices is reminiscent of the early days of linguistic fieldwork, where often the languages cannot be learned before the fieldworker arrives in the field. Much of the earlier phases of fieldwork are therefore constrained by limited fieldworker fluency in the local language(s), and often there are no professional interpreters available. While fieldworkers who already know one sign language before arriving in the field may have a head start over hearing nonsigners, the differences between sign languages can be considerable, as much as seen in the differences between spoken languages. If that challenge is combined with limited fluency in the spoken and written languages of the field region, that limited fluency in both modalities can compound the difficulties.

However, unlike spoken languages that are often transcribed using well-established conventional orthographies, or even phonological transcription systems such as the International Phonetic Alphabet (IPA) and variants of Pike's Americanist phonological transcription systems, sign languages are frequently transcribed using idiosyncratic systems developed for the specific research projects. Stokoe Notation (Stokoe et al. 1976/1965) and HamNoSys (Hamburg Sign Language Notation System) (Hanke 2004) are two (visual) phonological systems, and the Berkeley Transcription System is meant for transcribing at the level of meaning (Slobin et al. 2001), but differing transcription systems remain an issue affecting comparison of data. More recently, ELAN (EUDICO Linguistic Annotator) (available from the Max Planck Institute for Psycholinguistics in Nijmegen, The Netherlands) is an example of a well-developed set of shared software and transcription tools. ELAN is particularly good for developing tiered-transcription systems that can be tagged to video files, and is especially useful for close linguistic analysis. As mentioned above in 4.4, Sutton SignWriting is a sign writing system based on (visual) phonetic principles that can be applied even to new sign languages without the specific fonts already developed for particular sign languages. It still has a relatively limited number of users, however.

We continue to see in many accounts of sign language the practice of combining drawings of signs, glossing, and the use of translations of utterances; these techniques are easy to adopt and fairly accessible to nonspecialists. In many cases, photographs (sometimes with annotations) are also used. Where multimedia options are available, video clips have proved very effective at showing actual signs, but they do not allow for fully anonymous representation because the signers' faces usually need to be distinguishable in order to include the grammatical facial gestures and eye-gaze. With high definition (HD) video now commonly available even on mobile phones, video as a medium of documentation and analysis is now affordable and feasible for even the smallest of projects, though acquiring the necessary skills and techniques to work with this medium will remain as a constraining factor.

6 Recommendations for Practice in the Study of Sign Languages

Perhaps the first and most important recommendation to be made to those studying sign languages and Deaf communities is to be mindful of the history of exclusion and, in many cases, oppression of deaf people and sign languages in many parts of the world. Like the study of other minority and indigenous languages, the research choices have ideological implications, and the accounts produced can have strong ideological effects. Hearing researchers need to be particularly sensitive and responsive to how their actions and accounts may be received by others, especially the Deaf communities studied, but also Deaf communities at home, and by Deaf colleagues. Deaf researchers must also be careful not to project their own experiences, cultural associations, and linguistic assumptions into cases that may have superficial similarities possibly masking deeper, differing principles at play.

Informed consent can be particularly tricky when conducting research in signing communities where literacy may be limited or nearly nonexistent, or where the full implications of consent may not be fully understood due to cultural differences. Wherever possible (and it usually is), researchers should bring their findings back to the communities of study in accessible formats. This practice can increase the reliability and validity of the findings. However, issues of privacy and disclosure can be particularly problematic, especially when sharing linguistic data; revealing facial gestures and eye-gaze, so central to linguistic analysis of signing, also exposes the participants' faces, jeopardizing anonymity.

On a methodological note, to increase the ease and reliability of comparisons, North American scholars collecting and coding sign language data would do well to consider adopting the ELAN system used increasingly in international circles, especially in Europe (many European grants for sign language work require the use of ELAN). The tools are available free of charge, and can be downloaded from a number of European university websites.

Of course, many of the methodological issues addressed in Part V of this volume apply to the study of signing and Deaf communities; researchers would do well to review those, as well as more comprehensive handbooks on anthropological fieldwork (e.g., Bernard 2011).

Finally, a plea to those coining new analytic terms: please think very carefully before creating terms whose distinctive forms require *seeing* the terms in print. The use of novel orthography, such as atypical capitalization or the incorporation of various symbols within terms, has reached a point where the use of these terms is becoming increasingly cumbersome, especially during oral presentations in conferences or classrooms, and thereby impeding useful discussion (e.g., d/Deaf and h/Hearing, *D*/deaf (Eckert 2010); DeaF (McIlroy and Storbeck 2010)).

7 Future Directions

Extrapolations from the approaches and topics already indicated in 3 and 4 (above) will suggest many of the future directions of the anthropological studies of sign languages. In addition, we are likely to see more accounts of the emergence and historical change of sign languages as circumstances allow (e.g., RJ Senghas 2003; Senghas et al. 2005; Hoffman-Dilloway 2011; Haviland 2014). With language emergence and differentiation inevitably arise issues of language endangerment, especially during the phases when the linguistic community of signers is small.

The performativity of deafness and signing, as well as the autonomy and self-determination of Deaf and signing communities, are also areas needing further attention (cf. Padden and Humphries 2005, especially chapters 1 and 8). Theoretical application of deafnicity and Deaf sociality to the analysis of a wider range of cases is certainly warranted, and would likely be fruitful, especially cross-linguistically and cross-culturally.

Media studies and the effects of technology are yet another area with significant and unpredictable promise, though we see inklings of the potential in a recent review article (Lucas et al. 2013). What might be the implications of more broadly adopted sign writing systems or transcription? Signing is now possible via video telephony and Internet channels, even on handheld, mobile devices; but what will happen if and when signing becomes as "readable" as text and voice, or when digital avatars can be made to sign?

Related Topics

3 Gesture (Streeck); **7** Language Ideologies (Kroskrity); **12** Language, Sexuality, Heteroglossia, and Intersectionality (Leap); **24** Discrimination via Discourse (Wodak).

Notes

1 For a while, to avoid what at the time seemed inappropriate references to sound, some linguistic terms such as *chereme* and *allocher* were proposed, but these seemed more awkward than useful, so now many of the phonetic and phonological terms (such as *phoneme* and *allophone*) are typically applied to signs, too.
2 Note that to use Morse code or semaphore, one has to convert the written version of the spoken language into the encoded form. An English message in Morse code remains in English; a Spanish message in semaphore remains in Spanish.
3 The Rochester Method basically involves fingerspelling whole sentences letter-by-letter, and excluding the use of artificial or natural sign.
4 The use of small-caps indicates a gloss for a corresponding sign; this is common practice when writing about signs without using esoteric linguistic transcription. The glossed sign might not carry precisely the same meaning or connotation as the English (or other spoken language) word might indicate.
5 The academic categorizations of sign languages and their associated phenomena are not immune to these principles!
6 About every month or two, references to articles appear on the Lg-Policy List of the Consortium for Language Policy and Planning (www.ccat.sas.upenn.edu/plc/clpp/) that somehow address issues affecting a local sign language. Sometimes the articles announce progressive changes to public policies involving sign languages (especially in public education), but often they decry oversights that inadvertently limit the use of sign language, or even ill-informed policies that explicitly prohibit or discourage the use of local sign languages.
7 The term *CODA*, Children of Deaf Adults, is often used to refer to this population.

References

Bagga-Gupta, Sangeeta, and Lars-Åke Domfors. "Pedagogical Issues in Swedish Deaf Education." In *Many Ways to Be Deaf: International Variation in Deaf Communities*, edited by Leila Monaghan, Constanze Schmaling, Karen Nakamura, and Graham H. Turner, 67–88. Washington, DC: Gallaudet University Press, 2003.
Baynton, Douglas. *Forbidden Signs: American Sign Language and the Campaign Against Sign Language*. Chicago: Chicago University Press, 1996.
Bernard, H. Russell. *Methods in Cultural Anthropology: Qualitative and Quantitative Approaches, Fifth Edition*. Walnut Creek, CA: AltaMira Press, 2011.
Breivik, Jan-Kåre. *Deaf Identities in the Making: Local Lives, Transnational Connections*. Washington, DC: Gallaudet University Press, 2005.
De Clerck and A. M. Goedele. "Meeting Global Deaf Peers, Visiting Ideal Deaf Places: Deaf Ways of Education Leading to Empowerment, an Exploratory Case Study." *American Annals of The Deaf* 152(1): 5–19, 2007.
Devlieger, Patrick. "Culture–Based Concepts and Social Life of Disabled Persons in Sub–Saharan Africa: The Case of the Deaf." In *The Deaf Way: Perspectives from the International Conference on Deaf Culture*, edited by Carol J. Erting, Robert C. Johnson, and D. L. Smith, 85–93. Washington, DC: Gallaudet University Press, 1994.
Eckert, Richard Clark. "Toward a Theory of Deaf Ethnos: Deafnicity ≈ D/deaf (Hómaemon • Homóglosson • Homóthreskon)." *Journal of Deaf Studies and Deaf Education* 15(4): 317–333, 2010.
Erting, Carol. "Language Policy and Deaf Ethnicity in the United States." *Sign Language Studies* 19: 139–152, 1978.

Fischer, Susan. "Influences on Word Order Change in American Sign Language." In *Word Order and Word Order Change*, edited by C. N. Li, 1–25. Austin, TX: University of Texas Press, 1975.

———. "Sign Languages and Creoles." In *Understanding Language through Sign Language Research*, edited by Patricia Siple, 309–332. New York, NY: Academic Press, 1978.

Fjord, Lakshmi. "Voices Offstage: How Vision has Become a Symbol to Resist in an Audiology Lab in the US." *Visual Anthropology Review* 15(2): 121–138, 1999–2000.

———. *Contested Signs: Discursive Disputes in the Geography of Pediatric Cochlear Implants, Language, Kinship, and Embodiment*. PhD thesis, University of Virginia, 2001.

Foster, Susan B. "Social Alienation and Peer Identification: A Study of the Social Construction of Deafness." *Human Origins* 48(3): 226–235, 1989.

———. "Communication Experiences of Deaf people: An Ethnographic Account." In *Cultural and Language Diversity and the Deaf Experience*, edited by Ila Parasnis, 117–136. Cambridge: Cambridge University Press, 1996.

Friedner, Michele. "Producing 'Silent Brewmasters': Deaf Workers and Added Value in India's Coffee Cafés." *Anthropology of Work Review* 24(1): 39–50, 2013.

———. "The Church of Deaf Sociality: Deaf Churchgoing Practices and 'Sign Bread and Butter' in Bangalore, India." *Anthropology & Education Quarterly* 45(1): 39–53, 2014.

Frishberg, Nancy. "Arbitrariness and Iconicity: Historical Change in American Sign Language." *51*: 696–719, 1975.

Goffman, Erving. *The Presentation of Self in Everyday Life*. New York: Anchor/Doubleday, 1959.

———. *Stigma: Notes on the Management of Spoiled Identity*. Englewood Cliffs, NJ: Prentice-Hall, 1963.

Groce, Nora E. *Everyone Here Spoke Sign Language: Hereditary Deafness on Martha's Vineyard*. Cambridge, MA: Harvard University Press, 1985.

Gumperz, John J. "The Speech Community." In *International Encyclopedia of Social Science*, 381–386. New York: Macmillan, 1968.

Hanke, T. "HamNoSys: Representing Sign Language Data in Language Resources and Language Processing Contexts." In *LREC 2004 Workshop Proceedings: Representation and Processing of Sign Languages*, edited by Oliver Streiter and Chiara Vettori, 1–6. Paris: ELRA, 2004.

Haviland, John B. "(Mis)understanding and Obtuseness: 'Ethnolinguistic Borders' in a Miniscule Speech Community." *Journal of Linguistic Anthropology* 23(3): 160–191, 2014.

Hladek, G. A. "Cochlear Implants, the Deaf Culture, and Ethics: The Study of Disability, Informed Surrogate Consent, and Ethnocide." *Monash Bioethics Review* 21(1): 29–44, 2002.

Hoffmann-Dilloway, Erika. "Metasemiotic Regimentation in the Standardizations of Nepali Sign Language." *Journal of Linguistic Anthropology* 18(2): 192–213, 2008.

———. "Many Names for Mother: The Ethno-linguistic Politics of Deafness in Nepal." *South Asia: The Journal of South Asian Studies* 33(3): 421–441, 2010.

———. "Writing the Smile: Language Ideologies in, and through, Sign Language Scripts." *Language and Communication* 31(4): 435–355, 2011.

Hymes, Dell. "On Communicative Competence." Reprinted in *Linguistic Anthropology: A Reader*, edited by Alessandro Duranti, 53–73. Malden, MA: Blackwell Publishers, [1972], 2001.

Irvine, Judith T. and Susan Gal. "Language Ideology and Linguistic Differentiation." In *Regimes of Language: Ideologies, Politics, and Identities*, edited by Paul V. Kroskrity, 35–84. Santa Fe, NM: School of American Research Press, 2000.

Johnson, R. E. "Sign Language, Culture, and Community in a Traditional Yucatec Maya Village." *Sign Language Studies* 73 (1991): 461–74, 1991.

Klima, E. and Ursula Bellugi. *The Signs of Language*. Cambridge, MA: Harvard University Press, 1979.

Kukick, Don. "No." *Language & Communication* 23: 139–151, 2003.

Lane, Harlan. *When the Mind Hears: A History of the Deaf*. New York: Random House, 1984.

———. *The Mask of Benevolence: Disabling the Deaf Community*. New York: Knopf, 1992.

Lane, Harlan, Robert Hoffmeister, and Ben Bahan. *A Journey into the Deaf World*. San Diego, CA: DawnSignPress, 1996.

Lane, Harlan, Richard C. Pillard, and Ulf Hedberg. *The People of the Eye: Deaf Ethnicity and Ancestry*, Perspectives on Deafness series. Oxford: Oxford University Press, 2011.

LeMaster, Barbara. *The Maintenance and Loss of Female and Male Signs in the Dublin Deaf Community*. PhD thesis, University of California, Los Angeles, 1990.

———. "School Language and Shifts in Irish Deaf Identity." In *Many Ways to Be Deaf: International Variation in Deaf Communities*, edited by Leila Monaghan, Constanze Schmaling, Karen Nakamura, and Graham H. Turner, 153–72. Washington, DC: Gallaudet University Press, 2003.

Lewis, M. Paul, Gary F. Simons, and Charles D. Fennig (eds). *Ethnologue: Languages of the World, 17th ed.* Dallas, TX: SIL International. Online version: www.ethnologue.com, 2014.

Lucas, Ceil and Clayton Valli. "Language Contact in the American Deaf Community." In *The Sociolinguistics of the Deaf Community*, edited by Ceil Lucas, 11–40. San Diego, CA: Academic Press, 1989.

Lucas, Ceil and Susan Schatz. "Sociolinguistic Dynamics in American Deaf Communities: Peer Groups Versus Families." In *Many Ways to Be Deaf: International Variation in Deaf Communities*, edited by Leila Monaghan, Constanze Schmaling, Karen Nakamura, and Graham H. Turner, 141–152. Washington, DC: Gallaudet University Press, 2003.

Lucas, Ceil, Gene Mirus, Jeffrey Levi Palmer, Nicholas James Roessler, and Adam Frost. "The Effect of New Technologies on Sign Language Research." *Sign Language Studies* 13(4): 541–564, 2013.

Lucas, Ceil, R. Bayley, and Clayton Valli (eds). *Sociolinguistic Variation in American Sign Language*. Washington, DC: Gallaudet University Press, 2001.

MacDougall, Jennifer Paige. *Being Deaf in a Yucatec Maya Community: Communication and Identity Negotiation.* PhD thesis, McGill University, Montreal, Quebec, 2012.

Markowicz, H. and James C. Woodward. "Language and the maintenance of ethnic boundaries in the Deaf community." 1978. Reprinted in *How You Gonna Get to Heaven If You Can't Talk With Jesus: On Depathologizing Deafness*, edited by James C. Woodward, 3–9. Silver Spring, MD: TJ Publishers, 1982.

McIlroy, Guy, and Claudine Storbeck. "Development of Deaf Identity: An Ethnographic Study." *Journal of Deaf Studies and Deaf Education* 16(4): 494–511, 2011.

Monaghan, Leila. "A World's Eye View: Deaf Cultures in Global Perspective." In *Many Ways to Be Deaf: International Variation in Deaf Communities*, edited by Leila Monaghan, Constanze Schmaling, Karen Nakamura, and Graham H. Turner, 1–24. Washington, DC: Gallaudet University Press, 2003.

Monaghan, Leila, Constanze Schmaling, Karen Nakamura, and Graham Turner (eds). *Many Ways to be Deaf: International Variation in Deaf Communities*. Washington, DC: Gallaudet University Press, 2003.

Morford, Jill. "Insights to Language from the Study of Gesture: A Review of Research on the Gestural Communication of Non-Signing Deaf People." *Language and Communication* 16(2): 165–178, 1996.

Nakamura, Karen. *Deaf in Japan: Signing and the Politics of Identity*. Ithaca, NY: Cornell University Press, 2006.

Padden, Carol. "The Deaf Community and the Culture of Deaf People." In *Sign Language and the Deaf Community: Essays in Honor of William C. Stokoe*, edited by C. Baker and R. Battison, 89–103. Silver Spring, MD: National Association of the Deaf, 1980.

———. "From the Cultural to the Bicultural: The Modern Deaf Community." In *Cultural and Language Diversity and the Deaf Experience,* edited by Ila Parasnis, 79–98. Cambridge, UK: Cambridge University Press, 1996.

Padden, Carol, and Tom L. Humphries. *Deaf in America: Voices from a Culture*. Cambridge, MA: Harvard University Press, 1988.

———. *Inside Deaf Culture*. Cambridge, MA: Harvard University Press, 2005.

Parasnis, Ila (ed.). *Cultural and Language Diversity and the Deaf Experience*. Cambridge, UK: Cambridge University Press, 1996.

Pizer, Ginger, Keith Walters, and Richard P. Meier. " 'We Communicated That Way for a Reason': Language Practices and Language Ideologies among Hearing Adults whose Parents are Deaf." *Journal of Deaf Studies and Deaf Education* 18(1): 75–92, 2013.

Plann, Susan. *A Silent Minority: Deaf Education in Spain, 1550–1835*. Berkeley, CA: University of California Press, 1997.

Polich, Laura. *The Emergence of the Deaf Community in Nicaragua: "With Sign Language You Can Learn So Much."* Washington, DC: Gallaudet University Press, 2005.

Preston, Paul. *Mother Father Deaf: Living between Sound and Silence.* Cambridge, MA: Harvard University Press, 1994.

Reilly, Charles B. and Nipapon Reilly. *The Rising of Lotus Flowers: Self-Education by Deaf Children in Thai Boarding Schools,* The Sociolinguistics in Deaf Communities Series. Washington, DC: Gallaudet University Press, 2005.

Schein, Jerome. *At Home among Strangers*. Washington, DC: Gallaudet University Press, 1992.

Senghas, Ann. "Language Emergence: Clues from a New Bedouin Sign Language." *Current Biology* 15(12): R1–R3, 2005.

Senghas, Richard J. "New Ways to Be Deaf in Nicaragua: Changes in Language, Personhood, and Community." In *Many Ways to Be Deaf: International Variation in Deaf Communities*, edited by Leila Monaghan, Constanze Schmaling, Karen Nakamura, and Graham H. Turner, 260–282. Washington, DC: Gallaudet University Press, 2003.

Senghas, Richard J., Ann Senghas, and Jennie E. Pyers. "The Emergence of Nicaraguan Sign Language: Questions of Development, Acquisition, and Evolution." In *Biology and Knowledge Revisited: From Neurogenesis to Psychogenesis*, edited by Sue Taylor Parker, Jonas Langer, and Constance Milbrath, 287–306. Mahwah, NJ: Lawrence Erlbaum, 2005.

Slobin, Dan I., Nini Hoiting, Michelle Anthony, Yael Biederman, Marlon Kuntze, Reyna Lindert, Jennie Pyers, Helen Thumann, and Amy Weinberg. "Sign language transcription at the level of meaning components: The Berkeley Transcription System (BTS)." *Sign Language & Linguistics* 4(1/2): 63–104, 2001.

Solomon, Andrew. *Far from the Tree: Parents, Children, and the Search for Identity*. New York: Scribner, 2012.

Stokoe, William, Carl Croneberg, and Dorothy Casterline. *A Dictionary of American Sign Language on Linguistic Principles*. Silver Spring, MD: Linstok Press, 1965/1976.

Tylor, Edward B. *Researches into the Early History of Mankind and the Development of Early Civilization*. London: Murray, 1878.

Washabaugh, William. *Five Fingers for Survival*. Ann Arbor, MI: Karoma Press, 1986.

Weisberg, Roger, Josh Aronson, Mark Suozzo, and Brian Danitz. 2000. *Sound and Fury*. New York: Filmakers Library.

Woodward, James C. "Implications for Sociolinguistic Research among the Deaf." *Sign Language Studies* 1: 1–7, 1972.

———. "Language Continuum, a Different Point of View." *Sign Language Studies* 2(1): 81–83, 1973a.

———. "Some Characteristics of Pidgin Sign English." *Sign Language Studies* 3(1): 39–46, 1973b.

———. "Black Southern Signing." *Language and Society* 5: 211–218, 1976.

Woodward, James, and S. DeSantis. "Negative Incorporation in French and American Sign Language." *Language and Society* 6(3): 379–388, 1977a.

———. "Two to One It Happens: Dynamic Phonology in Two Sign Languages." *Sign Language Studies* 17: 329–346, 1977b.

Woodward, James C. and Carol Erting. "Synchronic Variation and Historical Change in American Sign Language." *Language Sciences* 17: 9–12, 1975.

Woodward, James C., Carol Erting, and S. Oliver. "Synchronic Variation and Historical Change in American Sign Language." *Sign Language Studies* 10: 43–52, 1976.

Further Reading

Breivik, Jan–Kåre. *Deaf Identities in the Making: Local Lives, Transnational Connections*. Washington, DC: Gallaudet University Press, 2005.
An ethnographic approach to local Norwegian situations that are linked to transnational phenomena and resonate with circumstances found in many other countries.

Eckert, Richard Clark. "Toward a Theory of Deaf Ethnos: Deafnicity ≈ D/deaf (Hómaemon • Homóglosson • Homóthreskon)." *Journal of Deaf Studies and Deaf Education* 15(4): 317–333, 2010.
A useful theoretical framing with practical application that explores linkages between communities of origin, linguistic communities, and communities of shared worldview/world order.

LeMaster, Barbara and Leila Monaghan. "Variation in Sign Languages." In *A Companion to Linguistic Anthropology*, edited by Alessandro Duranti, 141–65. Malden, MA: Blackwell, 2004.
A brief introduction to linguistic variation in sign languages, with examples.

Monaghan, Leila, Constanze Schmaling, Karen Nakamura, and Graham Turner (eds). *Many Ways to be Deaf: International Variation in Deaf Communities*. Washington, DC: Gallaudet University Press, 2003.
This volume provides a survey of sign languages and communities from 15 different countries, highlighting their commonalities and differences, and with a useful historical summary chapter by the primary editor.

Senghas, Richard J. and Leila Monaghan. "Signs of Their Times: Deaf Communities and the Culture of Language." *Annual Review of Anthropology* 31: 69–97, 2002.
A review article on this topic, focusing on the formative literature of the 1980s and 1990s.

18
New and Emergent Languages

Kathleen C. Riley

Introduction

Humans love to play with language. Re-arranging sound and sense, we pun and riff, alliterate and rhyme, as children playing house or as adults writing poems, ads, or chants. We create new codes (Pig latin, Esperanto . . .) and mix old codes in new ways (Chinglish, Franglais . . .). We craft new voices, styles, and registers, produce new genres, and construct new media for channeling our thoughts, emotions, and persuasions. Sometimes we transform language just for fun, sometimes our linguistic play has ulterior motives, and sometimes linguistic procreation erupts out of bare necessity.

Other chapters in this volume address some of the social, political, and cultural forces that promote communicative creativity and heterogeneity: nationalism, globalization, immigration, socialization, education, and technology. These authors also discuss some of the same new communicative effects of these sociocultural conditions: verbal performance, pidgins and creoles, language revitalization . . . . The goal of this chapter, however, is to look more generally at the forms, functions, meanings, contexts, and consequences of new systems of communication, especially those that have been developing in recent years.

Thus, I begin by presenting a brief overview of traditional perspectives on language change, then probe a number of the newer models used to understand emergent modes of communicating, and finally examine a couple of key research approaches and tantalizing topics for future study. Throughout this survey, I reflect on issues of disciplinary presumption and ideology, explore an array of research methods, and dwell here and there on particularly intriguing findings.

Historical Perspectives: Older Views on How New Languages Emerge

Beginning this section with the Biblical story of Babel seems hopelessly clichéd and yet how else to begin the story of the development of Western understanding of why humans have produced so many different ways of speaking? Once "we" (or most of us) came to accept that all humans are human, then the next Darwinian trend was to imagine that our species originally produced one way of speaking (as did Adam under orders from God), which generated over time, in Stammbaum fashion (unlike all at once as in the Bible), a multitude of languages. That is, we came to understand that communities of speakers, whether in isolation or in contact, over space and time produce new means of communicating. Historical-comparative linguistics (e.g., Bopp 1862) is the field of study that grew out of this basic assumption, with dialectology (e.g., Wright 1961) and linguistic anthropology (e.g., Boas 1911) not far behind.

These early scholars were less interested in the messy processes by which multiple codes come into being in specific settings among particular speakers around the world, preferring instead to identify homogeneous communities of speakers whose languages, presumably fixed at present, could be studied as evidence of some neatly chartable moments of isolation and transformation in the past. But, in reality, all language change has probably occurred in the past much as it does now, through idiosyncratic moments of creation and exchange constrained by social, cultural, and political forces that are not always easy to trace or categorize (see Lightfoot 2006 for a new approach to historical linguistics along these lines). That these transformations are now more apt to occur via Facebook than around water holes is no reason to assume that what we are doing at present is astronomically more complex or chaotic (or, depending on one's teleological perspective, more or less barbarous). We simply need to expand our understanding of the modes by which humans interact rather than assume we have evolved into qualitatively different sorts of communicators. And to do so, we need to interrogate some of the old terminology, and open our ears to new and emergent terms and the models they articulate. In the next section, I will do the latter, but first I wish to examine one deeply embedded communication model, based on containers and contents, that continues to influence our understanding of how new languages emerge.

Social scientists and linguists have long presumed that human communication is spatially, temporally, socially, and cognitively con(s)t(r)ained by various metaphorical vessels: contexts (Malinowski), communities (Saussure), domains (Fishman), settings (Hymes), frames (Goffman), chronotopes (Bakhtin), fields (Bourdieu), situations (Jakobson), and grammars (Chomsky). The communicative codes associated with these containers are variously called languages (Boas), dialects (Labov), pidgins and creoles (Mufwene), koines (Weinreich), styles (Irvine), registers (Ferguson), genres (Bakhtin), voices (Keane), and semiotic systems (Peirce).

Many of the older terms are useful and worth preserving, if only as shorthand, in order to facilitate the construction of more dynamic models of how new communicative modes are produced. It is worth remembering, however, that words sometimes shape our thinking and to question some of the presumptions hidden within them – for example, that nation-states are intrinsically linked to a single code (e.g., French is and ought to be spoken by citizens of France). Antidotes to the static notion of the vessel have been sought for some time by a number of scholars – for example, Duranti and Goodwin (1992) emphasize the fact that contexts do not simply shape the social texts found within them but are also shaped by on-going interactions among situated individuals and the meanings they produce.[1] Additionally, to discuss the constrained agency of the human interlocutors, who create and use codes within communicative contexts, scholars have come to employ a range of terms: not simply speakers and listeners, but also agents, social actors, positions, positionalities, roles, principals/authors/animators/figures, identities, and subjectivities. Finally, to focus on the dynamism of the codes themselves, scholars have coined or newly re-visioned other terms: heteroglossia, polyphony, styling, hybridity, syncretism, multimodality, dialogism, bivalency, enregisterment, intertextuality . . . (see below for more about these).

The point of this emergent jargon is not to obfuscate but to examine with more precision how new forms of communicating escape through the cracks in the old metaphoric vessels, through practice, interaction, and co-construction. The next section considers some of these new models and the terminology that accompanies them, while providing a few key examples of the developing systems of communication under examination.

Kathleen C. Riley

Critical Issues: Emergent Models of Language Emergence

New modes of communicating emerge because creatures capable of semiosis (i.e., sign-usage) interact within the semiotic (i.e., sign-invested) vessels into which they are born. However, these semiotic vessels would not exist had no prior semiotic individuals constructed the semiotic vessels using some prior means of semiosis. Given this particular chicken and egg dilemma, I have chosen to move back and forth somewhat arbitrarily between the egg (the semiotic vessel) and the chicken (the semiotic individual). I will also start out by employing somewhat conventional terminology in referring to the semiotic vessel as a multilingual society and the semiotic creature as a multilingual individual. However, at some point I will turn to using the terminology inspired by Bakhtin (heteroglossia, dialogism, multivocality, etc.) to discuss the dynamism of individuals and vessels. This is because my goal in this section is to lay out the emergent models for understanding how new semiotic codes emerge from this chicken and egg feedback loop.

Multilingual Practices and Shifting Languages

Since the inception of multilingual studies in the 1950s (in particular with the work of Haugen 1953 and Weinreich 1953), it has been standard operating procedure to distinguish between individual and societal multilingualism, while also investigating some of the new linguistic forms that materialize as a result of language contact. Thus, many volumes that cover the field (e.g., Auer and Li 2007; Bhatia and Ritchie 2012; Myers-Scotton 2006; Romaine 1989) begin with chapters on how individuals acquire and use more than one language in their lives, move on to chapters that examine how and why societies produce and maintain more than one language, and throughout provide some analysis of the meanings, forms, and functions of the new textual results. Zentella has articulated this three-part model in the following terms: "on the spot, in the head, and out of the mouth." "On the spot" refers to the social-cultural-political forces that impinge on the immediate speech situation; "in the head" to the communicative knowledge that the participants bring to the speech event; and "out of the mouth" to the communicative practices (systemic or not) that emerge from the interaction (1997: 82–83). Here, I begin with "the head," move on to "the spot," while always emphasizing how both individual agency and sociocultural structuration contribute to the emergence of new systems of communication "out of the mouth."

Psycho-neuro-cognitive approaches are designed to understand how multilingual individuals acquire, maintain, and employ their multiple languages (see Grosjean 1982 for a good introduction). To do so, research has been conducted on early and late bilingualism, simultaneous and sequential bilingualism, as well as fully functioning and aphasic multilinguals. Much of this research is grounded in the Chomskyan axiom that human brains are hard-wired for the acquisition and generation of language(s). While Chomsky himself was primarily interested in how language functions as an ideal and autonomous code, a number of psycholinguists became interested in how Universal Grammar shapes not only how we acquire and generate creative sentences in one language but also how we learn, store, and use multiple languages, thus sometimes mixing and producing new ones.

Most researchers in this field seem now to concur that the multilingual brain, in the process of acquiring and processing more than one set of phonological, morpho-syntactic, and/or pragmatic systems, manifests interlingual effects in how it generates new utterances. Additionally, researchers within this field sometimes explore the notion that multilinguals' "knowledge" of how languages are used and perceived in the world around them also affects when, where, how, and why they use their available codes (see the articles in the first section of Bhatia and Ritchie 2012).

Within (or at least influenced by) this cognitive approach, several models have been proposed for the examination of how and why speakers engage in code-mixing and code-switching. Heavily influenced by formal linguistics, Poplack (1980) formulated a series of grammatical constraints on when and where multilinguals switch codes within an utterance. Attempting to incorporate more of the social factors affecting "bilingual speech," Myers-Scotton (2006) proposed two models (first the Matrix Language Frame, followed by the 4M model), which both still primarily focus on the structural constraints governing multilingual usage, including not only strategic but also "proficiency-based" factors. Another key player in these debates is the psycholinguist Genesee (2001), who demonstrates that the code-mixing patterns of young bilinguals prove their growing linguistic proficiency rather than their incompetence.

Whether the multilingual practices that result from lexical borrowing, phonological and grammatical interference, and code-switching by individuals converge into new systems shared (more or less) by a speech community depends upon many variables but is by no means infrequent (Muysken 2012). These new systems may develop into recognizable linguistic varieties, as in the case of dialects (Labov 1972), koines (Siegel 1985), or creoles (see Mufwene's chapter in this volume). They may take the form of mixed codes with linguonyms such as Spanglish (Zentella 1997) and Nouchi (Newell 2009). They may take the form of unnamed but relatively systematic ways of code-switching, which sociolinguists have sought models to analyze (e.g., Blom and Gumperz's (1972) metaphoric Vs. situational code-switching; Auer's (1984) code-alternation; or Woolard's (1998) bivalency). They may also take the form of newly enregistered heteroglossic systems generated by particular communities of practice to index new identities and meanings – e.g., HipHop (Alim 2006). However, the story of the formation of these new systems is not simply a matter of cognitive structuring or individual competence and agency, but is the result of complex ethnohistories of contact and the social-cultural-political institutions and ideologies governing that contact.[2]

Thus, for some time now scholars have been conducting research into the socio-cultural-political causes and consequences of the multilingual construction of new systems of communicating. Working inwards from the macro context, they have modeled the forms that multilingual societies take, e.g., Ferguson's (1959) diglossic societies (Haiti, Switzerland . . .), Bourdieu's (1991) linguistic marketplace (Béarn Vs. Paris), and Irvine and Gal's (2000) formulation of fractal recursivity in contested nationalist settings (nineteenth-century Senegal and twentieth-century Macedonia). What has become clear is that in order to avoid hypostasizing both codes and communities of speakers, we need to take an ethnohistorical linguistic approach that contextualizes all present-day research with "ethnohistories of communication," i.e., careful analyses of how "communities of contact" (Silverstein 1997) have produced "language shift" in the broadest sense of the term (Errington 1998), i.e., transformations in how multiple languages are structured and used. In order to understand these processes, we must focus not only on the large-scale (large D) Discourses generated within formal, institutional domains (schools, courts, and temples), but also the everyday (small d) discourses in more intimate and informal domains (homes, streets, and playgrounds). In other words, we must focus on how macro-institutional forces and language ideologies (see Kroskrity's chapter in this volume) are indexed and negotiated through interactions on the ground and how these in turn affect or reflect the emergence of new discursive systems. In short, while we need to acknowledge both centripetal forces that contribute to homogeneous ways of communicating, we must also bear in mind the centrifugal forces that disrupt homogeneity and generate heterogeneity.

Many of the scholars interested in this approach have built on the classic contrast between power and solidarity (first formulated by Brown and Gilman 1960), and the metapragmatic signaling of identity and relationship. On the one hand, it is understood that prestige dialects are constructed via standardization and other institutional discourses as a way to project and impose the power of the elite, e.g., Parisian French (Riley 2011a) and Bahasa Indonesian (Errington 1998) – or, as in the case of the construction of Japanese women's language (Inoue 2006), submit to the power of the patriarchy. By contrast, nonstandard varieties have been forged as tools of resistance to mark and communicate comfort and solidarity in the face of elite domination, e.g., New York Puerto Ricans' self-regulating use of Spanish-English code-switching (Urciuoli 1996). A particularly large number of code-switching code studies have been undertaken in Africa, with Spitulnik's (1999) study of Town Bemba (a mix of Bemba, English, and other local languages) in Zambia and Swigart's (2001) study of Urban Wolof (a mix of Wolof and French) in Senegal. The phrase "acts of identity," which has been very influential in formulating how language intersects with identity politics, comes from LePage and Tabouret-Keller's (1985) study of Jamaicans' use of patois in London.

Such a straightforward power-solidarity axis has proven to be a relatively blunt tool, however, when faced with the real-world complexities of emergent modes of code-switching and style-shifting. Instead, new models have been framed that highlight the ways in which hybrid communicative systems emerge out of identity-indexing practices. Working with Bakhtin's (1981) notions of heteroglossia and dialogism, translinguistics and voice, Hill and Hill (1986) explored how individuals have contributed – code-switching utterance by code-switching utterance – to the construction of a "syncretic" language system in Mexico (a mix of Mexicano and Spanish), a system that was, however, beginning to give way at that time to the encroaching power of Spanish. Other scholars have been influenced by this work; for example, Makihara (2009) examined the heterogeneous practices and construction of a syncretic (Spanish and Rapanui) style on Easter Island, and Riley (2001) analyzed dialogic code-switching and language shift in the Marquesas. And a number of newer volumes contain research exploring the construction of new hybrid codes and heteroglossic practices by multilingual speakers in multilingual contexts (Auer and Li 2009; Bhatia and Ritchie 2012; Heller 2007; Martin-Jones et al. 2012).

Finally, emergent languages also arise out of the sociopolitical conditions that lead to language endangerment (see the chapter by Brittain and MacKenzie in this volume). That is, in reaction to the threat of language loss, some languages (most famously Hebrew) are not simply reclaimed and revitalized by their communities, but also (re)created: new vocabularies and genres are generated for use in new communicative domains, while dialectal variants are leveled in order to construct orthographies, standardized grammars, and/or new literacy practices. These in turn are used to teach the language, sometimes in the face of the elders' objections as they do not agree that this thing being learned is actually their language (Nevins 2013). In fact, prescriptivist language ideologies about what a language is and is not (e.g., the purist notion that no borrowing, calquing, or code-switching should be allowed) sometimes obstruct the maintenance of the language and contribute to language shift, i.e., the construction of a "new," mixed-up language such as Charabia in the Marquesas (Riley 2007).

Heteroglossic Play and Intertextual Performance

Play has traditionally been considered the small-scale, informal version of performance – the contexts are usually grander in performance, the audiences larger, the means more scripted, and the content more significant than in play. This is a very conventional reading of those two terms, however. In this section, I examine: how performance functions impromptu in everyday interactions (by chickens); how play can have a powerful impact on the public stage (the egg); and how both playful performance and performative play indexically reflect and implement emergent communicative systems. I look, first, at purposely invented codes (their forms, functions, and metapragmatic meanings); second, at various "cool" styles, registers, and voices and how these are used for the sake of humor and other forms of powerful stance-taking; and third, at various new communicative genres. In all of these, the role of heteroglossia (as discussed above) will be considered.

Invented languages abound: Gibberish, Verlan, Klingon ... (see Okrent 2009 for a survey). Some inventors say they create codes simply for their own private amusement (a number of websites exist for teaching people to create languages for fun). Indeed, Tolkien devised Elvish to give voice to an invented world he could not know would go so public. However, codes are also frequently invented at least in part for political reasons, e.g., on the one hand, to exclude others (peers, parents, the police, neighboring tribes ...) or, on the other hand, to be purposefully, sometimes globally, inclusive (e.g., Esperanto). Either way, the play code becomes emblem, index, and channel for those who use it to bond through performance – sometimes in everyday, goofy ways (e.g., children using Ubbi Dubbi at school) and sometimes for starkly ritual effect (e.g., Pentecostals speaking in tongues). And just as new media technologies and standardized codes were key to the emergence of nation-states (Anderson 2006), so have imagined or constructed languages (conlangs) been key to the emergence of imagined virtual communities (Manning 2009: 314–15).

New ways of expressing oneself, however, are not always so purposefully or consciously invented; in fact, speakers may only sometimes be aware that they are playing and performing. Individuals construct personal styles through complex interactive means: taking stances, interpellating their interlocutors, aligning themselves (or not) with others, indexing their affiliations, cueing how they feel about specific stuff, and generally engaging in acts of identity[3]; and yet they may not intend to be "performing." For instance, Johnstone (2009) traces how the Texas politician Barbara Jordan constructed through a variety of stance-taking discursive strategies the "Barbara Jordan style," i.e., a way of speaking for which she became well known and that indexed her informational truthfulness and "moral authority." Apparently she was unaware of having acquired and composed this style out of a mix of her mother's insistence on "correct English," her father's African-American preaching genre, her engagement in the college debate team, or her apprenticeship in legal discourse. Nevertheless, the stylistic features of influential individuals may shape the construction of whole dialects, e.g., Labov's (2001) analysis of vowel shift in Philadelphia.

Youth in particular are known for enregistering various new styles (or registers) – sometimes referred to as youthspeak or slang – i.e., age-based vernaculars that unite a generation in its vision, its feel, its sense of what's meaningful and relevant (i.e., cool). "Cool codes" seem to be made and acquired on the fly, through the air, among peers, by the media, or somehow else just come to be ... cool. The users, nonetheless, are constantly playing with and performing them, recycling and disseminating them, with various intentions and sometimes unexpected consequences. Two excellent examples are the kogul: adolescent Japanese girls who perform and disseminate their bad girl identities using syncretic orthographies and anti-establishment dress-styles (Miller 2004). Similarly, in a Midwestern suburb working-class high school girls construct new vowel variants to project their "burnout" identities (Eckert 1999).

Many new "cool" ways of speaking depend on borrowing contrastive codes (i.e., heteroglossia). As discussed above with respect to the emergence of code-switching codes, speakers may induct multiple codes in order to index ethnic identity, but these code-switching codes can also be used to performatively construct not only ethnicity, but also age, gender, class, urbanity, modernity, and cosmopolitanism (e.g., Gaudio's (2011) study of the use of "Broken English" to project global "Blackness" in Nigeria, and Mendoza-Denton's (2008) study of Chicanas' use of Spanish-accented English to affiliate appropriately as homegirls). Sometimes these youth codes signal urbanity and cosmopolitanism, whether or not the speakers actually live in cosmopolitan, urban centers: e.g., Marquesan youth on the island of Nuku Hiva in the middle of the Pacific

Ocean are as apt to play with multiple languages (French, Marquesan, English, Tahitian) as are multilingual youth in Montreal (Riley 2011b).

Depending on one's perspective, this heteroglossic borrowing can be considered an act of illicit appropriation or fun and games. Rampton (1995) coined the term "crossing" to explore the dynamics involved in taking on an "other's" voice or style. In his study of British youth groups who were constructing new codes out of bits and pieces from the repertoires of their friends of other ethnicities, bits to which they had no "natural" right, the rationale and interpersonal consequences were not necessarily negative. However, although the act of appropriating linguistic material may seem "cool" to those inside the frame, the very same moves may appear dumb or racist to those on the outside. Hill (1998) has initiated a large number of studies of the racializing impact of Euro-Americans' uses of various "mock" ethnic registers (Mock Spanish, Mock Chinese, etc.).

One final contribution to the study of how performance and play contribute to the development of new communicative systems is the research that has been done on emergent genres. Several excellent examples are the work of Hoffman in Morocco, Kuipers in Indonesia, and Ahearn in rural Nepal. Hoffman (2008) explains how Ishelin (Berber) women living on the plains of Morocco performed traditional Tashelhit songs in Arabic in formal settings for life-cycle rituals, while in informal rehearsal spaces they used both codes (Tashelhit and Arabic) constructing heteroglossic events and hybrid identities. On the island of Sumba in Indonesia, Kuipers (1998) analyzes how ritual speech has transformed not only the languages used, but also the forms, contexts, meanings, and acquisition of the genres in the larger postcolonial context; as the old forms no longer held the same power, new ways of performing were constructed. Ahearn (2001) has examined the development and impact of literacy in rural Nepal as young people have applied this new technology to the genre of "love letters" to explore changing notions of romantic love and life aspirations associated with modernity.

One more emergent genre emanating from the center of modernity is stand-up comedy. In the West, "humorous" ethnolinguistic play has been around for centuries (e.g., see Bakhtin (1984) on Rabelais), creating variously denigrating or resistant effects. However, the linguistic anthropological study of the heteroglossic voices and performative stylings of stand-up comedians in particular has begun to proliferate in the last twenty years, beginning with Woolard's (1987) work on code-switching comedians in Barcelona, Barrett's (1999) writing on the polyphony of African-American drag queens doing "white lady" talk, and Chun's (2009) work on Cho, a stand-up comic who has constructed her own heteroglossic performance style by mixing a consciously critical use of Mock Asian with voices from her own personal biography.

In my own analysis (Riley 2012) of the political polyphony of some of the comedy (e.g., Key and Peele) found on the global airwaves, I find that the boundary between formal and informal spaces and genres is growing more porous, that the mind is rediscovering intelligence in the body, and that some comedians are using embodied voices to question the structures and ideologies of our present lives. Sometimes, through the use of politically incorrect or offensive language (remember George Carlin?), these humorists construct a stance that metapragmatically communicates (like Bateson's playful kittens): "Though I'm biting you, this is not a bite. It is not real; it's truer than that." Through this humor, "we the people" (as opposed to Bakhtin's "folk") are exploring how signs refer, how interpretants remake intentions, and how agents weigh the impact of utterances through subtle interplay with an audience, sometimes producing new and regenerative ritual forms.

Current Contributions: Newer and Still Emergent Approaches

This section presents a brief introduction to two significant emergent approaches to studying how new languages develop out of dynamic ethnohistorical linguistic contexts on the one hand

and complex semiotic interactions on the other. First is the study of language socialization, i.e., how new languages emerge from the mouths of babes (and other novices), and second, the study of transidiomatic practices, i.e., how new codes emerge from translocal interactions. Both involve multimodal discourse analysis, so I will begin with a brief overview of this methodology as practiced by linguistic anthropologists.

Discourse analysis refers to a range of methods involving the collection and analysis of "natural" discourse (the definition of "natural" has expanded to mean any form of communication that happens: formal or informal, purposely performative or not, even if constructed by the research process, just so long as the constraining contextual forces are taken into analytic account). It is related to textual analysis (i.e., the study of written texts, originally literary), conversation analysis (i.e., the study of how everyday conversational moves are accomplished), and critical discourse analysis (i.e., the study of how everyday (little d) discourse reflects and affects the dominant (big D) discourses by which societies run). Linguistic anthropologists who practice discourse analysis (almost all do in one way or another) take both content and style into account (as do literary analysts), analyze minute discursive moves in real time (as do conversation analysts), and attend to the ideological forces that shape the discourse (as do critical discourse analysts). One aspect of discourse that is of particular interest is intertextuality, i.e., the ways in which bits of discourse may be decontextualized from their original contexts, and recontextualized in new contexts, resulting in recycled resonances that allow the politics and emotion of the original utterance to bleed into the new interaction. One other aspect of discourse analysis to be noted here is that discourse is now understood to involve many modes, so that more and more analysts may record and analyze not only language and speech but also writing, audio-visual material, embodied moves, and objects, for their communicative functions and values. Multimodal discourse analysis is at the heart of studying language socialization, transidiomatic practices, and the new codes they produce.

Language socialization is the study of how social practices and cultural knowledge (including language itself) are developed via social interaction (see the chapters on language socialization by Paugh and Stoll, in this volume). One of the key principles of this paradigm is that children and other novices do not merely reproduce the knowledge and practices of those worldly others with whom they interact. To the contrary, each generation works dialogically with the resources they are offered and the sanctions to which they are submitted, adds its own distinctive flavor to the values, voices, and behaviors being transmitted, creates new slangs, generates creoles, etc. In other words, the paradigm is particularly generative when applied to the study of multilingual situations and speakers because it synthesizes individual and societal approaches (see Baquedano-López and Garrett (2002) for a survey, and the collection edited by Bayley and Schecter (2003) for examples).

The oldest and most influential of these studies is Zentella's (1997) longitudinal, multigenerational examination of how and why New York Puerto Rican children learn to be more or less multilingual in varieties of Spanish and varieties of English, and how through the acquisition of code-switching practices they contribute to the variety of Spanglish spoken in their neighborhood. Similarly, Riley's (2001, 2007) language socialization study in the Marquesas has documented the construction of a code-switching code that mixes French and Marquesan (and some Tahitian and English), even in the midst of a movement to revitalize the "pure" form of Marquesan. Fader (2009) has studied the production of Yiddish English among Hasidim women in Brooklyn, focusing on how community beliefs (e.g., about gender roles, modernity, and the chosen people) affect the socialization process and thus the form these new variants take.

Several important studies of language socialization have been conducted in areas where creoles and creole continuums are still in the course of being generated. For example, Paugh (2012) looks carefully at how the peer socialization that occurs during children's play performances (as teachers, bus drivers, field laborers . . .) contributes to the construction of code-switching registers between the creole (Patwa) and the locally produced form of English. By contrast, Garrett's (2005) work in St Lucia has focused on the socialization practices that produce new heteroglossic registers such as swearing, and Kulick (1992) looks at the language ideologies in the village of Gapun, Papua New Guinea, that propel women in particular to engage in an emergent code-switching (Taiap and Tok Pisin) genre known as kros, a kind of angry, neighborly rant. By contrast, Schieffelin (1993) has reported the production of a multilingual caregiver register among Haitians in New York City, involving the instrumental use of English, French, and Kreyol, to promote comprehension and acquisition.

A number of multilingual socialization studies within school settings have also shed light on how multimodal socialization practices (the modes include embodied signs – posture, gestures, gaze – and technology-mediated forms – literacy, etc.) affect the process by which students influence the construction of new codes and genres. In California, Baquedana-López (1997) has examined how Mexican teachers have composed a narrative genre, called doctrina, to accomplish Catholic training in California. Moore (2006) compares two different forms of literacy produced among multilingual children in Cameroon studying Arabic at the mosque and French at the school. Several articles collected in Heller and Martin Jones' volume (2001) explore the distinctions between teaching colonial lingua francas (English, French, and Spanish) to urban elites in Africa, South America, and Asia compared with the production of a "safetalk" register within rural classrooms, where children are never expected to acquire the prestige code and the classroom socializing rituals. Using "safetalk" ensures that this will be so. Finally, Heller (2003) and Blackledge and Crease (2010) explore multilingualism in Canadian and British schools, specifically how immigrant students construct new heteroglossic practices in the interstices of the hegemonic forms of communication imposed within the classroom.

The other burgeoning approach to the study of emergent communicative systems has to do with transidiomatic practices (Jacquemet 2005) – i.e., the new forms of communicating that stem from the fact that new forms of transportation and information technology are allowing humans to live translocal lives and seek new syncretic ways to stay bonded. Many of these are multimodal, technology-mediated forms (see, for example, the chapter by LeBlanc-Wories in this volume on the relationship of language to media and technology), while others are simply the result of old technologies put to work in new translocal contexts (see also the chapters by Pujolar, by Jacquemet, and by Van Dijk on the linguistic impact of globalization).

First of all, new information technologies have produced new mediaticized spaces (Skype, Facebook, Youtube . . .), within which new codes have been developed to cross national and regional borders. One new set of registers includes the varieties of textese crafted for communication online or by cellphone – including not only acronyms and emoticons, but also emergent pragmatic rules for organizing interaction (e.g., Jones et al 2011). Another transidiomatic site for the creation of new languages is the world of virtual gaming – not only the "artificially" created codes needed to get started as a player, but also the codes that emerge naturally among players attempting to interact with each other outside the gaming platform (Boellstorff 2008). One new venue – the mini-video (6–7 seconds) of Vine – offers a brave new world for researching the construction of stereotyping memes across communities. And multimodal, multisited political action offers yet another instance of newly sprouted transidiomatic genres in need of investigation – from 350.org's connect-the-dots art project to the twitter orchestrated rounds of die-in actions following Eric Garner's murder.

By contrast, transidiomatic emergence may also be studied in somewhat traditionally local locales because the global world arrives wherever we are these days. For instance, Blommaert

(2013) looks at the effects of superdiversity but in a relocalized format by exploring the linguistic landscape of his own neighborhood in Belgium. In his case, emergent forms of heteroglossic signage index new relationships and channels of communication among new neighbors. Maryns (2006) studies how false narratives are constructed during multilingual asylum-seeking processes as a consequence of misreading and translation errors. Shankar (2009) studies how multilingual "Desi" youth in California use intertextual Bollywood references to index issues of gender and class. Spitulnik's (1997) work on the playful recycling of radio talk in everyday discourse exemplifies how intertextuality operates as a performative strategy for braiding hybrid urban identities. Finally, many multilingual socialization studies contribute to our understanding of how children build new ways of communicating within new translocal settings (e.g., García-Sánchez (2012) examines the generation of communicative systems for excluding immigrant students in southern Spain).

As Jacquemet (2005) has suggested, the emergence of these new "transidiomatic practices" calls for the reimagining of "communicative environments" on a global scale, as well as new research paradigms and multisited fieldwork methods. In particular, it means abandoning a dystopic vision of globalism as a centripetal, homogenizing force spelling the end of linguistic creativity. This is not to ignore the fact that powerful people, forces, and ideologies oppress peoples in marginal positions, but that opportunities for dialogic resistance frequently exist in the interstices. Language socialization is a never-ending process, and new cross-linguistic contacts construct new multilingual vessels (in situ or in virtu) for the performative construction of new heteroglossic codes. Methods for the study of these productive performances and the platforms for action that they spawn continue to be developed.

Future Directions, or Just Some Final (Emergent) Words in That Direction

A growing number of scholars now follow Bakhtin in making the point that "languages" never fully exist, i.e., as neatly bounded and fixed systems consisting of grammatical rules and lexicons that can be completely learned and used to communicate in perfectly regulated ways (see, for example, Alvarez-Cáccamo (1998)). For these researchers (and I count myself among them), languages only ever "exist" as social constructs through the tensions of social practice; in that case, as systems, all languages are always "emergent." That is, the sound contrasts, morphosyntactic formulations, semantic fields, and pragmatic strategies are constantly under negotiation in every site of interaction.[4] Thus, what actually emerges over time within communities of practice is not really a full-fledged code per se but more concretely a set of thoughts and opinions (a language ideology) about the languages, registers, styles, genres, voices . . . being used – whether they are im/proper, in/effective, un/meaningful, aesthetically pleasing or not – and whether the people who use them are lazy, crazy, funny, cruel, or cool.

Having clearly stated my bias here at the end, one may well wonder how I could have said yes to Nancy Bonvillain's kind invitation to write a chapter on "new and emergent languages". Yet I don't think it was foolhardy. In effect, if linguistic anthropologists are to have an object of study at all, we must identify that object and identify how it develops. Just as cultural anthropologists have wrung their hands for decades over "culture," so must we at least closely examine the notion of "language?" In effect, this chapter has allowed my ideas to emerge and take shape not only over the object itself (language), but also over all the ways in which new ones (or their simulacra) emerge and take shape.

While I disagree that distinctly bounded languages ever emerge from anyone's head (fully armed like Athena from Zeus'), I do believe that humans are language-making creatures. Sometimes we do it just for fun, other times to facilitate market exchange; sometimes to engender intimacy, other times to instantiate boundaries; sometimes to reach our gods, other times to master our servants; sometimes to resist arrest, other times to idolize pop stars. The list is endless and our research has only just begun.

What is clear is that all emergent codes and the emergent ideologies concerning them have human histories, social contexts, and moments in the sun (or the abyss) where others respond (or don't) as if they understand (or don't) and transmit aspects of these codes and ideologies about them (or don't). Languages created in a vacuum without any attempt made to use them with others (real or fictional) are not languages; they are just lists of words and rules. The ones that make it out into the light of day (actual or virtual) to play, if only for a moment, are the newly emergent languages.

Related Topics

6 Being in the Cloud (LeBlanc-Wories); **20** Language, Immigration, and the Nation-State (Pujolar); **22** Language in the Age of Globalization (Jacquemet); **24** Racism in the Press (Van Dijk).

Notes

1 See Riley (2013) for more about the ideological construction of this spatial metaphor and the need to explore the permeability of the community vessel. See also Blommaert et al.'s attempt to transform the notion of "scale" from a spatio-temporal context into a "qualitative feature of meaning making" (2015: 126).
2 Jourdan (2006) makes this clear in her discussion of how pidgins and creoles were created within particular, historically situated, work-based communities of practice (i.e., plantations in the Pacific, Atlantic, and Indian Oceans), in which both the cultures and the languages that gave voice to those cultures emerged (a process she calls "enlanguagement" (2006: 135)). This was the result of plantation workers' and overseers' prior language-culture systems, hegemonic structuring by plantation society, and specific interactions among individual agents in the interstices.
3 See Irvine's (2001) use of Bourdieu's (1979) notions of distinction, Goffman's (1981) ideas about footing and frames, and Silverstein's (1979) notions of language ideology in order to analyze how styles are semiotically produced; Agha (2005) took similar ideas about footing and style to develop his notion of enregisterment.
4 Auer and Pfänder (2011) offer a good summary of the difference between "emerging" and "emergent" grammars, the former being an artifact of Chomsky's models and the latter the product of the sort of thinking I am propounding here, i.e., that "grammar" constrains but does not determine usage because it is ever-transforming as a function of interaction. In doing so, they use the term "languaging" to discuss the process in which we are all always engaged in the course of producing new codes, which are never complete and autonomous (except in hindsight).

References

Agha, Asif (2005) Voice, Footing, Enregisterment. *Journal of Linguistic Anthropology* 15(1): 38–59.
Ahearn, Laura M. (2001) *Invitations to Love: Literacy, Love Letters, and Social Change in Nepal*. Ann Arbor: University of Michigan Press.
Alim, H. Samy (2006) *Roc the Mic Right: The Language of Hip Hop Culture*. New York: Routledge.
Alvarez-Cáccamo, Celso (1998) From "Switching Code" to "Code-Switching": Toward a Reconceptualisation of Communicative Codes. In Peter Auer (ed.) *Code-Switching in Conversation: Language, Interaction and Identity*, pp. 29–50. London: Routledge.
Anderson, Benedict (2006) *Imagined Communities: Reflections on the Origins and Spread of Nationalism*, rev. ed. London: Verso.
Auer, Peter (1984) *Bilingual Conversation*. Amsterdam: Benjamins.
Auer, Peter, and Wei Li (eds) (2007) *Handbook of Multilingualism and Multilingual Communication*. Berlin: De Gruyter Mouton.
Auer, Peter, and Stefan Pfänder (2011) Constructions: Emergent or Emerging? *Linguae and Litterae* 6: 1–21. Berlin: Walter de Gruyter.

Bakhtin, Mikhail M. (1981) *The Dialogic Imagination: Four Essays,* Michael Holquist (ed.), Caryl Emerson, and Michael Holquist (trans.). Austin: University of Texas Press.
Bakhtin, Mikhail M. (1984) *Rabelais and his World,* Hélène Iswolsky (trans.). Bloomington IN: Indiana University Press.
Baquedano-López, Patricia (1997) Creating Social Identities through Doctrina Narratives. *Issues in Applied Linguistics 8*(1): 27–45.
Baquedano-López, Patricia and Paul Garrett (2002) Language Socialization: Reproduction and Continuity, Transformation and Change. *Annual Review of Anthropology 31*: 339–361.
Barrett, Rusty (1999) Indexing Polyphonous Identity in the Speech of African American Drag Queens. In Mary Bucholtz, A. C. Liang, and Laurel A. Sutton (eds) *Reinventing Identities*, pp. 313–331. Oxford: Oxford University Press.
Bayley, Robert and Sandra R. Schecter (eds) (2003) *Language Socialization in Bilingual and Multilingual Societies.* Clevedon: Multilingual Matters.
Bhatia, Tej K. and William C. Ritchie (eds) (2012) *The Handbook of Bilingualism and Multilingualism.* Chichester, West Sussex: Wiley Blackwell.
Blackledge, Adrian and Angela Creese (2010) *Multilingualism: A Critical Perspective.* London: Continuum.
Blom, Jan-Petter and John Gumperz (1972) Social Meaning in Linguistic Structures: Code-Switching in Norway. In John Gumperz and Dell Hymes (eds), *Directions in Sociolinguistics,* pp. 407–434. New York: Holt, Rinehart and Winston.
Blommaert, Jan (2013) *Ethnography, Superdiversity and Linguistic Landscapes: Chronicles of Complexity.* Bristol: Multilingual Matters.
Blommaert, Jan, Elina Westinen, and Sirpa Leppänen (2015) Further Notes on Sociolinguistic Scales. *Intercultural Pragmatics 12*(1): 119–127.
Boas, Franz (1911) *Handbook of American Indian Languages.* Washington: US Government Printing Office.
Boellstorff, Tom (2008) *Coming of Age in Second Life.* Princeton: Princeton University Press.
Bopp, Franz (1862) *A Comparative Grammar of the Sanscrit, Zend, Greek, Latin, Lithuanian, Gothic, German, and Sclavonic Languages.* London: Williams.
Bourdieu, Pierre (1979) *Distinction.* Cambridge MA: Harvard University Press.
Bourdieu, Pierre (1991) *Language and Symbolic Power.* Cambridge, MA: Harvard University Press.
Brown, Roger, and Albert Gilman (1960) The Pronouns of Power and Solidarity. In T. A. Sebeok (ed.) *Style in Language,* pp. 253–276. Cambridge: MIT Press.
Chun, Elaine W. (2009) Ideologies of Legitimate Mockery: Margaret Cho's Revoicings of Mock Asian. In Angela Reyes and Adrienne Lo (eds) *Beyond Yellow English: Toward a Linguistic Anthropology of Asian Pacific America,* pp. 261–287. Oxford: Oxford University Press.
Duranti, Alessandro and Charles Goodwin (eds) (1992) *Rethinking Context: Language as an Interactve Phenomenon.* Cambridge: Cambridge University Press.
Eckert, Penelope (1999) *Variations and Social Practice: The Linguistic Construction of Social Meaning in Belton High.* Oxford: Blackwell.
Errington, J. Joseph (1998) *Shifting Languages: Interaction and Identity in Javanese Indonesia.* Cambridge: Cambridge University Press.
Fader, Ayala (2009) *Mitzvah Girls: Bringing Up the Next Generation of Hasidic Jews in Brooklyn.* Princeton: Princeton University Press.
Ferguson, Charles A. (1959) Diglossia. *Word 15*: 325–340.
García-Sánchez, Immaculada M. (2012) Language Socialization and Exclusion. In *Handbook of Language Socialization,* A. Duranti, E. Ochs, and B.B. Schieffelin (eds), pp. 391–419. Malden, MA: Blackwell.
Garrett, Paul (2005) What a Language is Good for: Language Socialization, Language Shift, and the Persistence of Code-Specific Genres in St. Lucia. *Language in Society 34*(3): 327–361.
Gaudio, Rudolf P. (2011) The Blackness of "Broken English." *Journal of Linguistic Anthropology 21*(2): 230–246.
Genesee, Fred (2008) Bilingual First Language Acquisition: Evidence from Montreal. Diversité urbaine, 9–26. http://id.erudit.org/iderudit/019559ar (consulted 12/23/14).
Goffman, Erving (1981). *Forms of Talk.* Philadelphia: University of Pennsylvania Press.
Grosjean, François (1982) *Life with Two Languages: An Introduction to Bilingualism.* Cambridge, MA: Harvard University Press.
Haugen, Einar (1953) *The Norwegian Language in America: A Study in Bilingual Behavior.* Philadelphia: University of Pennsylvania Press.
Heller, Monica (ed.) (2003) *Crosswords: Language, Education and Ethnicity in French Ontario.* Berlin: Mouton de Gruyter.

Heller, Monica (2007) *Bilingualism: A Social Approach*. London: Palgrave Macmillan.
Heller, Monica and Marilyn Martin-Jones (eds) (2001) *Voices of Authority: Education and Linguistic Difference*. Westport CT: Ablex.
Hill, Jane H. (1998) Language, Race, and White Public Space. *American Anthropologist* 100(3): 680–689.
Hill, Jane H. and Kenneth C. Hill (1986) *Speaking Mexicano*. Tucson: University of Arizona Press.
Hoffman, Katherine E. (2008) *We Share Walls: Language, Land, and Gender in Berber Morocco*. Malden MA: Blackwell Publishing.
Inoue, Miyako (2006) *Vicarious Language: Gender and Linguistic Modernity in Japan*. Berkeley: University of California Press.
Irvine, Judith (2001) Style as Distinctiveness: The Culture and Ideology of Linguistic Differentiation. In Rickford, John R. and Penelope Eckert (eds) *Style and Sociolinguistic Variation*, pp. 21–43. Cambridge: Cambridge University Press.
Irvine, Judith and Susan Gal (2000) Language Ideology and Linguistic Differentiation. In Paul V. Kroskrity (ed.) *Regimes of Language: Ideologies, Polities, and Identities*, pp. 35–84. Santa Fe, NM: School of American Research Press.
Jacquemet, Marco (2005) Transidiomatic Practices: Language and Power in the Age of globalization. *Language & Communication* 25: 257–277.
Johnstone, Barbara (2009) Stance, Style, and the Linguistic Individual. In Alexandra Jaffe (ed.) *Sociolinguistic Perspectives on Stance*, pp. 29–52. Oxford: Oxford University Press.
Jones, Graham M., Bambi B. Schieffelin, and Rachel E. Smith (2011) When Friends Who Talk Together Stalk Together: Online Gossip as Metacommunicaiton. In Crispin Thurlow and Kristine Mroczek (eds) *Digital Discourse: Language in the New Media*, pp. 26–47. Oxford: Oxford University Press.
Jourdan, Christine (2006) Pidgins and Creoles Genesis: An Anthropological Offering. In Christine Jourdan and Kevin Tuite (eds) *Language, Culture, and Society*, pp. 135–155. Cambridge: Cambridge University Press.
Kuipers, Joel C. (1998) *Language, Identity, and Marginality in Indonesia: The Changing Nature of Ritual Speech on the Island of Sumba*. Cambridge: Cambridge University Press.
Kulick, Don (1992) *Language Shift and Cultural Reproduction: Socialization, Self, and Syncretism in a Papua New Guinean Village*. Cambridge: Cambridge University Press.
Labov, William (1972) *Sociolinguistic Patterns*. Philadelphia: University of Pennsylvania Press.
Labov, William (2001) *Principles of Linguistic Change*, Vol. 2: *Social Factors*. Malden MA: Blackwell.
Le Page, Robert B., and Andrée Tabouret-Keller (1985) *Acts of Identity: Creole-based Approaches to Language and Ethnicity*. Cambridge: Cambridge University Press.
Lightfoot, David (2006) *How New Languages Emerge*. Cambridge: Cambridge University Press.
Makihara, Miki (2009) Heterogeneity in Linguistic Practice, Competence, and Ideology: Language and Community on Easter Island. In Neriko M. Doerr (ed.) *The Native Speaker Concept: Ethnographic Investigations of Native Speaker Effects*, pp. 249–275. Berlin: Mouton de Gruyter.
Manning, Paul (2009) Can the Avatar Speak? *Journal of Linguistic Anthropology* 19(2): 310–325.
Martin-Jones, Marilyn, Adrian Blackledge, and Angela Creese (eds) (2012) *The Routledge Handbook of Multilingualism*. New York: Routledge.
Maryns, Katrijn (2006) *The Asylum Speaker: Language in the Belgian Asylum Procedure*. Manchester: St. Jerome.
Mendoza-Denton (2008) *Homegirls: Language and Cultural Practice among Latina Youth Gangs*. Malden MA: Blackwell.
Miller, Laura (2004) Those Naughty Teenage Girls: Japanese Kogal, Slang, and Media Assessments. *Journal of Linguistic Anthropology* 14(2): 225–247.
Moore, Leslie (2006) Learning by Heart in Qur'anic and Public Schools in Northern Cameroon. Social Analysis. *The International Journal of Cultural and Social Practice* 50(3): 109–126.
Muysken, Pieter (2012) Two Linguistic Systems in Contact: Grammar, Phonology, and Lexicon. In Bhatia, Tej K., and William C. Ritchie (eds) *The Handbook of Bilingualism and Multilingualism*, pp. 193–215. Chichester, West Sussex: Wiley Blackwell.
Myers-Scotton, Carol (2006) *Multiple Voices: An Introduction to Bilingualism*. Malden MA: Blackwell.
Nevins, M. Eleanor (2013) *Lessons from Fort Apache: Beyond Language Endangerment and Maintenance*. Malden, MA: Wiley Blackwell.
Newell, Sasha (2009) Enregistering Modernity, Bluffing Criminality: How Nouchi Speech Reinvented (and Fractured) the Nation. *Journal of Linguistic Anthropology* 19(2): 157–184.
Paugh, Amy L. (2012) *Playing with Languages: Children and Change in a Caribbean Village*. New York: Berghahn Books.
Okrent, Arika (2009) *In the Land of Invented Languages: Esperanto Rock Stars, Klingon Poets, Loglan Lovers, and the Mad Dreamers who Tried to Build a Perfect Language*. New York: Spiegel & Grau.

Poplack, Shana (1980) Sometimes I'll Start a Sentence in Spanish y Termino en Español: Toward a Typology of Code-Switching. *Linguistics* 18(7–8): 581–618.
Rampton, Ben (1995) *Crossing: Language and Ethnicity among Adolescents*. London: Longman.
Riley, Kathleen C. (2001) *The Emergence of Dialogic Identities: Transforming Heteroglossia in the Marquesas, F. P.* Doctoral dissertation, CUNY Graduate Center.
Riley, Kathleen C. (2007) To Tangle or Not to Tangle: Shifting Language Ideologies and the Socialization of Charabia in the Marquesas, F.P. In Miki Makihara and Bambi B. Schieffelin (eds) *Consequences of Contact: Language Ideologies and Sociocultural Transformations in Pacific Societies*, pp. 70–95. New York: Oxford University Press.
Riley, Kathleen, C. (2011a) Language Socialization and Language Ideologies. In A. Duranti, E, Ochs, and B.B. Schieffelin (eds) *Handbook of Language Socialization*, pp. 493–514. Malden, MA: Blackwell.
Riley, Kathleen (2011b) Learning to Code-Switch in the 21st century: Towards an Understanding of Global Ideologies of Youthful Cosmopolitan Cool. AAA, Montreal, QC.
Riley, Kathleen (2012) Jumping on One Foot in Several Worlds at the same time: The Art and Politics of Ethnolinguistic Humor. San Francisco, CA: AAA.
Riley, Kathleen (2013) L'idéologie hétéroglossique et l'identité dialogique à Montréal. In C. Trimaille and J. M. Eloy (eds), *Idéologies linguistiques et discriminations, (Actes du colloque du Réseau Francophone de Sociolinguistique, Rennes, juin 2009*, pp. 59–83. Paris: Harmattan.
Romaine, Suzanne (1989) *Bilingualism*, 2nd ed. Oxford: Blackwell.
Schieffelin, Bambi B. (1993) Codeswitching and Language Socialization: Some Probable Relationships. In Judith F. Duchan, Rae M. Sonnenmeier, Lynne E. Hewitt (eds) *Pragmatics: From Theory to Practice*, pp. 20–42. Englewood Cliffs, NJ: Prentice-Hall.
Shankar, Shalini (2009) Reel to Real: Desi Teens' Linguistic Engagements with Bollywood. In Angela Reyes and Adrienne Lo (eds) *Beyond Yellow English: Toward a Linguistic Anthropology of Asian Pacific America*, pp. 309–324. Oxford: Oxford University Press.
Siegel, Jeff (1985) Koines and Koineization. *Language in Society* 14(3): 357–378.
Silverstein, Michael (1979) Language Structure and Linguistic Ideology. In R. Cline, W. Hanks, and C. Hofbauer (eds) The Elements: A Parasession on Linguistic Units and Levels, pp. 193–247. Chicago: Chicago Linguistic Society.
Silverstein, Michael (1997) Encountering Language and Languages of Encounter in North American Ethnohistory. *Journal of Linguistic Anthropology* 6(2): 126–144.
Spitulnik, Debra (1997) The Social Circulation of Media Discourse and the Mediation of Communities. *Journal of Linguistic Anthropology* 6(2): 161–187.
Spitulnik, Debra (1999) The Language of the City: Town Bemba as Urban Hybridity. *Journal of Linguistic Anthropology* 8(1): 30–59.
Swigart, Leigh (2001) The Limits of Legitimacy: Language Shift in a Changing Market. *Journal of Linguistic Anthropology* 10(1): 90–130.
Urciuoli, Bonnie (1996) *Exposing Prejudice: Puerto Rican Experiences of Language, Race, and Class*. Boulder CO: Westview Press.
Weinreich, Uriel (1953) *Languages in Contact: Findings and Problems*. New York: Linguistic Circle of New York.
Woolard, Kathryn (1987) Codeswitching and Comedy in Catalonia. *Pragmaties* l(1): 106–122.
Woolard, Kathryn (1998) Simultaneity and Bivalency as Strategies in Bilingualism. *Journal of Linguistic Anthropology* 8: 3–29.
Wright, Joseph (1961) *The English Dialect Dictionary, Being the Complete Vocabulary of All Dialect Words Still in Use, or Known to Have Been in Use during the Last Two Hundred Years*. London: Oxford University Press.
Zentella, Ana Celia (1997) Growing Up Bilingual: Puerto Rican Children in New York. Malden, MA: Blackwell Publishers.

Further Reading

Bhatia, Tej K. and William C. Ritchie (eds) (2012) *The Handbook of Bilingualism and Multilingualism*. Chichester, West Sussex: Wiley-Blackwell.
This handbook provides an introduction to how multilingualism, both social and individual, generates new systems of communicating.

Eckert, Penelope and John R. Rickford (eds) (2001) *Style and Sociolinguistic Variation*. Cambridge: Cambridge University Press.
This seminal set of essays by seasoned sociolinguists and linguistic anthropologists sheds light on how new "styles" are produced.

Lightfoot, David (2006) *How New Languages Emerge*. Cambridge: Cambridge University Press.
This text draws on theoretical linguistics to formulate a new historical linguistic approach to understanding how new languages emerge out of the tension between incremental changes in individuals' I-languages and society's "ambient" E-languages (E for external).

Reyes, Angela and Adrienne Lo (2009) *Beyond Yellow English. Toward a Linguistic Anthropology of Asian Pacific America*. Oxford: Oxford University Press.
This collection offers a range of studies that illustrate how immigration and language socialization (in this case of Asian peoples in North America) produce new transidiomatic practices (e.g., racial stereotyping and bilingual strategies) and new heteroglossic performance genres (from narratives to stand-up comedy).

Thurlow, Crispin and Kristine Mroczek (2011) *Digital Discourse: Language in the New Media*. Oxford: Oxford University Press.
This volume provides a great selection of studies of the emergent effects of new media on how we communicate, many of which provide insight into both the theory and methods needed for this new enterprise.

Part IV
Language and Local/Global Power

19

Language and Political Economy

Bonnie McElhinny

Introduction

One way to survey the study of language and political economy is to consider why language seems, more than linguistic anthropologists would like, to be left out of studies of political economy. This approach considers why language and economy have sometimes been taken to be opposed (e.g., in such formulations as base vs. superstructure), and then suggests strategies for overcoming the binary, theoretically and empirically. I will, below, briefly review these arguments. This article, however, takes a different approach; it asks why, at certain moments, debates about language are so central to discussions of political economy.[1] It argues that if we understand language as one means among many of making meaning, we can better grasp both why or how language does (or does not) matter in different ways, to different kinds of people, at different times. Language is one particularly important means for the construction of relations of social difference and social inequality, but not the only one and not always the most important one. This chapter is constructed around a loosely chronological account of how capitalism, as an uneven world system, has been linked to particular ways of understanding language in the production of inequality. In the template I was given for writing it, I was asked to offer an overview of historical perspectives, and then critical current themes and future directions. But this chronological approach combines these, by asking us to regard the history of work on language with a fresh eye, and to be richly attentive to the ways that current approaches, taken as critical, may occasionally be collusive in changing political situations, as some past linguistic ideas were. It suggests that a historical eye – one that asks "Why this, why now?" – needs to suffuse all of our analytic accounts.

There are extended debates on the relationship between linguistic ideologies, practices and political economic forces (Coulmas 1992, Eagleton 2007, Friedrich 1989). Briefly, one approach, often called the *base/superstructure* model, suggests that economic forces shape all else – religion, cultural expression, political life, religious expression, and forms of consciousness. This is the view often associated with Marx (1859). Engels (1890) protested that Marx's comments were often misread, that rather than saying that the economic element was the *only* determinant, he and Marx had argued that the ways that life was produced and reproduced were *ultimately* determining. Volosinov (1973), writing after the Russian Revolution of 1917, agreed. He critiqued earlier Marxists for ignoring language, but also linguists like Saussure for studying language as an abstract sign system, rather than as something involved in economic and other social struggles.[2] He argued, instead, that the study of language was a key site for understanding economic struggles. Williams (1973, 1977) offered an even more profound challenge to the base/superstructure distinction (see also Bourdieu 1977).

Gal's influential (1989) review of language and political economy argued that much sociolinguistic research since its origins in the 1960s could be seen as challenging both the separation of the linguistic sign from the material world, as well as the relationship of (socio)linguistic structures to individual or group strategies (p. 346). She argues that Gramsci, Volosinov and Williams show how language is central to how domination is achieved, and why subordinate groups accept the power of the dominant as legitimate. Gal notes, "Whether the term is hegemony, symbolic domination, oppositional culture, subjugated discourse, or heteroglossia, the central insight remains: Control of the representations of reality is not only a source of social power but therefore also a likely locus of conflict and struggle" (p. 348). (See Irvine 1989 for another useful review at the same time.) Scholars continue to debate these questions (compare Gal 2012, Heller 2010, and McGill 2013 for different positions on the relationship between base and superstructure and the relative independence of language ideologies).

Gal's (1989) article proceeds with a rich overview of a variety of different ways in which sociolinguistic research illuminates these struggles, through studies of sociolinguistic variation, commodified language, literacy, institutional language, the construction of national standards, struggles about language in colonial settings, expressive genres, and the ways anthropological discourse is itself a dominant discourse, and not just a site of criticism for it. Arguably, the most detailed and lengthy section of the review focuses on the role of language in state formation, including the elaboration of national standards and the role of education in constructing hegemonically legitimate linguistic varieties. She also notes that although sociolinguistics has excelled at *description* of linguistic variation, a key challenge for the field remains *explanation*, which could be done by more carefully locating "the role of language in colonization, capitalist expansion, state-formation, class relations and political economic dependence" (p. 349). We also need, she argued, to do more work on active resistance of subordinate groups (p. 354) (see also Huayhua, this volume). In this review, I take stock of some of the work in the twenty-five years since her review, noting the irony that her definitive review was published in 1989, often construed as a year marking the conclusion of a set of significant changes in the 1970s and 1980s, as the Berlin Wall fell, Western nations moved from more welfarist regimes to neoliberal states, Soviet and Chinese communist governments adopted a more marketized face and international agencies required more marked economic restructuring plans for countries seeking development aid (Harvey 2005).

Building on the imperative to further understand how legitimation of inequity occurs, as well as to challenge overly reductionist accounts of the manipulation of people by ruling class interests, a significant site for work in linguistic anthropology through the 1990s was a focus on ideology, which was seen as a way "to relate the micro-culture of communicative action to political economic considerations of power and social inequality" (Woolard 1998: 27). See Kroskrity, this volume, for a more detailed review. While the term "language ideologies" is useful precisely because it facilitates conversations amongst people who can have remarkably different approaches to linguistic study (see Woolard 1998), Philips (1998) cautioned that ideology should not be merely substituted for culture or worldview; because "[i]deology carries with it connotations of the exercise of power primarily because Marxist writings about ideology and reactions to them in the nineteenth century have given the term those connotations" (p. 213). Some explicit and implicit critiques of what a focus on language ideology can facilitate are evident in the recent concentration of work on language and materialism

(Shankar and Cavanaugh 2012; see also Holborrow 2015). Studies of language and materialism also, however, display a broad and ecumenical approach, with some studies attentive to power and inequity while others are not (see Eagleton 1989 for early notes on this).

The project of critical analysis does not stop with asserting the materiality of language; this is where the project of developing a critique of capitalism starts. This requires investigating precisely the kinds of dilemmas, challenges and contradictions thrown up in different places and times by, variously, mercantile, industrial, monopoly and finance capitalism that shape, and are shaped by, ideologies and practices of language, with an eye to analyzing the inequities created or rationalized by such ideologies and practices. This chapter, therefore, is organized historically rather than thematically, to see what kinds of questions arise at particular moments, and to think about continuities and discontinuities, with particular attention paid to the twentieth and early twenty-first century. I give more attention to the topics that have received least attention, as well as to building some linkages between literatures that are often taken as discrete. Such an approach certainly raises the question of how periodization is defined, and from whose perspective. These questions are helpful in a more historicizing account. Linguistic anthropology has taken as its objects of study a wide-ranging set of sites and people, but the approach itself is one developed within, and still largely articulated within, Western, and even American, institutions (witness the affiliation of authors published in the *Journal of Linguistic Anthropology*). A key step in historicizing studies more carefully is also deprovincializing them (Bauman and Briggs 2003, Chakrabarty 2000). This step is also a necessary first move in developing a more inclusive international dialogue – on which, more at the end.

Language and Colonialism

Edward Said has analyzed how both Marx and Williams fail to take into account the central role of European imperialism in shaping European capitalism, social formations and knowledge production. His book *Orientalism* (1978) catalyzed a new wave of studies of colonialism. Said argued that while military, political and economic policies had dominated academic studies of colonialism, his contribution was to consider the role that knowledge and culture play too. Said defines Orientalism as

> ... a way of coming to terms with the Orient that is based on the Orient's special place in European Western experience .... Orientalism expresses and represents that part culturally and even ideologically as a mode of discourse with supporting institutions, vocabulary, scholarship, imagery, doctrines, even colonial bureaucracies and colonial styles.
> *Said (1978: 1–2)*

In *Orientalism,* Said asks how a variety of disciplines, including, history, biology, political theory, economic theory and literature all come into the service of imperialism. Comparative linguistics attracts particular attention from him, for the ways it construes people as separate, and in distinct genealogical and hierarchical relationships to one another. Others have built on this work. For instance, Trautmann's superb trilogy (1997, 2005, 2006) of works on linguistic scholarship in British-occupied India looks at the ways British linguistic innovations, including the study of phonetics, were often indebted to Indian traditions of linguistic scholarship in ways that remain largely unacknowledged, as he traces the varying meanings of Aryan, notions that started out to elaborate ideas of kinship between Europeans and Indians, and were narrowed to focus on white superiority. As Gilmour writes, "the development of colonial linguistics was fundamental to strategies by which Westerners interpreted the world, categorized its peoples, and affirmed the superiority of their own position within it" (2006: 2). How did and does language study and instruction help construct, maintain and consolidate imperial power? What notions of language are developed in colonial and imperial settings? How do concepts of nation evolve with imperial rule?

Said's account begins with the first wave of European imperialism, a story that begins in the fifteenth century. There has been some critical and compelling work done on this period (Hanks 2010, Errington 2008, Mannheim 1991, Rafael 1988). For the purposes of considering how we can continue to deepen and broaden our historical approach, I will focus here on the second wave of European imperialism, co-extensive with a period of intensive nation-building and beginning at the end of the nineteenth century, when capitalism in Europe was facing one of its periodic crises (Hobsbawm 1987). The number of industrial producers and industrial economies was growing rapidly, and technological advances improved the output of industry, but because a significant market for consumption had not yet developed (strikingly, the advertising industry evolved in this period, as a way of identifying and creating needs), prices and profits dropped. Ideas of nation, standards and national language policy became extensively elaborated in this period, as governments used four strategies to address this crisis: (1) *protectionism*, insulating industries in the nation from competition, as well as developing domestic markets; (2) *scientific management*, detailed regulations for production processes and laborers' actions, in order to increase productivity (see Urciuoli and LaDousa 2013 on Taylorism and language); (3) *monopoly*, combining potential competitors to make it possible to raise prices without risk of competition; and (4) *imperialism*, formal conquest, annexation and administration of territories to control access to raw materials, markets, and people. The word *imperialism* was coined in British politics in the 1870s (Hobsbawm 1987: 60). Conquest of other countries helped alleviate class tensions produced by industrialization, in part by improving economic conditions at home and offering sites where dissatisfied Europeans could migrate to find economic opportunities, but also by encouraging the disenfranchised to identify with nation, and increasingly race, rather than focus on class divisions and conflict (Hobsbawm 1987: 69). Developing national, often monoglot, linguistic standards was part of this European nation-building. Hierarchized notions of racialized difference, which helped to rationalize colonial rule, were sharpened in a number of sciences of the time, including linguistics.

By 1914, one quarter of the world outside Europe and the Americas was divided into territories formally controlled by a handful of countries, specifically Britain, France, Germany, Italy, the Netherlands, Belgium, the United States and Japan (Hobsbawm 1987: 57–59). By the end of World War I, 85 percent of the world was colonized by Europe (Said 1978: 123). The earlier pre-industrial empires of Spain and Portugal were in some cases carved up by other imperial powers, and in others remained. Two major areas of the world, Africa and the Pacific, were comprehensively divided up. A number of studies have examined debates about what the languages of rule should be (the colonial language, a local language, a local lingua franca). Different colonial powers had different official approaches, though colonial officials, businessmen and missionaries often had conflicting views. Linguistics often played a key role in rationalizing racialized difference and colonial rule. For some helpful reviews see Errington (2008), Fabian (1986), and Gilmour (2006).

One of the domains of language and political economy perhaps best studied in the overall literatures is the development of European nations, and the forms of linguistic homogenization and standardization linked with these national movements at this same time. However, sociolinguistics has yet to take on a move more widely seen in colonial, post-colonial and anti-colonial studies: more fully integrating metropole and colony into one field (see Stoler and Cooper 1997). In other fields, this has meant not assuming nations as fully formed and shaping imperialism, but rather nations emerging in the context of imperialism. In linguistic anthropology, this could involve:

- tracing actors and ideologies from one site to another in one colonial domain (for instance, considering how French policy in Algeria and Vietnam was like and unlike policy in Brittany, and indeed shaped metropolitan policy);
- looking at linkages between disparate sites (for instance, exploring how English language instruction pioneered by US missionaries for nineteenth-century industrial education in Hawaiian schools was transplanted to the mainland as a model for the education of African-Americans, and Native Americans, and then returned to the Pacific during the US colonization of the Philippines);
- examining the import of the simultaneity of the codification of Spanish and its teaching in the early Spanish colonies;
- considering linkages between subaltern groups that drew on each other's resistance strategies, including linguistic ones, in thinking about overthrowing colonial rule (compare exchanges between Indian and Irish nationalists (Chandra 2012), or note how francophone activists in Canada in the 1960s compared themselves to Black nationalists elsewhere); and
- more carefully linking accounts of immigration related to various colonial developments and immigrant interactions with indigenous groups in complex imperial circuits.

Notions of race were, of course, not simply perpetuated by but critiqued in linguistic anthropology. A key challenge came from the work of Franz Boas and his students (Darnell 2001). In the United States, in the late nineteenth century, industrial capitalism was seen as tearing the fabric of rural society, large numbers of immigrants coming from southern and eastern European countries gave rise to eugenics movements for racial purification; there were backlashes against the achievements made by African-Americans after the Civil War era; wars continued between the US military and Natives defending territory; and the United States became involved in overseas colonialism in Guam, Hawaii, Panama, Puerto Rico, the Philippines and Samoa. Departments of American anthropology, which included linguistic study as one of four fields (alongside physical anthropology, ethnology and archaeology), were founded at the same time. A key figure in the professionalization of anthropology, and in establishing the field of linguistic anthropology as one of anthropology's four fields, was Franz Boas, a German-born Jew who moved to the United States in the late 1880s. At Columbia, he trained a number of anthropologists, including Ruth Benedict, Zora Neale Hurston, Alfred Kroeber, Robert Lowie, Margaret Mead and Edward Sapir, who played key roles in establishing anthropology as an intellectual field and who also fostered its growth at other universities like California, Berkeley, Chicago and Yale. Boas's work ranged widely: he wrote on the language and culture of Northwest Coast Indians, on the bodies and cultures of American immigrants, especially those from southern and eastern Europe, on the position of "Negroes" in American society and their cultural achievements in Africa, and on race-mixing. He critiqued eugenics, Nazi science, anti-Semitism, miscegenation statutes, and concepts of nationalism.[3] In Boas (1911) he separated notions of language, culture and race, arguing that each pursues a different historical trajectory. Such a notion directly critiqued ideas of nationalism (like Herder's) that described, and prescribed, these as unified. He challenged evolutionary ideas of "primitive" language, such as those evident in some of the accounts of missionary and comparative linguistics in southern Africa, arguing that this was a matter of European observers transferring their own analytic biases onto the perception of cultural material. Nonetheless, a biography by his former student, Melville Herskovits (1953), an illustrious anthropologist of the African diaspora, noted that "[m]atters of colonial rule touched him lightly" (p. 112). Bauman and Briggs (2003) eludicate Boas's theories of language and their role in challenging evolutionary concepts, but also, ultimately, show some of their limitations, arguing that "Boas's cosmopolitanism was friendly to capitalism", since he saw commerce, science and art as fostering ties that would bind mankind together, and he "denounced imperialism and colonialism, but he did so on cultural and political grounds; opposing them did not lead Boas to question the logic of capital" (p. 290).

The rivalries between the imperial powers eventually led to World War I (1914–1918). strikingly, some of the first clashes were between British, French and German colonial forces in Africa – which ended with the dismantling of the German, Austro-Hungarian, Russian, and Ottoman empires, the creation of many new European nations and significant transformation of the colonial landscape. Continuing capitalist crises led to both communist and fascist revolutions. Space here does not permit a full review of the ways that linguistic ideas forged in the Soviet Union and its satellites, and in communist China, questioned capitalism, class distinctions and Western imperialism, as other forms of expansionism were ratified. A number of these concepts also raised key questions about how to understand the relationship of language and political economy that were not evident in Western discussions until the 1960s (and, indeed, the translation of some of these works was key to many of the discussions that led to the rise of sociolinguistics at that time). Some key works that deserve further consideration, however, or that have already raised some significant questions, include: Brandist (2003), Lähteenmaki (2006), Stalin (1951), and Zhou (2004).

Language and Fascism

As Arendt (1968) argued in her landmark integration of European histories of anti-Semitism, imperialism and totalitarianism, fascism in Europe is a product of the second wave of European imperialism that began in the late nineteenth century, as well as of the form of nationalism, also shaped by imperialism, in which the equation between language = nation = race is taken to its most extreme and violent form. Fascism also tried to resolve, in the most isolationist, genocidal and racist way possible, the contradictions that imperialism raises: the creation of racial proximities and interactions, in spheres ranging from families and children to politics and trade, as well as shared languages, in the context of occupation and claims to racial superiority. A focus on imperialist glory, and national unity, helped redress class antagonisms arising in the wake of industrial capitalism, substituting notions of national/racial superiority for class consciousness and solidarity. Thomas (2014) argues that Italy, Germany and Japan did not become fascist because they were not modern, but because they were modern. Studying fascism helps us to examine contemporary forms of racism, and forms of discontent that are expressed, partially, as racism, and consider the dynamics under which a fascist politics might emerge now (see Eley 2013, Woodley 2012).

In a recent and superb master's thesis, Sheppard (2014) notes that there are two key questions to ask of linguistic ideologies and practices under fascist regimes: (1) how they draw on linguistic ideologies to elaborate notions of race and nation, and (2) how they go about "creating new sensibilities . . . as well as new subjectivities" (p. 1) (see also Faye 1964, Klemperer 2000, Orwell 1995). National Socialism in Germany has received the most attention, and so these notes also rely heavily on that case, without assuming it can be easily extrapolated to other sites.

The lack of a unified German state before 1871 meant the task of unification seemed more urgent for nationalists, especially in light of increasing German migration in the wake of industrialization's economic disruptions and the putative dangers of foreign influence linked to German's imperial presence in Africa and the Pacific (Townson 1992). Germany was hard-hit by World War I, with restrictions placed on its military forces, the surrender of European territory and all of its overseas colonies, and high expenses for reparations. Strikingly, it was in the context of this more extreme anxiety about national identity that Jews, a group seen as distinctively cosmopolitan and not attending to norms of nation states, were seen as threatening. National Socialism was seen as a response both to the problems with capitalism and the concerns about communism (Hutton 2005). However, as Sheppard notes, "What National Socialism promised then was not in the end a revision of the economic system in order to achieve a more equitable re-distribution of the goods of production . . . . Class distinctions would not disappear, but they would be reinterpreted . . . economic equality would be substituted with social egalitarianism . . . ." (2014: 16). The Nazi concept of the *Volksgemeinschaft* – "people's community" – was central to the definition of "Germany" in the interwar years, drawing its boundaries between "races" rather than classes.

Linguistic and other scholarship (especially biological and genetic) had a critical role to play in defining who was German, and who was not. Strikingly, though Said (1978) focuses on the development of comparative linguistics in France and England, it was Germany that was generally seen as the key and most influential site for the elaboration of this work. Some of the earliest articulations of the notion of *Volksgeist*, or "spirit of the people," or "national character," come from Herder and Humboldt, who were making sense of human diversity in the light of European expansion (Bauman and Briggs 2003). Herder focused more on global unity, while Humboldt's work on linguistic diversity argued for the different natures of different people, as well as the fact that certain languages were more successful than others in ways that easily led to hierarchized notions of difference. Philologist Jacob Grimm also studied contemporary diversity in order to reconstruct a unified golden age, with a single German people and a single German language (Bauman and Briggs 2003). Hutton's (2005) landmark work shows how ideologies of *Muttersprache*, "mother tongue," were the ideologies of language through which fascist ideas of kinship, national identity and unity were built. With the German empire lost after World War I, the concerns about the purity of Germany were focused intensively on the internal others, European Jews, who were all the more dangerous because their differences were sometimes racially "invisible." The dilemma, as raised even in *Mein Kampf*, was that there was no correspondence between the "racial" boundaries marked out by racial anthropology and linguistics; the task, therefore, was taken to be to make them congruent. But which should be prioritized? Hutton (2005) argues that eventually a division of labour emerged between a deterministic race theory based on genetics, and a voluntarist and teleological variety of linguistics.

There is significant work to do on how German fascism is like and unlike other fascisms, with the Italian and Spanish cases notably interacting with Catholicism in complex ways. In the Italian case, race was pre-empted by language as the primary determinant of membership, because of the need to forge a sense of shared identity from a highly regionalized population (Golino 1994, Sheppard 2014, Wodak and Richardson 2012), a project that focused the construction of the new Italian nation as the heir of imperial Rome.[4] Francoist Spain pursued yet another strategy in which the idea of "race", while invoked, had less to do with biology than traditional Spanish history, culture and language. Sheppard notes that the Spanish empire had only recently been lost, in 1898, and this gave rise to a notion of *hispanism*, a supernational notion which suggested that Spain's unique culture was embodied in Castilian, an argument that allowed Spain to lay claim to a cultural continuity, if not military oversight, with former colonies, as it was used to manage internal diversity (Guibernau 2004, Pinto 2004).

There are continuing debates about whether to understand imperial Japan as fascist, though Thomas (2014) argues, compellingly, that in Japan there was not a violent overthrow of the government, but a violent redefinition of it, in which rightwing leadership and ultra-rightwing popular movements embraced a new idea of the emperor to unify the nation, heal its dislocations and suppress the left. Strikingly, Thomas argues, this state of exception was coded as unexceptional, in contrast with Germany, so the ideological focus was on continuity and tradition, rather than temporal rupture. The ways in which this shaped Japanese linguistic study remains to be fully unpacked, though we can take some cues from the ways that Inoue (2006), working at a slightly earlier period, challenges histories of Japanese women's language as linked to time immemorial rather than particular moments of state and capitalist crisis.

Sociolinguistic work has begun to consider how histories of fascism are invoked – or often euphemized and erased – in contemporary European politics, and the implications of this. A recent edited collection (Wodak and Richardson 2012; see also Wodak, Khosravinik and Mral 2013 on the discourse of rightwing populism) looks at the ways that political 'rebranding' has taken place across Europe, wherein parties with fascist political predecessors in Austria, France, Germany, Portugal, Spain and the United Kingdom both orient towards, and simultaneously deny, any continuity with arguments and policies of previous movements (see Moralejo 2012 for a thoughtful review noting that fascist discourses may be better approached not as failures of democracy, but in economic terms, as evidence of crises in capitalism). Debates about citizenship and migration, integration and assimilation in Europe and elsewhere, as well as moral panics about terrorism and diversity, continue to both perpetuate and challenge homogenized notions of nation (for related reviews, see other chapters in this volume, including: Baugh, Van Dijk, Huayhua, Pujolar, Chun and Lo, and Wodak).

After World War II ended in 1945, many countries in Africa, Asia and the Pacific gained their political independence; others were incorporated in various, often still contested, ways. The United Nations Special Committee on Decolonization maintains a list of countries that remain under imperial control (countries some call non-decolonized), with the aim of helping to eradicate colonialism, though even this list is contentious (for instance, it excludes many indigenous groups in settler colonial states). Linguistic anthropology and sociolinguistics were central to language planning in the new nations that became independent after World War II (see, e.g., Fishman 1972, Fishman, Ferguson and Das Gupta 1968); this work deserves further attention, and further articulation with other critical accounts of development. Similarly, many other anthropologists participated in post-war development schemes. John Gumperz was part of a large project in India, and though he has written of the ways long-standing Indian linguistic traditions influenced his work, there is more to do on this and the impact of development more broadly on our field (cf. Gupta 2012 on American anthropologists and India during this period).

Language and the Cold War

After World War II, and the revelation of genocidal atrocities linked to fascist notions of race, language and nation, new ideas of race, nation and imperialism shaped international discussions. An emerging body of literature explores the way that Cold War antinomies between capitalism and communism shaped scientific and social scientific inquiry (Chomsky 1997, Cohen-Cole 2003, Martin-Nielsen 2009, 2010, Simpson 1994, Solovey and Cravens 2012). Some of this work has begun to consider how linguistics was shaped by the Cold War, though there is much more to be done, and much of the effort has thus far focused on the United States. We see the rise in this period of more universalist approaches to understanding language, which sociolinguists and linguistic anthropologists then challenge, especially from the 1960s forward. But it is important to note the ways that these approaches arose at least in part as a response to the genocidal concepts of language, race and difference that emerged in fascist discourses, and to historize them as well.

During World War II, language expertise came to be seen as strategic for a variety of military, political and economic ends. After the war, linguistics was funded as never before in the United States, with support passing from philanthropic organizatons to the government, and research being funded by the army, the navy, the air force, the National Institutes of Health and the National Science Foundation. Linguistics departments were founded, with significant government support. In 1946 there were no linguistics departments; by 1965 there were close to 30; by 1970 there were 135. Professional societies grew astronomically (the Linguistic Society of America quintupled between 1950 and 1970), and language teaching was also funded after the passage of the National Defense Education Act, designed to remedy the skills of American students in three strategic areas: mathematics, science and foreign languages (Martin-Nielsen 2010).

Linguistic research was key to projects ranging from code-breaking to information retrieval, but the defining project of linguistics in the post-war period was *machine translation*, which was meant to enable more rapid access to information written in "the languages of the scientifically creative cultures," a project in which the Soviet Union was reputed to be markedly ahead (Martin-Nielsen 2010: 142). Laboratories to study machine translation were established at universities like MIT, Berkeley and Georgetown, and in non-profit think tanks. This focus also helps explain the emergence of the centrality of syntax to linguistic inquiry: "The premise of postwar machine translation was to equip a computer with a set of formal rules which, when applied to an input text in one language (usually Russian or German), would produce an output translation in another language, usually English. These rules worked not by deciphering the meaning of the input text, but by using knowledge of syntactic structure to build an output translation . . . ." (Martin-Nielsen 2010: 142). Many linguists thus turned to the development of formal rule-based syntactic theories, and computational applications of these, as well as to thinking about discourse analysis. Two scholars notable in this regard were Zellig Harris, and his star student, Noam Chomsky. Both were immersed in, and significantly influenced by, socialist forms of Zionism (some of which might not be understood as Zionism now), and were thus thinking through the continuing implications of fascism, communism and toxic forms of nationalism in Europe. Both Harris and Chomsky were in departments and universities that benefited significantly from Cold War funding.

The Russian revolution led to significant debates about socialism and nationalism, and a dramatic change in the historical situation of the Jews (Harshav 1999). Jewish revolutionaries found themselves in a double bind, caught between those who had a vision for a better future and the populist aspirations of revolutionary groups, with some members arguing that pogroms were legitimate expressions of peasants' critique of oppressors. Massive migrations to escape pogroms had a significant impact on many aspects of American life, including linguistics. The families of Zellig Harris and Noam Chomsky were part of these immense population movements. Both began their careers with studies of Hebrew linguistics.

As an undergraduate at the University of Pennsylvania, Harris became a member of Avukah, a student socialist Zionist group that expanded with the anti-fascist, anti-Bolshevik events of the 1930s. The goal of the literate, educated, articulate radicals was to de-fool themselves, and then help de-fool others (Barsky 2010: 44). Significantly, by the mid-1940s, Avukah's leftist Zionist analysis mentioned the links between their work and a variey of other liberation struggles, seeing Black struggles against Jim Crow and Jewish struggles against anti-Semitism as analogous, and noting what could be learned to aid thinking about British colonialism in Palestine from critiques of British colonialism in India (Barsky 2010: 247–248). Harris and others engaged in a long-term, wide-ranging operation called the Frame of Reference project, which resulted in the posthumous publication of a book entitled *The Transformation of Capitalist Society* (1997).

The book aimed at moving out of capitalism by having more nearly equal allocations of resources, more efficient production and a lack of controlling and controlled behavior (Barsky 2010: 269). Science, and more reliable and rational linguistic communication, was seen as the solution. This led to Harris' support for logical theories of language and information, including structural linguistics and machine translation, work funded by the National Science Foundation, the Air Force Psychological Research Division, IBM and Bell Laboratories. Students were assigned various related projects in discourse analysis (e.g. investigating the linguistic techniques used in influential US magazines to slant discussions of the new Labour government in the United Kingdom). One talented student was assigned a linguistic analysis of Sidney Hook's writings from the time when he was a communist to when he became an anti-communist. That student was Noam Chomsky.

Scholars who are interested in sociolinguistic approaches are often puzzled by what they see as the paradox of Chomsky: a scholar who has generated some of the most searingly critical analyses of media and political discourse that exist, in books such as *Manufacturing Consent*, while regularly abjuring any social influence on language form. However, it is possible to see the ways that these are united in the way Chomsky understands human nature, language and freedom. In the aftermath of the extreme culturally relativist and genocidal policies associated with European fascism in the mid-twentieth century, new versions of linguistic thought emerged that downplayed difference. In Chomsky-influenced grammatical theory, the theory of human nature underlying the linguistic theory has strong liberal underpinnings; variations among humans are seen as fairly minor when compared with the overwhelming similarities that unite humans as a species (Otero 1988: 154). Rather than emphasizing rationality as the shared human trait (as eighteenth- and nineteenth-century liberal theorists did), Chomsky instead focuses on the human yearning for freedom as a critique of forms of behavioralist psychology that he saw as being used to control the masses (Chomsky 1959; Barsky 1997: 99). Chomsky has noted that he learned about the links between anarchism and classical liberalism from visits to the office of the Yiddish-language anarchist journal *Freie Arbeiter Stimme*, and after reading George Orwell, he became fascinated by the anarcho-syndicalist communes that had been set up during the Spanish Civil War as an example of a working libertarian society, the type of society that continues to remain his ideal (Barsky 1997: 26).

As linguists and other activists became increasingly uncomfortable with military patronage and American foreign policy, these frustrations were played out in discussions of linguistic theory, in debates Roy Harris has called *The Linguistics Wars* (see Martin-Nielsen 2010: 149). Martin-Nielsen notes that many critics of Chomsky's linguistics program argued that heavy military investment at MIT gave Chomsky and his MIT colleagues an unfair advantage. Sociolinguists and linguistic anthropologists, meanwhile, critiqued the lack of social context in formal linguistic theory, and the notions of competence and performance it assumed (see key works by John Gumperz, Dell Hymes, and William Labov – and see Murray 1994, for a significant and helpful sociological account of this period).

Both Harris and Chomsky were prepared for public critique and even imprisonment, though both were protected to some degree by tenured positions. During the Cold War period, however, other linguists were much more publicly assailed. Price (2004) draws on over 30,000 pages of FBI and other government documents to note "how the repressive post-war McCarthy era shaped and dulled what might have been a significant and vital anthropological critique of race, class and the inadequacies of global capitalism" (p. xi). The inability to read certain works by the Bakhtin circle until the late 1960s could be seen as one example of a Cold War effect (due to internal policy in the Soviet Union as well as international dynamics), but so too were critiques of certain scholars. Two linguistic anthropologists markedly affected were Melville Jacobs and Morris Swadesh.

Jacobs studied under Franz Boas, and was the author of 15 books, most of them documenting and preserving Native American languages of the Pacific Northwest. Jacobs, like Boas, was Jewish, and concerned about anti-Semitism, fascism and racism, including Japanese-American internship during World War II and bills to prevent racial intermarriage. His 1947 book with Bernhard Stern on general anthropology argued, as did many Boasians, for the plasticity of human behavior and criticized racism and the cultural biases of IQ tests. Jacobs was subjected to two public loyalty trials, and decades of FBI persecution and surveillance. In 1947 hearings on what was believed to be a ring of communist professors at the University of Washington, Jacobs was called in front of the Washington State Interim Committee on Un-American Activities. Price argues that afterwards, "[t]hroughout the 1950s and into the early 1960s Jacobs became more subdued in his academic writings on race, and his public appearances advocating racial equality occurred much less frequently" (Price 2004: 97).

Although Jacobs retained his tenured job, those like Morris Swadesh who were in more precarious academic positions lost theirs. Throughout the 1930s Swadesh studied more than twenty indigenous languages in Canada, the United States, and Mexico. His FBI file also recorded his marching in the May Day parade, a letter of protest to the New Jersey governor about the trial of six African-Americans accused of a murder, and participation in a rally in favour of Paul Robeson. Swadesh was an untenured professor who worked on a year-to-year contract. In 1949 he was suddenly notified that he would not be reappointed. He argued that this was a flagrant violation of academic freedom, and also evidence of anti-Semitic racism. He lost his job, however, and ultimately moved to Mexico in 1956. It was not just Swadesh, but those who were seen as supporting him who would be affected. Dell Hymes, in an interview with Price, speculated that Cold War politics could have played a role in Harvard's rejection of his tenure file, given subscriptions he had to leftwing journals, an invitation he arranged for Swadesh to give a talk, and his public attendance at meetings on how to revive the left (Price 2004: 343–344). Even avid critics of communism were not immune from persecution. McElhinny (2014) draws on documents shared by Price to review the surveillance of Roman Jakobson. In one interview with an FBI agent, Jakobson felt compelled to give the agent detailed critical quotations about himself in print in publications from Russia, satellite nations and China, to demonstrate his anti-communist stances. The kind of formal analysis, structuralism, which Jakobson centrally developed, is repeatedly labelled in these publications as bourgeois, reactionary and explicitly opposed to Marxism and materialist accounts. This work raises some important questions about which linguistic and anthropological interpretations might have been particularly feasible in the Cold War United States, and how these continue to shape accounts of language through the 1960s, and even now, including those with a more self-evidently sociological or anthropological bent.

Language and Neoliberalism

In much recent scholarship, globalization has been offered as an explanation for the changing ways that people understand interactions and social relations, though, as we have seen, global interactions are not new (see Jacquemet, this volume); we need, therefore, to capture more precisely what characterizes current interactions. Harvey (1989) conceptualizes globalization as changing experiences of space and time, shaped by the periodic crises of capitalist over-accumulation. He argues that in Western economies the Fordist regime of mass production of standardized items became so successful and efficient that it began to overproduce, leading to the lay-off of workers and a reduced demand for products. Companies moved operations to new countries to reduce costs. Serious discussions of productivity, efficiency and audit have proliferated for the same reason (Urciuoli and LaDousa 2013). A post-Fordist regime of flexible accumulation has emerged in its place, with a focus on adjustable labour processes and production arrangements, and consumption focused on niche markets vs. mass production, all of which have transnational implications. Changing notions of the global and local are underpinned by neoliberalism, defined as "a theory of political economic practices that proposes that human well-being can best be advanced by liberating individual entrepreneurial freedoms and skills within an institutional framework characterized by strong private property rights, free markets, and free trade" (Harvey 2005: 2); however, neoliberalism is not a description of social reality but a claim on the future (Fairclough 2000). Proponents of neoliberalism attempt to transform divisions of labour, welfare provisions, reproductive activities and "habits of the heart" (Harvey 2005: 3).

A number of recent works in sociolinguistic and linguistic anthropology (Block and Cameron 2002, Blommaert 2010, Coupland 2003, Heller 2003, Holborrow 2015, Leap and Boellstorff 2004, McElhinny 2007) consider the ways neoliberalization and globalization are leading to new ways of understanding language, as well as to the creation of new identities for workers, parents, students, citizens and consumers. In a pivotal collection, Heller and Duchêne (2012) argue that language plays a particularly central role at this moment because of its function in the regulation and legitimization of political economic spaces (p. 3). Language also plays a key role in a range of enterprises in which language may or may not be imagined as the primary work or commodity (see Heller 2010 on tourism, advertising, language teaching, translation, call centres and performance art). In this section, I will quickly review research on language and neoliberalism in four realms: definitions of personhood, labour, consumption and commodification, and nations.[5]

Personhood

The artist Jay Z was recently quoted as saying, "I am not a businessman, I am a business, man!" This comment neatly encapsulates the changes that neoliberalism might require in personhood – from a version where work is a portion of one's life to being all of one's life (Gershon 2011). "Language work, particularly in neoliberal regimes, presupposes the channeling of employee sociality and ... subjectivity into company interests" (Urciuoli and LaDousa 2013: 176). Soft skills, or the ability to align oneself with certain people, tasks or situations, become emphasized (Allan 2014, Bell 2013, Urciuoli 2008); putative lack of such skills can be used to blame workers rather than structural conditions for un- or under-employment. A view of personhood as responsible, autonomous, self-sufficient and entrepreneurial leads, simultaneously, to a celebration of choice and self-realization through consumption, as well as a focus on diseases of the will, or failures of self-control. As affect becomes commodified, a focus also emerges on parsing authenticity and sincerity (see essays in Gal and Woolard 2001), as well as other affective stances; a number of recent sociolinguistic studies have thus recently returned to examining language and emotion (see McElhinny 2010).

Linguistic anthropological and sociolinguistic studies in a variety of different sites have attempted to consider how and where neoliberal changes of heart are actively engineered, in both capitalist and former communist countries. This is evident in the attempt to engineer work sensibilities amongst welfare recipients in New Zealand (Kingfisher 2006), and in ways that the attitudes of US workers towards work conditions are managed, without better pay or working conditions (Ducey 2007), and in the emergence of new words for talking about self-responsibility (Inoue 2007). See also Richard and Rudnyckyj (2009) on how grassroots networks in Mexico forge solidary transnational networks with foreign donors and on how a Jakarta steel company attempted to use a spiritual practice to train workers in a manner that was more disciplined and emotionally open. Lempert (2006) reports on changes in the ideas of moral discipline among Tibetan Buddhist monks in India as neoliberal ideologies about civility take hold, and Matza (2009) on the deployment of neoliberal technologies in host–caller exchanges on a Moscow talk show. Wilce and Janigsen (2014) and Brison (2014) document the rise of new emotional pedagogies which are circulated internationally, with Brison noting some of the contradictions and continuities between pedagogies for elite children in Fijian that educate them in Christian ways for capitalist roles. Language, affect and self are managed in the restructuring of socialist states as well, from workers' interactions in the transition from Maoist planned economy to Dengist market economy (Yang 2006, 2007) to resumé workshops for workers in the Slovak Republic (Larson 2008).

Labour

From the end of World War II until the early 1970s, the old industrial mass-market capitalism in Western countries had large national markets for consumer goods (Gee et al. 1996). As markets became more heavily saturated with consumer goods, and industrial work moved to countries in the Global South, companies began to focus on creating new kinds of customers and new sorts of desires, and they retooled workforces accordingly (Urciuoli and LaDousa 2013). Communication and affect are increasingly central in service jobs in health care, education, finance, entertainment, and advertising, where for the workers and their clients the production of feelings of well-being and even passion are key (Hardt 1999). While older studies of language and work tended to emphasize talk in medical, legal, therapeutic, and educational professions in ways that largely neglected other work sites, the new research examines a wider range of occupations in the interests of studying tertiarization, and the rise of the significance of service work in countries from which industries have fled. Nonetheless language in the primary and secondary sectors (resource extraction/agriculture, and the processing of these products in factories and warehouses) remains a largely neglected topic in linguistic anthropology, a gap that perhaps shares the ideologies of institutions that do not perceive linguistic practice and form as part of their responsibility.

The rise of research on language and landscape, and language and environment, sometimes called ecolinguistics, explicitly addresses the impact of increasingly destructive practices in the primary sector, but sometimes only implicitly articulates these within political economic frameworks (Myerson and Rydin 1996, Muhlhausler and Peace 2006). Work reporting emergent trends examines how companies manage their image and publicity (Benson and Hirsch 2010, Benton and Short 1999); the linguistic training of previously marginalized workers for such industries (Bell 2013); clashes over the meaning of water and landscape, often within the context of privatization or shifts from uses for production to consumption/leisure (Strang 2004); and the transition from socialist land reform to neoliberal pastoralism (Zukosky 2008).

Sectors in which workers and clients are often in or from different regions, classes and nations, like call centres and domestic work, get particular, even fetishized, attention. Consider studies of the rise of communication factories (call centres), where the Fordist logic of the assembly line governs interactional routines, and certain personality traits are set as industry standards in England (Cameron 2000), francophone Canada (Roy 2003), India (Mirchandani 2012), and the Philippines (Salonga 2010). Heller (2010) insightfully argues that call centres attract such attention because they are symbols of the transition from industrial, white, masculine, working-class, first-world production to feminized, racialized, "off-shore" work. Domestic work is a counterpart in the realm of reproduction, and thus studies of paid caregiving have aroused particular interest because of the ways they highlight the interaction of the negative impact of structural adjustment policies in the Global South with the privatization of health, elder care and child care in the Global North and the tragic irony of Third World women supporting their own families by leaving them to care for wealthier households, which themselves become more multicultural and cross-class as a result (see, e.g., England and Stiell 1997, Lorente 2007). The provision of other forms of reproductive labour, previously understood as unpaid labour in many feminist analyses in the 1980s, has also become significantly more commodified (Ehrenreich and Hochschild 2002). See, for instance, Di Leonardo (1987) on paid greeting cards and the work of kinship, Hall (1995) on paying for sex talk, and Leidner (1993) on paying for the preparation and serving of food.

The linguistic regulation of migrants often changes in light of changing economies. Allan (2014) notes how Canada's earlier focus on the recruitment of agricultural and industrial labourers has been replaced by a focus on highly skilled professionals, who are nonetheless seen as requiring additional linguistic training for Canadian workplaces, a regulation that also serves to rationalize labour market exclusions of racialized workers from Asia and Africa, and workers from formerly socialist countries in Eastern Europe. Critiques of migrants or citizens deemed as "other" or "new" are linked to debates about colonialism and post-colonialism, and about assimilation and diversity, including discussions about whether new social formations should be understood as novel in their "superdiversity" or whether such notions reinscribe Western imperial and national attitudes. For discussions of the re-inscription of whiteness, see Hill (2008).

Commodities and Cosmopolitanism

Commodities are no longer only material goods (Urciuoli and La Dousa 2013). The increased attention to commodification of language is linked to capitalist expansion that requires management of communication across linguistic differences, technological changes demanding new literacy skills, the growth of the service sector, the need to add value to goods to sell products, and the development of niche markets as a response to market saturation markets (Heller 2010). The question of whether global phenomena are homogenizing ones is a particularly controversial question (Meyerhoff and Niedzielski 2003). Corporations ask how to sell products in a global marketplace, how to sell in multiple locations, how and whether to address the world, and how to accommodate linguistic and cultural differences while remaining internally coherent (Klein 2000: 115). Though some companies try to persuade the world to come to them – to speak their language and absorb their culture – and argue that an inability to get consumers to do this is a sign of corporate weakness, other companies focus on selling diversity (Abu-Laban and Gabriel 2002), and trying to distance themselves from any easy critique of Western imperialist practices (see Machin and van Leeuwen 2003).

One of the sharpest changes in corporate worlds over the last fifteen years is that many successful corporations now produce brands, rather than products. Klein (2000) argues that branding is not the same as advertising. Ads inform people about the existence of a product, arguing that their lives will be better if they use it. But now, she arguess, companies are advertising brands – a lifestyle, an experience – and penetrating into domains previously untouched by commercialism (see Gaudio 2003). Manning's (2010) semiotic review of brands is, however, wary of an argument that moves from more productivist to consumerist approaches. Considering the international variation in consumer desires that Western brands may not fully attend to, he warns that brands may reveal different things depending on whether they are approached as semiotic objects within an economy, or meta-semiotic objects that can reveal semiotic ideologies latent in economic categories (p. 46). For some recent ethnographic approaches to the analysis of brands see Bucholtz (2007), Shankar (2015), and Zhang (2007).

Nations: Scattered Hegemonies, Postnationalism, and Transnationalism

Over a decade ago Philips (1998) challenged linguists to move beyond strictly Gramscian approaches to hegemony in nationalist contexts to thinking about how language and power are organized across institutions and groups, both within a nation and transnationally. Feminist critics Grewal and Kaplan argue that a new conception of scattered hegemonies is needed to more fully acknowledge transnational flows and material conditions in diverse locations, in part to be able "to construct an effective opposition to current economic and cultural hegemonies that are taking new global forms" (1994: 17). To do this, we need to address a number of different hegemonic forces, which are also differently hegemonic: global economic structures, patriarchal nationalisms, "authentic" forms of tradition, local structures of domination, legal-juridical oppression, and even certain approaches to feminism and other forms of social critique (Grewal and Kaplan 1994: 17). A number of scholars (Besnier 2007, Gaudio 2009, Miskimmin 2007, Philips 2007, Yang 2007) have taken up ethnographic perspectives on language and "scattered hegemonies."

One of the sites at which studies of language global economy were most robustly developed in earlier studies was research in multilingualism (though Besnier 2007 has recently argued that even in these studies analysis often seems to stop at national boundaries). In bilingual or multilingual societies, in areas where national boundaries have been drawn and redrawn, in post-colonial contexts, and in diglossic linguistic situations, it is often the use of, or access to, certain languages that differentiates the speech of men and women, or more elite and less elite men and women. In colonial or post-colonial situations, access to economic and political power may depend on being able to speak the language of imperial, or former imperial, powers (see Haeri 2007, Hill 1987, Pavlenko et al. 2001, Weidman 2006). Indeed, the question most frequently debated in the emerging literature on language and globalization may be how best to understand the effects of cultural and linguistic imperialism, especially of English (Canagarajah 1999; Pennycook 2003).

New economic developments are seen by some to throw the political primacy of the nation-state into question, and by others to simply change its forms and functions. This may be articulated as post-nationalism (Heller 2011), as changing notions of publics, polities and publicity (Cody 2011), of sovereignty (Barker 2005) or of standards and standardization, shaped not just in national, or even settler colonial or post-colonial circumstances but also by transnational governmental bodies (Gal 2012) or transnational labour migration needs (Lorente 2012). New economic developments, however, may also be articulated as new or renewed claims to sovereignty from marginalized groups, sometimes linguistic minorities or indigenous groups, sometimes using the notion of nation, and with language often key to defining inclusions and exclusions (Frekko 2009, Galley 2009, Urla 2012).

Critical Issues and Future Directions

This review has suggested that studies of language and political economy can continue to deepen their attention to the distinctive political and economic forces in each historical period, to arrive at accounts that not only have more explanatory power, but can be more readily integrated with debates in other fields, and thus play a more pivotal role in scholarship and movements that resist inequities. It has offered a few critical moments in Western history and thought that have shaped the ways that knowledge is produced, and language is understood, in distinctive ways – without claiming that such forms of periodization will be universally useful. This review has suggested the ways in which linguistic analysis can be a critical – or collusive – tool in thinking about constructions of inequity. Even seemingly progressive approaches need to be evaluated not by comparison with past practices, but with attention to what current work they do. Gee et al. (1996) analyze the key words of the new work order evident in new capitalist texts, and consider whether ESL (English as a second language) classes and team meetings at a Silicon Valley company with a multilingual workforce, offered in the name of empowering workers to collaborate as a team, may work as a new form of surveillance and regulation. Holborrow (2015) considers when and how notions of "linguistic market" and "discourse-centred" approaches can reinforce neoliberal ways of centering economic understandings. McElhinny (2012) examines the congruence of the focus on communities of practice, a sociolinguistic concept developed in Silicon Valley, and strategies for industrial restructuring in a "knowledge economy."

Contemporary interest in imperialism, communism, fascism and the Cold War may be ways to challenge earlier silences (which themselves deserve analysis), as they are, also, results of contemporary interests in globalization, resurgent rightwing populism and totalitarianism, and an interest in spaces of hope (Harvey 2000). These interests, that is, at the moment are also part of a complicated reaction to new forms of globalization, and heightened attention to marketization that goes under the name of neoliberalism. Linguistic anthropology will continue to consider the impact of forces labeled "global" in a range of settings, but the field itself is subject to some of the same forces of globalization and internationalization as other forms of knowledge production. There are more international conferences, with a wider range of scholars. This is evident, too, in compendia: compare the contents of the first *Language and Gender Handbook* (Holmes and Meyerhoff 2003) with the new edition (Holmes, Meyerhoff and Ehrlich in press). Some conferences now travel: consider the origins of regular conferences on language and gender at Berkeley, which then evolved into the International Gender and Language Association, which now has a different conference site every two years and has been hosted in the UK, New Zealand, Brazil, and Canada. There are intensive debates about what internationalization of scholarly discourse might mean, and attempts to create broader conversations (in such initiatives as Déjà Lu, and the World Anthropological Network). Part of the task of linguistic anthropologists is not just to cover more sites and processes but to find ways to develop more fully collaborative conversations with scholars working in a range of traditions and attempting to move beyond imperial ways of interaction (Chen 2010).

Related Topics

7 Language Ideologies (Kroskrity); **8** Social Subordination and Language (Huayhua); **14** Discursive Practices, Linguistic Repertoire, and Racial Identities (Baugh); **15** Language and Racialization (Chun, Lo); **20** Language, Immigration, and the Nation-State (Pujolar); **21** Language and Nationalism (Haque); **22** Language in the Age of Globalization (Jacquemet); **24** Discrimination via Discourse (Wodak); **25** Racism in the Press (Van Dijk).

Notes

1. Some parts of this approach have been developed in rich conversations with Monica Heller, with whom I'm writing a forthcoming advanced textbook on linguistic anthropology for University of Toronto Press informed by similar formulations.
2. See Brandist (2015) for a thoughtful review of debates about authorship in the Bakthin circle, the role of Marxism, and differential receptions of the work by American liberal and British Marxist critics.
3. One of the articles which was most widely circulated, "Aryans and non-Aryans (1933)" was printed on tissue-thin paper for circulation by the anti-Nazi underground, the better to conceal it as it was circulated hand-to-hand (Herskovits 1953: 117).
4. Even critics of the fascist state, like Gramsci, could see some benefit to a unified national linguistic strategy that might, for example, unite a divided working class.
5. Two other key topics not reviewed here are the ways changing technologies articulate with notions of language, and the ways changing ideas of space and leisure are evident in new kinds of tourism.

References

Abu-Laban, Yasmeen and Christina Gabriel. (2002). *Selling Diversity: Immigration, Multiculturalism, Employment Equity and Globalization*. Toronto: University of Toronto Press.
Allan, Kori. (2014). Learning How to "Skill" the Self: Citizenship and Immigrant Integration in Toronto, Canada. Ph.D. dissertation, University of Toronto.
Arendt, Hannah. (1968). *The Origins of Totalitarianism*. Orlando: Harcourt.
Barker, Joanne (ed.). (2005). *Sovereignty Matters: Locations of Contestation and Possibility in Indigenous Struggles for Self-Determination*. Lincoln: University of Nebraska Press.
Barsky, Robert F. (1997). *Noam Chomsky: A Life of Dissent*. Cambridge, MA, London: MIT Press.
———. (2010). *Zellig Harris*. Cambridge, MA: MIT Press.
Bauman, Richard and Charles Briggs. (2003). *Voices of Modernity: Language Ideologies and the Politics of Inequality*. Cambridge: Cambridge University Press.
Bell, Lindsay. (2013). Diamonds as Development: Why Natural Resource Exploitation Fails to Improve the Human Condition. Ph.D. dissertation, University of Toronto.
Benson, Peter and Stuart Kirsch (eds). (2010). Corporate oxymorons: Entry points into the ethnography of capitalism. Special issue of *Dialectical Anthropology* 34(1), March 2010.
Benton, L. and J. R. Short (1999). *Environmental Discourse and Practice*. Oxford: Blackwell.
Besnier N. (2007). Language and gender research at the intersection of the global and local. *Gender and Language* 1(1): 67–78.
Block, David and D. Cameron (eds). (2002). *Globalization and Language Teaching*. London: Routledge.
Blommaert, Jan (2010). *The Sociolinguistics of Globalization*. Cambridge: Cambridge University Press.
Boas, Franz. (1911). Introduction. *Handbook of American Indian Languages*, vol. 1. Washington: Government Printing Office.
Bourdieu, Pierre. (1977). The economics of linguistic exchanges. *Social Science Information* 16(6): 645–668.
Brandist, Craig. (2003). The origins of Soviet sociolinguistics. *Journal of Sociolinguistics* 7(2): 213–231.
———. (2015). The Bakhtin Circle. *The Internet Encyclopedia of Philosophy*. www.iep.utm.edu/bakhtin. Accessed January 5, 2015.
Brison, Karen. (2014). Producing emotional selves through Pentecostal pedagogy in Fiji. Paper presented at AAA Meetings, Washington DC, December.
Bucholtz, Mary. (2007). Shop talk: Branding, consumption and gender in American middle-class youth interaction. In Bonnie McElhinny (ed.), *Words, Worlds, Material Girls: Language, Gender and Global Economies*, 371–402. Berlin: Mouton de Gruyter.
Cameron D. (2000). *Good to Talk? Living and Working in a Communication Culture*. London: Sage.
Canagarajah, Suresh. (1999). *Resisting Linguistic Imperialism in English Teaching*. Oxford: Oxford University Press.
Chakrabarty, Dipesh. (2000). *Deprovincializing Europe*. Princeton, NJ: Princeton University Press.
Chandra, Shefali. (2012). *The Sexual Life of English: Languages of Caste and Desire in Colonial India*. Durham, NC: Duke University Press.
Chen, Kuan-Hsing. (2010). *Asia as Method: Towards Deimperialization*. Durham, NC: Duke University Press.
Chomsky, Noam. (1987). Language and Freedom. In James Peck (ed.), *The Chomsky Reader*, 139–156. New York: Pantheon.
———. (1959). A review of B. F. Skinner's *Verbal Behavior*. *Language* 35(1): 26–58.
———. (1997). The Cold War and the University. In *The Cold War and the University: Toward an Intellectual History of the Post-War Years*. New York: New Press.
Cody, Francis. (2011). Publics and politics. *Annual Review of Anthropology* 40: 37–52.
Cohen-Cole, J. (2003). Thinking about Thinking in Cold War America. Ph.D. dissertation, Princeton University.
Coulmas, Florian. (1992). *Language and Economy*. Oxford: Blackwell.
Coupland N. (2003). Introduction. Sociolinguistics and globalization. *Journal of Sociolinguistics* 7(4): 465–72.
Darnell, Regna. (2001). *Invisible Genealogies: A History of Americanist Anthropology*. University of Nebraska Press.
Di Leonardo, Micaela. 1987. The female world of cards and holidays: Women, families and the work of kinship. *Signs* 12(3): 440–453.
Duchêne, Alexandre and Monica Heller (eds). (2012). *Language in Late Capitalism: Pride and Profit*. New York: Routledge.

Ducey A. (2007). More than a job: Meaning, affect, and training health care workers. In P. T. Clough with Jean Halley (eds), *The Affective Turn: Theorizing the Social*, 187–209. Durham, NC: Duke University Press

Eagleton, Terry. (1989). Base and superstructure in Raymond Williams. In Terry Eagleton (ed.), *Raymond Williams: Critical Perspectives*, 165–227. Cambridge: Polity Press.

———. (2007). *Ideology: An Introduction*. New York: Verso.

Ehrenreich, B. and A. Hochchild (eds) (2002). *Global Woman: Nannies, Maids and Sex Workers in the New Economy*. New York: Metropolitan Books.

Eley, Geoff. (2013). *Nazism as Fascism*. London: Routledge.

Engels, F. (1890). Letter to J. Bloch. *New International* 1(3): 81–85, September–October 1934.

England, K. and B. Stiell. (1997). "They think you're as stupid as your English is": Constructing foreign domestic workers in Toronto. *Environment & Planning A* 29(2): 195–215.

Errington, Joseph. (2008). *Linguistics in a Colonial World: A Story of Language, Meaning and Power*. Malden, MA: Blackwell.

Fabian, Johannes. (1986). *Language and Colonial Power*. Cambridge, Oxford: Cambridge University Press, Blackwell.

Fairclough, Norman. (2000). *New Labour, New Language*. London: Routledge.

Faye, Jean-Pierre. (1964). Langages totalitaires: fascistes et Nazis. *Cahiers Internationaux de sociologie*. Nouvelle Serie, no. *36* (January–June): 75–100.

Fishman, Joshua. (1972). *Language and Nationalism*. Rowley, MA: Newbury.

Fishman, Joshua, Charles Ferguson, and Jyotirindra Das Gupta (eds). (1968). *Language Problems of Developing Nations*. New York: John Wiley.

Frekko, Susan. (2009). "Normal" in Catalonia: Standard language, enregisterment, and the imagination of a national public. *Language in Society 38*: 71–93.

Friedrich, P. (1989). Language, ideology and political economy. *American Anthropologist 91*(2): 295–312.

Gal, Susan. (1989). Language and political economy. *Annual Review of Anthropology 18*: 345–367.

———. (2012). Sociolinguistic regimes and the management of "diversity". In Alexandre Duchêne and Monica Heller (eds), *Language in Late Capitalism: Pride and Profit*, 230–261. New York: Routledge.

Gal, Susan, and Kathryn Woolard (eds) (2001). *Languages and Publics: The Making of Authority*. Manchester, UK: St. Jerome.

Galley, Valerie. (2009). Reconciliation and the revitalization of indigenous languages. In Gregory Younging, Jonathan Dewar, and Mike de Gagne (eds), *Response, Responsibility and Renewal: Canada's Truth and Reconciliation Journey*, 219–236. Ottawa: Aboriginal Healing Foundation.

Gaudio, Rudolf. (2009). *Allah Made Us: Sexual Outlaws in an Islamic African City*. Oxford: Wiley-Blackwell.

———. (2003). Coffeetalk$_{TM}$: Starbucks and the commercialization of casual conversation. *Language in Society 32*: 659–691.

Gee J. P., G. Hull, and C. Lanshear (1996). *The New Work Order: Behind the Language of the New Capitalism*. Sydney: Allen & Unwin.

Gershon, Ilona. (2011). Neoliberal agency. *Current Anthropology 52*(4): 537–555.

Gilmour, Rachel. (2006). *Grammars of Colonialism: Representing Languages in Colonial South Africa*. Palgrave Macmillan.

Golino, Enzo. (1994). *Parola de duce: Il linguaggio del Fascismo*. Milan: Rizzoli.

Grewal, Inderpal and Caren Kaplan. (1994). Transnational feminist practices and questions of postmodernity. In Indepal Grewal and Caren Kaplan (eds), *Scattered Hegemonies: Postmodernity and Transnational Feminist Practices*, 1–36. Minneapolis: University of Minnesota Press.

Guibernau, Montserrat. (2004). *Catalan Nationalism: Francoism, Transition and Democracy*. New York: Routledge.

Gupta, Akhil. (2012). The United States and India: imperialism or irrelevance? Paper presented at AAA Conference, in panel on "Imperialism: An overdue "dialogue".

Haeri, Niloofar. (1997) *The Sociolinguistic Market of Cairo: Gender, class and education*. London: Kegan Paul International.

Hall, K. (1995). Lip service on the fantasy lines. In K. Hall and M Bucholtz (eds), *Gender Articulated: Language and the Socially Constructed Self*, 183–216. New York: Routledge.

Hanks, William. (2010). *Converting Words: Maya in the Age of the Cross*. Berkeley: University of California Press.

Hardt, Michael. 1999. Affective labor. *boundary 2 26*(2): 89–100.

Harris, Zellig. (1997). *The Transformation of Capitalist Society*. Lanham, MD: Rowman and Littlefield.

Harshav, Benjamin. (1999). *Language in the Time of Revolution*. Palo Alto: Stanford University Press.
Harvey, David. (1989). *The Condition of Postmodernity: An Inquiry into the Origins of Cultural Change*. Oxford: Wiley-Blackwell.
———. (2000). *Spaces of Hope*. Berkeley: University of California Press.
———. (2005). *A Brief History of Neoliberalism*. Oxford: Oxford University Press.
Heller, Monica. (2011). *Paths to Postnationalism: A Critical Ethnography of Language and Identity*. Oxford: Oxford University Press.
———. (2003). *Linguistic Minorities and Modernity: A Sociolinguistic Ethnography*. London: Longman.
———. (2010). The commodification of language. *Annual Review of Anthropology 39*: 101–114.
Heller, Monica and Alexandre Duchêne. (2012). Pride and profit: Changing discourses of language, capital and Nation-State. In Alexandre Duchêne and Monica Heller (eds), *Language in Late Capitalism: Pride and Profit*, 1–21. New York: Routledge.
Herskovits, Melville J. (1953). *Franz Boas: The Science of Man in the Making*. New York: Scribner's.
Hill, Jane. (2008). *The Everyday Language of White Racism*. Oxford: Wiley-Blackwell.
———. (1987). Women's speech in modern Mexicano. In Susan Philips, Susan Steele and Christine Tanz (eds), *Language, Gender and Sex in Comparative Perspective*, 121–162. Cambridge: Cambridge University Press.
Hobsbawm, Eric. (1975). *The Age of Capital. 1848–1875*. London: Cardinal.
———. (1987). *The Age of Empire. 1875–1914*. New York: Pantheon Books.
———. (1996). *The Age of Extremes: A History of the World, 1914–1991*. New York: Vintage Books.
Holborrow, Marnie. (2015). *Language and Neoliberalism*. New York: Routledge (Series on Language, Society and Political Economy).
Holmes, Janet and Miriam Meyerhoff. (2003). *The Language and Gender Handbook*, 1st ed. Oxford: Basil Blackwell.
Holmes, Janet, Miriam Meyerhoff, and Susan Ehrlich. In press. *The Language and Gender Handbook*, 2nd ed. Oxford: Basil Blackwell.
Hutton, Christopher. (2005). *Linguistics and the Third Reich: Mother-Tongue Fascism, Face, and the Science of Language*. London: Routledge.
Inoue, Miyako. (2006). *Vicarious language: Gender and linguistic modernity in Japan*. Berkeley: University of California Press.
———. (2007). Language and gender in an age of neoliberalism. *Gender and Language 1*(1): 79–92
Irvine, Judith T. (1989). When talk isn't cheap: Language and political economy. *American Ethnologist 16*: 248–267.
Kingfisher, Catherine. 2006. What D/discourse analysis can tell us about neoliberal constructions of (gendered) personhood: Some notes on commonsense and temporality. *Gender and Language 1*(1): 91–103.
Klein, Naomi. (2000). *No Logo: Taking Aim at the Brand Bullies*. Toronto: Vintage.
Klemperer, Victor. (2000 [1947]). *The Language of the Third Reich: LTI – Lingua Tertii Imperii. A Philologist's Notebook*. Martin Brady (trans.). London: The Athlone Press.
Lähteenmaki, Mika. (2006). Nikolai Marr and the idea of a unified language. *Language and Communication 26*: 285–295.
Larson, Jonathan. (2008). Ambiguous transparency: Resumé fetishism in a Slovak workshop. *Ethnos 73*(2): 189–216.
Leap, William and Tom Boellstorff (eds) (2004). *Speaking in Queer Tongues: Globalization and Gay Language*. University of Illinois Press.
Leidner R. (1993). *Fast Food, Fast Talk: Service Work and the Routinization of Everyday Life*. Berkeley: University of California Press.
Lempert M. (2006). Disciplinary theatrics: Public reprimand and the textual performance of affect at Sera Monastery, India. *Language and Communication 26*: 15–33.
Lorente, Beatriz. (2012). The making of "Workers of the World": Language and the labor brokerage state. In Alexandre Duchêne and Monica Heller (eds), *Language in Late Capitalism: Pride and Profit*, 183–206. New York: Routledge.
———. (2007). Mapping English linguistic capital: The case of Filipino Domestic Workers in Singapore. Ph.D thesis 260 pp., National University of Singapore.
Machin, David and Theo van Leeuwen. (2003). Global schemas and local discourses in Cosmopolitan. *Journal of Sociolinguistics 7*(4): 493–512.
Mannheim, Bruce. (1991). *The Language of the Inka since the European Invasion*. Austin: University of Texas Press.
Manning, Paul. (2010). The semiotics of brand. *Annual Review of Anthropology 39*: 33–49.

Martin-Nielsen, J. (2009). Private Knowledge, Public Tensions. Theory Commitment in Post-War American Linguistics. Ph.D. dissertation, University of Toronto.

———. (2010). "This war for men's minds": the birth of a human science in Cold War America. *History of the Human Sciences* 23(5): 131–155.

Marx, Karl. (2009 [1859, 1977]) 2009]. *A Contribution to the Critique of Political Economy*, Maurice Dobb (trans. and ed.) Ithaca, NY: Cornell University Press.

Matza T. (2009). Moscow's echo: Technologies of the self, publics, and politics on the Russian talk show. *Cultural Anthropology* 24(3): 489–522.

McElhinny, Bonnie. (2010). The audacity of affect: Gender, race and history in linguistic accounts of legitimacy and belonging. *Annual Review of Anthropology* 39: 309–328.

———. (2012). Silicon Valley sociolinguistics? Analyzing language, gender and *communities of practice* in the New Knowledge Economy. In Alexandre Duchêne and Monica Heller (eds) *Language in Late Capitalism: Pride and Profit*, 230–261. New York: Routledge.

———. (2014). Cutting the red thread: Roman Jakobson, the FBI and Cold War Linguistics. Presented at panel on "Why materiality matters? Language and social inequality in the new economy," American Association of Applied Linguistics, March 22–25, 2014, Portland. Oregon.

McElhinny, Bonnie (ed.) (2007). *Words, Worlds, Material Girls: Language and Gender in a Global Economy.* Berlin: Mouton de Gruyter.

McGill, Kenneth. (2013). Political economy and language: A review of some recent literature. *Journal of Linguistic Anthropology* 23(2): 84–101.

Meyerhoff, Miriam and Nancy Niedzielski. (2003). The globalisation of vernacular variation. *Journal of Sociolinguistics* 7(4): 534–555.

Mirchandani, Kiran. (2012). *Phone Clones: Authenticity Work in the Transnational Service Economy.* Ithaca, NY: Cornell University Press.

Miskimmin, Susanne. 2007. When Aboriginal equals "at risk": The impact of institutional discourse on Aboriginal Head Start families. In Bonnie McElhinny (ed.), *Words, Worlds and Material Girls: Language, Gender, Globalization,* 107–131. Berlin, New York: Mouton de Gruyter.

Moralejo, Ruben. (2012). Review of *Analyzing Fascist Discourse.* In R.Wodak and J. Richardson (eds) *Inter-stratal Tension: A Place to Review the Delicate Balance between Language and Reality.* www.interstratal tension.org/?p1610. Accessed Dec. 15, 2014.

Muhlhausler, Peter and Adrian Peace. (2006). Environmental discourses. *Annual Review of Anthropology* 35: 457–479.

Murray, Stephen. (1994). *Theory Groups and the Study of Language in North America. A Social History.* Amsterdam: John Benjamins.

Myerson, G. and Y. Rydin. (1996). *The Language of Environment: A New Rhetoric.* London: University College London Press.

Orwell, George. (1995). Politics and the English language. In Robert Jackall (ed.) *Propaganda*, 423–437. New York: New York University Press.

Otero, C. P. (ed.). (1988). *Language and Politics – Noam Chomsky.* Montreal: Black-Rose Books.

Pavlenko, Aneta, Adrian Blackledge, Ingrid Piller, and Marya Teutsch Dwyer (eds) (2001). *Multilingualism, Second Language Learning and Gender.* Berlin: Mouton de Gruyter.

Pennycook, Alistair. (2007). *Global Englishes and Transcultural Flows.* Sydney: Routledge.

Philips, Susan. (1998). Language ideologies in institutions of power: A commentary. In Bambi Schieffelin, Kathryn Woolard, and Paul Kroskrity (eds) *Language Ideologies: Practice and Theory*, 211–228. Oxford: Oxford University Press.

———. (2007). Symbolically central and materially marginal: Women's talk in a Tongan work group. In Bonnie McElhinny (ed.), *Words, Worlds, Material Girls: Language, Gender and Global Economies*, 41–76. Berlin: Mouton de Gruyter.

Pinto, D. (2004). Indoctrinating the youth of post-war Spain: A discourse analysis of a Fascist civics textbook. *Discourse & Society* 15(5), 649–667.

Price, David. (2004). *Threatening Anthropology: McCarthyism and the FBI's Surveillance of Activist Anthropologists.* Durham, NC: Duke University Press.

Rafael, V. (1988). *Contracting Colonialism: Translation and Christian Conversion in Tagalog Society under Early Spanish Rule.* Ithaca, NY: Cornell University Press.

Richard, A. and D. Rudnyckyj. (2009). Economies of affect. *Journal of the Royal Anthropological Institute* 15: 57–77.

Roy, Sylvie. (2003). Bilingualism and standardization in a Canadian call center: challenges for a linguistic minority community. In R. Bayley and S. Schecter (eds) *Language Socialization in Multilingual Societies*, 269–287. Clevedon, UK: Multilingual Matters.

Salonga, Aileen Olimba. (2010). Language and Situated Agency: An Exploration of the Dominant Linguistic and Communication Practices in the Philippine Offshore Call Centers. Ph.D. dissertation, National University of Singapore.

Said, Edward. (1978). *Orientalism*. London: Routledge and Kegan Paul.

Shankar, Shalini. 2015. *Advertising Diversity: Producing Language and Ethnicity in American Advertising*. Durham NC: Duke University Press.

Shankar, Shalini and Jillian Cavanaugh. (2012). Language and materiality in global capitalism. *Annual Review of Anthropology 41*: 355–69.

Sheppard, Emily Elizabeth. (2014). Making Sense of National Socialism: Linguistic Ideology and Linguistic Practices in Germany, 1933–1939. Master's thesis, Social Justice Education, University of Toronto.

Simpson, C. (1994). *Science of Coercion: Communication Research and Psychological Warfare 1945–1960*. Oxford: Oxford University Press.

Solovey, Mark and Hamilton Cravens (eds). 2012. *Cold War Social Science: Knowledge Production, Liberal Democracy and Human Nature*. New York: Palgrave Macmillan.

Stalin, Joseph. (1951). *Marxism and Linguistics*. New York: International Publishers.

Stoler, Ann Laura and Frederick Cooper. (1997). Between metropole and colony: Rethinking a research agenda. In F. Cooper and A. L. Stoler (eds), *Tensions of Empire: Colonial Cultures in a Bourgeois World*, 1–58. Berkeley: University of California Press.

Strang, Veronica. (2004). *The Meaning of Water*. Oxford: Berg.

Thomas, Julia Adeney. (2014). Visualizing Fascism: Japan's state of unexception. Paper presented for Workshop on "Visualizing Fascism", University of Toronto, November 21, 2014.

Townson, Michael. (1992). *Mother-Tongue and Fatherland: Language and Politics in Germany*. Manchester, UK: Manchester University Press.

Trautmann, Thomas. (1997). *Aryans and British India*. Berkeley: University of California Press.

Trautmann, Thomas R. (2006). *Languages and Nations: The Dravidian Proof in Colonial Madras*. Berkeley: University of California Press.

———. (2005). *The Aryan Debate*. New Delhi: Oxford University Press.

Urciuoli, Bonnie. (2008). Skills and selves in the new workplace. *American Ethnologist 35*(2): 211–22.

Urciuoli, Bonnie and Chaise LaDousa. (2013). Language management/labour. *Annual Review of Anthropology 42*: 175–90.

Urla, Jacqui. (2012). Total Quality Language Revival. In Alexandre Duchêne and Monica Heller (eds), *Language in Late Capitalism: Pride and Profit*, 73–92. New York: Routledge.

Volosinov, V. N. (1973). *Marxism and the Philosophy of Language*, Ladislav Matejka and I. R. Titunik (trans.). Cambridge, MA: Harvard University Press.

Weidman A. (2006). *Singing the Classical, Voicing the Modern: The Postcolonial Politics of Music in South India*. Durham, NC: Duke University Press.

Wilce, James and Janina Fenigsen. (2014). Emotion pedagogies: An emergent global phenomenon. Paper presented at AAA Meetings, Washington D.C., December.

Williams, R. (1973). Base and superstructure in Marxist culture theory. *New Left Review 82*: 3–16.

———. (1977) *Marxism and Literature*. Oxford: Oxford University Press.

Wodak, Ruth and John E. Richardson (eds). (2012). *Analysing Fascist Discourse. European Fascism in Talk and Text*. London: Routledge.

Wodak, Ruth, Majid Khosravink, and Brigitte Mral (eds). (2013). *Right-Wing Populism in Europe: Discourse and Politics*. London: Bloomsbury.

Woodley, Daniel. (2012). Radical right discourse contra state-based authoritarian populism: Neoliberalism, identity and exclusion after the crisis. In Ruth Wodak and John Richardon (eds), *Analysing Fascist Discourse*. London: Routledge.

Woolard, Kathryn. (1998). Introduction: Language ideology as a field of inquiry. In Bambi Schieffelin, Kathryn Woolard and Paul Kroskrity (eds) *Language Ideologies: Practice and Theory*, 3–50. Oxford: Oxford University Press.

Yang, Jie. (2007). "Re-employment Stars": Language, gender and neoliberal restructuring in China. In Bonnie McElhinny (ed.) *Words, Worlds, Material Girls: Language, Gender and Global Economies*, 73–102. Berlin: Mouton de Gruyter.

———. (2006). Ritualized Transition: Language, Gender and Neoliberal Restructuring in China. Ph.D. thesis, University of Toronto.

Zhang, Qing. (2007). Cosmopolitanism and linguistic capital in China: Language, gender and the transition to a globalized market economy in Beijing. In Bonnie McElhinny (ed.) *Words, Worlds, Material Girls: Language, Gender and Global Economies*, 403–423. Berlin: Mouton de Gruyter.

Zhou, Mingliang (ed.). (2004). *Language Policy in the People's Republic of China*. Boston: Kluwer.

Zukosky, Michael. (2008). A semantic shift from Socialist land reform to neoliberal pastoral development in China. *Studies in Language and Capitalism*. Issue 3–4: 93–109.

Further Reading

Said, Edward. (1978). *Orientalism*. New York: Vintage Books.
This book provided one of the earliest, most influential analyses of the ways imperialism has shaped Western knowledge production – see especially the chapter on comparative linguistics.

Hutton, Christopher. (1999). *Linguistics and the Third Reich: Mother-Tongue Fascism, Race, and the Science of Language*. London: Routledge.
Ground-breaking and nuanced study of the role that linguistics played in racial ideologies.

Errington, Joseph. (2007). *Linguistics in a Colonial World: A Story of Language, Meaning and Power*. New York: Blackwell.
Book-length survey of a significant sampling of existing research – especially strong on Spanish colonialism, philology, pidgins, and proto-national languages.

Duchêne, Alexandre and Monica Heller (eds). (2012). *Language in Late Capitalism: Pride and Profit*. New York: Routledge.
Collection on the changing significance of language and nation in late capitalism in a range of sites in Asia, Europe, Canada, and the United States.

McElhinny, Bonnie (ed.). (2007). *Words, Worlds, Material Girls: Language and Gender in a Global Economy*. Berlin: Mouton de Gruyter.
Studies of language, gender and sexuality in a range of African, Asian, European, North American sites and a Pacific Islander site, with attention to the changing meaning of hegemony, multilingualism, commodification, and history.

20

Language, Immigration, and the Nation-State

Joan Pujolar

1 Introduction

Historically, issues of migration have not featured centrally in anthropology or linguistic anthropology. The discipline was orientated towards studying eminently stable human groups as settled in specific territories. Some early anthropologists developed lengthy and sophisticated descriptions of their communities that sometimes obviated the fact that they were significantly affected by migration. The example of Margaret Mead is widely quoted as she silenced the significance of migration from the Papua-New Guinean groups she researched, even when it affected about half of the adult male population (see Brettell 2003). This state of affairs significantly changed, however, during the last decades of the twentieth century where issues of mobility and displacement, migration flows, and diasporic communities have attracted interest across the social sciences and the humanities. Interest in issues of migration has correspondingly increased, and sociolinguistic and linguistic anthropological research on migration has become an important area of the field, one that is seen as central to understand the role of languages, and linguistic ideologies, in contemporary social change.

In this chapter, I shall not provide a general overview of the field of language and migration but touch upon one dimension that I believe is central to it, which is the nation-state. Taken both as administrative apparatus and as the imagined community, the nation-state provides the means to examine both the experience and social conditions of immigrant communities, as well as the very perspective from which migration phenomena have been studied. To put it in another way, it is the nation-state that defines particular people as immigrants but also the angle from which they are supposed to be observed. This is, of course, problematic, and worth reflecting about. I will begin section 2 by briefly defining the scope of this chapter, which focuses on *immigration* and not on migration processes more generally. After this, I will present three key concepts of the field: community, integration, and linguistic capital. In section 3 I will provide examples of studies on immigration that exemplify the significance of these concepts in present-day immigration contexts. And in section 4 I will seek to bring all threads together into a reflection on how research on language and immigration is presently transforming the traditional fundamental principles of sociolinguistics and linguistic anthropology, particularly through the debates on multiliteracies and superdiversity.

Joan Pujolar

2 Definitions

2.1 Migration, Emigration, Immigration

In the social sciences "migration" refers generally to the process of people moving in search for work or specific resources, such as arable land, animals to hunt or, more recently, employment. It generally involves a change of residence to a new place seen as "away from home." The concepts of "emigration" and "immigration" are directly connected to it; but are different in a substantial and important way, basically as they pivot not on the persons but on the territories: "emigration" is the phenomenon as seen from the territories that migrants leave, "immigration" from those they settle in. Although these terms are not used in regular and consistent ways, each of the three tends to express slightly different orientations. "Migration" is more generic and is often applied to studies that take up the perspective of the people who move, and often while the moving is in progress or very recent. "Emigration" and "immigration," on the contrary, lean towards how migrants affect communities or how they are perceived or treated by their communities of origin or arrival.

So we may enter migration research with substantially different interests in mind that will determine the questions we ask. For example, we may wish to understand how displacement is experienced by particular groups, how they develop strategies to adjust and adapt to a new environment while struggling to maintain a sense of continuity with their former livelihoods and cultural practices. This is to adopt centrally the perspective of the migrant as she deals with new contexts where people have different ideologies, social hierarchies, allegiances, and social relations at all levels. This is very much about what it means to live between (or over) two worlds (or more). Alternatively, we may have an interest in understanding how migration is experienced and organized in the specific communities where people decide to leave, whether it is seasonal, temporal, or permanent as seen from the local perspective, and what investments the local community develops upon those who leave: do they expect remittances? Do they try to control migrants morally or economically? Do they endeavor to keep in contact? Do migrants play a role in local politics and cultural practices? And finally, receiving societies normally worry about the "impact" of incoming migrants on the multiple aspects of social and institutional life that they may allegedly unsettle, from how urban spaces are occupied or social services are used by immigrants, to what implications the new population has in the definition of citizenship and national identity. The keyword "integration" is commonly recruited to cover the full range of these possible "issues" connected with immigration. "Integration" generally carries an assumption that immigrants should somehow align themselves with the ways of the locals, such that it contributes to significantly steering research and political agendas in ways that are much more predefined, fixed, often biased than in the two previous perspectives.

2.2 Migration in Linguistic Anthropology

The linguistic anthropological perspective on migration basically focuses on the linguistic and sociolinguistic aspects of the process. It can therefore explore how the linguistic repertoire of migrants develops and changes as they move or after settling, and also how their experience is discursively constructed in different contexts and in relation to different issues. For example, Zentella's (1997) seminal work on Puerto Ricans in New York might be counted as a good example of a study where the perspective of the migrant community occupies center-stage. Although it may be classified as "immigration" research, in the sense that it focuses on a well-established migrant community, it is very much organized in terms of how New York Puerto

Ricans use different varieties of Spanish and English (including so-called Spanglish, when the two are highly hybridized), how they value their complex repertoire and how they use it as they adjust or react to a social and institutional environment characterized by racism, economic exploitation and urban/spatial segregation. On the other hand, Hill and Hill's (1986) classical ethnography of Nahuatl, communities in Mexico can be regarded as a good example of a study of a community affected by emigration, that is, by the classical processes of urbanization that attract the young to rapidly expanding cities across the globe. As has been the case with many linguistic minorities, for the Nahuatl emigration became associated with the adoption of the dominant language, Spanish, which was inextricably tied to the appropriation of new "modern" or "urban" ways of life. In this context, Nahuatl-Spanish bilingualism was founded on an unequal hierarchy in which Nahuatl ways of speaking became progressively obsolete as the younger generations were less fluent and less acquainted with the genres and grammatical structures associated with former Nahuatl social relations.

Immigration research is often particularly sensitive to the specific orientation of each researcher and the ways in which immigration issues are connected with their life trajectories. Researchers may come from migrant families themselves, or from places that have experienced social and political contentions around "immigration." Not that there is anything wrong with this, but it is important for researchers to be aware of the conditions that bring them to study immigration in specific ways. More often than not, these research interests are not strictly personal but social and institutional: "immigration" may be an established topic of interest for their government, their research institutions, specific professional groups, or society at large. And this political interest may even lie behind the grant that is funding the research in the first place, and may significantly inform the specific issues addressed and the research questions.

The linguistic dimension of immigration is overwhelmingly associated with issues of ethnicity, nationality, and citizenship; hence the stress on the "nation-state" in this chapter. When immigrants settle in a given place in (what are perceived to be) significant numbers, different social actors and institutions begin to comment and pose questions as to how the incomers should be "managed," and by doing so they refer implicitly or explicitly to ideas of what constitutes a community and how language is connected with community belonging. Not that this community must necessarily refer to the nation-state (see below for a comment on the notion of "community" in linguistic anthropology). But although the state is not the sole dimension of belonging, as we shall see, it represents the ultimate "older brother" that is often expected to "set things straight" in the neighborhood. And this usually involves policies through which nation-states can deeply affect the lives of immigrants: citizenship policies (work and residence permits), social services and healthcare, education, and so on. So for the time being, let us note this: linguistic anthropological research on immigration can basically be presented as a long contention on the ways in which language does or should constitute community belonging and the consequences thereof for all parties, and that this contention most often takes place in the public spaces and institutions that project the national community and its state institutions in multiple forms.

2.3 Keywords in the Sociolinguistics of Immigration: Community, Integration, and Linguistic Capital

Sociologist John Urry (2000) has pointed out that sociology often "parasites" its issues and concepts from social movements and contentions. One consequence of this is that sociologists cannot claim full control over many of their objects and concepts and must learn to live with their fuzzy boundaries, displacements, and the specific political investments of their own actors.

Pierre Bourdieu (1991) also provides pointed reflections on how the meaning of politically "hot" terms (such as "popular") follows the logic of the very contentions in which these terms are brought about. Raymond Williams (1985) argued that following the semantic variations of "keywords" provided a good perspective to understand social struggles and change. It follows from this that some of the terms and concepts we use to understand social problems are problematic themselves because they are precisely part of the social problem we intend to address and the object of contention amongst the social actors we intend to examine. In relation to immigration research, "community" and "integration" often constitute the focal point of this contradiction.

The concept of "community," i.e. "speech community," has a long history in sociolinguistics and linguistic anthropology. The concept was adopted and adapted from linguistics by redefining the object of study from "language" (as an abstract repertoire of lexicogrammatical resources) to "speech" (the actual practices of everyday communication). At first it was assumed that "speech communities" would be groups displaying the same forms of linguistic behavior. But the evidence of diversity found in the contexts studied led to widen the scope to those who somehow shared the same evaluations of language behavior even when their actual language use was not the same. In the long run, however, researchers increasingly found further difficulties in operationalizing the concept, as contentions on language norms and values (i.e. linguistic ideological struggles) are also common. Later, the notion of "community of practice" (Eckert and McConnell-Ginet 1992) was gradually regarded more favorably, not because the term "practices" is clearer than "speech," but basically because it gives researchers more flexibility to work out contextually, often together with the subjects, what constitutes the community under study (see Duranti 1997, Morgan 2004, and McElhinny 2012 for more detailed discussions of this idea's trajectory).

The heart of the matter is not so much to arrive at the "correct" definition of communities in the abstract or of any community in particular; but rather address the issue of how communities are brought into existence, how membership is defined, and what social actors and/or institutions have the power to decide what counts for the community; and, of course, what role language plays in all these processes.

"Integration" is a closely related notion that steers our gaze towards the social problems associated with community belonging. It brings up the fundamental issue that, in some contexts and moments, belonging or not belonging to a particular community may have important implications for specific actors, such as providing or denying access to resources and social relations. In the context of immigration research, "integration" refers to the multiple ramifications involved in belonging to the *national community* in whose territory immigrants have come to live. As a consequence, immigration and integration are by definition matters of state, namely the nation-state, the sovereign political unit that (re)presents itself as an expression of the nation and, at the same time, brings the nation into being by ruling it and by managing it. Immigration affects the very definition of the community that legitimizes the existence of the state. And given that, as Michel Foucault (1991) has argued, the prime mission of the state is to manage its population, it follows that immigration becomes a key object of *governmentality*, that is, the art of managing populations according to principles of rationality. So whenever we talk about integration, what we are actually doing is referring to the multiple interconnections between how members of a nation (and specially the social groups that identify with it) imagine themselves to be, and the ways in which the nation-state seeks to sustain its own sense of coherence by incorporating, or not, immigrant populations as subjects and objects of rule, as well as members of the national body. Most importantly, this means that "integration" cannot be treated as a simple technical concept, no matter how officially established its meaning might be for local institutions. Rather, it will typically be a central object of debate and struggle in immigration contexts.

Now language is almost invariably implicated in these contentions over national belonging, and we shall provide an array of examples below of what this means in practice. It is important to stress that issues of integration, despite their connections with national consciousness and state policy, do not just implicate national institutions and administrations. What makes integration an important issue is the fact that it pops up in multiple shapes and at multiple levels in the form of tensions in human relationships that visibly involve persons as members of specific ethnic or racial categories: exclusion, confrontation, ridicule, misunderstandings, segregation, marginalization, distrust, and hate can arise at the level of families, neighborhoods, youth cliques, school mates, workplaces, social services, commercial relations, private dealings, media representations, state legislation, police and judicial procedures, and so on. What is interesting, and sometimes deeply troubling, is to learn how nationalist and nation-state ideologies (with their linguistic components) hover like an omniscient big brother in the remotest corners of a city and the subtlest details of social relations and communicative practices of the contemporary citizen. If we contribute to understanding why and how this happens, we shall certainly do a big service for our fellow students and fellow humans.

Finally, the notion of "linguistic capital" needs to be explained in order to follow the explanations and interpretations of examples in the next section. The concept is borrowed from Bourdieu (1991), who devised a theoretical model that has become commonplace in much sociolinguistic research. It has allowed researchers to leave behind functionalist perspectives, whereby specific social practices were seen as simply contributing to specific forms of social organization, or behavioral perspectives whereby practices were seen as the expression of inner states (such as attitudes) that provided reactions to external stimuli. Bourdieu sees social actors basically as pursuing the accumulation of economic and cultural capital through social exchanges. From this perspective, any social artifact or social practice can be regarded as possessing a value that is open to negotiation in social fields operating in similar ways to markets. Seen from a linguistic viewpoint, language forms and linguistic practices have a *value* that depends in complex ways on the categories of speakers and social practices by which and in which they can be mobilized to conduct social exchanges. Thus, a standard register of a language used by the wealthier social classes in their social and professional lives acquires a higher social value than a "dialect" used by people connected to a rural economy. This means that societies have by definition a linguistic hierarchy, and hence we can begin to appreciate that immigrants, as they settle, characteristically enter a "socioeconomically charged" linguistic space. When they settle in a new context, the linguistic capital they possessed in their place of origin is, to put it in this way, *reevaluated* according to local hierarchies, most often *devaluated*, such that immigrants must somehow endeavor to acquire the linguistic capital that is locally needed to access symbolic and economic goods. This linguistic capital is supposed to play an important role in people's forms of socialization, so that it may determine their opportunities of access to specific social spaces, employment, and categories of people. As we shall see, the "nation-state" is again an important actor in the creation of the "market conditions" for the evaluation (and devaluation) of linguistic capital and hence provide a key element to understanding the linguistic challenges faced by immigrants.

3 The Linguistic Articulation of Immigration in Social Life

I am going to provide three examples of how anthropological research throws light on the ways in which nation-state linguistic ideologies constitute social practices at various levels affecting immigrants: 1) in Madrid schools (Spain), how teachers claim the right to monitor the language choices of Moroccan and Chinese students; 2) in New York, how the bilingual speech of

Latinos is constructed as problematic; and 3) amongst Filipino domestic workers in Singapore, whose English proficiency is constructed as an international commodity, both by the state of the Philippines and the Singaporean recruiting agencies.

3.1 Spanish as "Respeto"

The school is by far the most popular research context where issues of immigration are examined. Whether they are public or private, schools have a very direct link with state institutions that provide national curricula and hence project officially sanctioned ideas about how children become citizens, including the way in which citizenship is associated with the (national) legitimate language. Schools are also the context where the young population (i.e., that in which cultural reproduction is supposed to happen) is most accessible, that is, open to observation and evaluation in ways that are not unlike the routine observation and evaluation already carried out by teachers, inspectors, and other institutions. And finally, precisely because of these reasons, states themselves provide ample means for teacher training and research centers to continuously monitor and improve the conduct of education.

Linguistic anthropologist Luisa Martín Rojo (2013) has for many years conducted ethnographic observations in Madrid schools, particularly in classrooms with significant numbers of children whose parents have recently moved to Spain from all over the world. In the example provided, the main groups of newcomers were from Morocco and China, and respectively spoke popular Arabic or Amazigh and Mandarin or other Chinese languages. Transcript 1[1] will be used to illustrate one of the ways in which a teacher can act as agent of articulation of a specific linguistic regime connected with nation-state ideologies. In the segment, Lucía, the teacher, intervened to regulate the use of languages in the classroom, basically to prevent Moroccan students from speaking any of their home languages:

Transcript 1[1]

Lucía: *si aqui en clase yo les digo que no hablen en árabe porque ·· porqueeee claro ··*
but here in class I tell them not to talk in Arabic because ·· because of course ··

SiQing nooo · lo entiende · y es de mala educación
SiQing /the Chinese student/ doesn't understand · and it's rude.

Nadya: [*es que profe · mira*
[but teacher · look

Lucía: & *claro*
& of course

Researcher: & *a ver*
& let's see

Nadya: & *nosotras QUEREMOS↑ [hablamos español*
We WANT↑ [we talk in Spanish

Student 1: &*no*

Student 2: [*hablamos español*
we talk in Spanish

Fatima: =*pero*
=but

Nadya: *& un tiempo / no me acuerdo de esa palabra y hablo con ella {a Fátima} árabe*
            & once / I don't remember that word and I talk to her {pointing at Fátima} in Arabic

Lucía: *=pero es que- / pues NO lo dices o lo dices de otra manera- porque insistooo por*
            =but the thing is- / DON'T say it or say it otherwise because, I insist, for

            respeto a SiQingg
            respect towards SiQuing

Fátima: *[((TÚ NO PUEDES))*
            [((YOU CAN'T))

Lucía: *=no pue- / pues os estáis [calladas]*
            =you can'- / well then stay [quiet]

Fátima: *[((vamos))] / a respetarnos todos [profe]*
            [((let's))] all respect each other [teacher]

Lucía: *[por re-] pues por [respeto]*
            [for re-] / well for [respect]

Nadya: *[no solo] yoooo=*
            [not just] meee=

Lucía: *&no no / pero por respto a SiQuingg no debéis hablar en árabe=*
            &no no / but for respect for SiQing you mustn't talk in Arabic=

Fátima: *=sí*
            yes

Lucía: *=& EN CLASE [cuando]*
            & IN CLASS [when]

Nadya: *[sí y] TÚ también profe {se oyen risas}*
            [yes and] YOU too teacher {laughter is heard}

Nadya: *NO/NO / TÚ también tienes que RESPETAR profe*
            NO/NO / YOU too must show RESPECT teacher

Lucía: *pero si YO os respeto!*
            but I DO respect you.

Nadya: *no solo YO profe*
            not just ME teacher

Lucía: *yo os RESPECTO / pero si estás aquí para aprender español // [pues os tendré*
            I do RESPECT you / but if you are here to learn Spanish// [then I've got

            que decir que habléis español]
            to tell you to speak Spanish]

Nadya: { [بدات هي أي بدات هي ها ، راسي في لي كاتطلع .كاتعصبني] }
            {[ay, now I'm starting to get fed up / it's driving me mad]}

Lucía: *Eeh / ves? {risas}*
            Eeh / you see? {laughter}

> Nadya: *yo digoo / no sé profe / yo quiero habla árabe [(()*
>   I say / I don't know teacher / I wish to talk Arabic [(())
>
> Lucía: *pues- / sí] / pero hablas árabe cuando sales de aquí / Nadya*
>   But- / yes] / but you talk in Arabic when you walk out of here / Nadya
>
> Martín Rojo (2013: 11–13)

As we can appreciate, the event consisted of a metapragmatic discussion about what language it is appropriate to use in the classroom context. Moroccan student Nadya argued that she preferred to resort to Arabic at specific moments to get assistance from her Moroccan school mates. The teacher Lucía strongly opposed this idea, arguing that this excluded Chinese students; Fatima and Nadya disagreed.

When encountering circumstances like this it is important to appreciate that a high degree of ambivalence is very common. Although it is perfectly possible for a teacher to scold a class for using languages other than Spanish on the grounds that "this is Spain" (with which direct reference to the nation-state dimension would be made), such an argument is, rather, usually reached through a complex evaluation of different, more ambivalent events across many contexts. Thus, in another extract from the same context, Martín Rojo observes that the teacher also censured Moroccan girls because they grouped together in the playground and spoke Arabic. In this case, the problem was, reportedly, that they were not using opportunities to practice Spanish with Spanish-speaking school mates. When different arguments are brought out in different contexts there is a case for suspecting more unspoken, implicit motivations, often those of which the subjects involved are not fully aware. Martín Rojo further observes that the school operated with the logic of systematically displacing or hiding "other" languages from public view, such that the specific linguistic and cultural skills that foreign students brought in were never made collectively visible. Thus, while pedagogical principles generally encourage building on the children's experience to construct learning, in that context foreign children were required to shield from view all aspects of their linguistic and cultural background that was perceived as a threat to a public space operating in Spanish.

This is one of the many ways in which the value of linguistic capital is negotiated in ambivalent and nuanced ways. The argument explicitly offered by the teacher was expressed as a question of "respect," namely a matter of politeness referring to the need to leave the communication channel open for bystanders to participate. The same argument was often used by Spanish nationalists in Catalonia in the late 1970s to prevent people from using the local language, Catalan, in public spaces. There is evidence, however, that such linguistic regimentation is also applied to speakers of Latin American varieties of Spanish, which, as Corona et al. (2012) showed, were also treated as inappropriate for use in student exercises. In all cases, what we see is a negotiation about the specific linguistic resources that can eventually be mobilized in specific situations, which is one way of expressing how a given linguistic variety is evaluated in a given context. In this sense, Martín Rojo also points out in her work that the ideologies that support nation-state hegemony were much more generally accepted in the past, while now they are being increasingly contested, such that we find different types of linguistic capital in competition in different contexts. She considers that the disagreement expressed (albeit in backstage comments in Arabic) by Moroccan girls in this extract is an example of such contentions.

3.2 Spanish as Stigma: Growing up Bilingual in New York City

Ana-Celia Zentella's (1997) seminal work on the Spanish-speaking communities in the United States, and particularly on the Puerto Rican community in New York City, provides an excellent illustration of the linguistic challenges often faced by immigrants. Her research has three major strengths: 1) it is based on an extensive and intensive ethnography that focuses on people's daily lives across different contexts from the home to the neighborhood; 2) it has an unusual temporal dimension as she sustained her relationship with her research subjects over many years; and 3) it provides a wealth of description of bilingual talk that can then be analyzed in an adequately contextualized form.

Zentella's study basically focused on 20 families that lived in a small area of the city that she called "El Bloque," and complemented her participant observation with the audio and video recording of everyday talk. The main thrust of her research has to do with confronting the stigmatization suffered by Nuyoricans, a term NY Puerto Ricans used, half ironically, to refer to themselves; and she focuses in particular on the stigmatization of the speech of this community. This discredited linguistic reputation occurred at many levels and had important consequences: basically, it contributed to reinforcing racial stereotypes that portrayed Puerto Ricans as a community whose members generally failed to learn "proper" English, acquire educational qualifications, and, overall, integrate culturally and economically with American social life.

The linguistic stigmatization of Nuyoricans illustrates the multiple ways in which language in contemporary societies can be treated with discriminatory effects though not necessarily with discriminatory intentions. At the heart of the matter lie attitudes towards hybridity, that is, the fact that bilinguals use in a routine fashion resources connected with two languages *and* in ways that are unexpected from the point of view of monolinguals. Thus the speech of NY Puerto Ricans, Zentella observes, could be depicted as a faulty Spanish when their pronunciation or vocabulary did not coincide with that of Standard Peninsular Spanish, when they used "Barbarisms" (e.g. mainly expressions taken from English) or simply switched between Spanish and English for reasons of politeness or expressiveness. And their speech was also regarded as problematic when their English displayed traces of Spanish pronunciation or grammar. "Code-switching," or "Spanglish," as the community refers to it, is for Zentella the linguistic practice that best represents both the ways in which Puerto Ricans lived between and within the two linguistic spaces (Spanish and English) and also the ways in which this bilingualism was used to stigmatize them. Code-switching refers to the combination in speech of linguistic resources associated with different varieties. Zentella observes that all the bilingual features of Nuyoricans' speech were often taken by educators, authorities, and people in general as evidence that they did not properly master either of the two languages. Bilingual practices expressed from this viewpoint a "linguistic deficit," which was then used to justify or explain away the poor socio-economic conditions in which members of this community lived.

She counter-argues this stigma and the stereotypes by showing via her data that code-switching was overwhelmingly used as an expressive resource to produce conversational effects, negotiate speaker roles, produce changes of footing and generally signal a sense of belonging to "both worlds," i.e. to the Spanish- and English-speaking community. Transcripts 2 and 3 provide extracts from Zentella's analysis: with a sizable corpus of code-switching instances, she documented and classified them in different expressive functions, in these cases, "topic shift" and "quotations."

Transcript 2

Topic shift (n=73, 9%): The speaker marks a shift in topic with a shift in language, with no consistent link between topic and language.

Example: *vamo|h| a preguntar\e* / it's raining!
           let's go ask her

Transcript 3

Quotations, direct and indirect (n=70, 9%): The speaker recalls speech and reports it directly or indirectly, not necessarily in the language used by the person quoted.

Example: *él me dijo* / call the police / *pero yo dije no voy a llamar a la policía na(-da).*
  he told me   but I said I am not going to call the pólice nothin
  Zentella (1997: 94)

She also provides examples of future functions such as "Declarative/question shift," "Future referent check and/or bracket," "Checking," "Role shift," "Rhetorical ask and answer," and "Narrative frame break – evaluation or coda."

In short, NY Puerto Ricans spontaneously develop a bilingual repertoire that serves multiple and subtle expressive purposes but is regarded as problematic by official institutions around them and becomes generally stigmatized in the country. The ongoing debates on "Spanglish" – one of the ways to name and often disparage such bilingual registers – illustrates the fact that Puerto Ricans in the US confront a profoundly rooted monolingual ideology that regards the boundaries between languages as sacred and hence considers linguistic hybridity a kind of social malaise. In her study, Zentella documents the multiple experiences of Puerto Ricans at school and in social life, where they face these attitudes even when, in most cases, English is clearly their predominant everyday language and they speak it as fluently as anyone else. Their stigmatization affects their performance at school, and often in bilingual programs too because these are also inspired by a monolingual ideology that forces students to keep languages separate. A telling case was provided by a girl diagnosed with a speech disorder in which common features of Nuyoricans' bilingual style were taken as evidence of her problematic condition.

Zentella does not explicitly engage in a critique of the nation-state and the ideologies it constitutes, as such, but her work is sufficiently rich to bring it into this discussion. First, there is the obvious, though often invisible, problem of who gets categorized as an immigrant. As she pointedly documents, the Puerto Rican community is relatively old in New York, dating from the beginning of the twentieth century. The flow has never stopped for extended periods of time, which means that the community is characterized by the coexistence of longer-standing and more recent immigrants, who often roughly correspond with higher use of English or of Spanish. In any case, the scene begs the question of how long, or through how many generations, one's status as "immigrant" or member of an "immigrant-related" community endures socially, even when citizenship status is the same as those classified as "locals," given Puerto Rico's status as a US territory. The same question can of course be expanded to the wider Hispanic community in the United States, which includes people from very diverse backgrounds: Cuban exiles; local Chicanos; Spanish-speaking, native-born Americans in Texas and California; and new immigrants from Mexico and other Latin American countries. The term "Hispanic" itself thus provides not so much a description of a given human group, but actually a range of racial and cultural categories connected to people and practices that rest uneasily within the hegemonic images of what constitutes (US) American national identity. Indeed, as Zentella (2003) points out in later works, it is this culturally hegemonic (White) America that generally develops and disseminates stereotypes about Spanish speakers, their languages and the social and linguistic criteria by which they are to be judged. This is another way of saying that it is White America that is in control of the national linguistic economy and thus determines the value of the different forms of linguistic capital present in the territory. And the criteria of evaluation basically rely on the monolingual ideology that has been constitutive of the modern capitalist state, whereby national communities were homologous to language communities, speakers were monolingual, and languages were bounded structures and repertoires that suffered if "foreign" linguistic material "entered" their space.

3.3 Workers between States

Beatriz Lorente's (2007, 2012) study of the market in domestic workers in Singapore will allow us to exemplify added layers of complexity to the sociolinguistics of migration. First, in the increasingly globalized logics of markets and politics, states retain powerful means to act, despite having lost some degree of control. Second, immigration studies have traditionally been very "NATO-centered," but powerful migration flows take place outside these areas that require studying too. Third, a gender perspective on migration is also essential to understand how inequalities on a global scale operate in terms that connect access to wealth, race and gender, in complex ways.

Lorente (2007) studied the experiences in Singapore of foreign domestic workers (FDWs) from the Philippines, i.e. women working as house maids, or child or elderly carers. In Singapore, as in many industrialized countries, the fact that women have gone into paid employment has created a big demand for household assistants or "domestic workers," that is, workers that take up the types of (formerly unpaid) work that women used to perform in families. A local industry of "maid agencies" has developed in Singapore to act as brokers between the immigrants and their prospective employers. These agencies basically conduct standardized routines to screen candidates (commonly young Filipino or Indonesian women), establish wage levels and work conditions, publicize offers, liaise with employers, and manage visa procedures. An important characteristic of this arrangement is that most domestic workers get hired *before they leave* their homes. The Singaporean recruitment agencies in fact liaise with Philippine agencies, who, for profit, assist local Filipino workers to find employment abroad.

Language plays an important role in this process, as knowledge of English is used to establish the "value" of the domestic worker, which translates in turn into differences in wage level. Lorente (2007) observed that, in the context she studied, competence in English is not so much individualized as generalized to national groups, with Filipino women assumed to be most skilled. Correspondingly, Filipino women in principle earn slightly more than Indonesian or Sri Lankan women. Maid agencies construct these "nationality-based levels of English proficiency" based on stereotypes, and these linguistic stereotypes are commonly matched with other values related to modernity. Filipino FDWs are often marketed as ideal to work as tutors for children, and their association with English provides the grounds for additional positive stereotypes, such as their "quick ability to learn," being "competent, meticulous, more initiative, and hygienic," though accompanied by the drawbacks of a modern ethos: "bold and streetwise" (p. 133).

Lorente describes how this market-bound stereotyping is embodied in specific events that she calls "scripts of servitude." These scripts consist of videorecorded messages that act as a proxy for a job interview (and are actually often called "interviews"), in which the prospective worker (still living at home) addresses the prospective employer and displays her suitability, as shown in the transcript of the video below:

Transcript 4

Detsie: good afternoon / sir / madam // this is Detsie de Vera / 22 years old / single and came from the province of Union // I am one of the members of the *iglesia ni kristo* // we are four in the family // I have two brothers and one sister // my brother is already married and my little sister is still studying for her college // I have finished my bachelor of

secondary education / last 2002 / major in mathematics // though I don't have experience in going abroad / I can assure you that I can be a good maid / an honest / hardworking housemaid and babysitter of yours // I have experience or I was used to take care of my nephews and nieces especially when their parents are busy working because they are both working // so I need to prepare for their food / prepare for their clothes // that's why I can assure you that I can do anything though I am so small / I am just four feet and ten inches in height / I can do what other people can do // ma'am if you will choose me as one of your maids / I promise to do my very best just to serve you with all my heart // thank you
Lorente (2007: 145)

Lorente identifies the key features of these highly scripted events: They begin with a) a greeting in which terms of address are used expressing politeness and willingness to submit to hierarchy. This is followed by a self-descriptive section stating b) a list of personal details such as age, marital status, education, religion, origin, and so on, and c) former experience in matters connected with the work. Finally, d) a "service guarantee" is issued in the form of an assurance of willingness and capacity to serve before the closing formulas are delivered. The key issue, however, is not necessarily one of format but of process, i.e. the fact that these scripts are designed by maid agencies and imposed on both workers and employers as the terms under which the selection process is conducted, which in turn determines to a great extent how the labor relation is established. Additional important elements in this accord are the conditions that the worker would not engage in any form of sexual relationship, could not marry a local, had to undergo a pregnancy test every six months, had the right to little or no free time, no right to apply for citizenship in Singapore, and was often bound to the agency for many months as she had to pay a fee for the recruitment service (in the form of a loan).

The plight of FDWs in Singapore exemplifies the increasing complexity of immigration processes in the context of globalization, and its linguistic components. On the one hand, we see the emergence of an industry (e.g. maid agencies) devoted to the management of immigrant labor and even charged with control of the sexual practices of immigrants; here one might be tempted to argue that this exemplifies the ways in which neoliberal states withdraw from intervening in such spheres. Lorente, however, provides evidence to the contrary, that is, the increasing concern of nation-states to regulate and profit from such procedures. In this case, what we have are very active roles played by the states of both the Philippines and Singapore in developing the socioeconomic conditions that enable specific forms of labor relations and immigrant control to emerge. In the case of the Philippines, we have a decades-old process of steering national education, economic strategies, and foreign relations towards the production of a migrant workforce that can compete in specific contexts where cheap labor is in demand, so that the state can sustain itself via their remittances (Lorente 2012). In the case of Singapore, it is not just the fact that state regulations provide the framework in which "maid agencies" operate so that its own skilled women can enter paid employment. It also establishes the regulatory means that discriminates between different types of migrant workers, thus making "foreign maids" temporary "guestworkers" who are supposed to go back home when the contract expires, while it encourages more skilled workers to settle in the country and acquire regular work permits.

Moreover, although it can be argued that the position of English as an employment asset can be attributed to the international standing of this language, it is worth bearing in mind the multiple ways in which nation-states may also intervene in local linguistic economies. There is, first, the highly conscious policy developed by different Philippine governments over the years to promote the learning of English amongst the lower classes so that they can be more easily directed to find employment outside the country. Additionally, the Philippine state intervenes by forcing local agencies to require a minimum wage in employment contracts. Although such regulations can arguably be bypassed, they do have an impact on how Filipino women are marketed. On the other hand, the government of Singapore has also been very active for years promoting English as an official and public language to create cohesion in an eminently multiethnic country, at the same time that English helps the nation to participate in the global economy. So both the offer and demand for English in the market for domestic workers are very much state-driven and the whole picture provides a good example of how nation-states continue to intervene in linguistic markets, even in the context of globalization.

4 Immigrants, the State, and Social Inequalities

What these three examples demonstrate is not so much that nation-states fully determine the social standing of immigrant communities in their linguistic repertoires, but rather that they play a pivotal role in the production of the symbolic and economic conditions immigrants have to face. The first element is, obviously, by providing the fundamental ideological framework on the basis of which "immigrant" becomes a relevant category. The second is by virtue of the means that states usually have to bear directly on the living conditions of immigrants, typically through visas, residence and work permits, education, social and security services, and so on. The third is more indirectly through the conduct of actors, human or corporate, not necessarily bound to the state organically but who nevertheless act upon and contribute to reproduce the (official or unofficial) linguistic, cultural, social, racial, and sexual hierarchies that feature in that given context and have complex connections with the state, the most obvious being that the state's ruling classes commonly possess the most valued forms of economic, cultural, and linguistic capital, the official/hegemonic currency against which all other currencies are measured.

The situations shown have exemplified some of these hierarchies as they are projected in state institutions such as the school, in social life more generally, or in the service industry. It is worth pointing out, however, some of the dimensions that in many ways transcend local logics, such as racial difference and the sexual division of labor. Thus a language like Spanish may be dominant in one (state) context and a stigma in another; but in both Spain and the US linguistic dominance appears as a way to assert racial dominance. Additionally, the Filipino maids also remind us that migration is structured in terms of gender, with the paradox that female immigrant labor is mobilized to enable the more sexually "liberated" ways of life in industrialized societies, thus producing new forms of gender division of reproductive labor on a global scale, in which the English language plays a central role.

The examples presented also display the productivity of methodological diversity: while the three studies contain to different degrees excerpts of naturally occurring interaction, it is substantially different to carry out ethnography in a public space such as a school, or in private homes, or in work-related contexts. And it requires different interpretative modes to work with recordings of spontaneous interaction, with interviews, or scripted videos, and also with the kind of documentation enabling connection of the concrete experience of people with a wider framework of state policies at the sending and receiving end of migration, as Lorente does. It is, in any case, this methodological diversity that allows the progressive building of the wider picture of how migration contributes to structuring relationships of inequality in contemporary societies.

5 Directions in Immigration Research

Immigration research, sociolinguistic and otherwise, has undergone profound transformations in recent decades. In the 1980s the so-called "assimilation paradigm" was dominant, that is, the assumption that immigrants "naturally" assimilated to the host society in three generations, the third having largely forgotten or simply not learned the original family language. As sociologists (see for instance Urry 2000) and anthropologists (see Clifford 1997) became increasingly aware of the momentous social changes that were taking place due to increasing mobility, political and economic internationalization, the improvement of transport and the development of digital technologies, views on immigration have greatly changed. These changes have also been gradually taken up in the development of a critical sociolinguistics through the works of Cazden et al. (2011), Heller (2011), or Blommaert (2010), all of them deeply engaged in research where immigration features centrally. From this perspective, an article by Steven Vertovec (2001) is often quoted as symbolically representing this change of perspective whereby immigrants are increasingly capable of leading "transnational" lives, that is, sustaining networks of meaningful social participation both in the countries where they settle but also in their countries of origin or in previous contexts of residence. Cultural hybridity becomes, from this perspective, the expected pattern, not assimilation. Vertovec (2007) is also responsible for another seminal article that caused a lively debate in the sociolinguistics of the late 2000s. In this article, he posits the concept of "superdiversity" to argue that current research on immigration must cease to revolve around issues of ethnicity and take up its increasing complexity as immigrant communities are also themselves characterized by diversity: according to country of origin, channel of migration, legal status, cultural capital, access to employment, transnationalism, coexistence with other groups, local policies and service providers, and so on. Although this article was primarily focused on the British context and its traditional policies of multiculturalism, it has led to further theoretical and epistemological debates (see Blommaert and Rampton 2011) that hail a new sociolinguistics centrally concerned with change, mobility, and linguistic hybridity.

Related Topics

Readers interested in issues of immigration may also consider studying how the topic is constructed in the media – see **25** Racism in the Press (Van Dijk). The notion of Language Ideologies (**7** Kroskrity) is conceptually central to the topic too. Chapters **12–15** on intersectionalities, gender, race, and ethnicity are also directly relevant. Chapter **19** on Language and Political Economy (McElhinny) provides fundamental principles that elaborate the succinct theoretical overview provided here. Chapters **21** on Language and Nationalism (Haque), **22** on Language in the Age of Globalization (Jacquemet), and **24** on Discrimination via Discourse (Wodak) also touch on aspects that affect immigrants directly.

Notes

1 Transcription conventions (those of different authors have been adapted):

Arnaldo:	Interactional participant
Right (italics)	Speech and data not in English in the original
{ }	Comments made by the transcriber
&	Turn latched to previous turn
=	Maintaining of a participant's turn in an overlap
[ ]	Turn overlapping with similarly marked turn
-	Te-starts and self-interruptions without any pause
/	Short pause (0'5" seconds)
//	Long pause (0'5–1'5" seconds)

↑	Rising intonation
↓	Falling intonation
→	Intonation of suspension
RIGHT (all capital letters)	Loud talking
(( ))	Incomprehensible speech
pa'l	Syntactical phonetic phenomena between words
aa (doubled vowels)	Vowel lengthening
ss (doubled consonants)	Consonant lengthening
?	Questions (Also used for tag questions such as 'right?', 'eh?', 'you know?')
!	Exclamations

References

Blommaert, Jan. 2010. *The Sociolinguistics of Globalization*. Cambridge: Cambridge University Press.

Blommaert, Jan, and Ben Rampton. 2011. "Language and Superdiversity." *Diversities* 13(2): 1–22.

Bourdieu, Pierre. 1991. *Language and Symbolic Power*, edited by J. B. Thompson. Cambridge, MA: Polity Press.

Brettell, Caroline. 2003. *Anthropology and Migration: Essays on Transnationalism, Ethnicity, and Identity*. Walnut Creek (CA): Rowman Altamira.

Cazden, Courtney, Bill Cope, Norman Fairclough, Jim Gee, Mary Kalantzis, Gunther Kress, Allan Luke, Carmen Luke, Sarah Michaels, and Martin Nakata. 1996. "A Pedagogy of Multiliteracies: Designing Social Futures." *Harvard Educational Review* 66(1): 60–92.

Clifford, James. 1997. *Routes*. Cambridge, MA: Harvard University Press.

Corona, Víctor, Luci Nussbaum, and Virginia Unamuno. 2012. "The Emergence of New Linguistic Repertoires among Barcelona's Youth of Latin American Origin." *International Journal of Bilingual Education and Bilingualism* 16(2): 182–194.

Duranti, Alessandro. 1997. *Linguistic Anthropology*, vol. 1. Chichester: John Wiley & Sons.

Eckert, P. and S. McConnell-Ginet. 1992. "Think Practically and Look Locally: Language and Gender as Community Based Practice." *Annual Review of Anthropology* 21(1): 461–488.

Foucault, M. 1991. "Governmentality." In *The Foucault Effect: Studies in Governmentality. With Two Lectures by and an Interview with Michel Foucault*, 87–104. Hertfordshire: Harvester Wheatsheaf.

Heller, Monica. 2011. *Paths to Post-Nationalism: A Critical Ethnography of Language and Identity*. New York: Oxford University Press.

Hill, Jane H. and Kenneth C. Hill. 1986. *Speaking Mexicano: Dynamics of Syncretic Language in Central Mexico*. Tucson: University of Arizona Press.

Lorente, Beatriz P. 2007. "Mapping English Linguistic Capital: The Case of Filipino Domestic Workers in Singapore". Ph.D thesis, 260 pp. National University of Singapore.

Lorente, Beatriz P. 2012. "The Making of 'Workers of the World': Language and the Labor Brokerage State." In *Language and Late Capitalism: Pride and Profit*, edited by Alexandre Duchêne and Monica Heller, 183–206. New York: Routledge.

Martín Rojo, Luisa. 2013. "From Multilingual Practices to Social Processes." In *Multilingualism and Multimodality: Current Challenges for Educational Studies*, edited by Ingrid de Saint-Georges and Jean-Jacques Weber, 33–58. Rotterdam: Sense Publishers.

McElhinny, Bonnie. 2012. "Silicon Valley Sociolinguistics? Analyzing Language, Gender and Communities of Practice in the New Knowledge Economy." In *Language in Late Capitalism: Pride and Profit*, edited by Alexandre Duchêne and Monica Heller, 230–261. Critical Multilingualism series. New York: Taylor & Francis, Routledge.

Morgan, Marcyliena. 2004. "Speech Community." In *A Companion to Linguistic Anthropology*, edited by Alessandro Duranti, 3–22. Malden, MA: Blackwell.
Urry, John. 2000. *Sociology beyond Societies: Mobilities for the Twenty-First Century*, vol. 1. Routledge.
Vertovec, Steven. 2001. "Transnationalism and Identity." *Journal of Ethnic & Migration Studies* 27(4/10): 573–582.
Vertovec, Steven. 2007. "Superdiversity and its Implications." *Ethnic and Racial Studies* 30(6): 1024–1054.
Williams, Raymond. 1985. *Keywords: A Vocabulary of Culture and Society*. Oxford: Oxford University Press.
Zentella, A. C. 1997. *Growing Up Bilingual: Puerto Rican Children in New York*. Oxford: Blackwell.
Zentella, Ana Celia. 2003. " 'José Can You See?': Latin@ Responses to Racist Discourse." In *Bilingual Aesthetics: A New Sentimental Education*, edited by Doris Sommer, 51–66. New York: Palgrave.

21
Language and Nationalism

Eve Haque

Introduction

The role of language in nationalist projects cannot be outlined without a consideration of the various ways in which nationalism itself has been theorized. This is a large body of literature that continues to proliferate and generate new approaches to the question of nations and nationalism. In many of these approaches, language is seen as a central organizing element of nationalist projects, and in others, language is understood as one element of national culture. However, in all these cases, given the centrality of language to the generation of human community, the question of the specific role of language in nationalism remains.

Conventional scholarship on nationalism organizes theories of nations and nationalism into various schools of thought, the main and most recurrent being primordialism and modernism. Primordialists include those who argue that nations are part of a natural order, ancient and ubiquitous, with modern nations evolving from an enduring descent group. Modernists, on the other hand, treat the nation as a recent, socio-political fact derived from the processes of modernization. Responses to the modernist position give rise to two other schools of thought, which are perennialism and ethnosymbolism. Perennialists, although agreeing with the primordial nature of nations, deny its predestination and see nations as temporally continuous or recurrent in history. Ethnosymbolists, on the other hand, reject the 'continuism' of perennialists and give weight to the transformations of modernity, as well as underscoring the wider significance of the *ethnie* over the *longue durée* to explain the affective bases of nation formation (Ozkirimli, 2010). There are elaborations of the modernist school of thought extended into both the postcolonial and settler colonial context, in which the role of language is also significant. As a relatively recent approach, postmodernist theorizations of nationalism encompass a highly diverse category of scholars, who unpack the discursive construction of the nation, highlight the fragmentation of contemporary national identities, and unravel the gendered and racialized discourses of nation building. Increasingly postnationalist challenges to the nation-state from both supranationalist and subnationalist perspectives are emerging, and language also plays a key role in these movements.

Despite the impression of clearly delineated categories, it is important to note that in fact there is considerable overlap and contestation about these classifications. Further confusion also arises from the fact that there is little consensus on definitions of nations and nationalism across schools of thought as these may vary depending on the approaches taken. As well, the contingent nature of language is not always thoroughly theorized, and language is often given as a clearly bounded and defined category with stable characteristics. Ultimately, the role of language in nationalist projects is determined by the specific framework of nationalism under consideration; thus, in this chapter, I will detail the role of language in the various schools of thought outlined above.

Historical Perspectives

Primordialism

In the primordialist school of thought, language is a central element around which the nation is organized. Primordialism is commonly associated with the German Romantic era, and one of the names most famously connected with it is Johann Gottfried Herder (1744–1803), who is also credited with being the first to coin the term nationalism. In his prize-winning and influential essay of 1770, *Über den Ursprung der Sprache* (The Origin of Language), Herder links the ideas of reason and language, "Each nation speaks in the manner it thinks and thinks in the manner it speaks . . . . We cannot think without words" (cited in Barnard, 1965: 56). Herder believed that the sustaining and integrating power of language would lead to higher rates of social cohesion, the conscious fostering of a common linguistic medium, and the emergence of a Volk or a "people," which in turn would give rise to the community's consciousness of difference from those speaking another language (Barnard, 1965: 58). Herder believed that since diversity was the fundamental characteristic of the universal order, the world must be constituted of many nationalities, so the Volk was a natural division of the human race and endowed with its own language as the embodiment of its soul or character (Barnard, 1965: 58). This also meant that intermixture with other nationalities was to be avoided. The formulation of language and Volk meant a close association between language and politics, which led to a change in the understanding of nation. Thus, a nation was no longer a group of political citizens united under a political sovereign; rather, it was now a separate *natural* entity, whose claim to political recognition rested on the possession of a common language (Barnard, 1965: 59).

Johann Gottlieb Fichte (1762–1835) was one of the most famous disseminators of Herder's views, and built on them to develop his own theory of national superiority based on supposed linguistic purity. His contention was that German was superior to the French language because it was the original language, whereas French was inferior because it represented an adoption of foreign elements such as Latin (Edwards, 1985: 25). Thus, as the original German was superior to the bastardized French, it followed that the German nation was also superior to the French nation. As Fichte argued, the previous ancestry of those who spoke an original language was unimportant; rather, it was the continuity of the language that mattered most since "men are formed by language far more than language is formed by men" (Fichte cited in Edwards, 1985: 25).

Herder's ethnolinguistic formulation of the nation set the stage for what in the present day is more popularly known as the blood and belonging form of nation. In this category, groups who perceive themselves as possessing a common culture and language come together to make a political state, with "blood" and language the main criteria for belonging (Wright, 2004: 41). Germany and Japan are the classic examples of this formulation, as nation-states where the main organizing principle is the belief in a common cultural and linguistic heritage. Interestingly, despite Fichte's emphasis on the purity of the original language, what actually exists throughout the territory of the German state is a broad dialectical continuum and only in the written form is there a hegemonic standard (Wright, 2004: 41). Perhaps it is the weight given to "blood" belonging that allows for the tolerance of spoken dialectal difference; however, language is very important here because it is a more salient marker than blood and mother tongue is a key concept in this model. It is also clear that in this formulation of nation, one is born in, and cannot become assimilated into, the nation.

There are two advantages to primordial ethnolinguistic nationalism. The first is that as an organizing principle, it is easy to harness and promote since people can understand and respond to its emotional appeal. Furthermore, the promotion of a national language as a primordial marker of a people fits neatly with the promotion of oral and written nationalist imagery and the formation of a manageable political unit (Wright, 2000: 17). The challenges to ethnolinguistic nationalism, however, arise from the universalism and republicanism derived from the Enlightenment and the French and American Revolutions, exemplars of the modernist approach to nationalism.

Modernism

In the modernist account, nations arise out of very specific social, economic, and political circumstances. The modern nation-state emerges with the advent of modernization and the rise of the state alongside the entrenchment of the ideology of nationalism. In this school of thought, language plays a crucial unifying role in the rise of the modern nation, but this standard national language is not so much a primordial essential precursor to nation formation; rather, it emerges through the processes of modernity. Language as a unifying force in the formation of the modern nation-state can most famously be traced back to the French Revolution and the emergence of a national standard of French.

In the aftermath of the French Revolution in the late 18th century, the issue of linguistic unification became a key issue among the demands for a participatory and egalitarian political system. Charged with the preliminary task of carrying out the census, Abbé Grégoire lamented in his report of 1794 that most Frenchmen in fact did not speak the national language but, rather, spoke varieties of patois related to French, resulting in what he described as a "Tower of Babel." Based on his findings, Grégoire emphasized the political importance of linguistic unification and a common language as an integral part of the Revolution, in order that all citizens could, first, communicate with each other; second, be molded into a "national whole," and, finally, "to simplify the mechanism of the political machine and make it function more smoothly" (cited in Grillo, 1989: 24). Thus, the advocacy of linguistic unification was a practical, political, and philosophical Revolutionary effort to appropriate French as a language of state and literature from the upper classes and to transform it into French as the language of national identity and political participation for the broader citizenry. This signaled the congruence of the nation, state, and language as a shift away from sovereign power emanating from the king to sovereign power residing in the nation; a fundamentally constitutive moment of the modern nation-state. This move centralized the importance of education, whereby through mass access to teaching in the standardized national language, people would become informed citizens and be able to participate directly on equal terms in the political process. The Revolutionary model of linguistic uniformity in France has given rise to a present-day conceptual framework of integration, where assimilation is compelled through a hegemonic national monoculturalism and monolingualism, and the relationship between nationalism and the mono-ethnic state has become naturalized (Fishman, 1972).

Gellner (1983) builds on this model, with particular emphasis on the importance of communication in industrializing societies. Specifically, he highlights the material changes brought about by industrialization at the end of the 18th century as the main cause of the rise of the modern nation, with a shift from localized, feudal, agrarian societies to the modern, industrialized population with its literate, mobile, and occupationally specialized division of labor. It is in this move, where the substitutability of the worker – that is, the ability of the worker to move between increasingly complex and differentiated roles – became increasingly important to industrialized work, that Gellner locates the emergence of the modern nation-state and the need for cultural and linguistic standardization, out of which a literate and common culture could evolve. For Gellner, language has a central unitary role as the cement of modern society, but it is mass education to the national standard that is central to the production of fully "technologically competent" citizens. Thus, nationalism flourishes as education and a unified culture set a path to modernity, political legitimacy, and shared cultural and linguistic identity (Gellner, 1983: 55). Gellner's highly functionalist model, in which a homogeneous nation could be shaped on the basis of a strong state culture due to the requirements of industrialization, gives rise to his important insight that nationalism is primarily a political principle in which the "political and the national unit should be congruent" (Gellner, 1983: 4). Thus, in Gellner's functionalist account of the emergence of the modern nation-state, the standardized national language is accorded a central function as well.

In Benedict Anderson's oft-cited book, *Imagined Communities* (1983), nations are "imagined" out of particular historical and institutional practices. As he specifies, nations are imagined as a "deep horizontal comradeship," imagined as limited by the finite boundaries of the nation, and imagined as sovereign because of the passing of the divinely ordained, hierarchical, dynastic realm. Anderson explains that it is in the vacuum left in the era of the Enlightenment, with the advent of rationalist secularism, that the idea of the modern nation appears. He states that the emergence of a standardized national language through print capitalism – particularly newspapers – provided the technology for an "imagined linkage," which made it possible for growing numbers of people to relate themselves to others, even those they would never meet, in profoundly new ways (p. 40). Print capitalism's restless search for markets forced the production of text in the common words of the masses, which gave fixity to the language of publication and created unified fields of exchange and communications at a lower level than Latin but above the spoken vernaculars, becoming the dominant standard language of the nation (p. 47).

Anderson also emphasizes the affective role of language in nation formation, arguing that all languages seem to appear rooted in the past, and operate to create an image of *unisonance* and simultaneity that produces a contemporaneous community through such forms as the national anthem. It is in this way that the nation is conceived in language, not blood, and thereby anyone can be "invited" into the imagined community of the nation, which can present itself as simultaneously open and closed (Anderson, 1983: 133). The role of language, and here it is language as the strongly self-identifying mother tongue, is central in suturing together the past, present, and future of the nation in the imagination of the citizen. In the modernist framework, according to Anderson, a national standardized language that emerges out of functionalist needs and unification of the modernized country also serves a key role in binding together an imagined national community across the bounded geographical space of the nation.

Critical Issues and Topics

Perennialism

As a response to the modernist school of thought, perennialism is most often seen as the bridge between primordial and modernist models of nation building, whereby nations are deemed to be temporally continuous or recurrent throughout human history. Specifically, although particular nations may come and go, the nation as a form of collective human association and community endures. Adrian Hastings, as the most commonly cited scholar of perennialism, defines ethnicity as "a group of people with a shared cultural identity and spoken language," which are the building blocks of a nation, and nations themselves are self-conscious communities that emerge across ethnicities as a creation of human communication (Hastings, 1997: 20). Thus, in this formulation, language is a critical element of community formation. As Hastings argues, even in ancient worlds, oral languages became more stable as they took the form of written vernaculars. Consequently, increasingly larger numbers of people could communicate with each other, thereby expanding the vernacular as the universal language of religion, government, and education, and giving rise to what he calls a "proto-nation" (p. 20). For Hastings, this is exemplified in Christian nations, where he links the translation of the Bible into vernaculars – a process he traces back to the 2nd century (p. 195) – as a key catalyst in linguistic unification and the emergence of national consciousness (p. 24). As Hastings underscores, in most models of nationalism, arguments for or against the linguistic bases of nation formation usually focus on orality, whereas he maintains that in reality the recurrent literary bases of linguistic unification underlie the emergence of national consciousness. Hastings rejects Anderson's modernist thesis that the rise of nations could only happen when the influence of the sacred languages of religion declined; rather, as Hastings' reading of the Bible shows, Christianity has the use of the world's vernaculars inscribed into its origins, with neither Hebrew, Greek, nor Latin ever identified as a sacred language. Armenia is identified by Hastings as the first state to become Christian, in the late 3rd century, and notes the survival, into the present, of the Armenian national identity with that of the Armenian Bible, liturgy, and related literature (p. 198). He recognizes the Ethiopian case as a close parallel, where, in a people "as far removed from Enlightenment as conceivable," national identity was reinforced via vernacular literary traditions from the 14th century on and horizontal mass participation was ensured through the rites and music of the Ethiopian Orthodox Church (p. 151).

If Hastings emphasized the role of literary vernacularization as a key linguistic element in his perennialist account of nationalism, Joshua Fishman focused on the important role of language in forging ethnic ties, myths of origin, and familial metaphors in rousing popular support for nationalism. Defining nationalism as the organization of "elaborated beliefs, values, and behaviours that nationalities develop on behalf of their avowed ethnocultural self-interest" (Fishman, 1972: 4), he pointed to the built-in tension between the requirements of modernization and those of authentication. Fishman identified three main attributes of language that answered the political community's desire for a common cultural heritage alongside the need for modernization. The first was that language could offer a link with the glorious past, where the mother tongue signaled history itself, the second was language as a link to authenticity, and finally, language provided contrastive self-identification from others. Thus, Fishman was clear about both the primordial and modernist links between language and nationalism, which required that language use and language planning both encouraged and facilitated broader unity and deeper authenticity, as well as the various modern implementations of sociocultural and political-organizational integration (p. 66). As the accounts of both these key scholars show, perennialist formations of nationalism are located between, and informed by, primordialist and modernist theories of nation building.

Ethnosymbolism

Ethnosymbolism is another school of thought that emerges out of a critique of modernism and primordialism, as well as a rejection of the continuism of perennialists. Specifically, ethnosymbolists place greater emphasis than the perennialists to the transformations of modernity, even as weight is given to the importance of premodern ethnic formations in understanding the differences between contemporary nations. Therefore, myths, traditions, values and symbols, are deemed to be significant across the *longue durée* (i.e., a course of many centuries) to explain the intense group identification, or ethnic consciousness, of the nation. The emphasis on subjective elements of long-term ethnic identifications is a central element of this school of thought, so elements such as language become a symbolic resource in how the *ethnie*, or ethnic groups with shared myths, memories, and culture, maintain durable identities across temporal shifts and historical forces.

John A. Armstrong, one of the first theorists of ethnosymbolism, examined the significance of the *longue durée* for nationalism in his seminal book, *Nations before Nationalism* (1982). Tracing the genealogy of ethnic consciousness across various civilizations, he concludes that ethnic identification finds its meaning not in recognized group characteristics or territorial occupation, but rather by comparison to "strangers" or through exclusion. As Armstrong explains, this differentiation between group and stranger takes place through the "uncanny experience of confronting others," who "remained mute in response to . . . attempts at communication" (Armstrong, 1982: 5); in this way "large ethnic groupings came to recognize their own relatively close relationship" (p. 5). With this instrumental focus on the communicative aspects of language, Armstrong further elaborates that ethnic distinction through boundary mechanisms requires concentration on linguistic elements that act as "border guards" (p. 242). It is not, however, only the instrumental elements of language that interest Armstrong in the processes of ethnic formation; drawing on the work of linguist Otto Jespersen, he also clarifies that the "high affect" potential of language makes it significant for use in myths and symbols in order to cement affective attachments for ethnic formation.

With an analysis that focuses on premodern civilizations, Armstrong underlines the importance of different ways of life between the territorial fixed, or "sedentary," as opposed to the nomadic, as well as the significance of religion, particularly Islam and Christianity, to premodern ethnic formation. He argues that premodern ethnic alignments could emerge without recourse to linguistic affiliation as regional dialect continua were more the norm than were clear linguistic divisions. Acknowledging that it is with modernization that language becomes a more salient marker of ethnic group identification he nevertheless identifies religion and politics as the independent variables in relation to linguistic interaction within language families. Thus, language remains a symbolic resource for ethnic identification, with the significance of language "highly contingent" on political and religious forces in the premodern eras and most often a product rather than a cause of polity formation (Amstrong, 1982: 241). Ultimately, in the ethnosymbolist school of thought, language in both its instrumental and affective capacities is an important element of core ethnic grouping and identification but remains a factor that is dependent for its significance on political and religious allegiances across the eras.

Postcolonialism

If perennialism and ethnosymbolism are responses to the polarities of the modernist and primodialist schools of thought, postcolonial and settler colonial nationalisms can probably be understood best as elaborations and reactions to these two foundational approaches to the study of nationalism. Postcolonial nationalisms emerge in the aftermath of anti-imperial and anticolonial struggles to liberate entire regions of the global south from direct colonial rule. The project of nation building for independent postcolonial nations meant the need to create a distinct yet unified national culture and identity while also addressing the legacies of colonialism. These legacies included imposed arbitrary boundaries and borders, communities displaced from traditional homelands, the institution of hierarchies between groups, remnants of colonial bureaucratic and state structures, as well as colonial languages.

Partha Chatterjee is one notable scholar of postcolonial nationalisms who has tried to outline the specificities of nation building in the wake of colonial rule. Critiquing Anderson's assertion that the historical experience of nationalism in Europe and the Americas had provided a set of modular forms of nationalism from which the nationalist elites of Asia and Africa could choose, Chatterjee has argued that anticolonial nationalist movements were actually predicated on a *difference* from the modular forms of nationalism propagated by the modern West (Chatterjee, 1986, 2010: 25–26). He elaborates that anticolonial nationalisms operated by addressing both the "material" or "outside" domain of economy and statecraft, which often replicated Western models, as well as the "inner" domain of essential and national "cultural" identity. Thus, although the colonial state structures may have left a legacy in the postcolonial state as part of the material domain, the inner domain was where the fashioning of a non-Western, modern national culture took place. Chatterjee goes on to illustrate his point by outlining how the development of national culture in Bengal in fact began pre-independence in the emergence of unique forms of Bengali drama, literature, art, and schooling that escape the modular influences of European languages and literatures, despite colonial influences. As Chatterjee clarifies, the history of postcolonial nationalisms must account for more than just the material domain of the state as the site of contest with the colonial power; rather, the inner domain of national culture is the site of distinction and unification, as well as contestation, in the re-imagining of the postcolonial nation.

The establishment of postcolonial national culture centers the question of language in the nation building project and raises questions about how to contend with internal heteroglossia and colonial language/s. In particular, with language most often identified as the carrier of culture, the legacy of colonial languages remained, for the nation building project, a highly contested arena. This is best exemplified in the works of anticolonial Kenyan writer Ngugi wa Thiong'o, who argued that language is indistinguishable from culture as a collective memory bank of people's experience in history (Ngugi, 1986: 15), and vowed to stop writing in English and publish only in Gikuyu and Kiswahili as a rejection of the colonial legacy of English in Kenya. Similarly, anticolonial scholar Frantz Fanon also maintains that to speak a language is to assume a culture and therefore mastery of the colonial language was directly proportional to the power that the colonized subject could assume (Fanon 1967). This was the common case of colonial rule leaving a material world of bureaucracy and state structures organized through colonial practices and languages to the postindependence nation, now run by bilingual locals and elites who were invested to varying degrees in the maintenance of colonial languages and the privileges these accrued. Therefore, class hierarchies between groups as a legacy of colonial rule were often a factor in the identification of national and official languages for the postcolonial state. As well, in the interest of fostering national culture, the elevation of local languages as signs of national identity were also often marked by the legacy of colonial rule, as different ethnic communities vied for the recognition of their languages. Colonial rule had often left bordering mismatches between national/territorial ethnic communities or had led to ethnic group displacement, which in the postindependence era had ramifications for group recognition and therefore how different communities' languages fared.

These complexities in the wake of colonial rule meant that the role of languages – both local and colonial – in postcolonial nationalism could not be easily predicted or categorized. Thus, highly multilingual postindependence states have variable language policies. For example, India has developed a three-language formula, where Hindi and English are the official languages at the national level and each state designates an official language. South Africa recognizes

11 official languages including two colonial languages – English and Afrikaans – and nine Bantu languages. In Indonesia, however, only Bahasa Indonesian is the recognized official language despite the presence of hundreds of indigenous languages. These different formulations for recognition of both colonial and local/indigenous languages have emerged as different postcolonial states have been driven by different imperatives for nation building. These imperatives include balancing the need for language in its instrumental capacity for modernization, education, and local/global economic development with language in its symbolic capacity for group recognition, inclusion, and national unity. Ultimately, the role of language in postcolonial nationalism is as complex as its historical particularities and colonial legacies.

Settler Colonialism

Settler colonial states have also been called breakaway settler colonies (McClintock, 1992), Creole states (Anderson, 1983) or white settler societies (Stasiulus & Yuval-Davis, 1995), and theorizations of these nation-state forms as a separate category has exploded in the past decade (Veracini, 2010; Wolfe, 2006). Ronald Weitzer defines settler states as "founded by migrant groups who assume a super-ordinate position vis à vis native inhabitants and build self-sustaining states that are de jure or de facto independent from the mother country and organized around the settlers' political domination over the indigenous population" (Weitzer, 1990: 24). Thus the three pillars of establishing stable settler rule are: achieving autonomy from the metropole in molding social, political, and economic structures; the consolidation of control over indigenous populations and lands – often through violent and coercive means; and the maintenance of unity within the dominant settler populations (Weitzer, 1990; Stasiulus & Yuval-Davis 1995). States identified as settler nations include Canada, the United States, Australia, and Israel, among others.

In settler colonial nations, language is not used to differentiate from respective imperial metropoles; rather, the imperial language is that of the dominant settler group, who often share a common language and/or descent (Anderson, 1983: 50). In the "English dominant nations" (Herriman & Burnaby, 1996), a shared British colonial heritage in these settler states meant that English remains the prominent language in the colonizing process; thus, English was imposed on the indigenous population, which resulted in the denial, suppression, and neglect of indigenous languages, leading to catastrophic language loss. Technologies of language eradication include community displacement and dispossession, impoverishment, and colonial schooling, in particular, residential schooling. Residential schooling, best exemplified in the US and Canada, was a process of removing children from indigenous families in order to "civilize" them by imposing the settler language and completely prohibiting the use of indigenous languages in all contexts (Haig-Brown, 1998). Separated for months and years from their families and punished for any use of indigenous languages, entire generations of residential school victims suffered catastrophic language loss and shift into the dominant settler language. This legacy finds its contemporary expression in either a complete denial or anemic recognition of indigenous language rights, which has done very little to stem the tide of ongoing indigenous language loss and shift.

As settler nations became more established, migration from regions outside the metropole also expanded as labor for settling the nation was required, bringing speakers of other languages to the settler nation. The imperative of settler unity and domination, however, meant that any claims for an expanded, inclusive set of rights for other languages would most often be met with rejection or at best some form of lesser recognition, often couched as vague and underresourced cultural rights (Haque, 2012). This ensures that language shift out of the nondominant first language into the dominant settler language usually takes place within three generations (Curdt-Christiansen, 2009). Further, an emphasis on settler language competence for socioeconomic integration and mobility means that immigration processes increasingly emphasize settler language competence as a sorting mechanism for immigrant selection and admission; immigrants are increasingly made responsible for their own language training to shift into the dominant language (Haque, 2014).

Canada is an example of a white settler colonial nation that emerged out of the expansion of the second British empire at the end of the 19th century, giving rise to a settler population caught between their colonial location in relation to the metropole, yet colonizers in relation to the indigenous population, who suffered genocide and land dispossession at the direct hands of both French and English settlers. The historical complexity of two settler groups in the Canadian territory meant the establishment of a bilingual compromise in the quest for settler unity, which saw both English and French appointed as the official languages for the first time in 1969 (Haque, 2012). The present legacy of this settler bilingualism compromise has meant that claims for equal linguistic rights for indigenous languages and nonofficial languages continue to remain unrecognized. In short, the historical legacy and sociopolitical structuring of the three pillars of settler rule leads to the naturalization of the imperial language of the metropole as the dominant settler language in the settler colonial nation.

Postmodernism

Postmodern approaches to nationalism vary widely as postmodernism can be understood not only as a historical condition – that is, after modernism – but also as a philosophical and methodological approach that seeks to interrogate and deconstruct all-encompassing conceptions of nationalism (Ozkirimli, 2010: 216). As such, a postmodern approach would not attempt to outline an overarching grand theory of nationalism, as many of the previous approaches described above attempt to do; rather, the contingency, instability, and constructedness of national histories are the focus of postmodernist theorizations of nationalism. Scholars such as Craig Calhoun (1997) thus draw on Foucault's notion of discourse as "practices that form the object of which they speak" (Ozkirimli, 2010: 206) to define nationalism as a "'discursive formation," which is socially constituted and embedded in relations of power (Calhoun, 1997). For Calhoun, the discursive formation of nationalism gives rise to a "rhetoric of nation," which depends on a series of features, among them *culture* that includes "some combination of language" (Calhoun, 1997: 5). However, given the contingency of national histories and forces, the centrality of language as a feature of nationalism depends entirely on the social, political, and historical context out of which the particular nation emerges and so no definitive role of language in nation building can be predetermined.

Building on Calhoun's insight that the rhetoric of nation escapes definition in a single universal theory, other postmodern scholars have put forward the discursive construction of nationalism in terms of the nation as narration. Homi Bhabha (1990) exemplifies this approach and, given the emphasis on how relations of power are central in postmodern approaches to nation building, this also provides an opportunity to foreground minority and resistance counternarrations to the dominant national discourses. For Bhabha, these counternarrations emerge out of his approximation of a model of nation building that introduces notions of ambivalence, liminality, and resistance in order to destabilize the certainty of a linear and progressive national history and a homogeneous national subject. This model disrupts a finite conception of the nation and its "origins," and also ruptures the boundaries of the nation by highlighting the presence of different Others as not just outside the nation but also present within. Bhabha argues that an ambivalent and contentious liminal space emerges within the nation from tensions arising between the nationalist pedagogy of the official dominant narrative of the nation and the complex lived realities of performative daily life. Within this liminal space there is the possibility of supplementary strategies of resistance that eschew simple confrontation with and negation of dominant national narratives. Specifically, the different or "minority" Other can resist on the terrain of the dominant discourse by insinuating himself into the terms of the national narratives to rework the traditional narrations of the nation.

Bhabha illustrates this resistant strategy as he traces the role of language in nation building. He contends that the Other who speaks the "foreignness of language" (Bhabha, 1990: 315) can split the unisonant narrative of the nation. In his example, Bhabha argues that when the Turkish worker in Germany speaks a German word, the visibility of his difference changes the meanings of the words expressed. For example, when he asks for "coffee" in a bar, what the word signified to the barman was that he was asking for coffee in a bar where he should not be asking for coffee, that is, where he did not belong (p. 316). Thus, the very visibility of the Other makes his words opaque; the meaning of the words are no longer transparent, and they take on the meaning with which the visibility and foreignness of the "alien" imbues them, rendering him silent. Bhabha maintains that this silenced Other is the internal stranger whose languageless presence splits the unisonant nation space. Therefore, the presence of the silent Other does not evoke a harmonious patchwork of cultures; instead, it challenges the totality of national culture by bringing in his history of elsewhere and articulating a counternarration, albeit through silence, of cultural difference that disrupts the national history. Therefore, in Bhabha's postmodern model of nationalism, language can reveal the relation of the Other to the nation in ways that other universal models of nationalism cannot, creating space for counternarrations to the dominant national narrative. Although no singular model of postmodern nationalism can be outlined, Calhoun and Bhabha demonstrate the contingent nature and discursive contruction of nationalism in ways that can allow for a more complex accounting of the relationship between language, nation building, and the Other.

Postnationalism

Any overview of language and nationalism will require a brief discussion of the role of language in the postnational context, where the fundamental architecture of the nation-state is called into question in ways that can challenge issues of national sovereignty and unity (Pujolar, 2007). Although subnational movements have been around as long as nationalism, in the contemporary context a variety of factors are implicated in postnational processes, including demographic diversification due to increased migration, the expanding penetration of information and communication technologies, and, in particular, the increase in political and economic globalization (Pujolar, 2007).

It is important to note that postnationalism does not necessarily destabilize the hierarchies and essentialist ethnocultural dimensions of nation-state discourses, even when couched in the framework of universal rights and linguistic biodiversity (Muehlmann & Duchêne, 2007). Supranational and universalist declarations such as the *Universal Declaration of Linguistic Rights* or the *European Charter for Regional or Minority Languages* exemplify these essentializing tendencies as they prioritize the linguistic rights of those identified as historically established territorial minorities over the linguistic rights of those who are identified as im/migrants. Even movements for the maintenance of indigenous languages, whether from the perspectives of biodiversity or of indigenous ontologies, often reproduce the logic of territorialized linguistic rights and replicate the essentialisms and exclusions of nationalist thinking. Subnationalist movements, whether they lead to breakaway states or not, also tend to replicate these hierarchical and essentialist tendencies of the nation-state form. An excellent example is Quebec, where an important historical struggle for recognition of the rights of francophones has, in the present, evolved into a strong ethnolinguistic nationalism with an entrenched regime of language policing that targets, in particular, the cultural and linguistic choices of immigrant communities and their descendants through the development of increasingly exclusionary policies on language and culture.

Globalization in its many forms also has profound implications for the role of language in postnationalist contexts. The proliferation of communication technologies, as well as the economic and political effects of globalization, have all exacerbated the growth of major-scale regional languages such as Spanish, Mandarin, and Arabic; have entrenched language power blocs such as the Francophonie and the Hispanofonia (Pujolar, 2007: 86), and have led to the explosive expansion of English around the world. Globalization accelerates the commodification and consequent standardization of languages but, in the present, it is English in particular that has charged to the forefront as the international language of globalization, shifting both small and large languages in the global linguistic landscape. Whether English is seen as a force of linguistic imperialism (Phillipson, 1992), or the language of cosmopolitanism and opportunity (Crystal, 2003), or even as laden with the possibilities of indigenization and reclamation, there is no doubt that at this moment, no other language better exemplifies the postnationalist challenge to national sovereignty, even as it is concurrently mobilized in the service of replicating essentialist hierarchies of authenticity. Thus, although the role of language in postnationalist contexts may call into question issues of national sovereignty and unity, it may also serve to reproduce and reinforce essentialist and hierarchical characteristics of nation-state discourses.

Future Directions

These various models of nation building, although not exhaustive, trace some of the primary ways language has been accounted for in studies of nation and nationalism. Although the operation of language varies widely within each school of thought, as a primary element in the formation of human community, language continues to be a significant and constitutive aspect of nation formation. The communicative and symbolic functions of language provide means of achieving social cohesion and also of enabling political participation. Specifically, in both these functions language operates as a mode of national identification and exclusion, even as the boundaries and defining characteristics of national language/s require ongoing re/definition. As well, the historical and sociopolitical specificities of each national context reveal both the significance and particularities of linguistic convergence in the development of the nation-state (Wright, 2004). Even postnationalist challenges to conventional thinking about the role of language in nationalism can reproduce the essentialist and hierarchical logics of national identification and exclusion. Despite Chatterjee's (1986) important caveat that all nationalisms are not modular because of the various social and historical antecedents of particular nations, given the centripetal forces of language, the common element of language will continue to be significant across all models of nationalism.

Related Topics

19 Language and Political Economy (McElhinny); **20** Language, Immigration, and the Nation-State (Joan Pujolar); **22** Language in the Age of Globalization (Jacquemet).

References

Anderson, Benedict. (1983). *Imagined Communities*. London: Verso.
Armstrong, John, A. (1982). *Nations before Nationalism*. Chapel Hill: University of North Carolina Press.

Barnard, Frederick. M. (1965). *Herder's Social and Political Thought: From Enlightenment to Nationalism.* Oxford: Clarendon Press.
Bhabha, Homi, K. (1990). DissemiNation: Time, Narrative, and the Margins of the Modern Nation. In, Homi K. Bhabha (Ed.), *Nation and Narration*, pp. 291–320. London: Routledge.
Calhoun, Craig. (1997). *Nationalism.* Minneapolis, MN: University of Minnesota Press.
Chatterjee, Partha. (1986). *Nationalist Thought in a Colonial World: A Derivative Discourse?* London: Zed Books.
Chatterjee, Partha. (2010). *Empire and Nation: Selected Essays.* New York: Columbia University Press.
Crystal, David. (2003). *English as a Global Language.* Cambridge: Cambridge University Press.
Curdt-Christiansen & Xiao Lan. (2009). Invisible and Visible Language Planning: Ideological Factors in the Family Language Policy of Chinese Immigrant Families in Quebec. *Language Policy*, 8, 351–375.
Edwards, John R. (1985). *Language, Society and Identity.* Oxford: Basil Blackwell.
Fanon, Frantz. (1967). *Black Skin, White Masks.* New York: Grove Press.
Fishman, Joshua. A. (1972). Language and Nationalism: Two Integrative Essays. Rowley. MA: Newbury House.
Gellner. Ernst. (1983). *Nations and Nationalism: New Perspectives on the Past.* Oxford: Basil Blackwell.
Grillo, Ralph D. (1989). *Dominant Languages: Language and Hierarchy in Britain and France.* Cambridge: Cambridge University Press.
Haig-Brown, Celia. (1998). *Resistance and Renewal: Surviving the Indian Residential School.* Vancouver, BC: Arsenal Pulp Press.
Haque, Eve. (2012). *Multiculturalism within a Bilingual Framework: Language, Race and Belonging in Canada.* Toronto: University of Toronto Press.
Haque, Eve. (2014). Language Training and Labour Market Integration for Newcomers to Canada. In Valerie Preston, Robert Lathan, Leah Vosko, & Melisa Breton (Eds), *Challenges to Liberating Temporariness: Imagining Alternatives to Permanence as a Pathway for Social Inclusion.* Montreal: McGill–Queen's University Press.
Hastings, Adrian. (1997). *The Construction of Nationhood: Ethnicity, Religion and Nationalism.* Cambridge: Cambridge University Press.
Herriman, Michael & Barbara Burnaby. (1996). Introduction. In Michael Herriman, & Barbara Burnaby (Eds), *Language Policies in English Dominant Countries: Six Case Studies*, pp. 1–14. Philadelphia: Clevedon Multilingual Matters.
McLintock, Anne. (1992). The Angel of Progress: Pitfalls of the Term "Postcolonialism." *Social Text*: 1–15.
Muehlmann, Shaylih & Duchêne, Alexandre. (2007). Beyond the Nation-State: International Agencies as New Sites of Discourses on Bilingualism. In Monica Heller (Ed.), *Bilingualism: A Social Approach*, pp. 96–110. New York: Palgrave Macmillan.
Ngugi wa Thiong'o. (1986). *Decolonising the Mind.* Oxford: James Currey/Heinemann.
Ozkirimli, Umut. (2010). *Theories of Nationalism: A Critical Introduction*, 2nd edn. New York: Palgrave Macmillan.
Phillipson, Robert. (1992). *Linguistic Imperialism.* Oxford: Oxford University Press.
Pujolar, Joan. (2007). Bilingualism and the Nation State in the Post-national Era. In Monica Heller (Ed.), *Bilingualism: A Social Approach*, pp. 71–95. New York: Palgrave Macmillan.
Stasiulis, Daiva & Yuval-Davis, Nira. (1995). Introduction: Beyond Dichotomies – Gender, Race, Ethnicity and Class in Settler Societies. In Daiva Stasiulis & Nira Yuval-Davis (Eds), *Unsettling Settler Societies: Articulations of Gender, Race, Ethnicity and Class*, pp. 1–38. London: Sage.
Veracini, Lorenzo (2010). *Settler Colonialism: A Theoretical Overview.* Hampshire, UK: Palgrave Macmillan.
Weitzer, Ronald. (1990). *Transforming Settler States.* Berkeley: University of California Press.
Wolfe, Patrick. (2006). Settler Colonialism and the Elimination of the Native. *Journal of Genocide Research* 8(4), 387–409.
Wright, Sue. (2004). *Language Policy and Language Planning: From Nationalism to Globalisation.* New York: Palgrave Macmillan.

22
Language in the Age of Globalization

Marco Jacquemet

1 Introduction

In the late 1970s, multinational marketers, financial analysts, and social scientists began clamoring about the dawn of a new age, to be known as the age of globalization. In response, starting in the 1980s, multiple voices, particularly those of historians and political scientists, were raised to object to this characterization of late modernity and/or to critique its social importance. In particular, they pointed out that globalization was not an altogether new phenomenon, considering that the social, economic, and cultural flows that typify it have been shaping people's lives since imperial and colonial times (Kellner 1989). Although globalization is indeed a long-term historical evolution (Braudel 1996, Wallerstein 1974, 2004), it is undeniable that late modernity is experiencing globalization at an unprecedented scale and scope, mostly because of the high degree of space-time compression achieved by the increasing mobility of people, commodities, texts, and knowledge (Harvey 1989, Hannerz 1996, Clifford 1997, Tomlinson 2007). These movements do not happen against the background of a neutral space, but rather are shaped by relations of power and inequality conveyed through "global" languages that cross national boundaries and political allegiances (Blommaert 2009, Coupland 2010).

The novelty of the current wave of globalization is best understood as a development *within* globalization characterized by mobile, deterritorialized people and digital communication technologies playing the central role in organizing social life on a global scale (Appadurai 1996). As a result of these social and technological changes, we witness the growth of a novel, and generalized, global consciousness: people all over the world experience the speed and immediacy of global flows as significant factors in their ability to feel interconnected, to be part of a world where geographical, social, political, and linguistic entities seem to be losing their bounded nature.

As Appadurai (1996) conclusively established two decades ago, transnational migration and digital communication technologies are the two most important diacritics of postindustrial globalization, and where they intersect, we find novel communicative environments shaped by multiple languages transmitted over diverse, at times simultaneous, communicative channels.

Globalization makes a significant impact on language in two ways. First, as people move, they learn new languages, often while maintaining previous ones. The movement of people across borders thus creates multilingual speakers. Second, the movement across borders of resources – both material goods and intangible resources such as knowledge – increases the demand for people with multilingual capabilities. Globalization leads to multilingualism becoming more common and more valuable (Heller 2003).

In this light, contemporary studies of language and communication must address the progressive globalization of communicative practices and social formations that result from the increasing mobility of people, languages, and texts. Accelerating rates of migration around the world, accompanied by communication technologies that enable people to engage with others over multiple locations and channels, have inspired language scholars to study linguistic communities that are diffused and overlapping, in which groups of people, no longer territorially defined, think about themselves and communicate using an array of both face-to-face and long-distance media. As a corollary, these scholars are examining the ways social hierarchies and power asymmetries are reconfigured on a global scale (see Blommaert 2009, Rampton 1995, Fairclough 2002).

My own work is part of this movement in language scholarship and seeks to describe the communicative practices of networks of people exposed to deterritorialized flows and able to interact in different languages and semiotic codes using simultaneously a multiplicity of communicative channels, both near and distant. I use the term *transidioma* to describe these communicative practices at the intersection of mobile people and mobile texts.

After reviewing the literature on language and globalization and addressing critical and pressing issues in this field, this chapter will explore some of these transidiomas and will discuss how they will play an increasingly significant role in the communicative landscapes of the twenty-first century.

2 Historical Perspectives

Modern Western ideas about language originated during the Enlightenment, when the social world came to be seen as composed of bounded entities: clusters of people, confined within geographical and linguistic boundaries and structured by national imaginings of their social identity. These entities were seen as culturally, linguistically, and territorially uniform. Early modern philosophers of both the French Enlightenment (especially Condillac) and German Romanticism (especially Herder) identified a language with a people and a place and, consequently, understood peoplehood according to the criterion of linguistic and territorial unity.

Throughout the nineteenth and most of the twentieth centuries, the legacy of this linkage between territory, cultural tradition, and language pushed scholars interested in language to focus on the emergence of a national consciousness. A people came to be viewed as an "imagined community" held together by shared behavioral norms, beliefs, and values mediated by a common language spoken over a contiguous territory (Anderson 1983). According to Anderson, the creation of imagined communities became possible because of print capitalism. Capitalist entrepreneurs printed books and newspapers in the vernacular of the dominant classes (instead of using languages only preserved in writing, such as Latin) in order to maximize circulation. As a result, these vernaculars became the national language, allowing readers speaking various local varieties to understand each other. Anderson argued that the first nation-states were thus formed around their "national print-languages."

This modern national consciousness was an essential component of the social phenomenon that can be considered the antecedent of linguistic globalization: the imperial colonialism of the nineteenth century. During this period, colonizers' languages spread by means of economic and military conquest, by the emigration of colonists, by cultural influence (especially in regards to education), by the imposition of the "civilizing" influence of religion, and by the introduction of communication technologies (such as the telegraph) able to link distant lands and transmit messages in a common language (Graddol 1996, Crowley 2005). At the same time, as Cohn (1996) argues, the study of native languages became a necessary condition for the colonial project of control and command. As a result of all these factors, colonial encounters led to the emergence of new languages, refashioned the existent local languages (i.e. through lexicography and grammar-writing), and transformed communicative patterns and language relations (Pennycook 1998, Errington 2007).

In the twentieth century, the colonial geography of social and communicative relations evolved into the tense interactions of Cold War international relations and postcolonial movements. This period was marked by the increasing interest of the United States in wielding its political and military power overseas and by the migration of former colonial populations to their European metropolitan centers. These two developments gave rise to two distinct approaches in language studies.

After World War II, the US government took several steps to raise its global influence: foreign service and development agency personnel were engaged in implementing the Marshall Plan, the US Agency for International Development was created, and the US Information Agency brought foreign visitors to the United States. These and other governmental organizations, over time, encouraged academic disciplines to focus their research on a global scale. One strand in the study of language and globalization evolved from research performed at the US Department of State's Foreign Service Institute between 1946 and 1956. During those years, the institute hired a cohort of linguists and anthropologists for the specific purpose of training American diplomats about to be sent abroad. In 1955, Edward T. Hall joined the Foreign Service Institute in Washington, DC, and created, with Ray L. Birdwhistell, George L. Trager, and others, training programs for foreign service officers that focused on the intersection of culture and communication in bilateral exchanges. They explored the effects of space, time, and other nonverbal behavior on human interaction and developed the process of experiential training in intercultural, international settings. In this vein, they studied relationships between American and Japanese businessmen and the reaction of German civilians to American soldiers. This research found its academic home within the emerging departments of communication studies (mostly founded in the 1960s and 1970s) and in the field of international intercultural communication (IIC). Unfortunately, over the years this strand of research lost its linguistic focus and intellectual precision, producing works with a strong applied perspective but for the most part lacking ethnographic and theoretical sophistication (Leeds-Hurwitz 1990).

Meanwhile in Europe, starting in the 1950s, former colonial powers such as Britain and France experienced steady waves of migrants coming from colonized areas in search of economic opportunities. When these opportunities failed to provide migrants with social mobility and integration, a cohort of language scholars became increasingly concerned with the linguistic competence of these low-skilled workers and with the problematic nature of their interactions with the native population.

Sociolinguists, especially those interested in the ethnography of communication (Gumperz and Hymes 1964, 1972), elected to study intercultural communication by focusing on how the "local" community strived to maintain internal boundaries – and to separate themselves from outsiders – through code-switching, linguistic awareness, and ideological patrolling (see in particular Gumperz 1964, Blom and Gumperz 1972). They examined not only linguistic forms but also the nexus of language, power, and interaction to explore how migrants' communicative practices departed from the communicative style of the host country – even when migrants spoke the local language. European locals, who usually occupied the dominant position in interactions with migrants, perceived the migrants' unexpected ways of speaking, structuring information, and producing social meanings as communicative breakdowns. Such setbacks, as

Gumperz suggested (1982), ultimately contributed to larger social problems such as ethnic stereotyping and unequal access to information and opportunities.

This sociolinguistic perspective offered both academics and policymakers not only a means of understanding the role of language in producing social inequality but also ways of identifying causes of miscommunication and strategies for improving communication. Gumperz, for instance, served as a consultant for an educational BBC documentary, *Crosstalk* (1979), which addressed the subtleties of intercultural communication in multicultural workplaces in London. In addition, his work inspired other scholars to share, with nonacademic audiences, sociolinguistic insights into intercultural dynamics.

The work of sociolinguists such as Gumperz and Ferguson led most language scholars interested in the transnational nature of late modern communicative environments to focus on issues of multilingualism and its related practices, such as diglossia, code-switching, and code-mixing (Urciuoli 1991, Auer 1998, Woolard 2005, Blommaert 2010, Blommaert and Rampton 2011, Hall and Nilep forthcoming). These scholars have examined current multilingualism in the context of the postindustrial wave of migration, made up of transnational migrants (or "transmigrants") who sustain a multiplicity of involvements in both home and host countries, made possible by their networks of interpersonal relationships. Transmigrants develop a "triadic geography of belonging" (Vertovec 2007), composed of their relation to place of residence, their creation of myths of homeland, and their imagination of the diasporic community. Transmigrants thus develop multilingual practices that are necessarily fluid, mixed, and relatively unbounded.

Moreover, language scholars need to incorporate in language analysis the study of how people express themselves through communication technologies. Until recently, the study of electronic media had been neglected by language scholars, who left the subject to scholars in the fields of media/cultural studies (Gitlin 1983, Baudrillard 1984, Ang 1985, 1996, Morley 1986, 1992). Most of these media/cultural studies, however, disparaged fieldwork in favor of more abstract theoretical exercises, were overdependent on textual criticism, and suffered from inattention to linguistic detail. They neglected to analyze the indexical/pragmatic aspects of media communication and the global spread of media idioms (Murphy 1999). It was only in the first decade of the twenty-first century that, while media scholars finally acknowledged the need for an ethnographic perspective (Kraidy and Murphy 2004, Ginsburg et al. 2002), language scholars started using ethnographic methods to study how communication technologies (particularly computer-mediated communication) have provided speakers with distinct techniques and resources to generate speech and create meaning (Spitulnik 1996, Crystal 2000, Danet and Herring 2007).

3 Critical Issues and Topics

The study of communication in globalized settings has brought to the foreground a myriad of pressing issues. Within sociolinguistics, the following have been subject to particular scrutiny: 1) the discourse on language endangerment and creation; 2) the modern understanding of what constitutes a language, 3) the play between local and global scales, 4) the impact of media technologies on communicative practices, and 5) the political economy of linguistic globalization.

3.1 Language Endangerment and Creation

In studies of the link between language and globalization, we find two prominent and opposing strands, each built on the belief that diversity is desirable but differing in what *counts* as linguistic diversity (Billings 2014, see also Jacquemet 2005). One strand is distinguished by its dystopic vision, in which the spread of English and other global languages is seen as a force that is wiping out linguistic diversity through linguistic imperialism, causing languages to become endangered, lost, or even extinct (Phillipson 1992, Crystal 2000, Nettle and Romaine 2000). The second strand of literature presents a more optimistic perspective and explores how global cultural flows have made linguistic and communicative resources available locally for the creation of communicative mutations. This strand generated an impressive array of new concepts (discussed below) in an attempt to address the progressive globalization of communicative practices and social formations resulting from the increasing mobility of people, languages, and texts. Notwithstanding their optimism about language change, most studies in this strand recognize the asymmetrical power relations engendered by global flows.

Language scholars in the first strand believe that globalization – and the increased contact and power asymmetry between languages that it entails – leads to a severe reduction of the number of languages spoken around the world. According to recent estimates, most of the approximately 6,000 languages "alive" today are in serious danger of disappearing. Only 600 languages are "safe" and expected to survive very long (Dorian 1989, Nettle and Romaine 2000, Thomason 2001). This fact has prompted more than one linguist to declare a state of emergency, urging governments and scholars alike to attend to the ongoing "catastrophic destruction of the linguistic world" (Krauss 1992: 7).

In the 1990s, language scholars mobilized to promote the documentation and preservation of endangered languages through various agencies created for this purpose (such as the Linguistic Society of America's Committee on Endangered Languages and their Preservation, the Endangered Language Fund, and the International Clearing House for Endangered Languages) and pressure governmental bodies to take action against language death. This movement produced the 1996 Declaration of Universal Linguistic Rights, which sought to protect "the rights of language communities which are historically established in their own territory, the rights of language groups with different degrees of historicity and self-identification, and those of individuals living outside their community of origin" (from www.linguistic-declaration.org).

Today's ecolinguistic movement is "concerned about the future of the world's biological, cultural, and linguistic diversity" and believes that "unless action is taken to support and foster linguistic diversity, ... perhaps 50 percent of the extant oral languages – conceivably as many as 90 percent – may become extinct, or doomed to extinction" (quotes from www.terralingua.org).

Globalization is understood by the ecolinguistic movement as a destructive force, causing the penetration of a few dominant languages into fragile linguistic areas and widespread loss of oral languages. Because of this perspective, I characterize this movement as the dystopic strand in the debate over globalization and culture.

Language deaths may be sad events, but whether they warrant the ecolinguists' call to arms is often questionable. When a language disappears because its speakers are killed or forced to adopt a new language, ecolinguists (and others) are indeed justified in mobilizing a political response to this violence. But laments over endangered languages – including the media coverage that language deaths tend to receive – often reveal naive assumptions about language, its evolution, and its diversity.

The claim that a language has disappeared or is disappearing is in itself a problematic one. When did Latin die? Did Hebrew die and was it later resuscitated or has it always lived? Behind every declaration of the "death" of a language lies the assumption that this language had a fixed, immutable, and formal denotational structure and system of pragmatic use. It was a "standard" language, in other words, that maintained a recognizable structure over time. This implies, as Silverstein argued, a horizon of linguistic purity, origin, and isolation, free of any evidence of the "massive mutual interinfluencing of denotational codes under complex speech-community conditions even in precolonial, predocumentation eras." (1998: 409). There is ample evidence – left by missionaries, traders, anthropologists, and linguists – that many "endangered" languages have in fact seen various phases of evolution in just the past four centuries, rendering problematic the choice of a particular moment for codification of the linguistic norms and rules that must be saved. The standardization and teaching of a synchronic slice of the "heritage" language could be as damaging to its speakers as its obsolescence.

Ecolinguists draw an analogy between languages and biological species. They have produced a discourse centered on loss of cultural diversity, arguing that with language loss a large part of a culture will vanish forever. As Thomason writes in an otherwise excellent review of the field of language contact: "Every loss of a language deprives us of a window into the human mind and the human spirit; every language that dies deprives us of a unique repository of human experience and thought." (2001: 223)

This dystopic perspective reveals, as argued by Silverstein, a "most naive Whorfianism about culture and so-called 'world-view' " (1998: 422).[1] The "language as a living museum" argument (see Nettle and Romaine 2000) assumes that the denotational code defines the worldview. This argument is at odds with contemporary research on the nexus of language and culture, which shows that the language people speak does not determine the way they think and behave (Levinson and Gumperz 1996). Moreover, this perspective is blind to the emergence of new linguistic formations in pidgins, creoles, and other mixed languages.

In sum, the ecolinguistic view is rooted in a fundamentally flawed understanding of the relationship between language and culture, since it essentializes what a "language" is and how it determines its "culture," strips local speakers of agency, opposes "good" to "bad" languages, disregards the way "foreign" linguistic materials can be used to form new languages, and sensationalizes linguistic loss as social catastrophe.

Rather than lamenting the homogenizing forces of globalization, the opposing strand of scholarship points out the creative potential for language mixing, hybridization, and creolization that English and other global languages bring to local communicative environments. Some of the resulting communicative mutations include South Asian hip-hop (Pennycook 2007), African grassroots literature (Blommaert 2008), South African performances of identity (Higgins 2009), and Tanzanian beauty contests (Billings 2014). Studies of these mutations have shown that groups of speakers exposed to deterritorialized communicative flows employ English and other "imperial" or "dominant" linguistic materials for interactional and symbolic effect. In this strand of scholarship, globalizing processes offer opportunities for creative and empowering communicative practices to flourish. English, for instance, can be seen as a major positive force behind the evolution of new languages, including known pidgins and creoles (where, according to Thomason, English is "by a large margin the most frequent lexifier language," 2001: 164) and of new media idioms – such as global advertising, newscasts, religious tracts (Aravamudan 2001, 2006),[2] as well as netpidgins (such as "Euro-English").[3]

Another linguistic phenomenon associated with globalization is the emergence of new languages and new varieties of older ones. In the case of English, linguists have begun to talk about "Englishes" or "English languages" to acknowledge the emerging differences among the regions where English is the first or national language (Kachru 1982, 1986, Platt et al. 1984, Gorlach 1991, Smith and Forman 1997, Schneider 1997, McArthur 1998, Nero 2001).[4] Furthermore, in a recent review of contact languages, 507 "new" languages were listed, including 372 creoles and pidgins, and 135 mixed languages. There is strong documentation of many functioning creoles and mixed languages, from the Berbice Dutch Creole of Guyana (Kouwenberg 1994) to Michif, one of the languages of the Métis of Canada, to the Media Lengua of Ecuador

(Muysken 1997). In some cases pidgins and creoles have become national languages, as in the rise of Bislama from pidgin to the national language of Vanuatu (Crowley 1989), or the evolution of Tok Pisin in Papua New Guinea (Roumaine 1992). However, most of these languages are still not recognized as such by a discipline straight-jacketed by formalist notions of what constitutes a language.

3.2 The Nature of Language

Although scholarship in language studies traditionally conceptualized interaction as taking place in a single language, a growing body of research in sociocultural linguistics views multilingual interaction as a norm instead of an exception. As a consequence, it has questioned the very core of the modern understanding of what constitutes a language and how to define the boundaries between languages.

As discussed earlier, the majority of scholars interested in language in the nineteenth and twentieth centuries conceived of languages as bounded entities corresponding to specific peoples and places. Because of this, they failed to investigate the linguistic mutations resulting from communicative practices in the multiple crevasses, open spaces, and networked ensembles of contact zones.[5]

This situation is now evolving. Recent scholarship, as Hall and Nilep (forthcoming) pointed out, "has focused on linguistic hybridity instead of uniformity, movement instead of stasis, and borders instead of interiors." This shift has two profound consequences. First, the experience of de- and reterritorialization and the sociolinguistic disorder it entails require a serious reconceptualization of the connection between communication and shared knowledge. Because of the multilingual and multicultural nature of an increasing number of contemporary settings, scholars can no longer assume that such shared knowledge exists to provide a common ground from which to negotiate conflicts and agendas. The identification and establishment of common ground itself must be understood as a major challenge in the process of communication (Rampton 1998, Gee 1999).

Second, deterritorialization forces us to look at the ideological process of making and patrolling the boundary of a social formation that is no longer territorially confined. Linguistic anthropology has investigated the ideological formation of social identity through shared knowledge (Gumperz 1982), national consciousness (Gal 1979, Woolard 1989), and political activism (Urban and Sherzer 1991) within geographically bounded languages, but it must now raise the question of how groups of people no longer territorially defined think about their multiple voices and recombinant identities.

With these issues in mind, scholars writing about the "superdiversity" of language in digital environments and metropolitan areas (e.g. Blommaert and Rampton 2011) tend to approach social mixture as the norm and treat multilingualism as the default mode for interaction in the new global economy. Their research focuses on the border-crossing communicative practices and speakers who were marginalized in previous generations of scholarship. As Blommaert points out, an individual speaker's national identity and ethnolinguistic identity often do not match, and his or her ethnolinguistic identity must be understood as shaped by the impact of "spatial trajectories" on language acquisition (2003: 616). One of the consequences of globalization is that communicative practices and cultural knowledge, rather than marking an individual's point of origin, index an itinerary across linguistic communities, which can be traced through the speaker's linguistic mixtures and blends of accents, lexemes, speech styles, and genres.

This line of inquiry eventually calls into question the concept of language itself: in globalized environments, what counts is not what "language" one speaks but the capacity to make oneself understood by others (based on translinguistic semiotic forms) and be seen as a normal social being (based on socioculturally shared norms and values). In this logic, the ideological formations constituting what is "proper" language give way to concerns over semiotic understandings and intercultural codes of communicative behavior, rather than over shared knowledge.

In this logic, the study of multilingualism in transnational communities has generated an impressive array of new terminology to try to explain the increasingly unbounded nature of communicative practices through which speakers not only engage with their immediate surroundings (by developing locally appropriate cultural and communicative competencies), but also activate wider flows (allowing them to stay in touch with distant social realities and alternative social imaginations). Just in the first decade of the twenty-first century, language scholars, never too shy to create new words, have introduced the following terms: codemeshing (Canagarajah 2006), transidiomatic practices (Jacquemet 2005), truncated multilingualism (Blommaert et al. 2005), transnational heteroglossia (Bailey 2007), polylingualism (Jørgensen 2008), translanguaging (García 2009), plurilingualism (Canagarajah 2009), flexible bilingualism (Creese and Blackledge 2010), heterolingualism (Pratt et al. 2011), metrolingualism (Otsuji and Pennycook 2011), translingual practices (Canagarajah 2011), and transglossic language practices (Sultana et al. 2015). This impressive list of terms is evidence of a movement within language studies to develop new tools to analyze a transformed communicative landscape – tools that had never been needed in the traditional sociolinguistic studies which assumed that languages were bounded entities.

3.3 Local and Global Scales

As commodities, texts, people, and languages move through space and time, their significance and substance are reworked into locally based categories of meaning – in other words, global flows are reterritorialized according to local cultural practices. As Bollywood stories of arranged marriages and star-crossed lovers find a sympathetic audience with conservative Nigerian Muslims (Larkin 2008), or Hollywood romance movies are embraced by Nairobi's women as emblems of personal and financial independence (Spronk 2009), so the use of English and other global languages is recontextualized to reflect local ideologies, practices, and institutions. For instance, Pennycook (2007) traced how African-American hip-hop words mixed with local communicative practices in South Asia give birth to popular musical forms that both reference hip-hop roots and produce unmistakably local styles and performances. Similarly, Jacquemet (2005) illustrated how urban Albanian speakers utilized linguistic fragments from American pop music, Italian TV shows, and online advertising to produce linguistic mutations that index their cosmopolitanism and cultural self-fashionings (such as *don uorri*, a mutation out of the American syntagm "don't worry"). Along these same lines, Billings' study of Tanzanian beauty pageants (2014) shows how contestants use highly fragmented and nonstandard English speech as cultural capital to display their status and education.

The local adoption of transcultural communicative flows complexifies the relationship between these local practices and regional or global centers. Tanzanian beauty pageant speech or Albanian linguistic creations may have a very different reception in nonlocal settings, where they could be viewed as indexes of linguistic incompetence. This phenomenon reflects the tension between core and periphery: even in the periphery – in areas removed from centers of global power – values and standards for use of global languages are dictated by core, metropolitan desires to maintain class and race distinctions. The ability to speak a globally commodified language, such as English, in a way that is acceptable locally may indicate a "cosmopolitan" person in that peripheric setting, but that same manner of speaking may, in a global center, point to the inferior status of this speaker: her marked, "unorthodox" communicative style becomes an index of her outsider, marginalized status. Not all settings are endowed with the same power to set standards and determine value. As linguistic resources move from one locale to another and from the periphery to global centers, their functions and meanings shift in accordance with the contextually dominant linguistic ideology: "the English spoken by a middle-class person in Nairobi may not be (and is unlikely to be) perceived as a middle-class attribute in London or New York" (Blommaert 2010: 38).

In a world where the size and boundedness of social entities cannot be assumed to be fixed, *scale* becomes the best available spatial metaphor to understand the embedded nature and multiple planes of human interaction. Applied to the study of globalization, scale refers to the idea that a given human activity may have different meanings when viewed within contexts of varying geographic scope. Language use in a specific communicative event evokes multiple spatiotemporal scales, from the local to the national to the transnational, and participants in the event may evaluate communicative competence in very distinct, and at times opposing, ways, according to their scale of reference – as in the case mentioned above of the English spoken by a Nairobian. On the other hand, while a nonstandard variety of English developed and viewed positively in a given location (say, Nairobi) may be negatively indexed by dominant core groups, as we have discussed above, this same nonstandard variety may find a more sympathetic audience among people who have recently arrived in the metropole (for instance, other African migrants to London). Often, nonstandard speakers find social and political alliances and smoother lines of communication with other nonstandard speakers. A well-known fact about European Union meetings is that nonnative English speakers (Spaniards, Italians, Greeks, and so on) often happily and efficiently converse among themselves in an accented English that British native speakers find difficult to comprehend and interact with (EU interpreter/translator Diego Marani has written about this communicative situation in his blog *Europanto*, http://www.europanto.be/gram.en.html).

Finally, scales are organized in fundamentally stratified ways. By investigating the hierarchical organization of scales, scholars can better understand power and inequality at the heart of sociolinguistic life (Blommaert, Collins, and Slembrouck 2005, Blommaert 2003, 2010, Collins 2009). A logical next step for language scholarship would be to understand how "scalar" communicative competence works: how particular communicative routines can be successful in one scale of reference and a failure in a different one, according to the hierarchically layered communicative regimes.

3.4 Digital Communication Technologies

An understanding of scales is particularly relevant to the study of digital communication. These technologies can support communicative practices among people at multiple scalar levels. Digital communications can be produced by single individuals at home as well as by production teams spread over multiple continents. Likewise, the recipients of these communications can range from a neighborhood to a global market. Thanks to this multiscalar nature of digital communication technologies, people using these technologies confront expanded rules and resources for the construction of social identity and cultural belonging: "when the rapid, mass-mediated flow of images, scenarios, and emotions merges with the flow of deterritorialized audiences, the result is a recombination in the production of modern subjectivity" (Appadurai 1996: 39). When Moroccan families make videotapes of their weddings to send to relatives who migrated to Italy (Jacquemet 1996), when an international and diasporic community interacts simultaneously on Facebook and face-to-face (Jacquemet 2013), or when Pakistani taxi-drivers in Chicago listen to sermons recorded in mosques in Kabul or Teheran (Appadurai 1996), we witness the deployment of mobile media practices over multiple scales, creating multiple zones of transnational interactions. In these zones, a new, deterritorialized social identity takes shape, light-years away from the corporate logic of the nation-state. This new identity coagulates around a sentiment of belonging that can no longer be identified with a purely territorial dimension, and finds its expression in the creolized, mixed idioms of the transidioma (more below on this concept).

Moreover, the sampling and recontextualizing of media content, a capability specific to digital technologies, are becoming basic communicative practices in media cultures characterized by linguistic bricolage and by the increasing tendency to incorporate conversational speech styles into public discourse. This phenomenon gives rise to "dense interpenetration of local performances with styles of speech that are reflexively designed, produced, and disseminated though mass mediated institutional and/or electronic communication systems" (Rampton 1998: 423, 2006).

Digital communication technologies do much more than facilitate people's interactivity and mobility: they alter the very nature of this interactivity, transforming people's sense of place, belonging, and social relations. We are currently witnessing the emergence of digitally mediated communicative practices, occupying a space in the everyday flow of experience that is distinct yet integrated with face-to-face interactions of physical proximity. Digital communication technologies are transforming human experience in all its dimensions. These transformations can be observed in both social relations (now globalized and deterritorialized) and economic processes (with their shifting methods of production, delivery, and consumption). In addition, digital communication technologies produce not only new conveniences and entertainments, but also new anxieties – as in the discourse about information overload – and pathologies – as in the discourse about Internet addictions (Tomlinson 2007). In this context, few of the experiences with present-day electronic media have any historical counterparts beyond the last few decades.

Among these experiences, two phenomena in particular warrant further research: the layering of digital information over material environments (a phenomenon referred to as *augmented reality*) and the transformation of knowledge infrastructure as a result of digital automatisms for information storage, search, and retrieval. People nowadays are interfacing with digital devices in most current situations: to navigate in traffic, reach a destination, take a picture, seek out information, interact in a foreign language. In all these contexts, we witness the emergence of a new kind of machine–human interaction with its own linguistic rules, communicative modalities, and social norms. While this interaction has received some attention from social scientists (Boelstorff 2008), language scholars have yet to focus their analytical tools on the communicative aspects of these phenomena.

3.5 The Political Economy of Linguistic Globalization

One of the essential elements of globalization has been a transformation of the forms and processes of labor and their linguistic effects. Specifically, along with the movement toward globalization there has been a passage, especially salient in Western economies, from the hegemony of material, industrial labor to the hegemony of symbolic, postindustrial labor. The passage to a postindustrial system does not mean the disappearance of industrial production (which is now mostly concentrated in production centers in the global South characterized by extremely exploitative labor conditions). Instead, it marks a shift from labor-intensive production based on centralized coordination, requiring a single language easily understandable along a chain of command (Deleuze and Guattari's (1987) famous *order-words*), to a late capitalist regime where the value of production is substantially enhanced through the circulation of products (including semiotic products, from advertisements to social media content) on a global scale (Heller 2010).

In a globalized, postindustrial world where circulation plays a key economic role, the knowledge of multiple languages becomes not only a resource but also a global commodity.

Two strands of recent scholarship focus on language in the global economy. One strand looks at languages (and multilingualism) as essential commodities of the global economy. The production and manipulation of information and images, the necessity of communicating across languages and time-zones, and the need to be present in multiple markets provide communicative practices with added exchange value, turning them into commodities. The claim that communicative practices have become commodities is not just a metaphor: scholars can now trace the financial value of multilingual competence. For instance, in some Canadian call centers, the ability to speak both French and English is worth about a dollar an hour more pay than that received by monolingual English speakers (Heller 2010). Translators of written texts charge by the word. Consumers of "exotic" goods request performance of linguistic authenticity (as expressed, for instance, in the language on labels) as part of what they are buying (Cavanaugh and Shankar 2015).

The second strand looks at the role of language in the service economy. Language plays a crucial role in what has been termed "affective labor," that is, labor that forges interpersonal relationships through contact that can be direct (as in the service economy) or virtual (as in the production of entertainment). Health care workers, screenwriters, and flight attendants are examples of this affective labor. Their work results in a material product – such as a stitched wound, a script, or served food – but they also create affects, such as a sense of well-being in a patient, an emotional response in a viewer, or satisfaction in a traveler. In a global economy, affective labor is performed in densely multilingual environments where communicative competence needs to be based on intercultural knowledge. Expanding the global circulation of goods and people requires affective management based on effective communicative skills in mediation and transaction.

4 Current Contributions and Research

The transformed communicative landscape outlined above has important implications in at least two fields of sociolinguistic inquiry: literacy and mobility.

4.1 Studying Grassroots Literacy

In the world shaped by cultural globalization, developments in metropolitan cores have effects on their peripheries, but at the same time these peripheries play a role in complexifying normative understanding of this world. Grassroots literacy, i.e. the spontaneous emergence of written vernaculars not in conformity with nationally recognized standards, is a case in point, providing examples of ways that unorthodox codes, once inserted in global circulation through cell phones and internet, bring with them an added complexity to current understanding of language and communication.

Texts do not quickly or easily communicate the messages they contain: a text written in the margins of a nation-state using nonstandard spelling may be perfectly understandable at the local scale, but its meaning increasingly disappears in the widening gap between local practices and literacy orthodoxies at the national and international scales. As Blommaert notes, "What is perfectly appropriate writing in one place becomes a meaningless sign system in another. Texts may travel easily, but the system of use, value, and function in which they were produced usually does not travel with them" (2008: 6). On the other hand, while nation-states (and their educational policymakers) worry about writing standards and the decline of literacy skills, we find a growing gap between their national ideologies and the textual practices of globalized writers.

Further, the intensive use of online and mobile communication technologies opens a vast opportunity for forms of informal learning, offering users access to vocabularies, registers, genres, and styles, as well as cultural templates for practices. In spite of moral panics and public anxieties (including critical views on the effects of texting on literacy), people active in the communicative environment shaped by digital technologies are reading and writing more than ever before. Text messaging, instant messaging, chatting, blogging, and tweeting – all constitute platforms of literacy and literacy acquisition, although research has shown that most people do not think of their electronic or digital communications as "real" writing or reading (see Lenhart et al. 2008).

The newly created field of grassroots literacy studies (Blommaert 2008) seeks to investigate the forms and norms of what constitutes a text in a globalized world. Literacy scholars are now confronted by written products that do not look at all like polished text: instead, they are composed of broken sentences, incorporating visual features (such as the infamous smileys), abbreviations, and multimedia links. Of particular significance is the incorporation into these texts of *vernacular language* – that is, graphic replicas of spoken forms, including code-switching, colloquialisms, or other "impurities."

Take, for instance, the text messages sent by an undocumented Tunisian migrant to his Italian friend (as they were recorded in Giulia Bondi's documentary *Harraguantanamo*, produced in 2011, original text on the left):

Tchawe Joulya.je suis arrive` a Catania.je sais pas *ci en desson* la` ou *en pass* a Napoli.je vais te parle` *ci il a* de nouveau. *Tchawe* bella. :-* 6:55 04/04/2011	Ciao Giulia.i arrived in Catania I don't know if we disembark here or we go to Naples. i'm going to tell you if there's something new. Ciao bella.:-* 6:55 am 4/4/2011

In this text we found many features of grassroots literacy (in italics): graphic replicas of spoken words ("tchawe" for the Italian greeting "ciao," "desson" for the French third person singular present form of the verb descendre "descend," "ci il a" for the French construct "s'il y a"), lack of punctuation and proper spacing, and graphic signs (the emoticon). Two more text messages from the same corpus can further illustrate these features:

Senuit 21personnes *on feui* La police *ouvrire* le feu sur*1* 01:21 10/04/2011	Tonight 21 people escaped The police opened fire against one of them 1:21 am 4/10/2011

Hay ma belle, les personnes *qui'ils ont fewi ils ont rontres aujourdhui.me* la police *rufise ses rentres o sontre*. Ah ((je te monque.et oui)) 10:14 10/04/2011	Hey my beautiful, the people who escaped came back today. But the police is refusing to let them in or out. Well ((I'm teasing you. oh yes)) 10:14 am 4/10/2011

Of particular note in these two messages is their unstable morphology (feui/fewi), making it extremely difficult to analyze them and to reach conclusions on what constitutes their "language."

4.2 For a Sociolinguistics of Mobility: Superdiversity and Transidioma

Sophisticated technologies for rapid human mobility and electronic global communication – such as high-capacity airplanes, television cable lines and satellite link-ups, fixed and mobile telephony, and the Internet – are producing communicative environments where multiple languages and channels of interaction are simultaneously evoked by transnational speakers no longer anchored in clearly identifiable national languages (De Swaan 2001; Jacquemet 2005; Danet and Herring 2007; Pennycook 2007).

European language scholars working on this cluster of mobile people and mobile media are increasingly evoking the paradigm of "superdiversity" to refer to the vastly increased range of linguistic, religious, ethnic, and cultural resources characterizing late modern societies. The term was coined by Steve Vertovec in a review of demographic and socioeconomic changes in post-Cold War Britain: "Super-diversity underscores the fact that the new conjunctions and interactions of variables that have arisen over the past decade surpass the ways – in public discourse, policy debates and academic literature – that we usually understand diversity in Britain." (2007: 1–2)

As Blommaert and Rampton 2011 pointed out, superdiversity should be understood as *diversification of diversity* due to changes in migration patterns in Europe and elsewhere. This diversity cannot be understood in terms of multiculturalism (the presence of multiple cultures in one society) alone. At the basis of this shift are the changing patterns and itineraries of migration into Europe and the continued migration by the same people inside Europe: "More people are now moving from more places, through more places, to more places" (Vertovec 2010: 86). In effect, people bring with them ever more varied resources and experiences from different places in their everyday interactions and encounters with others and institutions.

The term "superdiversity" does have numerous limitations and a growing list of critics who object to its imprecise theoretical fuzziness, a lack of engagement with political theory, a metropolitan Eurocentric bias, and a neoliberal euphoric thrust, exemplified by the prefix "super." Nevertheless, this concept evokes the mutated reality of contemporary metropolitan life. The world is now full of settings where deterritorialized speakers use a mixture of languages in interacting with family, friends, and co-workers; read English and other "global" languages on their computer screens; watch local, regional, or global broadcasts; and access popular culture in a variety of languages. Such settings will become ever more widespread in the future and superdiversity will become the standard modality.

The usefulness of the concept of superdiversity is particularly evident if we extend its reach to the analysis of the communicative mutations resulting not only from complex migration flows but also from developments in the field of communication technologies The contemporary complexity of migration depends on, and is enabled by, communicative technologies that have made digital media accessible to everyone, via mobile phones and linked computers, producing an epochal transformation in access to knowledge infrastructure (just think of Google) and in long-distance interactions. Transcontinental travels, transnational moves, chain migrations, and diasporic networks have been greatly facilitated by these new technologies. In turn, migration and technological innovations result in mutated communicative repertoires and more complex forms of communication. Language scholars, however, have been slow to examine the intersection of mobile people and mobile texts. In the last decade, we find solid work on migration and language and also heightened attention to the linguistic analysis of electronic technologies, but there has been very little research that combines these two fields. Blommaert (2011) is a notable exception, as is Jørgensen et al. (2011).

In order to examine not only migrants' linguistic practices but also their (and others') digital interactions, I developed the concept of "transidioma/transidiomatic practices" (Jacquemet 2005, 2015). Through the concept of "transidioma" I seek to investigate the communicative practices of groups of people, no longer territorially defined, who use an array of both face-to-face and long-distance media, thus combining multilingual and multimedia digital communication.

Transidiomas are found in environments that are characterized by the co-presence of multilingual talk and digital media. No longer solely contained in areas of colonial and postcolonial contact, transidiomas flow through the multiple channels of electronic communication over the entire world, from contact zones, borderlands, and diasporic nets of relationships to the most remote and apparently isolated areas of the globe. Globalized settings are clearly transidiomatic. For instance, in Indian calling centers we find phone operators talking in English(es) with their long-distance customers, using the local language(s) to interact with management and co-workers, reading English and other "global" languages on their computer screens, and at times listening to American pop music. Other obviously transidiomatic settings include videoconferences by the personnel of multinational companies, multilingual social media, or the command centers of international military forces. In addition, I would argue that today most settings (from living rooms to hospital operating rooms to political meetings) experience a localized multilingualism, interacting with the digital technologies of contemporary communication.

Transidiomatic practices are most often employed by people with the linguistic and cognitive skills to operate in multiple, overlapping communicative frames. The codes they use to communicate depend on the contextual nature of their multisite interactions, but are necessarily mixed, translated, creolized. Transidiomatic practices are often the products of linguistic innovations grafted onto an English structure, but any number of other languages could be involved in these recombinations. The social world is increasingly composed of settings where speakers use a mixture of languages in interacting face-to-face with known and unknown people; these settings become "transidiomatic" when the participants *habitually* read English and/or other global languages on their computer screens, watch local, regional, or global broadcasts, listen to pop music in various languages, and interact via cellular phones with nonpresent contacts. In these environments, speakers use mobile, real-time communication devices (from laptops to cell phones to wi-fi enabled tablets) to enhance everyday social interactions, producing a massively fluid, layered communicative style that relies on access to multiple communicative channels to achieve its shape.

The focus here is on *habitus*: I do not claim that all multilingual settings are now transidiomatic, but for analytical purposes I want to flag the increasing number of communicative environments where we find that the co-mingling of localized, multilingual interactions and digitally mediated, distant communication is producing linguistic habits and communicative mutations that are redefining the entire field of language and communication studies.

The concept of transidioma challenges researchers to look at multiple linguistic forms, indexicalities, and power relations in mobile and media-saturated contexts, where different repertoires from various languages may be simultaneously activated, over a range of multiple channels, depending on the social desires and linguistic ideologies at play in a particular environment. These transidiomatic practices have been developing for a while, but they have become much more prevalent and pervasive due to recent developments in communication technology, making them the main force shaping communicative patterns in the early part of the twenty-first century.

Future Directions

Globalization today requires language scholars not only to conceptualize a "linguistics of contact" resulting from the "randomness and disorder of the flows of people, knowledge, texts and objects across social and geographical space, in the boundaries of inclusion and exclusion, and in fragmentation, indeterminacy and ambivalence" (Rampton 1998: 125, see also Pratt 1987, 1991), but also, more importantly, to examine communicative practices based on disorderly recombinations and language mixings occurring simultaneously in local and distant environments. In other words, it is time to conceptualize a linguistics of xenoglossic becoming, transidiomatic mixing, and communicative recombinations.

Finally, language and culture scholars need to focus on power-saturated environments, such as asylum hearings, multilingual communication in war operations, long-distance medical interpreting, or business teleconferences. In all these environments we find deep asymmetries among participants based on the intersectionality of status, role, multilinguistic communicative competence, and technological facility. This is the world that is awaiting our sociolinguistic analysis, a world where indexicalities and ideologies can no longer be solely embedded in national languages and international codes, but must also be found in the multiple transidiomatic practices of de/reterritorialized speakers. This paradigmatic shift should shape the analysis of cultural becoming, social mutations, and recombinant identities, and allow language scholars to begin to understand communication as the tactical deployment of transidiomatic practices by social formations able to imagine themselves, interact, and mutate while tossed about in a whirlpool of electronic, communicative turbulence.

Related Topics

6 Being in the Cloud (LeBlanc-Wories); **18** New and Emergent Languages (Riley); **20** Language, Immigration, and the Nation-State (Pujolar); **23** The Emergence of Creoles and Language Change (Mufwene); **28** Language Maintenance and Revitalization (Cowell); **30** The Politics of Language Endangerment (Meek).

Notes

1 A single quote will suffice: "When one or more languages are chosen for mega-communication, the small communication zones wither away, resulting in loss of culture." (Pattanayak 1996: 145)
2 "Far more practically efficacious than the productions of South Asia's admittedly talented Anglophone authors, guru English is the most globalized of South Asian cosmopolitanism, delivering neo-Orientalist wisdom in modernized idiom." (Aravamundan 2001: 27)
3 "Flipping through the Nettime reader, I noticed again and again, kinds of 'Euro-English', at once charming and strange. It's a temptation, as a native speaker, to think these usages are 'wrong'. But I think there's a better way of seeing it. What I think the net makes possible is the circulation of the very wide range of forms of English as a second language that have existed for some time, and which are, via the net, coming more and more in contact with each other. (. . .) When non-English language speakers start writing in English, elements of their native grammar and style come into English. This enriches English immeasurably, I think, so long as the way in which English is being used in a given non-native context is reasonably coherent. (. . .) A fantastic hybrid of ways of becoming in language. A wacky sidebar to the Sapir-Whorf hypothesis." (McKenzie Ward 1996, www.nettime.org/nettime.w3archive)
4 These varieties have also a great influence on "standard" English. For instance, as Holborow (1999: 191) noted, "the new words contributed not only by the media and the trading floor but also by the black slang which buzzes between Brooklyn, Trenchtown, Brixton, and Soweto."
5 For a critical reading of this tradition, see Woolard 1999.

References

Anderson, B. (1983) *Imagined Communities*. London: Verso.
Ang, I. (1985) *Watching Dallas: Soap Opera and the Melodramatic Imagination*. London: Methueun.
———. (1996) *Living Room Wars: Rethinking Media Audiences for a Postmodern World*. London: Routledge.
Appadurai, A. (1996) *Modernity at Large*. Minneapolis: Minnesota University Press
Aravamudan, S. (2001) Guru English. *Social Text 66, 19*(1): 19–44.
———. (2006) *Guru English*. Princeton University Press.

Auer, P. (1998) *Code-Switching in Conversation: Language, Interaction, and Identity*. London: Routledge.
Bailey, B. (2007) Heteroglossia and boundaries. In Heller, M. (ed.) *Bilingualism: A Social Approach*. London: Palgrave.
Baudrillard, J. (1984) *Simulations*. New York: Semiotext(e).
Billings, S. (2014) *Language, Globalization and the Making of a Tanzanian Beauty Queen*. Bristol: Multilingual Matters.
Blom, J.P. and Gumperz, J. (1972) Social Meaning in Linguistic Structures. In J. Gumperz and D. Hymes (eds.) *Directions in Socio-linguistics: the Ethnography of Communication*, 407–434. New York: Holt, Rinehart, and Winston.
Blommaert, J. (2003). Commentary: A sociolinguistics of globalization. *Journal of Sociolinguistics* 7: 607–623.
———. (2005) *Discourse: A Critical Introduction*. Cambridge: Cambridge University Press.
———. (2008) *Grassroots Literacy: Writing, Identity and Voice in Central Africa*. London: Routledge.
———. (2009) Language, asylum, and the national order. *Current Anthropology* 50(4): 415.
———. (2010) *The Sociolinguistics of Globalization*. Cambridge: Cambridge University Press.
Blommaert, J., Collins, J., and Slembrouck, S. (2005) Spaces of multilingualism. *Language and Communication* 25: 197–216.
Blommaert, J. and Rampton, B. (2011) Language and superdiversity. *Diversities* 13(2), 1–21.
Boellstorff, T. (2008) *Coming of Age in Second Life*. Princeton University Press.
Braudel, F. (1996) [1949] *The Mediterranean and the Mediterranean World in the Age of Philip II*. Berkeley: University of California Press.
Canagarajah, A. S. (2006). The place of world Englishes in composition: Pluralization continued. *College Composition and Communication* 57(4): 586–619.
———. (2009) The plurilingual tradition and the English language in South Asia. *AILA Review* 22(1): 5–22.
———. (2011) Codemeshing in academic writing: Identifying teachable strategies of translanguaging. *The Modern Language Journal* 95(iii): 401–417.
Cavanaugh, J. and Shankar, S. (eds) (2015) *Language and Materiality*. Oxford University Press.
Chouliaraki, L. and Fairclough, N. (1999) *Discourse in Late Modernity*. Edinburgh University Press.
Clifford, J. (1997) *Routes*. Cambridge, MA: Harvard University Press.
Cohn, B. (1996) *Colonialism and its Forms of Knowledge*. Princeton University Press.
Collins, J. (2009) *Globalization and Language Contact*. London: Continuum.
Creese, A. and Blackledge, A. (2010) Separate and flexible bilingualism in complementary schools: Multiple language practices in interrelationship. *Journal of Pragmatics* 43(5): 1196–1208.
Crowley, T. (1989) *Standard English and the Politics of Language*. Urbana: University of Illinois Press.
———. (2005). *Wars on Words: The Politics of Language in Ireland 1537–2004*. Oxford: Oxford University Press
Crystal, D. (1997) *English as a Global Language*. Cambridge University Press.
———. (2000) *Language Death*. Oxford University Press.
Danet, B. and Herring, S. (eds) (2007) *The Multilingual Internet*. Oxford: Oxford University Press.
De Swaan, A. (2001) *Words of the World*. Cambridge: Polity Press.
Deleuze, G. and Guattari, F. (1987) *A Thousand Plateaus: Capitalism and Schizophrenia 2*. Minneapolis: University of Minnesota Press.
Dorian, N. (ed.) (1989) *Investigating Obsolescence: Studies in Language Contraction and Death*. Cambridge University Press.
Errington, J. (2007) *Linguistics in a Colonial World: A Story of Language, Meaning, and Power*. Malden, MA: Blackwell.
Fairclough, N. (2002) Language in New Capitalism. *Discourse and Society*, 13(2): 163–166.
———. (2006) *Language and Globalization*. London: Routledge.
Ferguson, C. A. 1959. Diglossia. *Word* 15: 325–340.
Gal, S. (1979) *Language Shift: Social Determinants of Linguistic Change in Bilingual Austria*. New York: Academic Press.
García, O. (2009) Education, multilingualism and translanguaging in the 21st century. In Ajit Mohanty, Minati Panda, Robert Phillipson, Tove Skutnabb-Kangas (eds) *Multilingual Education for Social Justice: Globalising the Local*. New Delhi: Orient Blackswan.
Gee, J. (1999) *An Introduction to Discourse Analysis*. London: Routledge
Ginsburg, F., Abu-Lughod, L., and Larkin, B. (eds) (2002) *Media Worlds: Anthropology on New Terrains*. Berkeley: University of California Press.
Gitlin, T. (1983) *Inside Prime Time*. Berkeley: University of California Press.

Gorlach, M. (1991) *Englishes*. Amsterdam: Benjamins.
Graddol, D. (1996) Global English, global culture? In Goodman, S. and Graddol, D. (eds) *Redesigning English*. London: The Open University.
Gumperz, J. (1964) Linguistic and social interaction in two communities. *American Anthropologist 66*: 6.
———. (1982) *Discourse Strategies*. Cambridge University Press.
Gumperz, J. and Hymes, D. (eds) (1972) *Directions in Sociolinguistics*. New York: Holt, Rinehart, and Winston.
Gumperz, J. et al. (1979) *Crosstalk: A Study of Crosscultural Communication*. London: National Center for Industrial Language Training in association with the BBC.
Hall, K. and Nilep, C. (forthcoming). Code Switching, Identity, and Globalization. In Tannen, T., Hamilton, H., and Schiffrin, D. (eds), *Handbook of Discourse Analysis*, 2nd ed. Malden, MA: Blackwell-Wiley.
Hannerz, U. (1996) *Transnational Connections*. New York: Routledge.
Harvey, D. (1989) *The Condition of Postmodernity*. New York: Wiley.
Heller, M. (2003) Globalization, the new economy, and the commodification of language and identity. Special issue: Sociolinguistics and Globalization, *Journal of Sociolinguistics* 7(4): 473–492.
———. (2010) Commodification of language. *Annual Review of Anthropology 39*: 101–114.
Higgins, C. (2009) *English as a Local Language: Postcolonial Identities and Multilingual Practices*. Bristol: Multilingual Matters.
Holborow (1999) *The Politics of English*. London: Sage.
Jacquemet, M. (1996) From the Atlas to the Alps: Chronicle of a Moroccan migration. *Public Culture* 8(2): 377–388.
———. (2005) Transidiomatic practices: Language and power in the age of globalization. *Language and Communication 25*: 257–277.
———. (2013) Language, media, and digital landscapes. In Auer, P. and Stuckenbrok, A. (eds) *Language and Space: Applied Cases*. Berlin: De Gruyter Mouton.
———. (forthcoming) *Transidioma: Language and Power in the Age of Globalization*. London, New York: Blackwell-Wiley.
Jørgensen, J. N. (2008). Polylingual languaging around and among children and adolescents. *International Journal of Multilingualism* 5(3): 161–176.
Jørgensen, J. N., Karrebaek, M., Madsen, L., and Moller, J. (2011) Polylanguaging in superdiversity. *Diversities 13*(2): 22–37.
Kachru, B. (1982) *Other Tongue: English Across Cultures*. Urbana: University of Illinois Press.
———. (1986) *The Alchemy of English*. Oxford: Pergamon.
Kellner, D. (1989) *Critical Theory, Marxism and Modernity*. Cambridge: Cambridge University Press.
Kouwenberg, S. 1994. *Papiamentu*. Munich: Lincolm Europa
Kraidy, M. and Murphy, P. D. (2004) *Global Media Studies: An Ethnographic Perspective*. London: Routledge.
Krauss, M. (1992) The world's languages in crisis. In Hale et al. (eds) *Endangered Languages. Language* 68: 4–10.
Larkin, B. (2008) *Signal and Noise: Media, Infrastructure and Urban Culture in Nigeria*. Durham, NC: Duke University Press.
Leeds-Hurwitz, W. (1990) Notes in the history of intercultural communication: The Foreign Service Institute and the Mandate for Intercultural Training. *Quarterly Journal of Speech* 76(3): 262–281.
Lennhart, A., Arefeh, S., Smith, A., and Macgill, A. (2008). *Writing, Technology, and Teens*. Pew Internet and American Life Project.
Levinson, S. and Gumperz, J. (eds) (1996) *Rethinking Linguistic Relativity*. Cambridge: Cambridge University Press.
McArthur, T. (1998) *The English Languages*. Cambridge University Press.
Morley, D. (1986) *Family Television, Cultural Power, and Domestic Leisure*. London: Comedia.
———. (1992) *Television, Audiences, and Cultural Studies*. London: Routledge.
Murphy, P.D. (1999) Media cultural studies' uncomfortable embrace of ethnography. *Journal of Communication Inquiry* 23(3): 205–221.
Muysken, P. (1997) Media Lengua. In Thomason, S.G. (ed,) *Contact Languages: A Wider Perspective*. Amsterdam: Benjamins.
Nero, S. (2001) *Englishes in Contact*. Cresskill, NJ: Hampton Press.
Nettle, D. and Romaine, S. (2000) *Vanishing Voices: The Extinction of the World's Languages*. Oxford University Press.
Otsuji, E. and Pennycook, A. (2010) Metrolingualism: Fixity, fluidity, and language in flux. *International Journal of Multilingualism* 7(3): 240–254.

Pattanayak, D. (1996) Change, language and the developing world. In Coleman, H. and Cameron, L. (eds) *Change and Language*. Bristol: Multilingual Matters.
Pennycook, A. (1998) *English and the Discourses of Colonialism*. London: Routledge.
———. (2007) *Global Englishes and Transcultural Flows*. London: Routledge.
Phillipson, R. (1992) *Linguistic Imperialism*. Oxford University Press.
Platt, J. Weber, H. and Lian H. (1984) *The New Englishes*. London: Routledge.
Pratt, L. (1987) Linguistic Utopias. In Fabb et al. (eds) *The Linguistics of Writing*. Manchester University Press.
———. (1991) The Arts of the Contact Zone. *Profession*, *91*: 33–40
Pratt et al. (2011) Comparative Literature and Global Languascapes. In Behdad, A. and Thomas, D. (eds), *A Companion to Comparative Literature*. John Wiley & Sons, Ltd: Chichester, UK.
Rampton, B. (1995) *Crossing: Language and Ethnicity among Adolescents*. London: Longman.
———. (1998) Speech community. In Verschueren et al. (eds) *Handbook of Pragmatics*. Amsterdam: Benjamins
Rampton, B. (1998) Speech community. In Verschueren, J. Ostman, J. O. and Blommaert, J. (eds) *Handbook of Pragmatics*. Amsterdam: Benjamins.
Rampton, B. (2006) *Language in Late Modernity*. Cambridge: Cambridge University Press.
Roumaine, S. (1992) *Language, Education, and Development: Urban and Rural Tok Pisin in Papua New Guinea*. Oxford University Press.
Schneider, E. (ed.) (1997) *Englishes Around the World*. Amsterdam: Benjamins.
Silverstein, M. (1998) Contemporary transformations of local linguistic communities. *Annual Review of Anthropology* 27: 401–426.
Smith, L. E. and Forman, M. L. (1997) *World Englishes 2000*. Honolulu: University of Hawaii Press.
Spitulnik, D. (1996) The social circulation of media discourse and the mediation of communities. *Journal of Linguistic Anthropology* 6(2): 161–187.
Spronk, R. (2009) Media and the therapeutic ethos of romantic love in middle-class Nairobi. In J. Cole and L. M. Thomas (eds) *Love in Africa*. Chicago: University of Chicago Press.
Sultana, S., Dovchin S., and Pennycook, A. (2015) Transglossic language practices of young adults in Bangladesh and Mongolia. *International Journal of Multilingualism* 12(1): 93–108.
Thomason, S. (2001) *Language Contact: An Introduction*. Georgetown University Press.
Tomlinson, J. (2007) *The Culture of Speed: The Coming of Immediacy*. London: Sage.
Urban, G. and Sherzer, J. (eds) (1991) *Nation-States and Indians in Latin America*. Austin: Texas University Press.
Urciuoli, B. (1991) The political topography of Spanish and English: The view from a New York Puerto Rican neighborhood. *American Ethnologist* 18(2): 295–310.
Vertovec, S. (2007) Super-diversity and its implications. *Ethnic and Racial Studies* 30(6): 1024–1054.
———. (2010) Towards post–multiculturalism? Changing communities, contexts and conditions of diversity. *International Social Science Journal* 99: 83–95.
Wallerstein, I. (1974). *The Modern World – System I: Capitalist Agriculture and the Origins of the European World Economy in the Sixteenth Century*. New York: Academic Press.
———. (2004) *Historical Capitalism*. London: Verso.
Woolard, K. (1999) Simultaneity and bivalency as strategies in bilingualism. *Journal of Linguistic Anthropology* 8(1): 3–29.
———. (2005) Codeswitching. In Duranti, A. (ed.) *A Companion to Linguistic Anthropology*, 73–94. Malden, MA: Blackwell.

Further Reading

Blommaert, J. (2010) *The Sociolinguistics of Globalization*. Cambridge University Press.
In this book Jan Blommaert, one of the leading scholars in the field of language and globalization, explores how the world has become a complex web of villages, towns, neighborhoods and settlements connected by material and symbolic ties in often unpredictable ways. Through a study of locality, repertoires, competence, history and sociolinguistic inequality, Blommaert constructs a theory of changing language in a changing society.

Coupland, N. (ed.) (2010) *Handbook of Language and Globalization*. London: Routledge.
This edited volume has a broad scope and covers the main areas of the intersection between language and globalization: global multilingualism, world languages and language systems; global discourse in key domains and genres; and

language, values and markets under globalization. It does so by exploring an impressive breadth of topics including tourism, language teaching, social networking, terrorism, and religion.

Pennycook, A. (2006) *Global Englishes and Transcultural Flows.* London: Routledge.
This book explores the relationship between global Englishes (the spread and use of diverse forms of English within processes of globalization) and transcultural flows (the movements, changes and reuses of cultural forms in disparate contexts). Drawing on sociolinguistic and performative theory, this wide-ranging study focuses on the ways English is embedded in other linguistic contexts, including those of East Asia, Australia, West Africa, and the Pacific Islands.

Fairclough, N. 2006. *Language and Globalization.* London: Routledge.
In this book, Fairclough combines critical discourse analysis with cultural political economy to study the relationship between discourse and other dimensions of globalization. Using examples from a variety of countries such as the United States, Britain, Romania, Hungary, and Thailand, this work shows how the analysis of texts can be coherently integrated within political economic analysis. Fairclough incorporates topical issues such as the war on terror and the impact of the media on globalization into his discussion.

Crystal, D. 1997. *English as a Global Language.* Cambridge University Press.
This by now classic introduction to the world of global languages considers the history, present status, and future of English, focusing on its role as the leading international language. Aided by engaging facts and compelling figures, Crystal explores the international success of the English language and its 1500 million speakers.

23

The Emergence of Creoles and Language Change

Salikoko S. Mufwene

1 Introduction

From an evolutionary perspective, creoles have typically been discussed in relation to pidgins, from which they have allegedly evolved. This position has been disputed by, especially, Chaudenson (2001, 2003), Mufwene (2001, 2005, 2008), and DeGraff (2009), for reasons I discuss below. Much earlier, Alleyne (1971) had disputed the "baby talk" hypothesis, according to which pidgins had evolved from simplified, baby-like utterances produced by the non-Europeans with whom the Europeans came in contact. Alleyne argues that fossils of variants still evident in Haitian Creole, Saramaccan, and Sranan (e.g., *broko* 'break', *dede* 'died, dead') speak otherwise. I show below that the history of the European trade and exploitation colonization of the relevant territories also disputes the "baby talk" hypothesis and its alternative, the "foreigner talk" hypothesis, according to which the Europeans spoke to non-Europeans in trade colonies in reduced utterances, imitating those produced by their interlocutors.

Since the late 19th century, the study of creoles has been marked by a social bias according to which non-Europeans were incapable of learning European languages adequately (Mufwene, 2001, 2005, 2008; DeGraff, 2003, 2005). Creoles have also been stipulated as separate languages from their lexifiers and not genetically related to them (Thomason & Kaufman, 1988; Thomason, 2001), although most speakers of these new vernaculars say they speak the same European language (Mühlhäusler, 1985; Mufwene, 1988). The stipulation is disputed in part by the fact that the Romance languages, which, like creoles, would not be mutually intelligible with Vulgar Latin, are also by-products of language shift. I will avoid the bias by sometimes referring to creoles as *vernaculars* or as *language varieties*, thus leaving room for them to be treated as new, colonial nonstandard dialects of the relevant European languages, produced by populations that are predominantly of non-European descent. Evolutionarily, they are on a par with, for instance, the French vernaculars of Louisiana and Québec, except that these have been produced by predominantly French colonists. Lack of mutual intelligibility with, especially, their metropolitan lexifiers, which has often been invoked to justify the disfranchising of creoles from the relevant European genetic linguistic families, also applies, as variably, to some of these other colonial vernaculars.

The term *lexifier* is used in this chapter as a label of convenience for the language from which a creole has typically inherited the overwhelming part of its vocabulary. This practice is based on the assumption that a creole has inherited its grammar from sources other than its lexifier (Holm, 1988; Thomason & Kaufman, 1988; Thomason, 2001). However, although the basilect of a creole has a very different grammar from the standard variety of its lexifier (called *acrolect*), many of its grammatical features can be traced, at least partly, to some of the nonstandard varieties of its lexifier, to which its "creators" were exposed. This is in fact one of the strongest contributions of Sylvain (1936), ironically invoked by some creolists as a forerunner of the relexification hypothesis (see below). Also, although the term *creole* has been extrapolated to various contact vernaculars, including those with a non-European lexifier (cf. Kouwenberg & Singler, 2009), this chapter is restricted to those lexified by a European language. The reasons for this position are articulated below.

2 Historical Perspectives: What Are Creoles and Pidgins?

Strictly speaking, creoles and pidgins are new language varieties that developed out of contacts between colonial nonstandard varieties of a European language and several non-European languages around the Atlantic and in the Indian and Pacific Oceans during the 17th–19th centuries. *Pidgins* typically emerged in trade colonies, which developed around trade forts (as on the coast of West Africa) and on whaling ships (as in the South Pacific). They have reduced structures and restricted communicative functions: typically trade and whaling activities. Initially they served as non-native lingua francas to users who maintained their native vernaculars for their intra-ethnic interactions. Some pidgins have expanded into regular vernaculars, especially in urban settings, and are called *expanded pidgins*. Examples include Bislama and Tok Pisin (in Melanesia) and Nigerian and Cameroon Pidgin Englishes. Structurally, these are as complex as *creoles* (Féral, 1989; Jourdan, 1991, 2009), though their evolutionary trajectories are different (see below).

Creoles emerged typically in settlement colonies whose primary industry consisted of sugar cane or rice cultivation, for which non-indigenous, non-European slaves were employed, constituting the overwhelming majority of the plantation populations. Examples include Haitian, Mauritian, and Seychellois (lexified by French); Jamaican, Guyanese, and Hawaiian Creole, as well as Gullah in the United States (all lexified by English); and Saramaccan and Sranan in Surinam (lexified by English, with the former heavily influenced by Portuguese and the latter by Dutch). Creoles have also been singled out in Australia, although they are endogenous, as they were produced by Aboriginal, rather than exogenous, populations (Chaudenson, 1979).

Vernaculars such as Cape Verdian Crioulo (lexified by Portuguese) and Papiamentu in the Netherlands Antilles (apparently Portuguese-based but influenced by Spanish) suggest that the plantation industry is not as significant a factor as population growth (including rate of population replacement) and population structure (related to early segregation) in the identification of a colonial vernacular as a creole. These considerations help explain why Brazil, which engaged in sugar cane cultivation a century earlier than the Caribbean colonies but had a non-segregated population structure, did not produce a creole (Mufwene, 2005, 2008). Certainly, it is also disputable whether creoles can be singled out as a typological class, let alone a genetic one (see below).

Although Melanesian expanded pidgins are associated with sugar cane plantations, they need not be considered as creoles. According to Keesing (1988), they originated in trade and whaling settings and were adopted as lingua francas on the plantations (but cf. Baker, 1993), before they evolved into urban vernaculars and expanded their functions and structures. However, since the complexity of their grammars makes them comparable to creoles, they raise the question of whether only one evolutionary trajectory need produce the extreme kind of structural divergence from the lexifier that has been associated with these vernaculars. It remains debatable whether, in the first place, creoles can be defined by their structural features.

Even McWhorter (1998) had to posit a small subset of "creole prototypes" (refuted by DeGraff, 2001), to dodge the question of why creoles are like each other only on the family resemblance model (Mufwene, 2001, 2005, 2008). This state of affairs is inconsistent with typological classifications, which are predicated on classical categories: all members must share the feature or combination thereof that justifies grouping them together.

According to Chaudenson (1979, 2001, 2003), creoles have evolved by basilectalization away from the closer approximations of their lexifiers spoken by the earliest slaves. This account is grounded in the particular way in which plantation settlement colonies developed, originally settled in small homesteads whose populations were integrated and eventually becoming larger, racially segregated plantations, as economic capital increased.

Linguists have also typically considered as creoles the varieties that are structurally the most divergent from the acrolects, called basilects. According to Chaudenson, these evolved later in history, through imperfect approximations of already imperfect approximations.[1] The notion of ACROLECT should not be confused with that of LEXIFIER, because the lexifiers were typically nonstandard and most likely *koinés* (i.e., compromises between different dialects) of the relevant European languages.

It appears that, evolutionarily, creoles relate to expanded pidgins in a way that a half-empty bottle relates to a half-full bottle: different histories but similar outcomes. Interesting evidence for this may be found in Solomon Islands Pidgin. Jourdan (2009) reports recent "system-internal innovation[s]," consisting of English prepositions used predicatively and transitivized according to Pidgin's grammar, with the suffix *-im*, which make the vernacular more divergent from its lexifier and more similar to the indigenous substrate languages.

The position since the 19th century that creoles evolved from erstwhile pidgins by the acquisition of native speakers appears to have been prompted by the assumption that complex structures evolve from simpler ones. However, a diachronic examination of the morphosyntaxes of Indo-European languages such as English or French reveals a trend from more complex to simpler morphosyntax. Colonial history also disputes this traditional position. Creoles emerged in settings where contacts with Europeans and native speakers of the lexifiers could not have been as sporadic as in the trade settings that produced pidgins, certainly not during the homestead phase, when the non-European component of the settlement population was the minority and the populations were racially integrated, though not necessarily equal socially (Chaudenson, 2001; Mufwene, 1997, 2001, 2008). Geographically, our epistemological prototypes of creoles and pidgins developed in separate places, in plantation settlement colonies of the New World and the Indian Ocean for creoles and in Canton, the Pacific, and Oceania for pidgins (Mufwene, 2005, 2008). Moreover, the term *pidgin* was first used in print in 1807, in Canton (Baker & Mühlhäusler 1990), much later than the term *creole*, which had been coined in Latin America for locally born people of non-indigenous stock in the late 16th century. It was used in reference to a "corrupted" variety of Portuguese spoken in Senegal only in the late 17th century (La Courbe's *Premier voyage*, 1688: 192, cited by Arveiller, 1963). Its later extension to other colonial nonstandard varieties spoken primarily by descendants of non-Europeans may have been initiated by locally-born White colonists, who were proud to be identified as Creoles (given some rights they could claim to administer the colonies) and claimed to have maintained the European language intact, but dissociated themselves from the non-White Creoles (Stewart, 2007).

The etymology of the term *pidgin* points to *business English* in Canton, though the emergence of the term is probably also due to partial congruence between *business* and Cantonese *bei chin* 'give money' or 'pay' (Comrie et al., 1996: 146). Noteworthy is the fact that Canton was an important trade colony where no plantation industry developed and no variety has been identified as creole. Besides, the history below also suggests that the emergence of pidgins lexified by European languages may be a peculiarity of British colonial ventures in the 19th century. Pidgins lexified by other European languages are scant and are not attested before the 20th century.

Also bearing heavily on the position that creoles evolved from antecedent pidgins is the role played by interpreters in the early contacts between Europeans and non-Europeans (Bolton, 2000, 2002; Fayer, 2003; Mufwene, 2005, 2014). This is best documented in relation to China, where the interpreters (often identified as *linguists*) were also required power brokers in trade (Van Dyke, 2005). Further evidence comes from the colonization of Hawaii (Beechert, 1985), where interpreters, from the monarchy, played an important role in the spread of English in the Pacific. Additional evidence comes from the colonization of Africa, facilitated by interpreters all the way to the early 20th century (Fortbath, 1977; Reader, 1997; Austen, 1999; Austen & Derrick, 1999; Lawrance, et al., 2006; Kennedy, 2013). There is similar evidence about the colonization of the Americas, where interpreters were used in trade with Native Americans (Karttunen, 1994; Curtin, 1984; Gray & Fiering, 2000; Metcalf, 2005).

It appears that in the particular territories where pidgins lexified by European languages emerged, knowledge of the European language remained the privilege of a few who benefited from the trade, then operating as in today's globalized economic networks, between indigenous rulers and the foreigners, interfaced by experts who can carry on the transactions. The slave trade, which has figured centrally in the relevant literature, did not proceed in bazaar-style open markets (Mufwene 2014). The British East India Company traded exclusively with a guild of Chinese merchants (*Co-Hong*) in tea, porcelain, and silk.

There are thus plenty of reasons to question the traditional, ahistorical view that derives creoles from pidgins (*pace*, e.g., Siegel, 2008; Bakker, 2009). Although the Pacific illustrates the pidgin-to-expanded-pidgin evolutionary trajectory, this is not the one followed by creoles around the Atlantic and in the Indian Ocean, or even in Hawaii. Expanded pidgins are by-products of the replacement of trade colonization by exploitation colonization, whereas creoles emerged in territories that remained settlement colonies until independence. Barring disputable stipulations of some South and East Asian vernaculars as creoles, there is a neat ecological complementary distribution between creoles and expanded pidgins: settlement plantation colonies for creoles vs. former trade colonies for pidgins.

Also, although Bickerton (1981, 1984) presents Hawaii as typical of settings where creoles developed, it was rather exceptional compared to Atlantic and Indian Ocean settlement colonies (Mufwene, 2008). In Hawaii, Creole emerged in the city but Pidgin on the plantations (Roberts, 1998, 2004), whereas in the other territories creoles developed on the plantations. Caribbean cities produced closer approximations of the lexifier. Creoles spread to them after the abolition of slavery, when former slaves who did not want to continue working on the plantations migrated to the city.

History also suggests that even pidgins must have evolved gradually rather than abruptly. In the case of Africa, as trade intensified in the 18th century and there were fewer and fewer interpreters who had learned the European language in Europe, more and more linguistically less competent individuals assumed their function. Then the reduced structures associated with pidgins emerged, in a way similar to the basilectalization that produced creoles. Expanded pidgins of course arose by recomplexification, in response to the more diversified communicative needs of those who would use pidgins as vernaculars in the emergent multi-ethnic cities. Under indigenous substrate influence, this complexification furthered the structural divergence from the lexifier.

The often-invoked jargon or pre-pidgin stage in the emergence of creoles and pidgins has not been documented. The hypothesis is not consistent with the role of interpreters during the trade colonization of Africa and Asia up to the 19th century. According to Drechsel (2014), the same interpreters used a Maritime Polynesian Pidgin (MPP) in communicating with the Natives on the Pacific islands, from New Zealand to Hawaii. MPP had apparently been used as a lingua franca by Polynesians before they traded with the Europeans.

One should not ignore the fact that no French or Dutch pidgins emerged on the African coast comparable to Nigerian and Cameroon English pidgins. "Le français tirailleur," associated with African recruits in the French army since the 19th century, appears to be a stereotypical creation of the French colonizers themselves. The recruits hardly spoke it, though it has been kept in the French citizens' negative representation of Africans' inability to learn standard French competently (Vigouroux, 2013). Tai Boy in Vietnam emerged only in the 20th century, just like "l'abidjannais" in Southern Côte d'Ivoire, and was short-lived. No pidgin based on a colonial language other than English appears to have emerged in the Pacific. Unserdeutch, spoken in Papua New Guinea, and also known as Rabaul Creole German, is considered a creole. Pidgins appear to be by-products of British trade colonization, though the reason for this historical peculiarity is not yet clear. It also appears that they did not emerge before the late 18th century (based on some disputable attestations) or, more likely, the early 19th century. That is after Caribbean and Indian Ocean creoles had already emerged (Mufwene, 2014).

Supporting the above hypothesis is also the observation by Huber (1999) and Ostler (2005) that Portuguese, for which there is no evidence of pidginization in history (*pace* Whinnom, 1971), had functioned as a convenient lingua franca of trade and diplomacy along the African and Indian Ocean coasts, all the way to the Far East, until the 18th century, after the Dutch, the French, and the English confiscated some of the Portuguese colonies. The European slave trade with Africa appears to have been conducted in Portuguese, spoken by the *grumetes* (young sailors) and the children of the Portuguese "factors" or *lançados*, who acted both as intermediaries and as interpreters (Berlin 1998). Nigerian and Cameroon pidgins may thus have arisen for reasons that had little to do with the slave trade.

Hall's (1962, 1966) and Mühlhäusler's (1997) "life-cycle" hypothesis, according to which creoles are somewhere on an evolutionary trajectory proceeding from the lexifier to a jargon, then to a pidgin, possibly to a creole, and sometimes even to a postcreole, by decreolization (see also Schuchardt, 1914; Bloomfield, 1933, on the latter), appears to be inconsistent with history (Mufwene, 1994). The term *jargon* was used randomly by colonizers for any language variety they did not understand, not necessarily pidgins. The term and its meaning actually have a longer usage than the European colonization, dating from the 13th century (Mufwene, 1997). Neither Hall nor Mühlhäusler provide operational criteria for distinguishing their putative jargons from interlanguages, except that the latter are less stable. Even Plag's (2008, 2009) claim that creoles evolved from interlanguages does not redeem this traditional position, because all L2 learners go through interlanguages, which are individual but not communal varieties (DeGraff 1999, 2009; Mufwene 2008, 2010a). Also noteworthy is the fact that Black Creoles of the homestead phase appear to have spoken the relevant colonial koinés instead. In addition, several Hispanic American countries identify Creole populations who speak no creole vernaculars.

3 Critical Issues

3.1 How Many Creoles Are There?

Under whatever definition, it is not clear which contact-based vernaculars count as creoles and which do not, especially outside the Caribbean and the Indian Ocean. Hawaiian English

Creole is problematic because it evolved in the city, rather than on the plantations, where a pidgin emerged. It was also produced by contract laborers rather than slaves. Besides, there was no extensive multilingualism among the laborers, who consisted of Chinese, Japanese, Filipinos, Koreans, and "Portuguese," arrived at different periods, and lived in separate ethnic "houses." They continued to speak their ethnic vernaculars, in which they received instructions for work, and they resorted occasionally to Pidgin Hawaiian and later on to English, which they pidginized, for inter-ethnic communication. To date, their descendants have kept their ethnic identities, although most of them speak Hawaiian English (Creole) as their vernacular.

Kreol of Queensland is identified as such because it was produced by non-Europeans, primarily from Australia, who worked on sugar cane plantations. It is structurally close to Melanesian pidgins, which Baker (1993) claims evolved from it or its antecedent in New South Wales. Important structural differences between these Pacific varieties and those of the Atlantic and Indian Ocean make it futile to attempt to define creoles structurally (*pace* McWhorter, 1998; Bakker et al., 2011).

More difficult to accept as creoles are varieties such as Afrikaans, classified as such by Valkhoff (1966) but not by Hesseling (1897). The latter found it less divergent from Dutch than Negerhollands (now dead), which had been produced by African slaves who had worked on sugar cane plantations. Hans den Besten (Wouden, 2012), however, saw "creole features" in Afrikaans, capitalizing on the fact that the Dutch settlers had been in contact with non-European people, with whom they sometimes mixed, and Cape Dutch was restructured under their influence. Afrikaners do not think their language, now stipulated as separate from European Dutch, is a creole, no more than Louisiana White Creoles think they speak Créole, although their vernacular is very similar to Louisiana French Creole (see, e.g., Klingler, 2003), associated exclusively with Black Creoles and sugar cane cultivation.

There are also varieties spoken by descendants of non-Europeans in small, former endogenous Portuguese settlement colonies, from South Asia (e.g., Korlai in India) to Southeast and East Asia (e.g., Papia Kristang in Malaysia and Mecanese in Macau), which are called creoles. Their speakers are descendants of indigenous populations that had lived with the Portuguese, sometimes formed unions with them, converted to Christianity, and adopted their colonizer's language. The vernaculars are not associated with the plantation industry, nor do their features match those of our epistemological prototypes of creoles in the Caribbean and Indian Ocean. They just share with the latter the fact of being nonstandard vernaculars of European origins spoken by a non-European population. This brings up the issue of whether the race of the speakers is not really an important tacit reason why some "contact-based" vernaculars are called creoles (Mufwene, 2001, 2005, 2008; DeGraff, 2003, 2005).

On the other hand, some creolists have extrapolated the terms *creole* and *pidgin* to various varieties around the world that are not lexified by European languages but have been restructured in similar ways, "under contact conditions." Thus, new African languages such as Kikongo-Kituba, Lingala, and Sango in Central Africa, Kinubi in South Sudan and Kenya, Fanakalo in South Africa, and Hiri Motu in Papua New Guinea have been branded as creoles if they have native speakers, otherwise as pidgins. I have avoided that extrapolation in this chapter, though I believe it is easier to operationalize the concept PIDGIN (by invoking reduced communicative functions and structures) than CREOLE.

Some linguists, such as Bailey and Maroldt (1977) and Schlieben-Lange (1977), have gone even farther back in time and claimed that Middle English, for the former, and the Romance languages, for the latter, are creoles, since they are outcomes of language contact. The issue is whether there are any modern languages that do not owe at least part of their structures to language contact (Hjelmslev, 1938). How can the boundary be drawn between the kind of contact that produces a creole and the kind that does not? Are there any cases of language speciation that have nothing to do with language contact?

On the other hand, why did Bailey and Maroldt not go even farther back and claim that Old English was a creole? The Germanic populations that colonized England in the 5th century had spoken no English. The latter is indigenous to England. Old English appears to have emerged only in the 7th century, two centuries after the Germanic invasion. It may be argued that it was a Germanic koiné, out of the contact of the languages of the Jutes, Saxons, Angles, and perhaps Frisians. However, the names *England* 'land of the Angles' and *English* 'language of the Angles' suggest that one group prevailed, at least culturally, and their language won a Pyrrhic victory, just as in the case of creoles. An important difference is that it was not the socioeconomically subjugated people who shifted languages in the process. What seems more significant here is that language change and speciation were actuated by contacts with populations speaking different languages or dialects.

Overall, it is difficult to answer the question of how many creoles are spoken today, nor how many can be documented in history, because creolists do not have a common yardstick for determining which ones count as creoles and which do not. The inventories provided by Hancock (1977), Holm (1989), and Smith (1995) provide drastically different numbers!

3.2 Are Creoles Separate Languages from Their Lexifiers?

Another contentious issue about creoles is the traditional stipulation by linguists that creoles are separate languages from their lexifiers and related varieties spoken by descendants of Europeans in the same or other former colonies. Thus, the nonstandard French varieties spoken in Quebec and Louisiana, as well as on the Caribbean islands of St Barts and St Thomas, are considered dialects of French rather than creoles. Likewise Latin American nonstandard varieties of Spanish and Portuguese are not considered creoles (with the exception of Palenquero, spoken by a population of primarily African descent!), despite structural similarities that they exhibit with creoles of the same lexifiers, such as São Tomense, Principense (both spoken in the Bight of Biafra), and Cape Verdiano Crioulo for Portuguese.

Interestingly, African American Vernacular English is not considered a creole, perhaps because it shares its origins with American (White) Southern English or because their structures remain so closely similar. In any case, Holm (2004) claims that it is a semi-creole, though there are no structural features by which creoleness can be measured (Mufwene, 1986a, 2000). Gullah, spoken by a majority-Black population has been stipulated to be a creole (though its speakers think Creole is spoken only in Louisiana). Amish English is not, however, despite the fact that it has also diverged significantly from other White American Englishes. It is spoken by descendants of German-speaking Swiss! Ignoring Hjelmslev's (1938) and Posner's (1985) position that creoles are new dialects of European languages, creolists have adopted uncritically this socially based naming tradition in former European settlement colonies, identifying as creoles modifications of European languages produced and appropriated as vernaculars by non-European majorities.

It is striking that, in the first place, grammatical divergence must weigh so heavily in these stipulations. Genetic connections have typically been based on lexical, phonetic, and morphosyntactic correspondences. Proportionally, creoles share more lexical materials with their lexifiers (over 90 percent of their vocabularies) than English does with modern German or Dutch. And their grammatical features probably do not diverge more from those of their nonstandard lexifiers than those of English do from those of other Germanic languages. Besides, there is yet no yardstick for measuring global structural divergence from the lexifier or between any other languages.

Also, as noted above, contact has played as important a role in the speciation of Vulgar Latin into the Romance languages as in that of French and Portuguese into their respective creoles. Thomason and Kaufman's (1988) stipulation that the comparative method cannot be applied in the case of creoles is a foregone conclusion with no empirical basis (Mufwene, 2003, 2005, 2008). Ironically, it is invalidated indirectly by equally disputable attempts, based on the comparative method such as by Bakker et al. (2011), that connect creoles genetically in their own separate families.

Granted that the non-creole varieties are not as structurally divergent from their common lexifiers as the creole vernaculars, there is another explanation that weakens the traditional distinction. In the case of White American English varieties, for example, the majority of European immigrants, who were of non-English descent, shifted to English after the American Revolution, i.e., after its critical formative phase. This timing puts them in a situation comparable to that of more recent immigrants, with their children acquiring the extant variety natively and the immigrants themselves taking most of their xenolectal features with them to their graves. This is why continental European immigrants have exerted little influence on the grammar of American English, although their descendants are today the majority of the White American population (Mufwene, 2009a).

4 Current Contributions and Research

4.1 Creole "Genesis"

The central question here is: how did creoles emerge? The following hypotheses are the major ones competing today, although efforts have been made by some to integrate their insights: the substrate, the superstrate, and the universalist hypotheses.

Substratist positions are historically related to the *"baby talk" hypothesis*, which can be traced back to late 19th-century French creolists: Bertrand-Bocandé (1849), Baissac (1880), Adam (1883), and Vinson (1882). According to them, the languages previously spoken by the Africans enslaved on New World and Indian Ocean plantations exerted a strong influence on structures of the European languages they appropriated as their vernaculars. They also assumed African languages to be "primitive," "instinctive," in "natural" state, and simpler than the "cultivated" European languages. Creoles' systems allegedly reflected the mental inferiority of their producers.[2] The connection with "baby talk" is that, in order to be understood, the Europeans supposedly had to speak to the Africans like to babies (Bloomfield, 1933). More or less the same idea is to be found in the "foreigner talk" hypothesis (as explained above). Unsurprisingly, Maurice Delafosse (1904) claimed that "le petit nègre" was invented by the Africans, though history suggests otherwise.

The revival of the substrate hypothesis (without its racist component) has been attributed to Sylvain (1936). Although she recognizes significant influence from nonstandard French dialects, she concludes her book, surprisingly, with the statement that Haitian Creole is Ewe spoken with a French vocabulary. Over a decade later, Turner (1949), disputing American dialectologists' claim that there was virtually no trace of African languages in "Black English," highlighted some morphosyntactic similarities between "the Gullah dialect" and some West African (especially Kwa) languages. He then concluded that "Gullah is indebted to African sources" (p. 254), which stimulated more research on African substrate influence on African-American English (e.g., Dillard, 1972) and on Caribbean English creoles (e.g., Alleyne, 1980).

There are three main schools of the substrate hypothesis today. The first, led by Alleyne (1980, 1996) and Holm (1988) is closer to Turner's approach and is marked by what is also its main weakness: invocation of influences from diverse African languages without explaining what kinds of selection principles account for this seemingly random invocation of sources.

This criticism is not *ipso facto* an invalidation of substrate influence. It is both a call for a more principled account, one that can articulate the particular ecological factors that appear to have favored various individual influences (thus legitimating what was dubbed the "Cafeteria Principle"), and a reminder that the nature of such influences must be reassessed (Mufwene, 2001, 2008).

The second school, identified by its practitioners as the *relexification hypothesis* (RH), is fully articulated by Lefebvre (1998), who argues that Haitian Creole (HC) consists largely of French lexical entries spoken with the grammar of languages of the Fongbe group. Extended to other creoles, the position has been repeated in some of the contributions to Lefebvre et al. (2006), though some others (see especially Aboh, 2006 and Siegel 2006) dispute it, and almost all contributing to Lefebvre (2011) are more cautious. Objections to RH include the following: 1) Lefebvre's "comparative" approach has not taken into account several features that HC (also) shares with nonstandard French; 2) she downplays features that HC also shares with several other African languages that were represented in Haiti during the critical stages of its development, so it is not obvious why there is the exclusive focus on the Fongbe languages; 3) studies of naturalistic second language acquisition provide little evidence in support of RH, even if the emergence of creoles could at all be associated exclusively with adult L2-learners (Chaudenson, 2001, 2003); and 4) Lefebvre does not account convincingly for those cases where HC has selected structural options that are not consistent with those of Fongbe. Moreover, relexificationists assume, disputably, that languages of the Fongbe group are structurally identical in all respects and that no influence-related competition among them was involved. The most elaborate critique of RH is DeGraff (2002), which is complemented by various refined analyses of hybridized structures in Haitian by Aboh (2006, 2009, 2015). For contrary evidence from other creole-like languages, see especially Siegel (2006).

The least disputed version of the substrate hypothesis is Keesing's (1988), which shows that substrate languages may impose their structural features on the new, contact-induced varieties if they are typologically homogeneous, with most of them sharing the relevant features.[3] Thus, Melanesian pidgins are like (most of) their substrates in having DUAL/PLURAL and INCLUSIVE/EXCLUSIVE distinctions and a transitive marker on the verb. For other common features see especially Sankoff and Brown (1976), Keesing (1988), Sankoff (1993), and Jourdan (2009). Singler (1988) invokes a "homogeneity of the substrate" (see also Mufwene, 1986b) to account generally for substrate influence.

The Melanesian pidgins have not, however, inherited all the peculiarities of the substrate languages. For instance, they do not have their VSO major constituent order, nor do they have much of a numeral classifying system in the combination of *pela* with quantifiers. For an extensive discussion of substrate influence in Atlantic and Indian Ocean creoles, see Muysken and Smith (1986) and Mufwene (1993). For similar discussions about creoles and the like in the Pacific, see Lefebvre et al. (2006) and Lefebvre (2011).

Competing with the above genetic views has been the dialectologist, or superstrate, hypothesis, according to which the primary, if not the exclusive, sources of creoles' structural features are nonstandard varieties of their lexifiers. This position was first defended by Faine (1937), according to whom HC was essentially Norman French. It was espoused later by Hall (1958), who argues that

> the 'basic' relationship of Creole is with seventeenth-century French, with heavy carry-overs or survivals of African linguistic structure (on a more superficial structural level) from the previous language(s) of the earliest speakers of Negro Pidgin French; its 'lexical' relationship is with nineteenth- and twentieth-century French.
>
> *Hall (1958: 372)*

Chaudenson (2001, 2003) is more accommodating to substrate influence as a factor accounting for the more extensive structural divergence of creoles from their lexifiers compared to their non-creole colonial kin. Chaudenson's allowance for substrate influence is elaborated especially by Corne (1999), who articulates the most explicitly how feature selection can be driven by congruence, even if only partial, between the languages in contact. Although, unlike Pacific pidgins, the Atlantic and Indian Ocean French creoles did not typically emerge in settings that satisfied Singler's "homogeneity of the substrate" condition, partial structural congruence between the substrates and nonstandard French favored the selection of the particular features French creoles possess, for instance in the domain of time reference. Aboh (2006, 2015) has carried this approach farther with detailed analyses showing how structural traits can be hybridized in ways similar to biological gene recombination, in various aspects of the grammar. According to him, even transfers from the substrate languages were modified by the contact. One must then determine whether such substrate influence, which does not boil down to mere introduction of features from substrate languages (identified as "apports" by Allsopp, 1977), was facilitated by the numerical proportion of speakers of the relevant languages and/or by the time of the insertion of these in the feature pool. See Singler (1996, 2009) for such considerations regarding HC.

The *universalist hypotheses*, which stood as strong contenders to substrate hypotheses in the 1980s and 1990s, have forerunners in the 19th century. For instance, Adolfo Coelho (1880–1886) partly anticipated Bickerton's (1981, 1984, 1989) *language bioprogram hypothesis*, according to which creoles "owe their origin to the operation of psychological or physiological laws that are everywhere the same, and not to the influence of the former languages of the people among whom these dialects are found." Bickerton pushed things further in claiming that children, not adults, constructed creoles by fixing the parameters of these new language varieties in their default settings, as specified in Universal Grammar (UG). To account for cross-creole structural differences, Bickerton (1984: 176–177) invokes a "Pidginization Index" (PI) that includes the following factors: the proportion of the native to non-native speakers during the initial stages of colonization, the duration of the early stage, the rate of increase of the slave population after that initial stage, the kind of social contacts between the native speakers of the lexifier and the learners, and whether or not the contact between the two groups continued after the formation of the new language variety. These factors, which are included in Mufwene's (2001) ecological approach, were simply not anchored in the actual history of the colonization of the different creole-speaking territories.

Some nagging questions with Bickerton's position include the following: Do structures really support the claim that they were produced primarily by children (DeGraff, 1999; Roberts, 1998)? Is his intuitively sound PI consistent with his hypothesis that creoles emerged abruptly, over one generation, from an antecedent macaronic pidgin? Is the "abrupt creolization" hypothesis consistent with the socioeconomic histories of the relevant territories? How can we explain similarities between abrupt creoles and expanded pidgins when the structural expansion and stabilization of the latter is not necessarily associated with restructuring by children (Meyerhoff, 2009)? Is there convincing evidence for assuming that adult speech is less controlled by UG than child language is? If so, how can an adult learn and speak any other language at all?

Not all universalists have invoked children as critical agents in the emergence of creoles. For instance, Sankoff (1979) and Mühlhäusler (1981) make allowance for UG to operate in adults, too. Few creolists nowadays subscribe exclusively to one genetic account, as evidenced by the contributions to Mufwene (1993) and Lefebvre (2011). The "complementary hypothesis" (Baker & Corne, 1986; Corne, 1999; DeGraff, 2009; Hancock, 1986; Mufwene, 1986b, 2001) seems to be an adequate alternative, provided we can articulate the ecological conditions under which the competing influences (between the substrate and lexifier languages, and within each group) may converge or prevail upon each other. Aboh (2015) articulates in fine detail how competition and selection operate during the restructuring of the lexifier under the influence of some specific substrate languages. Schuchardt (1909, 1914) anticipated this language-mixing account in his discussions of the genesis of the Mediterranean Lingua Franca and of Saramaccan.

It is also noteworthy that the traditional claim that creoles emerged abruptly, within one generation, from a pidgin ancestor, has increasingly been disputed by, e.g., Chaudenson (1979, 2001, 2003), Arends (1989, 1995), Singler (1996, 2009), and Mufwene (1996–2008, 2010a). Baker (1995) argues that even pidgins developed their characteristic features gradually. Overall, the oldest documentary evidence shows more similarities between the new vernaculars and their lexifiers than do the later texts. The gradualist scenario is consistent with the gradual way in which plantation colonies evolved, having started from homestead settings settled by small integrated groups in which the slaves were in the minority and interacted regularly with the European colonists; shortage of capital made it difficult to import more slaves. The colonial populations then grew, albeit slowly, more by birth than by (forced) immigration (Mufwene, 2001, 2005, 2008).

Still, the future of research on the emergence of creoles has some issues to address. Knowledge of the nonstandard lexifiers from which they evolved remains limited, though more research is now underway and much of the scholarship on the dialectology of the relevant European languages is becoming useful. There are few comprehensive and integrated descriptions of creoles' structures, especially from a diachronic perspective, which makes it difficult to determine globally how the competing influences interacted among themselves and how the features selected from diverse sources became integrated into new systems. Other issues remain up in the air, for instance, regarding the markedness model that is the most adequate to account for the selection of features into creoles' systems. Can there really be an ecology-independent, universal scale of markedness that can account for the selection of particular features into the structures of particular creoles? If so, how can one explain why even creoles that, for all practical purposes, evolved from the same lexifier do not have identical structures, e.g., Gullah, and Guyanese and Jamaican Creoles?

4.2 Genetic Creolistics and Language Change

Creoles have typically been treated as historical anomalies, being contact-based and with mixed systems. Only exceptionally has it been claimed that they can help us better understand how languages change and can speciate into new ones. They remind us that language or dialect contact is a common actuator of change. To wit, the birth of English is a by-product of language contact primarily between the different Germanic languages that were brought to England from continental Europe, although students of Celtic Englishes argue that the Celts too contributed to the emergence of Old English on their land. In addition, various changes in the history of English in England have involved the Danelaw, the Norse rule, and the Norman Conquest. Changes in British English within the last half-millennium can also be associated with population movements within England. The emergence of varieties such as Irish and Scots Englishes also has everything to do with language contact.

Likewise, the speciation of Vulgar Latin into so many Romance languages stemmed both from variation among the Celtic languages spoken by the populations that shifted to Latin and from differences between the other languages with which the numerous emergent neo-Latin varieties came in contact, e.g., Frankish in nothern Gaul and Arabic and Moorish in Iberia. Thus, the emergence of creoles, outside Europe, is a repetition of history in kind, especially with naturalistic language learning being the dominant mode of language appropriation.

Creoles have also been prompting us to reconsider the way changes have been discussed in historical linguistics: A→B in the environment of C. Discussions of the emergence of creoles have made us more aware of variation in the feature pool, which provides the apparently more accurate statement of how competition was resolved: B was selected over A in the environment of C. This brings up the actuation question: what led the B variant to prevail over the A variant? Indeed, the consequences of such a shift in the conceptualization of change may take us all the way back to Grimm's Law, as explained below.

No justification has been provided for assuming that Proto-Indo-European (PIE) was one single language and as monolithic as a biological organism. Rather, we can assume that like modern languages, if it were really a single language, PIE must have varied internally. If it were a cluster of related languages, like some language clusters today (e.g., Kikongo in central Africa and Quechua in South America), some aspects of its system are likely to have varied. Thus, instead of the typical formulation $b^h > b > p > \phi$ for part of Grimm's Law, one can argue that these consonants were variants of each other in PIE, with some dialects or languages preferring one or the other. As the Indo-Europeans dispersed to Europe and South Asia, the original competition was resolved in different ways, leaving some room for the pre-IE populations that they encountered to have contributed to differing selections from among the variants.

Alternatively, the pre–IE languages may have introduced some of the variants, which subsequently were selected over the PIE obstruents. This competition-and-selection alternative appears to be evolutionarily more plausible than the traditional account, especially because it brings us closer to addressing the question of why this specific change occurred. From the point of view of language speciation, one may argue that the dispersal led the separated groups to strengthen their respective preferences, probably under the influence of the populations with which they came to coexist.

5 Future Directions

The debate on "creole genesis" informs genetic/historical linguistics on the relevance of the varying external-ecology not only to the actuation question and to language change and speciation but also to language vitality (Mufwene, 2005, 2008). A concomitant of the emergence of creoles around the Atlantic and in the Indian Oceans was the loss of heritage languages among the (descendants of) the enslaved Africans. The cause of this is language shift, which was concurrent with the appropriation of the European language.

Language shift, which results in language loss, was also a concomitant of the emergence of the Romance languages, as of Irish and Scots Englishes, though in these cases, involving endogenous language contact, the shift was more gradual. Language shift happens when opportunities for using one's heritage vernacular decrease to zero and/or when speakers cannot remember the heritage language when an opportunity does arise. The speed at which a population experiences the shift varies from one contact setting to another, apparently faster in exogenous colonies with a high level of societal multilingualism and population-mixing than in others. The contract laborers of Hawaii maintained their heritage languages longer than the Atlantic and Indian Ocean slaves precisely because of this difference in population structure, although in both cases the laborers had been transported to an exogenous setting.

On the other hand, although European colonists and immigrants also migrated to exogenous colonies, they lost their heritage languages more slowly than the African slaves, simply because they remained for a long time, into the 19th century in the Americas, in segregated mini-national colonies. They shifted to the dominant languages only after they integrated the economically and politically dominant population, for instance, the Anglos in English colonies or the Portuguese in Brazil.

The language-shift factor also explains why the influence of continental European languages on American English is way below what it could have been if continental Europeans had been integrated since the 17th century and had constituted the White American majority since then (Mufwene, 2009a). Additionally, it highlights the role of children as agents of selection (DeGraff, 1999) in a contact setting. Being better learners and wanting to be integrated in the linguistically and culturally dominant population, the children of immigrants weeded out a large proportion of the features their parents could have contributed to the host country's vernacular.

Genetic creolistics makes historical linguists and historical dialectologists more aware of population movements and language contact as ecological factors that generate new feature pools, by introducing new elements, reweighting the variants, or modifying their distribution. One can also invoke periodization and population structure (viz. integration vs. segregation, notwithstanding disparities in demographic size) to explain why different subgroups have not exerted the same (extents of) influences on the languages they have appropriated. This accounts for differences between the influences of the substrate languages spoken by the African slaves and those of the languages spoken by Americans of continental European descent on American Englishes.

We must also revisit the distinction between externally and internally-motivated language change. Since languages have no separate existence from their speakers/signers, they must be distinguished from the mental and anatomical infrastructures that enable them. Thus the mind and the anatomy count as the most immediate ecologies, which, combined with the personalities of speakers/signers, shape our idiolects and the ways in which we contribute to restructuring our communal languages. This relation of languages to speakers/signers suggests that there are probably few fundamental structural changes that are not externally motivated, contrary to the tradition that has acknowledged as such only contact-induced changes. The reasons for this conclusion include the following: 1) learning, which is naturally imperfect, may introduce new variants of forms or rules; 2) pressures to communicate new ideas or nuance one's statements may introduce new variants by modifying current meanings or structures; 3) dynamics of mutual accommodations between idiolects may in some cases offset the balance of power among the variants and thereby produce changes in the system; and 4) knowledge of another language can influence the speaker's/signer's performance, especially if that other language is ecologically favored, say, by how much more frequently it is used, by the number or prestige of its speakers, or by the fondness that speakers of the changing language have for it.

The only changes that are internally motivated are those that are consequences of other changes that have already affected the system. For instance, while it is not clear that the construction *be going to* was coopted as an alternative for expressing the FUTURE tense/mood because of some language-internal reason, its contraction to *be gonna* in some dialects or even *gon* in African American English was internally motivated. The latter change appears to be an analogical evolution similar to the morphophonological reduction of, for instance, *will, will not,* and *shall not* to, respectively, PRONOUN'*ll, won't,* and *shan't.* An extreme conclusion is that, since languages have no agency independent of their speakers/signers, all changes are externally motivated.

The list of insights that genetic creolistics can contribute to historical linguistics and historical dialectology remains open. The primary reason for this ignorance is the assumption of "creole exceptionalism" (DeGraff, 2003, 2005), which has deterred linguists from identifying ways in which the scholarship on creoles can inspire research on language change. Rejecting "creole exceptionalism" would entail at least questioning the ideological stipulation that creoles cannot be grouped genetically with their lexifiers, even if they are considered as separate languages. Acknowledging the role of substrate influence as a possible actuator of change in non-creole languages can also benefit from controversies about it in the emergence of creoles, just like the latter may help refine discourse on transfers or interference in language acquisition (Schumann, 1978; Andersen, 1983; Lefebvre, et al., 2006; Lefebvre, 2011; Mufwene, 2010a). No less interesting is the light that genetic creolistics can shed on speculations regarding the evolution of language (Bickerton, 1990, 1995, 2010; Botha, 2006; Mufwene, 2008, 2009b, 2010b; Hurford, 2012). Perhaps the time has finally come when creoles can influence more conspicuously the way linguists and other scholars study language.

Related Topics

18 New and Emergent Languages (Riley); **19** Language and Political Economy (McElhinny); **20** Language, Immigration, and the Nation-State (Pujolar); **21** Language and Nationalism (Haque); **22** Language in the Age of Globalization (Jacquemet).

Acknowledgments

I am grateful to Nancy Bonvillain for facing my delays in completing this essay with a lot of patience and for her very helpful feedback to my first draft. I am solely responsible for the remaining shortcomings.

Notes

1. Since there are no features that are particularly creole and the relevant vernaculars have been disenfranchised typically because of the particular social history of their emergence, one may ask why the whole basilect-to-acrolect continuum is not characterized as creole. After all, some structural features of the colonial acrolects have also diverged from their metropolitan counterparts, reflecting language contact or conservatism. However, the elite associated with the colonial acrolects would feel insulted, while the distinction between creole and non-creole colonial varieties would become more elusive.
2. This assumption would also be repeated by Delafosse (1904), who encouraged the French army officers to speak to African recruits in broken French, the ancestor of the mythical "français tirailleur."
3. These expanded pidgins are brought back into the discussion here not because they should be considered as creoles but for other reasons discussed elsewhere.

References

Aboh, Enoch. 2006. The role of the syntax-semantics interface. In Claire Lefebvre, Lydia White, & Christine Jourdan (eds) *L2 acquisition and creole genesis*, pp. 221–252. Amsterdam: Benjamins.
Aboh, Enoch & Norval Smith (eds) 2009. *Complex processes in new languages*. Amsterdam: Benjamins.
Aboh, Enoch 2015. *The emergence of hybrid grammars: Insights into language contact, language change, and language creation*. Cambridge: Cambridge University Press.
Adam, Lucien. 1883. *Les idiomes négro-aryens et malayo-aryens: essai d'hybridologie linguistique*. Paris: Maisonneuve.
Alleyne, Mervyn C. 1971. Acculturation and the cultural matrix of creolization. In Dell Hymes (ed.) *Pidginization and cre of languages*, pp. 169–186. Cambridge: Cambridge University Press.
Alleyne, Mervyn C. 1980. *Comparative Afro-American: An historical-comparative study of English-based Afro-American dialects of the New World*. Ann Arbor: Karoma.
Alleyne, Mervyn C. 1996. *Syntaxe historique créole*. Paris: Karthala.
Allsopp, Richard. 1977. Africanisms in the idioms of Caribbean English. In P. F. Kotey & H. Der-Houssikia (eds) *Language and linguistics problems in Africa*, pp. 429–441. Columbia: Hornbeam Press.
Andersen, Roger (ed.). 1983. *Pidginization and creolization as language acquisition*. Rowley, MA: Newbury House.
Arends, Jacques. 1989. Syntactic developments in Sranan: Creolization as a gradual process. Doctoral thesis, University of Nijmegen.

Arends, Jacques (ed.) 1995. *The early stages of creolization.* Amsterdam: Benjamins.
Arends, Jacques, Pieter Muysken, & Norval Smith (eds). 1995. *Pidgins and creoles: An introduction.* Amsterdam: Benjamins.
Arveiller, Raymond. 1963. *Contribution à l'étude des termes de voyage en français (1505–1722).* Paris: D'Artrey.
Austen, Ralph A. (ed. 1999). *In search of Sunjata: The Mande oral epic as history, literature, and performance.* Bloomington: Indiana University Press.
Austen, Ralph A. & Jonathan Derrick. 1999. *Middlemen of the Cameroons Rivers: The Duala and their hinterland c. 1600-c. 1960.* Cambridge: Cambridge University Press.
Bailey, Charles, N. James, & K. Maroldt 1977. The French lineage of English. In Jürgen M. Meisel (ed.) *Pidgins – creoles – languages in contact,* pp. 21–53. Tübingen: Narr.
Baissac, Charles. 1880. *Etude sur le patois créole mauricien.* Nancy: Imprimerie Berger-Levrault.
Baker, Phillip. 1993. Australian influence on Melanesian Pidgin English. *Te Reo 36:* 3–67.
Baker, Phillip. 1995. Some developmental inferences from the historical studies of pidgins and creoles. In Jacques Arends (ed.) *The early stages of creolization,* pp. 1–24. Amsterdam: Benjamins.
Baker, Phillip & Chris Corne, 1986. Universals, substrata and the Indian Ocean creoles. In Pieter Muysken & Norval Smith (eds). *Substrata versus universals in creole genesis.* pp. 163–183. Amsterdam: Benjamins.
Baker, Phillip & Peter Mühlhäusler. 1990. From business to pidgin. *Journal of Asian Pacific Communication 1:* 87–115.
Bakker, Peter. 2009. Pidgins versus creoles and pidgincreoles. In Silvia Kouwenberg & John V. Singler (eds) *The handbook of pidgin and creole studies,* pp. 130–157. Malden, MA: Wiley-Blackwell.
Bakker, Peter, Aymeric Daval-Markussen, Mikael Parkvall, & Ingo Plag. 2011. Creoles are typologically distinct from non-creoles. *Journal of Pidgin and Creole Languages 26:* 5–42.
Beechert, Edward D. 1985. *Working in Hawaii: A labor history.* Honolulu: University of Hawaii Press.
Berlin, Ira. 1998. *Many thousands gone: The first two centuries of slavery in North America.* Cambridge, MA: Harvard University Press.
Bertrand-Bocandé, Emmanuel. 1849. Notes sur la Guinée portugaise ou Sénégambie méridionale. *Bulletin de la Société de Géographie 12:* 57–93.
Bickerton, Derek. 1981. *Roots of language.* Ann Arbor: Karoma.
Bickerton, Derek. 1984. The language bioprogram hypothesis. *Behavioral and Brain Sciences 7:* 173–221.
Bickerton, Derek. 1990. *Language and species.* Chicago: University of Chicago Press.
Bickerton, Derek. 1995. *Language and human behavior.* Seattle: University of Washington Press.
Bickerton, Derek. 1999. How to acquire language without positive evidence: What acquisitionists can learn from creoles. In Michel DeGraff (ed.) *Language creation and language change: Creolization, diachrony, and development,* pp. 49–74. Cambridge, MA: MIT Press.
Bickerton, Derek. 2010. *Adam's tongue: How humans made language, how language made humans.* New York: Hill and Wang.
Bloomfield, Leonard. 1933. *Language.* New York: Holt, Rinehart and Winston.
Bolton, Kingsley. 2000. Language and hybridization: Pidgin tales from the China coast. *Interventions 5:* 35–52.
Bolton, Kingsley. 2002. Chinese Englishes: From Canton jargon to global English. *World Englishes 21:* 181–199.
Botha, Rudolf. 2006. Pidgin languages as a putative window on language evolution. *Language & Communication 26:* 1–14.
Chaudenson, Robert. 1979. *Les créoles français.* Paris: Fernand Nathan.
Chaudenson, Robert. 2001. *Creolization of language and culture.* London: Routledge.
Chaudenson, Robert. 2003. *La créolisation: théorie, applications, implications.* Paris: L'Harmattan.
Coelho, Adolfo. 1880–1886. Os dialectos romanicos ou neolatinos na Africa, Asia, e America. *Bolletin da Sociedada de Geografia de Lisboa.*
Comrie, Bernard, Stephen Matthews, & Maria Polinsky (eds.). 1996. *The atlas of languages: The origin and development of languages throughout the world.* New York: Facts on File.
Corne, Chris. 1999. *From French to Creole: The development of new vernaculars in the French colonial world.* London: University of Westminster Press.
Curtin, Phillip D. 1984. *Cross-cultural trade in world history.* Cambridge: Cambridge University Press.
DeGraff, Michel. 1999. Creolization, language change, and language acquisition: A prolegomenon. In Michel DeGraff (ed.) *Language creation and language change: Creolization, diachrony, and development,* pp. 1–46. Cambridge, MA: MIT Press.
DeGraff, Michel (ed.). 1999. *Language creation and language change: Creolization, diachrony, and development.* Cambridge, MA: MIT Press.

DeGraff, Michel. 2001. On the origin of creoles: A Cartesian critique of neo-Darwinian linguistics. *Linguistic Typology* 5: 213–310.
DeGraff, Michel. 2002. Relexification: A reevaluation. *Anthropological Linguistics* 44: 321–414.
DeGraff, Michel. 2003. Against creole exceptionalism: Discussion note. *Language* 79: 391–410.
DeGraff, Michel. 2005. Linguists' most dangerous myth: The fallacy of creole exceptionalism. *Language in Society* 34: 533–591.
DeGraff, Michel. 2009. Language acquisition in creolization and, thus, language change: Some Cartesian-uniformitarian boundary conditions. *Language and Linguistics Compass* 3(4): 888–971.
Delafosse, Maurice. 1904. *Vocabulaires comparatifs de plus de 60 langues ou dialectes parlés à la Côte d'Ivoire et dans les régions limitrophes: avec des notes linguistiques et ethnologiques, une bibliographie et une carte*, Paris: E. Leroux.
Dillard, J. L. 1972. *Black English: Its history and usage in the United States*. New York: Random House.
Drechsel, Emanuel J. 2014. *Language contact in the earlier colonial Pacific: Maritime Polynesian Pidgin before Pidgin English*. Cambridge: Cambridge University Press.
Faine, Jules. 1937. *Philologie créole: études historiques et étymologiques sur la langue créole d'Haïti*. Port-au-Prince: Imprimerie de l'Etat.
Fayer, Joan. 2003. African interpreters in the Atlantic slave trade. *American Anthropologist* 45: 281–295.
Féral, Carole de. 1989. *Pidgin-English du Cameroun*. Paris: Peters/SELAF.
Fortbath, Peter. 1977. *The River Congo: The discovery, exploration, and exploitation of the world's most dramatic river*. Boston: Houghton Mifflin Co.
Gray, Edward G. & Norman Fiering (eds) 2000. *The language encounter in the Americas 1492–1800*. New York: Berghahn Books.
Hall, Robert A., Jr. 1958. Creole languages and genetic relationships. *Word* 14: 367–373.
Hall, Robert A., Jr. 1962. The life-cycle of pidgin languages. *Lingua* 11: 151–156.
Hall, Robert A., Jr. 1966. *Pidgin and creole languages*. Ithaca, NY: Cornell University Press.
Hancock, Ian F. 1977. Appendix: Repertory of pidgin and creole languages. In Albert Valdman (ed.) *Pidgin and creole linguistics*, pp. 362–391. Bloomington: Indiana University Press.
Hancock, Ian. 1986. The domestic hypothesis, diffusion and componentiality: An account of Atlantic Anglophone creole origins. In Pieter Muysken & Norval Smith (eds) *Substrata versus universals in creole genesis*, pp. 71–102. Amsterdam: Benjamins.
Hesseling, Dirk Christiaan. 1897. Het Hollands in Zuid Afrika. *De Gids* 61: 148–62. Translated as "Dutch in South Africa", in T. L. Markey & P. Roberge (eds). *On the origin and formation of creoles: A miscellany of articles*, pp. 1–22. Ann Arbor: Karoma.
Hjelmslev, Louis. 1938. Etudes sur la notion de parenté linguistique. Première étude: relations de parenté de langues créoles. *Revue des Etudes Indo-Européennes* 1: 271–286.
Holm, John. 1988. *Pidgins and creoles*. Vol. 1: *Theory and structure*. Cambridge: Cambridge University Press.
Holm, John. 1989. *Pidgins and creoles*. Vol. 2: *Reference survey*. Cambridge: Cambridge University Press.
Holm, John. 2004. *Languages in contact: The partial restructuring of vernaculars*. Cambridge: Cambridge University Press.
Huber, Magnus. 1999. Atlantic creoles and the Lower Guinea Coast: A case against Afrogenesis. In Magnus Huber & Mikael Parkvall (eds) *Spreading the word: The issue of diffusion among the Atlantic creoles*, pp. 81–110. London: University of Westminster Press.
Hurford, James R. 2012. *The origins of grammar: Language in the light of evolution*. Cambridge: Cambridge University Press.
Jourdan, Christine. 1991. Pidgins and creoles: The blurring of categories. *Annual Review of Anthropology* 20: 187–209.
Jourdan, Christine. 2009. Complexification or regularization of paradigms: The case of prepositional verbs in Solomon Islands Pijin. In Enoch Aboh & Norval Smith (eds) *Complex processes in new languages*, pp. 159–170. Amsterdam: Benjamins.
Karttunen, Frances. 1994. *Between worlds: Interpreters, guides, and survivors*. New Brunswick, NJ: Rutgers University Press.
Keesing, Roger M. 1988. *Melanesian Pidgin and the Oceanic substrate*. Stanford: Stanford University Press.
Kennedy, Dane. 2013. *The last blank spaces: Exploring Africa and Australia*. Cambridge, MA: Harvard University Press.
Klingler, Thomas A. 2003. *If I could turn my tongue like that: The creole language of Pointe Coupée Parish, Louisiana*. Baton Rouge: Louisiana State University.
Kouwenberg, Silvia & John V. Singler (eds) 2009. *The handbook of pidgin and creole studies*. Malden, MA: Wiley-Blackwell.

Lawrance, Benjamin, Emily Lynn Osborn, & Richard L. Roberts (eds). 2006. *Intermediaries, interpreters, and clerks: African employees in the making of colonial Africa*. Madison: University of Wisconsin Press.

Lefebvre, Claire.1998. *Creole genesis and the acquisition of grammar: The case of Haitian Creole*. Cambridge: Cambridge University Press.

Lefebvre, Claire, Lydia White & Christine Jourdan (eds). 2006. *L2 acquisition and creole genesis*. Amsterdam: Benjamins.

Lefebvre, Claire (ed.). 2011. *Creoles, their substrates, and language typology*. Amsterdam: Benjamins.

McWhorter, John H. 1998. Identifying the creole prototype: Vindicating a typological class. *Language* 74: 788–818.

Metcalf, Alida C. 2005. *Go-betweens and the colonization of Brazil, 1500–1600*. Austin: University of Texas Press.

Meyerhoff, Miriam. 2009. Forging Pacific pidgin and creole syntax: Substrate, discourse, and inherent variability. In Silvia Kouwenberg & John V. Singler (eds), *The handbook of pidgin and creole studies*, pp. 48–73. Malden, MA: Wiley-Blackwell.

Mufwene, Salikoko S. 1986a. Les langues créoles peuvent-elles être définies sans allusion à leur histoire? *Etudes Créoles* 9: 135–50.

Mufwene, Salikoko S. 1986b. The universalist and substrate hypotheses complement one another. In Pieter, Muysken & Norval Smith (eds) *Substrata versus universals in creole genesis*, pp. 129–162. Amsterdam: Benjamins.

Mufwene, Salikoko S. 1988. Why study pidgins and creoles? Column. *Journal of Pidgin and Creole Languages* 3: 265–76.

Mufwene, Salikoko S. 1994. On decreolization: The case of Gullah. In Marcyliena Morgan (ed.) *Language, loyalty, and identity in creole situations*, pp. 63–99. Los Angeles: Center for Afro-American Studies.

Mufwene, Salikoko S. 1996. The Founder Principle in creole genesis. *Diachronica* 13: 83–134.

Mufwene, Salikoko S. 1997. Jargons, pidgins, creoles, and koinés: What are they? In Arthur K. Spears & Donald Winford (eds) *Pidgins and creoles: Structure and status*, pp. 35–70. Amsterdam: Benjamins.

Mufwene, Salikoko S. 2000. Creolization is a social, not a structural, process. In Ingrid Neumann-Holzschuh, & Edgar Schneider (eds) *Degrees of restructuring in creole languages*, pp. 65–84. Amsterdam: John Benjamins.

Mufwene, Salikoko S. 2001. *The ecology of language evolution*. Cambridge: Cambridge University Press.

Mufwene, Salikoko S. 2003. Genetic linguistics and genetic creolistics. *Journal of Pidgin and Creole Languages* 18: 273–288.

Mufwene, Salikoko S. 2005. *Créoles, écologie sociale, évolution linguistique*. Paris: L'Harmattan.

Mufwene, Salikoko S. 2008. *Language evolution: Contact, competition and change*. London: Continuum.

Mufwene, Salikoko S. 2009a. The indigenization of English in North America. In Thomas Hoffmann & Lucia Siebers (eds) *World Englishes: Problems, properties, prospects*, pp. 353–368. Amsterdam: Benjamins.

Mufwene, Salikoko S. 2009b. The evolution of language: Hints from creoles. In James Minett & William S-Y Wang (eds) *Language, Evolution, and the Brain*, pp. 1–33. Hong Kong: City University of Hong Kong Press.

Mufwene, Salikoko S. 2010a. SLA and the emergence of creoles. *Studies in Second Language Acquisition 32*: 359–400.

Mufwene, Salikoko S. 2010b. 'Protolanguage' and the evolution of linguistic diversity. In Zhongwei Shen et al. (eds) *The joy of research II: A festschrift in honor of Professor William S-Y Wang on his seventy-fifth birthday*, pp. 283–310. Shanghai Jiaoyu Chubanshe (Education Press).

Mufwene, Salikoko S. 2014. Globalisation économique mondiale des XVIIe–XVIIIe siècles, émergence des créoles, et vitalité langagière. In Arnaud Carpooran & Yannick Bosquet-Ballah (eds) *Langues créoles, mondialisation et éducation*, Proceedings of the 13th Colloquium of the Comité International des Etudes Créoles, Mauritius 2012, pp. 23–79. St. Louis, Mauritius: Creole Speaking Unit.

Mufwene, Salikoko S. (ed.). 1993. *Africanisms in Afro-American language varieties*. Athens: University of Georgia Press.

Mühlhäusler, Peter. 1981. The development of the category of number in Tok Pisin. In Pieter Muysken (ed.) *Generative studies on creole languages*, pp. 35–84. Dordrecht: Foris.

Mühlhäusler, Peter. 1985. The number of pidgin Englishes in the Pacific. *Papers in Pidgin and Creole Linguistics*, no.1 Pacific Linguistics A-72: 25–51.

Mühlhäusler, Peter. 1997. *Pidgin and creole linguistics*. London: University of Westminster Press.

Muysken, Pieter, & Norval Smith (eds). 1986. *Substrata versus universals in creole genesis*. Amsterdam: Benjamins.

Ostler, Nicholas. 2005. *Empires of the word: A language history of the world*. New York: Harper Collins.
Plag, Ingo. 2008. Creoles as interlanguages: Syntactic structures. *Journal of Pidgin and Creole Languages 23*: 307–328.
Plag, Ingo. 2009. Creoles as interlanguages: Phonology. *Journal of Pidgin and Creole Languages 24*: 119–138.
Posner, Rebecca. 1985. Creolization as typological change: Some examples from Romance syntax. *Diachronica 2*: 167–88.
Reader, John. 1997. *Africa: Biography of a continent*. New York: Alfred Knopf.
Roberts, Sarah J. 1998. The role of diffusion in the genesis of Hawaiian Creole. *Language 74*: 1–39.
Roberts, Sarah J. 2004. The Emergence of Hawai'i Creole English in the Early 20th century: The Sociohistorical Context of Creole Genesis. Doctoral dissertation, Stanford University.
Sankoff, Gillian. 1979. The genesis of a language. In Hill, Kenneth C. (ed.) *The genesis of language*, pp. 23–47. Ann Arbor: Karoma.
Sankoff, Gillian 1993. Focus in Tok Pisin. In Francis Byrne, & Donald Winford (eds.) *Focus and grammatical relations in creole language*, pp. 117–140.
Sankoff, Gillian & Penelope Brown. 1976. The origins of syntax in discourse: A case study of Tok Pisin relatives. *Language 52*: 631–666.
Schlieben-Lange, Brigitte. 1977. L'origine des langues romanes: un cas de créolisation? In Jürgen Meisel (ed.), *Langues en contact – pidgins – créoles – Languages in contact*, pp. 81–101. Tübingen: Gunter Narr.
Schuchardt, Hugo. 1909. Die Lingua Franca. *Zeitschrift für Romanische Philologie 33*: 441–461.
Schuchardt, Hugo. 1914. *Die Sprache der Saramakkaneger in Surinam*. Amsterdam: Johannes Muller.
Schumann, John. 1978. *The pidginization process: A model for language acquisition*. Rowley, MA: Newbury House.
Siegel, Jeff. 2006. Links between SLA and creole studies: Past and present. In Claire Lefebvre, Lydia White & Christine Jourdan (eds) *L2 acquisition and creole genesis*, pp. 15–46. Amsterdam: Benjamins.
Siegel, Jeff. 2008. *The emergence of pidgin and creole languages*. Oxford: Oxford University Press.
Singler, John V. 1988. The homogeneity of the substrate as a factor in pidgin/creole genesis. *Language 64*: 27–51.
Singler, John V. 1996. Theories of creole genesis, sociohistorical considerations, and the evaluation of evidence: The case of Haitian Creole and the relexification hypothesis. *Journal of Pidgin and Creole Languages 11*: 185–230.
Singler, John V. 2009. The sociohistorical context of creole genesis. In Silvia Kouwenberg & John V. Singler (eds) *The handbook of pidgin and creole studies*, pp. 332–358. Malden, MA: Wiley-Blackwell.
Smith, Norval. 1995. An annotated list of pidgins, creoles, and mixed languages. In Jacques Arends, Pieter Muysken & Norval Smith (eds) *Pidgins and creoles: An introduction*, pp. 331–374. Amsterdam: Benjamins.
Stewart, Charles (ed.). 2007. *Creolization: History, ethnography, theory*. Walnut Creek, CA: Left Coast Press.
Sylvain, Susanne. 1936. *Le créole haïtien: morphologie et syntaxe*. Wettern, Belgium: Imprimerie De Meester.
Thomason, Sarah G. 2001. *Language contact: An introduction*. Washington, DC: Georgetown University Press.
Thomason, Sarah G. & Terrence Kaufman 1988. *Language contact, creolization, and genetic linguistics*. Berkeley: University of California Press.
Turner, Lorenzo Dow. 1949. *Africanisms in the Gullah dialect*. Chicago: University of Chicago Press.
Valkhoff, Marius F. 1966. *Studies in Portuguese and creole – with special reference to South Africa*. Johannesburg: Witwatersrand University Press.
Van Dyke, Paul A. 2005. *The Canton trade: Life and Enterprise on the China coast, 1700–1845*. Hong Kong: Hong Kong University Press.
Vigouroux, Cécile B. 2013. Francophonie. *Annual Review of Anthropology 42*: 379–397.
Vinson, Julien. 1882. Créole. *Dictionnaire des sciences anthropologiques et ethnologiques*. Paris.
Whinnom, Keith. 1965. The origin of the European-based pidgins and creoles. *Orbis 14*: 509–527.
Whinnom, Keith. 1971. Linguistic hybridization and the "special case" of pidgins and creoles. In Dell Hymes (ed.) *Pidginization and creolization of languages*, pp. 91–115. Cambridge University Press.
Wouden, Ton van der (ed.). 2012. *Roots of Afrikaans: Selected writings of Hans den Besten*. Amsterdam: John Benjamins.

24
Discrimination via Discourse

Ruth Wodak

1 Introduction/Definitions[1]

The starting point for a discourse analytical approach to the complex phenomenon of discrimination is to realize that *racism*, as a *social practice* and as an *ideology*, manifests itself discursively and thus through a range of discursive and material practices. On the one hand, discriminatory opinions, stereotypes, prejudices and beliefs are produced and reproduced by means of discourse; and through discourse, discriminatory exclusionary practices are prepared, implemented, justified and legitimated. On the other hand, discourse offers a space in which to criticize, delegitimate and argue against racist opinions and practices, that is, to pursue anti-racist strategies.

In his seminal book *Prejudice in Discourse,* Teun A. van Dijk (1984) focuses in great detail on the "rationalization and justification of discriminatory acts against minority groups." He labels the categories used to rationalize prejudice against minority groups as *"the 7 D's of Discrimination."* These are *dominance, differentiation, distance, diffusion, diversion, depersonalization* or *destruction,* and *daily discrimination.* These strategies serve in various ways to legitimize and enact the distinction of 'the other,' for example, by dominating minority groups, by excluding them from social activities, and even by destroying and murdering them (van Dijk 1984: 40).

The *public management of 'inclusion' and 'exclusion'* via a range of policy papers and laws is a question of 'grading' and 'scales', ranging from explicit legal and economic restrictions to implicit discursive negotiations and decisions. I assume that 'inclusion/exclusion' of, and related discriminatory practices against, migrant groups change due to different criteria of how insiders and outsiders are defined in each instance. In this way, various topologies, criteria, or group memberships are arbitrarily constructed, which sometimes include a certain group, and sometimes do not, depending on sociopolitical and situational contexts and political interests as well as necessities (Wodak 2007a,b,c).

Thus, a specific migrant status (coming from a certain host country) may serve as a criterion for exclusion; sometimes, however, language competence is defined as salient. Foreigners or migrants arrive from different countries, with different motives and goals, with various educational backgrounds, religious and political affiliations, and cultural (gendered) traditions. Specifically, right-wing populist rhetoric seems to merge all foreigners into one homogeneous group that symbolizes the negative 'other.'[2] Furthermore, a specific job qualification may mean inclusion, despite the respective migrant coming from an otherwise excluded country; in other cases, religion and gender are regarded as criteria that discriminate against specific groups.[3] The mere use of certain labels manifests the fluidity of definitions and membership categories. Recent research on the British press, for example, has illustrated that the semantic concepts of 'migrant,' 'refugee' and 'asylum seeker' have become conflated and that all of these concepts are sometimes used in contemporary media to label all "foreigners who are not welcome," always defined anew in a context-dependent way.[4] Such multifaceted processes necessarily call for an interdisciplinary approach that integrates historical, socio-political, and socio-psychological and discourse analytic approaches in a more general problem-oriented framework.[5]

Discrimination implies *deprivation of access* through means of explicit or symbolic power (in Pierre Bourdieu's sense) implemented by the social elites: access to participation, citizenship, the media, information, language learning, power positions, certain organizations, jobs, housing, education, etc. Moreover, debates about immigration and nationhood are crucially linked to assumptions about place. 'Our' culture belongs 'here' within the bounded homeland, whilst the culture of 'foreigners' belongs 'elsewhere.'[6] The theme of place is particularly threatening to groups who are seen to have no 'natural' homeland, such as the Romani or other diasporic communities today, or the Jews in the first half of the twentieth century. Religion as a central condition for inclusion/exclusion and discrimination, frequently triggered by indexical markers such as the 'headscarf' worn by Muslim women, has become dominant in some EU countries only in recent years.[7]

Powerful elites frequently justify such exclusion in various ways. Reference is then made, explicitly or implicitly, to status, belonging, ethnicity or gender, by discursively creating ever new topologies: modern and global forms of discrimination and exclusion can, I claim, be most acutely symbolized by somebody having or not having a 'passport' to enter the countries of their choice. Hence, acquisition of citizenship becomes a legal means for inclusion, which, however, does not guarantee that migrants or refugees become accepted members of the respective host country once they have legally become citizens.

In this paper, I cannot elaborate and explain in all its facets the complex phenomenon of discrimination against autochtonous, linguistic or sexual minorities, foreigners, and specific ethnic and/or religious groups.[8] Rather, I restrict myself in what follows to discussing and elaborating several important dimensions of discrimination and *othering* via text, image and talk, i.e., via manifold written, oral and visual discursive practices: below, I focus briefly on three manifestations of the *rhetoric of exclusion* (i.e., discriminatory rhetoric), while having to neglect many other linguistic *expressions* of discrimination for reasons of space (such as explicit hate speech; word plays; comparative dimensions across various public spaces; and so forth):[9] on the *discursive construction of in-groups and out-groups*, which relates to *strategies of positive self- and negative-other presentation*; on *strategies of justification and legitimation* of exclusionary practices through *argumentative devices*; and, thirdly, on the *denial of racism* that frequently accompanies and introduces discriminatory rhetoric. Finally, I will illustrate some of these discursive practices with one example from the Viennese election campaign in October 2010 by analyzing a poster from the Austrian Freedom Party (Freiheitliche Partei Österreich; FPÖ)[10] as this integrates many elements of extreme right-wing ideology and related discursive practices. The debate about this poster is typical regarding the so-called *strategy of provocation* and the *strategy of calculated ambivalence*, which both emerged in the past two decades (since 1986) in the propaganda launched by the FPÖ (Engel & Wodak 2013; Wodak & Richardson 2013a; Wodak et al. 2013b).

At this point, it is important to emphasise that such exclusionary and discriminatory discursive practices are, of course, not new but have been part and parcel of manipulative and persuasive rhetoric and propaganda for centuries,[11] have accompanied, or indeed prepared the ground for, physical violence, struggles, and wars. Thus, we should not be surprised that such discursive practices still exist and continue to be employed; rather, it is salient to investigate continuities and changes, for example during and after crises, during and after wars, and during election campaigns, from governing parties and from the opposition (in democratic systems).[12] Moreover, it is salient, I believe, for social scientists, historians, and so forth to be aware not only of the possible mobilizing effects of such discursive practices but also of the context-dependent, complex and intricate linguistic forms that are employed, while exploiting all available communicative channels (such as new social media). Of course, new modes of resistance to discrimination and exclusion via social media should also be analysed systematically and in detail in order to understand the challenging and rapid socio-political changes with which our globalised world is currently confronted.[13]

2 Historical and Current Socio-political Perspectives

The European Union Context

Before embarking on a discussion of the salient characteristics of discrimination via text and talk, it is important to recall the European legal framework that defines and regulates discrimination, thus accounting for David Goldberg's – quite controversial but legitimate – claim that "the state is inherently contradictory and internally fractured, consisting not only of agencies and bureaucracies, legislatures and courts, but also of norms and principles, individuals and institutions" (2002: 7). In Goldberg's view, there is no singular modern state, and no singular racialized state. On the contrary, he claims that both are intertwined, the "histories of the former at once accountable in terms of the projected spatialities and temporalities of the latter" (p. 7). It is important, therefore, to acknowledge – as Goldberg states – that modern states are racial in their modernity and modern in their racial quality. Taking this view further, it becomes obvious that the rhetoric of discrimination and exclusion has, on the one hand, to be analysed in its specific historical context; on the other, transnational and global patterns also have to (and can) be detected and deconstructed. In this chapter, I thus attempt to point to general developments and tendencies while also presenting an in-depth analysis of a contextualized example.

In 2000, the European Union (EU) adopted two directives (Sugarman & Butler 2011): the *Employment Equality Directive* prohibited discrimination on the basis of sexual orientation, religious belief, age, and disability in the area of employment; the *Racial Equality Directive* prohibited discrimination on the basis of race or ethnicity in the context of employment, but also in accessing the welfare system and social security, and goods and services. These directives imply a significant expansion of the scope of non-discrimination law by the EU, which recognises explicitly that in order to allow individuals to reach their full potential in the employment market, it is also essential to guarantee them equal access to areas such as health, education and housing.

In 2004, the *Gender Goods and Services Directive* expanded the scope of sex discrimination to the area of goods and services. Protection on the grounds of gender does not, however, quite match the scope of protection under the *Racial Equality Directive* since the *Gender Social Security Directive* guarantees equal treatment in relation to social security only, and not to the broader welfare system, such as social protection and access to healthcare and education. Although sexual orientation, religious belief, disability and age are protected grounds only in the context of employment, a proposal to extend protection on these grounds to the area of accessing goods and services (known as a '*Horizontal Directive*') is currently being debated in the EU institutions.[14]

Human Rights Charter and Access to Citizenship

It is quite remarkable, I believe, that the original treaties of the European Communities did not contain any reference to human rights or their protection, in spite of the aftermath of World War II. It was not believed in the early 1950s that the creation of an area of free trade in Europe could have any impact relevant to human rights. As cases began to appear, however, before the European Court of Justice (ECJ), alleging human rights breaches caused by Community law, the ECJ developed a body of judge-made law known as the *'general principles' of Community Law* (Sugarman & Butler 2011: 6). In recognising that its policies could have an impact on human rights and in an effort to make citizens feel 'closer' to the EU, the EU and its Member States proclaimed the *EU Charter of Fundamental Rights* in 2000. The Charter contains a list of human rights, inspired by the rights stated in the constitutions of the Member States, the European Convention on Human Rights (ECHR) and universal human rights treaties, such as the UN Convention on the Rights of the Child. The Charter, as adopted in 2000, was merely a 'declaration,' which means that it was not legally binding, although the European Commission stated that its proposals would be in compliance. When the Treaty of Lisbon entered into force in 2009, it altered the status of the Charter of Fundamental Rights to make it a legally binding document (see also Wodak 2011a). As a result, the institutions of the EU are bound to comply with it. EU Member States also comply with the Charter, but only when implementing EU law.[15] It remains to be seen how well these laws are implemented in all EU Member States and beyond; or how far changes and adaptations occur when recontextualising such legislation nationally or even locally (Wodak & Fairclough 2010). Thus, it is relevant to recognise the dialectics between the scale of the EU and national or even regional entities, i.e., to be aware that

> the insistence on rights locally, at least normatively, is at once also the realization of rights more generally, tentatively more globally. . . . If rights are generalizations from local practice and local embodiments of generalized extensions, then my right – the right of those like me, of "my people" – at once contains the kernel of the rights (or their restriction and lack) for all.
> *Goldberg (2002: 273)*

Along this vein, it is important to discuss and investigate policies of exclusion with respect to citizenship (Bauböck & Faist 2010). In general, we can perceive nation-states as 'imagined communities' (Anderson 1985), which are also (re)produced in everyday lives by banal forms of nationalism (Billig 1995). This banal nationalism, for example, uses specific forms of *deixis*[16] in newspapers and in political rhetoric, so that 'here' is assumed to be the national homeland, and 'us,' by inference, the members of the imagined national community. The *banal nationalism* of nation-states is vague about who exactly 'we' are: sometimes the particular 'we' of the nation means the general 'we' of all 'reasonable people' (Billig 1995). In other cases the 'we' is very clearly defined and restricted to membership of certain groups (see below). Nation-states, however, also have laws that enable discrimination to be practised with precision: Typically, as already hinted at above, nation-states will have laws that discriminate between those who are permitted citizenship of the state and those who are not. Similarly, they will have laws that grant residency to some non-citizens but not others, often linked nowadays to restrictive language tests (de Cillia & Wodak 2006, Wodak 2011b).

3 Relevant Methodologies of Analysis

The study of discriminatory practices necessarily implies qualitative in-depth analysis as traditional methods of measurement encounter huge obstacles when trying to account for racist, antisemitic or xenophobic attitudes. Indeed, much research has provided ample evidence that more educated people understate their prejudiced beliefs;[17] moreover, the ideological value of tolerance is widespread in contemporary capitalist societies, so that the explicit promulgation of exclusionary politics conflicts with the generally accepted values of liberalism.[18] Hence, discriminatory utterances tend to be '*coded*' in official rhetoric so as to avoid sanctions; *linguistic cues* such as *insinuations* are frequently only comprehensible to insiders. Indeed, the very terms 'discrimination,' 'exclusion' or 'prejudice' carry negative connotations. Few would admit in public or when interviewed to agreeing with the exclusion of, or prejudice or discrimination against, minority groups. This is why opinion polls and interviews are inherently doomed to fail when investigating racist belief systems. Usually people deny these beliefs and try to present themselves in a positive way as they are aware that such opinions are taboo or might even be associated with extremist right-wing political affiliations. This is also why the study of exclusionary rhetoric has tended to attract critical analysts, who do not take what people say at face value but seek to examine the – often latent – ideological/discriminatory, complex nature of discourse. This means studying how discursive practices can accomplish exclusion in its many facets without the explicitly acknowledged intention of actors; exclusion becomes 'normality' and thus acceptable, and integrated into all dimensions of our societies.

3.1 Positive Self- and Negative Other-Presentation

According to Reisigl and Wodak (2001: 1), racism/discrimination/exclusion manifests itself discursively: "racist opinions and beliefs are produced and reproduced by means of discourse . . . through discourse, discriminatory exclusionary practices are prepared, promulgated and legitimized." The construction of in- and out-groups necessarily implies the use of *strategies of positive self-presentation and the negative presentation of others*.[19] In this paper, I focus on five types of discursive strategies, which are all involved in positive self- and negative other-presentation. These discursive strategies underpin the justification/legitimisation of inclusion/exclusion and the constructions of identities. '*Strategy*' generally means a (more or less accurate and more or less intentional) plan of practices, including discursive practices, adopted to achieve a particular social, political, psychological or linguistic goal.[20] Heuristically, I distinguish between five questions:

1   How are persons, objects, phenomena/events, processes and actions named and referred to linguistically?
2   What characteristics, qualities and features are attributed to social actors, objects, phenomena/events and processes?
3   What arguments are employed in the discourse in question?
4   From what perspective are these nominations, attributions and arguments expressed?
5   Are the respective utterances articulated overtly; are they intensified or mitigated?

Table 24.1 summarizes the five strategies and some of the related linguistic, pragmatic, rhetorical and argumentative means used in specific genres and contexts to realise the respective strategies.

4 Important Dimensions

4.1 The Denial of Exclusion and Racism

Linked to positive self-presentation and the construction of positive group and collective identities is the denial of racism. Recall the well-known examples of justification discourses, such

Table 24.1 A selection of discursive strategies (adapted from Reisigl & Wodak 2009: p. 95)

Strategy	Objectives	Devices
referential / nomination	discursive construction of social actors, objects/ phenomena/events and processes/actions	• membership categorization devices, deictics, anthroponyms, etc. • tropes such as metaphors, metonymies, and synecdoches (*pars pro toto, totum pro parte*) • verbs and nouns used to denote processes and actions
predication	discursive qualification of social actors, objects/ phenomena/events and processes/actions (more or less positively or negatively)	• stereotypical evaluative attributions of negative or positive traits (e.g., in the form of adjectives, appositions, prepositional phrases, relative clauses, conjunctional clauses, infinitive clauses and participial clauses or groups) • explicit predicates or predicative nouns/ adjectives/pronouns • collocations • explicit comparisons, similes, metaphors, and other rhetorical figures (including metonymies, hyperboles, litotes, euphemisms) • allusions, evocations, presuppositions/ implicatures
argumentation	justification and questioning of claims of truth and normative rightness	• topoi (formal or content-related) • fallacies
perspectivization, framing or discourse representation	positioning speaker's or writer's point of view and expressing involvement or distance	• deictics • direct, indirect, or free indirect speech • quotation marks, discourse markers/particles • metaphors • animating prosody
intensification, mitigation	modifying (intensifying or mitigating) the illocutionary force and thus the epistemic or deontic status of utterances	• diminutives or augmentatives • (modal) particles, tag questions, subjunctives, hesitations, vague expressions, etc. • hyperboles, litotes • indirect speech acts (e.g., question instead of assertion) • verbs of saying, feeling, thinking

as 'I have nothing against . . . , but,' 'my best friends are . . . , but,' 'we are tolerant, but,' 'we would like to help, but the boot is full,' etc. All these discursive utterances, labelled as *'disclaimers,'* manifest the *'denial of racism or exclusion'* and emphasize *positive self-presentation* (see above; van Dijk 1989). By and large, speakers in such debates seek to justify the practice of exclusion without employing related overt discriminatory rhetoric.

Such overt denials of prejudice basically involve two presuppositions. First, they presuppose the existence of 'real' prejudice. In this regard, the existence of extreme, outwardly fascist groups enables defenders of mainstream racism/exclusion/discrimination to present their own rhetoric as being unprejudiced – by comparison. Second, speakers, in denying prejudice, will claim that their criticisms of minority group members are 'factual,' 'objective,' and 'reasonable,' rather than being based upon irrational feelings, and will accordingly employ a range of discursive strategies of legitimisation (Billig 2005). Speakers can, of course, use similar denials of prejudice and arguments of reasonableness when talking about different forms of discrimination, such as sexism, racism, antisemitism or religious discrimination. Additionally, each type of exclusionary practice will integrate particular themes, stereotypes and argumentative devices (*topoi*), all contributing to the *syncretic nature of mainstream discriminatory discourse*.

4.2 Justification and Legitimation Discourses: The Logic of Argumentation

Positive self- and negative other-presentation requires the explicit or implicit (coded) use of justification and legitimation strategies; the latter imply the usually strategic and manipulative application of specific argumentation schemes as well as topoi and fallacies (Reisigl & Wodak 2009: 102). Within argumentation theory, '*topoi*' can be described as parts of argumentation, which belong to the required premises. They are the formal or content-related *warrants* or 'conclusion rules' that connect the argument(s) with the conclusion, the claim. As such, they justify the transition from the argument(s) to the conclusion (Kienpointner 1996: 194). Topoi are not always expressed explicitly, but can always be made explicit as conditional or causal paraphrases such as 'if x, then y' or 'y, because x.'[21]

Argumentation schemes are reasonable or fallacious. If the latter is the case, we label them *fallacies*. There are rules for rational disputes and constructive argument, which allow the discerning of reasonable topoi from fallacies.[22] These rules include the freedom to argue, the obligation to give reasons, correct references to the previous discourse by the antagonist, the obligation to 'matter-of factness,' the correct references to implicit premises, the respect of shared standpoints, the use of plausible arguments and schemes of argumentation, logical validity, the acceptance of the discussion's results, and clarity of expression and correct interpretation. If these rules are flouted, fallacies occur. However, as Reisigl and Wodak (2009: 102) admit, it is not always easy to distinguish precisely without contextual knowledge whether an argumentation scheme has been employed as reasonable topos or as fallacy.

In debates about immigration and religious difference or in media reporting, speakers/writers will often employ arguments about 'culture,' depicting it as an essentially bounded entity whose integrity is threatened by the presence of residents supposedly belonging to a different 'culture' and thus not being willing to learn and adopt 'our' conventions and norms, i.e., to assimilate; in these argumentative sequences, deictic elements acquire salience and culture is regarded as a static entity that somebody either knows about or not; has or does not have. Culture is thus essentialised in such debates (see above). For example, van Leeuwen and Wodak (1999) observed regimes of exclusion and discrimination when analysing official rejection letters by the magistrate of the city of Vienna, denying 'family reunion,' i.e., rejecting applications of migrants who had already settled in the host country to have their families come and join them. Indeed, in the latter case, a number of moral and rational legitimation strategies were employed that were used to justify exclusion by referring to statistics or to moral values (ethics, humanitarianism, religion, etc.). The *topos of culture* was particularly salient in this case.

When analysing discriminatory and exclusionary rhetoric in post-war Europe, four factors typically have to be taken into account, albeit realised linguistically in context-dependent ways:[23] a) exclusionary practices occur in situations of differential power; b) the powerful actors need not possess a conscious goal or intention; indeed, they may deny that any discrimination/exclusion has occurred; c) the powerful actors consider their own actions 'reasonable' and 'natural' and d) the actions that lead to exclusion are usually conducted through 'coded' language; overt exclusionary language is rarely to be observed.

5 Current Contributions and Research: A Discourse-Historical Analysis of the FPÖ's Discriminatory Rhetoric

5.1 Socio-political and Historical Context

In their political discourse in general and especially in their past election campaigns, the FPÖ (the Austrian Freedom Party)[24] has developed a specific discursive pattern that has led to much discussion in the media as well as in academic work. So far, research has provided evidence that similar discursive practices and argumentation schemata emerge time and again, albeit with certain variations.

Since Jörg Haider's 1986 coup to gain leadership of the FPÖ, all its election campaigns have successfully combined traditional and innovative means of election campaigning (events both small and large, including speeches and other performances by the top candidates in public spaces, beer tents and discotheques, posters, advertisements, party-run newspapers, media appearances, distribution of printed materials, etc.), as well as the new social media (the internet, brochures designed to look like comic books, a rap song specifically written for and performed by the party leader).[25] This has effectively opened up avenues for communication with diverse target groups and created a whole network of texts and images intertwined with each other. The contents distributed by such means include open and covert constructions of marginalising and discriminatory statements that draw on xenophobic, Islamophobic, antisemitic, homophobic and other resentments. Examples from earlier election campaigns include the slogans *'Daham statt Islam'*[26] in 2006 and *'Abendland in Christenhand'*[27] in 2009. While such statements regularly test the boundaries of the socially acceptable and legally permissible, it is rare for a slogan to cross the legal boundaries of the freedom of speech, although moral thresholds defined by mainstream society are often violated. The FPÖ-MP Susanne Winter, for instance, was tried and convicted[28] by a criminal court of justice for hate incitement (*'Verhetzung'*) and the vilification of religious teachings,[29] because she had used her speech at a New Year's meeting of the FPÖ to claim that the founder of Islamic religion had written the Koran during epileptic fits and had also been a paedophile.

It is through precisely this *strategy of provocation* that the FPÖ has placed the general public, but especially its political competitors, in a dilemma: Even if it is one of the basic rules of politics that any reaction raises the attention given to a political adversary and should therefore be avoided, the principle 'By remaining silent, we agree' also applies here. There are, however, statements that cannot be left unchallenged – these, of course, are precisely those that the FPÖ launches intentionally in order to provoke and set the agenda.

The by now predictable response to such reactions on the part of the FPÖ is, in turn, an integral part of the campaigns themselves and is used to reinforce the FPÖ's status as a victim, inviting voters through a strengthened sense of group identity against a common enemy on the outside (see, for example, Haider's poster slogan 1994: *'Sie sind gegen ihn, weil er für Euch ist'*).[30] Thus, reaction and counter-reaction can lead to an escalation of the debate that virtually guarantees the FPÖ unanimous attention, a process through which the party succeeds in dominating the political agenda.

In the following, I first provide a brief history of the FPÖ in post-war Austria; then I summarise some important characteristics of the Vienna election campaign in 2010. These two sections provide the broad historical and socio-political contexts that both allow embedding and contextualising of the immediate event. Finally I analyse and interpret a specific FPÖ poster using the background of the contextual information and the linguistic methodology provided above. In this way, the so-called *'Four-Level-Context' Model* of the *Discourse-Historical Approach* to Critical Discourse Analysis serves to make the analysis and interpretation both transparent and retroductable (see Wodak 2001, 2011a). The first level is descriptive, while the other three develop the Discourse-Historical Approach to meaning in 'context':

1. the immediate, language or text internal co-text;
2. the intertextual and interdiscursive relationship between utterances, texts, genres, and discourses;
3. the extralinguistic social/sociological variables and institutional frames of a specific 'context of situation';
4. the broader socio-political and historical contexts, which the discursive practices are embedded in and related to (Wodak 2001: 67).

These four levels of context illustrate that discourses, genres and socio-political contexts are dependent on each other, i.e., linked in a dialectical relationship.

5.2 The Austrian Freedom Party

In 1949, 'liberals' with a strong German National orientation and not much of a classical liberal tradition (see Bailer-Galanda & Neugebauer 1997: 326), who felt unable to support either the Social Democrats (SPÖ) or the Christian Conservative People's Party (ÖVP), founded the VdU (*Verband der Unabhängigen* – Association of Independents). This party became the electoral home for many former Austrian Nazis. The FPÖ, founded in 1956, was the successor party to the VdU, retaining an explicit attachment to a so-called 'German cultural community.'[31]

In the 1949 parliamentary elections, the VdU won 12% of the national vote, making it the third-strongest party. Soon thereafter the VdU called for the abolition of all laws governing de-nazification procedures. The argument that the VdU employed to this end rested above all on the reversal of the perpetrator–victim dichotomy: the real victims were not those persecuted by the Nazi regime, but rather former members of the NSDAP (*Nationalsozialistische Deutsche Arbeiterpartei* – National Socialist German Workers' Party), who were now being singled out.

Accordingly, the VdU used a "grotesque conception of fascism" (Manoschek 2002: 6), based on a crude view of totalitarianism, "to attack the de-nazification policies of the government and to equate Nazism with other political systems" (p. 6). Hence, "when the VdU spoke about fascism, it mentioned neither National Socialism nor the Holocaust, at best indicating the 'positive aspects' of German fascism, such as – infamously – full employment and economic growth" (p. 6), thereby allowing for a revival of Austrian 'pro-fascist' sentiment on a national scale and making such sentiments a significant element of the country's political agenda and of public discourses for many years to come.

Given the early VdU ideology, as well as the fact that the party was a conglomerate of members sharing a very broad spectrum of views on the role of an Austrian 'third political force,' it did not take long before the party entered a significant crisis, resulting in an even stronger pan-Germanist and pro-fascist agenda coming to the fore. It was amidst this crisis that the Freedom Party of Austria (FPÖ) was established in 1955–56, clearly being "funded as a German nationalist party of the far right, in which former, seriously incriminated National Socialists took the leading functions" (Schiedel & Neugebauer 2002: 16). For example, the first FPÖ chairman, Anton Reintaller, had once been "a member of the National Steering Committee of the Austrian NSDAP and the SS-Brigadenführer, and held the position of Minister of Agriculture in the first Nazi-led Austrian government' (p. 16).

In its more than fifty-year history, the FPÖ has, therefore, never been a 'liberal' party in the European sense, although there were always tensions between more liberal and more conservative members of the party. For instance, in 1986 Jörg Haider was elected as leader of the party, unseating Norbert Steger, who belonged to the liberal wing. Since then, the FPÖ has progressively gained votes, reaching 26.9% of all the votes cast in the Austrian elections of October 1999 (1,244,087 voters). Throughout the 1990s, the FPÖ's party policy and politics became conspicuously more anti-immigrant, anti-European Union and widely populist, resembling Le Pen's Front National in France.

From 4 February 2000, the FPÖ constituted part of the Austrian government, having formed a coalition with the conservative ÖVP. This development caused a major upheaval internationally and nationally, and led to the so-called 'sanctions' against the Austrian government by the 14 other Member States of the European Union. In September 2000, the sanctions were lifted due to a report of the three 'Wise Men' appointed by the European Commission to investigate the situation in Austria and recommend how a face-saving solution could be found. Nevertheless, the report stated that the FPÖ should be regarded as a "right wing extremist populist party, a right wing populist party with radical elements."

In May 2005, a section of the FPÖ splintered off to form a new party, the *Bündnis Zukunft Österreich* (Association for the Future of Austria – BZÖ). Haider, a chief architect of the BZÖ's creation, remained regional governor in Carinthia, but Peter Westenthaler took over the leadership of the party. Heinz-Christian Strache, in many ways emulating the younger Haider, took over the far more right-wing, traditional FPÖ. The FPÖ continues to thrive on explicit xenophobia, pan-Germanic sentiments, antisemitism and Islamophobia, in contrast to the BZÖ, which has continued its more economically oriented populist programme with – sometimes – relatively subtle xenophobic and antisemitic subtexts.[32] In the 2006 parliamentary elections, the SPÖ (*Sozialdemokratische Partei Österreichs* – Social Democratic Party of Austria) gained the majority in Austria after having been in opposition for six years. The BZÖ proportion of the vote was reduced to 5%, securing only seven seats in parliament; the FPÖ attracted around 11% of the vote and was also represented in parliament.

Since 2006, however, the FPÖ under the leadership of Heinz-Christian Strache has achieved 17.5% in national elections (2008), and almost 26% in the most recent Vienna municipal elections (2010). While the FPÖ's extreme right-wing nationalist base (some of whom are former Nazis) constitutes only a small portion of the electorate, it is still catered to deliberately through a *strategy of calculated ambivalence* about questions of war guilt, the Holocaust, Nazi ideology, xenophobia and racism.

5.3 The Vienna Election Campaign 2010

The summer of 2010, leading to the local election set for 10 October, saw a poster campaign featuring subjects that in various ways did not correspond to the familiar patterns: one of them read "*Wir geben unseren Wienerinnen und Wienern ENDLICH SICHERHEIT*"[33] and featured the front-runner H. C. Strache in conversation with a woman and a man in police uniform. The discourse of security, which the target audience of people living in Vienna very likely associated with this poster, comprises both a theme related to the number of police officers in Vienna in general and to the number of officers in the field in particular, as well as a second theme positing that criminality can be virtually equated with certain groups of offenders from foreign countries. Put in these terms, the poster's subject did indeed conform to the usual topics raised by the FPÖ, but it lacked the usual rhymes and did not constitute a discursive provocation. Such a provocation was, however, delivered by a poster first spread across the city in mid-August 2010 (see Figure 24.1).

Ruth Wodak

Figure 24.1 Poster used by the FPÖ in the Vienna election campaign of 2010. http://www.hcstrache.at/home/?id=48, picture 63, June 6, 2013, © FPÖ; see also http://www.helge.at/2010/08/reines-wiener-blut. (Credit: © Helge Fahrenberger)

The poster is situated in the action field of political advertising. The social actors involved are the politician Heinz-Christian Strache, the Austrian Freedom Party FPÖ (both on a national and a local, i.e., Viennese, level), the Viennese we-group with its "Viennese blood," foreigners referred to by objectifying and nominalizing metonymy, i.e., '*Fremdes*' ('the Foreign' [foreignness]), and the Viennese voters who are asked to vote for Strache and the FPÖ. Indirectly, political opponents are of course presupposed, since a democratic election always includes more than one option and the comparative "more courage" implies that there must also be political competitors with "less courage."

Very bright overall, the poster predominantly uses white, blue (the traditional colour of the party, derived from the cornflower, also known as blue-bottle, worn by the German Nationalists of the nineteenth century) and red (the second colour of the party logo, not discernible in a black-and-white reproduction: The letter Ö is printed in red, F and P are both blue).[34] Red is also the colour of the slogan used on the right-hand side of this poster. The call to vote for the party in the upcoming election, spread across the foot of the poster, is printed in white over a blue background and provides some cohesion for the different elements of the poster (van Leeuwen 2011). The representation of the man, born in 1969, is youthful, casual, clean and healthy: a spotless white shirt, unbuttoned at the top, no jacket or tie, brilliant blue eyes and white teeth, a tanned complexion, dense brown hair with only a touch of grey at the temples; he smiles self-confidently from the poster's surface.

At the top, on the poster's right, we find the party logo, consisting of two elements: the party acronym FPÖ and the predication '*Die soziale Heimatpartei*,' meaning 'The Social Homeland

Party.' The logo thus emphasizes the self-presentation of the party as liberal, social and homeland oriented. These three predications also fulfil the important principle of multiple addressing as the party acronym satisfies both traditional FPÖ voters and the whole party. The attribute "social" is a positive signal to socialist voters who are dissatisfied with current policies of the governing social democratic party. The compound *'Heimatpartei'* with its specifying predication *'Heimat'* obviously fishes in the water of conservatives and nationalists. The German flag-word *'Heimat'* is intended to evoke patriotic feelings of belonging to the local community, oriented towards traditional rural values.

Beneath the logo, on the right, there is a rhyme in red letters: 'More COURAGE for our "Viennese blood"'; in German: *'Mehr MUT für unser "Wiener Blut"'*. And slightly beneath the rhyme, in black, is: "Too much of the Foreign is not good for anybody." (*"Zu viel Fremdes tut niemandem gut."*).

The rhyming speech act is an elliptical appeal and request in slogan-like nominal style, constructing a 'we-group' that is characterized by its *blood*. The blood is thus specified as having the quality of being 'Viennese': the biologizing metaphor of blood with its localizing predication 'Viennese' is certainly ambiguous. Its use follows the above mentioned principle of *calculated ambivalence*, which allows for manifold convenient readings (see Reisigl 2002: 170ff, Engel & Wodak 2009, 2013).

Blood stands firstly for biological descent, kinship and ancestry. The opposition of "our Viennese blood" and the depersonalizing metonymy "too much of the Foreign" contributes to the both naturalizing and homogenizing construction of a Viennese we-group that seems endangered by 'too' many foreign immigrants. The producers of the poster, however, took precautions against such a literal biologist reading of "Viennese blood" – which implies that they were obviously conscious of the intended biologising meaning. By framing the phrase in quotation marks, the authors attempt to indicate distance from the literal meaning (perspectivation strategy). In this sense, the inverted commas mitigate the potentially racist meaning of the appeal/request.

Secondly, "Viennese blood" implies Viennese culture, since *"Wiener Blut"* – and this is the third meaning intertextually recoverable from the collocation – is the title of the well-known waltz and operetta by Johann Strauss (Jr). Strauss and his music are clear identity markers for a specific Austrian and particularly Viennese culture. Thus, the red and black catchphrases construct a dichotomy between the Viennese and foreign culture, the latter a threat to the former. In the Discourse-Historical Approach, however, it is necessary to look at the respective text of Strauss' operetta and reconstruct the intertextual links. The refrain starts as follows: *"Wiener Blut, / Wiener Blut! Eign'er Saft, / Voller Kraft, / Voller Glut. / Wiener Blut, / selt'nes Gut, / Du erhebst, / Du belebst / Unser'n Mut!"* ("Viennese blood, / Viennese blood! / Special sap / full of force, / full of fire. / Viennese blood, / exceptional good; / You turn on, / You liven up / Our courage!"). When contextualising these lines within the plot of the operetta, listeners probably realise that boiling "Viennese blood" is considered to be responsible for various love affairs; moreover, that several of the operetta's protagonists are 'blue-blooded,' i.e., aristocrats. In addition, it becomes obvious that the FPÖ's demand for 'more courage' is linked intertextually to the libretto of the operetta, where "Viennese blood" is said to 'liven up our courage.' However, it is also obvious that the FPÖ poster recontextualizes 'courage' and "Viennese blood" quite differently: audacity, for example, is no longer connected to amorous passion.

Indeed, the request for "more courage for our Viennese blood" presupposes that, nowadays, political opponents are not brave enough to engage in protection of the "Viennese essence." Hence, the appeal suggests that the FPÖ – in contrast to the other political parties – is ready to protect this "Viennese essence" against "too much of the Foreign"; and this 'fact' further implies that the party deserves to be elected. The ellipsis at the bottom of the poster concludes with the claim: "Therefore, Yes for HC Strache." (*"Deshalb Ja zu HC Strache."*). The claim is visually supplemented by a circle marked with a hand-drawn red cross.

In sum, the salient message of the poster condenses the following argumentation scheme: "You should vote Strache and the FPÖ, because he and his party are more courageous than their political opponents and will protect our "Viennese blood" against "too much of the Foreign." The statement "Too much of the Foreign is not good for anybody" takes the form of a generalizing assertive speech act. The assertion refers to the relationship between "Own" and "Foreign," suggesting that the "Own" can be exposed to – only – a certain amount of any "Foreign." At this point, one question remains: What do Strache and the FPÖ consider being "too much of the Foreign"? The answer is not explicitly given in the poster, but it can be found in other election campaign material with anti-foreigner and particularly anti-Muslim statements and sentiments.

Such indirect and implicit triggering of 'xenophobic' anxieties by the construction of unreal frightening scenarios is a well-known strategy of the FPÖ[35] and permits the denial of any accusations of racism. The fearmongering of the FPÖ had its intended effect: in the Vienna election, the FPÖ achieved 25.8% of the votes – 11% more than in 2005. In a public opinion poll after the election, 68% of the respondents who voted for the FPÖ argued that they did so because the FPÖ engages actively against migration (see Köhler & Wodak 2011: 73).

Indeed, the FPÖ did reject all criticism and produced in response a new advertisement, on the topic 'What do we mean by "Too much of the Foreign is not good for anybody."'[36] On the surface, this creates the appearance of a rational discourse; the content of its arguments, however, are recognisable as a mixture of insinuations and indirect statements, formulated as conditional clauses, which makes it almost impossible to reject them directly. The arguments brought forth in this poster do, however, clarify what is meant by "the Foreign." On the one hand, they attack the FPÖ's main political opponent, the SPÖ, for its alleged political position regarding immigration and integration. On the other hand, they focus specifically on religion, in particular on Islam.

6 Future Directions

The rise of right-wing populist movements in recent years – and, related to this phenomenon, the frequently repeated requests for more discrimination against out-groups in increasingly blatant and explicit rhetoric – would not have been possible without massive media support. This does not, of course, imply that all newspapers share the same positions; although some tabloids, of course, do.

Hence, leading populist politicians have to be – and usually are – media-savvy. Anthropologist André Gingrich (2002) rightly describes such a leader as "a man/woman for all seasons."

On the other hand, they intentionally provoke the media by violating publicly accepted liberal norms. In this way, the media are forced into a 'no-win' situation: if they do not report a scandalous racist remark, they might be perceived as endorsing it. If they do write about this, they explicitly reproduce the xenophobic utterance. A predictable dynamic is triggered that allows right-wing populist parties to set the agenda and distract the media from other important news as any new scandal would be publicised immediately, in great detail. The dynamic consists of several stages:

The scandal is first denied; once some evidence is produced, the scandal is re-defined and equated with entirely different phenomena. Predictably, the provocateur then claims the right of freedom of speech for themselves, as a justificatory strategy: "Why can't one be critical?" or "It must be permitted to criticise Turks, Roma, Muslims, Jews...!" or "*We* dare say what everybody thinks," and so forth. Such utterances, of course, immediately trigger another debate – unrelated to the original scandal – about freedom of speech and political correctness. Simultaneously, victimhood is claimed by the original provocateur, and the event is dramatised and exaggerated. This leads to the construction of a conspiracy: somebody must be 'pulling the strings' against the original producer of the scandal: scapegoats (Muslims, Jews, Turks, Roma, foreigners, and so forth) are quickly discovered. Once the accused member of the respective minority finally receives a chance to present substantial counter-evidence, a new scandal is launched. Possibly, a 'quasi-apology' might follow, should 'misunderstandings' have occurred; and the entire process starts all over again.

This dynamic implies that right-wing populist parties strategically manage to frame media debates; other parties and politicians are thus forced to react and respond to endless newly staged scandals. Few opportunities remain to present other agendas, frames, values and counter-arguments. In this way, right-wing populist parties in Europe and beyond succeed in dominating the media and public debates; moreover, in this way, the dissemination of discriminating rhetoric persists and is continuously (re)produced.

Related Topics

7 Language Ideologies (Kroskrity); **14** Discursive Practices, Linguistic Repertoire, and Racial Identities (Baugh); **15** Language and Racialization (Chun, Lo); **25** Racism in the Press (Van Dijk).

Notes

1 I am very grateful to the peer-reviewed journal *Zeitgeschichte* for allowing me to reprint a shortened and revised as well as updated version of the paper 'Discourse and Discrimination: Theories and Methodologies' (2013) as chapter for this volume.
2 See Harrison & Bruter 2011; Matouschek et al. 1995; Pelinka & Wodak, 2001; Reisigl 2002, 2005; Reisigl & Wodak 2000, 2001, 2009; Rydgren 2005; Wodak & Pelinka 2002; Wodak & Richardson 2013; Wodak, KhosraviNik, & Mral 2013; Wodak 2015.
3 See Flam & Beauzamy, 2011; Pedwell 2007 for gender-related dimensions.
4 See Baker et al. 2008; Delanty et al. 2011a.
5 See Delanty et al. 2011a; Jones & Krzyżanowski 2011; Krzyżanowski & Wodak 2007; Wodak 2008a,b; 2009, for theoretical and methodological elaborations of the concepts of 'identity' and 'belonging'. There, I draw on the results of the 5th EU framework project XENOPHOB in which I was the PI of the Viennese team involved in the discourse analysis of political speeches and party programmes of right-wing populist parties (across the European Union) and of the focus group data of migrant participants. See Krzyżanowski & Wodak (2009) for more details of the specific Austrian case.
6 See Billig 2005; Delanty 2011a; Schweitzer 2012.
7 See Adorno 1973; Hall 1989; Krzyżanowski & Wodak 2009; Matouschek, Wodak & Januschek 1995; Reisigl 2002, 2005; Reisigl & Wodak 2000; Richardson & Wodak 2009a,b; Taguieff 1987; Wallerstein 1994; Wiewiorka 1994.
8 See, for example, Jiwani & Richardson 2011; Pelinka, Bischof, Stögner, 2009; Poliakov 1993.
9 See Chilton 2004; Billig 1978, 2005; KhosraviNik 2009, 2010a,b; Reisigl & Wodak 2000, 2001; Richardson 2004; van Dijk, 2005a, b; Wodak 2007a, b, c; 2008a, b; 2009, 2011a, 2015; for extensive overviews. In this chapter I can only point to some linguistic manifestations in the brief illustration of exclusionary rhetoric in one example. I have to refer readers to the many detailed linguistic analyses in the huge body of literature referred to above.
10 See also Köhler & Wodak 2011; Wodak & Köhler 2010 for more extensive examples and analysis.
11 See, for example, the vast literature on propaganda and manipulation in general; and specific research on the propaganda in the Third Reich (Römer 1989; Judt 2007).

12 See Triandafyllidou et al. 2009; Stråth & Wodak 2009; Wodak & Richardson 2012; Judt 2007.
13 See Schweitzer 2012 for manifold examples of exclusionary practices and rhetoric as well as conspiracy theories created by conservative new social and traditional media and instrumentalised by many politicians of the US 'Tea Party' Movement, all intended to disqualify and denounce the Obama government and President Obama directly. As Schweitzer is able to illustrate in her in-depth investigation, the Tea Party movement has changed significantly from its inception in the nineteenth century and is now manifested across various different groups and also individuals in a range of different ways. Thus, the libertarian movement of Ron Paul, for example, is to be distinguished from Sarah Palin's much more radically nativist and 'homeland' oriented followers which again differ in their rhetoric and ideologies from the fiercely antisemitic and racist groups surrounding Fox TV and their 'infamous' moderators, Glen Beck and Rush Limbaugh. Current global developments therefore draw on traditional antisemitic world conspiracy stereotypes and prejudices (Adorno 1973; Wiewiorka 1994; Wodak 2007b, 2011c). These developments, of course, provide ever more reason to involve historians in the research of identity politics and the politics of exclusion (cf. Conze & Sommer 2004; Nipperdey & Rurüp 2004).
14 For more details see Sugarman & Butler, 2011: 9ff.
15 For further elaborations and exceptions, see Sugarman & Butler 2010.
16 In pragmatics and linguistics, *deixis* (Greek for 'display, demonstration or reference') is a process whereby expressions rely utterly on context. The 'origo' is the context to which the reference is made – in other words, the viewpoint that must be understood in order to interpret the utterance. A word that depends on deictic clues is called a 'deictic' or a 'deictic word'. Pro-forms are generally considered to be deictics, but a finer distinction is often made between grammatical person/personal pro-forms such as 'I,' 'you' and 'it,' and pro-forms that refer to places and times such as 'now,' 'then,' 'here,' 'there.' In most texts, the term 'deictic' implies the latter but not necessarily the former. (In philosophical logic, the former and latter are collectively called 'indexicals.') In the context of 'inclusion/exclusion,' deictic units are frequently used to construct boundaries and groups (inside-outside; us and them).
17 See Kovàcs 2010; Wodak 2011c.
18 See, for example, the extensive discussion on methods of measuring racist and antisemitic opinions in post-war Europe; Wodak et al. 1990; Billig 1978, 1991.
19 Here, I draw on the Discourse-Historical Approach in Critical Discourse Analysis, best summarized in Reisigl & Wodak (2001, 2009) and Wodak (2001, 2011a), which was first developed to study antisemitic rhetoric in post-war Austria (Wodak et al. 1990).
20 All these strategies are defined by numerous categories and examples in Reisigl & Wodak (2001: 31–90). It would be impossible owing to space restrictions to define and illustrate all these linguistic devices in this paper.
21 For more details, see Reisigl & Wodak (2001: 69–80) and Toulmin (1969).
22 See the pragma-dialectical approach of van Eemeren & Grootendorst (1992).
23 See Billig 2005.
24 See Wodak & Pelinka 2002 for elaborate analyses of the right-wing populist Austrian Freedom Party and the so-called Haider Phenomenon.
25 See http://www.hcstrache.at/.
26 Literally a rhymed form of 'At home instead of Islam'. German '*Daham*' is a dialectal form of '*daheim*' ('at home'). In Viennese dialect, diphthongs are monophthongised. The use of very simple rhymes is part of a trademark/brand of FPÖ campaigns (see Wodak & Reisigl 2015 for an extensive analysis).
27 Literally, 'The Occident in Christian hands.'
28 Oberlandesgericht Graz, 17.06.2009.
29 § 283 section 2 and § 188 *Österreichisches Strafgesetzbuch*.
30 Literally 'They are against him, because he is for you.' Poster of the FPÖ in the national election campaign, October 1994, see http://www.demokratiezentrum.org/bildstrategien/personen.html?index21&dimension.
31 For further political and historical information about the FPÖ as successor party to the former NSDAP, see Bailer-Galanda & Neugebauer 1997.
32 Richardson & Wodak 2009a, b.
33 Literally 'We FINALLY give SAFETY to our women and men of Vienna.'
34 See Kress & van Leeuwen (1996), and van Leeuwen (2011) for a general discussion of visual design and the salience of choice of colour.
35 Cf. Wodak & Reisigl 2015; Wodak & Köhler 2010; Wodak 2015.
36 Accessible at www.hcstrachemediaordner/g10,14110782715,0830.jpg.

References

Adorno, Theodor W. *Studien zum autoritären Charakter*. (Frankfurt 1973).
Bailer-Galanda, Brigitte & Wolfgang Neugebauer. *Haider und die Freiheitlichen in Österreich*. (Berlin 1997).
Anderson, Benedict. *Imagined Communities*. (London 1985).
Baker, Paul, Costas Gabrielatos, Majid KhosraviNik, Michal Krzyżanowski, Tony Mcenery & Ruth Wodak. 'A methodological synergy. CDA and corpus linguistics: Analysing racist discourses,' *Discourse & Society* 19(3): 273–306. (2008).
Bauböck, Rainer & Thomas Faist (eds). *Diaspora and Transnationalism*. (Amsterdam 2010).
Billig, Michael. *Fascists. A Social Psychological Analysis of the National Front*. (London 1978).
Billig, Michael. *Ideology and Opinions*. (London 1991).
Billig, Michael. *Banal Nationalism*. (London 1995).
Billig, Michael. 'Discourse and discrimination,' in: K. Brown (ed.) *Elsevier Encyclopedia of Language and Linguistics*, 2nd ed. (Oxford 2005).
Chilton, Paul. *Analyzing Political Discourse*. (London 2004).
Conze, Werner & Antje Sommer. 'Rasse,' in: Otto Brunner, Werner Conze & Reinhart Koselleck (eds) *Geschichtliche Grundbegriffe. Historisches Lexikon zur politisch-sozialen Sprache in* Deutschland, pp. 135–178. Vol. 5: Pro – Soz. (First Publication 1984. Publication for Research with attached corrections 2004). (Stuttgart 1984/2004).
De Cillia, Rudolf & Ruth Wodak. *Ist Österreich ein 'deutsches' Land? Anmerkungen zur Sprachenpolitik der Zweiten Republik*. (Innsbruck 2006).
Delanty, Gerard. 'Dilemmas of secularism: Europe, religion and the problem of pluralism,' in: Gerard Delanty et al. (eds) *Migration, Identity, and Belonging*, pp. 78–100. (Liverpool 2011a).
Delanty, Gerard, Ruth Wodak & Paul Jones (eds). *Migration, Identity, and Belonging*, 2nd rev. ed. (Liverpool 2011b).
Engel, Jakob & Ruth Wodak. 'Kalkulierte Ambivalenz, "Störungen" und das "Gedankenjahr": Die Causen Siegfried Kampl und John Gudenus,' in: Rudolf de Cillia & Ruth Wodak (eds) *Gedenken im "Gedankenjahr": zur diskursiven Konstruktion österreichischer Identitäten im Jubiläumsjahr*, pp. 79–100. (Innsbruck 2009).
Engel, Jakob & Ruth Wodak. 'Calculated ambivalence and Holocaust denial in Austria,' in: Ruth Wodak & John E. Richardson (eds), *Analyzing Fascist Discourse. Fascism in* Text and Talk, pp. 73–96. (London 2013).
Flam, Helena & Brigitte Beauzamy. 'Symbolic violence,' in: Delanty et al. *Migration, Identity, and Belonging*, 2nd rev. ed., pp. 221–240 (Liverpool 2011).
Gingrich, Andre. 'A man for all seasons,' in: Ruth Wodak & Anton Pelinka (eds) *The Haider Phenomenon in Austria*, pp. 67–95. (New Brunswick 2002).
Goldberg, David. *The Racial State*. (Oxford 2002).
Hall, Stuart. 'Rassismus als ideologischer Diskurs.' *Das Argument 178*: 913–921. (1989).
Harrison, Sarah & Michael Bruter. *Mapping Extreme Right Ideology*. (Basingstoke 2011).
Jiwani, Yasmin & John E. Richardson. 'Discourse, ethnicity and racism,' in: Teun A. van Dijk (ed.) *Discourse Studies. A multidisciplinary introduction*, pp. 241–262. (London 2011).
Jones, Paul & Michał Krzyżanowski. 'Identity, belonging and migration: Beyond Describing "Others,"' in: Delanty et al. (eds) *Migration, Identity and Belonging*, pp. 38–53. (Liverpool 2011).
Judt, Tony. *Postwar*. (London 2007).
KhosraviNik, Majid. 'The representation of refugees, asylum seekers and immigrants in British newspapers during the Balkan conflict (1999) and the British general election (2005).' *Discourse & Society* 20(4): 477–498. (2009).
KhosraviNik, Majid. 'The representation of refugees, asylum seekers and immigrants in the British newspapers: a critical discourse analysis.' *Journal of Language and Politics* 8(3): 1–29. (2010a).
KhosraviNik, Majid. 'Actor descriptions, action attributions, and argumentation: towards a systematization of CDA analytical categories in the representation of social groups.' *Critical Discourse Studies* 7(1): 55–72. (2010b).
Kienpointner, Manfred. *Vernünftig argumentieren. Regeln und Techniken der Diskussion*. (Hamburg 1996).
Kovàcs, Andrew. *The Stranger at Hand*. (Louvain 2010).
Köhler, Katharina & Ruth Wodak. 'Mitbürger, Fremde und "echte Wiener" – Ein- und Ausgrenzungen über Sprache. Diskursive Konstruktion von Macht und Ungleichheit am Beispiel des Wiener Wahlkampfes 2010.' *Deutschunterricht* 6: 64–73. (2011).

Kress, Gunther & Theo van Leeuwen. *Reading Images. The Grammar of Visual Design.* (London 1996).
Krzyżanowski, Michał & Ruth Wodak. 'Multiple/collective identities, migration and belonging. Voices of Migrants,' in: Carmen Caldas-Coulthard & Rick Iedema (eds) *Identity Troubles*, pp. 95–119. (Basingstoke 2007).
Krzyżanowski, Michał & Ruth Wodak. *Politics of Exclusion: Institutional and Everyday Discrimination in Austria.* (New Brunswick 2009).
Manoschek, Walter. 'FPÖ, ÖVP and Austria's Nazi past,' in: Ruth Wodak & Anton Pelinka (eds) *The Haider Phenomenon in Austria*, pp. 3–17. (New Brunswick 2002).
Matouschek, Bernd, Ruth Wodak & Franz Januschek. *Notwendige Maßnahmen gegen Fremde.* (Vienna 1995).
Nipperdey, Thomas & Rolf Rürup. 'Antisemitismus,' in: Otto Brunner, Werner Conze & Reinhart Koselleck (eds) *Geschichtliche Grundbegriffe: historisches Lexikon zur politisch-sozialen Sprache in Deutschland*, pp. 129–153. Vol. 1: A–D. (Stuttgart 2004).
Pedwell, Carolyn. 'Tracing the "Anorexic" and the "Veiled Woman": Towards a relational Approach.' *New Working Papers Series* 20. (Newcastle 2007).
Pelinka, Anton, Karin Bischof & Karin Stögner (eds). *Handbook of Prejudice.* (Amherst 2009).
Pelinka, Anton & Ruth Wodak (eds). *'Dreck am Stecken.' Politik der Ausgrenzung.* (Vienna 2001).
Poliakov, Leon. *Der arische Mythos. Zu den Quellen von Rassismus und Nationalismus.* (Hamburg 1993).
Reisigl, Martin. '"Dem Volk aufs Maul schauen, nach dem Mund reden und angst und bange machen" – Von populistischen Anrufungen, Anbiederungen und Agitationsweisen in der Sprache österreichischer Politikerinnen' in: Walter Eismann (ed.), *Rechtspopulismus in Europa. Österreichische Krankheit oder europäische Normalität?* pp. 149–198. (Vienna 2002).
Reisigl, Martin. 'Argumentation in Political Discourse,' in: Keith Brown (ed.) *Elsevier Encyclopedia of Language and Linguistics.* 2nd rev. ed. (Oxford 2005).
Reisigl, Martin & Ruth Wodak. 'The Discourse-Historical Approach in CDA,' in: Ruth Wodak & Michael Meyer (eds) *Methods of CDA*, pp. 87–121. 2nd rev. ed. (London 2009).
Reisigl, Martin & Ruth Wodak. *Discourse and Discrimination.* (London 2001).
Reisigl, Martin & Ruth Wodak. '"Austria first." A discourse-historical analysis of the Austrian "Anti-foreigner Petition" in 1992 and 1993,' in: Martin Reisigl & Ruth Wodak (eds) *The Semiotics of Racism. Approaches in Critical Discourse Analysis*, pp. 269–303. (Vienna 2000).
Richardson, John E. *(Mis)Representing Islam.* (Amsterdam 2004).
Richardson, John E. & Ruth Wodak. 'The impact of visual racism: Visual arguments in political leaflets of Austrian and British far-right parties.' *Controversia* 2: 45–77. (2009a)
Richardson, John E. & Ruth Wodak. 'Recontextualising fascist ideologies of the past: right-wing discourses on employment and nativism in Austria and the United Kingdom.' *Critical Discourse Studies* 6(4): 251–267. (2009b).
Römer Ruth. *Sprachwissenschaft und Rassenideologie in Deutschland.* 2nd ed. (Munich 1989).
Rydgren, Jens (ed.). *Moments of Exclusion.* (New York 2005).
Schiedel, Herbert & Neugebauer, Wolfgang. 'Jörg Haider, die FPÖ und der Antisemitismus,' in: Pelinka, Anton & Wodak, Ruth (eds) *Dreck am Stecken. Politik der Ausgrenzung*, pp. 11–32. (Vienna: Czernin).
Schweitzer, Eva C. *Tea Party. Die weiße Wut.* (Munich 2012).
Sugarman, David & Mark Butler. *Handbook of European non-descrimination law.* (Vienna 2011, Fundamental Rights Agency (FRA)).
Stråth, Bo & Ruth Wodak. 'Europe-Discourse-Politics-Media-History: Constructing Crises,' in: Anna Triandafyllidou, Ruth Wodak & Michał Krzyżanowski (eds) *European Public Sphere and the Media: Europe in Crisis*, pp. 15–33. (Basingstoke 2009).
Taguieff, Pierre A. *La Force du Préjugé. Essai sur le racisme et ses doubles.* (Paris 1987).
Toulmin, Stefan. *The Uses of Argument.* (Cambridge 1969).
Triandafyllidou, Anna, Ruth Wodak & Michał Krzyżanowski (eds). *European Public Sphere and the Media: Europe in Crisis.* (Basingstoke 2009).
Van Dijk, Teun A. *Prejudice in Discourse.* (Amsterdam 1984).
Van Dijk, Teun A. 'The denial of racism,' in: Ruth Wodak (ed.). *Language, Power and Ideology.* (Amsterdam 1989).
Van Dijk, Teun A. 'Contextual knowledge management in discourse production. A CDA perspective,' in: Ruth Wodak & Paul Chilton (eds) *A New Agenda in (Critical) Discourse Analysis*, pp. 71–100. (Amsterdam 2005a).
Van Dijk, Teun A. *Racism and Discourse in Spain and Latin America.* (Amsterdam 2005b).

Van Eemeren, Frans & Rob Grootendorst. *Argumentation, Communication and Fallacies: A Pragma-Dialectical Perspective.* (Hillsdale 1992).
Van Leeuwen, Theo. *The Language of Colour.* (London 2011).
Van Leeuwen, Theo & Ruth Wodak. 'Legitimizing immigration control: A discourse-historical analysis.' *Discourse Studies* 1(1): 83–118. (1999).
Wallerstein, I. *The Capitalist World-Economy.* (Cambridge 1994).
Wiewiorka, Michel. 'Racism in Europe: unity and diversity,' in: A. Rattansi & S. Westwood (eds) *Racism, Modernity and Identity. On the Western* Front, pp. 173–188. (Cambridge 1994).
Wodak, Ruth, Johanna Pelikan, Peter Nowak, Helmut Gruber, Rudolf de Cillia & Richard Mitten. *'Wir sind alle unschuldige Täter!' Diskurshistorische Studien zum Nachkriegsantisemitismus.* (Frankfurt/Main 1990).
Wodak, Ruth. 'The discourse historical approach,' in: Ruth Wodak & Michael Meyer (eds). *Methods of CDA*, pp. 63–95. (London 2001).
Wodak, Ruth. 'Discourses in European Union organizations: Aspects of access, participation, and exclusion.' *TEXT and TALK*, 65(6): 655–680. (2007a).
Wodak, Ruth. 'Turning the tables: Anti-Semitic discourse in Post-war Austria,' in: Teun A. van Dijk (ed.). *Discourse Studies*, pp. 350–375. (London 2007b).
Wodak, Ruth. 'Pragmatics and critical discourse analysis. A cross-disciplinary analysis.' *Pragmatics and Cognition.* 15(1): 203–225. (2007c)
Wodak, Ruth. 'Controversial issues in feminist critical discourse analysis,' in: K. Harrington, L. Litosseliti, H. Sauntson & J. Sunderland (eds) *Gender and Language. Research Methodologies*, pp. 193–210. (Basingstoke 2008).
Wodak, Ruth. 'Prejudice and discourse,' in: Anton Pelinka, Karin Bischof & Karin Stögner (eds.). *Handbook of Prejudice*, pp. 409–443. (Amherst 2009).
Wodak, Ruth & Katharina Köhler. 'Wer oder was ist "fremd"? Diskurshistorische Analyse fremdenfeindlicher Rhetorik in Österreich.' *Sozialwissenschaftliche Studien* 1: 33–55. (2010).
Wodak, Ruth & Norman Fairclough. 'Recontextualizing European higher education policies: the cases of Austria and Romania'. *Critical Discourse Studies* 7(1): 19–40. (2010).
Wodak, Ruth. *The Discourse of Politics in Action: Politics as Usual*, 2nd rev. ed. (Basingstoke 2011a).
Wodak, Ruth. 'Old and new demagoguery. The rhetoric of exclusion.' www.opendemocracy.net/ruth-wodak/old-and-new-demagoguery-rhetoric-of-exclusion, published on-line. (May 5, 2011b).
Wodak, Ruth. 'Suppression of the Nazi past, coded languages, and discourses of silence: Applying the discourse-historical approach to post-war anti-Semitism in Austria,' in: Willibald Steinmetz (ed.) *Political Languages in the Age of Extremes*, pp. 351–379. (Oxford 2011c).
Wodak, Ruth. '"Us" and "them": inclusion/exclusion – discrimination via discourse,' in: Gerard Delanty, Ruth Wodak & Paul Jones (eds) *Migration, Identity, and Belonging*, pp. 54–77. (Liverpool 2011d).
Wodak, Ruth. *The Politics of Fear. What Right-wing Populist Discourses Mean.* (London 2015).
Wodak, Ruth & Martin Reisigl. 'Discourse and Racism,' in: Heidi Hamilton, Deborah Tannen & Deborah Schiffrin (eds) *Handbook in Discourse Studies*, 2nd rev. ed. (Oxford 2015).
Wodak, Ruth & John E. Richardson (eds). *Analysing Fascist Discourse. Fascism in* Text and Talk. (London 2013a).
Wodak, Ruth, Majid KhosraviNik & Brigitte Mral (eds). *Rightwing Populism in Europe. Discourse and Politics.* (London 2013b).
Wodak, Ruth & Anton Pelinka (eds). *The Haider Phenomenon in Austria.* (New Brunswick 2002).

25
Racism in the Press

Teun A. van Dijk

1 Introduction

This article presents a multidisciplinary account of the role of the mass media, and especially the press, in the daily reproduction of "white" racism in multicultural society. After a definition of racism as a system of social domination, controlled by the symbolic elites, the article summarizes the ways news production and news report structures presuppose, confirm, and reproduce the shared ethnic prejudices and ideologies on which the system is based.

2 Racism

Racism is defined here as a specific social system of domination in which ethnic groups and their members in various ways abuse their power in their interaction with other ethnic groups and their members (for detail, see Van Dijk, 1993). Historically, this has been especially the case for the domination by "whites" (Europeans and groups of European descent) of "non-whites," such as people of African, Asian or Indigenous/Native American descent, so we shall focus here on "white racism."

The system of racism consists of two major subsystems, a cognitive and an interactional one, better known as prejudice and discrimination, respectively. However, whereas traditionally prejudice is often seen as individual bigotry, it is here understood as a form of social cognition, as a system of negative attitudes about ethnic others shared by members of the dominant group (see Augoustinos, 2001; Dovidio, Glick & Rudman 2005).

These attitudes are based on, and organized by, a more general and fundamental racist ideology, featuring notions of superiority and priority of the dominant ethnic ingroup, and of inferiority of the dominated ethnic outgroup.

Racist ideology and the more specific negative attitudes (prejudices) it controls not only serve as the cognitive aspect of white group identity, but also as a legitimation of its power abuse in the many forms of 'everyday racism' (Essed, 1991) or discriminatory interaction – that is, the observable manifestation of the system of racism in everyday life (for general introductions to the study of racism, see, e.g., Garner, 2009; Rattansi, 2007).

3 Historical Perspective

Racism as a system of ethnic or racial domination is not limited to Europeans. Yet its most widespread and consequential form has been the "white" racism as invented and practiced by Europeans, e.g., from the legitimization of slavery and colonialism, until eugenics, the Holocaust, and current discrimination against non-European immigrants (of the vast number of histories of racism, see, e.g., Allen, 1994; Bjørgo & Witte, 1993; Hannaford, 1996). Indeed, white prejudice against non-Europeans, based on the idea of the superiority of the white "race," goes back to Antiquity (Isaac 2004).

4 Critical Issues and Topic: The Discursive Reproduction of Racism

Ethnic prejudice, as the cognitive basis of discrimination, is not innate but learned, as is the case for all social attitudes and ideologies. It is learned by various forms of socialization within the dominant ingroup, especially by public discourse and interpersonal conversations influenced by such public discourse. Especially influential are the text and talk of politics, the mass media (including the internet), and education, where systematic attention is being paid to ethnic others, such as ethnic minorities or immigrants. Among the many forms of the discursive reproduction of racism, this article focuses on the role of the press in multicultural societies.

This discourse analytical study of racism not only has a cognitive and a discursive dimension but also an important social one, thus defining the triangular, multidisciplinary approach of this article. Dominant discourse in society, such as that of politics, the media, and education (including research), are controlled by social groups with specific privileges and power of access (Van Dijk, 2008b). Not anybody can speak in Parliament or Congress, write in the newspaper or in a textbook. The groups who do have special access to public discourse will be called the 'symbolic elites' (Van Dijk, 1993). They control public communication and thus influence, discursively, the beliefs of the dominant group and its members, in a very complex sociocognitive manner that will not be detailed here. It is important that, also along a social dimension, racism is not reduced to individual acts of everyday discrimination, but a form of systematic power abuse in everyday interaction, legitimated by the prejudices reproduced by the prevalent discourse of symbolic elites, who control epistemic and doxastic institutions such as those of politics, the media, and education.

Discourse has a specific role in the reproduction of racism. On the one hand, it is a form of social interaction among others. Hence, if racism is expressed as a form of discriminatory social interaction, this also applies to discourse, as is the case for prejudiced text and talk. On the other hand, we have assumed that ethnic prejudice and ideology are not innate but learned, and that such acquisition is largely discursive. So racist discourse is itself a form of power abuse and at the same time reproduces and legitimates the sociocognitive basis, the prejudices, of all forms of discriminatory action (including discourse) in society (for studies on racism and discourse, see, e.g., Blommaert & Verschueren, 1998; Jäger, 1992; Reisigl & Wodak, 2001; Wetherell & Potter 1992; Wodak & Van Dijk, 2000).

5 Current Contributions and Research: The Press

Much, if not most, of what white people know about ethnic minorities or immigrants they find out from the mass media, especially the press, television, and the internet. To focus the discussion of this article, it will concern itself especially with the written press, today still a major source of information of the symbolic elites, also on politics and other media, and inextricably related to public debate and policies on ethnic affairs.

To understand the role of the press in the reproduction of racism, it is crucial not to limit the study to a simple content analysis of racial slurs or stereotypical topics in news and opinion articles, but engage in multidisciplinary study of press discourse and its cognitive and societal contexts (for books on racism in the press, see, e.g., Campbell, 2010; Cottle, 2000; Downing & Husband, 2005; Jäger & Link, 1993; Jiwani, 2006; Richardson, 2004; Van Dijk, 1991; Wilson, Gutiérrez & Chao, 2003).

5.1 The Context of News Production

In contemporary discourse studies it is crucial, first of all, to analyze not only texts but also their contexts, that is, the communicative situation as participants construe it in their minds as a specific type of mental model: context models (Van Dijk, 2008a). Indeed, the "same" text or talk may be racist in one communicative situation and not in another. Therefore, we also need to examine the production context of the various discourse genres of the press, featuring, e.g.:

- Setting (Time, Place)
- Participants (and their Identities, Roles, and Relations)
- Type of Communicative Action
- Aim and Goals of the Communicative Action
- Knowledge, Attitudes, and Ideologies of the Participants

This means that journalists during newsgathering and news production have a context model in mind with these categories controlling all their discursive and communicative conduct. Thus, in their context model they represent the following relevant knowledge of the communicative situation:

i) where they are (as shown in the byline);
ii) date and time (to meet a deadline);
iii) that they are now acting in their identity as journalists and in their role of reporter or interviewer, and in a specific relation with their editors, on the one hand, or their news sources or news actors, on the other;
iv) engaging in a specific kind of communicative interaction (e.g., a phone interview, assisting at a press conference, consulting the internet, etc.);
v) with the aim of gathering information or writing a news article, and informing the public, and
vi) with specific knowledge and attitudes about minorities, immigrants, or specific issues (such as immigration or quotas).

Since a white journalist writes not only in their identity as a journalist, but also, at least marginally, is aware of being a member of an ethnic group, all these activities and contexts may also be permeated by the influence of the ethnic attitudes of the journalist (a dimension often neglected in other studies of news production – see, e.g., Tuchman, 1978). In other words, in all phases of the production of discourse in the press, the ethnic identity of the journalist and other participants plays a fundamental role.

This will show, among other things, in the sources they find reliable and credible (typically symbolic elites of their own ethnic group – i.e., mostly white authorities for white journalists), which they will therefore approach with greater probability, in what incoming information they select and focus on, and in whose point of view is likely to be favored in news writing. Thus, in our fieldwork among journalists in Amsterdam we found that press releases of minority groups were seldom found reliable, credible, or otherwise interesting, and were routinely discarded in favor of official (white) sources, such as the government, the police, or experts (Van Dijk, 1991).

The same is true for interviews with ethnically different sources or news actors, who may suffer bias – if only due to the attitude that such sources by definition favor their own group, an assumption seldom made in interviews with white authorities.

Finally, whereas many phases of the production of news discourse may already be ethnically biased, the same will be the case for the actual production of news reports, depending again on the knowledge, attitudes, and ideologies of the journalist – or, rather, as dominant in the newspaper. Detailed 'epistemic analyses' of news about ethnically different groups may reveal that lacking knowledge about the Others, as well as about their social and cultural context, may be one of the sources of biased reporting.

5.2 Structures of News

As suggested, it is not surprising that in such a biased production context the product, such as the news, editorials, columns, or feature articles, in many ways show ethnic bias. Let us therefore systematically examine some structures of news in the press and how these may be affected by such bias (for structures of news, see Bell, 1991; Van Dijk, 1988; Richardson, 2007).

5.2.1 Topics

The meaning of discourse is globally organized by macropropositions defining the topic, gist, or upshot of discourse (Van Dijk, 1980). Topics, as subjectively construed by the participants, are crucial for the production, comprehension, memory, and reproduction of discourse. In news production they represent the 'plan' a journalist has for the writing of a news report, and in the reception of news, it is the information readers tend to remember best – as we shall see below (Van Dijk & Kintsch, 1983).

News discourse, in general, may be about any public issue in the domains of society, politics, culture, sports, or entertainment. Yet, depending on the political orientation of a newspaper, some issues, and hence some topics, have more probability and more space, than others. For instance, as is the case for all polarized ideological discourse (Van Dijk, 1998), we read more about terrorism of Others against Us, than of Our forms of power abuse (such as colonialism, oppression, wars, etc.) against Them. The same is true for the coverage of immigrants and minorities. Research shows that news about ethnic Others is semantically less diverse than news about Us, and typically prefers to focus on topics such as:

- immigration as a problem or a threat, and once Others have immigrated
- integration problems, e.g., due to cultural (linguistic, religious, etc.) differences
- deviance and crime.

Controlled by underlying racist ideologies and specific ethnic attitudes, the Others and their actions are thus globally represented as Different, Deviant, and a Threat.

By the logic of polarized underlying ideologies, the representation of Our own ingroup, and its actors and institutions, is usually neutral or positive: We are portrayed as helping, supporting, or tolerating the Others, in our own or in their own countries. At the same time, the corollary of the 'ideological square' (Van Dijk, 1998) is that whereas the news will seldom report many positive stories about the Others – except in specific domains, such as sport and entertainment – it also tends to ignore or mitigate negative topics about Us. So, topics on Our prejudices and racism are rare, unless committed by an Outgroup within the Ingroup, such as the Extreme Right, neo-Nazis, football hooligans, etc. Racism or xenophobia of the mainstream elites is largely ignored or denied. We see that macrostructures also define at least some of the aspects of what is usually rather vaguely described as the overall 'framing' of news.

5.2.2 Headlines and Leads

Of the schematic organization of news, the Summary, consisting of Headline and Lead, plays a crucial role precisely because they are the preferred textual categories for expression of topics. They strategically function for readers as explicit instructions on how to construe the overall meaning, macrostructure, or topics of news reports.

Although normatively and theoretically expressing the most important topic of a news report, headlines may also focus on other aspects of the news so as to manipulate the attention, understanding, and memory of the readers. Thus, an account of an otherwise largely peaceful demonstration may typically focus on the violence of a small group of demonstrators. Similarly, the headlines of the coverage of 'race riots' focus on black violence rather than on police violence. Stories about religious differences, e.g., on Muslim women, focus on Their deviance, such as wearing a hijab, rather than on Our prejudices, intolerance, or xenophobia.

5.2.3 Local Semantics

Overall semantic macrostructures of discourse not only define its topics but are typically expressed prominently (first, on top, and in larger type) in headlines. They also, and by definition, organize the local meanings of words and sentences of text and talk, as well as the processes of understanding and memory.

Local meanings of discourse are characterized by many properties, only some of which have been systematically studied in linguistics, such as modalities, metaphors, and presuppositions. Others are (still) ignored or unknown in mainstream research, as are the ways persons, actions, or events are described, implications, generalizations vs. specifications, functional relations, amount of detail, granularity, perspective and point of view, and so on.

For the analysis of news on minorities and immigrants, such local semantic analysis is especially relevant because at this level we encounter the more subtle ways news about Others may be biased. Thus, among many other characteristics of news about immigrants and minorities, research has shown the following semantic properties of news about Others:

- News events are generally described from the perspective of Us – i.e., our government, police, etc.
- Others tend to be described rather as group members than as individuals.
- The negative actions of Others are described with more detail, and those of Us with less detail.
- Negative attributes of Others (e.g., their violence) may be 'falsely' presupposed, and hence obliquely asserted, that is, even when there is no evidence of such negative characteristics.
- Negative attributes of Others are often implied when explicit assertion would appear too blatant.
- Our own negative actions against Them, if any, are described with modalities of necessity, that is, as inevitable – as is the case with police actions, limiting immigration, or expulsion of immigrants.
- Metaphors tend to emphasize the threatening nature of Others, as is stereotypically the case for the arrival of 'waves' of immigrants.

5.2.4 Local Syntax

Sentence syntax may vary in many ways in the expression of underlying semantic or pragmatic meanings, thus focusing on specific aspects of these propositions rather than on others. The ways agents of actions may be hidden or made less prominent by using passive constructions or nominalizations are well known. This is typically the case for negative actions of Our government, police, agencies, or authorities, against the Others. Thus, news may be about discrimination or xenophobia, without mentioning who exactly discriminates, or pretends to fear immigrants or minorities (Fowler, 1991; Fowler, Hodge, Kress & Trew, 1979).

5.2.5 The Lexicon

The ideological logic of negative Other presentation obviously also affects lexical choice. The Others can be described in many ways, some of which have more or less negative implications. Classic examples of biased political coverage describe Others in terms of terrorists, rebels, or freedom fighters, depending on Our ideological perspective.

The same is true for minorities or immigrants – as is well known from the long historical debate about, and the lexical development of, such expressions as *Negroes, Blacks, Afro-Americans* and *African Americans,* in media and politics, and more offensive words in less public contexts (see, e.g., Essed, 1997).

Similarly, both in the United States as well as in Europe, immigrants may variously be described as *migrants, immigrants, ethnic minorities,* in more formal discourse, and as foreigners (*Ausländer, buitenlanders, extracommunitari,* etc.), in less formal text and talk, depending on the country and the language. More typical of negative reporting is the lexical emphasis on breaking the law when words such as *illegals* are used. The British tabloid press is lexically most explicitly racist in describing poor immigrants or refugees as *scroungers,* and related negative words.

5.2.6 Quotations

News is largely produced on the basis of discourses by various sources, such as news actors, commentators, witnesses, or declarations and press releases of institutions. More or less explicitly, these sources may be directly or indirectly quoted – one of the ways the production of news is shown in the text. As may be expected on the basis of news production routines, elites tend to be quoted more than nonelites. Obviously the same applies to Our sources rather than Their sources – signaling not only which sources are more available or more sought after, but especially which sources are found to be more reliable. Thus, ethnic events are defined by Us, and seldom by Them. If Others are allowed to speak, they never speak alone – although that is quite common for Our own speakers. Besides the overall perspective of the report, such biased citation patterns further emphasize Our dominant definition of ethnic affairs.

6 Reception of Biased News

A multidisciplinary study of racism in the press is not limited to an inquiry into news production routines and news structures, but obviously also needs to examine the effects of such news on the public at large.

Though reception studies are notoriously difficult, if not problematic, and typically met with extensive debate in the field of journalism, current insights in cognitive and social psychology provide at least a basis for a more explicit approach to this issue. Thus, we generally know what discourses and what properties of discourse tend to be understood and memorized best (Graber, 1988; Jensen, 1986; Larson, 1983).

One basic finding is that, all other things being equal, memory for discourse depends on the combined influences of text or talk itself, on the one hand, and on the properties (interest, knowledge, attitudes, aims, etc.) of the recipients, on the other. Indeed, the same news report may be read, understood, represented, and remembered differently by different readers. Roughly, those with more interest in, and knowledge about, immigration tend to remember stories better than others. Basic insights of cognitive and social psychology predict that readers with negative attitudes or racist ideologies will focus on, and better remember, negative aspects of stories on immigrants or minorities — thus finding confirmation of their own prejudices.

Yet, discourse processing and hence the production of the *mental models* in memory (Johnson-Laird, 1983; Van Dijk & Kintsch, 1983) that define our interpretation of news reports, are also influenced by the structure of the news reports themselves. This is especially the case for those readers who do not (yet) have strong attitudes or ideologies about minorities or immigrants.

It is at this point that the structures summarized above, overall tending to focus on negative attributes of the Others, may manipulate readers to construe "preferred readings," that is, mental models of events that are rather in line with the discursively expressed intentions of the journalist.

Thus, negative overall topics, as expressed by biased headlines, will contribute to the construction of overall negative macrostructures controlling the lower-level microstructures of the mental model that represents people's understanding of news reports. The same is true for the many types of local negative descriptions — which in their own way influence the local structures of the mental model.

For instance, the use of the ubiquitous metaphor of "waves" of immigrants does not merely signify that there are many immigrants, but at the same time activates generic knowledge about waves as large and threatening quantities of water in which "We" may drown. Since mental models are multimodal, such a metaphorical interpretation may thus feature fears of "'drowning" in immigrants. Fieldwork among autochthonous people in Amsterdam, talking about "foreigners" in their neighborhood, shows that these are indeed the kinds of meanings associated with immigration as represented by the mass media.

6.1 From Mental Models to Socially Shared Attitudes and Ideologies

Finally, as explained above, racism is not a question of individual bias and bigotry. Despite significant individual variation, racism is a form of social domination of one group by another group — and needs to be described and explained at a collective, societal level.

Thus, whereas mental models are personal, ad hoc and contextual, and dependent on the specific interests, knowledge, opinions, and experiences (old models) of individual readers, readers tend to generalize their mental models and abstract more generic attitudes about immigrants and their properties. In-group members communicate with others on immigration in daily conversations, and may also read about the experiences (mental models) and attitudes of others in the press. It is in this way that ingroup members are "ethnically socialized," by adopting (or sometimes opposing) dominant attitudes.

Given the ubiquitous influence of the mass media, including the press, in the field of stories on minorities and immigrants, their dominant discourses are more likely to influence mental models, and indirectly socially shared generic attitudes about the Others. This is especially the case when there are no other, competitive, different, public discourses about the Others, or when the personal experiences of readers are systematically inconsistent with media discourse.

It follows, then, that the dominant (negative) definition of minorities and immigrants in the press – as well as in politics, as represented in the press – most likely has a powerful influence on the formation and confirmation of public attitudes – and more fundamental ideologies – on immigration or ethnic affairs. It is in this way that public discourse, as social practice, not only itself may be a form of discrimination, but even more fundamentally plays a role in the reproduction of the system of racism, by discursively producing or reproducing ethnic prejudices, generalized and abstracted from negative mental models of ethnic events as described in news reports (Van Dijk, 1987).

Related Topics

7 Language Ideologies (Kroskrity); **14** Discursive Practices, Linguistic Repertoire, and Racial Identities (Baugh); **15** Language and Racialization (Chun, Lo); **24** Discrimination via Discourse (Wodak).

References

Allen, T. W. (1994). *The invention of the white race*. London: Verso.
Augoustinos, M. (Ed.). (2001). *Understanding prejudice, racism, and social conflict*. London Thousand Oaks, CA: Sage.
Bell, A. (1991). *The language of news media*. Oxford, UK, Cambridge, MA: Blackwell.
Bjørgo, T. & Witte, R. (Eds). (1993). *Racist violence in* Europe. New York: St. Martin's Press, Macmillan Press.
Blommaert, J. & Verschueren, J. (1998). *Debating diversity: Analyzing the discourse of tolerance*. New York: Routledge.
Campbell, C. P. (Ed.). (2010). *Race and news. Critical perspectives*. New York: Routledge.
Cottle, S. (Ed.). (2000). *Ethnic minorities and the media*. Buckingham, UK: Open University Press.
Dovidio, J. F., Glick, P. & Rudman, L. A. (Eds). (2005). *On the Nature of prejudice: Fifty years after Allport*. Malden, MA: Blackwell.
Downing, J. D. H. & Husband, C. (2005). *Representing race. Racisms, ethnicities and media*. London: Sage.
Essed, P. (1991). *Understanding everyday racism: An interdisciplinary theory*. Thousand Oaks, CA: Sage.
Essed, P. (1997). Racial intimidation: Sociopolitical implications of the usage of racist slurs. In: S. H. Riggins (Ed.), *The language and politics of exclusion: Others in discourse* (pp. 131–152). Thousand Oaks, CA: Sage.
Fowler, R. (1991). *Language in the news. Discourse and ideology in the press*. London, New York: Routledge.
Fowler, R., Hodge, B., Kress, G. & Trew, T. (1979). *Language and control*. London: Routledge & Kegan Paul.
Garner, S. (2009). *Racisms. An introduction*. Los Angeles: Sage.
Graber, D. A. (1988). *Processing the news*, 2nd ed. New York: Longman.
Hannaford, I. (1996). *Race. The history of an idea in the West*. Woodrow Wilson Center Press.
Isaac, B. H. (2004). *The invention of racism in classical antiquity*. Princeton, NJ: Princeton University Press.
Jäger, S. (1992). *BrandSätze. Rassismus im Alltag.* ('Brandsätze' – Inflammatory Comments / 'Firebombs'. *Racism in everyday life*). DISS-Studien. Duisburg: DISS.
Jäger, S. & Link, J. (1993). *Die vierte Gewalt. Rassismus und die Medien*. (The Fourth Power. Racism and the Media). Duisburg: DISS.
Jensen, K. (1986). *Making sense of the news: Towards a theory and an empirical model of reception for the study of mass communication*. Aarhus: Aarhus University Press.
Jiwani, Y. (2006). *Discourses of denial. Mediations of race, gender, and violence*. Vancouver: UBC Press.
Johnson-Laird, P. N. (1983). *Mental models*. Cambridge: Cambridge University Press.
Larson, C. U. (1983). *Persuasion. Reception and responsibility*. Belmont, CA: Wadsworth.
Rattansi, A. (2007). *Racism. A very short introduction*. Oxford, New York: Oxford University Press.
Reisigl, M. & Wodak, R. (Eds). (2001). *Discourse and discrimination. Rhetorics of racism and antisemitism*. London, New York: Routledge.
Richardson, J. E. (2004). *(Mis)representing Islam. The racism and rhetoric of British broadsheet newspapers*. Amsterdam, Philadelphia, PA: John Benjamins.

Richardson, J. E. (2007). *Analysing newspapers. An approach from critical discourse analysis.* New York: Palgrave Macmillan.
Tuchman, G. (1978). *Making news: A study in the construction of reality.* New York: Free Press.
Van Dijk, T. A. (1980). *Macrostructures. An interdisciplinary study of global structures in discourse, interaction, and cognition.* Hillsdale, NJ: Erlbaum.
Van Dijk, T. A. (1987). *Communicating racism. Ethnic prejudice in thought and talk.* Newbury Park: Sage.
Van Dijk, T. A. (1988). *News as discourse.* Hillsdale, NJ: Erlbaum.
Van Dijk, T. A. (1991). *Racism and the press.* London, New York: Routledge.
Van Dijk, T. A. (1993). *Elite discourse and racism.* Thousand Oaks, CA: Sage.
Van Dijk, T. A. (1998). *Ideology: A multidisciplinary approach.* London, UK: Sage.
Van Dijk, T. A. (2008a). *Discourse and context. A sociocognitive approach.* Cambridge: Cambridge University Press.
Van Dijk, T. A. (2008b). *Discourse and power.* Houndmills: Palgrave-Macmillan.
Van Dijk, T. A. & Kintsch, W. (1983). *Strategies of discourse comprehension.* New York, Toronto: Academic Press.
Wetherell, M. & Potter, J. (1992). *Mapping the language of racism: Discourse and the legitimation of exploitation.* New York: Columbia University Press.
Wilson, C. C., Gutiérrez, F. & Chao, L. M. (2003). *Racism, sexism, and the media. The rise of class communication in multicultural America.* Thousand Oaks, CA: Sage.
Wodak, R. & Van Dijk, T. A. (Eds). (2000). *Racism at the Top. Parliamentary Discourses on Ethnic Issues in Six European States.* Klagenfurt, Austria: Drava Verlag.

26
Legal Discourse

John M. Conley

Introduction

Since its beginnings in the 1970s, the study of legal discourse has evolved into a sprawling field, with contributions from sociolinguists, conversation analysts, rhetoricians, discourse analysts of multiple persuasions, and lawyers with varying degrees of linguistic training. Little of this work has been done by linguistic anthropologists, though. To illustrate the point, I have just finished co-editing a book about legal discourse called *Lay-Legal Communication: Textual Travels in the Law* (Heffer, Rock, and Conley 2013). Of 21 contributors, only three (including myself and my co-author, Jean Cadigan) are anthropologists; the rest are from such fields as linguistics, pragmatics, communication, and criminal justice studies. There have always been exceptions to this generalization, and there is evidence that things are changing in a significant way. Nonetheless, it is fair to say that linguistic anthropology is a relative latecomer to the legal arena.

This is surprising, given that law was among anthropology's earliest ethnographic topics (e.g., Malinowski's (1985 [orig. 1926]) *Crime and Custom in Savage Society*) and was the subject of some of the classic ethnographies of the twentieth century (e.g., Gluckman's (1955) *The Judicial Process Among the Barotse* and Bohannan's (1989 [orig. 1957]) *Justice and Judgment Among the Tiv*). Language, of course, has always been a core focus of anthropology. But the two interests have rarely come together: until recently legal ethnographies have contained little actual discourse, while linguistic anthropology has rarely ventured into legal contexts (see Goldman 1986, 1993).

To define *legal discourse* as I will use it in this chapter, I begin with *discourse*. At one level, "discourse refers to connected segments of speech or writing" (Conley and O'Barr 2005: 6), any unit of language beyond the single sentence or utterance. In another, more abstract sense, discourse refers to "the broad range of discussion that takes place within a society about an issue or a set of issues" (Conley and O'Barr 2005: 7). Legal discourse then becomes speech or writing that occurs within legal processes and practices, very broadly construed, as well as higher-level discussion about law and issues related to law – also broadly construed. Thus, legal discourse in the first sense includes what lawyers, judges, and witnesses say and write in court cases. It also includes all the speech and writing that occurs "in the shadow of the law," in law-influenced settings as diverse as mediation, negotiation, bureaucratic service encounters, and obtaining informed consent to medical procedures. In its second sense, the term encompasses scholarly writing about law-related topics, media accounts, public debate, and commentary, and much more. And the term in both senses is cross-cultural, not bound to any particular society's definition of what constitutes law or legal process.

I will focus throughout this chapter on the related questions of what distinguishes a linguistic anthropological approach to legal discourse from other perspectives, and whether those distinguishing characteristics make a significant difference in the resulting analysis. That is, what can linguistic anthropologists contribute that others might not, and does it matter? I will illustrate the point with reference to several historical examples, review some significant contemporary examples of linguistic anthropologists working on legal discourse, comment on the practical significance of such work, and conclude with some thoughts about future directions.

Historical Perspectives

One way to appreciate the relative paucity of anthropological work on law is to examine the role of law in two books that have been influential in defining the field of linguistic anthropology: Alessandro Duranti's (1997) *Linguistic Anthropology,* part of the Cambridge Textbooks in Linguistics series, and continually reprinted; and an anthology that Duranti (2006) edited several years later, *A Companion to Linguistic Anthropology.* The words *law* and *legal* do not appear in the index to either book. The concluding chapter to the 1997 text hints at legal discourse, in sections devoted to "Public and Private Language" and "Language in Society" (Duranti 1997: 334–337). Under the former heading, for example, Duranti asks, in reference to language as a "public resource," "how can we ensure that we can still control it, bend it to our needs, that we as individuals are not crushed under the weight of the socially shared code?" Although Duranti does not do so explicitly, these are certainly questions that we might want to ask about legal discourse.

The later edited volume does not list legal discourse as the topic of any of its 22 chapters. However, Susan Philips' chapter on "Law and Social Inequality" (Philips 2006) is largely devoted to discourse that is, at a minimum, law-related. In her introduction, Philips (2006: 475–476) defines several concepts that are central to the operation of legal systems: symbolic capital, "authoritative speech," the relative reliability of different forms of evidence, and "power relations, or relations of dominance and subordination." She then briefly reviews her own prior work on how professionals dominate discourse in such bureaucratic settings as "classrooms, courtrooms, and clinics" (Philips 2006: 478) and the attendant consequences for social inequality. Her next topic is "gender, inequality, and language" (Philips 2006: 480), a subject that William O'Barr and I had begun to explore in the courtroom in the 1970s (Conley, O'Barr, and Lind 1978). Her final two topics are "language and political economy" (Philips 2006: 483), which, she shows, has been of concern to linguistic anthropologists since the 1950s, and "the colonial transformation of language and social inequality" (Philips 2006: 486), also a matter of long-standing interest among linguistic anthropologists. Language and political economy necessarily implicates law, albeit indirectly, since many of the status distinctions that result from language differences are encoded in law, enforced by a legal system, or manifest in legal proceedings. The relationship among colonialism, language, and law is more explicit since, as Philips observes, "colonialism entailed the introduction and imposition of the key institutional and ideological complexes or discourses of European religion, education, law, and media" (Philips 2006: 488).

The point of discussing these two significant books is twofold. First, both show that linguistic anthropology has been reticent in claiming legal discourse as a topic of interest and priority. But second, and notwithstanding that reticence, linguistic anthropologists have long had a great deal to say about matters that comprise or relate to legal discourse in both its ground-level and broader societal senses.

In fact, Philips herself has done extensive anthropological work on legal discourse. In an excellent but hard-to-find 1988 paper with the intriguing subtitle of "Acquiring the 'Cant,'" Philips investigated how law students – typically 22-year-olds just out of a generalist undergraduate education – were socialized into a manner of speaking that seems utterly foreign to most of the rest of the American speech community (Philips 1988). Then, in a 1998 book entitled *Ideology in the Language of Judges*, she used detailed analysis of discourse to refute the notion that Anglo-American judges are neutral arbiters who sit above the fray (Philips 1998). Instead, as she showed, judges are active and often dominant participants in many aspects of the adversary process, using such linguistic devices as turn control to move the unfolding legal discourse in directions they prefer. Here again, the subtitle says it all: *How Judges Practice Law, Politics and Courtroom Control.*

Philips' 1988 paper represents one of the first efforts by a linguistic anthropologist to deal directly with legal discourse. O'Barr and I had begun to write about the power of language in the courtroom in the late 1970s and early 1980s (e.g., Conley, O'Barr, and Lind 1978), but our perspective then was not fundamentally anthropological. Initially, our work was strongly influenced by conversation analysis, with its intensive focus on the evidence available from the discourse itself. In collaboration with social psychologists, we also conducted controlled experiments to determine the effect of language variation on jurors, something that is outside the ethnographic tradition.

Nonetheless, because we are anthropologists, we were drawn to the cultural context from which our linguistic evidence emerged. Even in our earliest work, we sought to understand the relationship between language and power. By the late 1980s, we had begun to investigate the differences between lay and professional understandings of what constitutes an adequate legal narrative. Our interest in this issue led us to conduct an ethnographic study of small claims courts around the United States in which we did participant observation in courtrooms, interviewed and conversed with litigants and judges, and conducted intensive qualitative analysis of recorded legal discourse. This research was the subject of our 1990 book *Rules Versus Relationships: The Ethnography of Legal Discourse* (Conley and O'Barr 1990), in which we argued for a fundamental distinction between the "rule-oriented" worldview of those who had been exposed to the culture of law and business and the "relational" outlook of those who had not. Rule-oriented narratives describe problems in terms of the violation of specified rules (not always the same as those the law recognizes) and demand concrete forms of redress, whereas relational ones focus on the violation of broader social norms and seek remedies that would mend torn social relations.

Some of the most significant earlier work on legal discourse has involved *language ideology* (used more-or-less synonymously with *ideology of language* and *linguistic ideology*). (For the purposes of this chapter I will define "contemporary" work as having been done within the last 10 years – since 2004 – and everything else as "early" or "earlier.") In everyday usage, the word *ideology* suggests a body of ideas, a philosophy, or an outlook. It often has political connotations, as in "Marxist ideology" or "conservative ideology." Applying everyday thinking to the term *language ideology* yields a definition along the lines of "a body of ideas about language," with a particular focus on political contexts. Although the scholarly definitions of both ideology and language ideology are endlessly debated, the most common social science usages do not differ materially from their everyday counterparts.

In a widely cited definition of language ideologies, Alan Rumsey (1990: 346) has characterized them as "shared bodies of commonsense notions about the nature of language in the world" – in other words, ideas about language held by groups of people. Judith Irvine and Susan Gal (2000: 35) extend this minimalist definition to encompass the relationship between language and society:

395

"the ideas with which participants and observers frame their understandings of linguistic varieties and map those understandings onto people, events, and activities that are significant to them." The linguistic anthropologist John Haviland (2003: 764) glosses these two formulations, elegantly and helpfully, as "what ideas the people we work with (and, indeed, we ourselves) have regarding what language is or what language is good for." In an elaboration that sets up the obvious connection with law, many definitions have focused explicitly on power. Irvine (1989: 255, emphasis added), for example, has defined language ideology as "the cultural system of ideas about social and linguistic relationships, *together with their loading of moral and political interests.*" Haviland's (2003: 764) version is "ideas about language and its place in social arrangements or its use and usability for social and political ends." And in a definition that presumes awareness and intent, Michael Silverstein (1979: 193) has proposed "sets of beliefs about language articulated by users as a rationalization or justification of perceived language structure and use."

Two illustrations of linguistic anthropology focused on language ideology in legal contexts are Susan Hirsch's (1998) book about Kenyan divorce courts, *Pronouncing & Persevering: Gender and the Discourses of Disputing in an African Islamic Court*, and Haviland's (2003) *American Anthropologist* article about an Oregon murder trial, "Ideologies of Language: Some Reflections on Language and US Law." Hirsch (1998) did ethnographic research in the Kadhi's Courts of coastal Kenya, in which an Islamic judge, or kadhi, is empowered by the state to apply Islamic law in certain cases (including divorce) that involve Muslim parties. Her title captures an ideological contrast between "a Muslim husband pronouncing divorce and his persevering wife silently accepting the decree" (Hirsch 1998: 2). In this stereotype, the husband's authority to pronounce both reflects and reaffirms his autonomy and agency, whereas women, "devoid of agency" (Hirsch 1998: 1), in language and in fact, "are expected to endure marital hardships without complaint and to accept divorce in the same spirit" (Hirsch 1998: 3).

Lacking the power to pronounce, wives who find themselves in intolerable marriages must go before the kadhi and make a case. There they confront a seemingly irreconcilable dilemma. Women should personify a cultural ideal of respect, honor, and modesty, which includes shielding private matters from public scrutiny; instead of making public complaints about marital troubles, one perseveres quietly. But a parallel cultural ideal – guaranteed by Islam and Islamic law – exalts the concepts of justice and rights. The obvious quandary is that in order to achieve her rights as a wife, a woman puts at risk the very qualities that make her deserving of such rights. But women regularly bring and win divorce cases, meaning that they somehow walk this exceedingly fine line.

The solution seems to lie in the ability to negotiate a minefield of culturally significant and often conflicting language ideologies. Specifically, women invoke ideologies that index, or point to, themselves as proper wives, while at the same time stepping outside the traditional bounds of propriety to assert their rights. As Hirsch (1998: 219) puts it, "Swahili women who complain in court embody a contradiction. Through their participation in cases and mediations, they generally stand in gross violation of appropriate speech, and yet, in so many dialogues, they are also routinely depicted as compliant wives."

Haviland's (2003) paper involves an Oregon murder trial in which he served as an expert witness (a particularly compelling form of participant observation). The defendant was convicted of killing a fellow migrant agricultural worker in a field outside the camp where they lived. The critical linguistic feature of the trial was that none of the witnesses to the events in question spoke English. Almost all were native speakers of Mixtec, and few had meaningful competence in Spanish. Nonetheless, the only translator provided by the court was a native speaker of Cuban Spanish (which is quite different from Mexican Spanish), who knew no Mixtec.

Haviland's account focuses on some beliefs about language that were critical to the outcome of the trial. The first (Haviland 2003: 767) is the notion of "referential transparency," or "the assumption that expressions in one language can be unproblematically rendered into propositions and translated 'verbatim' into another." This belief, or ideology, rests on the fallacy that "the truth-functional core of what someone says can be decoupled from the actual saying itself." In fact, no one language can be mapped directly onto another in "verbatim" fashion. Nonetheless, the judge relied on referential transparency and its underlying fallacy to instruct the translator as well as to instruct the jury about how to deal with the translations. Haviland also analyzes the role that several other comparably absurd language ideologies played in the trial, including the belief that English is not only a standard language, but "is also somehow in the repertoire of skills of a 'standard person', one who is socially and, perhaps, morally whole or 'normal.'" There is a powerful negative implication: those who do not speak English are "abnormal" or "substandard."

Haviland's analysis is both powerful and depressing. It is powerful because he is able to explain some otherwise impenetrable things that happened in this trial and that regularly happen in multilingual trials across the United States: judges instructing interpreters to "translate the responses of the witness verbatim, word for word;" or instructing the jury that the interpreter's "verbatim" translation of a witness' answers – presumably bereft of any commentary, paraphrases, or, ironically, "interpretation" – was to be their sole source of evidence; or permitting a prosecutor to browbeat and demean a witness who could speak neither English nor Spanish. But despite the power of his insights, Haviland (2003: 773) concludes on a discouraging note. He admits that his readers will inevitably expect "a triumphal cry for linguistic anthropology as an antidote to bad theories of language." But he concedes that he has no practical solutions, and in that he is probably right.

Hirsch's book and Haviland's article share features that mark them as works of linguistic *anthropology*. First, both projects involve ethnography, and in particular participant observation of events. In both cases, the authors focus on legal discourse as a cultural practice, with its production simultaneously reflecting and helping to constitute broader cultural values. Finally, both use language ideology as a core concept. That concept is not unique to anthropology, as it is a matter of interest across the spectrum of discourse studies. But the way in which both authors emphasize its *power* implications is clearly anthropological, since the exercise, maintenance, and subversion of power have long been central concerns in political and legal anthropology. I turn next to a more general discussion of what might distinguish the linguistic anthropology of legal discourse from other approaches.

Critical Issues and Topics

What's Unique about Linguistic Anthropology?

In considering the special value that linguistic anthropology might bring to the study of legal discourse, it is useful to review how linguistic anthropologists define their field. Most definitions stress both orientation and the methods. With respect to orientation, Duranti defines linguistic anthropology in his foundational textbook as "*the study of language as a cultural resource and speaking as a cultural practice*" (Duranti 1997: 2 [emphasis in original]). Elaborating, he continues:

> This means that linguistic anthropologists see the subject of their study, that is, *speakers*, first and above all as *social actors*, that is, members of particular, interestingly complex, communities, each organized in a variety of social institutions and through a network of intersecting but not necessarily overlapping sets of expectations, beliefs, and moral values about the world.
>
> *Duranti 1997: 2 [emphasis in original]*

Finally, he emphasizes that what ultimately distinguishes linguistic anthropologists from other linguists is "their focus on language as a set of symbolic resources that enter the constitution of social fabric and the individual representation of actual or possible worlds." This focus in turn allows linguistic anthropologists to address issues that have long been of special interest to anthropology generally, including several that are particularly salient in legal discourse: "the politics of representation, the constitution of authority, the legitimation of power, the cultural basis of racism and ethnic conflict . . . [and] the relationship between ritual performance and forms of social control" (Duranti 1997: 2–3)

With respect to method, one important contribution of linguistic anthropology is simply its cross-cultural focus. Most analysis of legal discourse has been done by Westerners working in their home countries and in their native languages. Many linguistic anthropologists – including me – have done the same. But almost everyone who has studied legal discourse in non-Western contexts or languages is a linguistic anthropologist: Hirsch and Haviland, for example. Thus, to the extent that there is comparative legal discourse analysis, it is linguistic anthropologists who have done most of it.

Ethnography based on participant observation is also characteristic of most anthropological research, including linguistic anthropology. Think again of Hirsch and Haviland, and the work that O'Barr and I did in small claims court. But ethnography is no longer the sole property of anthropology, and has not been for some time. To cite but one example, Douglas Maynard, a sociologist and conversation analyst, relied heavily on ethnography in *Good News, Bad News* (Maynard 2003), his excellent work on communications between professionals and patients in medical clinics.

What may be nearly unique to linguistic anthropology, though, is the multi-level nature of its ethnography. That is, few discourse analysts of other persuasions have combined the thick description of traditional ethnography, with its focus on culture as a set of symbolic resources, with the fine-grained analysis of text. To quote Duranti once more, linguistic anthropologists "connect the micro-level phenomena analyzable through recordings and transcripts with the often invisible background of people's relations as mediated by particular histories, including institutional ones" (Duranti 1997: 8). In the end, this enables an unusually rich understanding, not just of how speakers do the work of talk, but of how they use talk to do the work of social action.

What Difference Does This Make to the Study of Legal Discourse?

An initial response to this question is that the perspective of linguistic anthropology need not make any difference at all. Others do ethnography, and everyone who does discourse analysis does the fine-grained study of recorded and transcribed text. But it has made a difference, perhaps because the multi-level, connective approach I have described is driven by the experience of anthropology. Linguistic anthropologists always look at the world in this way; others might, but rarely do.

To illustrate this difference, consider two examples of excellent legal discourse work done by sociologists practicing conversation analysis. The first is J. Maxwell Atkinson and Paul Drew's (1979) *Order in Court,* one of the first exemplars of rigorous legal discourse analysis, and a book that has exerted significant influence on the field. The project is based on transcripts of British court proceedings, with much of the material relating to Catholic–Protestant violence in Northern Ireland in the late 1960s. Atkinson and Drew use these legal texts to explore issues that have long been of special interest to conversation analysts, including turn-taking, opening and organizing a proceeding (i.e., generating "order in court"), managing accusations, and offering justifications and excuses.

The project has obvious real-world implications, as evidenced by the final chapter's discussion of policy and reform implications. Nonetheless, consistent with the norms of conversation analysis and its antecedents in ethnomethodology, Atkinson and Drew (1979: 22) emphasize that the analyst's task is "not to stipulate what rules members *really* were 'following' or 'governed by', but to locate rules that they might be 'orienting to' and using in producing a recognizable orderliness in some setting." While acknowledging that many ethnomethodologists were ethnographers (including Erving Goffman, who coined the former term as a result of his work on the Chicago Jury Project), they argue nonetheless for a fundamental distinction between ethnography and conversation analysis, and seek to identify "some of the advantages conversation analysis has over ethnography" (Atkinson and Drew 1979: 33). Moreover, culture is nowhere to be found.

Linguistic anthropologists are, as I will discuss shortly, perfectly comfortable with this idea of *emergent* rules. But most, I think, would resist the idea that searching texts for emergent rules is sufficient in itself. In addition, there must be a more holistic consideration of the social action that discourse – and especially legal discourse – helps to constitute. To a linguistic anthropologist, the analysis of discourse may be the core of ethnography, but it is not the entirety of it.

Another milestone in the conversation analysis of legal discourse is Gregory Matoesian's (1993) *Reproducing Rape: Domination through Talk in the Courtroom*, a study of three rape trials in the US Midwest. Matoesian (1993: 23) roots his method in the early work of Goffman and Harold Garfinkel and calls it "the sociology of talk." The book is closely attendant to the broader social context of the trials, with an introductory chapter on "The Social Facticity of Rape." It is also intensely focused on courtroom talk as a means of producing and exercising power, and of disempowering the alleged victim. Indeed, its most compelling chapter is called "Talk and Power in the Rape Trial," a mind-opening and profoundly disturbing revelation about the power implications of otherwise routine cross-examination techniques in the rape context.

Yet despite all these affinities with linguistic anthropology – the social context, the emphasis on power, the scrutiny of talk as action – Matoesian's work is different. Not better, not worse, but different. For one thing, it is not ethnographic. This is not a criticism, just a fact: Matoesian analyzed publicly available court transcripts and, in one case, a tape recording that he transcribed. He augmented his analyses with ethnographic interviews of some participants, which he found to be "a rich mine of information" (Matoesian 1993: 60), but he, like Atkinson and Drew before him, takes care to point out ethnography's limited utility. Moreover, culture is nowhere to be found. It is not in the index, and Matoeisan does not employ the concept in drawing connections between the trial and its social context.

These two examples are intended to illustrate the point that linguistic anthropology makes a difference in the analysis of legal discourse. In its fine-grained study of talk in search of emergent rules, it overlaps significantly with conversation analysis and other methods of discourse analysis rooted on sociolinguistics and allied fields. But its defining characteristics also include a multi-level ethnographic method, a focus on talk as social action, and an abiding interest in discourse as simultaneously reflective, constitutive, and subversive of cultural norms and values. Other methods of discourse analysis often share some of these characteristics, but not all of them, all the time.

One further "historical" example from linguistic anthropology that confirms this point is Laurence Goldman's (1986) study of cases involving illicit premarital sex in village courts in the Huli society of Papua New Guinea. Like Matoesian, Goldman did fine-grained analysis of actual trial talk about sexual encounters. His analytical conclusions are in many respects strikingly similar: in particular, both researchers found power and coercion in the ostensibly mundane details of question-and-answer sequences. But Goldman's work was both ethnographic and cross-cultural, and it led him to challenge widely accepted cultural ideas about gender relations, in Huli society and elsewhere.

Current Contributions and Research

In this section I will briefly review several more current examples – one book by a senior scholar and three very recent papers by more junior authors – of the linguistic anthropology of legal discourse, in an effort to illustrate the special contributions that our discipline can make. The first is *The Language of Law School: Learning to "Think Like a Lawyer,"* by Elizabeth Mertz (2007), who is both an anthropologist and a lawyer. Her research site is the first-year law school classroom in several American law schools, and her objective is to investigate law students' initial exposure to "thinking like a lawyer." Lawyers claim this process as their intellectual hallmark, often describing it in terms of a logical rigor that stands in stark contrast to the sloppy emotionalism of the nonlegal world. Critics, on the other hand, have derided "thinking like a lawyer" as nothing more than a superficial language game that mystifies the simple and thereby reinforces the legal profession's unwarranted monopoly power – merely "acquiring the 'cant,'" as Philips (1988) put it. Critical legal theorists have also questioned the deeper effects of the process on students, arguing that legal education strips students of the values they bring to law school while subtly inculcating new and troubling ones that may undermine empathy for people and their problems.

Working in the ethnomethodological tradition, Mertz initially steps back from such questions and asks what thinking like a lawyer actually means in practice. What happens, linguistically, when law professors set out to teach student beginners how to do it? How do the students respond? What apparent rules and structures emerge when one explores the linguistic details of classroom interactions? In a nod in the direction of the Whorfian tradition, she explores the thought processes that are connected to the language of teaching law – a possible "deeper message about how the world operates, about what kind of knowledge counts, about how to proceed" (Mertz 2007: 23). This, in turn, provokes a further round of original thinking about the nature of the law itself and the prospects for change in legal education. Throughout, Mertz gives special attention to the concepts of language ideology and text, shedding new light on the ways in which legal practice depends on entextualization, reentextualization, and the management of the fuzzy text–context boundary.

What distinguishes Mertz's work as anthropological? First, it is ethnographic, in fact a multi-sited ethnography. Mertz and her collaborators attended, observed (making notes), recorded, transcribed, and coded an entire first-year class at eight American law schools chosen for their diverse locations and relative prestige. Moreover, Mertz herself was a "native" participant observer, having been through the process herself as both law student and law teacher. Second, her ultimate focus is on understanding the *culture* of legal practice and the role of law schools as sites and agents of acculturation. Her legal discourse analysis is directed very specifically at the question of how the language of law school works to reproduce the power relations at the core of the social fabric of law in practice.

Finally, Mertz's suggestions about the possibilities for change are also fundamentally anthropological. Many, many people in legal education have been arguing for some time that legal values (or, colloquially, "legal culture") are in decline, that law school plays a critical role in this decline, and that the law school experience must therefore be reformed. But Mertz is the first, to my knowledge, to connect the social practice of language with these broader concerns. By discovering the specific ways in which language functions as an essential constituent of legal culture, she is in a position to identify the points at which things are going wrong, and to suggest concrete changes. To me, her ability to appreciate language as a cultural resource is indispensable, and it derives from her anthropological sensibilities.

Next is Shonna Trinch's (2013) linguistic ethnography of how Latina women report rape to legal authorities when seeking protective orders against their husbands or partners. As in much of the linguistic anthropology of legal discourse literature, Trinch emphasizes the themes of culture and ideology. Her analytical starting point is a widespread cultural stereotype according to which Latina women would be expected to show shame, stigma, fear, and isolation. Yet the narratives that these women co-produced with their legal interlocutors, "situated in a larger cultural and political context yet created locally within a particular speech setting" (Trinch 2013: 290), reflect a different reality. The women were "well-dressed, composed, and few cried at all . . . [n]or did their narratives in any way suggest that because they were some man's wife they were required *by culture* to submit to his will" (Trinch 2013: 293 [emphasis in original]).

Exploring the origins of the cultural stereotype, Trinch discovers narratives of rape that have traveled through law, literature, and media. These narratives have been influential in defining the ideologically salient categories of "victim" and "survivor" and in shaping the interaction of those categories with the legal concept of rape. Trinch's contribution here is to challenge and disrupt the stereotype with evidence drawn from women's own narratives. Her ambition, largely realized, is to "travel with women who have been sexually assaulted to new discursive territories where we can develop a richer understanding of rape . . . [and] see, in women's words, what they do afterwards, and how they themselves move forward after rape" (Trinch 2013: 303).

The second example is Hadi Deeb's (2013) analysis of the California Supreme Court oral arguments in an important case about same-sex couples' right to marry. The court ultimately ruled that prior state restrictions on same-sex marriage violated the state constitution and were thus invalid and unenforceable.

Oral arguments in appellate cases follow the submission of written briefs and involve unscripted, often-intense give-and-take between the judges (here, the seven justices of the California Supreme Court) and the parties' lawyers (there are no witnesses). Lawyers begin with prepared statements but are usually interrupted by questions almost immediately. They rarely get to finish an answer before the next question. As happened here, the judges often interrupt each other with follow-up questions. Questions tend to be argumentative and frequently involve hypotheticals intended to test the strength and limits of the lawyers' positions.

Deeb uses video recordings of the arguments to conduct a detailed and sophisticated analysis of both the linguistic and visual aspects of the proceedings, and situates that analysis in its broader cultural context. Using principles developed in other anthropological and linguistic settings, he dissects "a series of stance-taking displays" in which speakers – both lawyers and judges – make and comment on arguments and punctuate the "complex weave and flow" of the discourse (Deeb 2013: 46). In an unusually vivid and persuasive example, he shows speakers using a repertoire of gestures to comment on such key legal concepts as joining, excluding, and allowing. The result is a demonstration of "the integration of pragmatic displays with the words that participants used to take, and tie, blended stances toward the case and one another" (Deeb 2013: 57).

Deeb then uses this analysis to illuminate "the relationship between communication among participants within a courtroom and the surrounding social context." Thus, he interprets the gestural display of one of the justices as "target[ing] social indexes of a sexual minority" (Deeb 2013: 57). On a theoretical level, he sees his findings as complementing "insights from existing linguistic-anthropological scholarship on how legal language helps define group identities" (Deeb 2013: 57). Deeb cites specific connections to the work of Haviland, Hirsch, and Philips, discussed earlier in this chapter, as well as to Richard Bauman's (1975) seminal "Verbal Art as Performance," Michael Silverstein's (1998) work on ideology, and Justin Richland's (2008) ethnography of Hopi tribal courts.

The final example is Robin Conley's (2013) ethnographic study of decision making by jurors in Texas death penalty cases. Her analysis and findings have a good deal in common with Deeb's, though her focus is on trials rather than appeals. Her research is based on classic ethnography: she traveled throughout Texas, attending capital murder cases; sitting in on lawyers' meetings; talking formally and informally with prosecutors, defense lawyers, defendants, and court and prison personnel; and finding and interviewing jurors in the weeks after they rendered their verdicts. This article focuses on the transcripts of trials and juror interviews.

Like Deeb, Conley sees the courtroom – here, the trial courtroom – as an arena of intense verbal and visual communication. She emphasizes the "embodied experience" of participants, noting that "[t]he legal subject in practice . . . whether a defendant or juror, is intersubjectively and bodily entwined with others throughout the course of a trial" (Conley 2013: 506). She sees a fundamental conflict between this experience of intimacy between the defendant and the jurors and the jurors' duty, conveyed to them in the judge's instructions, to put aside empathy and emotion and decide the defendant's fate on the basis of a rational assessment of the evidence. In simplest terms, how do jurors manage to decide to kill another human being who has been sitting ten feet away from them every day for a week or more?

Conley discovers potential answers in the details of language. Working with the language of the judge's instructions, the testimony from the witness stand, and the lawyers' arguments, jurors develop linguistic strategies to overcome the impact of their shared embodied experience with the defendant and ultimately to distance themselves from the life-or-death decision they must make. Specific strategies she identifies include the manipulation of deictic references to the defendant and the construction of agency in ways that mitigate jurors' personal responsibility. Her conclusions combine microlinguistic analysis, an understanding of the local culture of the Texas capital trial, and an appreciation of broader culture contexts in a way that is uniquely and strikingly anthropological.

All three of these recent papers illustrate the difference that the anthropological perspective can make to the analysis of legal discourse. All three are ethnographic: Trinch's and Conley's in the traditional way, Deeb's in an unconventional yet recognizable way. Most importantly, all three analyze legal discourse in a way that is faithful to Duranti's definition of linguistic anthropology: *"the study of language as a cultural resource and speaking as a cultural practice"* (Duranti 1997: 2 [emphasis in original]). Trinch sees the potential of the rape narratives she studies to challenge and change broader cultural stereotypes about rape and its victims. Deeb connects communication in the appellate courtroom to broader cultural issues, in particular the definition of social identities. And Conley embeds her microlinguistic analysis in multiple layers of cultural context, from the local environment of the trial to legal culture more generally, and ultimately to pervasive social norms. Again, others may generate similar insights, but to anthropologists they are the first priority.

Recommendations for Practice

Looking ahead, I have three specific recommendations for the practice of legal discourse analysis by linguistic anthropologists. The first is: do more of it. As I have noted throughout this chapter, linguistic anthropology can make unique contributions to understanding legal discourse and its broader significance. But linguistic anthropologists have, until recently, been bit players in this endeavor. So I hope that more linguistic anthropologists will turn their attention to law and legal processes.

My second recommendation – and this will sound odd, directed at anthropologists – is to be more cross-cultural. Legal anthropology has followed a trajectory of starting out in small-scale societies (see the references above to Malinowski, Gluckman, and Bohannan), then turning its lens on the legal systems of Western countries, and then returning to a global perspective. The linguistic anthropology of law seems to be following a slightly different path. Earlier work involved a mix of Western (O'Barr and J. M. Conley) and traditional (Hirsch) sites, as well as projects that examined cross-cultural interactions in Western legal systems (Haviland, for example). The most recent work in the field (as illustrated by the previous section) seems to be largely focused on problems in the US legal system. This is good: turning anthropology's critical perspective on any system can only be illuminating. But at the same time, anthropology is by its nature a global enterprise, and linguistic anthropologists studying law should not forget that.

A recent example that illustrates the point is Justin Richland's (2008) ethnography of Hopi justice, *Arguing with Tradition: The Language of Law in Hopi Tribal Courts*. Though set within the boundaries of the United States, the project is in fact about the emergence of a new culture of tribal law, and with it a new conception of tribal sovereignty. In an intriguing irony, Richland's micro-analysis of Hopi courtroom discourse shows how each evocation of tradition – conventionally, something excavated from a static past – in fact contributes to cultural change, helping to shape a continually evolving sense of Hopi justice. The details of discourse also suggest an unexpected reversal of the arrow of agency in the relationship between the Hopi and the U.S. legal systems: rather than simply reacting and adapting, the Hopi system is exporting its values to its nominal suzerain. It is inconceivable to me that these insights could have been produced by anyone other than an anthropologist.

My third recommendation is that in studying legal discourse, linguistic anthropologists should strive to be more applied. The decline of the "public anthropologist" has been a source of great angst in recent years. Even as our core concept of culture gets hijacked by just about everyone, it is rare to see anthropologists shaping public debate about important issues. The legal arena presents an opportunity to change that.

All of the projects I have reviewed in this chapter have yielded powerful theoretical insights, new ways of looking at law and legal practice. But all of them also have important implications (whether or not realized) for the pursuit of justice. Recall that Haviland did his ethnographic work while serving as an expert witness; similarly, Richland has advised Hopi legal officials, while Conley has shared her insights with defense lawyers seeking to understand how jurors reason. I turn next to some evidence that this trend may be accelerating.

Future Directions

A possible model for the future practice of the linguistic anthropology of law emerged at the 2013 Annual Meeting of the American Anthropological Association. The Society for Linguistic Anthropology sponsored a half-day panel entitled, "Engaging Language: Linguistic Anthropologists as Agents of Social Change." Five of the twelve wide-ranging presentations dealt explicitly with law and legal discourse: "Occupying Language: Challenging Linguistic Inequality with Anthro-Political Linguistics," by Ana Zentella; "The Linguistic Anthropologist/ Sociolinguist as Expert Witness: English-Only in the Workplace Rules," by Keith Walters; "Interrogating Abuse: Linguistic-Anthropological Interventions in a Child Molestation Case," by Mary Bucholtz and colleagues; "Ethnographers Can Make Better Lawyers: Engaging Law School Reformers with Linguistic Anthropological Research," by Joon-Beom Chu; and "Linguistic Ideologies and Dehumanization in U.S. Legal Practice," by Robin Conley. As the titles suggest, in each instance linguistic anthropologists brought their unique perspective – ethnographically based and culture-focused – to bear on a real-world legal problem, to creative and productive effect. My concluding thought is that both linguistic anthropology and the legal world would benefit enormously from more such work.

Related Topics

8 Language Ideologies (Kroskrity); **19** Language and Political Economy (McElhinny); **22** Language in the Age of Globalization (Jacquemet);

References

Atkinson, J. Maxwell, and Paul Drew. 1979. *Order in Court*. Atlantic Highlands, NJ: Humanities Press.
Bauman, Richard. 1975. Verbal Art as Performance. *American Anthropologist* 77(2): 290-311.
Bohannan, Paul. 1989 (orig. 1957). *Justice and Judgment Among the Tiv*, 3rd ed. Prospect Heights, IL: Waveland Press.
Conley, John M., William M. O'Barr and E. Allen Lind. 1978. The Power of Language: Presentational Style in the Courtroom. *Duke Law Journal* 27: 41-64.
Conley, John M., and William M. O'Barr. 1990. *Rules versus Relationships: The Ethnography of Legal Discourse*. Chicago: University of Chicago Press.
Conley, John M., and William M. O'Barr. 2005. *Just Words: Law, Language and Power*, 2nd ed. Chicago: University of Chicago Press.
Conley, Robin H. 2013. Living with the Decision that Someone Will Die: Linguistic Distance and Empathy in Jurors' Death Penalty Decisions. *Language in Society* 42: 503–526.
Deeb, Hadi Nicholas. 2013. Boiling Down to the M-Word at the California Supreme Court. *Journal of Linguistic Anthropology* 23: 41–64.
Duranti, Alessandro. 1997. *Linguistic Anthropology*. Cambridge: Cambridge University Press.
Duranti, Alessandro (Ed.). 2006. *A Companion to Linguistic Anthropology*. Malden, MA: Blackwell.
Gluckman, Max. 1955. *The Judicial Process among the Barotse of Northern Rhodesia (Zambia)*. Manchester, UK: Manchester University Press.
Goldman, Laurence R. 1986. A Case of "Questions" and Questions of "Case." *Text* 6: 345–392.
Goldman, Laurence R. 1993. *The Culture of Coincidence: Accident and Absolute Liability in Huli*. New York: Clarendon Press.
Haviland, John B. 2003. Ideologies of Language: Some Reflections on Language and U.S. law. *American Anthropologist* 105(4): 764–774.
Heffer, Chris, Frances Rock and John Conley. 2013. *Lay-Legal Communication: Textual Travels in the Law*. New York: Oxford University Press.
Hirsch, Susan F. 1998. *Pronouncing & Persevering: Gender and the Discourses of Disputing in an African Islamic Court*. Chicago: University of Chicago Press.
Irvine, Judith T. 1989. When Talk Isn't Cheap: Language and Political Economy. *American Ethnologist* 16: 248–267.
Irvine, Judith T., and Susan Gal. 2000. Language Ideology and Linguistic Differentiation. In Paul V. Kroskrity (Ed.) *Regimes of Language: Ideologies, Polities, and Identities*. Santa Fe, NM: School of American Research Press.
Malinowski, Bronislaw. 1985 (orig. 1926). *Crime and Custom in Savage Society*. Totowa, NJ: Rowman and Allanheld.
Maynard, Douglas W. 2003. *Good News, Bad News: Conversational Order in Everyday Talk and Clinical Settings*. Chicago: University of Chicago Press.
Matoesian, Gregory M. 1993. *Reproducing Rape: Domination through Talk in the Courtroom*. Chicago: University of Chicago Press.
Mertz, Elizabeth. 2007. *The Language of Law School: Learning to "Think Like a Lawyer."* Oxford: Oxford University Press.
Philips, Susan. 1988. The Language Socialization of Lawyers: Acquiring the "Cant." In George Spindler (Ed.) *Doing the Ethnography of Schooling: Educational Anthropology in Action*. Prospect Heights, IL: Waveland.
Philips, Susan. 1998. *Ideology in the Language of Judges: How Judges Practice Law, Politics, and Courtroom Control*. Oxford: Oxford University Press.
Philips, Susan. 2006. Language and Social Inequality. In Alessandro Duranti (Ed.) *A Companion to Linguistic Anthropology*. Malden, MA: Blackwell.
Richland, Justin. 2008. *Arguing with Tradition: The Language of Law in Hopi Tribal Courts*. Chicago: University of Chicago Press.
Rumsey, Alan. 1990. Wording, Meaning and Linguistic Ideology. *American Anthropologist* 92(2): 346–361.

Silverstein, Michael. 1979. Language Structure and Linguistic Ideology. In Paul R. Clyne, William F. Hanks and Carol L. Hofbauer (Eds) *A Parasession on Linguistic Units and Levels*. Chicago: Chicago Linguistic Society.
Silverstein, Michael. 1998. The Uses and Utility of Ideology: A Commentary. In Bambi B. Schieffelin, Kathryn A. Woolard and Paul V. Kroskrity (Eds) *Language Ideologies: Practice and Theory*. New York: Oxford University Press.
Trinch, Shonna. 2013. Recalling Rape: Moving Beyond What We Know. In Chris Heffer, Frances Rock and John Conley (Eds) *Lay-Legal Communication: Textual Travels in the Law*. New York: Oxford University Press.

Further Reading

Philips, Susan. 1998. *Ideology in the Language of Judges: How Judges Practice Law, Politics and Courtroom Control*. Oxford: Oxford University Press.
Richland, Justin. 2008. *Arguing with Tradition: The Language of Law in Hopi Tribal Courts*. Chicago: University of Chicago Press.
Schieffelin, Bambi B., Kathryn A. Woolard and Paul V. Kroskrity (Eds). 1998. *Language Ideologies: Practice and Theory*. New York: Oxford University Press.

27
The Language of Transitional Justice

Susan F. Hirsch

Introduction

In the second half of the twentieth century, instances of horrific mass violence, such as state-sponsored genocides in Guatemala and Rwanda and civil wars in the former Yugoslavia and Sierra Leone, left survivors and the world community with the responsibility of responding to the "world's worst crimes" while also rebuilding shattered lives and societies. Dated to the Nuremberg trials after World War II, transitional justice comprises legal and quasi-legal mechanisms of delivering justice after significant sociopolitical upheaval and violence, such as a period of dictatorship or political repression, civil or international war, or mass violence from another source (Minow 1998, Teitel 2000). A burgeoning set of practitioners, notably lawyers and NGO workers in postconflict settings, are prime movers of what is sometimes called the transitional justice industry. The study of transitional justice is a large and growing scholarly field, most often associated with political science, international relations, law, and sociolegal studies. The proliferation of multiple forms of transitional justice in the 1990s, including international tribunals, national trials, truth and reconciliation commissions (TRCs), and a wide array of locally meaningful rituals and performances aimed at providing culturally relevant justice and reconciliation makes it both a relatively new phenomenon for anthropological study and one characterized by widely varying and emergent forms.

Transitional justice is also the subject of considerable controversy. It is not surprising that controversy would arise over whether any of the practices of transitional justice could accomplish the daunting tasks of redressing the harm of mass violence or healing devastated societies. Conventional methods of anthropological linguistics can help to explain why many participants are dissatisfied with transitional justice processes, especially those held in formal legal settings, and why approaches designed to be less formal, such as TRCs, also fall short. As a broader controversy, the past twenty years of efforts in the name of transitional justice have emphasized Western liberal legal approaches and, in so doing, have triggered reactions critical of the hegemonic role of powerful international actors, who are accused of shaping transitional justice in self-serving ways. Recent scholarship in anthropological linguistics, particularly semiotics, can illuminate this controversy and account for why it is unlikely to fade.

Defining Transitional Justice

A foundational text defines transitional justice "as the conception of justice associated with periods of political change, characterized by legal responses to confront the wrongdoing of repressive predecessor regimes" (Teitel 2003: 69), yet both parts of the term have come in for criticism. The word "transition" implies an expectation of movement or change, either transition toward democracy or transition away from violence, each of which are difficult to apprehend and achieve. As for "justice," is it assumed to mean accountability and punishment, or are other incarnations, such as public apology or reparations, acceptable substitutes? Rather than dwell on definitions, this chapter takes an expansive view, which allows for exploration of scholarship about a wide range of processes.

Post-Nuremberg transitional justice was characterized by national trials and tribunals (e.g., those held in Latin America in the 1970s), and it expanded onto an international scale in the 1990s with the creation of several United Nations-sponsored ad hoc tribunals and courts.[1] Regional human rights courts also handle transitional justice cases, and in 2001 the International Criminal Court (ICC) was established in The Hague to provide, when no other venue is possible, a permanent UN-linked site to try perpetrators accused of war crimes, crimes against humanity, and genocide. The same time frame saw the establishment of TRCs; the prototype and widely celebrated version was mounted in South Africa in 1994 (see, e.g., Ross 2003, Wilson 2001). Not all of the many subsequent TRCs achieved the same level of acclaim (Avruch and Vejarano 2002, Hayner 2002). Typically, transitional justice includes several elements, namely, establishing the truth or an account of what happened, determining responsibility for harm, punishing those responsible, and fostering reconciliation or some means of addressing social rupture (Kerr and Mobekk 2007, Minow 1998). The challenges of accomplishing these aims on a mass scale or in formal settings, especially in international courts situated far from where violence occurred, led to recognition of other forms of transitional justice, such as reconciliation rituals and other "performative symbolic and ritual gestures" (Okello 2012, Wagner-Pacifici and Hall 2012).[2]

Outline of This Chapter

Language is at the heart of transitional justice, but anthropological linguists have only begun to examine it. As explained in the next section, scholarly studies of law and language that focused on courts are precursors to contemporary studies of transitional justice. The section entitled Critical Ideas and Topics considers five areas: Accounting for Past Harm; Special Concern for Victims; Transition through Speech Acts; Culture, Ritual, and Transition; and Framing Discourses. The ever-widening variation in post-1990 transitional justice – from formal legal contexts to TRCs to everyday practices – means that an array of anthropological scholarship informs contemporary studies. The Current Contributions and Research section highlights just three as forms of transitional justice: semiotic approaches; apologies; and rituals, embodiment, and silence. Two later sections describe the multiple methods used to study transitional justice, and the practical problems that emerge, especially for individuals, that could be addressed using insights from linguistic anthropology. These and other practical problems could be among the directions for future study, which are described in the chapter's penultimate section. The concluding section returns to the topic of the controversy over the hegemonic role of Western liberal legal discourse in transitional justice. Recent attention to law's extraordinary discursive power helps explain why this controversy is likely to continue, even as individual survivors exercise agency in ever more creative ways in response to mass violence.

Historical Perspectives

The post-World War II trials held in Nuremberg and Tokyo were unprecedented and controversial in that many people viewed them as "victors' justice," given the control over the proceedings exerted by the United States and their allies (see, e.g., Bass 2000, Kerr and Mobekk 2007). Over a decade later, philosopher Hannah Arendt drew attention to the linguistic features of transitional justice in her journalistic reporting of the trial of Adolf Eichmann in Jerusalem (Arendt 1963). Arendt's account highlighted how the trial's focus on the defendants, rather than the victims, exposed the "banality of evil," as narrated through their dispassionate testimony. Although not a systematic linguistic analysis, Arendt's popular depiction of the Eichmann trial became a touchstone for scholars and practitioners interested in how narratives of atrocity are developed through formal legal proceedings. As she demonstrated, the trial testimony failed to include many stories, including those of victims and survivors. As a philosopher, Arendt emphasized the crucial importance of public deliberation to democracy and thus was deeply sensitive to the public's interpretation of the Eichmann trial.

The literature on law and language generates theoretical questions and methodological approaches that are particularly insightful, as they elucidate the micro-level dynamics of the courtroom, which is one venue for transitional justice (see, e.g., Conley and O'Barr 1998, Matoesian 1993, 2001). These studies explicate the conventions of courtroom discourse, for instance, the pre-allocation of turns at talk and the question-and-answer format, as well as the effects of these peculiarities on participants as well as on outcomes (Mertz 1994). The linguistic study of alternative dispute resolution highlights the contrast between formal and informal disputing processes and thus offers approaches pertinent to examining truth commissions and other quasi-legal forums. The foundational literature in law and language also drew attention to gender and power, which has influenced subsequent studies.

Critical Issues and Topics

Each of the following critical issues and topics emerges out of concerns over the adequacy of particular transitional justice initiatives; at the same time they reflect significant areas for developing theories on the role of language in transitional justice.

Accounting for Past Harm

Many transitional justice initiatives are designed to produce an account of the violence, with the assumption that such accounts must be developed, presented, and acknowledged in a relatively public setting in order to achieve justice or some other beneficial result. Accounting for past harm raises questions, however: What should an account include? Who should present it? In what context? How widely should it be disseminated? Accounts of mass atrocity tend to be shaped by victors, often the government in power. They usually produce "master narratives" that acknowledge the horror of the past, when vilified enemies committed atrocities, while also paving the way for a peaceful future with the state as guardian against violence. In the delicate balance of recounting horrific crimes, blaming those responsible, and creating or restoring social bonds between members of a severely divided society, narratives that counter a simplistic master story, or present too complex a story, can be drowned out or marginalized (Cobb 2013). For instance, narratives that recount any violence committed by the victorious regime are frequently omitted. Similarly, in situations where one political party or ethnic group predominated in using violence against another, stories of how "victims" were also violent, or the reasons behind perpetrators' violence, are deemed counterproductive to reconciliation. Narratives from perpetrators or bystanders are treated as less important than those from victimized survivors. The marginalization of some stories exposes the inherent partiality of all the accounts of what happened.

In legal contexts where attributing blame is a primary purpose, stories are often carefully crafted, especially by lawyers. Mertz and Yovel (2005: 86) assert, "The imposition of legal frames moves litigant narratives away from more emotional and relational stories toward accounts organized around theories of cause-and-effect and responsibility that respond to the requirements of legal rules." Even relatively straightforward criminal proceedings ignore many aspects of what happened. In the case of an extremely complex situation where rape, genocide, and other crimes were perpetrated on a mass scale, a narrow explanatory narrative might effectively attribute blame, but it would necessarily fail to reflect multiple perspectives and parallel stories. Furthermore, the constraints of courtroom language and strategy make it difficult to reconcile contradictions in the stories told by previously warring parties (see, e.g., Wilson 2011).

The linguistic constraints of formal legal contexts led to the endorsement of TRCs and other quasi-legal forums, yet conventions for interaction in those settings are also limiting. The trauma of recounting particular events and the instability inherent in mass violence can make it difficult for narrators to follow the usual convention of recounting a story chronologically (Hirsch 2007). Accounts of atrocity are told for multiple purposes, including as a balance against silencing, as sacrament, and as carnivalistic expression, although not all of these are welcome in any particular transitional justice setting (Phelps 2004). Trial courts and TRCs serve as sites for such accounts, yet they cannot control whether an account will stand as the "truth" of what happened, whether other narratives that express different perspectives will emerge, and how these accounts will circulate in the future (Savelsberg and King 2011).

Special Concern for Victims

The widespread belief that narrating mass violence is necessary for transition to a stable society provokes deeper questions about whether the pain of violence can ever be adequately described. Scarry (1985) argues that speech fails as a vehicle for an individual's experience of violence. Simpson similarly argues that, for victims, the inability to articulate the harm was inextricably part of the experience of violence itself, and consequently the inability to recount their experiences may be a lasting effect (Simpson 2007). By contrast, legal proceedings and other forms of transitional justice are organized under the assumption that victims have a strong desire to speak about their experiences and that narrating the harm might have therapeutic effects, as well as legal consequence (Ross 2003).

The assumption that victims want to tell their stories, coupled with the concern that doing so might be difficult, has fueled attention to victims in the policies of transitional justice settings, such as courts and TRCs (Hirsch 2009, Mertus 2004). For instance, the ICC has a separate Victims' Unit that conducts outreach to victims and prepares them for courtroom proceedings. Concern over the retraumatization or revictimization that can occur during testimony has led courts to provide therapists and other assistance (see Koomen 2013, Matoesian 1993, on revictimization). Future research might determine whether this increased effort has had appreciable linguistic effects.

With respect to mass violence French (2012: 343) argues that "some actors lost more than others" and thus warrant special attention. By occupying a special status, however, individual victims risk being treated as emblematic of a group whose members might in fact hold diverse perspectives (French 2012). Their diversity could extend to their level of interest in recounting experiences of violence or in seeking justice at all (Stover 2005). As well, victims vary in their reactions to participating in courts and other transitional justice settings. Some experiences are negative precisely because those who testified did not feel that their stories were heard or taken seriously (Mertus 2004, Ross 2003, Stover 2005). Although granted special status, victims might not be experiencing the empowerment imagined by those who advocated for their participation (French 2009).

Transition through Speech Acts

Depending on where and how they are offered, accounts of harm can be instrumental in allocating responsibility for crimes. Relatedly, blaming is a significant speech act associated with many forms of transitional justice, as is admission of guilt or confession. Both blaming and confession were central elements of *gacaca*, a form of local transitional justice instituted after the Rwandan genocide to adjudicate tens of thousands of alleged perpetrators of genocide and other crimes (Burnet 2012, Clark 2010). Based loosely on a "traditional" approach to resolving more minor conflicts, *gacaca* was reconfigured by the post-1994 Rwandan government and implemented across the country. During *gacaca* hearings, which are public and often held in the open air, alleged perpetrators are encouraged to engage in truth-telling about their participation in the genocide, and community members are asked to confirm or challenge their statements. Locally elected judges determine responsibility and mete out sentences. Even though thousands of *gacaca* trials were conducted, given the scale of the violence, not everyone would have a direct experience of blaming or confessing. In other conflicts, the prevalence of amnesties as part of the conflict resolution process made confession a less likely speech act as part of transitional justice.

Several speech acts that are rare in formal legal settings, such as apology and forgiveness, are the intended outcomes of other types of transitional justice. Expressions of remorse and forgiveness during the South African TRC were thought to encourage reconciliation. Similarly, truth-telling followed by acknowledgement or forgiveness are speech acts central to a form of local transitional justice in northern Uganda called *mato oput* (Anyeko, Baines, Komakech, Ojok, Ogora, and Victor 2012). The centrality of speech acts to these processes begs questions always asked of speech acts: What are the "felicity conditions" that make a speech act effective? Who determines whether the conditions have been met? The classic problem of meeting the "felicity conditions" of speech acts is exacerbated by the extraordinary circumstances of mass violence. For instance, what are the challenges in determining the sincerity of an accused person who apologizes for the murder of one's family member? How does the specter of retaliation shape understandings of whether "felicity conditions" have been met (Burnet 2012)? Although the South African TRC established some principles for evaluating speech in transitional justice settings, cultural, linguistic, and institutional differences can make it difficult to determine whether any particular act is acceptable to those involved or furthers reconciliation.

Culture, Ritual, and Transition

The contexts for transitional justice vary considerably with respect to the conventions of interaction that typify each. Increasingly, political struggles over transitional justice refer to the linguistic features of available contexts. As studies of courtroom discourse would predict, some participants in tribunals or trials express frustration that the formality of the context felt foreign or threatening (Mertus 2004, Stover 2005). Even the multilingual nature of international trials can be off-putting, at the same time as interpretation enhances the goal of involving a broader audience. Less formal contexts might be equally unfamiliar; the South African TRC relied on many new conventions for speaking about violence based, in part, on the concept of *ubuntu*, a

Bantu-language concept that invokes the interconnectedness of community members, who are assumed to share common humanity, and the embrace of reconciliation as a response to violence or conflict (Murithi 2012). The value system underlying *ubuntu* offers an approach to reconciliation that requires passing through the following stages central to the South Africa TRC: "acknowledgement of guilt, showing remorse and repenting, asking for and giving forgiveness, and paying compensation or reparation as a prelude to reconciliation" (Murithi 2012: 202).

Whether formal proceedings are unsatisfying to victims or otherwise inadequate, the sheer scale of mass crimes can preclude bringing every accused perpetrator before a court or TRC. The concern that some people will miss justice entirely combines with the concern that certain contexts offer unfamiliar justice for victims. Such concerns have fueled efforts to identify culturally recognizable justice, such as *gacaca* mentioned above. Moreover, the emphasis on blame and punishment in courts and some TRCs is viewed by critics as standing in the way of societal healing or reconciliation, the ultimate goal of transitional justice. One difficulty in adopting already existing, grassroots justice is that, because these institutions or rituals were not created with such massive infractions in mind, adaptation is imperative. For instance, *mato oput* was one of several rituals of the Acholi people that was redesigned to address destructive violence in northern Uganda (Allen 2006, Clarke 2009). The ritual emphasized welcoming alleged perpetrators back into the community through rituals of healing, rebirth, and forgiveness, using culturally recognized conventions for apology, repentance, forgiveness, and reconciliation. Those who supported the rituals as substitutes for national or international prosecution insisted that local linguistic and cultural practices would promote individual and societal healing. Yet, as neo-traditions, the legitimacy of these rituals is easily questioned, particularly in culturally diverse communities or those that were severely destabilized (Allen 2006, Hirsch 2009). Certain rituals are also vulnerable to criticism – internal and external – for not conforming to human rights discourse and standards, particularly concerning gender and age.

In addition to publically recognized rituals – regardless of their origin or level of endorsement – individuals and groups of people spontaneously create their own locally meaningful ritualized responses, as will be discussed in the Current Contributions and Research section.

Framing Discourses

The discourse of human rights – powerful in both its moral message and global reach – provides the frame for the international institutions that seek accountability for mass atrocity in the name of humanity (Ojara 2012). More broadly, the discourse of Western liberal legalism underpins international human rights, humanitarianism, and criminal law, and shapes the micro-level discourse of many transitional justice proceedings (Clarke 2009, Drumbl 2007). This framing role is especially evident in international prosecutions; however, national-level trials generally use similar discursive conventions. Moreover, the power of Western liberal legalism means that, even in local contexts, the speech of many parties is influenced in subtle ways.

Kagoro (2011) argues that transitional justice provides the wrong frame in African contexts and endorses a broader, restorative 'global justice' "that has juridical and material dimensions, a culture of accountability that looks at internal mechanisms as well as external reparations by multinational corporations and developed nations complicit in Africa's conflicts, political repression and human rights violations" and contrasts sharply with Western legal liberalism's narrow frame (Kagoro 2011: 18). Clarke (2009) confirms the concern expressed about Western liberal legal approaches, particularly in African nations where prominent international prosecutions have been mounted and challenged, at the same time as structural violence and external causes remain unaddressed. Criticism of Western liberal legalism as a discursive frame that fails to scrutinize the West's complicity is increasing at the same time as that frame is becoming more pervasive and powerful.

Current Contributions and Research

New venues for transitional justice continue to emerge, such as national institutions that invoke universal jurisdiction or prosecute internal infractions that rise to the level of crimes against humanity. Comparison across different institutions and cases is increasingly possible, as is longitudinal study. At the same time as other disciplines have made a quantitative turn in the study of transitional justice (see, e.g., Olsen, Payne, and Reiter 2010, van der Merwe, Baxter, and Chapman 2009), in-depth studies of language in these contexts is warranted. This section highlights three areas of research from among many.

Treating Accounts as Texts

Accounts of past violence produced through transitional justice bear the contradictory burden of revealing the "truth" of what happened and also being constructed – implicitly and explicitly – through those processes. Ross (2003) was among the first scholars to note that accounts of violence were shaped by the South African TRC process itself, as well as by factors such as gender and age. The influence of transitional justice on accounts begins early as human rights workers or legal personnel conduct "outreach" among survivors. For instance, "ambivalent or contradictory" memories were policed out of narratives collected through the outreach of Cambodia's Extraordinary Chamber (Manning 2012).

French's study of the reports produced after the Guatemalan truth commission is notable in demonstrating how the final accounts were divested of key aspects of the meaning present in their original telling: "survivor testimonies are disciplined into particular institutionally supported forms that further erase ways of meaningful telling and knowing among structurally subordinated groups, further re-inscribing their marginalization in an unintended way" (French 2009: 100). Far from being a transparent window on truth, narrative bears culturally specific messages that reports fail to include. Parallelism, repetition, and metaphor convey considerable meaning about the teller's experience yet reports rarely include them (French 2009: 102). Survivors' stories are distorted when reports focus on referential aspects of testimony, rather than pragmatic aspects that come through reported speech and evidentials. For example, fear of the Guatemalan authorities was evident in how survivors quoted them during testimony; however, this aspect of their persecutors' speech is absent in the historical record (French 2009: 103). The realization that accounts of past violence are entextualized through politicized processes leads French to argue for a semiotic approach that will focus "on the forms such narratives take, the contexts of their production, and their ongoing local, national, and transnational circulation" (French 2012: 344).

An important, albeit controversial, manner in which accounts circulate is as histories of particular conflicts. The history written through an international legal proceeding has to contend with testimony from deeply partisan perspectives. Arguing that multiple discursive approaches to history – beyond partisan accounts – are part of the trial process, Wilson counters conventional wisdom by refusing to conclude "that the pursuit of justice and the writing of history are inherently irreconcilable" (Wilson 2011: 19). Accounts circulating as history are readily repurposed to explain conflict or to justify strategies in the present or future. Savelsberg and King (2011) draw attention to how media accounts of legal responses to specific atrocities (e.g., the My Lai massacre) shape collective memory and vice versa.

Accounts of violence that are produced with no references to public discourse outside the court or TRC have little chance of creating the conditions for reconciliation (Mazzei 2011). The absence of international legal attention can invigorate "narratives of victimhood" that publicize and memorialize using other means (Chiwengo 2008: 92). The public telling of stories about the past can have significant influence on those who did not experience it, and the knowledge about the past created through formal instances of transitional justice operates in relation to other circulating discourses and is repeatedly renegotiated in conversation (Achugar, Fernández, and Morales 2013) and in various media.

Apologies and Their Many Effects

Research on apologies has grown apace with the expanding use of this staple speech act in transitional justice initiatives. Individual apologies are frequently offered during testimony in TRCs, and these have been scrutinized for their adherence to "felicity conditions," such as the apologizer's sincerity. Public apology has been an especially fertile area for linguistic analysis (see, generally, Harris, Grainger, and Mullany 2006). *The Age of Apology* describes the many instances of public apology during the post-Cold War era (e.g., President Clinton's apology to African Americans for slavery; Pope John Paul II's apology related to the Holocaust) and makes a case for the difficulty of producing an efficacious public apology (Gibney, Howerd-Hassmann, Coicaud, and Steiner 2008). For instance, in the absence of material recompense, a verbal apology can be dismissed as insincere or merely symbolic, and many linguistic tactics can be used to feign the appearance of apology without incurring its negative effects, such as losing face or assuming responsibility. Powerful leaders are especially adept at these tactics (James 2008). They might, for instance, express "regret" and use other non-performative verbs, when they endeavor to reshape social relations, while preserving their own image (Kampf 2009). The increase in apologies sets up a norm, yet following a pattern by rote can also cast doubt on a speaker's sincerity. Celermajer (2013) argues that the heightened scrutiny of sincerity that is used to judge individual apologies is misplaced when applied to collective transition rituals, which operate with a different logic.

Much of the research on apology in transitional justice assesses whether any particular apology fosters the transition of the conflictual relationship, ideally moving it toward reconciliation. Apologies are generally embedded in larger rituals that have the distinct aims of purification (of the offender's past), humiliation (of the offender), and settlement (i.e., restored relations) (Kampf and Löwenheim 2012). Noting the scholarly focus on the illocutionary functions of apology, Renner (2011) urges attention to apology's perlocutionary aspects, particularly its effects on those who are not the intended recipients. A series of apologies between Czech and German officials broke the "taboo of silence" on certain issues, such as the Czech expulsion of Sudeten Germans after World War II, and thereby created not only a public outcry among Czechs not ready for this admission but also new calls for reparations as well as symbolic transitional justice. Coining the phrase "pioneer apologies," Renner delineates the sensitivity of apologies to their immediate historical context and the diversity of their effects on a wider array of actors than usually considered.

Justice as Performance, Embodiment, and Silence

At the same time as liberal legal approaches extend their reach through the ICC, regional and national courts, and TRCs, an ever-widening variety of approaches to the quest for justice has emerged in local contexts and includes memorials, everyday acts of remembrance and collective memory, reconciliation rituals, and the silent embodiment of understandings about past events (see, e.g., Das 2007, French 2012: 348). These local, idiosyncratic responses to violence are evidence of human creativity and experimentation in the face of massive social upheaval. For example, efforts to address the anticommunist massacres in Indonesia in the 1960s highlight local sense-making through spirit possession (Steedly 1993), state-sponsored formal dance performances (Larasati 2013), and community construction of a park as a monument and performance site (Dwyer 2011). Linguistic and paralinguistic scripts and improvisations that have long been of interest in anthropological linguistics are evident in these rituals and sites, where participants not only make sense of past events but also struggle over present-day relations of power and difference, such as gender, ethnicity, and political allegiances. While acknowledging new contributions to this literature, this section highlights recent scholarship on silence as a key element of the embodiment and performance of transitional justice in local contexts.

Even in places where efforts have been made to encourage narrative, testimony, and dialogue toward reconciliation, silence is a common response to mass violence and to transitional justice initiatives. As Nee and Uvin (2010) found, silence was a more palatable option than formal trials, dialogue, or traditional mediation for Burundians who were asked how past violence should be addressed. Yet, silence should not be interpreted as representing either denial of what happened or lack of participation in justice efforts (Burnet 2012, Dwyer 2009). Burnet's research in Rwanda demonstrates how the victorious government amplified master narratives that contrasted with the experiences of many Rwandan women, who, in turn, experienced "amplified silence." The result is an inability to bridge the divisions of the past through speech. For some residents of Sarajevo, silence about the violence in the former Yugoslavia is not erasure but rather has the strategic effects of demanding and producing normalcy, making a moral claim on those who witness a person's silent presence, and also protesting against particular narratives (Eastmond and Selimovic 2012: 505–506). From this perspective silence displays agency and should not be understood as ceding the opportunity to settle accounts in the future.

Reminding scholars that speech and silence are neither opposites nor one-dimensional, Dwyer describes local responses to the Indonesian genocide of 1965–66 shaped through decades of political repression: "silence is not an even fog barricading events and emotions from view, but a variegated landscape that Balinese navigate with what knowledge and caution they can muster, sometimes drawing on local notions of how speech is channeled and dammed and sometimes moving blindly, the certainty that one can find direction on a shifting social topography undermined in the experience of terror" (Dwyer 2009: 135).

Main Research Methods

Discourse analysis and related approaches in conversation analysis and the ethnography of speaking have been used to explore the micro-dynamics of interaction in the contexts where transitional justice is sought, especially trials, TRCs, and local rituals. Solid findings in the language and law literature illuminate the constraints of formal legal settings, especially for laypersons, and the power relations negotiated through interaction. *Speech act theory* directs attention to key linguistic forms, such as blaming, apology, forgiveness, and confession, that might spark movement toward both accountability and reconciliation. *Narrative analysis* has been a significant approach, given the centrality of truth-telling and creating accounts in most transitional justice settings. It was the recognition that stories and other utterances in transitional justice settings bear the influence of power dynamics that led to *semiotic approaches* and the attention to entextualization. Understanding how the language of transitional justice – in its many forms – becomes invested with ideological or political significance is a critically important aim that begins to explain the criticisms leveled against some approaches.

Many studies combine linguistic analysis with ethnography, especially those that examine transitional justice outside legal institutions. Research on transitional justice places heavy demands on researchers. Even in so-called postconflict societies tension can be high, and the politics of conducting research requires special vigilance. Protection of informants is paramount and might require shielding them from the retraumatization of narrating violence. Researchers must guard against furthering the aims of powerful actors who might, for instance, benefit if one particular account of violence is privileged or if silence is interpreted as lack of interest in past violence or in seeking justice (Dwyer 2009). Burnet (2012) makes the poignant observation that ethnographers need to "descend into the ordinary" of survivors' lives to feel the culturally shaped sensations of their interlocutors, such as holding back tears or silently refusing to comment.

Recommendations for Practice

Insights from linguistic anthropology can be useful to policy makers, human rights practitioners, and legal personnel as they work to develop and improve institutions of transitional justice. Findings about the effects of formal proceedings on the language and experience of participants can help to create a more hospitable atmosphere, especially for those with special needs, such as children, victims of sexual assault, linguistically marginalized persons, and those suffering from trauma or stigma. A semiotic perspective on the construction of stories could enhance understanding among those who work with witnesses, and perhaps counter, through explanation, the frequent criticism that witness accounts have an "inauthentic" or "rehearsed" quality. Relatedly, such an analysis can also help to explain why stories told during trials, TRCs, and local memorial events can sometimes sound as though they had been tailored for an international audience expecting Western liberal legal discourse.

Application of research findings could help ensure that transitional justice better promotes healing and stability for individuals and societies. Although memorials serve an important public function, they can traumatize people who were involved in the conflict and others with similar experiences. Based on a study of a museum display of the internment of Japanese-Americans in concentration camps, to which victims of the Nazi Holocaust took exception, Schiffrin (2001) describes multiple ways in which linguistic anthropologists could reduce negative reactions by translating and contextualizing materials.

Urging experimentation with different speech settings, Simpson concludes that "finding an inclusive procedure or set of procedures in the long term through which even those 'truths' and stories which seem utterly incompatible or incongruent with the dynamics of peace and reconciliation (as defined by new regimes), and which often stretch into the unknown territory of the as yet unspeakable, is arguably crucial to the long-term prospects of a stable democratic government" (Simpson 2007: 100).

Future Directions

Future research, which will no doubt examine transitioning societies as they move further from the time of mass violence, might explore the following questions: How do people think about and tell stories of violence over time? Do their narratives change? How is transitional justice spoken about or memorialized? How is meaning made of returns to violence after transitional justice? The extent to which reconciliation is an outcome warrants study; however, the linguistic challenge is significant (Moon 2008). What counts as evidence of reconciliation? Is it verbal? A handshake? Silent co-existence sustained over time? Novel speech or perhaps very ordinary-sounding interaction? The exploration of these questions through linguistic analysis will need to pay careful attention to culture and context.

Anthropologists will no doubt continue to identify myriad ways in which people deal with a violent past through locally meaningful rituals and the mundane behaviors of everyday life. Understanding transitional justice in these forms might require not only careful attention to local cultural context but also to globally circulating discourses of traumatism and therapy, humanitarianism, and religious healing that can blend with, augment, or eclipse the discourse of transitional justice. Linguistic anthropologists can help to tease out the relations among these discourses and frictions that result from their co-terminous production, especially when the formal institutions of transitional justice fail to deliver what they promise.

Conclusion

The friction between two discourses – transitional justice and the previously mentioned, broader notion of global justice that focuses on restoring relationships and exposing global power dynamics – is especially intense when the topic is the relatively new ICC. The ICC is criticized not only for its narrow legalistic approach to the cause of conflicts but also for focusing attention on less powerful countries in a neo-colonial fashion that is the antithesis of global justice. The ICC's prosecution of African political leaders has led to calls to ignore or reconfigure the court's jurisdiction. At first glance this challenge could be interpreted as undermining an emblematic institution of transitional justice. However, Richland's "theory of jurisdiction" would suggest that, through public debates over the ICC, "the force, authority, and legitimacy" of the court is made manifest, even as its jurisdiction is challenged (Richland 2013: 211). Drawing on semiotics, Richland argues: "[t]hat this is true suggests the extent to which the actors engaging each other in and through the language of law are always already speaking law's social force into existence, and doing so in ways that simultaneously presuppose, and make unavailable for critical assessment, the grounding source of that power" (Richland 2013: 214). Debates over prosecuting alleged perpetrators of twenty-first century atrocities will continue to speak the nascent ICC into being and to grant legitimacy to it and similar institutions of transitional justice. At the same time people seeking justice and healing after mass violence will continue to engage in ever more creative responses that may or may not be understood as justice. Although we can hope for a reduction in the atrocities that demand redress, transitional justice appears poised to remain a site of local, national, international, and transnational struggle – and that struggle will take place through language.

Related Topics

22 Language in the Age of Globalization (Jacquemet); **24** Discrimination via Discourse (Wodak); **26** Legal Discourse (Conley).

Notes

1 These include the International Criminal Tribunal for the former Yugoslavia; the International Criminal Tribunal for Rwanda; the Special Court for Sierra Leone; and the Extraordinary Chambers of the Cambodian Courts.
2 Transitional justice is also pursued through political lustration and memorializations of many types, although these fall beyond the scope of this chapter.

References

Achugar, Mariana, Amparo Fernández, and Nicolás Morales. 2013. Re/constructing the past: How young people remember the Uruguayan dictatorship. *Discourse & Society* 24(3): 265–288.

Allen, Tim. 2006. *Trial Justice: The International Criminal Court and the Lord's Resistance Army*. London, New York: Zed Books.

Anyeko, Ketty, Erin Baines, Emon Komakech, Boniface Ojok, Lino Owor Ogora, and Letha Victor. 2012. 'The Cooling of Hearts': Community Truth-Telling in Northern Uganda. *Human Rights Review* 13(1): 107–124.

Arendt, Hannah. 1963. *Eichmann in Jerusalem: A Report on the Banality of Evil*. New York: Viking Press.

Avruch, Kevin, and Beatriz Vejarano. 2002. Truth and Reconciliation Commissions: A Review Essay and Annotated Bibliography. *OJPCR: The Online Journal of Peace and Conflict Resolution* 4(2): 37–76.

Bass, Gary Jonathan. 2000. *Stay the Hand of Vengeance: The Politics of War Crimes Tribunals*. Princeton Studies in International History and Politics. Princeton, NJ: Princeton University Press.

Burnet, Jennie E. 2012. *Genocide Lives in Us: Women, Memory, and Silence in Rwanda*. Women in Africa and the Diaspora. Madison, WI: University of Wisconsin Press.

Celermajer, Danielle. 2013. Mere Ritual? Displacing the Myth of Sincerity in Transitional Rituals. *International Journal of Transitional Justice* 7(2): 286–305.

Chiwengo, Ngwarsungu. 2008. When Wounds and Corpses Fail to Speak: Narratives of Violence and Rape in Congo (DRC). *Comparative Studies of South Asia, Africa and the Middle East* 28(1): 78–92.

Clark, Philip. 2010. *The Gacaca Courts, Post-Genocide Justice and Reconciliation in Rwanda: Justice without Lawyers*. Cambridge Studies in Law and Society. Cambridge, New York: Cambridge University Press.

Clarke, Kamari Maxine. 2009. *Fictions of Justice: The International Criminal Court and the Challenges of Legal Pluralism in Sub-Saharan Africa*. New York: Cambridge University Press.

Cobb, Sara B. 2013. *Speaking of Violence: The Politics and Poetics of Narrative Dynamics in Conflict Resolution*. Explorations in Narrative Psychology. New York: Oxford University Press.

Conley, John M., and William M. O'Barr. 1998. *Just Words: Law, Language, and Power*. Language and Legal Discourse. Chicago: University of Chicago Press.

Das, Veena. 2007. *Life and Words: Violence and the Descent into the Ordinary*. Berkeley: University of California Press.

Drumbl, Mark A. 2007. *Atrocity, Punishment, and International Law*. Cambridge: Cambridge University Press.

Dwyer, Leslie. 2009. A Politics of Silences: Violence, Memory, and Treacherous Speech in Post-1965 Bali. In A. L. Hinton and K. L. O'Neill (eds) *Genocide: Truth, Memory, and Representation*. Durham, NC: Duke University Press.

Dwyer, Leslie. 2011. Building a Monument: Intimate Politics of "Reconciliation" in Post-1965 Bali. In A. L. Hinton (ed.) *Transitional Justice: Global Mechanisms and Local Realities after Genocide and Mass Violence*. New Brunswick, NJ: Rutgers University Press.

Eastmond, Marita, and Johanna Mannergren Selimovic. 2012. Silence as Possibility in Postwar Everyday Life. *International Journal of Transitional Justice* 6(3): 502–524.

French, Brigittine M. 2009. Technologies of Telling: Discourse, Transparency, and Erasure in Guatemalan Truth Commission Testimony. *Journal of Human Rights* 8(1): 92–109.

French, Brigittine M. 2012. The Semiotics of Collective Memories. *Annual Review of Anthropology* 41(1): 337–353.

Gibney, Mark, Rhoda Howerd-Hassmann, Jean-Marc Coicaud, and Niklaus Steiner (eds). 2008. *The Age of Apology: Facing up to the Past*. Pennsylvania Studies in Human Rights. Philadelphia: University of Pennsylvania Press.

Harris, Sandra, Karen Grainger, and Louise Mullany. 2006. The Pragmatics of Political Apologies. *Discourse & Society* 17(6): 715–737.

Hayner, Priscilla. 2002. *Unspeakable Truths: Facing the Challenge of Truth Commissions*. New York: Routledge.

Hirsch, Susan F. 2007. Writing Ethnography after Tragedy: Toward Therapeutic Transformations. *PoLAR: Political and Legal Anthropology Review* 30(1): 151–179.

Hirsch, Susan F. 2009. The Victim Deserving of Global Justice: Power, Culture, and Recovering Individuals. In K. M. Clarke and M. Goodale (eds) *Mirrors of Justice: Law, Power, and the Making of History*. Cambridge: Cambridge University Press.

James, Matt. 2008. Wrestling with the Past: Apologies, Quasi-apologies, and Non-apologies in Canada. In M. Gibney et al. (eds) *The Age of Apology*. Philadelphia: Pennsylvania University Press.

Kagoro, Brian. 2011. The Paradox of Alien Knowledge, Narrative and Praxis: Transitional Justice and the Politics of Agenda Setting in Africa. In *Where Law Meets Reality: Forging African Transitional Justice*. Cape Town [etc.]: Pambazuka Press.

Kampf, Zohar. 2009. Public (Non-) Apologies: The Discourse of Minimizing Responsibility. *Journal of Pragmatics* 41(11): 2257–2270.

Kampf, Zohar, and Nava Löwenheim. 2012. Rituals of Apology in the Global Arena. *Security Dialogue* 43(1): 43–60.

Kerr, Rachel, and Eirin Mobekk. 2007. *Peace and Justice: Seeking Accountability after War*. Cambridge: Polity Press.

Koomen, Jonneke. 2013. "Without These Women, the Tribunal Cannot Do Anything": The Politics of Witness Testimony on Sexual Violence at the International Criminal Tribunal for Rwanda. *Signs: Journal of Women in Culture & Society* 38(2): 253–277.

Larasati, Rachmi Diyah. 2013. *The Dance that Makes you Vanish: Cultural Reconstruction in Post-Genocide Indonesia, Difference Incorporated*. Minneapolis, Minnesota: University of Minnesota Press.

Manning, Peter. 2012. Governing Memory: Justice, Reconciliation and Outreach at the Extraordinary Chambers in the Courts of Cambodia. *Memory Studies* 5(2): 165–181.

Matoesian, Gregory. 1993. *Reproducing Rape: Domination through Talk in the Courtroom*. Chicago: University of Chicago Press.

Matoesian, Gregory M. 2001. *Law and the Language of Identity: Discourse in the William Kennedy Smith Rape Trial*. Oxford, New York: Oxford University Press.

Mazzei, Julie M. 2011. Finding Shame in Truth: The Importance of Public Engagement in Truth Commissions. *Human Rights Quarterly* 33(2): 431–452.

Mertus, Julie. 2004. Shouting from the Bottom of the Well: The Impact of International Trials for Wartime Rape on Women's Agency. *International Feminist Journal of Politics* 6(1): 110–128.

Mertz, Elizabeth. 1994. Legal Language: Pragmatics, Poetics and Social Power. *Annual Review of Anthropology* 23: 435–455.

Mertz, Elizabeth, and Jonathan Yovel. 2005. D. Herman, M. Jahn and M. L. Ryan (eds), *Courtroom Narrative*, pp. 86–88. *Routledge Encyclopedia of Narrative Theory*. London: Routledge.

Minow, Martha. 1998. *Between Vengeance and Forgiveness: Facing History after Genocide and Mass Violence*. Boston: Beacon.

Moon, Claire. 2008. *Narrating Political Reconciliation: South Africa's Truth and Reconciliation Commission*. Lanham: Lexington Books.

Murithi, Tim. 2012. Towards African Models of Transitional Justice. In M. C. Okello, C. Dolan, U. Whande, N. Mncwabe, L. Onegi and S. Oola (eds) *Where Law Meets Reality: Forging African Transitional Justice*, Cape Town [etc.]: Pambazuka Press.

Nee, Ann, and Peter Uvin. 2010. Silence and Dialogue: Burundians' Alternatives to Transitional Justice. In *Localizing Transitional Justice: Interventions and Priorities after Mass Violence*. Stanford, CA: Stanford University Press.

Ojara, Pius. 2012. Deconstruction and Demonization: The Role of Language in Transitional Justice. In M. C. Okello, C. Dolan, U. Whande, N. Mncwabe, L. Onegi and S. Oola (eds). *Where Law Meets Reality: Forging African Transitional Justice*. Cape Town: Pambazuka Press.

Okello, Moses Chrispus et al. (eds). 2012. *Where Law Meets Reality: Forging African Transitional Justice*. Cape Town: Pambazuka Press.

Olsen, Tricia D., Leigh A. Payne, and Andrew G. Reiter. 2010. *Transitional Justice in Balance: Comparing Processes, Weighing Efficacy*. Washington, D.C.: U.S. Institute of Peace.

Phelps, Teresa Godwin. 2004. *Shattered Voices: Language, Violence, and the Work of Truth Commissions*. Pennsylvania Studies in Human Rights. Philadelphia: University of Pennsylvania Press.

Renner, Judith. 2011. "I'm Sorry for Apologising": Czech and German Apologies and their Perlocutionary Effects. *Review of International Studies* 37(04): 1579–1597.

Richland, Justin B. 2013. Jurisdiction: Grounding Law in Language. *Annual Review of Anthropology* 42(1).

Ross, Fiona C. 2003. *Bearing Witness: Women and the Truth and Reconciliation Commission in South Africa*. London, Sterling, VA: Pluto Press.

Savelsberg, Joachim J., and Ryan D. King. 2011. R. D. King (ed.) *American Memories: Atrocities and the Law*. Rose Series in Sociology. New York: Russell Sage Foundation.

Scarry, Elaine. 1985. *The Body in Pain: The Making and Unmaking of the World*. New York: Oxford University Press.

Schiffrin, Deborah. 2001. Language and Public Memorial: "America's Concentration Camps." *Discourse & Society* 12(4): 505–534.

Simpson, Kirk. 2007. Voices Silenced, Voices Rediscovered: Victims of Violence and the Reclamation of Language in Transitional Societies. *International Journal of Law in Context* 3(02): 89–103.

Steedly, Mary Margaret. 1993. *Hanging without a Rope: Narrative Experience in Colonial and Postcolonial Karoland*. Princeton Studies in Culture/Power/History. Princeton, NJ: Princeton University Press.
Stover, Eric. 2005. *The Witnesses: War Crimes and the Promise of Justice in the Hague*. Pennsylvania Studies in Human Rights. Philadelphia: University of Pennsylvania Press.
Teitel, Ruti G. 2000. *Transitional Justice*. Oxford, New York: Oxford University Press.
Teitel, Ruti G. 2003. Transitional Justice Genealogy. *Harvard Human Rights Journal* 16.
Van der Merwe, Hugo, Victoria Baxter, and Audrey R. Chapman (eds). 2009. *Assessing the Impact of Transitional Justice: Challenges for Empirical Research*. Washington, D.C.: United States Institute of Peace.
Wagner-Pacifici, Robin, and Meredith Hall. 2012. Resolution of Social Conflict. *Annual Review of Sociology* 38(1): 181–199.
Wilson, Richard Ashby. 2001. *The Politics of Truth and Reconciliation in South Africa: Legitimizing the Post-apartheid State*. Cambridge Studies in Law and Society. Cambridge, New York: Cambridge University Press.
Wilson, Richard Ashby. 2011. *Writing History in International Criminal Trials*. Cambridge, New York: Cambridge University Press.

Further Reading

Das, Veena. 2007. *Life and Words: Violence and the Descent into the Ordinary*. Berkeley: University of California Press.
Hinton, Alexander. 2010. *Transitional Justice: Global Mechanisms and Local Realities after Genocide and Mass Violence*. Genocide, Political Violence, Human Rights Series. New Brunswick, NJ: Rutgers University Press.
Shaw, Rosalind, Lars Waldorf, and Pierre Hazan (eds). 2010. *Localizing Transitional Justice: Interventions and Priorities after Mass Violence*. Stanford: Stanford University Press.
Teitel, Ruti G. 2000. *Transitional Justice*. Oxford, New York: Oxford University Press.

28
Language Maintenance and Revitalization

Andrew Cowell

Introduction/Definitions

Language maintenance and revitalization (henceforth LMR) are two related activities. Unlike most of the other topics in this handbook, these are fundamentally fields of practice. A great deal of research has been done on these two topics, but the vast majority of it is designed to improve practice. In fact, a great deal of the work in this area is done by individuals in Education and Applied Linguistics.

The term 'language maintenance' is normally used in situations where community members still speak their language on a daily basis, and transmission is still occurring in the home, but where signs of incipient language shift and/or loss are present. In these situations, *knowledge* of the language is not the central problem; rather, the issue is diminishing *usage*. In this article, 'shift' refers to changes in the daily patterns of language use in an entire community – most commonly, using a competing language more and more frequently to the detriment of the community language. The term 'loss' refers to changes in language proficiency among individuals or across generations due to diminished frequency or domains of usage. These losses typically involve diminished vocabulary, loss of less common and/or more complex grammatical patterns, and diminished range of speech registers. Language maintenance strategies generally involve social, political, and economic responses, including language planning and promotion, which are designed to change the 'language ecology' (Haugen 1972, Mühlhäusler 1992) of a community such that domains of usage are maintained or expanded. These responses typically also target the language ideologies within the community, since they have crucial influence on the frequency of language usage.

The term 'language revitalization' is used in situations where in-home transmission of a language has ceased. For the younger members of the community at least, the problem in these cases is *knowledge* of the language. For this reason, language revitalization strategies always include as one of their components a focus on second (henceforth L2) language teaching and learning. In many situations, revitalization efforts can still draw on language knowledge existing among the older members of the community, but in the most extreme cases this may not be so. Language revitalization efforts must also confront problems of usage: intergenerational transmission ceases due to extremely reduced usage of a language in a community, at least among the child-bearing generation, and usage may have virtually ceased among the entire community. In such settings, getting younger L2 learners to actually put their newly acquired knowledge of the language into regular usage can be a daunting challenge.

In this article, the initial discussion will focus on recovery of language knowledge, in revitalization contexts. These processes are well understood in their general outlines, and have been implemented widely in the world. Because they are narrowly focused on language per se as a code for communication, they are relatively easier to implement than processes that seek to address issues of language ecology, ideology, and usage. The latter force one to confront the much broader array of social, economic, and political factors that govern language in its richest sense, as a cultural implement for living in the world.

Historical Perspectives

The field of LMR is quite new, and the anthropological component is newer still. Language promotion projects were widespread in nineteenth-century Europe, linked to Romanticism and Nationalism, and language revitalization efforts occurred in locations such as Israel and Ireland, with varying success. Language scholars were often key participants in these projects. However, the academic study of LMR projects per se within the fields of linguistics and anthropology, and more particularly the effort to critically evaluate and improve on the methods used and to begin intervening in such projects as expert practitioners, expanded globally and became formalized primarily in the 1990s. The impetus for this was the recognition of rapidly increasing language shift and endangerment around the world. This recognition began in earnest in the 1970s and 1980s, both in academia (Krauss 1992), and among many minority and indigenous communities, particularly in North America, Australia, and Polynesia. A debate began about possible and appropriate responses to endangerment. One possible response is to try to maintain or revive everyday usage of endangered languages. It is this effort that gave birth to the field of LMR. One of the most widely cited early contributions to the field was Fishman 1991, and Hinton and Hale 2001 is also widely cited. Since that time, research and publications on the topic have greatly expanded. Among LMR projects themselves, long-term efforts with Irish, Welsh, and Scots Gaelic have drawn much attention. Two of the most widely cited recent programs are those of the Māori in New Zealand/Aotearoa, and of the Native Hawaiians (early summaries of both are in Hinton and Hale 2001).

The first researchers involved in this field were primarily linguists, and as a result larger sociocultural issues surrounding LMR were often given little attention or ignored. Early approaches tended to treat LMR from a narrowly linguistic perspective. This led to a number of weaknesses in academic understanding and in the development of specific projects. More recently, anthropological approaches have become much more prominent, leading to major re-evaluations of both theory and practice. Most fundamentally, these include a recognition that language shift is a symptom of broader and deeper socio-cultural shifts, which must be addressed in order for LMR projects to have chances of long-term success.

Critical Issues and Topics

The central issue in the field is the question of how broadly language endangerment is the same from language to language, and thus how broadly a general set of methodologies can be applied to address this problem. Early contributions to the field, such as Fishman 1991, tended to assume a fair amount of uniformity, so that a single 'grid' could be applied to evaluate conditions and responses. With increasing research, the vast differences between language situations have been recognized, and increasing attention has been paid to local ethnography in LMR.

A second issue is the study and development of effective methodologies for imparting language knowledge. There is much debate over the value of home-based as opposed to formalized, school-based approaches, as well as over specific methodologies within these categories.

A third issue is how to increase actual usage of languages by speakers, as opposed to increasing speaker knowledge. Many earlier responses to language endangerment have assumed that a language is being *prevented* from being used, due to lack of a writing system, unavailability of government services in the language, or actual prohibitions. In the case of situations such as boarding schools, where a language is literally banned from use, this can indeed be the case. Much recent research, however, shows that language shift now most typically occurs because speakers find another language more useful and/or prestigious, not because they are directly prohibited from using their language. Thus giving speakers the *right* to speak their language via legal means, or increased *possibilities* of speaking it via the development of literacy or government services in the language does not necessarily affect their *need* or *motivation* to use it and identify with it when the overall language ecology and ideologies in a community make some other language more dominant and attractive.

The problem of speaker motivations is now increasingly understood as the most crucial barrier to successful LMR. Motivations are directly tied to language ecology and ideology. The latter always reflect underlying socio-cultural conditions, including politics and economics. Thus LMR is fundamentally an anthropological, political, and economic problem, not a linguistic one. Since language shift and loss are symptoms of broader and deeper shifts in a community, attempts to address the symptom through language-specific interventions, without addressing the underlying causes, are unlikely to be successful. At the same time, language-specific interventions can begin to alter language ecologies and ideologies on their own, increasing knowledge, utility, and prestige of a language. Two key questions confront practitioners of LMR: first, are these language-specific interventions ever sufficient to reverse language shift on their own?; and secondly, if not, how can such approaches be combined with socio-cultural and socio-economic action in order to allow indigenous and minority language communities to flourish, in all aspects of life, with their language?

These questions raise two final issues. The first question is whether language shift should be resisted at all (Ladefoged 1992). Individuals in communities seek fundamentally to survive and prosper. As part of their daily practice and interactions, they make large numbers of instrumental evaluations and choices about how best to do this. These choices, aggregated over the community and over time, can lead to language shift. If, in fact, the current language is less efficacious within the language ecology of the community, so that the community is shifting languages in order to maintain or increase survival and prosperity, then why try to reverse that shift? There are a number of responses. Typically, individual choices about language usage and shift are not truly "free" choices, but are heavily influenced by socio-cultural and socio-economic inequalities and oppression. Most generally, language shift usually indicates socio-economic and socio-cultural stress on a community, which may or may not actually be alleviated by the shift. Efforts to maintain the language, in the context of broader community revitalization measures, may serve to alter or reinvigorate internal community organization, identity, processes, and resources in ways that actually provide a more effective response to the stresses.

Secondly, even if LMR is desirable, a number of scholars have argued that it is in fact impossible or at least extremely difficult (Edwards 2007). The socio-cultural forces driving shift are so powerful and pervasive, and perhaps so embedded in global processes of transformation, that local, language-specific resistance will be futile, and the smaller the speaker community, the more impossible the resistance will be in the absence of near-complete isolation. The most common response is that in an increasingly globalized world, the desire for stronger forms of local identity may actually increase, and language has always been one of the most powerful markers of identity. If this is true, LMR is likely to be primarily a bottom-up popular movement, however, rather than a top-down planned or expert-assisted process.

Current Contributions and Research/Practice

Home-Based Revitalization Strategies

Revitalization techniques can be divided into home- and school-based strategies. One home-based strategy is self-paced and self-motivated language learning by individuals, for usage in the home and transmission to children. While there are examples of this process being effective for selected individuals, most people lack the time, self-discipline, or ability to learn a language independently as adults, outside of formalized instruction settings, to a point of high proficiency. Thus this approach on its own is unlikely to be effective for *community* language revitalization in the classic sense of return to fluent usage and home-based transmission. On the other hand, it can be very valuable for raising the status of the language in the community and beginning to alter language ideologies, building support for more intensive or formalized programs.

A modified version of such home approaches are Master-Apprentice programs, pioneered by Leanne Hinton in California, and since used in many locations in the world (Hinton et al. 2002). The basic approach is for two individuals to spend several hours together per day, using only the target language, as they go about daily activities. The focus is much more on immersion into the language than on formalized instruction. One major advantage of this approach is that apprentices acquire vocabulary and structures immediately useful for daily life. Such programs also serve to (re)ideologize the language as a useful tool for social interaction, rather than merely an abstract form of knowledge. These programs often involve payments to the participants, sometimes in lieu of other jobs. They also normally involve some form of administrative oversight and guidance for the participants, offering them special interaction techniques and activities to facilitate learning. The programs can be supplemented by more formalized instruction for the apprentice. Successful versions normally run for at least a year, often longer. In this manner, apprentices can attain high proficiency in the target language. Successful programs also often provide symbolic community support and encouragement to the team(s) in the form of ongoing or periodic special recognition, honors, opportunities to play meaningful roles in social or ceremonial events, and similar positive feedback. In general, programs involving multiple pairs working simultaneously, with chances for broader interaction among the pairs, are preferable to only one or two pairs.

One obstacle to the success of these programs is unstable funding and inadequate administrative guidance. Loss of funding to pay the pairs is an obvious problem, but in addition, without regular oversight and encouragement, pairs can gradually lose momentum and slip more and more into the dominant language, or become stalled at a certain stage of learning, continually engaging in the same limited set of activities. Because such programs require a great deal of emotional and intellectual commitment on the part of both members of the pair, lack of community moral support and positive feedback (including opportunities to use the language in ways that provide symbolic capital) can also be very damaging. Finally, due to socio-economic pressures on many minority communities (job loss, elder care needs, transportation limitations), maintaining pairs over long time periods can be challenging.

The primary weakness of Master-Apprentice programs is that even when effective, they produce only limited numbers of fluent speakers. They also rely on a method that places high burdens of motivation and creativity on the individual Masters and Apprentices, and may involve extensive additional time commitments that conflict with other aspects of daily lives.

School-Based Revitalization Strategies

School-based approaches vary in their intensity. At the lowest level are language classes using methodologies similar to "foreign" language programs. This method is almost never effective on its own at producing highly proficient speakers. Even in the case of languages such as French or German, with long traditions of classroom teaching, very few American college or university programs can produce fluent speakers in four years without the aid of study abroad (i.e. immersion) opportunities. Such programs can, however, produce speakers who, with access to immersion situations, can attain fluency very rapidly. The same is true for high-quality university programs in minority/indigenous languages. At K-12 levels, high-quality, language class-based learning can be an effective feeder into immersion opportunities, provided the language is still used in some places or by some age groups as a daily language. But there is little evidence that K-12 foreign language teaching on its own, as actually practiced in real schools, can produce fluent speakers of endangered L2 indigenous or heritage languages.

More intensive than language classes are bilingual programs, in which two different languages are used for classroom instruction, typically a target indigenous/local language and a national language. This obviously offers more intensive exposure to the target L2. Recent research suggests, however, that where the target language is used for less than 50 percent of instruction (or even perhaps less than 80 per cent), full competency in that language is unlikely to be acquired, at least in revitalization (as opposed to maintenance) situations – and moreover, full competency in all registers of the national language, particularly "academic" ones, may also be impeded (May and Hill 2008).

Most intensive are preschool language 'nests' and immersion programs. In language nests, the target language is normally used 100 percent of the time, and the focus is on language acquisition. In immersion schools, the target language is used at least 80 percent of the time and up to 100 percent. The goal of these schools is comprehensive education, but through the medium of the target language. Typically however, the schools have a secondary goal of culturally sensitive education that attempts to validate the local community and draw on its cultural resources to enhance learning. Such immersion schools, at least for indigenous languages, were originally pioneered by Māori language revival workers and educators in New Zealand (King 2001), and soon copied by Native Hawaiians (Wilson and Kamanā 2001). The model has since spread widely around the world. There is ample research to show that in true immersion schools of this sort, students can acquire full fluency in the target language, in all registers. Moreover, once the second/national language is introduced, the students are able to transfer language skills to it from the target language with relative ease, and often test at least as well in the L2 as comparable students from the same community attending monolingual schools in that language, while also achieving higher graduation rates (Johnson and Legato 2006; Wilson, Kamanā, and Rawlins 2006). It is clear, however, that the L2 does need to be formally taught at some point, especially the more "academic" registers: these are not necessarily fully acquired by students simply as a by-product of being surrounded by the language outside the school (May and Hill 2008).

The key advantages of immersion programs are that they can produce relatively large numbers of fluent speakers, and that for the teachers and students involved, the domains where the language is used are part of their daily existence anyway, and thus not additive burdens. In addition, once in operation, immersion schools provide for a routinization of language learning that does not impose as high an individual burden on either teacher or student as Master-Apprentice programs. Additionally, the schools create an obvious new domain for language usage, and can contribute to greatly raising the status of the language in the community.

There are a number of obstacles to the success of immersion schools. These include shortages of financial and human resources, especially lack of trained teachers of an appropriate age; factors of economies of scale, which make such programs incrementally more expensive, especially in smaller language communities; legal and political impediments imposed at regional or national levels; demographic problems such as widely dispersed speakers and situations where speakers are a minority in any given community; and parental hesitations, especially with regard to their children adequately acquiring the national language, along with lack of reinforcement in the home when the parents are not speakers. Students must also remain in the schools eight or more years to fully acquire the language.

Immersion schools do have a number of potential weaknesses if not supplemented by other language initiatives: the language can be ideologized as primarily a school language, whose usage is limited to that domain; students can be isolated from remaining fluent elder speakers, leading to two different varieties of the language in the community, one used for daily home purposes by elders, and one used for school purposes by young people and a few teachers (with the latter often employing many neologisms completely unknown to older speakers); and the language can be ideologized as a type of abstract knowledge, *known* but not necessarily *used* outside the school, or even *in* the school outside of formal classroom settings.

From Knowledge to Usage: The Issue of Language Ambivalence

It is clear that several of the above strategies *can* produce fluent speakers of endangered languages. These language-focused efforts may, however, be seen as begging the larger questions of language ecology and social conditions. After all, when language shift begins, language *knowledge* and ability are not issues in most cases. The shift occurs because speakers find decreasing reasons to actually *use* the language in question, due to changes in language ecology, which reflect even deeper social and cultural changes. With the exception of some boarding school situations, problems of language acquisition and ability are rarely the cause of language shift – they are the result of it. Thus, going in the opposite direction, addressing issues of acquisition and ability alone is unlikely to cause a reversal of language shift.

For effective revitalization, regular usage must develop within the home and community, and then the language must be transmitted in the home. No type of language revitalization strategy among those described so far has shown good, proven results in moving from ability to usage. This is because the strategies tend to address language itself, rather than the larger socio-cultural conditions that led to language shift, and which are often still in place. Certainly in Hawaii a number of L2 learners have begun raising their children with Hawaiian as an L1 home language, but that number is certainly less than 10 percent of those with knowledge of the language. Given how recently the program began, it is too early to tell if and how much this number will increase; most speakers are still in their early twenties or younger, and have not yet had children. Nevertheless, even within immersion schools, there is a tendency in at least some schools for older students (grades 7–12) to use English increasingly, as well as Hawaiian among themselves, outside the school, or even outside of class.

The reason for this behavior, in immersion-based revitalization settings, is that there are typically relatively limited domains for usage outside the schools, so even immersion school students find themselves using English heavily in daily life. The result in many cases is ambivalence towards the language. Very often, this ambivalence involves a contrast between affective attitudes towards the language, where it is highly valued as a form of knowledge and a symbol of identity, and judgments based on use-value, which often lead to negative evaluations of the daily utility of the language. More generally in LMR settings, it is common to find large differences between overtly expressed attitudes regarding a heritage language (often highly favorable – see Fishman 1997) and actual language behavior, as measured by criteria such as daily usage, or effort committed to learning the language. It is especially important for outside consultants to recognize this potential gap between overt meta-linguistic attitudes and linguistic behavior, and not be misled by overly rosy expressed attitudes.

In summary, language shift occurs due to declines in the utility and status of a language. Unless the local language ecology is changed so that status and utility increase again, there is little reason to expect shift to reverse, no matter how much language acquisition occurs. Gaps between increased *knowledge* and actual *usage* reflect lagging (or unchanged) language ecology conditions, and thus lags in utility and status. In many cases where revitalization strategies have failed due to inadequate interest or commitment from sufficient numbers of members of the community, this failure can be understood in terms of ambivalence specifically, and problems in language ecology and ideology more generally.

Ideological Clarification

Due to the existence of language ambivalence, the process of 'ideological clarification' is highly desirable at the initiation of LMR projects. This involves frank discussions about the attitudes and goals of the community, in a context that attempts to look realistically at language ecology, reasons for language shift, and the possibilities for effective response to that shift in the context of available community resources. In the abstract (in response to surveys, for example), many individuals in revitalization contexts will indicate that their goal for their language is fluency among all in the community. When confronted with specific choices on the allocation of community and individual time and money, however, many people may be unwilling to commit the necessary resources to achieve the abstract goal. In general, most people vastly underestimate the time required to reach high proficiency in a language, and this is especially the case for heritage languages, since people often feel they have a 'genetic' ability to speak or quickly learn their heritage language. To give another example, a fairly common sentiment in Native American communities is that parents want children to know their tribal heritage language (fluently if possible), but would actually be quite content for the children to speak English or French as their everyday language. This preference mirrors the current situation of many Native American elders, who are fluent in their tribal language, but use French or English as their common daily language. Of course, the fluency of these elders is due to their having grown up in a setting where the tribal language was also the daily language; there is no way for the children of today to acquire such fluency if the daily language of the community is to be English or French. In summary, language ideology is a complex subject, and language ideologies within endangerment settings are if anything even more complex, and not uncommonly contradictory.

From Core Activism to Community Success

The very decision to initiate LMR efforts illustrates an incipient positive shift in language attitudes, and possibly in language ecology. The efforts themselves can contribute to additional positive shifts. Among younger Hawaiians, there is now a new-found prestige associated with the ability to speak Hawaiian. A key obstacle facing revitalization efforts that remains unresolved, however, is how to expand the interest and energy (and impressive achievements) of the few – the core revivalists – to the many – the broader population. Language ecologies function differently for different segments of communities, and language attitudes are equally variable. Impressive revival efforts may occur within a minority of the language community, while the majority may remain merely supportive from a distance (happy to see the language 'doing better,' but also happy that someone else is doing this). In many cases, there are one or two successful, long-running immersion schools in a language community (Blackfoot, Navajo, Mohawk), yet little or no expansion of such programs has occurred. Unless the majority of the community is willing to embrace revived acquisition and especially usage, the revitalization effort faces great long-term obstacles. Most revival movements are too recent to judge whether the energy of a minority can achieve a tipping point where the language is revitalized among the majority in the community. The longest-term revitalization effort is in Ireland, and certainly such a tipping point remains very distant at present. On the other hand, within the Aanaar Saami community (and perhaps other Saami languages), this tip seems to have occurred recently, and quite rapidly, though in a community where language retention was much better than in Ireland.

Language Maintenance

By definition, language maintenance involves a situation where language knowledge is not yet a problem, and thus where language acquisition is also not yet problematic. Rather, most typically, domain loss has begun to occur, or new domains (the internet, for example) have arisen where the language is disadvantaged. Other common signs of incipient language shift are failure of some younger members of the community to acquire the language, or incomplete acquisition (language loss), with unsuccessful acquisition of the full range of registers, structure, or vocabulary. While in some cases (especially these latter ones), school-based or other strategies may be needed to reinvigorate acquisition, the principal focus in maintenance situations is the need to address and reverse changes in language ecology and the status and utility of the language. These changes are what drive the shift away from the language, and only by addressing them is this shift likely to be reversed. In this respect at least, language maintenance and language revitalization share similar concerns.

There are a number of arguments in favor of language maintenance, many of which have been expressed in the context of the language endangerment literature, but they are equally applicable to situations of maintenance: issues of human rights, including linguistic rights; the value of linguistic and cultural diversity and the role of languages in forming ethnic identities; forms of knowledge intimately or perhaps even inextricably tied to specific languages and communities; the value of languages as foci of linguistic, social, and cognitive research; and the intellectual and historical achievement, which any language embodies. For maintenance efforts specifically, a much more immediate argument is that the more fully children acquire their L1, the more easily they are able to acquire an L2 as well, and conversely, failure to acquire LI fully can inhibit acquisition of L2.

Once leaders or communities make a commitment to language maintenance, there are a number of status-raising techniques that can be used. One of the most common of these is the introduction of writing, since literacy is often associated with high status, especially in diglossic situations. This also creates new domains of usage for the language. A related strategy is development of religious materials in the language, since in many communities the religious domain has very high status. Thus a number of communities, such as the Sakun in Nigeria, have specifically requested Bible translations so that Christian religious practice can be shifted into the local language (Michael Thomas, pers. comm.).

Direct promotion and raising of the visibility of the language can also be used: advertisements, posters and the like; language awards; honoring of speakers; naming of streets, buildings, and other sites using the local language; and installation of signs indicating these names. Conversely, efforts to eliminate negative pressures on the language from external (often governmental) sources can obviously be extremely important, with the most obvious steps being passage of laws to recognize and protect the language.

In addition to targeting high-status domains, generalized domain increase is probably the most common target of language policy and planning initiatives. One key domain is education, with many communities requesting use or expansion of their language in the education system. Another common target domain is public services. Especially in relatively large minority-language communities in Europe, the right to receive government services in one's own language has been a key demand. Media is also another common target domain. Strategies include: subsidies for publication of books or production of films; prizes for writers, songwriters, or film-makers; government subsidies for dubbing or subtitling movie and television productions from outside the language community; and efforts to insure translations into the local language (such as Catalan) rather than having to rely on Spanish translations, are examples of this kind of approach. Unfortunately, actual implementation of policies existing on paper remains problematic. These strategies can also be used within smaller communities ('Bambi' dubbed into Arapaho, 'Star Wars' into Navajo), but in these cases, the effort is more often symbolic, since economies of scale prevent the regular dubbing of enough material to truly maintain the utility of the local language in this domain.

All of the above efforts help generate social capital for a language. Ideally, this is easily convertible into economic capital. Private enterprise, however, is one of the hardest domains for LMR efforts to penetrate. Education, government services, or subsidized media are all amenable to political pressure. Governments are often willing to accept additional expenditures at the margins to benefit subgroups of citizens and voters. Private businesses and corporations are much less willing to increase expenditures at the margin unless clear benefits (i.e. more customers) will accrue. Thus one of the key areas of current research and practice is potential linkages between minority languages and economic profitability, such as through cultural tourism.

Conversely, a system that requires relatively little subsidy is the internet, an area where little research has been done regarding language maintenance, but which has great potential to reinforce minority language communities, especially those that may be highly dispersed or heavily intermingled with national-language speakers. The internet can be used to deliver language instruction, but it is likely more important as a new domain for language use. This can range from Wikipedias in indigenous languages, of which there are now dozens, to texting, Facebook pages and 'apps' that are language-specific. The Hawaiian *Leo Ki* web initiative, which began in the 1990s, was a key early example of this process, as are the websites for East Cree in Canada, which again seek to create on-line communities (http://www.eastcree.org/cree/nc/). One Cree site seeks to explain and overcome differences between various dialects, and even different Cree languages, in order to foster a greater sense of common language awareness, and thus a larger language community (http://www.atlas-ling.ca/#). In the case of very large communities, especially in Europe, there are a plethora of internet sites and communities.

Main Research Methods

LMR is a fundamental example of applied linguistic anthropology. Researchers are often direct participants in efforts to produce specific changes within communities, not just to study the changes. In other cases researchers may not be direct participants, but they still seek to provide applied understanding of how to best accomplish the goals of LMR, including measurements of the effectiveness of projects. A third, newer type of approach is much more theoretical in its orientations: the study of the socio-cultural and linguistic processes that surround and arise from LMR efforts (see Meek 2010). The ways in which communities attempt to confront and change language ideologies through direct intervention provide extremely interesting examples of social process. In all cases, participant/observation ethnographic methodology is central.

Each of these approaches raises problems. For the third approach, many communities are resistant to studies and projects that do not contribute some specific results applicable to the community. Such feelings may be exacerbated when the focus of the study is an LMR effort: the community is struggling with the language, often in the context of a shortage of adequate applied expertise in linguistics and anthropology, so the presence of a researcher who is perceived as simply documenting the struggle, without contributing directly to the success of the project, can lead to negative feelings.

Effective evaluations of community and academic efforts can also be problematic, due to the interests of both the community and the researcher. In the case of both, grant money has frequently been obtained for the purpose of LMR and often both parties hope to continue obtaining such funding. In a field highly driven by 'on the ground' social outcomes and changes, there is a powerful incentive to over-report good results and under-report poor ones. Academics with long experience in this field are aware of pervasive 'cherry-picking' of good results and the production of "feel-good" stories that do not match the reality of the situation.

Even where an academic researcher may not be directly involved as a collaborator, communities are often resistant to evaluation efforts. LMR is extremely difficult, with high failure rates so far. Language shift is often a traumatic experience for communities. The demand for positive news is very high, and reporting of negatives can be extremely discouraging to all concerned, potentially even threatening community willingness to continue projects. The popular media, in particular, is full of misleading stories of language revival, which largely celebrate the effort and good intentions of the moment, with virtually no critical evaluation of results.

In addition to participant observation, other methodologies are used. Surveys and interviews are often employed, but must be treated with care (see 'ideological clarification' and 'language ambivalence' above). Language documentation methodologies are central to many projects. Education progress and outcomes assessments, via testing, are a growing and desperately needed component of this field: there remains a major shortage of such critical, quantitative evaluation. Teacher training and curriculum development are also often key contributions from academic practitioners.

Recommendations for Practice

Currently, the biggest gap in this field is the availability of language skills testing before, during, and after specific LMR projects, as well as actual language usage measurements. A great deal of work relies on self-reporting by speakers and learners, often in terms of vague criteria. Where language ideologies are positive, there are strong incentives to over-state knowledge and usage, and the opposite is also true.

Related to this is a need for better outside evaluation by granting agencies of the overall results of projects. Practitioners of LMR are aware that quite large amounts of grant money are devoted to unrealistic, predictably ineffective, or poorly carried out projects. This is not unexpected: the field itself is relatively new; the tasks involved (socio-cultural and ideological manipulation) are enormously difficult to achieve in any kind of planned way; the success of projects ultimately hinges on the totality of day-to-day, moment-by-moment behavior and motivation of the majority of individuals in a community, making change much harder to achieve than in the case of medical interventions, economic loan programs, targeted human resource development, or many other projects where relatively discrete locations, individuals, or behaviors are involved; and LMR involves collaborations between academic personnel and communities, where the production of academic knowledge is not the primary goal.

Finally, the tension between activism and academic study that most LMR work involves needs to be much more carefully examined and considered from theoretical perspectives.

Future Directions

There is no reason that LMR must be conceived only in terms of the classic goal of first-language fluency within the community. Given the large number of obstacles facing many communities around the world, it appears likely that LMR efforts will fail in quite a number of cases, at least in terms of this goal. It may be more reasonable for communities to set a goal of continued use of the language in just a few domains. These can often be domains with high symbolic value (prayers, songs, ceremonies, personal introductions, personal names, place names). In many Native American communities, these are precisely the last domains where the language is currently used. With such limited usage, there is no way that fluent speakers can continue to be produced, so the language in these domains may either be memorized or highly formulaic in the future, or limited sets of vocabulary and structure specific to the target domain might be learned. Alternately, these domains could come to use a simplified version of the language, learned by certain individuals especially involved in the domains, though possibly not by all, or most, of the community.

Another domain that might be a focus is basic familiarity with vocabulary and common phrases, perhaps taught in school. Fluency is not needed for languages to retain high symbolic value, nor to maintain at least some links to the linguistic past. Where large amounts of natural discourse have been recorded, another potential goal would be passive access (perhaps enhanced by subtitles, bilingual editions, and annotations), which would allow traditional narratives, speeches, and other genres to remain alive for future generations.

While many or most communities would likely be disappointed at the thought of their language becoming a Latin or an Old English, those languages and literatures continue to play a vibrant role in modern culture, even millennia after their speakers have passed away. This is not to suggest that this is the necessary or only future of endangered languages but a more diverse and realistic discussion of possible futures would often be beneficial, and indeed, can actually invigorate language efforts. When the only goal under discussion is fluency for all members of the community, or return to daily usage of the local language, a combination of ambivalence about the goals, and despair at the likelihood of reaching them given current conditions, can lead to gloom, mourning, and frustration. This can actually debilitate potentially useful language maintenance and documentation efforts in communities where classical revitalization faces overwhelming obstacles.

Emerging new technologies will almost certainly play an increasing role in LMR efforts. The use of the technologies themselves is proliferating rapidly, from learning software for Navajo, Chitimacha, and other languages, produced by the private company Rosetta Stone, to the use of sites such as YouTube and Facebook by numerous individuals. The potential for new domains of usage and entire new communities organized around and through these means is enormous.

Finally, it may be that the classic goals of LMR are impossible except in a few exceptional circumstances – this remains to be seen. More narrowly, attempting to accomplish these goals as part of direct interventions in which academic researchers from a formal field called 'LMR' play a major role may prove to be a vast over-estimation of the potential of academic expertise to effect social change, especially in a domain where the issue that must be confronted involves collective individual behaviors dispersed across the entire realm of social life.

Related Topics

7 Language Ideologies (Kroskrity); **8** Social Subordination and Language (Huayhua); **9** Language Socialization (Paugh); **10** Studying Language Acquisition in Different Linguistic and Cultural Settings (Stoll); **11** Language Socialization and Marginalization (García-Sánchez); **19** Language and Political Economy (McElhinny); **22** Language in the Age of Globalization (Jacquemet); **29** Language Endangerment and Revitalization Strategies (Brittain, MacKenzie); **30** The Politics of Language Endangerment (Meek).

References

Edwards, John, 2007. "Language Revitalization and its Discontents: An Essay and Review of *Saving Languages: An Introduction to Language Revitalization.*" *Canadian Journal of Applied Linguistics* 10(1): 101–120.
Fishman, Joshua, 1991. *Reversing Language Shift. Theoretical and Empirical Foundations of Assistance to Threatened Languages.* Clevedon: Multilingual Matters.
Fishman, Joshua, 1997. *In Praise of the Beloved Language: A Comparative View of Positive Ethnolinguistic Consciousness.* Berlin: Mouton de Gruyter.
Haugen, Einar, 1972. *The Ecology of Language: Essays by Einar Haugen.* Selected and introduced by Anwar S. Dil. Stanford: Stanford University Press.
Hinton, Leanne and Hale, Alan, 2001. *The Green Book of Language Revitalization in Practice.* San Diego: Academic Press.
Hinton, Leanne, with Vera, M., Steel, N. and Advocates for Indigenous California Language Survival, 2002. *How to Keep your Language Alive: A Commonsense Approach to One-on-One Language Learning.* Berkeley: Heyday Books.
Johnson, F.T. and Legato, Jennifer, 2006. "Tséhtsooí Diné Bi'ólta'." *Journal of American Indian Education* 54(2): 26–33.
King, J., 2001. "Te Kōhanga Reo: Māori Language Revitalization." In Hinton and Hale 2001: 119–128.
Krauss, Michael, 1992. "The World's Languages in Crisis." *Language* 68: 410.
Ladefoged, Peter, 1992. "Another View of Endangered Languages." *Language* 68: 809–811.
May, Stephen and Hill, Richard, 2008. "Māori-medium Education: Current Issues and Challenges." In Nancy H. Hornberger (ed.) *Can Schools Save Indigenous Languages? Policy and Practice on Four Continents.* Basingstoke, UK: Palgrave Macmillan: 66–98.
Meek, Barbra, 2010. *We Are Our Language: An Ethnography of Language Revitalization in a Northern Athabaskan Community.* Tucson: University of Arizona Press.
Mühlhäusler, Peter, 1992. "Preserving Language or Language Ecologies? A Top Down Approach to Language Survival." *Oceanic Linguistics* 31(2): 163–180.
Olthuis, Marja-Liisa, Kivelä, Suvi, and Skutnabb-Kangas, Tove, 2013. *Revitalizing Indigenous Languages: How to Recreate a Lost Generation.* Bristol: Multilingual Matters.
Wilson, W.H. and Kamanā, K., 2001. "'Mai Loko Mai o ka 'I'ini: Proceeding from a dream' – the 'Aha Pūnana Leo Connection in Hawaiian Language Revitalization." In Hinton and Hale 2001: 147–176.
Wilson, W.H, Kamanā, Kauanoe, and Rawlins, Nāmaka, 2006. "Nāwahī Hawaiian Laboratory School." *Journal of American Indian Education* 45(2): 42–44.

Further Reading and Resources

There are dozens and perhaps hundreds of websites devoted to the LMR. One that is especially recommended for Native American languages is: www2.nau.edu/jar/TIL.html.

An earlier text that provides a world-wide perspective on LMR from an applied, community-oriented perspective is Hinton and Hale 2001.

A more recent book that covers one particular LMR project in detail (Aanaar Saami in northern Scandinavia), again with a very applied, community-oriented perspective, but also includes numerous "info boxes" at the end with extensive references to virtually every major sub-topic within LMR, is Olthuis, Kivelä, and Skutnabb-Kangas 2013.

A classic academic study of LMR is Grenoble, L.A. and Whaley, L.J. 2006. *Saving Languages: An Introduction to Language Revitalization* (New York: Cambridge University Press).

A recent book that looks carefully at the anthropological issues surrounding LMR in one community in Canada is Meek 2010.

29

Languages Endangerment and Revitalization Strategies

Julie Brittain and Marguerite MacKenzie

1 Introduction

Linguists believe that there are between 6,000 and 7,000 living languages in the world today (Grenoble and Whaley 2006). At least half of these are endangered and are not predicted to survive the twenty-first century (Crystal 2000). When a language ceases to be spoken, it is referred to as a *dead* (or *extinct*) language.[1] A living language is a dynamic system of communication, which is transmitted from generation to generation, changing over time as it adapts to meet new communicative needs. Generally speaking, a language is considered *endangered* when the likelihood arises of it ceasing to be used in this manner. The downward slide from full vitality toward death is referred to as *language decline*. Death is not the inevitable end point of decline, but it is a possibility if the process is not arrested. In this chapter we present an overview of the causes of, and responses to, language decline. We focus on the issues we feel best able to address given our experience and training, referring the reader onward to the relevant literature for those issues that have been dealt with comprehensively by other authors.[2] We begin with a word about what we mean when we use the term "endangered" with reference to languages.

A commonly used measure of language vitality is the five-way classification system developed by Kincade (1991: 160–163).[3] This system, and others that exist, make divisions based primarily on speaker numbers. Endangered languages occupy the mid-point on Kincade's scale. Below we present David Crystal's summary of Kincade's classification system:

> *viable languages:* have population bases that are sufficiently large and thriving to mean that no threat to long-term survival is likely;
>
> *viable but small languages:* have more than approx. 1,000 speakers, and are spoken in communities that are isolated or with a strong internal organization, and aware of the way their language is a marker of identity;
>
> *endangered languages:* are spoken by enough people to make survival a possibility, but only in favourable circumstances and with enough community support;
>
> *nearly extinct languages:* are thought to be beyond the possibility of survival, usually because they are spoken by just a few elderly people;

> *extinct languages*: are those where the last fluent speaker has died, and there is no sign of any revival.
>
> Crystal (2000: 20–21)

Of these five categories, only *viable* languages are not threatened. We will use the term *endangered* in a broader sense to refer to languages that are *viable but small*, *endangered* or *nearly extinct*. We mean, quite generally, any living language that is not indisputibly *viable*. We take Cree, for example, with 87,000 speakers (Statistics Canada 2006), to be *viable but small* and thus endangered to some degree. Although Cree has many more than 1,000 speakers, we consider it to be a *small* language by virtue of the fact it is generally spoken in isolated communities by people who are "aware of the way their language is a marker of identity". As Brittain and MacKenzie (2012) explain, Cree cannot be described as a *viable* language, nor does it fit well into the *endangered* category.

Kincade's classification reveals the correlation that exists between speaker numbers and language vitality: the lower the speaker numbers, the more endangered the language. Generally speaking, this is true, though, as we will see in section 5, speaker numbers are not the only factor considered in determining the vitality of a given language. It will suffice to say for the moment that there are languages that have several millions of speakers yet face an uncertain future. For example, although there are an estimated 4.25 million speakers of Tibetan living in the People's Republic of China (henceforth China), concern has been expressed over the future of this language (among others, Tournadre 2003) as it faces considerable pressure from Mandarin Chinese. Although legislation exists to prioritize Tibetan in much of the territory in which Tibetans live (e.g., in the Tibetan Autonomous Region), in practice, increasingly, Mandarin is widely used as the principal language of education, commerce, and the work place. Conversely, there are languages that have relatively low speaker numbers that are not necessarily (highly) endangered (e.g., Cree): each situation is unique and must be evaluated in light of the constellation of circumstances affecting the people who speak it. This fact notwithstanding, speaker numbers are important, so let us consider the conditions under which a language would lose speakers.

Broadly speaking, this happens either when speakers of a given language fall victim to some catastrophic event resulting in loss of life (e.g., genocide or famine), or when people abandon the language they grew up speaking in favour of a new language.[4] This latter scenario, referred to as *language shift* (Fishman 1991), is the most common underlying cause of language decline today. Most, if not all, cases of language shift involve moving from a small language to one that is larger (in speaker numbers). It is not immediately obvious why people would go to the trouble of replacing one language with another, but in identifying the underlying causes of language shift, we uncover the strategies required to *revitalize* declining languages. We provide more in-depth discussion of these two related issues in section 4. Over the past several decades that language loss has become a focus of concern, strategies have been developed to address the issue: *language maintenance* strategies are designed to halt language decline, preventing further loss, and *language revitalization* strategies, with a rather more ambitious goal, are aimed at reversing decline, moving a language from a state of endangerment to one less precarious. While technically maintenance and revitalization strategies can be differentiated in terms of projected outcome, in practice they are often the same. For this reason we do not distinguish between the two; we will refer to any set of measures employed to address language decline as revitalization strategies.

2 Historical Perspectives

As long ago as 1925, in the first issue of the journal *Language*, the American linguist Leonard Bloomfield made reference to the loss of the indigenous languages of America:

> ... one may mention the American Indian languages, which are disappearing forever, more rapidly than they can be recorded ...
>
> *Bloomfield (1925: 4)*

The principal response to language loss in the early twentieth century was documentation, the compilation of dictionaries, grammars and texts for specific languages (and, where relevant, their various dialects).[5] To this day, documentation remains the cornerstone of language revitalization; more generally, within the discipline of linguistics high priority is given to the goal of documenting every human language. The more endangered a language is, however, the more urgent is the need to document it.

In the 1970s a more organized and creative response to language loss evolved in many parts of the world (Janse 2003, Wurm 2001). To documentation as a response were added a variety of new strategies aimed at turning around the fate of declining languages. These new approaches to saving languages laid the foundation for the relative proliferation of organizations and projects that have characterized the field from the 1990s onwards. Wurm (2001: 8) observes:

> About 1970, there started a re-awakening of a feeling of ethnic identity among speakers of small and minority languages in quite a few parts of the world, with speakers of such languages taking an increasing interest in them, and being more and more concerned about their preservation and maintenance. This coincided in the 1970s and later, with a change of attitudes of speakers of dominant metropolitan languages, and government policies guided by them, from negative to positive or at least neutral in several important areas in the world, such as Australia, Japan, Canada, parts of Europe, (e.g. Britain), Scandinavia, the former Soviet Union after the collapse of communism (in particular in Siberia), and quite recently also in Italy.

Joshua Fishman, founder and editor of the *International Journal of the Sociology of Language*, was an early contributor to the field, publishing a number of influential works (Fishman 1987, 1991, 2000). Other early contributions came from Denison (1977), Dorian (1977, 1981, 1986) and Edwards (1985). Dorian (1989) brings together the work of a number of researchers in the field, more than a third of whom tackle the difficult subject of how the grammars of declining languages change (*language obsolescence*). By the 1980s, work highlighting the plight of specific endangered languages was appearing, drawing attention to the scale of the problem and to the need for an organized response (among others, Elmendorf 1981, Schmidt 1985). With the 1990s and the advent of the internet came a venue well suited to the fast-moving target that is the study of endangered languages, and the founding of many of the major not-for-profit advocacy organizations.[6] In 1995, in the United States, the Endangered Languages Fund (ELF, www.endangeredlanguagefund.org) was instituted; 1996 saw the creation in the United Kingdom of the Foundation for Endangered Languages (FEL, www.ogmios.org); Terralingua (www.terralingua.org), the focus of which is the preservation of biological and cultural diversity in general (language included), was founded in 1996. The 1990s also saw the beginning of legal action to protect the rights of speakers of endangered languages. The idea of linguistic rights was first formalized in the *Universal Declaration of Human Rights*, which was adopted by the United Nations General Assembly in Paris on December 10, 1948 in reaction to the events of the Second World War.[7] A number of other important documents have since been formulated, notably the 1996 *Barcelona Universal Declaration on Linguistic Rights*. As any quick search of the internet reveals, there are now a large number of bodies devoted to saving endangered languages, many of which are grassroots community-based organizations.

We conclude this section with a brief mention of one of the earliest and still one of the most prominent associations involved in saving languages: SIL International (henceforth SIL). Founded in 1934, SIL is a Christian missionary organization, the principal goal of which is to translate the Bible into every language. As the basic toolkit of the translator is a dictionary and a grammar, SIL was one of the earliest to specialize in language documentation. It is now a leader in the development of tools for language documentation and translation, and is, consequently, prominent in the field of language revitalization. The SIL on-line inventory of the world's languages, *Ethnologue* (www.ethnologue.com), has become the de facto global watchdog of language vitality. Contemporary linguistic enquiry is a science and, like all scientists, linguists are motivated to pursue knowledge in their field simply for the sake of contributing to the pool of scholarship. The scientific community in general is uneasy with motivations other than this. It is not surprising, then, that the prominent role a religiously motivated organization like SIL occupies in the field of language revitalization is the subject of ongoing debate within the linguistic community.[8]

3 Critical Issues and Topics

The first, and arguably the most important, question to address in discussing endangered languages is: Why should we care about language loss? If we see language shift as merely the replacement of one system of communication with another, there is no case to be made for revitalization. Language shift is, however, much more than this, as language and culture are so intimately bound to one another. Cree writer and director Jules Koostachin explores this interconnectedness in her 2010 documentary film *Remembering Inninimowin*, which provides a very personal perspective on language loss.[9] Reflecting on the film-making process, Koostachin (2013: 76) observes: "Inninimowin carries the traditional knowledge, customary laws, identity, spirituality, and everything that is sacred to the Inninuwak [the Cree people]; it embraces our ancient stories, our ceremonial practices, and the ancestral teachings originating from the Mushkegowuk area". More generally, it is not difficult to make the case that any reduction of the world's linguistic diversity is an impoverishment of our common heritage as a species; among others, see Crystal (2000: 27–67), Hale (1992a, 1992b, 1998), Hinton (1994, 2001), Mithun (1998), Nettle and Romaine (2000: 10–23) and Woodbury (1998).

Other issues and topics we regard as critical we deal with in subsequent sections of this chapter. In section 4 we discuss the causes of language decline, and responses to it (revitalization strategies). In section 5 we provide a brief overview of methodological frameworks used to assess language vitality, and we conclude, in section 6, by making five recommendations for future action in the field.

4 Current Contributions and Research

Causes of Language Shift

Language death is not a phenomenon unique to the contemporary world. We know from historical records that many once vibrant languages are no longer spoken (Ancient Greek, Latin, Ancient Egyptian, etc.). Language death is normal, in other words. What is unprecedented is the current scale of the phenomenon, the alarming rate at which linguistic diversity is diminishing. An urgent question to address must then be: What are the causes of language shift?

Let us first rule out the possibility that some languages are intrinsically better than others, and that language shift is the result of people choosing to replace an "inferior" language with one that is "superior". Although languages differ from one another in terms of vocabularies and grammars, all languages are equally good systems of communication: this is taken to be axiomatic within the field of linguistics.[10] We might prefer one make of car over another because we favour a more powerful, fuel-efficient engine, but we take "the machinery" of each language, the inventory of words and the grammar rules by which these are assembled into meaningful utterances, to be optimally designed for the purpose of communication. No language falls into decline because it is not a very good language, just as no language thrives because it is. Let us consider what factors contribute to a language becoming very successful – having hundreds of millions of speakers. In doing so we can see how, in the absence of these factors, a language can lose ground.

The most successful three languages in the world today are Mandarin Chinese with 848 million speakers, Spanish with 399 million, and English with 335 million.[11] Each of these languages has at least one nation to call its own: respectively, these are China, Spain and England. All three languages are also spoken by millions of people in other countries and in many cases they enjoy official language status, so they are used for government administration, education, commerce, and so on. As official languages they accrue support and prestige that advantages them even further over any smaller competing languages. Mandarin, Spanish and English coexist with smaller languages in many countries. Most Cree speakers, for example, are now bilingual in English, one of Canada's two official languages. The larger official language opens the door to further education and to a wider range of employment and business opportunities. The smaller Aboriginal language, which is not the language of wider communication in Canada, can be used in fewer contexts, even while, we stress, it is no less good, intrinsically, than English or any other language. People move themselves and their children toward the larger language for pragmatic reasons, to secure equal access to opportunities. The smaller language may lose ground as it comes to be used in a diminishing number of everyday situations (*domains*). To exacerbate the problem, while the smaller language often faces decline in an environment of linguistic diversity, the larger language thrives in its role as regional lingua franca. The geographical area occupied by an endangered language, by contrast, never coincides with the national boundaries of a country; such languages coexist with one or more larger languages. From this it follows that endangered languages tend not to have official status. In cases where an endangered language is an official language, official status is likely to have been designated in an effort to revitalize a declining language that is a significant marker of national identity. A good example of this latter situation is Irish (Gaelic), the first official language of the Republic of Ireland.[12]

Language shift is a particular problem for populations who are bilingual in languages of unequal vitality, as in the case of speakers of small (endangered) languages where the second language is a larger language of wider communication (e.g., Cree-English bilinguals). In these situations of unequal competition, the smaller language is not necessarily doomed to marginalization, but the potential certainly exists as the domains in which it is used are encroached on by the larger language. In sum, language shift tends to occur in situations where more than one language is available, and people make the shift when they come to perceive that the larger language affords them wider access to opportunities. Although the decision to shift may appear to be voluntary, it is in fact made in direct reaction to external pressure. No language shift is entirely voluntary.

People shift from one language to another because the new language is, very generally speaking, more beneficial to them in some way. Hinton (2001: 3) observes that a language "that is not a language of government, nor a language of education, nor a language of commerce or of wider communication is a language whose very existence is threatened in the modern world". The people who speak smaller languages may come to perceive them as a hindrance to their advancement in the world, or to that of their children. In theory, a language can be lost within a single generation if there is widespread displacement of it in the home environment and children are raised in a new language. This breakdown in *intergenerational transmission* can result in rapid language shift. A language that is no longer learned by children is referred to as *moribund* (Krauss 1992); moribund languages are in a serious state of decline. In Wurm's (1998) system of language vitality classification, the next step after *moribund* is *extinct*.

In some cases it is very obvious that the decision to shift is made under extreme duress. The suppression of language, an important marker of national or cultural identity, is a tool commonly wielded in the colonial context where the goal is to oppress and assimilate "troublesome minorities". The notorious residential school system of Canada, for example, created an abusive environment in which Indigenous Canadians were forced to stop speaking their languages and to adopt instead English or French (*Report of the Royal Commission on Aboriginal Peoples*, 1996).[13] An estimated 150,000 First Nations, Inuit and Métis children were forced to attend the 130 schools that operated in Canada throughout the nineteenth and twentieth centuries, the last closing in 1996 (*A history of residential schools in Canada*, CBC documentary, 2008).[14] As Koostachin (2013: 75) points out, the term "language loss" fails to describe the devastating impact of the residential school system on Canada's Aboriginal languages: this is not language loss but language severance, a deliberate and abrupt cut in transmission.[15] The psychological trauma suffered by survivors of residential schools reverberates down through the generations, a legacy that continues to feed the decline of the country's Aboriginal languages. It is this legacy that is explored by Koostachin in *Remembering Inninimowin*. As a young child she left the Cree-speaking community into which she was born, and moved south to Ottawa with her family. Although her mother's first language was Cree, she was a survivor of a residential school, and chose to raise her children in English. Her feelings toward her own language and culture came to be so intimately bound up with the abusive environment of the school that she decided not to pass the language on to her children. This family's story is a common one: we have heard similar personal stories told by Inuit elders in Labrador, now among the last few hundreds of speakers of the dialect of Inuktitut that is unique to the region. While in these cases the decision not to pass the language on to the next generation ostensibly lies with the speaker, coercion lies at the root of the decision.

In practice, language shift is likely to be the result of more than one factor, some quite obvious, others perhaps harder to articulate. In some cases speakers of a language for which little formal documentation exists may undervalue their language, perhaps feeling that it "has no grammar". Just about any library you search through is likely to have at least one shelf full of English grammars, but there are still languages that have not been documented, and for these there is no book of rules. A commonly held misconception is that if there is no grammar book for a given language, there is no grammar. The fact is, there is no such thing as a language that does not have a grammar. The grammar is the mental set of rules a speaker uses to produce and understand his or her language. When these rules are presented in book form, we refer to the book as "a grammar". The absence of a grammar book can be taken by a speaker as evidence that his or her language is structurally deficient. While this seems unlikely to be a sufficient catalyst to shift languages, it can be a contributing factor that stacks the odds against the survival of the smaller language. For this reason, we feel it is important to create written grammars and dictionaries for endangered languages, and to make oral literatures available as written texts, in the original language, and in translation to reach a wider audience. A well-documented language that has a literature of its own acquires prestige among its speakers as well as among members of the dominant culture who do not speak the language.

We close this discussion by considering two situations that encourage language shift, which have arisen as people have become more mobile. We see this in situations of urban migration, with movement occurring from smaller communities that speak an endangered language to urban centres where the language of the dominant culture prevails. The new arrivals are motivated to adopt the language of the culture into which they move. We also see the conditions for language shift displayed in what we will call "two-language homes". Take the case of a home where one parent is a Mandarin speaker, the other a French speaker – if this family lives in Germany, the language of the home, in which the children will be raised, will be German. This is the only practical solution in this situation. When the two parental languages are endangered, however, the shift contributes to decline. Drawing again on examples we are aware of in Canada, a speaker of Cree and a speaker of Ojibwe (both are Algonquian) who share a home, for example, are more likely to adopt English as the home language than either Aboriginal language, creating an English environment for their children. In Newfoundland we find the end result of this process: in the Mi'kmaq community of Miawpukek, the shift to English began during the twentieth century with the marriage of (mostly) non-native men and Mi'kmaq women. This created English-medium households, a situation that resulted in the decline of the Aboriginal language to the point that today there remain only two elderly fluent speakers in the community (Jeddore 2000).

Having considered some of the principal causes of language shift, we now turn our attention to some of the measures that can be taken to revitalize a declining language.

Responses to Language Decline

It is the fundamental right of the speaker to determine what becomes of his or her language and so the decision to address language decline comes in the first place from the speech community. Careful planning, tailoring the response to the specifics of the situation, is then crucial, with time running out and financial and human resources generally being scarce. We have already discussed documentation as an important tool in the fight to save languages. As this work has been the focus of our professional lives, we begin this section by making some additional observations on the importance of good documentation. We then discuss a number of other revitalization strategies that are often implemented in tandem with documentation. We recommend to the reader Grenoble and Whaley (1998), as well as chapter 3 of Grenoble and Whaley (2006: 50–68).

Good documentation of a language, in all the principal dialects involves the creation of a comprehensive dictionary and grammar. Additionally, as many different kinds of texts as possible should be recorded. We use the term "text" broadly to refer to any linguistic performance, whether written or captured in audio-visual format.[16] Ideally, a record should be made of all the many different ways people use language. Thorough documentation takes years to complete and requires collaboration between speakers and linguists, the latter usually bringing to a project funding, training (for members of the speech community), access to technology, and access to the wider community of language activists. If documentation is thorough, even if a language dies, the record that survives allows for scholarly study. It also opens up the possibility of language revival – bringing an extinct or moribund language back into everyday usage – a process that is referred to as *language reclamation*. The best-known and most successful case of language reclamation is Modern Hebrew, which was revived from moribund to become Israel's first language. A smaller-scale and more recent example is the reclamation of the Massachusetts language Wôpanâak (Eastern Algonquian), which was initiated in the 1990s with the establishment of the Wôpanâak Language Reclamation Project, a collaboration of the Wôpanâak Nation and linguists at the Massachusetts Institute of Technology.[17]

Next we consider the *total immersion* model of revitalization, an appropriate strategy to apply in the case of languages that have become moribund. Total immersion programs create an environment in which the endangered language is used exclusively, allowing the re-establishment, albeit on a small scale, of intergenerational transmission. Early childhood language immersion programs, so-called *language nests*, take advantage of the fact that children are proficient language learners (Krashen 1998). Hinton (2011: 298–299) provides a comprehensive overview of the history of language nests, beginning with their first implementation in the late 1970s and early 1980s in New Zealand and Hawaii. One of a number of strategies employed in the revitalization of Mâori (Austronesian, New Zealand), the Mâori *Te Kôhanga Reo* program (King 2001) has been the inspiration for numerous similar programs (Hawaiian *Pûnana Leo*). Andersen and Johns (2005) describe a language nest program initiated in 2001 in the Labrador community of Hopedale. The nest was one of several initiatives adopted by the community in an effort to reverse language shift for Labrador Inuttitut, a moribund dialect of Inuktitut. Although a good language nest is guaranteed to produce young speakers of the endangered language, careful planning and long term investment is required to ensure that the children have life-long opportunities to use the language; ideally they will go through all levels of education in the language, and then go on to use it in their place of employment. Committing to a program like this is, clearly, a serious undertaking that requires expertise and funding.

The Master-Apprentice program, developed in 1992 to address critical decline among the languages of California, focuses on the adult as the language learner. This now widely adopted model is essentially a one-on-one language immersion program where fluent speakers (masters) are partnered with committed learners (apprentices) for a set number of hours a week in an immersion environment fashioned out of everyday life. The ultimate goal is for the apprentice to become fluent enough to pass the language on in their own home, to re-establish intergenerational transmission. The Mentor-Apprentice Program offered by the First Peoples' Cultural Council Language Program in the Canadian province of British Columbia is a good example of this model.[18] The COOL project (Cayuga: Our Oral Legacy), which supports the highly endangered Iroquoian language Cayuga (spoken in Ontario), offers both language nests and Master-Apprentice programs.[19] Clearly, these two strategies complement one another and are best offered in tandem with one another.

For less critically endangered languages, partial immersion or bilingual programs are appropriate. In this model, school children are offered education in the smaller language some of the time – for a certain number of hours per week throughout their schooling, say, or for all classes in just the first few years. The rest of the time, the language of instruction is the larger language, the wider language of communication. We find such arrangements in a number of Cree-Innu-Naskapi communities in Canada, for example.[20] In these programs, the home is still regarded as the environment in which the child learns the language so the child is presumed to be starting his or her education already speaking it. In situations where the home does not offer a learning environment, the endangered language should be offered as a second language. A problem we have noticed is that, in situations of language decline, within a single community there can be significant variation in the extent to which the smaller language is used in the home. In homes where a shift from, say, Cree to English is underway, children can arrive in a Cree-medium class unable to cope and will quickly fall behind through no fault of their own. In short, within a single community it is often the case that the partial bilingual model is appropriate for some children, while others need to learn the language as a second language. It is crucial, in our opinion, that both systems be made available and for educators in bilingual communities to assess the language skills of children entering school so they can be streamed into the appropriate system. The creation of these assessment tools is usually a collaborative effort between community educators and academic linguists and educators.

5 Main Research Methods

A methodological framework is required in order to systematically identify types of language endangerment, and measure the extent of decline. We began this chapter (section 1) by considering Kincade's five-way classification system, according to which Mandarin Chinese, English and Spanish, the world's top three languages, are clearly viable. But what tools do we have at our disposal to determine degrees of language endangerment? How do we distinguish between Kincade's languages that are *small but viable, endangered,* and *nearly extinct*? And how do we make finer distinctions within each of these categories? We have already noted that absolute speaker numbers provide no more than an approximation as to language vitality. We need a systematic way to measure degrees of decline in order to design the most effective response. As Grenoble and Whaley (2006: 3) put it, "[a] language spoken by several thousand individuals on a daily basis presents a much different set of options for revitalization than a language that has a dozen native speakers who rarely use it". UNESCO (2003) recommends assessing language vitality by investigating the following nine areas:

1. intergenerational transmission;
2. absolute numbers;
3. proportion of speakers within total population;
4. trends in existing language domains;
5. response to new domains and media;
6. materials for language education and literacy;
7. governmental and institutional language policies, including official status and use;
8. community members' attitudes toward their own language;
9. amount and quality of documentation.

UNESCO 2003, as presented in Grenoble and Whaley (2006: 4)

We touch on some of these issues in this chapter but we refer the reader to Grenoble and Whaley 2006: 3–13 for comprehensive discussion of all nine criteria.

6 Recommendations for Practice and Future Directions

We close our discussion of endangered languages and revitalization with five recommendations for future practice.

Technology

Technology offers significant potential for the promotion of small languages. To maintain language vitality the focus must be on youth, who are also the primary users and developers of technology. The language should be available in forms that are accessible and appealing to everyone, but the focus, we suggest, should be on young people. Over the past 45 years dictionaries for the various dialects of East Cree and Innu have evolved from unpublished word lists to comprehensive published print versions, and these are now available as downloadable apps that are updated on a continual basis. Accompanying images and sound files that illustrate dialect pronunciations allow speakers with low literacy skills to search for words via English or French and to simultaneously read and hear new words. In the 2013 launch of the 27,000 word Innu dictionary in the Innu community of Sheshatshiu, Labrador, high school students were introduced to the book version and the app version. Although the students welcomed both forms of the dictionary, it was the app that captured their interest. Using the kinds of technologies young people are comfortable with to make the language accessible should, we feel, be a focus in the future.

Speaker Language Activists

We would also like to see many more speakers (and "semi-speakers") of small languages becoming language activists – the people who lead language revitalization projects.[21] There are at present not nearly enough opportunities for these important people to undertake the training they need to assume this responsibility. Speakers have more credibility within their own communities than the academic linguists, generally community outsiders, who tend to head the revitalization teams. There are not many speaker activists because so few places exist offering appropriate training programs. An example of the kind of program we would like to see more of is the *Community Linguist Certificate* offered by the *Canadian Indigenous Languages and Literacy Development Institute* (CILLDI), an initiative established at the University of Alberta in 2000. Participants require no previous knowledge of linguistics, but will be "speakers or semi-speakers of their Indigenous language, and they will have an abiding interest in preventing the loss of their language".[22] Another model program of this type is the *Certificate in Aboriginal Language Revitalization*, a community–university initiative offered by the University of Victoria's Department of Linguistics and the First Nations *En'owkin Centre*.[23] The kind of training an academic linguist undergoes, with its focus on mastering theories of linguistic analysis, requires a commitment of years, usually culminating in a Ph.D. The academic linguist may be schooled in the theory and practice of revitalization strategies, but this is generally viewed as a secondary area of specialization. The speaker activist only requires a basic knowledge of formal linguistics. Committing to a regular linguistics program would not only be a waste of time, it would not provide the appropriate training. In any language revitalization project, there will always be a role for the academic linguist as consultant, but ideally the speaker activist will lead the project.

The Primacy of Literacy

We also recommend taking a critical look at the current attention focused on literacy in promoting endangered languages. Documentation work generally presupposes either a community that is already (partially) literate, or one that will become literate. The language is not only recorded for posterity, but so that speakers can use the materials that are the end result of the work as reading material and models for writing. Literacy is viewed as an important tool in the fight against language loss. The promotion of literacy, however, can be very costly, diverting scarce funds away from initiatives that could promote the spoken language. This is especially a danger where the revitalization project relies heavily on the school system. If there is no common writing system, the materials will have to be produced multiple times, in each of the community orthographies. A common writing system allows for the economic production of materials, but it is not always feasible to pursue this goal. Writing systems tend to serve as markers of community or dialect identity and selecting one to the exclusion of the rest can generate hostility. The need to have a system that covers as much territory as possible must always be balanced against the strength of community feelings on the subject. A great deal of energy has been expended on bringing consistency to communities that use more than one writing system, and to creating systems for languages that have none. Care must be taken to ensure that the time and energy expended on creating, refining, or teaching a writing system does not detract from the primary goal of revitalization, which is to ensure that people use the language to speak to each other. It may, we suggest, be time to look to developing models that focus more on promoting the spoken language.

Improving the Promotion of Literacy

If literacy is indeed the goal, we recommend improving literacy promotion by producing more materials. We have found that, for example, in programs where Cree and Innu literacy is the goal, there is not enough reading material available to achieve the objectives. Production should be centralized to ensure that literacy materials reach the people who need them quickly and at a reasonable cost. One model that might be explored is to have a series of templates for a given language family into which specific languages, and dialects, can insert their own materials. For example, an Algonquian literacy materials organization could provide templates for all the languages/dialects in the family. Culture-appropriate illustrations and themes could be shared, and adaptations could be made as necessary. In order to make such a model work, a well-articulated policy or procedure should be developed to ensure contributors be properly acknowledged for their work.

The Promotion of Bilingualism

Finally, we would like to see the implementation of a campaign to raise awareness among populations who are bilingual in an endangered language and a larger language (e.g., Cree-English) as to the advantages of raising bilingual children. It is often felt that children raised in two languages become confused, learning neither well, and that it is better to expose them to just one. Bilingualism is frequently the scapegoat where any concern is raised over academic achievement in the schools. The (Quebec) Cree School Board recently overhauled their Cree-English bilingual education system to reduce the students' exposure to Cree in the classroom (Faries et al. 2010). Community decisions like this bolster parents' decisions to choose the larger language as the exclusive home language. A substantial body of research shows, however, that one language is not learned at the expense of another and that, moreover, bilingualism appears to enhance cognitive capacity: as early as 1985 Hakuta and Diaz found strong correlations between the degree to which an individual is bilingual and how well he or she scored in cognitive ability tests. Numerous subsequent studies have found that bilingual children perform cognitive tasks significantly better than their monolingual peers; Leikin (2012), for example, finds that early bilingualism in particular, combined with bilingual education, is a strong predictor of enhanced general and mathematical creativity in children. The results of this research should be made widely available, in an accessible format, to speakers of endangered languages. There would of course be no better person to communicate this information than the language activist community member.

Related Topics

21 Language and Nationalism (Haque); **28** Language Maintenance and Revitalization (Cowell); **30** The Politics of Language Endangerment (Meek).

Notes

1. We refer to languages being "spoken" in a general sense. It is not our intention in choosing this term to exclude from consideration the many sign languages that exist.
2. We have both worked (for the past 45 years for MacKenzie, the past 25 for Brittain) alongside speakers of the eastern-most dialects of the Cree-Innu-Naskapi dialect complex: East Cree and Naskapi, which are spoken in northern Quebec, and the Innu dialects of Labrador and Quebec's Lower North Shore.

With speaker numbers in the neighbourhood of 98,000 (Statistics Canada 2006), the language as a whole is not endangered but many of the individual dialects are in decline (Brittain and MacKenzie 2012).
3 Similar models have been developed by Wurm (1998), whose categories are *potentially endangered, endangered, seriously endangered, moribund,* and *extinct.* Bauman (1980) identifies *flourishing, enduring, declining, obsolescent,* and *extinct.*
4 For further discussion of language decline resulting from mass speaker death, we refer the reader to Crystal (2000: 70-76).
5 See also Wintermans (2009) who describes discussions held at the 1st International Congress of Linguists (1928, The Hague) on the topic of organizing what he refers to as "a global strategy for endangered languages". Lack of agreement among the participating organizations led to the endeavor eventually being shelved, but the fact that the discussions took place documents awareness of the issue in 1920s Europe.
6 Crystal (2000: 167-69) lists some of the major organizations.
7 The full text is available at http://www.un.org/en/documents/udhr last accessed June 1, 2015.
8 Epps and Ladley (2009) and Dobrin (2009) provide an excellent overview of this debate in particular, and of the issue of ethics in the field in general.
9 *Inninimowin* (Cree) is referred to in the linguistic literature as Swampy Cree. Koostachin's home community of Attawapiskat is in northern Ontario.
10 We refer the reader to David Crystal's excellent overview of this important issue (Crystal 2010: 6-7).
11 http://www.ethnologue.com/statistics/size last accessed June 1, 2015.
12 Although Irish is spoken by relatively few Irish people as a first language (between 50,000 and 60,000 according to Crystal 2010), thanks to its official status it is spoken as a second language by in excess of 1.6 million of the country's 4.5 million people.
13 Canada. (1996). Report of the Royal Commission on Aboriginal Peoples. Vol. 3, Gathering Strength. Ottawa: Indian and Northern Affairs Canada, pp. 563–580. http://publications.gc.ca/site/archivee-archived.html?url=http://publications.gc.ca/collections/Collection/R32-192-2000E.pdf last accessed June 1, 2015.
14 http://www.cbc.ca/news/canada/a-history-of-residential-schools-in-canada-1.702280 last accessed June 1, 2015.
15 Mi'kmaq (Algonquian) poet, the late Rita Joe, herself a residential school survivor, articulates the language loss she experienced in like manner: in her poem *I lost my talk* (Joe 1989), language is something that is taken from her in a deliberate act.
16 Many languages still do not have an orthography, and many speech communities have a stronger tradition of oral rather than written narrative.
17 http://www.wrlp.org last accessed June 1, 2015.
18 http://www.fpcc.ca/language/Programs/Master-Apprentice.aspx last accessed June 1, 2015.
19 http://cayugalanguage.ca/index.php?optioncom_contentandviewarticleandid48andItemid86 last accessed June 1, 2015.
20 At the Naskapi Jimmy Sandy Memorial School (Kawawachikamach, Quebec), for example, the language of instruction is Naskapi from pre-kindergarten to grade three. Instruction in English begins in a repeated grade three transition year, continuing through to secondary five. From grade three to secondary three, students take Naskapi language classes. Cf. http://www.cqsb.qc.ca/jsms last accessed June 1, 2015.
21 By "semi-speakers" we mean members of an endangered speech community who are what Hale (2001: 385) refers to as "less-than-fully-fluent" speakers. Also referred to as "passive bilinguals", they are unable to speak the language with any degree of fluency (and sometimes don't speak at all), but have comprehension skills. Passive bilinguals have acquired some knowledge of the vocabulary and grammar of the language and are, typically, highly motivated to support it.
22 http://www.cilldi.ualberta.ca/CommunityLinguistCertificate last accessed June 1, 2015.
23 http://www.uvcs.uvic.ca/aspnet/Program/Detail/?codeCALR last accessed June 1, 2015.

References

Andersen, Catharyn and Alana Johns. (2005). Labrador Inuttitut: Speaking into the future. *Inuit Studies* 29(1–2), 187–205.
Bauman, James A. (1980). *A guide to issues in Indian language retention*. Washington: Center for Applied Linguistics.

Bloomfield, Leonard. (1925). Why a Linguistic Society? *Language* 1(1), 1–5.
Brittain, Julie and Marguerite MacKenzie. (2012). *The future of Cree*. Web publication, posted at www.eastcree.org/cree/en/resources/readings/publications last accessed June 1, 2015.
Crystal, David. (2000). *Language death*. Cambridge: Cambridge University Press.
Crystal, David. (2010). *The Cambridge encyclopedia of language*, 3rd ed. New York: Cambridge University Press.
Denison, Norman. (1977). Language death or language suicide? *International Journal of the Sociology of Language* 12, 13–22.
Dobrin, Lise M. (2009). SIL International and the disciplinary culture of linguistics: Introduction. *Language* 85(3), 618–619.
Dorian, Nancy, C. (1977). The problem of the semi-speaker in language death. *International Journal of the Sociology of Language* 12, 23–32.
Dorian, Nancy C. (1981). *Language death: The life cycle of a Scottish Gaelic dialect*. Philadelphia: University of Pennsylvania Press.
Dorian, Nancy C. (1986). Abrupt transmission failure in obsolescing languages: how sudden the "tip" to the dominant language communities and families. In V. Nikiforidu, M. Van Clay, M. Niepokuj, and D. Feder (eds). *Proceedings of the Twelfth Annual Meeting of the Berkeley Linguistics Society*. Berkeley Linguistics Society, 72–83.
Dorian, Nancy C. (ed.). (1989). *Investigation obsolescence: studies in language contraction and death*. Cambridge: Cambridge University Press.
Edwards, John. (1985). *Language, society and identity*. Oxford: Blackwell.
Elmendorf, William W. (1981). Last speakers and language change: Two Californian cases. *Anthropological Linguistics* 23(1), 36–49.
Epps, Patience and Herb Ladley. (2009). Syntax, souls, or speakers? On SIL and community language development. *Language* 85(3), 640–646.
Faries, Emily, Julie Brittain, Elizabeth Chiskamish, Serge Demers, Nadine Dostaler, Marie-Odile Junker, Marguerite MacKenzie, Lori Morris, Susan Pashagumskum, and Susan Runnels. (2010). *Research report: Cree School Board language of instruction evaluation*. Chisasibi, Quebec: Cree School Board of Quebec. 476 pp.
Fishman, Joshua A. (1987). Language spread and language policy for endangered languages. In *Proceedings of the Georgetown University Round Table on Language and Linguistics*. Washington: Georgetown University Press, 1–15.
Fishman, Joshua A. (1991). *Reversing language shift: theoretical and empirical foundations of assistance to threatened languages*. Multilingual Matters, vol. 76. Clevedon, Philadelphia: Multilingual Matters.
Fishman, Joshua A. (2000). *Can threatened languages be saved?* Clevedon, Philadelphia: Multilingual Matters.
Grenoble, Lenore A. and Lindsay J. Whaley (eds). (1998). *Endangered languages: Language loss and community response*. Cambridge: Cambridge University Press.
Grenoble, Lenore A. and Lindsay J. Whaley. (2006). *Saving languages: An introduction to language revitalization*. New York, Cambridge: Cambridge University Press.
Hakuta Kenji and Rafael M. Diaz. (1985). The relationship between degree of bilingualism and cognitive ability: a critical discussion and some new longitudinal data. In K. E. Nelson (ed.) *Children's Language* 5. Erlbaum, 320–344.
Hale, Ken. (1992a). On endangered languages and the safeguarding of diversity. *Language* 68, 1–3.
Hale, Ken. (1992b). Language endangerment and the human value of linguistic diversity. *Language* 68, 35–42.
Hale, Ken. (1998). On endangered languages and the importance of linguistic diversity. In Grenoble and Whaley (eds), 192–216.
Hale, Ken. (2001). The Navajo language: III. In Hinton, L. and Hale, K. (eds), 385–388.
Hinton, Leanne. (1994). *Flutes of Fire. Essays on California Indian languages*. Berkeley, California: Heyday Press.
Hinton, Leanne. (2001). Language revitalization: an overview. In Hinton and Hale (eds.), 3–18.
Hinton, Leanne. (2011). Revitalization of endangered languages. In P. K. Austin and J. Sallabank (eds) *The Cambridge handbook of endangered languages*. Cambridge, UK: Cambridge University Press, 291–311.
Hinton, Leanne and Ken Hale (eds). (2001) *The green book of language revitalization in practice*. San Diego: Academic Press.
Janse, Mark. (2003). Introduction: language death and language maintenance: Problems and prospects. In *Language death and language maintenance: Theoretical, practical and descriptive approaches*. Current Issues in Linguistic Theory 240. Amsterdam: John Benjamins, ix–xvii.

Jeddore, Roderick J. (2000)."Investigating community perceptions of the Mi'kmaq language and culture on the First Nations reserve of Miawpukek." M.Ed. thesis, University of Saskatchewan.
Joe, Rita. (1989). *Canadian Woman Studies* 10(2/3), 28.
Kincade, M. Dale. (1991). The decline of native languages in Canada. In R. H. Robins and E. M. Uhlenbeck (eds), *Endangered languages*, Oxford and New York: Berg, 157–176.
King, Jeanette. (2001). *Te Kôhanga Reo: Mâori language revitalization*. In Hinton and Hale (eds), 119–128.
Koostachin, Jules. (2013). Remembering Inninimowin: The Language of the Human Beings. *Canadian Journal of Law and Society* 27(01), 75–80.
Krashen, S. (1998). Heritage language development: Some practical arguments. In S. D. Krashen, L. Tse and J. McQuillan (eds), Heritage language development. Culver City, CA: Language Education Associates, 3–13.
Krauss, Michael. (1992). The world's languages in crisis. *Language* 68, 4–10.
Leikin, Mark. (2012). The effect of bilingualism on creativity: Developmental and educational perspectives. *International Journal of Bilingualism* 17(4), 431–447.
Mithun, Marianne. (1998). The significance of diversity in language endangerment and preservation. In Grenoble and Whaley (eds), 163–191.
Nettle, Daniel and Suzanne Romaine. (2000). *Vanishing voices: The extinction of the world's languages*. Oxford: Oxford University Press.
Schmidt, Annette. (1985). *Young people's Dyirbal: an example of language death from Australia*. Cambridge: Cambridge University Press.
Statistics Canada. 2006. www12.statcan.ca/census-recensement/2006/as-sa/97-558/p19-eng.cfm#01, accessed June 13, 2014.
Tournadre, Nicolas. (2003). The dynamics of Tibetan-Chinese bilingualism: The current situation and future prospects. *China Perspectives* 45, 30–36.
UNESCO. 2003. *Language vitality and endangerment*. http://www.unesco.org/new/fileadmin/MULTIMEDIA/HQ/CLT/pdf/Language_vitality_and_endangerment_EN.pdf last accessed June 1, 2015.
Wintermans, Vincent. (2009). An early attempt to prepare a global strategy for endangered languages: CIPL, IIIC and the "primitive languages in process of extinction" (1928–1929). In *Endangered languages and history: Proceedings of the conference of the Fund for Endangered Languages (FEL)* 13(24–26), 124–132.
Woodbury, Anthony C. 1998. Documenting rhetorical, aesthetic, and expressive loss in language shift. In Grenoble and Whaley 1998, 234–258.
Wurm, Stephen A. (2001). Estudios de Sociolingüística 2(2), 1–12.
Wurm, Stephen A. (1998). Methods of language maintenance and revival, with selected cases of language endangerment in the world. In K. Matsumura (ed.) *Studies in endangered languages* (Papers from the international Symposium on Endangered Languages, Tokyo, 18–20 November 1995.) Tokyo: Hiyuzi Syobo, 191–211.

Further Reading

Crystal, David. (2000). *Language death*. Cambridge: Cambridge University Press.
Grenoble, Lenore A., and Lindsay J. Whaley. (2006). *Saving Languages: An introduction to language revitalization*. New York, Cambridge: Cambridge University Press.
Hinton, Leanne and Ken Hale (eds). (2001). *The green book of language revitalization in practice*. San Diego: Academic Press.
Nettle, Daniel and Suzanne Romaine. (2000). *Vanishing voices: The extinction of the world's languages*. Oxford: Oxford University Press.

30
The Politics of Language Endangerment

Barbra A. Meek

> Theories and models of analysis are particularly fraught with the tensions of expectations.
> *Philips (2011: 19)*

1 Introduction

In the quote above, Lisa Philips was reflecting on the contrast between the multilingual realities of First Nations peoples historically and the scholarly expectation of community monolingualism that plagues the historical record. These same expectations, grounded in a politics of domination and a discourse of modernity, continue to inflect the conceptualization of indigenous language practices, most apparently in the phrase language endangerment. The goal of this chapter is to unpack this phrase across a range of actors, discourses, and agendas. I hope to show how language endangerment is the quintessential anthropological fact, produced at the intersection[s] of cultural classification systems ... and a world that is dynamic and heterogeneous (Carse 2014: 391). Furthermore, like genetic facts (Marks 2012), studies of language endangerment provide anthropology with an opportunity to provoke a more nuanced conceptualization of the recursive relationship between its various dichotomies: the biological (physical/somatic) and the anthropological (discursive/ideological)(Carse 2014), or, more classically, the emotional – ethical and the scientific – analytic (cf. Friedrich 1989) – the material or physical experience and expression entwined through discourse and remembering.

Language endangerment has been a rallying phrase and a growing concern for the past few decades, alongside its counterpoint language revitalization, the response to endangerment and impending extinction. National Public Radio, the New York Times, and AOL.com have publicized stories on endangered languages in the past year or so. Panels at major conferences regularly address the issues and challenges of language endangerment (e.g. an AILA World Congress 2014 panel entitled "A world of indigenous languages: rights, access, and education," organized by Gillian Wigglesworth and Teresa McCarty). Publications, from ethnographies (Nevins 2013a) to new journals (such as *Documenting Endangered Languages*) continue to find an audience. Much of the broad, popular appeal of language endangerment hinges on alignments with intersecting social justice issues, biodiversity, and human rights. Within anthropology, however, the intellectual gravitas of language endangerment remains marginal and fraught with the tensions of expectations.[1]

As I currently reside in a department that values historical theoretical scholarship, part of language endangerment's banality might be explained by the very real purpose and execution such investigations entail. Yet it would be remiss, if not unethical these days, to merely document and theorize the death of a language without providing some kind of support for its potential phoenix-like resurgence or for its immediate growth, with the caveat that such language agendas or projects are already underway locally. In my experience, most scholars would not even have access to an endangered variety if an individual or individuals of a language community (Silverstein 1998) were not similarly motivated to preserve, to maintain, or to revitalize the shifting practices that university scholars intend to investigate. As Granadillo and Orcutt-Gachiri note in their introduction to their edited volume on language endangerment, '[w]e [university scholars] provide tools for the communities but are fully aware that it is the communities' choice whether to pursue activities to attempt to reverse language loss. We feel that communities are the only ones that can determine which path is the right one for them (2011: 12). People personally experiencing linguistic practices in shift, from a marginal to a dominant variety, may find discoursing about the situation, reflecting on their theories of language, and extrapolating from observation to patterned practice, a curiously odd response to the transformative process at hand. That is, for many affected by such drastic and rapid linguistic transformations (as implied by the label endangered language), there is an expectation that scholars (in this case, anthropologists) will provide assistance, not simply as public orators or political advocates, but as researchers who have skills that can be applied to local community projects. The expectation is that the university scholar will not only document people's practices and beliefs for his or her own theoretical accoutrement, but that he or she will work with people to develop and innovate new practices, methods, and skills for achieving some nondisciplinary goal, perhaps even to generate new speakers (including the university expert). This expectation is in stark contrast to the expectations of the institution(s) that mediate scholarly life. As anthropologists we are expected to make new theoretical contributions, not new language lesson plans or new speakers.

Thus, the theories and models that frame language endangerment investigations are fraught with the tedium of practical concerns, such that their theoretical significance is lost amidst the tensions of expectations across those of the people experiencing the change and striving for linguistic survival, those of the people striving for scholarly success and academic recognition, and those of the various institutions striving for (financial) success and (public) recognition. They are tensions arising at the intersection of expectations grounded in different politics and different economies (moral and market, local and global, individual and institutional). Like the distinction between the biological and the anthropological, the dichotomous treatments discussed below – between real-world action and academic modeling, or entextualized material and political discourse, or speaking bodies and extrapolated grammars – are most interestingly understood in a recursive relationship, where anthropological and linguistic facts are made manifest in a cacophony of human action and expectation. This exploration of the production of anthropological and linguistic facts vis-à-vis language endangerment begins with salvage ethnography and the Americanist tradition.

2 Historical Perspectives: Salvage Ethnography and the Americanist Tradition

According to Regna Darnell, '[t]here is an Americanist commitment to preserving the knowledge encoded in oral traditions so that it shall not be lost from the permanent record of human achievement . . . ' The contemporary concern over 'endangered languages' among linguists and anthropologists is rooted in this Americanist experience (1999: 46). Language endangerment thus sits squarely within the Americanist tradition. Entailed as well is the practice of salvage ethnography, a practice that marks the beginning of the documentation of the end of indigenous (language) practices. While similar approaches and motivations for documentation were undertaken in other colonial contexts, the salvage approach gained disciplinary traction in North America through Franz Boas, the founder of American anthropology and its Americanist Tradition (Valentine and Darnell 1999). Americanist anthropology was assumed from the start to be a salvage operation (Fogelson 1999: 81). Raymond Fogelson traces the origin of this operation back to Thomas Jefferson and his fascination with American Indian languages (1999, 77–78). As operations of great modernist proportions, salvage efforts were instituted in order to preserve the practices, beliefs, and knowledge of the colonized populations that colonial administrators, and their governments, were intent on dominating either through assimilation or genocide. Such documentary steps also provided a way in which to count, to geographically locate, and to classify indigenous populations. It was an operation with two material endpoints: bodies and texts.

In the United States, such efforts were undertaken by the Bureau of (American) Ethnology (BAE), which in 1881 merged with the US Geological Survey. Under the direction of John Wesley Powell, the BAE's second director, this department became the organization to carry out this national directive. Powell, an adherent of the racial-biological classification and evolutionary system of the day, used language (primarily word lists) as an instrument to identify and classify indigenous populations, along with Gallatin's 1836 map of tribes (Powell 1880, 1991[1891]). Boas, by contrast, argued that the entire linguistic system required documentation, from sounds to texts, and that such documentation required a standard nomenclature derived from all languages, not only Indo-European varieties. To that end, he established standards for linguistic description and a nomenclature for documenting grammars (Boas 1991[1911]). The motivation for such attention to grammar was two-fold: to discover the histories of indigenous groups (migration and contact) and to reveal the complexities of indigenous languages and, by extrapolation, indigenous mental life, language being one of the most important manifestations of mental life (Boas 1991[1911]: 63). Counter to Powell and other contemporaries, Boas' goal was to discover systems of classification based on universal units of comparison and to explain variation in relation to socio-historical context rather than some essential biological difference. However, both Powell and Boas 'faced considerable pressures to define culture in observable, preferably materially preservable, form' (Darnell 1999: 48) and both assumed the demise of American Indian languages and cultures (Nevins 2013a, 125–127).

Like Powell, Boas was a product of his time and his institutional environment. Having founded the first department of anthropology at Columbia University and being responsible for the training of the first generations of American anthropologists, he had his own expectations about what to preserve and how to preserve/represent the object of his preservationist attention, mediated in part by his own disciplinary training and intellectual interest. In their 1999 article, anthropologists Charles Briggs and Richard Bauman reveal the critical part Boas played 'in determining what would be rendered as "laws and stories," the form and content of the corpus, the discursive frames in which it would be placed, and what sorts of authority would accrue to the texts', through an analysis of Boas' written exchanges with George Hunt and editorial excisions of Hunt's textual efforts (Briggs and Bauman 1999: 480; see also Bauman and Briggs 2003). In particular, they detail the ways in which Boas managed the texts of these individually collected narratives in order to represent a more globally generic Kwakiutl culture, rather than the particular circumstances of their telling and the narrators who performed them. They argue that it is in these sleights of Boas' hand, and pen, that the construction of modernity persisted (Briggs and Bauman (1999: 481). For Boas, the authentic object for collection and preservation was not the unmodified object of original elicitation, but the unadulterated yet progressively arranged version that would meet the expectations of its modern (English-literate), white public and naturalize the authority of the anthropologist.

Enmeshed in these early projects are the politics of the nation financing these salvage expeditions and the personal politics of individuals charged with conducting the research. Masked by the analytic (classificatory) approaches of these researchers, and the transparency of biological difference that they assumed in their enumerative and documentary efforts, the social-political complexity within and across indigenous groups became buried under the weight of modernity and its reigning voices, their own voices silenced in these acts of entextualization and enumeration.

3 Critical Topics: Language Shift, Inequality, and Voice

In the mid-twentieth century, new voices arose in the academy, articulating with the Civil Rights movements in the United States and defining linguistic anthropology as the study of language as social action. Dell Hymes, along with colleagues such as Erving Goffman, John Gumperz, and William Labov, and his then students (such as Judith Irvine, Susan Philips, Joel Sherzer, and Elinor Ochs), recognized the significance of speech in the politics of everyday life. Hymes, building off the Boasian Americanist tradition, developed the textual tradition into the field of ethnopoetics (Webster and Kroskrity 2013). This development emphasized the stylistic elements of narrative in performance, across individuals, across narrative iterations and modalities, across contexts, and so forth. It expanded the textual tradition of the Boasian school in order to encompass all possible dimensions of narrative. In this analytic expansion, Hymes was also concerned with narrative inequality (as were his influential predecessors). However, his concern with inequality drew attention to individual speakers (or narrators) and their voices. As Blommaert notes, 'ultimately, what ethnopoetics does is to show voice, to visualize the particular ways – often deviant from hegemonic norms – in which subjects produce meaning' (Blommaert 2009: 271). Or, as Webster and Kroskrity summarize, 'Hymesian "voice" is both a creative and a political accomplishment' (2013: 3).

With respect to marginalized groups, especially indigenous communities and linguistic practice in Native North America, Hymes believed ethnopoetics and anthropological research generally could, and should, provide an opportunity for voice. He also recognized the political complexity within these communities: '[speech communities] are found to prefer one language for a purpose as against another, to acquire some languages and give up others because of their suitability for certain purposes'. No government can afford to assume the equality of all the languages in its domain (Hymes 1996: 56). Similarly, research on language in practice often reflected this observation, documenting one particular variety at the exclusion of others, and certainly excluding the complex code-interchanges that littered the speech of multilingual communities. While recognizing this complexity, '. . . language is in large part what users have made of it. Navajo is what it is partly because it is a human language, partly because it is the language of the Navajo' (1996: 26), Hymes' research often privileged a singular language for the entextualization and the performance of narrative. In fact, one might beg to differ with Hymes' claim that '[l]anguages may disappear through the destruction of their speakers, but not through the publication of linguistic papers and maps' (Hymes 1996: 29). If we take languages to mean linguistic varieties and repertoires of speech communities and acknowledge that the material resources produced by scholars are always only partial representations of these linguistic environments, then when no speakers remain (or only partially recollect past linguistic practices and knowledge) and the project is to revitalize or renew a language, such publications (and maps) will determine, or at least constrain, the range of knowledge (linguistic and otherwise) that is retrievable. Thus, while no direct connection may exist between the documents produced by scholars and the endangerment (or destruction) of a language, indirect connections can certainly be found between the representational strategies of voice and the opportunities for recreation or renewal that they may offer.

Developing further Hymes' concern with inequality and language, scholars such as Susan Philips, Susan Gal, and Jane H. Hill elaborated relationships between linguistic practice and social inequality within their own research and scholarship, often in the guise of a Bourdieuian political economy of language. Philips (1983), for example, examined the sociolinguistic environment of Warm Springs students' interactional expectations. She revealed that these students were socialized into different styles of interaction and learning than the institutional style promoted and positively evaluated by the teachers in their classrooms and practiced by non-Indian students. Gal, studying language shift in Austria, showed that the sociolinguistic patterns she discovered in a Hungarian-speaking community resulted from different ideological orientations and economic opportunities, aligning with sex roles and status expectations (Gal 1979). On the other hand, her analysis of causatives and narrow users' innovations in the field-defining volume *Language Obsolescence: Studies in Language Contraction and Death*, showed that even in shifting repertoires, where opportunities for acquisition may be diminished, grammatical word formation knowledge was productive across users, though variable (Gal 1989a). While younger generations were shifting away from conventional lexical items and grammatical patterns, the interactional expectations of the sociolinguistic environment stimulated new linguistic forms. More importantly, her work reveals the importance of investigating the tensions and conflicts surrounding linguistic practice, from the interactional to the political and ideological: '[m]ore broadly this suggests that we should examine the linguistic changes occurring during language shift not only through the metaphor of death and decay that the "pastoral" tradition provides, but also through an image of conflict and competition between differing forces – cognitive, interactional, symbolic – whose effects on the details of linguistic practice are sometimes contradictory' (Gal 1989a: 330). Similarly, in a commentary on Gal's chapter, Woolard (1989: 365) emphasizes the need for researchers to best begin by anchoring [their] generalizations in speakers' activities. Finally, Jane and Kenneth Hill in their extensive study of Mexicano (Nahuatl) reveal a relationship between individuals' practices (linguistic, social, economic) and their ideological orientations to Spanish and Mexicano along a continuum of power and solidarity (Hill and Hill 1986). Like Gal, Hill 1989 shows how, even in linguistic repertoires indicative of language shift, speakers exhibit a full range of expression, whether through calquing, innovative word formation, or some other creative development. While contemporary studies of language endangerment have transitioned from a concern with generalizable patterns and an emphasis on language (grammar) to the political, economic, and social conditions affecting the sociolinguistic environment and linguistic variation, these field-defining studies foregrounded this transition and on-going concerns with power, inequality, and political economy.

In examining the relationship between language and political economy, Susan Gal (1989b: 348) identified two points of contact, the first pertaining to inequality and the control of representations as 'a source of social power, . . . [and] a likely locus of conflict and struggle', and the second attending to interpersonal power relations and 'the exercise of institutional power in which language is also a constitutive element' (1989b: 349–351). Both points are concerned with how language participates in the valuing and evaluation of human diversity (cf. Hymes 1996). Given the central role of institutions in managing power and inequality, it is not surprising that they have played a significant role in both creating the situation for language endangerment (e.g. through boarding and residential schooling in the United States and Canada; see Hinton and Meek, forthcoming) and defining the unequal relations between members of minority language communities and supporters of majority language practices. This attention to the social complexities of situations of endangerment distinguishes contemporary studies of language endangerment from previous eras.

4 Current Contributions and Research: Beyond Language Endangerment – Politics and Ideologies

... ideology ... is an inevitable component of all politics ... in maintaining or achieving asymmetrical and exploitative relations of power, that is, in distorting or obfuscating or constricting possible understandings, possible imaginings of the self, and dialogic and other human relations (Friedrich 1989: 301–302).

Transitioning from attempts to develop a diagnostic framework for identifying and remedying endangered languages, contemporary linguistic anthropological research on language endangerment has begun to examine the ideological aspects of endangered language scenarios, considering not only the politics between polities but within them as well, and the layers of contestation surrounding issues of endangerment and the scaling of power and authority in the sanctioning of expertise, competence, and access. In their introduction to an edited volume on Native American ideologies, Kroskrity and Field point out that beliefs and feelings about language – and those about particular languages – are indeed an acknowledged part of the processes of language shift and language death that threaten many non-state-supported languages (2009: 4). Investigations of beliefs and feelings about language range from a concern with discourses of endangerment and linguistic entitlement (e.g., Cavanaugh 2009, Duchêne and Heller 2007, Hill 2002, Kroskrity 2011, Moore et al. 2010, Muehlmann 2012, Swinehart and Graber 2012) to practices of scholarly documentation (e.g., Kroskrity 2013a, b, Moore 2006, Nevins 2013b, Webster 2013) and textual and performative habits of representation and evaluation (e.g., Bender 2002, Carr and Meek 2013, Jaffe 2013, Kroskrity 2012, Makihara 2013, Meek 2010, Nevins 2013a, Patrick 2003). This research also crosscuts domains of practice – national, institutional, and individual – in their examinations of the social work that such endangered language projects envision, execute, and accomplish. Because there has been an abundance of research and writing in this arena, the rest of this section will focus on a few select pieces to demonstrate these dimensions and their entanglements with the tensions of expectations.

The politics of people affect the vitalities of language (Perley 2011), whether through institutional position or individual commitment. In *Defying Maliseet Language Death*, Bernard Perley provides an intimate portrait of his own heritage aboriginal language, a language his mother acquired as a first language but that he did not. It is a familiar portrait of language death in many ways. And yet Perley points out that language death is more than just the fragmented aftermath of colonial injustice. Instead he argues that individuals play as much of a role in the state of a language as the history they have endured. He demonstrates ethnographically that individual agency has as much impact on language change and endangerment as the colonial regimes that implement policy. In particular, Perley shows how the relationships of people to each other and to language affect the vitality of practice associated with particular languages (English, French, and most especially Maliseet). Whether as writing, reading, conversing, narrating, performing, or lamenting, each practice creates and indexes a unique relationship between an individual and the (linguistic) practice enacted – as a kindergartner learning to identify letters and sounds or a fourth-grader learning to write a prayer, as a councilman performing an introduction in Maliseet or a fluent First Nations leader sitting silently in attendance, as director of a university program or an anthropologist in training conducting fieldwork, as a young woman flirting in a bar or a politician describing his constituency to her – all of these people have unique, if overlapping, relationships and commitments to the vitality of Maliseet. Such individual experiences and expectations affect opportunities for speaking, and thus affect the vitalities of language. Finally, in recognizing individual agency, Perley recommends that language suicide is a more appropriate term for describing what is happening to the Maliseet language, rather than the less person-centered phrase of language death, or language endangerment.

In Urla's ethnography (2012), *Reclaiming Basque*, she similarly examines the impact of individual actions on the vitalities of language by carefully detailing the history of Basque language movements and the discourses encompassing them. She is equally concerned, however, with the politics of institutions and the role that statistical discourse has played in more recent iterations. She shows how enumeration of any sort is a (Foucauldian) governmental technology of power, wherein a regime of truth gets discursively drawn and transforms a political problem into a technical one (Urla 2012: 113). Such processes have dominated the public and popular discourse on language endangerment, providing truthful and thus unquestionable portraits of dying languages for the interested consumer and potential investor. From politics to business, Urla demonstrates how contemporary discourses of language revival are drawing on managerial rhetoric. In provocative illustration, chapter six ends with this observation: 'It was not without a sense of irony that one of my language-advocate friends gestured to the book on her nightstand that she and her fellow scholar/activist colleagues had decided to read: it was not Fanon; it was not Fishman. It was a translation of management guru Steven Covey's *Seven Habits of Highly Effective People*' (Urla 2012: 168).

In a similar fashion, Brigittine French's ethnography of Mayan linguistics in Guatemala sheds light on the politics of language in its most seminal sense, investigating historically and ethnographically the role of Mayan language politics in the modernist struggle for state recognition through traditional practices. She notes that [i]ndeed, the few but important victories Maya leaders have won involve the state's recognition of difference based upon the cultural distinctiveness of Mayan languages and their provisional inclusion in the Guatemalan national community (French 2010: 5). While similar ethnolinguistic nation-building efforts can be found elsewhere, French builds her ethnography in conversation with Bauman and Briggs' *Voices of Modernity* (2003), arguing that their analytic framework, in particular, direct[s] analytic attention to the construction of modernity and tradition as one of the most important ways through which language forms and collective identities become linked (French 2010: 10). In almost explicit demonstration of a modernist construction, French shares a statement from a Mayan linguist and leader of the Maya ethnonationalist movement, Dr Demetrio Cojtí: 'The Mayanist movement is at once predominantly conservative on the cultural plane and predominantly innovative and revolutionary on the political and economic plane. For that reason it is said that the Maya movement's path leads not only to Tikal (traditionalism) but also to New York and Tokyo (modernism)' (cited in French 2010: 11). To investigate the unfolding of these twin processes of modernity, French focuses on metalinguistic discourse and the scholarly regimentation of language, Mayan varieties and Spanish. Similarly to Hill and Hill's analysis of the relationship between Mexicano and Spanish, French describes a corresponding distribution of labor and ideological similitude, where Spanish aligns with progress and the indigenous language with tradition. Most strikingly, she shows how the seemingly benign act of documenting a grammar becomes a political act of recognition and resistance. She discusses how the first international linguists (Summer Institute of Linguistics or SIL) to begin documenting Mayan languages were aligned with the Guatemalan government's agenda toward indigenous peoples, i.e. to assimilate these populations into Spanish dominance and the state. Indigenous Maya linguists eventually began to repudiate SIL's approach, and the state's, developing their own system of documentation and representation, which did not rely on or emphasize the sameness of grammar between Spanish and Mayan varieties. Instead, these linguists and their supporters (Proyecto Lingüístico Francisco Marroquín – PLFM)) developed 'a new orthography for Mayan languages . . . that would consolidate Mayan linguistic struggles for self-determination around linguistic difference . . .' In effect, the PLFM created a process for attaining a regimentation of the sound systems of Mayan languages, which would establish linguistic difference on a scientific and rational basis, and which would pave the way for making assertions of cultural difference by native speakers/analysts (French 2010: 56–57). Complicating this further, local norms regarding linguistic practice reveal gendered and age-graded divisions that challenge the generic Pan-Mayan stance toward unification through language; not everyone speaks the same way, nor should they. While many linguistic anthropologists have written critically about the historical antecedents to contemporary documentary efforts (see citations above), French has demonstrated the significance and the complexity of these efforts and their negotiation for the indigenous communities involved. She also highlights a disciplinary distinction that may require a bit more reflection: where does linguistic anthropology (or anthropological linguistics) end and applied linguistics begin, and how are, or should, those conducting basic research on endangered languages be involved in these applied efforts, and their underlying politics?

5 Recommendations for Practice, Part 1: On Applied Efforts and Collaboration

Many, if not all, of the ethnographies on language endangerment and revitalization have grown out of interactions and collaborations with indigenous communities, committed individual speakers, and supportive governments (such as Paul Kroskrity's work with Rosalie Bethel, Marybeth Nevin's work with Rebekah Moody and the Ndee Biyati' Apache language project, and my work with Leda Jules, Aboriginal Language Services, and the Kaska Tribal Council). These collaborations and the labor provided are critical elements of the research, not merely as best practices for conducting research but as an epistemological necessity. For example, Nevins' multiple and diverse collaborations provide the basis for her ethnography, an investigation of language advocacy efforts on the Fort Apache reservation and their intended and unintended effects (Nevins 2013a). She argues that research must attend to the diversity of responses, innovation, and the success of apparent failures (2013a: 224) in order to 'make sense of the situation that [a] community finds itself in' (Nevins and Nevins 2012: 147–148), and that ethnography can help reframe the 'noise' of community critique of language programs into alternate claims to authority and into alternate definitions of community that are themselves germane to the ongoing relevance of indigenous languages (2013a: 9); see also Ahlers 2014, Debenport 2010, 2011). Granadillo and Orcutt-Gachiri reach a similar conclusion: '. . . every situation of language endangerment carries with it effects that cannot be foreseen' (2011: 5) and calls for a need to make ethnographic fieldwork a standard component of language endangerment research. The growing expectation across diverse participants in indigenous language advocacy is that of labor, in spite of conflicting political commitments.

Another development has been the push to involve academic institutions in these pursuits. Morgan (2005) has detailed the involvement of Michigan State University in ongoing efforts to revitalize Anishinaabegmowin (Ojibwe languages) and the challenges indigenous language programs at the university-level can face. Baldwin and Olds (2007; see also Leonard 2011) demonstrate the usefulness of collaboration across institutions, yet at the same time emphasize the importance of tribal control. They discuss the Myaamia Project, created among those with a vested interest in the continuation and survival of [Myaamia] community's traditional language and culture (2007: 285). This includes non-Native scholars and institutions, such as the University of Miami in Ohio. However, the objectives for the project are determined in relation to the applicability they have for the community. Thus, they distinguish between essential (reconstructing their traditional lunar calendar) and nonessential research (establishing a genetic relationship to Ohio's prehistoric mound builders), the ultimate goal being the renewal of Myaamia and the restoration of a traditional worldview. Investigating similarly entwined linguistic and cultural revitalization efforts, Michelle Jacob (2013) elucidates the politics of Yakama revitalization and the steps that individual tribal members took to overcome certain collaborative obstacles, including establishing an NGO in order to circumvent tribal politics and government control.

Within academic fields that study language, scholars have begun to articulate more explicitly their interdependent relationships with language communities and the need to develop research projects that benefit both the scholar and the community (see, e.g., Ahlers 2009). In a recent festschrift in Jane Hill's honor, Bischoff, Cole, Fountain, and Miyashita (2013) elaborate on the intersection of documentary linguistics, endangered languages, and social justice, a theme exemplified in several of the chapters in this volume. In Bischoff et al. (2013), Stacey Oberly, for example, provides a study of prosody in five elder speakers of Southern Ute, arguing that such linguistic documentation and analytic work is necessary for language preservation and revitalization in order to sound Ute. Colleen Fitzgerald, in her analysis of Tohono O'odham high vowels, works with an extensive data set collected over multiple generations and suggests that (past and present) phonological documentation serves both the needs of linguists and the needs of communities of speakers of endangered languages. Bischoff and Fountain's chapter on a grass roots project of web-based language archiving for the Coeur d'Alene language community demonstrates some of the complicated political and practical terrain that such projects encounter. This chapter focuses in particular on the challenge of how to make readily available legacy materials and other documentation without external funding and without technical expertise (Bischoff et al. 2013: 177). Additional challenges arose around issues of appropriate access and orthographic conventions. Despite such challenges, the authors encourage the development of such projects because '[t]echnologies such as web development have the potential to support the expression of local knowledge in ways that serve the needs of community members, academics, and policy makers without excluding local voices from the conversation' (Bischoff et al. 2013: 197). Finally, in Paul Kroskrity's chapter on Native American languages and narrative discrimination, he examines the logic with which scholars Anna Gayton and Stanley Newman negatively assessed the features of Yokuts and Western Mono narratives. He shows that such assessments are an especially appropriate site for understanding the professional and entitled language ideologies that further contributed to the discursive marginalization of [indigenous] narrative traditions (2013a: 323; see also Kroskrity 2011, 2012, 2013b). He concludes by pointing out that it is the disciplinary expectations of these scholars that constrained narrative representations and ultimately marginalized the verbal artistry of the two language communities being documented. Thus, as evidenced by each of these cases, any and all collaboration is a political act with – for better and for worse – social and economic effects.

6 Recommendations for Practice, Part 2: On Discrimination and Linguistic Racism

The sciences of humankind have developed in the matrix of a certain relationship between one part of the world and the rest. Anthropology has been fairly described as the study of colored people by whites (Hymes 1996: 59).

As mentioned above, the Hymesian tradition brought with it an attention to inequality in practice, such as unequal distributions of power, unequal access, and unequal standards of evaluation (Blommaert 2009, McCarty, Collins and Hopson 2011, Webster and Kroskrity 2013). Recently scholars working within language endangerment have begun to reconsider Hymes' concern with inequality, focusing especially on narrative inequality, or what Paul Kroskrity has termed narrative or discursive discrimination. This shift has in part emerged as a result of prominent scholars writing about linguistic racism in white public spaces (see Bischoff et al. 2013). But, it has also emerged in relation to the reclamation of control by marginalized groups. For language endangerment, this turn has meant increased attention to, if not actual privileging of, the agendas of indigenous language communities. As mentioned above, collaboration and advocacy have become the norm for much of the research being carried out on language endangerment. Alongside this shift has been a renewed interest in the subtle ways in which language figures in acts of discrimination and marginalization, as discourses of difference (processes of enfigurement) and as contestations over membership/participation (boundary-making processes). These areas are mutually constitutive. Processes of enfigurement socialize novices into certain sets of expectations (of appearance, of performance, of norms and standards, and so forth). Boundary-making processes rely on enfiguring processes in order to define the limits of inclusion (from membership to nonmembership). Of course, both processes are dynamic, meaning that they are interactionally negotiated, contested, realized, and they are temporally fluid (recursive and emergent), meaning that they become anchored only through discursive acts but are not themselves inherently linked to a particular place or time. What is most illuminating about this research are the ways in which expectations inflect and complicate enfigurement and boundary-making, provoking certain evaluations and undermining others. Understanding expectations is central to understanding our own habits of discrimination (evaluation) in perpetuating racialized inequalities.

Narratives and their entextualized antecedents exemplify these processes. Much of the current scholarship on narratives in endangered language contexts has emphasized the variability of expectation and evaluation within community practice (see Kroskrity 2012 for examples). Recognition of this variability has in part arisen due to efforts at revitalization that involve efforts to perform linguistically and become subject to evaluation. Another approach has been to examine closely the epistemological proclivities of earlier documentarians. For example, Kroskrity (2013a, b) has analyzed the evaluative habits of two earlier academic researchers, who documented indigenous central California narratives. Their evaluative scale relied on the following negative features: lexical deficiency, lack of figurative language, simplicity, redundancy, lack of explication, lack of variation (repetitive), lack of formal structure (Kroskrity 2013a: 325). Each of these features predisposes the reviewer to a negative evaluation of the narratives. Webster (2011) presents a similar scene for Navajo author and poet Blackhorse Mitchell. Published in 1963, his novel, *Miracle Hill*, received a supportive yet disdainful introduction by literary critic T. D. Allen, describing Mitchell's style of writing as primitive with a tangled grammar (Webster 2011: 65), an evaluation that then reverberated through later book reviews (2011: 67–69). As Webster highlights, because Navajo English is spoken and written by marginalized peoples, it can always be dismissed or devalued by outside assumptions concerning 'standard' English and 'aesthetic principles' . . . The expectations for Navajo English are for an English that is 'primitive' and 'incompetent' . . . What is not taken seriously is that Mitchell might be doing something with his use of Navajo English besides mere documentation (Webster 2011: 66). Similar misinterpretations of form appear in both of these examples. Meek (2011) considers how forms in practice that deviate from expert listener expectations, position actors differently, resulting yet again in the ongoing marginalization of indigenous ways of speaking. In her case, she traces the popular, public representations of American Indian speech in film (especially children's media) in the classroom, where teachers and other expert evaluators are primed to interpret First

Nations students' linguistic performances as remedial. All three of these cases illustrate the subtle ways in which experts' own social milieus and habits of expertise predispose them to negative evaluations of already marginalized indigenous practices.

Expert expectations and evaluations of indigenous performance are not the only arenas in which acts of discrimination creep in. In Feliciano-Santos' ethnographic research on Taíno language renewal (2011), she focuses on the establishment of relatedness through interaction, especially in terms of the development and manufacturing of Taínoness. These efforts include explicit political acts as well as more subtle interactional moments. As part of this reconfiguration of Taínoness, language figures centrally because it is one of the key features recognized by governments, institutions, and people as signifying some authentic indigenous identity. This movement also destabilizes popular and historical conceptions of Puerto Ricanness. Intimately linked to understandings of authenticity and citizenship, the reclamation of a Taíno image, along with the revitalization of associated linguistic and cultural practices, reframes and at times fragments these nationally-circulating representations of the ideal Puerto Rican citizen. In particular, her analysis of classroom interactions, language workshops, and protests reveal how people incorporate new individuals and distance others from their projects, interactionally defining interlocutors as either being or not being Taíno. The endangered language, in form and in interaction, participates in enfiguring individuals as Indian while also establishing them as (potential) members at certain moments (classroom lessons on heritage) and excluding them at others (protests at archaeological sites).

Before I conclude, consider this excerpt from Kroskrity:

> As for narrative *discrimination*, I think it is an especially appropriate tool for understanding how linguistic and cultural experts – ones who are overtly advocates of the languages/cultures they describe – can be recruited to participate in racializing projects that are much larger than their individual contributions . . . discursive discrimination may play a further role in emphasizing the inevitability of imposing standards and the ease with which attempts to appreciate the narrative conventions of others' *are saturated with discursive expectations and evaluations, typically located at the level of practical consciousness, that often prevent an informed understanding or a constructive representation* . . . Academic scholars may be experts capable of focusing a bright light on the limited regions of their expertise . . . but they are elsewhere common-sense social (i.e. national) actors who are likely to (re-)produce familiar cultural patterns stored in their practical consciousness.
>
> *Kroskrity (2013b: 335; emphasis added)*

Like Nevins' call to do ethnography as part of language endangerment research, Kroskrity also encourages us to consider the limits of expertise and its mediation in familiar cultural patterns stored in their [our] practical consciousness.

7 Future Directions: Language Endangerment in the Twenty-first Century

There are multiple cultural meanings and vested interests in genetic facts, and to confront their concealment is the start of an anthropological understanding of the science of human heredity (Marks 2012: 259).

The quote above prompts us to poke at the cultural underbelly of biological facts, reminiscent of previous social theorists' conceptualizations of representations as social facts (Rabinow 1986). For studies of language, genetic facts also constitute in part linguistic facts, such that exchanging genetic for linguistic produces a statement that similarly resonates with linguistic anthropological approaches to human behavior, that is, an attention to processes of concealment and investment. As shown above, much of the current research on language endangerment is concerned with the multiple cultural meanings and vested interests entailed in the diagnostics of endangerment and contemporary projects of language revitalization.

Yet, what exactly is language endangerment? Is it language change gone awry or language contact at its most extreme? Is it a dimension of linguistic racism? In a review of literature on language death, Salikoko Mufwene (2004), a linguist at the University of Chicago, broadened the question to include language birth and argued for a deeper temporal gaze, pointing out that '[t]he overemphasis on worldwide economic globalization as the primary cause of language loss has prevented any fruitful comparison between, on the one hand, recent and current evolutions and, on the other, what must have occurred during the earliest political and economic hegemonies in the history of mankind' (Mufwene 2004: 202). That is, language endangerment is part of a continuum that involves the emergence of new varieties and the recognition of the political-economic circumstances of language change. Of course, Susan Gal and Kathryn Woolard made similar appeals (Dorian 1998). Thus, while languages change, dialects shift, new linguistic varieties emerge and fade, the distinguishing feature of language endangerment is the political scenario that undergirds the existential trajectory of the languages considered endangered. As Mufwene (2004) also notes, much of the research on language endangerment has focused primarily on the indigenous languages of European ex-colonies and on minority languages of the European Union. If we expand our gaze further still by including anthropological research on language shift, small languages and small communities (Dorian 1998), regardless of their history of contact with European nations, reveal the significance of politics in understanding language endangerment, including language revitalization. The politics of contact remain in the foreground, whether as the result of direct acts of colonization or more subtle forms of global incorporation and the opening of new markets

This is not a new point. Duchêne and Heller, in the introduction to their co-edited volume (2007) on discourses of language endangerment, highlight the significance of the political-economic context within which discourses of endangerment have arisen. Discourses about language endangerment are circumscribed by the politics of difference and the stabilization of diversity within the nation state. They are discourses about maintaining a status quo of difference. Duchêne and Heller conclude by posing the following: 'Rather than assuming we must save languages, perhaps we should be asking instead who benefits and who loses from understanding languages the way we do, what is at stake for whom, and *how and why language serves as a terrain for competition*' (2007: 11). This statement concisely defines the conception of politics that has framed this chapter. The history of language endangerment research demonstrates how politics is the coordination of – including conflict over – particular sets of interests and investments that begin to delineate, configure, and constrain the vastness of linguistic practice and human diversity. It is the relationship between social relations, patterns of practice, and systems (including histories) of inequality in the coordination and recognition of groups; in other words, it is the management of diversity in the coordination of resemblance (assimilation).

Within the political scenario of endangerment, then, one of the crucial elements affecting the (assignment of) status of a(n) (indigenous) language is the vision of the ruling class, a nation's government, or the academy; what are their mission(s)? What role does language play (and which language(s)) in the development of the mission? How will the mission be executed, and what consequences will its execution have for nonofficial languages? This national, institutional dimension might begin as (economic) policy (or war) but is merely the political tip. Another significant dimension is the interpretation and implementation of policy; how will languages be represented? Which varieties will be documented? Who will assess and regulate the production of these materials and how will they be used, and by whom? Federally regulated expectations come into play at this stage, with all the complications that carrying out a mandate, or a vision, entails. Authority must be established and technocratic tools of regimentation devised (cf. Partridge 2012); teachers trained and curriculum materials produced, modified, expanded, or simplified. Finally, individual participation in, and responses to, the politics of governance becomes the final dimension that distinguishes processes of language endangerment from other investigations of language change. Contemporary studies of the politics of language endangerment critically explore these questions, ranging in their attention to nations, institutions, and individuals. They all variously show how the social-political life of a language is the most critical component for predicting its trajectory and possible future iteration(s). Or, more simply, what people expect and do with a language will determine its status, its state, and its future.

Acknowledgments

I am especially grateful to Nancy Bonvillain for her incredible patience and support of this chapter, and to Georgia Ennis for her feedback. All errors are my own.

Related Topics

7 Language Ideologies (Kroskrity); **8** Social Subordination and Language (Huayhua) **18** New and Emergent Languages (Riley); **21** Language and Nationalism (Haque); **28** Language Maintenance and Revitalization (Cowell); **29** Language Endangerment and Revitalization Strategies (Brittain, MacKenzie).

Note

1 An advanced search of AAA journals on the anthrosource site (www.anthrosource.net) for the phrase, language endangerment, resulted in 7 hits, only two of which were research articles; endangered languages resulted in 5 hits, one of which was a research-length article, and language shift resulted in 12 hits. The search parameters were all journals and anywhere in the article for the exact phrase. For comparison, bilingualism resulted in 30 hits; indigeneity, 48 entries; schizophrenia, 24 entries; biodiversity, 21 entries; fashion, 88 entries; tourism, 185 entries.

References

Ahlers, Jocelyn. 2009. The Many Meanings of Collaboration: Fieldwork with the Elem Pomo. *Language & Communication* 29(3): 230–243.
Ahlers, Jocelyn. 2014. Linguistic Variation and Time Travel: Barrier, or Border-crossing? *Language & Communication* 38: 33–43.
Baldwin, Daryl and Julie Olds. 2007. Miami Indian Language and Cultural Research at Miami University. In *Beyond Red Power: American Indian Politics and Activism since 1900*, edited by Daniel M. Cobb and Loretta Fowler, 280–290. Santa Fe: School for Advanced Research.
Bauman, Richard and Charles Briggs. 2003. *Voices of Modernity: Language Ideologies and the Politics of Inequality*. Cambridge: Cambridge University Press.
Bender, Margaret. 2002. *Signs of Cherokee Culture: Sequoyah's Syllabary in Eastern Cherokee life*. Chapel Hill: University of North Carolina Press.
Bischoff, Shannon T., Deborah Cole, Amy V. Fountain, and Mizuki Miyashita. 2013. *The Persistence of Language: Constructing and Confronting the Past and Present in the Voices of Jane H. Hill*. Amsterdam, Philadelphia: John Benjamins.
Bischoff, Shannon T. and Amy V. Fountain. 2013. A Case-study in Grass Roots Development of Web Resources for Language workers: The Coeur d'Alene Archive and Online Language Resources (CAOLR). In Bischoff et al., 175–200.

Blommaert, Jan. 2009. Ethnography and Democracy: Hymes' Political Theory of Language. *Text and Talk* 29(3): 257–276.

Boas, Franz. 1991[1911]. *Introduction to the Handbook of American Indian Languages*. Lincoln: University of Nebraska Press.

Briggs, Charles and Richard Bauman. 1999. The Foundation of all Future Researches: Franz Boas, Native American Texts, and the Construction of Modernity. *American Quarterly* 51(3): 479–528.

Carr, Gerald L. and Barbra A. Meek. 2013. The Poetics of Language Revitalization: Text, Performance, and Change. *Journal of Folklore Research* 50(1–3): 191–216.

Carse, Ashley. 2014. The Year 2013 in Sociocultural Anthropology: Cultures of Circulation and Anthropological Facts. *American Anthropologist* 116(2): 390–403.

Cavanaugh, Jillian. 2009. *Living Memory: The Social Aesthetics of Language in a Northern Italian Town*. Malden, MA: Wiley-Blackwell.

Darnell, Regna. 1999. Theorizing American Anthropology: Continuities Form the B.A.E. to the Boasians. In Valentine and Darnell, 38–51.

Debenport, Erin. 2010. The Potential Complexity of Universal Ownership: Cultural Property, Textual Circulation, and Linguistic Fieldwork. *Language & Communication* 30: 204–210.

Debenport, Erin. 2011. As the Rez Turns: Anomalies within and beyond the Boundaries of a Pueblo Community. *American Indian Culture and Research Journal* 35(2): 87–109.

Dorian, Nancy C. 1989. *Investigating Language Obsolescence: Studies in Language Contraction and Death*. Cambridge: Cambridge University Press.

Dorian, Nancy J. 1998. Western Language Ideologies and Small Language Prospects. In *Endangered Languages: Language Loss and Community Response*, edited by Lenore A. Grenoble and Lindsay J. Whaley, 3–21. Cambridge: Cambridge University Press.

Duchêne, Alexandre and Monica Heller (eds) 2007. *Discourses of Endangerment: Ideology and Interest in the defence of Languages*. London and New York: Continuum.

Feliciano-Santos, Sherina. 2011. An inconceivable indigeneity: The historical, cultural, and interactional dimensions of Puerto Rican Taíno activism. Ph.D. dissertation, University of Michigan.

Fogelson, Raymond D. 1999. Nationalism and the Americanist Tradition. In *Theorizing the Americanist Tradition*, edited by Lisa Philips Valentine and Regna Darnell, 75–83. Toronto: University of Toronto Press.

French, Brigittine. 2010. *Maya Ethnolinguistic Identity: Violence, Cultural Rights, and Modernity in Highland Guatemala*. Tucson: University of Arizona Press.

Friedrich, Paul. 1989. Language, Ideology and Political Economy. *American Anthropologist* 91(2): 295–312.

Gal, Susan. 1979. *Language Shift, Social Dimensions of Linguistic Change in Bilingual Austria*. New York: Academic Press.

Gal, Susan. 1989a. Lexical Innovation and Loss: The Use and Value of Restricted Hungarian. In Dorian (ed.), 313–334.

Gal, Susan. 1989b. Language and political economy. *Annual Review of Anthropology* 18: 345–367.

Granadillo, Tania and Heidi A. Orcutt–Gachiri. 2011. *Ethnographic Contributions to the Study of Endangered Languages*. Tucson: University of Arizona Press.

Hill, Jane H. 1989. The Social Functions of Relativization in Obsolescent and Non–obsolescent Languages. In Dorian, 149–166.

Hill, Jane H. 2002. Expert Rhetorics in Advocacy for Endangered Languages: Who is Listening and what do they Hear? *Journal of Linguistic Anthropology* 12: 119–133.

Hill, Jane H. and Kenneth C. Hill. 1986. *Speaking Mexicano*. Tucson: University of Arizona Press.

Hinton, Leanne and Barbra A. Meek. Forthcoming. Language Acquisition, Shift, and Revitalization Processes in the U.S., Canada, and Far North. In *The Handbook of Indigenous Language Revitalization in the Americas*, edited by Serafin M. Coronel-Molina and Teresa L. McCarty. New York: Routledge.

Hymes, Dell. 1996. Speech and Language: On the Origins and Foundations of Inequality among Speakers. In *Ethnography, Linguistics, Narrative Inequality: Toward an Understanding of Voice*, edited by Dell Hymes, 25–62. London and Bristol, PA: Taylor & Francis.

Jacob, Michelle M. 2013. *Yakama Rising: Indigenous Cultural Revitalization, Activism, and Healing*. Tucson: University of Arizona Press.

Jaffe, Alexandra. 2013. Minority Language Learning and Communicative Competence: Models of Identity and Participation in Corsican Adult Language Courses. *Language & Communication* 33: 450–462.

Kroskrity, Paul V. 2011. Facing the Rhetoric of Language Endangerment: Voicing the Consequences of Linguistic Racism. *Journal of Linguistic Anthropology* 21(2): 179–192.

Kroskrity, Paul V. 2012. *Telling Stories in the Face of Danger: Language Renewal in Native American Communities*. Norman: University of Oklahoma Press.

Kroskrity, Paul V. 2013a. Narrative Discriminations in Central California's Indigenous Narrative Traditions: Relativism or (Covert) Racism? In Bischoff et. al., 321–338.

Kroskrity, Paul V. 2013b. Discursive Discriminations in the Representation of Western Mono and Yokuts Stories: Confronting Narrative Inequality and Listening to Indigenous Voices in Central California. *Journal of Folklore Research* 50(1–3): 145–174.

Kroskrity, Paul V. and Margaret C. Field. 2009. *Native American Language Ideologies: Beliefs, Practices, and Struggles in Indian Country*. Tucson: University of Arizona Press.

Leonard, Wesley Y. 2011. Challenging Extinction through Modern Miami Language Practices. *American Indian Culture and Research Journal* 35(2): 135–160.

Makihara, Miki. 2013. Language, Competence, Use, Ideology, and Community on Rapa Nui. *Language & Communication* 33: 439–449.

Marks, Jonathan. 2012. The Nature/Culture of Genetic Facts. *Annual Review of Anthropology* 42: 247–67.

McCarty, Teresa, James Collins, and Rodney K. Hopson. 2011. Dell Hymes and the New Language Policy Studies: An Update from an Underdeveloped Country. *Anthropology and Education Quarterly* 42(4): 335–363.

Meek, Barbra A. 2010. *We Are Our Language: An Ethnography of Language Revitalization in a Northern Athabaskan Community*. Tucson: University of Arizona Press.

Meek, Barbra A. 2011. Failing American Indian Languages. *American Indian Culture and Research Journal* 35(2): 43–60.

Moore, Robert. 2006. Disappearing, Inc.: Glimpsing the Sublime in the Politics of Access to Endangered Languages. *Language & Communication* 26: 296–315.

Moore, Robert, Sari Pietikäinen, and Jan Blommaert. 2010. Counting the Losses: Numbers as the Language of Language Endangerment. *Sociolinguistic Studies* 4(1): 1–26.

Morgan, Mindy. 2005. Redefining the Ojibwe Language Classroom: Indigenous Language Programs within Large Research Universities. *Anthropology and Education Quarterly* 36(1): 96–103.

Muehlmann, Shaylih. 2012. Rhizomes and other Uncountables: The Malaise of Enumeration in Mexico's Colorado River Delta. *American Ethnologist* 39(2): 339–353.

Mufwene, Salikoko. 2004. Language Birth and Death. *Annual Review of Anthropology* 33: 201–222.

Nevins, M. Eleanor. 2013a. *Lessons from Fort Apache: Beyond Language Endangerment and Maintenance*. Wiley-Blackwell.

Nevins, M. Eleanor. 2013b. Grow with That, Walk with That: Hymes, Dialogicality, and Text Collections. *Journal of Folklore Research* 50(1–3): 79–116.

Nevins, M. Eleanor and Thomas J. Nevins. 2012. They Don't Know how to Ask: Pedagogy, Storytelling, and the Ironies of Language Endangerment on the White Mountain Apache Reservation. In Kroskrity, 129–150.

Partridge, Damani J. 2012. *Hypersexuality and Headscarves: Race, Sex, and Citizenship in the New Germany*. Bloomington: Indiana University Press.

Patrick, Donna. 2003. *Language, Politics, and Social Interaction in an Inuit Community*. Berlin: Mouton de Gruyter.

Perley, Bernard C. 2011. *Defying Maliseet Language Death: Emergent Vitalities of Language, Culture, and Identity in Eastern Canada*. Lincoln: University of Nebraska Press.

Philips, Lisa. 2011. Unexpected Languages: Multilingualism and Contact in Eighteenth- and Nineteenth-Century North America. *American Indian Culture and Research Journal* 35(2): 19–41.

Philips, Susan. 1983. *The Invisible Culture*. New York: Longman.

Powell, John Wesley. 1880. *Introduction to the Study of Indian Languages: with Words, Phrases and Sentences to be Collected*. Washington: Govt. Print. Off.

Powell, John Wesley. 1991[1891]. *Indian Linguistic Families of America North of Mexico*. Lincoln: University of Nebraska Press.

Rabinow, Paul. 1986. Representations are Social Facts: Modernity and Post-Modernity in Anthropology. In *Writing Culture: the Poetics and Politics of Ethnography*, edited by James Clifford and George E. Marcus, 234–261. Berkeley: University of California Press.

Silverstein, Michael. 1998. Contemporary Transformations of Local Linguistic Communities. *Annual Review of Anthropology* 27: 401–426.

Swinehart, Karl and Kathryn Graber. 2011/2012. Tongue-tied Territories: Languages and Publics in Stateless Nations. *Language & Communication* 32: 95–97.

Urla, Jacqueline. 2012. *Reclaiming Basque: Language, Nation, and Cultural Activism*. Reno and Las Vegas: University of Nevada Press.

Valentine, Lisa Philips and Regna Darnell (eds) 1999. *Theorizing the Americanist Tradition*. Toronto: University of Toronto Press.

Webster, Anthony. 2011. "Please read loose": Intimate Grammars and Unexpected Languages in Contemporary Navajo Literature. *American Indian Culture and Research Journal* 35(2): 61–86.

Webster, Anthony K. 2013. "The validity of Navajo is in its sounds": On Hymes, Navajo Poetry, Punning, and the Recognition of Voice. *Journal of Folklore Research* 50(1–3): 117–144.

Webster, Anthony and Paul V. Kroskrity. 2013. Introducing ethnopoetics: Hymes's legacy. *Journal of Folklore Research* 50(1–3): 1–11.

Woolard, Kathryn. 1989. Language Convergence and Language Death as Social processes. In Dorian, 355–368.

Further Reading

Dorian, Nancy C. 1989. *Investigating Language Obsolescence: Studies in Language Contraction and Death*. Cambridge: Cambridge University Press.
This edited volume defined the field of language endangerment across disciplines.

Grenoble, Lenore and Lindsay Whaley. 1998. *Endangered Languages: Language Loss and Community Response*. Cambridge: Cambridge University Press.
This edited volume extended the purview of language endangerment beyond grammar.

Grenoble, Lenore and Lindsay Whaley. 2005. *Saving Languages: An Introduction to Language Revitalization*. Cambridge: Cambridge University Press.
This book covers the how-to's of language revitalization and the ethics of research with endangered language communities.

Duchêne, Alexandre and Monica Heller. 2007. *Discourses of Endangerment: Ideology and Interest in the Defence of Languages*. London, New York: Continuum.
This edited collection presents the policies and politics encompassing a range of cases of language endangerment from aboriginal languages to French, Spanish, and English.

Index

9-month revolution 149

Aanaar Saami community 427
Abe, H. 180–1, 187
Aboh, E. 356–8
Aboriginal Australian languages 68–76
academic English 77
academic institutions 454–5
accommodations 82
accounts of past violence 408–9; treated as texts 412–13
Acholi people 411
acquisition corpora 143–7, 154
acrolects 350
acts of identity 266; ethnoracial 221, 222–3
'addressee' role 52–7
affective labour 339
Africa 234–5, 351, 353
African American drag queens 199, 222
African American English (AAE) 224, 226
African American Vernacular English 354
African Americans: black power salutes at 1968 Olympics 206–7; 'nigger' terminology 217; Zimmerman murder trial 215–16
Afrikaans 353
agency 98; children's and language socialization 132
Agha, A. 185, 185–6, 187
Aguaruna 19
Ahearn, L.M. 268
AIDS activism 182
Alexander, M. 213
Alim, H.S. 222–3
Allan, K. 292
Allen, T.D. 456
Alleyne, M.C. 348
allocentric orientation 21
ambivalence, language 425–6

American Anthropological Association (AAA) Statement on Ethics and Principles of Professional Responsibility 84–7
American Sign Language (ASL) 248, 253
American South 209
Americanist tradition 448–50
Amish English 354
analytic scales 161–3
anarcho-syndicalist communes 288
Andean household visiting programme 109–24
Anderson, B. 320, 330
Ando 17
Anglo-Irish working-class girls 195–6
animals 119–20
'animator' role 51–7
anonymity 86
anticolonial nationalisms 323
Apartheid Museum, Johannesburg 214–15
aphasics 239
apologies 413
Appadurai, A. 329
apps 441–2
archived data 86, 87
Arendt, H. 284, 408
argumentation 371, 372
Armenia 321
Armstrong, J.A. 322
artificial sign languages 247, 248
Asian Americans 226
assimilation paradigm 313–14
Athapascan community 130
Atkins, J. 62
Atkinson, J.M. 398–9
Atran, S. 16
attitudes, socially shared 390–1
audio-visual recordings 143–6
augmented reality 338
Australian Aboriginal languages 68–76

463

Index

Austrian Freedom Party (FPÖ) 367, 373–8
authenticity 321
'author' role 51–7
autism 164
Avukah 287
awareness 95, 96, 101–2
Axelrod, M. 101

baby talk 127–8, 152, 153
'baby talk' hypothesis of creole evolution 348, 355
bad subjects 161
Bakhtin, M. 181–2
Baldwin, D. 454–5
banal nationalism 369
Bangladeshi girls 194–5
Baquedano-López, P. 166, 270
Barcelona Universal Declaration of Linguistic Rights 326, 333, 435
Barrett, R. 199, 222
base-four system 23
base/superstructure model 279–80
basic kin terms 69
basilects 350
Basque 453
Basso, K.H. 225
Bateson, G. 29
Bauman, R. 284, 449
Bavin, E.L. 152–3
Bechar-Israeli, A. 82
Bengal 323
Berlin, B. 14, 15, 18
Bernstein-Ratner, N. 153
Bhabha, H. 325–6
Bickerton, D. 357
bilingualism: promotion of 443; *see also* immersion programmes
Billings, S. 336
Bininj Gunwok 68–72, 73, 74–6
biology 16–19
Birdwhistell, R.L. 29, 331
Bischoff, S.T. 455
black power salutes 206–7
blame/blaming 409, 410
Blommaert, J. 270–1, 335, 339
blood: blood and belonging formulation of nation 318–19; FPÖ political advertising 377–8
Bloomfield, L. 95, 96–7, 434–5
Boas, F. 3, 95, 96, 234, 449–50; lexical categories 13, 15; nationalism 283–4; race and primitive languages 221

body: justice as embodiment 413–14; living body and gesture 30, 32–3
Boellstorff, T. 84
Bondi, G. 340
Bosavi 165–6
Bourdieu, P. 32, 304, 305
brain damage 239
brands 292
Briggs, C. 284, 449
Brown, C.H. 17
Brown, D. 65
Brown, P. 152
Bucholtz, M. 165, 192, 196, 222, 226, 227
Bündnis Zukunft Österreich (BZÖ) 375
Bureau of American Ethnology (BAE) 449
Burnet, J.E. 414
burnouts 196
Burundi 414
Butler, J. 192
buying of Spanish 49–51
'bystander' role 52–7

calculated ambivalence strategy 375, 377
Calhoun, C. 325
California 166, 270; Native American groups 100; Supreme Court 401
call centres 291, 339, 342
Cameron, D. 193, 194, 199, 202
Cameroon 131, 270
Canada 292, 325; Cree websites 428; residential school system 324, 438
Canadian Indigenous Languages and Literacy Development Institute (CILLDI) 442
Canton 350–1
capitalism: language and political economy 279–300; print capitalism 320, 330
Carapana 17
Carlos, J. 206–7
Castoriadis, C. 44
Catalan 308
categorical speech perception 149
Catholic catechism classes 166
Cekaite, A. 132
Certificate in Aboriginal Language Revitalization 442
Chafe, W. 241
Charter of Fundamental Rights 369
Chatterjee, P. 323
Chaudenson, R. 348–50, 358–9
Chierchia, G. 47
child-directed speech (CDS) 127–8, 152, 153
CHILDES 146–7, 154

children: agency and creole genesis 360; agency and language socialization 132; individual variation 144; participation in language socialization research 134; peer cultures 163, 164–5, 168–9, 170; selection of target children 144, 146; *see also* language acquisition, language socialization
China 434
Chinese (Mandarin) 150, 434, 437
Chinese immigrants in Madrid 306–8
Chintang 150
chlorinated water 115, 116
Chomsky, N. 4, 5, 95, 97, 264, 287, 288
Christianity 321; Evangelical Christians 165–6
'Chuchiku' song 47–8
Chun, E. 227
citizenship: access to 369; laws 168
civil wars 406; *see also* transitional justice
Clarke, K.M. 411
class: gender and other sociocultural identities 194–6; intersectionality 177, 179–80; SES and language acquisition 146, 151–2
cleanliness inspection programme 109–24
cloud, the 80–91
clustering algorithm 147
Coates, J. 193
cochlear implants 252, 254
code-mixing 265
code-switching 102, 265, 266, 309–10
Coelho, A. 357
cognition: gesture as cultural cognition 35; and motion 33; semantic categorization and 13–26
cognitive revolution 1, 5
Cohen, L. 182–3
Cojtí, D. 453
Cold War 331; language and 286–9
collaborations 454–5
collective imagination 38
Collins, J. 102
colonialism 102, 286, 330–1; creoles and pidgins 349–51; language and 281–4; legacies of 322–3; settler colonialism 317, 324–5; *see also* postcolonialism
colour terminology 14–16, 19–20, 23
comedy, stand-up 268
commodification of language 292, 339
communication technologies 329–30, 332, 337–8, 340
communicative mutations 334
communism 286–9
community 185, 304; collaboration between scholars and language communities 455;

communities of practice 196–9, 304; EPM 88, 89; imagined communities 320, 330; language maintenance and revitalization 426–7
Community Linguist Certificate 442
community ostracism 163, 165–6
'competent' membership 159–61
competition 356, 358–9
complementary hypothesis 357–8
computer-mediated communication (CMC) 82–3
conceptualization 30, 35
concern for victims 409–10
concerted action 6
conferences, international 294
confession 410
Conklin, H.C. 15
Conley, J.M. 395
Conley, R. 402
constitutive material practice, language as 1, 6–7
constructivist theories 140
consultants 77
consumption 292
contact signing 248
containers 263
context: contextual variation in recordings 144–5; news production 386–7; studying marginalization across contexts and analytic scales 161–3;
contextualization cues 237
conversation analysis (CA) 31, 209, 213–14, 395; analyzing interactive discourse 234–5, 237, 238–9, 241–2; gender and identity 192; legal discourse 398–9; transcription system 240
conversational style 193–4
COOL project 440
coolness 196; youth cool codes 267–8
cooperative principle 48–9
core activism 426–7
core and periphery 336–7
Corne, C. 357
corpora 143–7, 154
correlational sociolinguistics 97
Corsican 100
cosmopolitanism 292
Coupland, N. 102
covert linguistic racism 103
Cree 434, 436, 437, 440, 443; East Cree 441; websites 428
'creepy ass cracker' 215–16
Crenshaw, K. 179
creole exceptionalism 360

Index

creoles 269–70, 334–5, 348–65; emergence 355–8; genetic creolistics and language change 358–9; number of 352–4; separate languages from lexifiers 354–5
critical discourse analysis (CDA) 96, 209–10
critical sociolinguistics 314
cross-context perspective 162–3
Cross-Cultural Survey 13–14
cross-culturality 398, 402–3
cross-sectional studies 142, 146–7
crossing 223, 268
Crosstalk 332
crying 197
Crystal, D. 433–4
cultural hybridity 314
cultural models of deafness 252
cultural signs 226
culturally problematic subjectivities 161
culture 3–4, 28; differences in input 151; EPM 88, 89; FPÖ and Viennese culture 377–8; gesture and 28, 35; language and postcolonial national culture 322–4; language socialization and marginalization 160–1; logic of argumentation 372; recognition of culture(s) of signing communities 251; ritual and transition 410–11
Czech-German apologies 413

Dabrowska, E. 152
Daga 17
D'Andrade, R. 19, 63, 67
Danehy, J.J. 235–6
Danet, B. 82
Dani 19–20
Darnell, R. 448
Davies, J. 201
deaf sociality 255
deafness 250–1; models of 252–3; terms associated with 249–50; *see also* sign languages
deafnicity 255
death penalty cases 402
Declaration of Universal Linguistic Rights 326, 333, 435
Deeb, H. 401, 402
deficit ideologies 164
DeGraff 348, 350, 352, 353, 356–7, 360
Delaware school administrators 216
Delhi 181–4
de-nazification policies 374
denial of exclusion and racism 370–2
depictive gestures 31
deprivation of access 367

desire: intersectionality and social difference 185–7; racialization of 184–5
deterritorialization 335
dialect geography 2
dialogue 237–9
diary studies 142–3
diasporas 131–2
Diaz, R.M. 443
difference: intersectionality, desire and 185–7; marginalization as a production of 163, 164–5, 168–9, 170
difference model of language and gender 193
digital communication technologies 329–30, 332, 337–8, 340
diplomat training 331
disability studies 164
discourse 393; discourses of language endangerment 458; discursive practices, linguistic repertoire and racial identities 206–19; discursive reproduction of racism 385; framing discourses 411–12; language and gender discourses 193–4; legal 393–405; nationalism as a discursive formation 325
discourse analysis 209, 213, 269, 414; discrimination 366–83; FPÖ's discriminatory rhetoric 373–8; interactive discourse 234–46; online communities 80–91
discrimination 161, 384; denial of exclusion and racism 370–2; discourse analysis 366–83; logic of argumentation 372; politics of language endangerment 455–7; racial *see* racism
discursive forms 46
distinctive ethnoracial language 221–2
distributional variation 144, 145–6
divorce courts 396
documentation 212–13, 435, 439
domains of language use 427–8, 430
domestic work 291–2; foreign domestic workers 306, 311–13
dominance model of language and gender 193
Dominica 129–30
Dorian, N.C. 435
double consciousness 45
double entendre 178–9
double negatives 99, 224
drag queens, African American 199, 222
Drew, P. 398–9
Du Bois, J.W. 240–1
DuBois, W.E.B. 45, 221
Duchêne, A. 458
Duranti, A. 263, 394, 397–8, 402
dwelling perspective 33

Dwyer, L. 414
dyadic terms 73–4, 74–5

e-language (linguistic behaviour) 5
early predispositions for language 148–9
East Cree 441
eating-based interactions 133
'eavesdropper' role 52–7
Eckert, P. 196
Eckert, R.C. 255
ecolinguistics 291, 333–4
ecological perspective on gesture 34
ecology 358, 359
education 428; access to 211–12; deaf education 253–4; educational institutions and marginalization 163–4, 168–9, 170; gender structures in educational settings 201; school-based revitalization strategies 130–1, 424–5
Edwards, J.A. 239
Efron, D. 29
egocentric orientation 21
Ehrlich, S. 201
Eichmann, A., trial of 408
ELAN system 256, 257
election poster campaign 375–8
embodiment, justice as 413–14
emergent genres 268
emergent languages 262–76; globalization and 333, 334–5
emergent models of language emergence 264–8
emergent rules 399
emergent structures 37
emic perspective 63–4
emigration 302
Employment Equality Directive 368
enaction 33
endangered languages *see* language endangerment
Endangered Languages Fund (ELF) 435
Engels, F. 279
English 325, 397, 437; academic 77; African American (AAE) 224, 226; African American Vernacular 354; Amish 354; Filipino domestic workers in Singapore 311–13; global 77; globalization and 334; historical changes in 358; international language of globalization 327; and kinship 62–3; language change 358; Middle 353–4; Old 354, 430; Standard American English 224, 226; White American varieties 355
English dominant nations 324
English Only movement 166

English-as-a-second-language (ESL) learners/classes 132, 294
Enlightenment 28, 330
enregistered voice 185–7
entextualized voice 185–7
environment: environment-centred perspectives 21; factors in language acquisition 150–4
environmentally coupled gestures 36–7
erasure 253
ergative case 152–3
Erickson, F. 235–6
Errington, J. 99, 100
eternal dependent model of deafness 252
ethics, research 84–7
Ethiopia 321
ethnic bias 386–91
ethnicity 221, 255, 321
ethnocentrism 62–3
ethnography 398, 415; and communities of practice 196–9; discourse analysis and 81, 82; signing practices 254–5
ethnography of speaking 5–6, 15, 97
ethnohistories of communication 265
ethnolects 223–4
Ethnologue 436
ethnopoetics 450
Ethnopragmatic Method (EPM) 87–90
ethnosymbolism 317, 321–2
Eurocentrism 62–3
Europe: imperialism 282, 284; migration to from former colonies 331–2
European Charter for Regional or Minority Languages 326
European Union 337; Charter of Fundamental Rights 369; and discrimination 368–9; and the FPÖ 375
evaluation by granting agencies 429–30
Evangelical Christians 165–6
Evans, N. 67, 69, 70, 72, 74
exclusion 366–7; denial of 370–2; marginalization as in migration settings 163, 166–70
expanded pidgins 349, 351
experiments 147–8
externally motivated language change 360
extinct languages 433, 434

Fader, A. 131, 165, 166, 269
fallacies 372
family bias 146
family visits 111
Fanon, F. 323

Index

Fanshel, D. 235–6
fascism 374; language and 284–6
father 66, 67, 69–70
father's father 70–2, 74–6
feature pool 357, 359–60
Feliciano-Santos, S. 457
felicity conditions 410, 413
feminist theory 177, 179–80
Fenson, L. 144
Fernald, A. 151–2, 153
Fichte, J.G. 318
Field, M.C. 452
'figure' role 51–7
Filipino domestic workers in Singapore 306, 311–13
fingerspelling 248–9
Fishman, J. 321, 435
Fitzgerald, C. 455
flames 83
Floyd, K. 82
Foley, W.A. 16
folk biology 16–19
folk taxonomy 13, 14–19
food-related interactions 133
foreign domestic workers (FDWs) 306, 311–13
foreign language-type programmes for language revitalization 424
foreign service officer training 331
Fort Apache reservation 454
Foundation for Endangered Languages (FEL) 435
Fountain, A.V. 455
Four-Level-Context Model of the Discourse-Historical Approach to Critical Discourse Analysis 373–4
fractal recursivity 253
Frame of Reference project 287–8
framing discourses 411–12
français tirailleur, le 352
France 319
Freiheitliche Partei Österreich (FPÖ) 367, 373–8
French, B. 409, 412, 453–4
French 2, 100, 318, 319, 325
French Revolution 319
Friedman, D. 130–1
Friedner, M. 255
Friedrich, P. 452
Fries, C. 238
functionalism 320
fundamental neural response categories 15–16

gacaca 410
Gaelic 101, 437

Gal, S. 102, 253, 280, 395–6, 451
Galician 101
Gandhi, M. 212, 215
Gapun, Papua New Guinea 126–7
garbage disposal 119–20
García-Sánchez, I.M. 134, 165, 167–70
Garde, M. 68–72, 73
Garrett, P. 129, 270
Gauteng, South Africa 184–5
gay men 178, 181–5
Gayton, A. 455
Gee, J.P. 294
Gellner, E. 99–100, 319–20
Gelman, R. 144–5
gender 177, 179–80; CDA and gender inequality 209; heterogeneity of gender identities 196–9; interplay with other sociocultural identities 194–6; interplay of sexuality and 199–200; language, identity and 191–205; structures 201
Gender Goods and Services Directive 368
Gender Social Security Directive 368
Genesee, F. 265
genetic creolistics 358–9, 360–1
genocides 406; *see also* transitional justice
genres, emergent 268
Georgetown Transcription System 240
German 318
Germany 318; apologies between Czech and German officials 413; National Socialism 284–5; Turkish-German Powergirls 197–8, 199
gesture 27–43, 249
Global English 77
global justice 411, 416
global scales 336–7
globalization 23, 289–90, 294, 327; language in the age of 329–47
Goffman, E. 51–2
Goldberg, D. 368, 369
Goldman, L. 399–400
Gomez de Garcia, J. 101
Goodenough, W. 66–7
Goodwin, C. 36–7, 239, 263
Goodwin, M.H. 165
governmentality 304
gradualism 358
grammar 148, 149, 238; Americanist tradition and documenting 449; importance of written grammars 438; universal 5, 357
Granadillo, T. 448
granting agencies, evaluation by 429–30
grassroots literacy 339–40
Greenberg, J.H. 14, 23

Grégoire, Abbé 319
Grenoble, L.A. 441
Grewal, I. 293
Grice, P. 48
growth stages 17
Guatemala: Mayan languages 453–4; truth commission 412
Gullah 354
Gumperz, J. 5, 97, 236, 331–2; transcription system 241
Guugu Yimithirr 21

habitus 32, 34, 127, 342
Haider, J. 373, 375
Haitian Creole 356
Hakuta, K. 443
Halberstam, J. 180, 183
Hall, E.T. 331
Hall, K. 192, 199–200
Hall, R.A., jr 352, 356
hands 33–4; washing 116–18; *see also* gesture
Hanunoo 15
Harding, S. 49
Harraguantanamo 340
Harris, Z. 287–8
Hart, B. 151
Harvey, D. 289–90
Hasidic Jews 131, 166
Hastings, A. 321
Haviland, J. 255, 396–7
Hawaii 351, 425; *Leo Ki* web initiative 428
Hawaiian English Creole 352–3
Hayward, R. 23
He, A.W. 131
headlines 388
health clinic 169
hearer roles 51–7
Heath, C. 32
Heath, S.B. 126, 163–4, 209
Heidegger, M. 32, 33
Heider, E. 19–20
Heine, S.J. 17–18
Heller, M. 270, 458
Henrich, J. 17–18
Herder, J.G. 285, 318
heritage language socialization 131–2
heteroglossia 177–90
heteroglossic play 266–8
high-density studies 146
Hill, J. 99, 103, 224, 266, 303, 451
Hill, K. 266, 303, 451
Hinton, L. 423, 437, 440

Hip Hop 215
Hirsch, S. 396
Hispanics 310
hispanism 285
history, accounts of past violence circulating as 412
Hitler, A. 214
Hockett, C.F. 235–6
Hoff, E. 145
Hoff-Ginsberg, E. 151
Hoffman, K.E. 268
Hoffman-Dilloway, E. 255–6
Holborrow, M. 294
Holt, R. 83
home-based revitalization strategies 423–4
homesigns 249
Hook, S. 288
Hopi justice system 403
horizontal identities 253
hospitality 111, 113, 114, 121
household visiting programme 109–24
Howard, K.M. 130, 134
Huanta peasants narrative 49–51
Huli society, Papua New Guinea 399–400
human–machine interaction 338
human nature 288
human rights 369, 411, 435
Human Speechome Project 146
human universals 65, 66–7
Humboldt, W. von 285
Hunn, E. 18
Hunt, G. 449
Hurston, Z.N. 234
Hutchby, I. 83
Hutton, C. 285
hygiene habits 109–24
Hymes, D. 5, 97, 289, 331, 332, 450, 455–6

i-language (grammar) 5
iconization 253
identity: acts of identity 221, 222–3, 266; creation online 82; discursive practices, linguistic repertoire and racial identities 206–19; globalization and 335, 338; interplay of gender with other sociocultural identities 194–6; language, gender and 191–205; language ideologies and construction of 102–3
ideological clarification 426
ideological sites 101
ideology 280–1; discursive processes and ideological production/disruption 224–5; ethnolect as 223–4; language endangerment,

politics and 452–4; language ideologies *see* language ideologies; sign languages and 253, 254–5; socially shared ideologies 390–1
Ilgar 72–3
image schemata 35
imagined communities 320, 330
imitation 149
immersion programmes 424–5; partial 424, 440; total 439–40
immigrants 292; descriptions in the press 389; language socialization 131; marginalization as sociocultural and sociopolitical exclusion 163, 166–70; the state and social inequalities 313; Turkish-German Powergirls 197–8, 199
immigration: defining 302; language, nation-state and 301–16; linguistic articulation of immigration in social life 305–13; settler nations 324–5; *see also* migration
imperialism 282, 284; *see also* colonialism
implicature 45, 48–51
implicit reference 226
inclusion 366–7
incremental comparisons 144
indexicality 128, 192, 199–200; indexical indeterminacy 225–6
India 212, 281, 323; gay men 181–4
indirect indexicality 192
individual style 267
individual variation 144
Indonesia 324; genocide 414
Indonesian standard language 99–100
industrial revolution 211
industrialization 319–20
inequality: immigrants, the state and social inequalities 313; language shift, voice and 450–2; narrative inequality 455–7
informed consent 257
Innu 441
input 140–1, 150–4; amount of 151–2; type of 152–4
inspection of households 109–24
institutional policies and practices: gender identity 201; language socialization and marginalization 163–4, 168–9, 170
integration 302, 304–5
intellectual revolutions 1–9
interaction research 29, 30–2
interactional affordances 169–70
interactional lamination 45, 51–7
interactional sociolinguistics 236–7
interactionism 6

interactions: analysis of interactive discourse 234–46; language acquisition and 141, 145, 152–3; medium of interaction 83–4; multimodal 36–8
intercontextual variability 170
intergenerational transmission 438
interlocutors 88, 89
intermediaries 352
internally motivated language change 360
International Association of Dialogue Analysis 237
International Criminal Court (ICC) 407, 409, 416
international conferences 294
internet 428
Internet Relay Chat (IRC) 82
interpreters 351–2
intersectionality 177–90; desire, social difference and 185–7; gender and other identities 194–200; as queer linguistics 187–8
intertextuality 269; heteroglossic play and intertextual performance 266–8
intracontextual variability 170
invented codes 267
inverted Spanglish 226
Ireland 427
Irish (Gaelic) 101, 437
Irvine, J. 54–5, 96, 102, 253, 395–6
Italy 285
item-based learning 143
Iwaidja 72–3

Jacobs, M. 288–9
Jacquemet, M. 336
Jaffe, A. 100
Jakobson, R. 4, 289
Japan 285–6, 318; Tokyo *see* Tokyo
jargon 352
Jaworski, A. 102
Jay Z 290
Jeantel, R. 215–16
Jefferson, G. 237, 240
Jefferson, T. 449
Jews 285, 287; Hasidic 131, 166
jocks 196
Johnstone, B. 267
joint attention 149
joint imagining 38
Jordan, B. 267
Journal of Computer-Mediated Communication 82
Journal of Linguistic Anthropology 235
judges 395

jurisdiction 416
jurors' decision making 402
justification discourses 370–1, 372

Kagoro, B. 411
Kaluli language socialization 126, 127–8, 151
Kam Muang 130
Kaplan, C. 293
Kaska 130
Kattan, S. 131
Kay, P. 14, 15, 20
Keane, W. 110
Keim, I. 197–8, 199
Kempton, W. 20
Kendon, A. 30–1
Kenyan divorce courts 396
Khan, S. 182–3
Kiesling, S. 194
Kincade, M.D. 433–4
King, M.L. 212
kinship 62–79
kitchens, Andean 110; cleanliness 118–19
Kitzinger, C. 199
Klein, N. 292
Klein, W. 131–2
knowledge-usage gaps 425–6
Koostachin, J. 436, 438
Kreol of Queensland 353
Kroeber, A.L. 3–4
Kroskrity, P.V. 95, 100, 452, 455, 456, 457
Ku Klux Klan 207, 208
Kuipers, J.C. 268
Kulick, D. 126–7, 160–1, 270
Kutsch Lojenga, C. 23
Kwakiutl 15
Kwéyòl 129

labour 291–2; affective 339
Labov, W. 5, 97, 235–6
Labrador Inuttitut 440
Lachler, J. 101
Lake Piwiray narrative 52–7
Lakhota Sioux 185–7
Lakoff, R. 193
lamination, pragmatic 45, 51–7
Langer, S. 46
language acquisition 125–6; in different linguistic and cultural settings 140–58; factors affecting the acquisition process 148–54
language activists 442
language ambivalence 425–6
language bioprogram hypothesis 357

language creation *see* emergent language, new languages
language death 452–3
language decline 433
Language and Dialogue 237
language endangerment 266, 421, 422; globalization and 332–4; politics of 447–62; and revitalization strategies 433–46; *see also* language maintenance, language revitalization
language ideologies 129, 223, 280–1; emergence, elaboration and application 95–108; and legal discourse 395–7
language loss 359, 420
language maintenance 427–8, 434
language maintenance and revitalization (LMR) 420–32
language nests 424, 440
language policy: sign languages 253–4; standardized languages 98, 99–100, 223–4, 319–20
language reclamation 439
language renewal 103–4
language revitalization 101, 103–4; home-based strategies 423–4; language endangerment and revitalization strategies 433–46; language maintenance and (LMR) 420–32; school-based strategies 130–1, 424–5; Ukraine 130–1
language shift 420, 421, 425, 426, 434, 436; causes of 436–9; creoles and 359–60; inequality and voice 450–2; issues for language maintenance and revitalization 422–3; language-learning children and 129–30; multilingual practices and 264–6
language socialization 125–39; 'competent' membership as an idealized endpoint of 159–61; and marginalization 159–74; and new languages 269–70; trajectories of 160–1, 162–3, 163–7
language-specific interventions 422
language standardization 98, 99–100, 223–4, 319–20
language subordination process 99
language vitality: Kincade's classification system 433–4; UNESCO approach to assessing 441
Latin 358, 430
Latinos 213; Latina women reporting rape 401
latrines 112–13, 117, 118, 120, 121
law schools 400
Lawson, R. 196–7
leads and headlines 338
leet speak 85–6, 87
Lefebvre, C. 356

Index

legal discourse 393–405
legitimation discourses 372
Leibniz, G.W. 76
Leikin, M. 443
Leo Ki web initiative 428
'lesbian bars' 180–1
Levinson, S. 21, 62
lexical choice 389
lexical universals 64–77
lexifiers 348–9, 350; creoles as separate languages from 354–5
Lienhardt, G. 15
life-cycle hypothesis 352
linguistic anthropology: defining 397–8; intellectual revolutions 1–9; uniqueness 397–8
linguistic capital 305
linguistic characteristics 150
linguistic racism 103, 455–7
linguistic relativism (Sapir-Whorf hypothesis) 3, 19
linguistic repertoires 206–19
linguistic rights 435
linguistics departments 287
Lippi-Green, R. 99
literacy: deaf education 253–4; grassroots 339–40; production of materials 443; revitalizing endangered languages 442–3
living body 30, 32–3
Lo, A. 225
local cultural practices 336–7
local semantics 388
local syntax 389
Loether, C. 101
Lofty Baradyal Nadjamerrek 68
Lomax, A. 213
Lomax, J. 213
long-term memory 149
longitudinal studies: language acquisition 142–7; marginalization 162–3
longue durée 322
Lorente, B. 311–13
Lucy, J.A. 20

Mabry, E.A. 83
MacArthur-Bates Communicative Development Inventories 142
MacDougall, J.P. 255
machine translation 287
macho discourse 201
macro-micro relations 162
MacWhinney, B. 146
Madrid schools 305, 306–8

maid agencies 311–12
mainstreaming 254
Makihara, M. 100–1, 130
Malinowski, B. 234
Maliseet 452–3
Mallery, G. 28–9
management theory 453
Mandarin Chinese 150, 434, 437
Mandela, N. 212
Mangual Figueroa, A. 166–7
Manning, P. 292
manual alphabets 248–9
Mâori 440
marginalization 159–74; case study of Moroccan immigrant children in Spain 165, 167–70; as trajectories of language socialization 163–7
Maritime Polynesian Pidgin (MPP) 352
markedness model 358
Marquesas 269
Martin, T. 215–16
Martin-Jones, M. 270
Martin-Nielsen, J. 288
Martín Rojo, L. 306–8
Marx, K. 279
Maryns, K. 271
mass media 104, 227; language maintenance 428; racism in the press 384–92; right-wing populist parties and 378–9
mass violence 406; *see also* transitional justice
Master–Apprentice programmes 423–4, 440
master narratives 408–9
materialism 280–1
mato oput 410, 411
Matoesian, G. 399
Max Planck Institute for Psycholinguistics 21, 22
maximum diversity sampling 147
Mayan languages 453–4
Maynard, D. 398
McConnell-Ginet, S. 47
McDaniel, C.K. 14
McElhinny, B. 294
McEwan-Fujita, E. 101
Mead, G.H. 29
Mead, M. 301
media *see* mass media
mediatizing processes 227
medical models of deafness 252
medium of interaction 83–4
Meek, B.A. 130, 456–7
Meetmarket 184–5
Mehan, H. 164

Melanesian pidgins 349, 356
memorials 415
memory, long-term 149
mental models 390
Merleau-Ponty, M. 32, 33
Merrifield, W. 15
Mertz, E. 400–1, 409
metaphor 28–9
metaphorical vessels 263
Mexican immigrant children 166
Mexico 99, 266, 303
Michigan State University 454
micro-macro relations 162
Middle English 353–4
migration 438–9; defining 302; to Europe from former colonies 331–2; and globalization 329–30, 331–2, 340–2; language, immigration and the nation-state 301–16; linguistic anthropological perspective 302–3; urban 438–9; *see also* immigration
Mi'kmaq community 439
Milani, T. 184–5
milestones 148–9
Minks, A. 132
Mitchell, B. 456
mixed racial heritage 211
mobility: sociolinguistics of 340–2; *see also* migration
models of deafness 252–3
Modern Hebrew 439
modernism 317, 319–20
Moerman, M. 237
monologue narrative 234
monopoly 282
Moore, L. 131, 270
Morgan, M. 225, 454
moribund languages 438
Moroccan immigrants in Spain: marginalization 165, 167–70; Spanish as '*Respeto*' 306–8
mother 66, 67, 69–70
motherese 127–8, 152, 153
mother's mother 70–2, 74–6
motivations, speakers' 422
Muang community 130
Mufwene, S. xiii, 263, 343, 458
Mühlhäusler, P. 352
multi-level ethnography 398
multilingual socialization 129–31
multilingualism 126, 293, 332, 335–6; and language shift 264–6; language socialization 129–32
multimodal discourse analysis 269

multimodal interaction 36–8
multiplicity of language ideologies 99–101
Munsell colour chart 14, 24
Murdock, G.P. 14
Myaamia Project 454–5
Myers-Scotton, C. 265
myths 322

Nahuatl communities, Mexico 99, 303
name strategy 20
narration, nation as 325–6
narrative analysis 414
narrative inequality/discrimination 455–7
narratives of victimhood 413
Nash, J. 180
Naskapi 440, 443, 444
nation building 282–3, 323
nation-states 293, 369; language, immigration and 301–16
national consciousness 330–1
National Socialism 284–5
national standardized languages 98, 99–100, 223–4, 319–20
national superiority 318
nationalism 254; banal 369; language and 317–28
Native Americans 3, 211, 426, 430; *see also under individual languages/communities*
nativist theories 140
Natural Core Model 18–19
natural semantic metalanguage (NSM) 63, 64–5, 88
natural sign languages 248
naturalistic/observational research 29, 142–7
nature of language 335–6
nature vs nurture debate 19, 125, 140, 141
Navajo English 456
nearly extinct languages 433, 434
Neds 196–7
negative other-presentation 370–2
Neogrammarians 1–2
neoliberalism 289–93
nerds 196
neurophenomenology 33
Nevins, M.E. 454
New Delhi 'Centre' NGO 199–200
new languages: and emergent languages 262–76; globalization and 333, 334–5
New Latino Diaspora, Pennsylvania 166–7
New York Puerto Ricans 127, 269, 302–3, 305–6, 308–11
Newman, S. 455

473

Index

news 386–91; context of production 386–7; reception of biased news 389–91; structures of 387–9
Ngugi wa Thiong'o 323
'nigger' terminology 217
nine-month revolution 149
nonliberal religious communities 163, 165–6
Norenzayan, A. 17–18
Norman, P. 206, 207
normative trajectories 160–1
not-for-profit advocacy organizations 435
novice–expert relationship 127
NSM approach 63, 64–5, 88
numbers of speakers 434, 437
numeral systems 23
Nuñez, R. 35
Nuremberg Trials 406, 408

Obama, B. 223
O'Barr, W.M. 395
Oberly, S. 455
observational/naturalistic research 29, 142–7
Ochs, E. 192; children with autism 164; language acquisition 145, 151; language socialization 125, 126, 127–8, 133, 159–60
official status designation 437
Old English 354, 430
Olds, J. 454–5
Olympic Games 206–7
Ong, W. 209
online communities 80–91
online personal advertisements 184–5
oral traditions 212
orality 321
Orcutt-Gachiri, H.A. 448
Oregon murder trial 396–7
Orientalism 281
orientation of linguistic anthropology 397–8
orthography 255–6
other: biased news and others 387–91; negative other-presentation 370–2; postmodern approaches to nationalism 325–6
Otthenheimer, H.J. 87
'outsiders inside' 168–70
'overhearer' role 52–7

Paccagnella, M. 82
paid caregiving 291–2, 306, 311–13
paintings 214
Papua New Guinea 126–7, 165–6, 399–400
paradoxes of marginalization 171
Parks, M.R. 82

partial immersion (bilingual) programmes 424, 440
participation frameworks 51–7
patios, Andean 112–13
patriline 74
pattern recognition 149
Patwa 129–30
Paugh, A.L. 129–30, 132, 269–70
peer cultures 163, 164–5, 168–9, 170
peer socialization 132
Peirce, C.S. 4, 97
pencil test 214–15
penetrative sex 181–4
Pennycook, A. 336
perennialism 317, 320–1
performance: gender and sexual identities 192, 202; intertextual 266–8; justice as 413–14
performative subject 222–3
Perley, B. 452–3
personal advertisements 184–5
personal hygiene 116, 118
personhood 290–1
Peru: household inspection programme 109–24; Quechua speakers *see* Quechua speakers
phenomenology 32
Philippines: Filipino domestic workers in Singapore 306, 311–13; role in the market for domestic workers 312–13
Philips, L. 447
Philips, S. 163, 394–5, 451
philologists 1–2
Pichler, P. 194–6
Pidginization Index (PI) 357
pidgins 334–5, 348, 349–52, 353
pioneer apologies 413
Pitjantjatjara 63
Pittenger, R.E. 235–6
Pizer, G. 254
Plains Sign Language 28
plantations 349
plants 19
play 132, 169; heteroglossic 266–8
pointing 32, 149
Polich, L. 252
political advertising 375–8
political economy: language and 279–300; of linguistic globalization 338–9
political 'rebranding' 286
politics 322; of language endangerment 447–62
Poplack, S. 265
population centred view of language 1, 6–7
population structure 349, 359–60

Index

Portuguese 352
positionality 98–9
positive identity practices 165
positive self-representation 370–2
postcolonialism 317, 322–4
postindustrial production 289–90, 338–9
postmodernism 317, 325–6
postnationalism 293, 317, 326–7
Powdermaker, H. 234–5
Powell, J.W. 449
power 161, 451; buying of Spanish by Chechua speakers 49–51; CDA and power dynamics 209–10; and solidarity 265–6
power-saturated environments 343
Powergirls 197–8, 199
practice: approach to gesture 34, 36; communities of 196–9, 304; practice turn in the social sciences 36
pragmatic lamination 45, 51–7
preferred readings 390
prejudice 384; *see also* discrimination
premarital sex, illicit 399–400
presentational forms 46
press: racism in the 384–92; *see also* mass media
presupposition 45, 47–8
Price, D. 288, 289
'primitive language' 283
primordialism 317, 318–19
'principal' role 51–7
print capitalism 320, 330
private enterprise 428
process orientation 162
production format of utterances 52
production regimes 289–90, 338–9
professional communities 37–8
project evaluation by granting agencies 429–30
protectionism 282
Proto-Indo-European (PIE) 359
provocation strategy 373
Proyecto Lingüístic Francisco Marroquín (PLFM) 454
psycho-neuro-cognitive approaches 264
public debate 403
public services 428
Puerto Ricans in New York 127, 269, 302–3, 305–6, 308–11
purism 102
Pye, C. 153

quantity, conversational maxim of 48–9, 51
Quebec 326–7; Cree School Board 443
Quechua speakers: social imaginary in narratives and songs 44–61; social subordination 109–24
queer linguistics 187–8
'queer' terminology 216–17
queerness, heteroglossic 183–4
questionnaires 142
Quintilianus, M.F. 28
quotations 389
quotative verbs 31–2

race 177, 179–80, 283; discursive practices, linguistic repertoire and racial identities 206–19
race talk 224
Racial Equity Directive 368
racialization: erotic desire 184–5; language and 220–33
racism 207–8, 211–12; denial of 370–2; discourse analysis of discrimination 366–83; discursive reproduction of 385; linguistic 103, 455–7; in the press 384–92
radical translator problem 15
Rampton, B. 268
Rap 215
Rapa Nui 100–1, 130
rape: reporting by Latina women 401; trials 399
reason 318
reception of biased news 389–91
reconciliation 415–16; *see also* truth and reconciliation commissions (TRCs)
recordings, audio-visual 143–6; recording schemes 145–6
'Redskins' football team 211
referential transparency 396–7
regularity of sound change 1–2
Reintaller, A. 374
Reisigl, M. 370, 371, 372
relational invariance 4
relational worldview 395
relexification hypothesis (RH) 356
religion 321, 322; community ostracism by nonliberal religious communities 163, 165–6; language maintenance or revitalization and religious materials 427, 436; language socialization and religious identity 131; *see also* Christianity
Remembering Inninimowin 436, 438
Renner, J. 413
repetition 152–3
research ethics 84–7
residential schooling 324, 438
respect 306–8

475

Index

revitalization strategies *see* language revitalization
rezu 'identity' 180–1
rhetoric: discriminatory 367–8, 370–8; of nation 325
Richland, J. 403, 416
right-wing populist parties 286, 378–9; FPÖ 367, 373–8
Riley, K. 130, 269
Risley, T.R. 151
ritual 410–11
role reversal 149
roles, speaker and hearer 51–7
Romance languages 348, 353–4, 358
Rosa, J. 226
Ross, F.C. 412
Rovee-Collier, C. 149
rule-oriented worldview 395
Rumsey, A. 395
Russian 2, 65–6
Russian revolution 287
Rwanda 414; genocide hearings 410

Sacks, H. 237
safe sex 182–3
safetalk 270
Saffran, J.R. 149
Said, E. 281–2, 285
salt tax protest 215
salvage ethnography 448–50
same-sex marriage 401
Samoa 126, 127–8, 151
sampling issues 142–8
Santa Ana, O. 213
Santa Barbara Discourse Transcription system 240–1
Sapir, E. 3–4, 19
Sapir-Whorf hypothesis 3, 19
Sarajevo 414
Saussure, F. de 2
scales: analytic 161–3; local and global 336–7
scattered hegemonies 293
Schegloff, E. 237
Schieffelin, B. 151, 270; language socialization 125, 126, 127–8, 133, 159–60, 160–1; marginalization 160–1, 165–6
Schneider, D. 63
scholars: collaboration with language communities 455; expectations of 448
school-based revitalization strategies 130–1, 424–5
scientific management 282
scientific observer 63–4

Scottish masculinities 196–7
scripts of servitude 311–12
Second Life 84
selection 355, 357–60
selection of target children 144, 146
self-paced/self-motivated language learning 423
self-presentation, positive 370–2
semantic categorization 13–26
semantic molecules 64–5
semantic primes 64, 65
semantics, local 388
semiotic approaches 414–15
semiotic models of communication 97
semiotic vessels 264
service economy 339
servitude, scripts of 311–12
settlement colonies 349
settler colonialism 317, 324–5
sex, as semantic component 65–6
sexual assault 201
sexual encounters: gay men in Delhi 181–4; illicit premarital sex in Huli society 399–400
sexuality: interplay of gender and 199–200; language, heteroglossia, intersectionality and 177–90
shaming 128–9
Shankar, S. 227, 271
Shatz, M. 144–5
Sheppard, E.E. 284, 285
Shinjuku Ni-choome 'lesbian bars' 180–1
Shoshoni 17, 101
Shultz, J. 235–6
sign languages 28–9, 247–61; language variation in 251–2; linguistic recognition 250; recognition of culture(s) of signing communities 251; types 247–9
silence 413–14
Silverstein, M. 6, 95, 97, 101, 333–4
Simon, T. 153
Simpson, K. 415
Singapore 306, 311–13
slavery 212–13, 215
smells 22
Smith, T. 206–7
Smitherman, G. 223
Snow, C. 146, 152
social capital 427–8
social constructionism 191–202
social difference *see* difference
social embeddedness of language 1, 5–6

social imaginary 44–61; implicature 45, 48–51; pragmatic lamination 45, 51–7; presupposition 45, 47–8
social inequalities *see* inequality
social media 81, 214, 270
social ontology 6
social order 128
social subordination 109–24
sociality 255
socialization, language *see* language socialization
socially shared attitudes and ideologies 390–1
socio-economic status (SES) *see* class
sociology of language 210
sociology of talk 399
soft skills 290
solidarity 265–6
Solomon, A. 252–3
South Africa 212, 214–15, 323–4; *Meetmarket* 184–5; truth and reconciliation commission 410–11, 412
Southern Peruvian Quechua *see* Quechua speakers
Sozialdemokratische Partei Österreichs (SPÖ) 375, 378
Spain 285; immigrants in Madrid schools 305, 306–8; Moroccan immigrant children 165, 167–70, 306–8
Spanglish 309–10; inverted 226
Spanish 437, 453–4; Quechua speakers, power and 49–51; as '*Respeto*' in Madrid schools 305, 306–8; as stigma for New York Puerto Ricans 308–11
spatial orientation 21–2
speaker activists 442
speakers: awareness 95, 96, 101–2; motivations 422; numbers of 434, 437; roles 51–7
special concern for victims 409–10
speciation 354–5, 358–9
speech acts 414; transition through 410
speech communities *see* community
Spitulnik, D. 271
St Lucia 129
Stahl, D. 145
stand-up comedy 268
Standard American English 224, 226
Standard Thai 130
standardized languages 98, 99–100, 223–4, 319–20
state: formation 280; inherently contradictory and internally fractured 368; language, immigration and nation-states 301–16
statistical learning 149

status-raising techniques 427–8
stereotype threat 213
stereotyping, market-bound 311–12
Sterponi, L. 132
stigmatization 308–11
Stokoe, W. 248, 250
Stoll, S. 152–3
Strache, H.-C. 375, 376, 378
Strauss, J. 377
Street, J. 152
structuralism 4, 221, 289
structure: discovery of 1, 2–4; emergent structures 37
style, gesture 29
subnationalist movements 326–7
subordination, social 109–24
substrate hypothesis 355–6
Summer Institute of Linguistics (SIL) 436, 453
superdiversity 314, 335, 340–1
superstrate hypothesis 356
suppression of language 438
Sutton Sign Writing (SW) system 255–6
Swadesh, M. 288, 289
Swahili 101
Sweetser, E. 35
Sylvain, S. 349, 355
symbolic elites 385
symbolic gestures, racial 206–7
symbols 322
synchronic linguistics 2
synchronic philology 3
syntax, local 389

tableware 118–19
Taiap 126–7
Taíno language renewal 457
Talmy, S. 132
Tannen, D. 236–7
Tanzania 101
Tarahumara 20
taste 22
Taxonomic Hierarchy Model 18
teachers' role in marginalization 170
teasing 194–6
technical terminology 76–7
techniques du corps 34
technology: apps 441–2; digital communication technologies 329–30, 332, 337–8, 340
templates 443
tensions of expectations 447–8, 452–4
Terralingua 435
Tewa 102

Index

Texas death penalty cases 402
Thadani, G. 182–3
'things that are common to all mankind' 66–7
'thinking like a lawyer' 400
Thomas, J.A. 285–6
Thomason, S. 334
Tibetan 434
Tima 16, 22
time 1–2; metaphorization of 35
Tok Pisin 126–7
Tokyo: 'lesbian bars' 180–1; post-World War II trials 408
Tomasello, M. 143, 145
topics, news 387–8
topoi 372
total immersion programmes 439–40
toughness 196–7; femininities 194–5, 197–9
trade colonies 349, 351
Trager, G.L. 331
trajectories of language socialization 162–3; marginalization as 163–7; normative 160–1
transcription: analyzing interactive discourse 235, 239–41; sign languages 256
transidiomas/transidiomatic practices 270–1, 330, 341–2
transitional justice 406–19
transnational migrants (transmigrants) 332
transnationalism 293, 314
Trautmann, T.R. 281
Trechter, S. 185–7
tribal law 403
Trinch, S. 401, 402
truth and reconciliation commissions (TRCs) 406, 407, 410–11
Turkish-German Powergirls 197–8, 199
Turner, L.D. 355
two-language homes 439
Tylor, E. 28, 248
Tzeltal 19, 152

ubuntu 410–11
Uganda 410, 411
Ukraine 130–1
understanding, technical terminology and 76–7
unequal competition 437
UNESCO 441
uniqueness of linguistic anthropology 397–8
United Nations 407; Special Committee on Decolonization 286
United States of America (US) 212; Cold War 286–9; colonialism 283; communities of practice 196; Foreign Service Institute 331;
global influence 331; growth of linguistics 286–7
Universal Declaration of Human Rights 435
Universal Declaration of Linguistic Rights 326, 333, 435
universal grammar 5, 357
universal semantic modules 64
universalism 28; creole genesis 357–8
universals 150, 214; human 65, 66–7; lexical and kinship 64–77
Uqhupata village 110, 111–22
urban migration 438–9
Urciuoli, B. 224
Urla, J. 453
Urry, J. 303
usage: increasing 422; usage-based theories of acquisition 140

Van Dijk, T.A. 366
variation in sign languages 251–2
verbal art 44–61
Verband der Unabhängigen (VdU) 374
verbatim principle 86
verbs 152; kinship 68–73; quotative 31–2
vernaculars 321, 330, 340, 348; *see also* creoles
vertical identities 252–3
Vertovec, S. 314, 341
viable but small languages 433, 434
viable languages 433, 434
victimhood, narratives of 413
victims, special concern for 409–10
Vienna Election Campaign 2010 375–8
Vinning, D. 178
virtual gaming 270
virtual worlds 84
visita domiciliaria programme 109–24
visual representations 214
voice 450–2
Volk (people) 318
Volksgeist 285
Volosinov, V.N. 279–80

Wallace, A.F.C. 62
Warm Springs 451
water quality 115, 116
Webster, A. 456
WEIRD people 17–18
Weitzer, R. 324
Werner, O. 19
West, D. 215–16
Westenthaler, P. 375
Western liberal legalism 411–12

Whaley, L.J. 441
White American English varieties 355
white superiority 385
Whorf, B. 3, 19
Wiener Blut (Strauss) 377
Williams, R. 6, 304
Wilson, R.A. 412
Winter, S. 373
Wodak, R. 370, 371, 372
Woodward, J.C. 250
Wôpanâak (Eastern Algonquin) 439
work 291–2
working-class girls 194–6
World War I 284, 285
World War II 286, 287

Wortham, S. 226
writing 212; language maintenance 427; in sign language 255–6
writing systems 442–3
Wurm, S.A. 435

youth: cool codes 267–8; European Americans 226; peer cultures 163, 164–5, 168–9, 170
Yovel, J. 409
Yucatec 20
Yuval-Davis, N. 179, 184

Zentella, A.C. 126, 127, 264, 269, 302–3, 308–11
Zimmerman, G., murder trial of 215–16

eBooks
from Taylor & Francis
Helping you to choose the right eBooks for your Library

Add to your library's digital collection today with Taylor & Francis eBooks. We have over 50,000 eBooks in the Humanities, Social Sciences, Behavioural Sciences, Built Environment and Law, from leading imprints, including Routledge, Focal Press and Psychology Press.

Choose from a range of subject packages or create your own!

Benefits for you
- Free MARC records
- COUNTER-compliant usage statistics
- Flexible purchase and pricing options
- All titles DRM-free.

Benefits for your user
- Off-site, anytime access via Athens or referring URL
- Print or copy pages or chapters
- Full content search
- Bookmark, highlight and annotate text
- Access to thousands of pages of quality research at the click of a button.

Free Trials Available
We offer free trials to qualifying academic, corporate and government customers.

eCollections
Choose from over 30 subject eCollections, including:

Archaeology	Language Learning
Architecture	Law
Asian Studies	Literature
Business & Management	Media & Communication
Classical Studies	Middle East Studies
Construction	Music
Creative & Media Arts	Philosophy
Criminology & Criminal Justice	Planning
Economics	Politics
Education	Psychology & Mental Health
Energy	Religion
Engineering	Security
English Language & Linguistics	Social Work
Environment & Sustainability	Sociology
Geography	Sport
Health Studies	Theatre & Performance
History	Tourism, Hospitality & Events

For more information, pricing enquiries or to order a free trial, please contact your local sales team:
www.tandfebooks.com/page/sales

www.tandfebooks.com